TAR HEEL
CATHOLICS

A History of Catholicism in North Carolina

William F. Powers

University Press of America,® Inc.
Lanham · Boulder · New York · Toronto · Oxford

Library of Congress Control Number: 2003110067
ISBN 0-7618-2598-3 (clothbound : alk. ppr.)
ISBN 0-7618-2599-1 (paperback : alk. ppr.)

For Monsignor Gerald L. Lewis

Ad Multos Annos

Contents

Leo XIII once remarked to Cardinal Manning: "It has been too much the fashion in writing history to omit what is unpleasant. If the historians of the last century had written the Gospels, for example, we might never have heard of the fall of Peter or the treachery of Judas."
• Cardinal James Gibbons, *The Ambassador of Christ*, 1896

Preface

My first contact with the Catholic Church in North Carolina occurred in 1979. Wanting to engage in some volunteer activity during the summer, and also to expose our young children to the idea of serving others, my wife, Ann, and I replied to a notice in the *National Catholic Reporter* looking for "migrant ministers" for the Diocese of Raleigh. After a telephone interview with the program director, Sister Evelyn Mattern, we were accepted and assigned to work in the tobacco warehouse city of Wilson where we lived with the pastor in the rectory of St. Alphonsus Church, one of the last surviving African American parishes in the state.

On one occasion during the orientation program at the Raleigh Catholic Center, Bishop Joseph Gossman, still a young man as bishops go, babysat our eight-year-old son, Billy, and our six-year-old daughter, Amy, while Mom and Dad attended a workshop. In Wilson, since there were no other children in the program, Billy and Amy played with the black children of the neighborhood and the Mexican children in the migrant housing. Coming from an affluent Long Island, New York community, North Carolina was for the children an experience that had a profound impact on their lives. Both of them have learned Spanish, spent considerable time in Latin America, and entered service careers.

Throughout the course of two months we traveled out to the rural camps, some consisting of black men and others of Mexican families. Our assignment was to do what we could to help the people, including driving them to town to apply for food stamps or to go to a clinic. On one occasion I visited in the hospital a young man who had fallen off the back of a truck. Here he was, far from his Mexican home, laid up with a fractured skull, looking up at a stranger who spoke but imperfect Spanish.

Back home in New York, Ann and I resumed our college teaching positions and our children returned to their classes. Although we did not return to North Carolina for many years, the state had captured our imagination. As retirement neared, we made several exploratory visits to Chapel Hill and decided to make it our new home. During the process of leaving a long term career and home state, I got the idea of writing a history of the church in North Carolina and wrote to Bishop Gossman. His Vicar General, Father Gerald L. Lewis, responded, welcoming the idea. It turned out that Father, later Monsignor, Lewis, had a strong personal interest in the history of the church and had penned brief histories himself on the occasion of diocesan anniversaries. From beginning to end, without ever putting any restrictions on my work, Father Lewis was supportive. He also read a complete draft of the manuscript and made a number of valuable suggestions. Were it not for him, I doubt if this book could have been written, and it is with warm gratitude that I dedicate it to him.

Much of the research took place in the small room in the Catholic Center that houses the diocesan archives. There, Bradley Blake, the archivist, served as gracious host and competent guide. It was during dozens of visits to the archives over the course of several years that the Church's past, like a ship gradually emerging from the fog, came to life.

Other archivists were helpful as well, especially Johanna Mims of the Charlotte Diocese, Father Paschal Baumstein, O.S.B. of Belmont Abbey, Sister Mary Andrew Ray, R.S.M. of the Sisters of Mercy Belmont Community, and Brother Kevin Dargan, MM of Maryknoll. Librarians at the North Carolina Collection in the Wilson Library on the University of North Carolina campus in Chapel Hill were invariably friendly professionals. George Cobb, Cynthia Barnes and Sherill Beason of the Charlotte Diocese helped locate maps and photos, as did John Strange, editor of the *NC Catholic*.

However, the real flavor of the church was communicated to this outsider by a number of North Carolina priests, religious, and lay men and women. They welcomed a stranger into their homes or were interviewed by phone, candidly sharing their experiences and perspectives. It was through my contact with them that life was breathed into archival documents. As for the clergy with whom I spoke, two pioneers have already gone to their reward — Monsignor James E. McSweeney and Father Charles Mulholland. Other priests to whom I owe a debt of gratitude include Msgrs. James R. Jones, Joseph Showfety, and Thomas P. Hadden, and Fathers J. Paul Byron, Roberto Keenan, George M. Kloster, Joseph G. Vetter, Bernard E Shlesinger, Mark J. Betti, Donald F. Staib, Donald Baribeau, M.S., and Daniel Quackenbush, O.F.M.Conv. Father Stephen C. Worsley, himself a skilled historian, made available to me his extensive collection of materials and shared with me his views on the early history of the church in the state.

The women religious include Sister Dolores Glick, M.H.S.H., Sister Rosemary McNamara, S.U., Sister Loretta Jean Schorr, C.D.P., and Sister Lois MacGillivray, S.N.J.M. Others who broadened my sense of the church in various sections of a vast state were Don and Marion Kaple, Paul and Karen Fredette, Fran Salone-Pelletier and Jean Pelletier, Sue and Vince Vilcinskas, John Ranalli, Julian Miller, Hedwig "Margie" Hewett, Sharon Roberts, Matt Doyle, Hazel Moore, and the late Mary Dowling

A special acknowledgement is due to Terry Jackson, D. Min., director of the Office of Evangelization of the Diocese of Raleigh. Not only was Terry a valued source of information, but he became a good friend as well. What otherwise might have been rather impersonal visits to diocesan headquarters, were transformed into much needed occasions of personal renewal.

Leaving the best for last, Ann, my wife of more than thirty years, has been not only a skillful editor who has read and critiqued every word of this book, but a loving support and companion. Research and writing are fundamentally solitary occupations; a partner like Ann is an antidote to loneliness.

Although these and other generous men and women had input, I accept full responsibility for what is recorded here.

Chapel Hill, North Carolina
December 2002

The Author expresses his gratitude to Bishop F. Gossman of the Diocese of Raleigh for authorizing the use of funds from the Nanny Gary trust to help defray the costs of preparing the manuscript for publication.

Photo Credits
Most of the photos appear through the courtesy of the Raleigh Diocese Archives, the Charlotte Diocese Archives, the *NC Catholic* and the *Catholic News & Herald*. Several from the Vicariate Apostolic period are the property of the Belmont Abbey Archives. The photograph of the Sister of Mercy is the property of the Sisters of Mercy, Belmont Community. The photograph of William Gaston is from the North Carolina Collection of the University of North Carolina, Chapel Hill. Acknowledgement is made of individual photos by Blackstone Studios, John G. Hemmer, Ray Rouser, the US Navy, Charles Cooper, Paul A. Fredette and Burnis Batchelor. The author photo is by Lifetouch Church Portraits.

Introduction

The story of Roman Catholicism in North Carolina is one of three centuries of frustration followed by three decades of rapid growth. Like a tree that seemed to be dead and then burst into bloom, the Church has seen its branches spread from the ocean to the mountains. Nevertheless, problems persist, not the least of which is the shortage of clergy, a situation aggravated by the clergy abuse scandals of 2002.

Admittedly starting from a small base, the Catholic population of the state has doubled and then doubled again since the 1960's. New churches in Charlotte and Raleigh are no sooner built than they prove to be too small. Even in rural areas, traditionally uncongenial to Catholics, an influx of Latinos has energized formerly sleepy country churches.

But hidden behind today's prosperity is yesterday's struggle. Just as it is difficult to believe the depth of racial discrimination that pervaded the state until recently, so also is it difficult to believe that anti-Catholicism profoundly infected Southern life until well into the 20th century. Indeed, as is explained in Chapter Five, until 1835, the North Carolina state constitution excluded Catholics from public office. The dramatic change in sentiment in the state is suggested by the fact that in the year 2000, a Catholic was elected governor with barely a ripple of comment as to his religious affiliation.

In light of the improved conditions in North Carolina, both with reference to the oppression of African Americans and to the venom of anti-Catholicism, it may seem indelicate to dig up the decaying bones of our misguided ancestors. But history is important, as embarrassing and distasteful as aspects of it may be. To live in the light of truth is to acknowledge the dark corners of the past as well as to celebrate the glories.

The majority of today's 300,000 North Carolina Catholics are newcomers, part of a new invasion of the Tar Heel State. This time, unlike in the Civil War, the invaders have remained and proceeded to transform the local culture, not unlike the barbarians who in the fourth century changed the Roman world, or the Europeans, who in the seventeenth century overwhelmed the indigenous populations of North America. The contemporary invaders are not soldiers with guns, but rather three categories of peaceful migrants, each coming for distinct reasons. Despite their different places of origin, languages, and economic status, many find themselves converging on the same Catholic churches.

One contingent of new arrivals is young professional families, attracted by the career prospects that present themselves in an expanding economy. They buy homes, look for good schools for their children, and troop off to mass each Sunday, finding the church an anchor of respectability and a source of consolation in an often stressful new world. A second group is comprised of well educated, affluent retirees drawn by milder winters, lower taxes, and ample golf courses. They offer their talents as parish volunteers and find in the church a family-like community. The final regiment of the silent army consists of Mexicans, Vietnamese, Koreans, and other refugees from poorer or war-ravaged countries who, like waves of immigrants before them, grasp the lower rungs of the economic ladder and seek from the church a linguistic and cultural base on which to ground themselves.

Many of the recent arrivals come from areas with large Catholic populations and are unaware of the long winter that preceded the present springtime of the Church in North Carolina. A fortunate few come to know Catholic "old timers," men and women who lived through the lean days, when Catholics were looked upon askance like the practitioners of some exotic cult. Their numbers were always small, but their tenacity was strong. Clinging to their faith in a hostile environment, they huddled around their priest, and if they were lucky, attended a school where sisters taught them their catechism along with the ABCs. As late as 1950, there were scarcely 20,000 Catholics in the entire state, ½ of 1% of the population.

By contrast, today several parishes have upwards of 10,000 members each. One of them is St. Matthew, a fifteen-year-old congregation in a developing Charlotte neighborhood. Unless it is split, St. Matthew will soon have as many Catholics as there were in the entire state 60 years ago. Furthermore, St. Matthew is typical of hundreds of Catholic parishes on the outer ring of scores of American cities. Located across Ballantyne Commons Parkway from a sprawling Target store that anchors a regional shopping center, St. Matthew itself is like a religious Target or Wal-Mart, a superstore of the spiritual, a magnet for thousands of restless "shoppers." Less than a mile away, office parks are cathedral-like in their own right, with arches spanning the entrances to the headquarters of business empires. In all directions, the raw earth has been churned up for the scores of housing developments that shelter in fragile prosperity the families that power the North Carolina economy. For its part, St. Matthew is a proud participant in this maelstrom of seemingly ceaseless growth. It boasts that it is the largest Catholic church in the Carolinas.

In the recently completed church that seats 2,000 worshipers, smartly dressed worshipers pray that the bubble of success not burst. Near the small Eucharistic chapel behind the main sanctuary is a note-book in which people can write intentions for which they request prayers. In the neat handwriting that suggests a parochial school educa-tion, a woman has written, "That Tom may find a job soon, a good job."

Far to the east of Charlotte, Pamlico County lies in the coastal region of the state, hugged by the Neuse River and Pamlico Sound. Whereas the city of Charlotte alone has more than a dozen Catholic churches, there are none in all of Pamlico County. Until recently, none was needed. Now, however, the little fishing village of Oriental has attracted two categories of Catholics: Northern retirees, tanned from days spent cruising on their boats and Mexicans, tanned from their days laboring in the fields or walking to the seafood processing plants where they work for minimum wage. For these two diverse populations, the Oriental United Methodist Church serves as temporary home. Once a week, a priest drives the thirty miles from the nearest Catholic church, St. Paul in New Bern. He celebrates mass in Spanish, the reasoning being that the English-speaking people could drive to New Bern for liturgy if they wanted to, whereas the poor Hispanics could not.

These are typical scenes from the Catholic Church in North Carolina today. The present book is an effort to reconstruct the past from which the contemporary church has emerged. Some of the guiding questions are: What were the conditions in which Catholics lived at a given period of time? How was their communal life organized? What was their relationship to the larger political and cultural world? What strategies did Church leaders use to advance the Church's cause? How did what was going on in the larger Church impact on its North Carolina branch?

The story of Catholicism in North Carolina is especially intriguing because it was the last state in the union to be raised to the status of a diocese, a development that occurred in 1924. Not coinci-dentally, North Carolina long had the distinction of being the state with the lowest percentage of Catholics in its population. Even today, bishops cannot resist referring to their "missionary diocese," a term which conjures up images of far-off Africa and Asia. In fact, as will be seen in Chapter Seven, North Carolina's most famous priest, Father Thomas Price, after twenty-five years of trying to convert North Carolinians, went off to China where he had considerably more success. The question must be addressed: Why was North Carolina so resistant to the Roman Catholic Church?

Originally, North Carolina was lumped together with South Carolina and Georgia as a single diocese. Chapters Four and Five relate the story of the first, and arguably the greatest bishop North Carolina has ever had, John England. In the 1820s, enamored of the American Constitution, he wrote a Constitution for the Catholic Church and had it ratified by the scattered communities of his vast jurisdiction. England instituted a form of "democratic" church in North Carolina that expired with him in 1842, and would not be revived for more than a century.

John England was deeply involved in the national debate over slavery. Unfortunately, in line with most other contemporary Catholics, he defended the institution. As if in punishment for its cowardice, the Catholic Church in North Carolina was virtually destroyed during the Civil War. Chapter Six relates the experience of Bishop, later Cardinal, Gibbons as he worked to reestablish the church in the rubble, depression, and bitterness that followed the War Between the States.

Gibbons was like a passing meteor in North Carolina, quickly moving on to more prestigious posts. On the other hand, Leo Haid, abbot of the Benedictine monastery at Belmont, governed the church in the state for thirty-six years, the longest tenure by far of any bishop, and one of the most contentious. Chapter Seven shows how much Haid accomplished and how little he was appreciated. At his death in 1924, the Diocese of Raleigh was born. Chapter Eight tells how the early bishops attempted to develop a church, which at its inception counted but 6,000 members in the entire state.

By 1972, the state's Catholic population had increased to 70,000, leading to the establishment of a second diocese, Charlotte. Chapter Ten relates how a post-Vatican Council II diocese was organized, under the leadership of a kindly, down-to-earth bishop, Michael Begley.

Not only are most of the Catholic lay people "outsiders," but so also have been the majority of priests and sisters who have worked in the state. As a mission territory, the Church in North Carolina has had to rely on men and women willing to accept the hardships of ministering in an area that yielded few rewards. While Chapter Nine recounts the lives of some of the pioneering diocesan priests who labored under the harsh conditions that prevailed in the first half of the 20th century, Chapter Eleven relates the contributions of their counterparts, members of religious orders, particularly women religious, who were often overlooked.

As is true of the Catholic Church throughout America, so in North Carolina, race and ethnicity were significant factors. Chapter Twelve examines the status of African Americans, Latinos, and other minority groups in the increasingly diverse church.

The book begins with the conflicted career of Bishop Vincent Waters, whose twenty-nine year tenure bridged the pre and post Vatican II periods, and stands as the pivotal period in the Church's history. Chapter One describes Waters' participation in the Civil Rights movement of the 1950s, how without his seeking such attention, he was catapulted to national attention in the early days of the struggle to eliminate racial segregation. Chapter Two describes the often abrasive and authoritarian style he employed in his single-minded determination to develop the Church in the state. Chapter Three shows the unfortunate fact that many of the priests and nuns initially attracted to North Carolina because of admiration of Waters' stand on Civil Rights, in their anguish at his resistance to the reforms of Vatican II, called on him to resign.

Indeed, monumental changes have taken place in the Church in the past forty years, not just changes that can be seen, such as revised rituals and nuns not wearing habits, but in the invisible world of ideas. The Catholic Church, which sometimes uses the image of a "rock" to suggest how strong it is, found itself "rocked" as never in its history, not by enemies out to destroy it, but by its own members out to restore it. Chapter Thirteen describes how the new vision has been incorporated into contemporary church structures, most particularly through the implementation of the concept of collegiality, the acknowledgement that all church members have a right to participate in decision-making.

William Gaston (1778-1844) was so prominent a public figure in his day that a city, a county, and a lake have been named in his honor. He authored the official state song, served on the state Supreme Court, and guided the constitutional reform that lifted the ban on Catholics holding public office. Gaston might also be considered the Father of North Carolina Catholicism. He served as legal advisor, friend, and host to Bishop England, contributed generously to building the state's first Catholic churches, and was the loving widowed father of his children. Despite the fact that Gaston and his family seldom had the ministrations of a priest and never in their lives belonged to the type of faith community that Catholics today take for granted, he persevered unwaveringly in the faith.

What would Judge Gaston think were he to visit St. Matthew Church in Charlotte and see that enormous structure filled with 2,000 Catholics? What would he make of the mass conducted in Spanish just down the sea road from his New Bern home? Without doubt he would be pleased that the Church that he loved was prospering in the state that he loved.

Chronology

1775   Alexander Gaston of New Bern marries Margaret Sharpe, an English Catholic, forming the first known Catholic family in the state.

1778   William Gaston is born in New Bern.

1820   Diocese of Charleston, South Carolina, is established, embracing South Carolina, North Carolina, and Georgia. John England is appointed bishop.

1821   Bishop England makes his first trip through North Carolina, visiting Wilmington, New Bern, Washington, Edenton, Raleigh, Fayetteville, and other settlements.

1822   Father Anthony O'Hannan is the first priest assigned to North Carolina. Rome approves Bishop England's "Constitution."

1828   The first Mass is celebrated in a Catholic church in the state -- the unfinished St. John in Washington.

1829   The first parishes are established in the state -- in Fayetteville and Washington.

1835   Gaston is instrumental in amending state constitution to allow Catholics to hold public office.

1840   Bishop England writes letters to U.S. Secretary of State defending slavery.

1842   Bishop England dies at the age of fifty-five.

1844   Gaston dies in Raleigh at the age of sixty-five. The
        Church of St. Paul is dedicated in New Bern by Bishop
        Ignatius Reynolds, England's successor.

1847   St. Thomas Church in Wilmington is dedicated.

1851   St. Peter Church in Charlotte is dedicated.

1858   Bishop Patrick Lynch heads the diocese of Charleston and
        during the Civil War is emissary for the Confederacy.

1868   Vicariate Apostolic of North Carolina is established with
        Bishop James Gibbons as first Vicar.

1869   Gibbons visits the young convert-author Frances Fisher
        (Christian Reid) in Salisbury. The Sisters of Mercy open a
        school in Wilmington.

1871   Newton Grove doctor, John Carr Monk, and his family are
        received into the Church by Gibbons.

1872   Gibbons is transferred to Richmond, Virginia, and North
        Carolina's few hundred Catholics are left in a state of drift.

1886   Thomas Frederick Price, first native-born North Carolina
        diocesan priest, is ordained in Wilmington.

1888   Leo Haid, O.S.B., abbot of newly established Belmont
        Abbey, is appointed Vicar Apostolic.

1891   Christopher Dennen begins forty-four year tenure as
        Wilmington pastor.

1892   The Sisters of Mercy locate their motherhouse in Belmont.

1897   Father Price opens an orphanage at Nazareth, near Raleigh,
        and begins effort to establish a community of priests for
        converting the American South.

1904   Michael Irwin becomes Newton Grove pastor. In 1928 he is transferred to New Bern where he dies in 1952.

1905   Isaac Kannon, immigrant from Lebanon, arrives in North Carolina. Eventually he and others are instrumental in founding St. Eugene parish, Wendell, one of many North Carolina churches established by Lebanese Catholics.

1906   William F. O'Brien founds Immaculate Conception parish in Durham where he remains until his death in 1960.

1910   Creation of the diocese-like *abbatia nullius* by the Belmont Benedictines angers the diocesan clergy. Father Price leaves North Carolina to establish Maryknoll.

1917   Josephite priests begin serving in black parishes.

1924   Abbot Haid dies and the Diocese of Raleigh is established.

1925   William Hafey of Baltimore is appointed the first bishop of Raleigh and uses the newly constructed Sacred Heart Church as his cathedral.

1937   Andrew Graves, SJ begins his forty-seven-year ministry in sparsely populated mountain area. Bishop Hafey is transferred to Scranton, Pennsylvania and succeeded by Eugene J. McGuinness.

1944   Bishop McGuinness is transferred to Oklahoma City.

1945   Vincent S. Waters is appointed third bishop of Raleigh.

1953   With substantial media attention, Bishop Waters integrates the Newton Grove parishes.

1958   Thomas P. Hadden is the first African American ordained a priest for Raleigh.

1959   Joseph L. Howze, the second African American priest for
        North Carolina is ordained. In 1972 he is named auxiliary
        bishop of Natchez-Jackson, Mississippi. In 1977 he
        becomes the first African American to head an American
        diocese in the 20th century.

1969   Post-Vatican II conflict culminates in a number of Raleigh
        priests calling on Bishop Waters to resign.

1972   The Charlotte Diocese is established with Michael J.
        Begley as bishop. *Centro Catolico Hispano*, the first
        Catholic program for Hispanics in North Carolina, is
        opened in Charlotte

1974   Bishop Waters dies as the Raleigh Diocese celebrates its
        fiftieth anniversary.

1975   F. Joseph Gossman becomes fourth bishop of Raleigh.
        Pastoral letter: *This Land is Home to Me*, is issued by
        Bishop Begley and other Appalachian region bishops.

1982   The Seventh Diocesan Assembly continues the process of
        organizing the church in Charlotte. Bishop Gossman issues
        "The Collegial Church."

1984   At age 75, Bishop Begley retires and is succeeded by John
        F. Donoghue as bishop of Charlotte. Three women
        religious are appointed administrators of parishes in the
        diocese of Raleigh.

1992   John Riedy is named the first lay Chancellor of the
        Raleigh Diocese.

1993   Bishop Donoghue is transferred to Atlanta and succeeded
        by William G. Curlin.

2002   Development campaign raises $57 million for the Raleigh
        Diocese. Clergy sex scandal affects both dioceses.
        Reaching age 75, Bishop Curlin resigns.

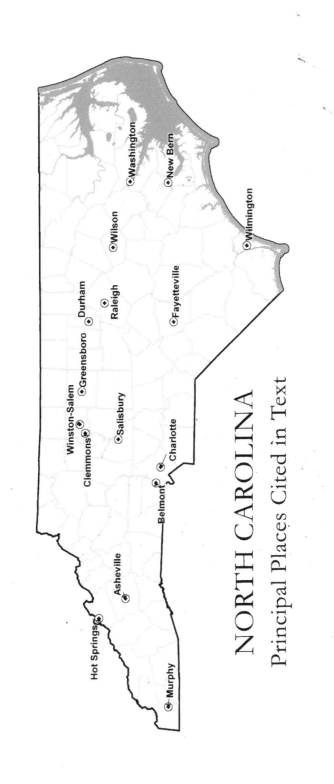

NORTH CAROLINA
Principal Places Cited in Text

Part I

The Bridge to the Modern World

Vincent S. Waters' tenure as bishop of Raleigh (1945-1974) was the linchpin that bound together the two major periods in the history of the Catholic Church in North Carolina. What preceded him was struggle and failure; what followed him has been growth and success. In his own life there were elements of both. Because of the significance of Waters for Catholicism in the state, separate chapters will be devoted to three major features of his career, namely, his role in the civil rights movement, his contributions to the development of the church, and his resistance to the changes unleashed by the Second Vatican Council.

*   *.   *

When the history of the Catholic Church in North Carolina is written, Bishop Waters will be the dominant figure because of his vision and dedication.

• Michael J. Begley, Bishop of Charlotte, 1974

Chapter One

Bishop Waters & Civil Rights

There is no segregation of races to be tolerated in any Catholic Church in the Diocese of Raleigh. The pastors are charged with the carrying out of this teaching and shall tolerate nothing to the contrary. Otherwise, all special churches for Negroes will be abolished immediately as lending weight to the false notion that the Catholic Church, the Mystical Body of Christ, is divided.

---Bishop Vincent S. Waters, June 12, 1953

Nineteen fifty-three was a good time to be an American and an especially good time to be an American Catholic. Although the Korean War produced daily lists of casualties and there was anxiety about the atomic bomb threat posed by the Soviet Union, Dwight D. Eisenhower presided over the prosperous, self-assured nation that had won World War II and was experiencing a period of unprecedented economic expansion. The Baby Boom then at its peak attested to the confidence families had in the future. Schools were crowded, suburbs spreading inexorably across the landscape, marriages stable, crime rates low, and that new wonder, television, was bringing happy faces into more and more living rooms.

Participating in the spirit of optimism was the Catholic Church, moving rapidly out of its defensive immigrant status into the American mainstream. On May 29 that year, a *New York Times* article on the Catholic Church bore the headline: "Big '52 Gains in US." The Catholic population passed 30,000,000 and for the seventh consecutive year conversions exceeded 100,000. More than 45,000 priests ministered to the growing flock.

That same month, Francis Cardinal Spellman officiated at the wedding of Eunice Kennedy and Sargent Shriver at New York's St. Patrick's Cathedral. Among the ushers were the bride's three brothers,

Senator John F. Kennedy, Robert, and Edward. The Cardinal himself had just been honored by the Catholic War Veterans as "America's Outstanding Citizen." In Washington, the Catholic senator, Joseph McCarthy, continued his controversial campaign to ferret out communists from positions of power and influence. Supporting his efforts, the *Pilot*, weekly publication of the Boston Archdiocese, criticized Harvard University for not dismissing faculty members who, as former communists, had supported "the cause of tyranny." Catholics were growing in numbers, power, pride, and patriotism.

Not far from Harvard, a young Boston University divinity student was completing his doctoral studies, planning his wedding, and preparing to assume a pastorate in Montgomery, Alabama. Martin Luther King, Jr. never dreamed that the following year he would be thrust into national prominence as he assumed a leadership role in the Montgomery bus boycott sparked by the refusal of Rosa Parks to relinquish her seat to a white man.

In 1953 there was no Civil Rights movement, only entrenched patterns of racial segregation which, by and large, were accepted as part of the American way of life. Though there were some cracks in the wall of complacency -- The United States Army had been integrated and Jackie Robinson was playing baseball with the Brooklyn Dodgers -- there was no national consciousness, no mobilization of forces to overthrow the legacy of suppression and rejection, no media spotlight to illuminate the darker corners of a thriving nation. Yet, one place where such a spotlight began to beam was the quiet rural town of Newton Grove, North Carolina. In hindsight, the confrontation in Newton Grove would be seen as a prelude to the Civil Rights movement.

Early on the morning of Sunday, May 31, 1953, Vincent S. Waters, the 49-year-old Catholic bishop of Raleigh, drove the fifty miles down State Road 50 determined to force a hostile white congregation to permit black Catholics to worship with them. A man who acknowledged that he had been prejudiced in his younger years, now risked bodily harm and the rejection of his parishioners in order to bring about a change which he had become convinced was just. However, for Waters, the issue was also one of authority. Consistent with his personality and his understanding of his role as bishop, he was adamant in his insistence that he be obeyed. Having received reports that the Newton Grove priests were wavering on enforcing his order that the black church be closed and its members absorbed into the white congregation, he decided to do something unprecedented. He would make a surprise personal appearance and do the job himself.

This forthright action would gain for the usually media-shy Waters widespread attention. Hundreds of newspaper articles would relate the story of what happened that hot Sunday morning, and Waters would become the darling of liberal Catholics who rejoiced in the fact that one of their bishops had assumed leadership in the cause of racial justice. The man who for eight years had been hardly known outside his own jurisdiction, one of the least populous Catholic dioceses in the country, would now be a national celebrity.

Paradoxically, as will be seen in Chapter Three, fifteen years later Bishop Waters would have a second media moment, one in which some of the same people who had cheered him earlier would then castigate him as a rigid reactionary who opposed the liberalizing momentum unleashed by the Second Vatican Council. This issue was brought to a head when Waters' intransigence to change prompted a number of his own priests, men attracted to serve in North Carolina because of the reputation the bishop had gained in his civil rights movement, to call for his resignation. As one Raleigh priest sadly put it, "Our hero had turned into Nero."

Vincent Waters, who served as bishop of Raleigh from 1945 to 1974, is not only a pivotal figure in the history of the Catholic Church in North Carolina, but a man who is representative of the tensions which enveloped the Catholic Church in general during the second half of the Twentieth Century. Change was crashing like a tidal wave across a church which for centuries had prided itself in holding fast to practices and ideas which many had come to consider impediments to growth rather than symbols of stability. The institution was being challenged to reform itself while holding fast to what was essential. But what was essential? What should be changed? Conflicting visions of what the Catholic Church should be like clashed on every level of church life.

Due to the dominating presence of Vincent Waters, North Carolina was one arena in which the universal church's agonizing process of renewal was experienced with special intensity. Waters was a man who could inspire highly motivated men and women to flock to North Carolina at a time when the state was seen as fertile mission territory for Catholicism and, subsequently, could drive out some of those same men and women when they failed to accept his style of leadership.

Waters embodied the ambivalence which characterized the church. He was a man standing on a bridge between two worlds. One leg was securely anchored in past, while the other searched for a foothold in the future. To understand Vincent Waters is to grasp something of the mentality which characterized highly committed churchmen of an age now past, men who in hindsight seem rigid and narrow minded, but who exhibited a tough, uncompromising spirit which for the time and place in which they lived might have been appropriate. In any case, Vincent Waters left behind a church which was both firmly established and deeply fragmented.

Early Life of Vincent S. Waters

Most of the priests and all of the early bishops of North Carolina had been outsiders, men viewed by the Protestant majority in the state as representatives of an alien faith with little understanding of southern culture. This charge could not be leveled against Vincent Waters, a man who referred frequently to his southern roots in an effort to win credibility among North Carolinians, Catholics and non-Catholics alike.

Waters was born August 15, 1904, in Roanoke, Virginia, a small city set in the mountains in the western part of the state.[1] In this peaceful setting, where the loudest sound was that of a steam-powered locomotive hauling a string of freight cars through town, Waters was shaped by two powerful forces. On the one hand, he took on the taciturn, cautious, wary characteristics of a mountaineer, a man who embraced isolation and privacy like a black bear, silently roaming the woods secure in the knowledge of his strength. On the other hand, he was a Catholic in a Protestant world, an outsider in his own native place, not fully accepted in the close knit world of the Appalachian region, which held to its ancient rural ways even as the rest of the country moved confidently into the industrial age. Like many other Catholics of the region, Waters embraced his religion with all his heart. It would be his consolation, the bedrock of his identity.

What gave special zest to the life of a young Catholic like Vincent Waters was the sense of being a pioneer on the frontier of faith, one of a small band of true believers who were challenged to preserve their religion in the face of great difficulties. Often the pastor of St. Andrew's parish in Roanoke would remind his congregation of working class families that they lived in an area where the Catholic Church had not yet gained a substantial footing. In fact, until well into the twentieth century, much of the South, including the Appalachian region and all of North Carolina, were officially designated as mission lands by Rome and eligible for financial assistance from more affluent areas of the church. As recently as the year 2000, a man raised in Charlotte, North Carolina said that when he was a child, Catholics were as exotic as Jews.[2]

The Waters' family beginnings in the United States were typical of how the country was settled and how Catholicism was introduced to an area like Roanoke. In 1850, probably attracted by work on the railroad as it pushed its way further and further into the interior, John Waters, a redheaded Irish immigrant, ventured into what was then the Virginia wilderness and, rather than moving on to a more hospitable area as did most of his fellow immigrants, he established a home, linking himself to the local culture through marriage. As the Civil War ended, the man who would be the bishop's paternal grandfather, married Mary Bell, "a hard shell Southern Baptist" widow, who had lost her husband at the Battle of Seven Pines. Although the religious divide between Catholics and Baptists was wide and deep, Mary converted to the religion of her new husband and a Catholic family was begun.

Vincent's own parents, Michael Bernard Waters and Mary Francis Crowley Waters, were part of the small, mostly Irish American Catholic community, attending mass regularly, socializing with other Catholics, and sending their five children to the parochial school which by this time had been established in the parish. Although Vincent's mother did not live to see her son ordained a priest, his father, a railroad machinist, lived to age ninety, not only attending his son's priestly ordination but his consecration as bishop as well. After this latter event, father and son traveled to Rome for an audience with Pope Pius XII. Addressing the young prelate and his aging father, the pope commented that it was the first time he had received a bishop who brought along his father.[3]

The depth of commitment of the Waters family to the Catholic religion is further demonstrated by the fact that one of Vincent's three sisters, Elizabeth, became a medical missionary with the religious name Sister Mary Michael.[4] Also, young Vincent grew up with a family mentor and role model in the person of his paternal uncle, Thomas Waters, a priest and later a monsignor of the Richmond, Virginia diocese. It was he who financed his nephew's education and in time channeled the younger cleric's career along the path that would lead to his eventual elevation to the episcopacy.

After attending St. Andrew's parochial school in Roanoke, young Waters journeyed by train through the foothills of the Southern Appalachians to the village of Belmont near Charlotte, where Benedictine monks conducted a school for boys consisting of high school and the first two years of college. The rural, monastic setting of Belmont Abbey College was such that the students might have been in medieval Europe. For the most part, the monks were German born or of German descent, men who had with their bare hands transformed a dilapidated farm into an impressive monastic complex. By attending Belmont Abbey College for six highly impressionable years (1920-1926), Vincent Waters was not only linking himself with North Carolina Catholicism but absorbing an understanding of that religion which placed the highest value on discipline, hard work, and unwavering loyalty to Rome.[5]

Further linking the adolescent Waters with the church which eventually he would lead, was the fact that Leo Haid, the president of the college and abbot of Belmont Abbey, was also the head of the Catholic Church in North Carolina. This unusual arrangement had come about in 1887 when it was decided that the few Catholics in the state could not support a bishop. Abbot Haid, as head of the only financially viable institution within the state, had been asked to assume the position of bishop for what was then the Vicariate Apostolic of North Carolina. By the time Vincent Waters arrived in Belmont, Leo Haid had been abbot and bishop for more than thirty years. Photographs show a tall, gaunt man with deep set eyes and a long white beard. In an age before media generated heroes, Leo Haid was as impressive and awesome a figure as most young Catholics were likely to see. Attending liturgical services in the abbey church, Waters would witness the deference paid to Haid by the other monks as the aging prelate presided from the episcopal throne.

All this changed in 1924. When Waters and the other students returned from their summer vacation they found an abbey in mourning, for Leo Haid had died on July 24th. Furthermore, there was considerable speculation as to the future of the church in the state. Since Haid had been bishop of North Carolina for thirty seven years, few Catholics could remember a time when Belmont had not been church headquarters or when the abbot and his fellow monks had not controlled church administration.

Some of the uncertainty was ended just before Christmas when it was announced that the diocese of Raleigh had been established. However, continuing concern about the financial condition of a diocese with only twenty diocesan priests and fewer than 6,000 Catholics resulted in the installation of a bishop being delayed for an additional six months. It would be Waters, named third bishop of Raleigh twenty three years later, who would shepherd the Catholic Church in North Carolina from its initial precarious missionary status into a state of financial, if not spiritual well being.[6]

But first the young Waters had to become a priest, a calling that flowed smoothly from his family and educational background. Upon being accepted as a seminarian by Bishop Andrew J. Brennan of his home diocese of Richmond, Waters was assigned in 1926 to St. Mary's Seminary in Baltimore, Maryland, the oldest and largest school for the training of priests in the United States.[7]

After two years of studying philosophy at St. Mary's, Waters was tapped for an assignment that would have a major impact on his life, including the likelihood that he would enter church administration and be selected as a bishop. Impressed by the student's ability and possibly recommended by Vincent's uncle, who now held several key positions in the diocese, Bishop Brennan sent Waters to Rome for his theological studies.

So, in the summer of 1928, the son of a humble family from the mountains of Virginia sailed to Europe. In one sense his world was expanding, but in a more significant way it became more constricted as he came more totally under the sway of the Rome-based church. Living at the North American College in the shadow of the Vatican, Waters conformed to the strict regimen to which students for the priesthood were subjected, including wearing their dress-like cassocks at all times, avoiding theatrical performances, spending hours in prayer each day and attending classes taught in Latin, a language which he would love and promote even after it had ceased to be the universally prescribed language of Catholic worship.

The Question of Prejudice

And Rome itself had its power. If the Abbey Church at Belmont seemed impressive, St. Peter's and the other churches of Rome were overwhelming. If Abbot Haid had been an awe-inspiring figure, how much more so Pope Pius XI. Vincent Waters may have come from and would return to an area where the Catholic Church was poor and despised, but his four years as a student in Rome, at the very heart of the ancient church, reinforced his commitment to a life of service to that church. This commitment would be his greatest strength and also, as shall be seen, the source of many of his problems as a bishop.

One lesson which Waters learned in Rome was not part of the seminary curriculum but would be critical to his work in North Carolina, in particular to his decision to integrate the state's churches and schools. Although a man who guarded his privacy, at a 1955 Liturgical Conference in Worcester, Massachusetts, Waters told the following story when asked if he himself had ever been prejudiced. The story consisted of encounters which he had had with two black men.[8]

The first experience occurred in Baltimore when, as a young seminarian, Vincent boarded a street car only to have a black man sit down beside him. Having lived his entire life in a segregated world, Waters was so uncomfortable that he immediately got off the car. He wrestled internally with this event for several years, his Southern heart in conflict with what his Christian faith told him was the correct way to think and behave.

The second experience transformed his perspective on race. It happened that a young black man had traveled north from Florida in search of employment. When he arrived in Philadelphia, he was standing outside a Catholic school wondering if there might be any work for him there, when one of the nuns came out and spoke to him. She asked him if he would like to attend the school. The man said that not only was he black, but he was not a Catholic. In a kindly manner, the sister said that there were others like him in the school already. In time, impressed with the love and generosity of the nuns, the man became a Catholic. Furthermore, he was so enthusiastic about his newfound religion that he announced that he wanted to become a priest.

After speaking with several priests, and being informed that it was not likely that any American bishop would accept him, the man decided on a bold strategy. He had been told that an order of priests based in Rome was accepting black candidates. With little more than his determination, the man obtained accommodations in steerage on a ship bound for Europe. During the voyage he attended and served the masses of several priests who were also journeying across the ocean. When they heard his tale, the priests took up a collection to help the impoverished man reach his destination.

Once in Rome, he naively knocked on the door of the mother house of the community which he had heard accepted black candidates. With no letters of   introduction and completely unknown to the priests there, he was turned away. Eventually, after several other failed attempts, the man was referred to the North American College where he was given employment in the kitchen. It was in this context that Waters became acquainted with the man and learned his story. He was so impressed that his feelings toward blacks were transformed.

What is particularly revealing about this experience is the reason Waters gave for his change of heart. He told his audience that he had come to believe that any black man he met might become a Catholic, even a priest. Waters was first, last, and always a Catholic. For him, the main objective of contact with people was the hope that they would join the church, an unabashedly sectarian viewpoint. In his world, there were only Catholics and people who might become Catholics.

Apprenticeship in Virginia

As was the practice with men studying in Rome, Vincent Waters was ordained a priest midway through his final year of studies. Together with North American College classmates from a number of dioceses, the 27-year-old made his final commitment to the service of the church in the Eternal City on December 8, 1931. As a simplex priest, that is, one who has been ordained but who has not yet undertaken priestly duties, Waters spent the final six months as a student in Rome, returning to Virginia in the summer of 1932. With the nation now in the throes of the Great Depression, Waters reverently celebrated his first solemn mass in Roanoke surrounded by family and friends, not a few of them deeply worried about their financial futures.

Preparation and preliminaries over, Waters undertook his ministry. For thirteen years he worked in Virginia prior to his appointment as third bishop of Raleigh. His first assignment was as assistant to Monsignor Edward Tearney, pastor of Holy Cross Church in Lynchburg, a city somewhat smaller than and situated fifty miles east of Roanoke. Here, for four years Waters served his clerical apprenticeship, becoming familiar with the priestly routines and solidifying his clerical identity. As was true of every novice priest, much of his time was spent saying mass, hearing confessions, instructing couples for marriage, vis-

iting the sick, training altar boys, and teaching catechism to school children. As a preview of the situation he would encounter in North
Carolina, most Sundays he traveled to mission churches in Bedford City
and Oak Ridge. Parishes all over the south had as many as half a dozen
missions, tiny churches in small towns where mass would be celebrated
on occasion for groups of Catholics, sometimes no more than two or
three families in a congregation.

Perhaps Lynchburg brought back memories of Rome, since
both are cities built on seven hills. However, it is not likely that much
time was spent reminiscing. Nor was there time for appreciating the historical riches of Lynchburg, including the house which Thomas
Jefferson had designed and where the statesman stayed when he visited
his plantation in the area. Waters may never have wandered reflective-
ly up and down the rows of tombstones in the city cemetery, final rest-
ing place for more than 2,000 Confederate soldiers, mute reminders of
the conflict which seventy years before had nearly torn the nation in
two. Subsequently, Waters would reveal an interest in history, but only
in so far as it concerned the Catholic Church.

Like most priests, Waters ministered mainly to those who were
already Catholic, with little time for outreach. However, motivated by
the prevailing Catholic belief that "outside the Church there is no salvation," he was anxious to "save" as many people as possible by bringing them into the Catholic fold. As it turned out, his bishop had other
plans for the young cleric, plans that would not only delay this dream of
being a missionary but take him out of parish life and away from direct
service to people. Paradoxically, what seemed like a seven-year detour
in fulfilling his dream increased the likelihood that Waters would be
appointed a bishop, a position which would offer enhanced opportunities for implementing a substantial push for conversions. In 1936,
impressed with the priest's intelligence and energy, Bishop Brennan
appointed Waters his personal secretary and chancellor of the Richmond
diocese.[9]

In these positions, Waters learned every aspect of diocesan
administration and became increasingly influential in the church. He
accompanied his bishop to meetings, attended him at visitations to
parishes, wrote his correspondence, and became his indispensable aide.

However, Waters did not limit himself to these administrative
tasks. For example, in 1941, he coordinated the annual meeting of the
Catholic Conference of the South held that year in Richmond. The

objective of the organization was the development of Catholicity --black and white-- in the South, including the training of leadership, both black and white. The very sparse black Catholic leadership on which Waters exerted an influence included Richmond's first black priest, Theophilus Brown, and Joseph Howze, who would become the nation's second black bishop. In 1977, Howze said that his meeting with Waters "was an act of Divine Providence."[10]

Waters' desire to be released from his desk job and to get back to what he considered the principal work of a priest was granted in 1943 with his appointment as director of the Diocesan Mission Fathers. With two other priests, he set to work evangelizing the state, preaching in the churches, consulting with parish clergy, and designing inquiry programs for non-Catholics. Most of all, he attempted to instill in all the priests a missionary orientation. If theirs was a mission diocese, then they must see themselves as missionaries, just as truly so as if they were in China or Africa.[11]

Then, less than two years later in March 1945, Waters' life was abruptly transformed. Nominated by his mentor bishop, at the age of forty Vincent Waters was named bishop of Raleigh. After his consecration in the Richmond Cathedral on May 15, he moved to North Carolina where he would spend the rest of his life.

A Reluctant Civil Rights Champion

Immediately upon arriving in Raleigh, Waters undertook a whirlwind tour of his far-flung diocese, getting to know his small band of priests and motivating them, as he had the priests in Virginia, to join him in a multifaceted mission outreach program. These activities, to be discussed in Chapter Two, were what the new bishop saw as his primary responsibility. At no time did Waters envision himself as a champion of human rights or as a civil rights leader. Yet, that would be the role that would be thrust on him and which would gain him national attention. It would also, serendipitously, help him marshal resources for his goal of a stronger Catholic Church in North Carolina.

The setting for his accidental projection into prominence was a most unlikely place, a nondescript little parish in the tobacco fields of Sampson County. Waters would have preferred to have avoided the incident, to have dodged the media spotlight, to have continued his work of developing the church. Yet, fate had other plans for the unsmiling prelate who drove into Newton Grove shortly after 7 a.m. on the last day of May 1953.[12]

On one side of what would subsequently be called Irwin Drive, named for Monsignor Michael A. Irwin, a long-time pastor of the parish, several buildings were lined up like sentinels. In the center was a large house flanked by white frame churches, each with its accompanying small rural schoolhouse. The ensemble was completed by a convent for the six Sisters of Mercy who staffed the parochial schools. Two of the sisters taught the thirty-six boys and girls enrolled in the black school, while the other four instructed the seventy-one white students in the other building. The central house, a rambling Victorian with a rickety front porch, was the residence of the Redemptorist priests who staffed the churches, Holy Redeemer for white Catholics and St. Benedict for blacks. For more than seventy years, even before the founding of St. Benedict, the two groups of Catholics had been united by faith but divided by race.[13]

The original nineteenth century church was indeed integrated in the sense that several pews were set aside for black parishioners, who received Communion after the whites. Then, in 1921, Mother Katharine Drexel, a major benefactor of the church in Newton Grove, provided a grant for the construction of a hall "to be used as a place of instruction for Colored People and where they may gather to hear lectures and have appropriate entertainments."[14] It was not Drexel's idea that the hall be used as a church, but in 1939, as part of the movement all over the South to reach out more vigorously to blacks, the hall was converted into a worship space and called St. Benedict. The Redemptorist Fathers, who had assumed responsibility for the Newton Grove parish in 1928 with the reassignment of Monsignor Irwin, believed that blacks could be served more effectively if they had their own church.

It had long been observed with envy that black Protestant churches were thriving centers of religious and social life. It was hoped that similar centers of black Catholic life could be developed. In particular, it was expected that parochial schools, open to Protestant children, would be conduits for channeling young converts into the church. With this vision, numerous communities of men and women made a major commitment of personnel and funds. The prevailing wisdom was that in the rigidly segregated South, separate black churches were advisable.

This was the situation when Bishop Waters became bishop in 1945, one with which he was never comfortable. In 1953 he acted. Although there had been no public expression of dissatisfaction with the segregated arrangement, he ordered that St. Benedict be closed and its members admitted to Holy Redeemer.

What motivated Waters to take such a provocative step? There were three interrelated motivating factors:

1) The bishop had become increasingly uncomfortable with the race-based structure of the diocese. Every city and larger town had separate churches and schools for whites and blacks. At first, Waters gave no indication that he objected to the situation.[15] However, as he had more and more contact with Catholics outside the South, in particular at the meetings of the American hierarchy, he began to question the morality of the arrangement. By 1951, he was expressing his concern in a pastoral letter.[16]

2) The Newton Grove situation was especially glaring, since the two churches were within sight of one another. There could be no arguing, as was done with reference to Raleigh, Wilmington, Wilson, and elsewhere, that the churches were located for neighborhood convenience. Furthermore, the size of the congregations in Newton Grove did not justify two churches. There were about 350 white and fewer than 100 black parishioners.[17]

3) The bishop chaffed at the independence from his control of the religious order priests who staffed Newton Grove and a number of other black parishes. On the one hand, the churches staffed by religious orders were not costing the impoverished diocese any money or personnel. On the other hand, the orders were wont to remind the bishop of their largesse. So, the Newton Grove pastor regularly reported that his community poured thousands of dollars each year into the parish. The catch was that, on the books, the money was listed as "loans" to the diocese. This subsidizing of the parish also was used to justify not paying the annual diocesan assessment on which Waters depended for his many projects.[18]

The Crisis Grows

What became "The Newton Grove Affair" began calmly enough when on April 19, 1953, Waters sent a letter to the Rev. Timothy Sullivan, the Redemptorist pastor, instructing him to merge the two churches on Memorial Day weekend, little more than a month away. When Father Sullivan announced the order from the pulpit, some of the outraged white parishioners contacted the local newspapers. Aware of how volatile the race situation was and anticipating a possible violent confrontation, the national news media picked up the item and Newton

Grove was no longer the local church matter which Waters intended it to be.

As the fated weekend approached, media attention intensified. On May 21, an Associated Press release describing the situation had been sent out, and on the following day *The New York Times* ran an article headed: "Whites in Catholic Church, Newton Grove, protest Bishop Waters order to admit Negroes."[19]

A few days later, the Raleigh paper ran a lengthy article accompanied by pictures of the Holy Redeemer church and of Dr. John C. Monk, the revered founder of the church. Dr. Monk's nephew, also John Monk, was quoted as saying that "the time is not right" for integration. Monk added that his brother, Dr. H. L. Monk of Salisbury, North Carolina had offered to lend financial support in "carrying it to the Supreme Court." D.D. Herring, the proprietor of a grocery store in Newton Grove, a Protestant married to a Catholic, said that "his children will not go to church with colored people." He added, "I think a lot of colored folks, but they ought to have their own churches."[20]

On the 27th, the AP reported that Waters had sent a form letter to Newton Grove church members who had written to him. He told the rebellious parishioners that his concern was for the souls of the members of the two churches and that souls have neither "race nor color."

Nowhere in the press accounts is there any intimation that Waters intended to go personally to Newton Grove. In fact, the Rev. George E. Lynch, the diocesan chancellor and Bishop Waters' close associate, was quoted as saying, "We think it is going to work out. We are going to let the situation take care of itself."[21] However, when Lynch said this, Waters was making his annual retreat at a Catholic facility at Southern Pines, North Carolina. Certainly, as the bishop prayed alone in the little chapel and walked in silence the beautiful grounds, he was thinking about the racial storm which inadvertently he had unleashed. Although he had gone on retreat with no intention of going to Newton Grove, when he returned to Raleigh he decided that the matter had escalated to such an extent that his personal participation was necessary.

At the time, Father Lynch was in residence at the diocesan orphanage called Nazareth, located a short distance from the episcopal residence on Western Blvd. Lynch was to accompany his boss to Newton Grove. Besides apprehension about a situation universally described as dangerous, both men were hungry, observing the rule that required priests to fast from food and drink before celebrating Mass.

Shortly after six a.m., the Bishop drove up to Nazareth and signaled to Lynch to get in. The weather had been unseasonably hot, and already perspiration moistened the clerical collars of the priests as they moved out onto the nearly empty road and headed south.

A Witness to History

One man had seen the two priests depart that morning. Floyd McKay Pope was already at work in the orphanage kitchen preparing breakfast for the nuns and children. Thirty years later Pope would tell his story, not only of that morning but of the fifty years he had worked for the Catholic church. Bishop Waters knew Pope well. Because it was for black men like him that the bishop was risking his life, Pope's story is worth repetition.[22]

The association of the Pope family with the Catholic Church extended back to 1896, when a young priest, Thomas Frederick Price, knocked on the door of Floyd's grandmother's small house across the road from a farm which Price had just bought. He told the surprised woman that he was going to build an orphanage there and that that he was looking for someone to do the laundry. Times were hard and work scarce, especially for black people living on the outskirts of Raleigh which, although the state capitol, was little more than a sleepy small town with minimal economic activity. Attracted to the priest's enthusiasm, yet skeptical, the woman agreed. For the rest of her life she worked in the Nazareth laundry witnessing Price's dream take shape.[23]

Pope's mother followed his grandmother as a domestic worker at Nazareth, which for nearly a century would be home to hundreds of boys and girls. However, although the two women devoted their lives to the church, they themselves never became Catholics, influenced as they were by the prevailing anti Catholicism. As Pope explained it: "It was the bad publicity that the Catholic Church was getting all over the South, in Raleigh and everywhere else that the black folks took up and kinda believed."

Pope himself began what would be his lifetime work in the kitchen in 1933, twelve years before Waters became the bishop. Continuing to reside in the family home across the road, Floyd walked to the orphanage in the dark each morning in order to heat the large pots of water in which he would make the oatmeal for the children's breakfast. In the afternoon, those same pots would be used to boil potatoes.

From infancy, Floyd had been brought to the orphanage by his mother. The Sisters of Mercy who staffed the institution during most of

its existence, held and spoke to and loved the little boy. In this environment of acceptance, Pope became a Catholic at the age of ten, explaining that his generation "learned about the prejudice and the lies that the
southern white ignorant mind was telling about the white Catholics."
Pope remained faithful to the church despite the fact that, by his own
account, he was exploited, required to work seven days a week and not
even given time off to attend Sunday mass. But he saw the nuns working just as long hours as he did and the priests traveling great distances
to their mission stations. As Pope recalled in old age, "In those days
people did not think of days off and vacations. They just worked."

    With reference to Newton Grove, and clearly embellishing his
account with some retrospective exaggeration, Pope said that "the
whole of Raleigh was nervous, the whole South was nervous, the whole
country was nervous because the old Catholic families in the state, in
New Bern, in Wilmington, in Newton Grove, all staunch Catholics,
couldn't see mixing black and white and they blocked the integration."

    Looking out the kitchen door, Pope saw Waters and Lynch
drive away. He knew where they were going and experienced a mixture
of pride and apprehension. Years later, as a philosophical elder, the
cook, reflected that what Waters did that Sunday in 1953, "was one of
the greatest things he ever did. He could have been shot and killed even
by his own people." Concluding his appraisal with characteristic hyperbole, Pope said that "the black folks here thought that Bishop Waters
was one of the greatest men for this state for what he did by integrating
and fighting for the Blacks. He did something like Martin Luther King.
He was a white man that did it for them."

Confronting White Anger

    Aware that there might be trouble that morning in Newton
Grove, Father Sullivan and his assistant, Father Edward McDonough,
had risen early and were preparing to go over to church together for the
7:30 a.m. mass. Despite the rumors to the contrary, they planned to obey
orders and integrate the church. For the first time in many years, there
would be no services held at St. Benedict. The members of the now
shuttered building were told to go to Holy Redeemer. However, the
black Catholics with whom the priests had spoken had expressed apprehension. Most were humble workers, schooled all their lives in submis-
sion to the racist social rules. Not prepared for conflict and doubtful that
the effort at integration would succeed, many told the priests that they

would not risk their lives or those of their children by attempting to attend a service in the white church.

When the dust-covered black car pulled up into the driveway beside the rectory, the Newton Grove priests were startled to see Bishop Waters emerge. Without any polite small talk, the bishop announced that he himself would say the early mass and preach at the later ones. He was taking full command; there would be no waffling or compromise.

In part resentful that Waters didn't trust them but also relieved that the burden of responsibility had been lifted from them, the Redemptorists accompanied the bishop to the church, where he vested in silence in the humid sacristy. Waiting for the white altar boy to ring the bell signaling the start of mass, the bishop leaned against the vesting case, his hands gripping the cloth-covered chalice to be used for the wine during the mass. Finally, promptly at 7:30, the bishop stepped out into the sanctuary, genuflected before the altar, and ascended the three steps. Smoothing the white altar cloth with the palms of his hands, his episcopal ring glistening on his finger, Waters kissed the altar as prescribed, turned around, and took a quick look out into the body of the church as he descended the steps for the Prayers at the Foot of the Altar. Facing him were fourteen whites and twenty blacks, all of them aware that history was being made and equally aware of the risks that they took. At least, they now realized, the bishop who had precipitated the crisis had joined them in the danger.

The mass proceeded without incident. Near at hand stood Father Lynch, accustomed to assisting his superior during liturgical ceremonies and to fretting over details. Today, nervously clasping and unclasping his hands, he cast occasional glances at the congregation as Waters recited the familiar Latin prayers. Through the open windows, cars could be heard arriving accompanied by voices spreading the word that the bishop was saying the mass. The little congregation became more tense as Waters moved from the altar to the pulpit.

In the liturgical calendar it was Trinity Sunday, which falls each year the week after Pentecost. At the time, Catholic priests did not always preach "homilies" based on the assigned reading of the day. They gave "sermons," which might or might not be related to the readings. Not that most parishioners would notice, since the Scripture readings were in Latin. The one exception was that on Sundays, after reading the Gospel in Latin at the altar, the priest would then repeat it in

English from the pulpit. For Catholics not following the mass in an English language missal, this would be the only Bible text they would hear. What the bishop read to the congregation included the words of Jesus,

> *"All power in heaven and on earth has been given to me. Go, there-*
> *fore, and make disciples of all nations, baptizing them in the name of*
> *the Father, and of the Son, and of the Holy Spirit, teaching them to*
> *observe all that I have commanded you. And behold, I am with you*
> *always, until the end of the world."* (Matt. 28:19-20)

Some insight can be gained into the mind of Waters by noting the way in which he reflected on these words. Rather than using them to encourage the brave people sitting before him, the bishop resorted to the imagery of sin, death, and hell, suggesting perhaps his belief that human behavior could best be guided by fear. Waters referred to segregated parishes as the product of "darkness" and said that the time had come for the "light of truth" to be thrown on the immoral system. But what was the "truth"? Waters' answer to this question, although perhaps theologically defensible, could be of little practical help to those interested in changing the social order. What Waters said was, "No matter under what guise he may present himself or what means he might use, there is only one enemy of mankind, of the Church, and of the individual Catholic: that enemy is Satan."

This sermon was vintage Waters. Satan as the enemy was a frequent theme of his letters and sermons, obviously a deeply held conviction and one that was likely to resonate well with people deep in the Bible Belt. However, this otherworldly mind set effectively excluded Waters from significant leadership in the emerging national civil rights movement. As courageous as he might be, he did not point, as would Martin Luther King, to the need for legal and cultural change in the here and now. He also did not extend the issue beyond that of Catholics accepting one another as equals in church. Although certainly the bishop advocated equality in all phases of American society, this is not what he preached. A man reared within the confines of a socially exclusionary Catholic world, he wanted to extend that world, not link it with the much larger world which included Protestants and others. His task as shepherd was to protect his flock from danger, not lead it into the broader pasture of American society.

As Waters continued with the mass, the number of people out-side increased. In the minds of those whites who opposed integrating the church, Waters was the enemy, the one responsible for disturbing their way of life. The crowd, mostly men and including the vice president of the Holy Name Society, shouted threats at those who thought to enter the church. One man was seen writing down the names of those who dared to enter the building. The intimidation would be effective. Only nine black and three white parishioners attended the second mass, conducted by Father Lynch. At the final mass at 11, the only attendees were a dozen white Catholics.

The presence of newspaper reporters further inflamed the crowd, some angry that outsiders were observing what they considered their private concern, others anxious to gain media attention for their cause. An Associated Press photographer who snapped a picture of the scene was pursued by a group of white men in an unsuccessful attempt to destroy his film.

Gaining Access to the Bishop

After the last mass, the irate protesters, getting hungry and feeling frustrated, marched across the grass to the rectory intent on see-ing the bishop. As Father Lynch stood at the door, two or three men rushed the priest. Several women screamed and ran off the porch. Lynch managed to stem the surge after the men had driven him back into the vestibule. Bracing a hand against the door and calling for calm, the priest eventually quieted the crowd and the men were admitted in twos to see the bishop. To all, Waters made the same point: segregation was wrong and would be ended. He said that the order did not come from him; it came from the Bible. One participant, a local farmer, described how the men had to walk down a long, dark corridor to the room where Waters received them, like a king in his throne room. The setting may well have been selected to evoke a sense of awe and respect.

Although there had been no serious violence, the newspapers embellished the event, adding details and further elevating the heroic stature of Waters. For example, one paper spoke of "two burly deputy sheriffs" intervening to prevent violence. It also stated that a group composed almost entirely of church members "stoned the church build-ing, harassed Bishop Waters, manhandled two priests in a brief hand to hand struggle, and threatened news reporters and photographers."[24] Another paper carried two photos of the crowd at the rectory door, accompanied by the heading, "Crowd Attempts to Force an Audience with Bishop."[25]

Although Bishop Waters insisted that for years there had been no segregation in the Catholic churches in North Carolina, the dual church system put the lie to his technically true statement. Now he had taken an unprecedented step, adding action to words. Newton Grove was the first merger of any church, Catholic or Protestant, in the state. Its significance was attested to by the scores of articles which appeared in newspapers throughout the country during the ensuing days. This attention to what was widely described as a breakthrough event elevated tiny Newton Grove into a symbol of victory in the war for racial justice which had just been declared.

Effect of Integration on Newton Grove Catholicism

However, although the symbolic value of Newton Grove was substantial and catapulted Waters to national prominence, the effect on the town itself was devastating. The Sunday following the confrontation very few people attended mass. When a reporter asked what had become of the woman who ran shouting happily from last week's desegregated service, defying the crowd and her friends, he was told: "She'll not be here. Her husband beat the hell out of her."

For their part, the black Catholics, who were supposedly the beneficiaries of the action, quietly drifted away. They had lost something precious, namely their own church with its choir, parish organizations, and leadership. A social network had been destroyed, replaced only with hatred and rejection. Many white Catholics as well became alienated from a church which they felt had betrayed them. The parish of Holy Redeemer virtually collapsed. Its schools were closed because of low enrollment, the Redemptorist priests withdrew, and bitterness simmered beneath the surface for decades. For those directly involved, the triumph of Newton Grove was a pyrrhic victory.

As if to obliterate all traces of the affair, the very name of the parish was changed. Changed once again. At its founding in the 1870's, it had been called St. Mark. Then in 1939, to honor the presence of the Redemptorists, more formally the Congregation of the Holy Redeemer, the parish was rededicated as Holy Redeemer. A jewel in the crown of the Redemptorist missionary efforts, the order invested thousands of dollars each year in Holy Redeemer parish and assigned several priests at a time to staff it. But, as soon as the dust had settled behind the departing priests, the parish became Our Lady of Guadalupe, a name which would prove to be prophetic. Today the majority of the parishioners are Latinos, mainly Mexican farm and factory workers. They sing and pray in Spanish, honoring their patron, unaware of the events half a century before which brought their church to national attention.

A Mandate Without Consultation

Although the outcome was heralded as progressive and in the broader sweep of history contributed to the dismantling of the Jim Crow system, the process by which the churches in Newton Grove were merged can be questioned. That process was a simple one -- issue an order and expect it to be obeyed. Bishop Waters consulted no one in Newton Grove. In particular, the black Catholics had no voice in the matter or even warning that their church was to be closed. No discussion was held with the Redemptorist priests whose ministry was to be so radically affected. No effort was made to identify white Catholics who might be supportive of an integrated congregation.[26] No provision was made to prepare the local community for a move that would disrupt deeply ingrained patterns of thought and behavior. It may be that Waters felt that his incisive, authoritarian approach was the only one that would work, that dialog and consultation would lead nowhere. However, he never verbalized this explanation. All he said was: "I have given an order and expect it to be obeyed."[27]

Although the situations are not completely comparable, a contrast might be noted between Bishop Waters' approach in Newton Grove in 1953 and that of Martin Luther King, Jr. the following year in Montgomery, Alabama. When asked to assume leadership in the bus boycott, the first thing King did was to call a meeting of the black leaders of the city. All voices were listened to, all points of view considered. What emerged was consensus -- and strength. With a broad coalition behind it, the boycott was successful.

The Pastoral Letter on Race

Placed in the spotlight by the Newton Grove incident, Bishop Waters felt the need to elaborate his position on race. Consequently, on June 12 he issued a six-page single-spaced letter to be read in all North Carolina Catholic churches on June 19. This pastoral letter, better than any other document, reveals not only the bishop's ideas on the issue at hand, but how his mind worked.

For one thing, race is not mentioned until the fourth page of the letter. Before that, using the imagery of the Mystical Body, Waters explains that all parts of the body must be connected under Christ, the Head, and the bishops, who are Christ's surrogates. Step by step, the case is built that the unity of the church is contingent upon obedience to legitimate church authority. Waters himself was motivated by such an appeal to the ecclesiastical chain of command and obviously felt that this was the most effective argument to use in dealing with the laity. Obedience was the crucial issue. As an example, he refers to the Church law requiring Catholics to abstain from meat every Friday, arguing that although this rule might be difficult, Catholics observed it "because of the Church's authority binding them under pain of serious sin."

In two sections of the letter, Waters takes a defensive tone. First, to emphasize that the message of the pastoral is not some new teaching, he refers to the letter he had issued two years earlier in which he had said that no Catholic institution was to be segregated.[28] However, that earlier letter had not been accompanied by action. Catholics might hear the principles stated, but as long as there was no enforcement, there was no real threat to their way of life.

Secondly, Waters distances himself from the network of diocesan race-based churches and schools by attributing their existence to his predecessors, who had invited religious orders into the diocese to establish Negro missions. The implication is that he never would have done such a thing and that he is about to dismantle the system. As it turned out, even at the time of Waters' death twenty years later, the process of eliminating segregated facilities had not been completed. It had became clear that the matter was not as simple as it might have seemed. Paradoxically, black Catholics did not want to lose their churches; it was too high a price to pay for a dubious integration.

Furthermore, although Waters must have known that, in the light of Newton Grove, his letter would be reported widely in the press, he does not expand the issue beyond that of integrating Catholic churches. There is no reference in the letter to basic justice, no tone of sensitivity to the plight of oppressed black Americans, no call for dismantling the all-pervasive system of racial segregation.

The Media Reaction

It might be argued in Waters' defense, that it was after all 1953, a time when even a whisper of reform was viewed as incendiary. What the bishop did was break the taboo that existing race arrangements were not to be questioned in any way. There was the fear that any slight breach in the wall would lead to ever more significant changes until the whole edifice collapsed. In such a context, Bishop Waters' letter was revolutionary. This is precisely how the media saw it, and this is how it was received by civil rights leaders throughout the country.[29]

Twice *Time* covered the issue. In the second article, which included a picture of the bishop, Waters was quoted as saying, "our faith is a cure for the virus of prejudice," words, which though quotable, reflect the man's consistent sectarian perspective. Nevertheless, in the early 1950s, Waters stood alone as an American southern bishop who took a stand against segregation.

Delighted to have such a spokesman, integrationists touted his praises. The Jesuit weekly, *America*, said that "the influence of such a forthright attitude on the part of a Catholic prelate extends far beyond the confines of the Catholic Church." The July 1953 *Interracial Review* said: "We believe that Bishop Waters' historical pastoral is another milestone in the crusade for interracial justice." The news agency of the American Catholic bishops said that Waters' letter would serve as a powerful force for good "in nations where communists use the US Negro problem as an example of American exploitation of minority groups."

Black publications joined the parade. An editorial in AFRO said: "We doff our hats to Bishop Waters, a genuine Christian, who is willing to stand up and fight for the doctrine of brotherhood. Unfortunately, men of his caliber are all too few on the American religious scene." A southern Protestant leader termed Waters' statement "the most important thing that has ever happened" in the South's religious history. The Minneapolis *Spokesman*, a black newspaper, said: "In the eyes of Negroes the [Catholic] Church gained a new place in their esteem."

The legendary champion of interracial justice, the Reverend John LaFarge, heaped praise on Waters citing the bishop's "firmness and kindness" in "bringing most of the malcontents over to his side." Later in the year, at a solemn high mass marking the second annual observance of interracial Sunday held at Fordham University in New York, a newspaper picture of "four prominent figures in the interracial movement" showed LaFarge, Waters, and two others. The bishop preached at the service.[30]

Despite the uninvited adulation, Waters was well aware that many would not heed his words, that his letter would not work some kind of magic, that the task of social transformation was only beginning. With an uncharacteristic soft touch, the bishop concluded his letter with the words, "My only sorrow is the fear that I shall not convince you of the wiles of Satan. But I shall be able to convince you if I love you enough, and if you love me enough you will understand." There can be no doubt but that Waters loved the church and yearned to fashion in North Carolina a Catholic people that reflected ever more perfectly the love of God. Perhaps he could have loved them more warmly or embraced them more firmly. But that was not his way. Whether it was the lack of a personal love relationship in his life, or a twist in his personality, or simply the aloof, authoritarian style which characterized many bishops at the time, it is clear that when Waters said "love me," he meant "obey me."

Integration of Schools and Hospitals

Although the pastoral, like the incident in Newton Grove, gained widespread attention, it was soon noted that Waters did not immediately order the integration of parochial schools. Even after the 1954 Supreme Court decision declaring school segregation unconstitutional, Waters was slow to take action, aware that as soon as black children were permitted to enroll in a previously white school, many of the white children would be withdrawn. This is precisely what happened in Newton Grove, where the year following the merger of the churches only six students enrolled in the one school that was opened. Although none of the six were black, the white parents did not want to take any chances. Needless to say, the school did not survive the year.

There was nothing which Waters loved more than the parochial schools. His dream was that of the American Catholic bishops at the time: every Catholic child in a Catholic school. As much as he favored integration, he could not bring himself to take a step which was certain to result in the collapse of the already fragile private school system.[31]

In September 1954, Waters did open Catholic hospitals and *high* schools to Negroes. A letter to school principals said directly, "At this time the mandate does not apply to the elementary schools or colleges." Responding immediately, Cathedral Latin Catholic High School in Raleigh accepted three black girls. At the same time, the two high schools in Charlotte also enrolled several black pupils.[32]

The letter to the superintendents of the four Catholic hospitals: Mercy in Charlotte, St. Joseph's in Asheville, St. Luke's in New Bern, and St. Joseph's in Southern Pines said that they were to "open all facilities of our Catholic hospitals to Catholic Negroes ... and non-Catholic Negroes as far as extra room may permit."

Conclusion

It is difficult in the Twenty-first Century to imagine just how totally and seemingly intractably the system of racial segregation gripped the South throughout the first half of the Twentieth Century. Even after the United States government ordered the dismantling of the American version of apartheid, a largely white supremacist culture devised a creative and cynical array of stratagems to circumvent the law. In this context, what today might seem like very small actions and timid words by a Catholic bishop were truly bold and risky. They contributed significantly to the protracted and painful process of change. The columnist Ralph McGill wrote of Protestants and Catholics alike feeling "the tremors from the Carolina hills" and quoted a Protestant leader as saying: "This is the pebble which will start the avalanche."

Although a reluctant hero, Waters did indeed inadvertently start the avalanche to be propelled forward by a man who, the year after Newton Grove, would prove a much more exciting champion, quickly relegating Waters to the media shadows. Martin Luther King, Jr., even deeper in the bowels of the racist south, in Alabama, undertook the crusade that would transform the American social landscape. His actions would be much more dramatic than those of Bishop Waters at Newton Grove and his spoken and written words more inspiring than those of a pastoral letter.

Nevertheless, it was Waters who came first, and who, for all his limited vision and flawed public relations skills, made many hearts beat with hope at a time when there was so little in which to hope. Without intending to do so, he lit the small flame which others would fan into a mighty blaze.

With a certain ironic justice, Bishop Vincent Waters is buried in the Newton Grove parish cemetery, a few yards from where he had been taunted by parishioners for his stand on racial justice.

Chapter Two

The Dream: A Church in Every County

As Thanksgiving approached in 1924, twin six-year olds, Lawrence and Clarence Hill, arrived at Nazareth, the Catholic orphanage located just outside Raleigh. The boys looked so much alike that the sisters who staffed the institution could not tell them one from the other. For their part, the boys huddled together in the chill afternoon, the loss of their parents almost too much to endure.

For thirteen years the brothers lived at Nazareth observing the rules which guided every move the children made, saying their prayers in the chapel morning and evening, attending the little school which the sisters conducted.

Then, having gone on to college and the seminary, on Thanksgiving Day, 1946 the boys returned to Nazareth as priests. On that day, Father Clarence celebrated his first high mass, assisted by his brother, Father Lawrence, who had been ordained a year earlier.

With perhaps a smile on his face, Bishop Waters sent Father Lawrence to the church of St. Lawrence in Asheville. For his part, the newly ordained Father Clarence went off to the Home Mission Apostolate, based at Whiteville, three hundred miles southeast of the mountain parish of his brother. For years the twin priests working in all parts of the state, were asked "Which one are you?" by friendly colleagues.[1]

*　　*　　*　　*

There were two distinct periods in the Waters years as bishop of North Carolina. The first was characterized by struggles which produced growth and success, the second by struggles which ended in criticism and disappointment. Chapter One related the widely praised role of Bishop Waters in the cause of racial justice, the most visible and nationally significant dimension of that early phase. The present chapter will examine several other aspects of his work during the Forties, Fifties and early Sixties, local initiatives aimed at expanding and strengthening the Catholic institutional presence in the state. They include: building churches, enlisting lay participation, forming priests, and expanding the parochial school network.

Chapter Three will consider the problems which soured the bishop's final years as the Catholic Church underwent the stressful process of reform that was unleashed by Vatican Council II.

*   *   *

On June 9, 1945, just four days after his installation as bishop, Vincent Waters undertook an exhaustive tour of the eastern section of the state, logging over 2,000 miles and visiting fifty-two churches and missions within two weeks. He then turned west and in short order added another 3,000 miles to the odometer of his Oldsmobile. Day after day he traveled to the far reaches of the state. At times, too far from home to return to Raleigh, he lodged overnight with one of his priests. Marking his map and noting where there were churches and asking the priests dozens of questions and checking their books, Waters quickly familiarized himself with North Carolina. Over the course of the next thirty years, he would make it his own.[2]

World War II had ended and the country was returning to peacetime pursuits. Ration books and civil defense paraphernalia were cast aside and economic production redirected from military needs to long-deferred consumer goods. The sound of hammers resounded throughout the nation as houses and schools were constructed for millions of demobilized servicemen and their families. Dreams put on hold during the grim days of the Depression and the bloody years of war were revived. One of those dreams was for churches. In North Carolina, even Catholics, small clusters of men and women clinging to their religious identity in a state slow to share in the nation's prosperity and with little sympathy for adherents of the church of Rome, wanted their own places of worship. As if on cue, along came this young bishop with a plan to make their dreams come true.

On November 14, 1945, in his first trip out of the South since being named a bishop, Waters traveled to Washington, DC for the semiannual meeting of the American Catholic bishops. From his days as secretary to Bishop Brennan of Richmond, he was acquainted with many of his new peers. There were congratulations and friendly slaps on the back. But the well-wishes of the veteran prelates were edged with a knowledge that their tall colleague was facing a daunting challenge. Raleigh was a diocese covering a vast area with fewer than 15,000 Catholics in the entire state. It was the frontier. Buried in the cultural darkness of the Deep South, burdened with stereotypes and poverty, its population had been taught by fundamentalist preachers that the Pope was antichrist and the Catholic religion the instrument of the Devil.

On a very pragmatic level there were but paltry financial resources available, no matter how anxious Waters might be to build churches and schools. The most promising hope was the Catholic Church Extension Society, the organization which Waters was well aware had financed many of the churches in North Carolina. Since its inception in 1905, Extension, which collected money from Catholics all over the country, had been making grants for the construction of modest but serviceable churches in mission areas all over America. To this day scores of churches in many states carry plaques attesting to the bounty of the Extension Society.

Wasting no time, the week after the Washington meeting Waters boarded a train once again, sitting up through the night on an uncomfortable seat watching small towns flash by in the darkness, as he planned his presentation to the Extension Society leaders in their Chicago headquarters. These men were not unfamiliar with zealous bishops and their impassioned appeals. A sympathetic ear but no commitments was what Waters received.

The commitment would come a few months later when at yet another meeting, this time a gathering in New Orleans of the bishops of southern dioceses, a challenge was presented which sent a jolt of excitement through the heart of the usually stoic Waters. Bishop William D. O'Brien, who served as President of the Extension Society for nearly forty years, made the following offer to the bishops: "For each five thousand dollars your dioceses will pledge through the Extension Society to build a church or chapel, the Catholic Church Extension Society will donate another five thousand." Waters went up to O'Brien after the meeting and said, "I'm afraid you are going to be sorry for that statement." To which O'Brien replied, "Oh, no I'm not." Waters concluded the conversation with the words, "Well, you will be hearing from me soon!"[3]

True to his word, just a few months later at the annual meeting of Extension, Waters took O'Brien aside and removed a check from his pocket saying, "Remember your promise to double our money? Well, here's $30,000 for six churches that I hope to build very soon down in North Carolina, and I shall be calling on Extension for $60,000."

Within days of that encounter, Waters received in the mail six certificates worth $10,000 each, payable on demand for building six churches. By mid 1949, churches had been constructed in High Point, Blowing Rock, Jacksonville, Wendell, Mooresville, and Bayboro. Very small churches for sure, and simply furnished, but concrete witness in these towns to an emerging Catholic presence. These frame structures, like so many in the state, were mission outposts usually with only a handful of Catholics. A priest would celebrate mass in these buildings perhaps once or twice a month. The rest of the time they were mute sentinels with a simple sign outside the front door announcing the presence of Catholics in the town.

How did Waters gather so much money in so little time? His answer was that big ideas achieve big results, that even people of modest means can be inspired and rise to the challenge. When Waters told local communities that their $5,000 would earn another $5,000, the money was forthcoming; people wanted their church.

Building Churches, Raising Spirits

North Carolina consists of an even one hundred counties. In the coastal region some are small, the result of jockeying for political power during the colonial period. The original settlements, strung along the water highways which linked them to the outside world, became concerned as pioneers pushed inland, establishing new population centers and threatening the hegemony which the older towns had enjoyed. Additional counties meant additional votes in the legislature. Over the course of more than a century, as the central piedmont region and the mountains to the west were settled, counties were added until the current configuration was fixed with the establishment of Hoke and Avery counties in 1911.[4]

When Waters became bishop of Raleigh, there were Catholic churches in half of the hundred counties. One of his goals, a rallying call to his priests and people as well as to himself, was to establish a church in every county. And so year by year new churches were constructed, more counties ticked off. In the early years, all the buildings were small frame structures, similar to the omnipresent Baptist churches which dot the Carolina landscape like daisies in a summer meadow. In later years, the churches would be constructed of stone and brick and be much larger, now rivaling the substantial Methodist, Presbyterian, and Episcopal churches whose spires dominated the downtown skylines of the larger towns. When Waters died in 1974, three quarters of the North Carolina counties had at least one Catholic church.[5]

The pace of building new churches and schools was especially dramatic during the first decade of Waters' tenure. Between 1945 and 1956, he constructed five high schools, over thirty grade schools, and fifty three churches. A magazine article referred to the "unbounded drive and zeal for the conversion of his diocese" of the "tall, lean man of fifty-two" who headed the most sparsely Catholic diocese in the country.[6]

Challenges Facing the Bishop

A major difficulty in introducing a Catholic presence to remote areas has been the requirement that clergy be male, highly educated, and celibate. As will be seen in Chapter Four, much of the success of Protestant denominations, the Baptists in particular, can be attributed to their less rigorous requirements for ministry. For Catholic bishops in mission areas like North Carolina, one of the most time-consuming and expensive occupations has been recruiting and retaining priests. In this regard, Bishop Waters had great difficulty simply maintaining the number of priests he had when he arrived. **Table I** shows that in the eleven years between 1945 and 1956, the number of diocesan priests increased by one, from 87 to 88. And, as noted above, this was the period during which dozens of new churches were being built. For the most part, there were no priests available to be pastors of these churches; they became missions of the existing parishes, with the overworked priests attempting to provide services in more and more locations.

Table I. **Statistical Profile of North Carolina, 1945-1975**

Year	Diocesan Priests	Order Priests	Total Priests	Seminarians	Converts	Catholic Population
1945	87	78	165	21	433	13,954
1946	86	67	153	20	481	14,109
1947	87	70	157	31	512	16,409
1948	86	77	163	28	511	17,602
1949	85	79	166	31	512	20,060
1950	90	77	169	30	611	22,067
1951	92	76	168	36	597	26,164
1952	94	76	170	31	574	28,600
1953	83	68	161	37	584	32,831
1954	88	77	165	47	769	32,498
1955	88	80	168	42	752	35,060
1956	88	82	170	41	721	31,889
1957	95	72	167	33	659	33,734
1958	88	80	168	34	600	35,323
1959	105	72	177	39	593	37,409
1960	104	69	173	39	519	41,910
1961	113	69	182	31	548	45,148
1962	110	68	178	29	510	45,947
1963	107	68	175	32	543	48,429
1964	111	60	171	30	560	49,954
1965*	126	54	180	27	536	53,242
1966	109	64	173	25	524	56,010
1967	107	68	175	20	516	59,400
1968	101	65	166	17	398	61,211
1969	98	64	162	11	386	63,639
1970	98	57	155	8	437	66,928
1971	92	63	155	8	354	69,428
1972	91	68	159	9	359	69,428
1973	74	66	140	10	322	70,923
1974	79	78	157	N/A	436	74,002
1975	78	76	154	N/A	452	77,834

"Order" priests include externs, i.e., all priests not incardinated into diocese.
* Number of diocesan priests for 1965 clearly not correct; probably a typo.
1945-1971: Data is from *Raleigh Diocesan Census.*
1972-1975: Data is a combination of Raleigh & Charlotte dioceses and taken from *Official Catholic Directory*, which discontinued listing number of seminarians.

The ordination of the Hill twins, related at the head of this chapter, contributed to Waters' dream that North Carolina itself would produce increasing numbers of vocations, lessening the need to rely on candidates from other sections of the country. As it would turn out, the state has never become self sufficient with regards to clergy. To this day, the majority of both the diocesan and religious order priests come from outside North Carolina.

Another problem Waters encountered was the vast expanse of the state. Although, as will be seen, earlier bishops had labored under even more arduous physical conditions, Waters was a hands-on bishop determined to be in direct contact with every corner of the diocese. What he had to contend with, in the era before the Interstate Highway system, was a state which stretched 543 miles west to east. North Carolina politicians are wont to allude to this distance with the phrase "from Murphy to Manteo," referring to the westernmost and easternmost towns. Murphy in Cherokee County, where North Carolina borders Tennessee and Georgia, has the small Catholic parish of St. William. During the summer the church fills to overflowing when visitors to the beautiful mountain region overwhelm the small year-round population. On the other end of the state, tiny Manteo, located on Roanoke Island, where Sir Walter Raleigh's "Lost Colony" mysteriously disappeared in 1587, does not have a Catholic church. However, it is not actually the easternmost town anyway, paired with Murphy more for the sake of alliteration than geography.

The towns on the Outer Banks, bathed by the Atlantic Ocean and threatened by hurricanes, are further east across a bridge from Roanoke Island. For more than 100 miles, a long string of narrow islands serve as a fragile shield for the mainland. Today, the Outer Banks is home to one of the largest Catholic parishes in the eastern part of the state, certainly the longest. Thanks to affluent sun-seeking Northerners who have retirement or vacation homes there, Holy Redeemer parish thrives. In summer, the pastor spends much of his time recruiting vacationing and retired priests to celebrate some of the Sunday masses offered in a variety of venues.[7]

Sleek bridges speed vacationers to the Outer Banks. Early in Bishop Waters' time, only slow-moving ferries linked the mainland with quiet fishing villages, some of whose residents claimed to have witnessed the first flight of Wilbur and Orville Wright on the sands of Kitty Hawk in 1903. By coincidence, a Catholic outpost was established in

1939 on a site in Kill Devil Hills in the shadow of the memorial to the pioneering aviators. A small, unheated building had been constructed on a tract of land deeded to the diocese by one of the two Catholic families on the islands at that time. Here mass was offered during the summer for half a dozen Catholics. In winter, services were held at Tuiford's funeral home in Manteo, where it is said the coffins outnumbered the worshipers. The thousand square mile territory remained a mission of Holy Family parish in Elizabeth City until 1953, when Bishop Waters assigned Father James R. Jones to be the first resident pastor. At the time, there were still fewer than 100 Catholic residents during the winter months.[8]

North to south the state's distances are considerable as well, with Roanoke Rapids near the Virginia border some two hundred road miles from Southport, the southernmost coastal town. Each of these towns had a parish when Waters arrived, and each was visited by him shortly thereafter.

Although scores of small towns like Roanoke Rapids and Southport dot the North Carolina landscape, they are overshadowed by Charlotte and Raleigh, the major population and economic centers of the state. According to the 2000 Federal Census, Charlotte had a population of 540,828 and Raleigh 276,093. Although both cities had grown by over 30% during the decade since 1990, their suburban areas have been growing even faster. For example, Cary, a Raleigh suburb, grew by 115%. The Cary parish, St. Michael the Archangel, with more than 3,000 registered families, has almost as many Catholics as there were in the whole state when Waters became bishop. The city of Charlotte, has more Catholic parishes today than there were in the entire state until the Twentieth Century. One of those parishes, St. Matthew, with over 10,000 parishioners, has twice as many Catholics as there were in North Carolina in 1907.[9]

The situation was quite different in 1945. Charlotte's emergence as the self proclaimed "Queen City" was two decades off. Still, it already had three Catholic churches, the only city in the state with so many. One of them was for black Catholics. For its part, Raleigh had but two churches, Sacred Heart Cathedral for white Catholics, and St. Monica for black Catholics. As late as the 1970s, the number of Catholic churches was somewhat deceptive, since even small towns maintained racially separate facilities. As has been indicated in Chapter

One, Bishop Waters was not comfortable with this situation but for the sake of expediency was slow to dismantle it.[10]

Enlisting the Laity

Although the post Vatican II Catholic Church of the mid-Sixties elevated the status of lay people and promoted ecumenism, Bishop Waters took a step in 1946, which at least superficially anticipated those developments by twenty years. He established the North Carolina Catholic Laymen's Association (NCCLA) with the goal of creating "better understanding between Catholics and non-Catholics."[11] Within months, more than a thousand members had been enrolled from virtually every parish of the state, a remarkable achievement considering the fact that there were only 13,000 Catholics in North Carolina at the time.

At the first meeting of the board of directors, Edward MacClements of Charlotte was elected president of the NCCLA. It was understood that the initial officers were to serve only until the association could hold a statewide convention, at which delegates elected by each parish would choose their leaders in a more democratic fashion.[12] The fledging organization promptly secured the services of Dale Francis, a professional journalist and convert of Waters', to serve as its Executive Secretary. Francis had worked with the *Dayton Herald-Journal* and now, together with his wife, Barbara, was to devote two years to constructing one of the most impressive lay organizations for the era of any diocese in the United States.

The inaugural project of the NCCLA was modest enough. More than 1,500 Catholic books, sent to North Carolina from throughout the country in response to an appeal, were donated to public libraries all over the state. It was hoped that accurate information would counteract widespread myths about the church. With the same goal in mind, Dale Francis became a featured speaker on radio broadcasts sponsored by the Conference of Christians and Jews. As a layman with recognizable credentials, he became increasingly prominent as a spokesperson for the church. Francis's capstone contribution was to serve as founding editor of the diocesan newspaper, the *North Carolina Catholic*, the first issue of which appeared October 6, 1946.[13]

Recalling that there were at most 7,000 adult Catholics in the state, it is remarkable that 25,000 copies of the 12-page inaugural issue of the newspaper were printed and distributed free of charge through all the parishes of the diocese. The entire back page was an appeal for subscriptions at $4 per year. As was to be expected, Bishop Waters urged every Catholic family to subscribe, promoting the weekly as not only a source of information but as a prime vehicle for the transmission of Catholic doctrine.[14]

The *NC Catholic* Shapes its Identity

As was true of all diocesan projects during the seemingly endless period of financial constraints, the fledgling newspaper was produced on a shoestring. In fact, the *NC Catholic* was assembled each week by three people, Dale and Barbara Francis and a typist. Their material came from three sources: syndicated articles, news items coaxed from far flung parishes, and editorials written by Francis.

Certainly to fill space as well as to instruct and inspire, much of each early issue consisted of lengthy articles, such as the series of convert stories titled, "Why I Became a Catholic," the serialization of books, including Hilaire Belloc's *How the Reformation Came About*, and Virginia Sobotka's *The Life of St. Francis of Assisi*. To some extent, the pages of nearly unbroken print made the *NC Catholic* look more like a journal than a newspaper.

As remains true today, parishes were encouraged to submit material. Often what appeared was more suitable for a parish bulletin than a diocesan paper. On one occasion, perhaps embarrassed by the poor quality of the items published, Francis said that the notices about barbecues and novenas communicated the vitality of the Catholic communities.

As far as editorials were concerned, Francis wrote energetically about the evils of the day, in particular what was invariably termed "atheistic Communism." Certainly the most distinctive feature of Catholic journalism after World War II was its championing of morality and its militant anti-Communism. The constant drumbeat for personal and societal morality served to show just how vigorously Catholics, often stereotyped as drunkards and gamblers, were upholders of decency and clean living. The near fanatical condemnation of Communism emphasized the patriotism of Catholics, still suspected of being un-American because of their allegiance to a "foreign power," namely the pope. Any Protestants chancing to read the *NC Catholic* could not fail to be impressed by the vigorous waving of the banners of morality and loyalty.

Diocesan and National Leadership

Although Bishop Waters was constantly on the move, both within the diocese and beyond, the *NC Catholic* was not used primarily as a vehicle for publicizing his activities. Budget constraints did not permit a reporter or photographer to accompany him. However, the paper does suggest the range of his efforts to promote the church and his emergence as a leader in the American hierarchy. The lead article in the very first issue reported that no fewer than three conferences had been held at Nazareth the previous week, featuring what the headline touted as "nationally known Catholics" as speakers. Each of the one-day meetings drew a distinct segment of the professional staff working in southern parishes. Religious sisters attended the Institute for Teachers; some clergy participated in the Annual Conference for Priests in White Work; other clergy, mainly belonging to religious orders, gathered for the Conference for Priests in Colored Work. Over the three days, hundreds of priests and sisters converged on Raleigh. Each group was welcomed by Waters.[15]

Early in 1947, Waters participated in the nationwide observance of the Church Unity Octave held at the National Shrine of the Immaculate Conception in Washington, DC. His "stirring sermon" reflected what the union of Christian churches meant to most Catholics at the time. Employing the theme of the Good Shepherd, Waters urged Catholics to pray for "the return to the fold of non-Catholics" and for the chief shepherd (the pope) who sends out other shepherds (the bishops) "to round up the straying sheep." In the lengthy sermon, Waters worked the image of shepherd and sheep from many angles, stressing that the goal was the return of everyone else to the Catholic fold.[16]

Clearly such a message would not be received warmly by Protestants, certainly not the Baptists who dominated the culture of North Carolina.[17] The tone and perspective does reveal what would remain the position of Waters even after the Vatican Council encouraged a more open and respectful view of other Christian denominations. In line with his discomfort with ecumenical activities, for many years Waters forbade his priests from participating in local associations of clergy, fearful that such collaboration might compromise the Catholic claim to be "the one, true Church."[18]

The Church's understanding of itself was explained by the Rev. Robert Wilken, Ph.D., at a Newman Club supper at the University of North Carolina, Chapel Hill in 1960.[19] Wilken, at the time editor of the diocesan newspaper, said that for Catholics the question of truth and the intellect comes foremost. On the other hand, Protestants tend to give primacy to the will and the emotions "and frequently were confused at the constant insistence of Catholics for TRUTH." He went on to say that Protestants, stressing freedom of thought, "think us weird when we insist that certain positions are 'true' or 'false.'" Using birth control and divorce as examples, Wilken said that for "a strong majority outside the Catholic Church, morality, as well as dogmatic truths, are susceptible to change. Catholic insistence on a 'core of unchanging truths' brings puzzled frowns."

It was often more than puzzled frowns that greeted the insistence of Father Wilken and Bishop Waters that Catholics possessed "core truths." On the contrary, Protestants typically viewed Catholicism as having strayed from the "core truths" by encumbering religion with such non-scriptural beliefs and practices as the infallibility of the pope and near idolatrous devotion to Mary.[20] Although virulent anti-Catholic sentiment had largely subsided by mid-Twentieth Century, it flared up anew when John F. Kennedy was nominated for the presidency in 1960. Paradoxically, it was the warm regard in which Kennedy was held by Americans, particularly after his assassination in 1963, that moderated expressions of anti-Catholicism throughout the country. Also, the open, unassuming manner of Pope John XXIII (1958-1963) won over many Protestants to a more sympathetic view of the Catholic Church.

The Clericalization of the Church

After one year as editor of the *NC Catholic*, Dale Francis was replaced by a young priest, Frederick A. Koch, who in his inaugural editorial "A Change of Hands" gave no explanation for Francis' departure.[21] From this point until well into the administration of Bishop Waters' successor, a priest would serve as editor of the diocesan paper. Although Waters may have felt that a priest could be controlled more easily than a lay person, Rev. Charles Mulholland boasted that while he served as editor he would often slip "liberal" material into the paper. Such behavior may explain Mulholland's short tenure as editor.[22]

Although the diocesan paper quickly passed from lay to clerical control, it continued to be touted as a creation of the lay people of the diocese. The NCCLA itself remained in existence throughout the Waters era but exercised little power and sponsored few significant projects. Superficially, it looked like Bishop Waters was progressive in his encouragement of lay initiative, but in fact the church during his years was overwhelmingly clerical in its leadership. All significant diocesan and parish posts were held by priests. Despite this situation, many priests complained that they were called upon to implement policies, seldom to propose or discuss them. As might be said today, Bishop Waters micromanaged the diocese. His understanding of the episcopate was that the bishop was responsible only to God and the Pope, that he was the general and the priests subordinate officers. As to the laity, their role was to "pray, pay, and obey."

The Missionary Apostolate

Despite his initiatives with regard to lay participation, Waters' primary objective was the formation of a corps of priests that embodied his own vision of the church in North Carolina, namely, that it was a missionary frontier pushing its way slowly into new territory, bringing the Catholic message to men and women who had never heard it proclaimed accurately, completely, and enthusiastically. With this goal in mind, Bishop Waters introduced the Missionary Apostolate, a program that would be his signature contribution to the church in the state.

As Waters envisioned it, the Missionary Apostolate consisted of four dimensions: a Summer Census taken by seminarians, the Apostolic Year for newly ordained priests, the Trailer Apostolate on which priests worked during the summer, and a year round Mission Band. Each will be considered here individually.

1) The Summer Census Project

Despite his rather overbearing manner and no nonsense approach to ministry, there was a romantic streak in Vincent Waters as well, or at least he was able to evoke in young men the vision of heroic service to Christ and the Church. On "begging tours" to the North, where he not only recounted the financial condition of his struggling diocese but also the dire need for priests, Waters touched the hearts of a number of young men. In particular, the decade after World War II was an unprecedented period for religious vocations all over the country. Monasteries and seminaries were full to capacity with Catholics who could imagine nothing more worthwhile than dedicating their lives to "saving souls." One story, repeated over and over by Waters was that, proportionate to the population, there were more Catholics in China than in North Carolina, and more priests. Whether accurate or not, the image was striking, that of a vast territory in the United States itself which, from a Catholic point of view, was a field ready for harvest. The first contact of Waters' recruits with that "China in America" was taking the summer census.[23]

Waters knew that idealism by itself was no substitute for exposure to the reality of life in North Carolina. Accordingly, he instituted a summer program which required that students live and work together, get a taste of priestly life, and test their readiness for a commitment to such a ministry. Under the hot Carolina sun many men decided that such a life was not for them. Others fell in love with the area and with such a priesthood.

The census project got under way when, in the summer of 1946, eight Raleigh seminarians spent four weeks in upstate New York learning the mission system which had been developed by the diocese of Buffalo. The following summer, eleven seminarians, including those who had gone to New York the previous year, inaugurated the program in North Carolina taking a census of the see city of Raleigh. In light of the population expansion that has occurred since 1947, it is hard to believe that the students visited every house in Raleigh over the course of six weeks.[24]

Despite their inexperience and the lack of professional assistance, the students planned and executed the census with considerable skill. In the initial Raleigh program, large street maps were obtained and the city divided into districts. Day after day the students knocked on hundreds of doors, returning each evening to their headquarters in the cathedral rectory where they marked off the districts as they were completed, shading the maps in different colors to represent predominantly black and predominantly white areas. In subsequent years, as the process became more refined, the seminarians put pins in the maps to indicate where Catholics lived -- white pins for white parishioners and black pins for black parishioners. Eventually, becoming even more precise, yellow pins were used to signify nonpracticing Catholics.

As they went door to door dressed in their black suits, the students on that first census became more and more enthusiastic. They were filling out cards indicating that a majority of the people of Raleigh -- in particular the Negroes -- were anxious to receive literature on the teachings of the church. Only later did they learn that the apparent readiness to accept more information was merely a feature of Southern culture. Black people in particular did not say "No" to white men.

During much of the 21-year period that the summer census was conducted, racial segregation characterized life in the southern states. From the log entries, it is clear that the seminarians, most of whom were Northerners and some of whom were black, accepted the rigid separation of the races as an unfortunate but unalterable aspect of life.

The first mention of Negro seminarians was in the report of the 1953 census in Charlotte. The subtle wording of the log reveals the social reality, namely that the Negro seminarians "were very kindly received *in the Negro areas*" (emphasis added). Two years later, while taking the census in Fayetteville, the Negro seminarians were not able to eat in the same restaurant as their white colleagues. The problem was resolved by hiring a cook to prepare meals for all the young men in the local convent. In 1957, as the students prepared to take the census in the town of Lincolnton, a black seminarian was "not welcome" at the motel where the other seminarians stayed. Lodging for him was arranged "at a home for colored teachers on the other side of town."

The Reflections of Future Bishop Joseph Howze

Despite the pervasive anti-black discrimination which the students encountered and the fact that the civil rights movement was beginning to gather momentum, the tone and content of the 1958 entry in the log, written by Joseph L. Howze, a black deacon, is striking. Howze prefaces his report of that summer's census with a two-page reflection on the project in general, now in its eleventh year. Aware that the log would be read by seminarians taking the census in subsequent years, Howze presents a vision to the students which avoids anger, transcends race, and attempts to motivate them to a more profound understanding of the Christian life. While his words reflect both his youth and a pre-Vatican Council perspective, they are worth attending to, especially since Joseph Howze was destined to become a bishop. The following is an excerpt from Howze's entry in the census log:

> After a Raleigh seminarian has been taking census in our missionary diocese for a couple of weeks, and has experienced the task of finding few Catholics in an area where he has to cope with Protestant and anti-Catholic propaganda, he is likely to become a little discouraged when the first fervor of his Apostolic zeal has waned. To go from house to house for a period of three weeks without finding a Catholic and seeing no reasonable indication that there is even a conversion in sight can be a little disheartening to a seminarian who

has dreamt of doing great apostolic work. Then again the seminarian is confronted with that peculiar heresy that is becoming daily more widespread, and which the seminarian hears from almost every non-Catholic who says that all churches are good, and that it doesn't matter what religion a man chooses as long as he leads a good and clean life. A non-Catholic with this attitude is more detrimental to our work than an openly antagonistic one. His apathy and indifference to a true religion encourages him and his associates to be satisfied with the status quo, and he sees no reason to investigate further the claims of other denominations.

Added to all this, the seminarian is likely to be taking census in an area where such noisy propagandists as Jehovah Witnesses are at the same time passing out literature. All of this and more can create a disturbing problem for a seminarian who is trying to keep his fervor alive during a religious survey on a hot dusty road.

Howze did not know that within two months of his writing these words Pope Pius XII's nineteen-year reign would come to an end and that his successor, Pope John XXIII, would throw open the windows of the Catholic Church to modern thought, ending the four-hundred-year defensiveness which had followed the trauma of the Protestant Reformation. It is quite likely that, as the perspectives and expectations of the seminarians changed, the admonitions of Howze seemed quaint pieties from a period of time rapidly dissolving.

Not that there had not been discontent even before Howze's effort to revive flagging spirits. For example, the students complained that the pastors were not as supportive of their work as they would like. As a matter of fact, pastors had no say as to participation in the census. They were simply told by Waters to house, feed, and supervise as many as forty students. So, what might have been for them a tranquil summer was abruptly transformed into a period of high demand activity.

There was also veiled criticism of the bishop himself for not authorizing the use of more ecumenically sensitive literature. Further, the students complained about the inadequacies of the orientation program held before the commencement of each year's census. Such sentiments were prelude to the abrupt termination of the program.

The Census Project Collapses

The log report for 1967, the final year of the summer census program, reveals obliquely that the discord bubbling up in the Catholic church in general and in North Carolina in particular had infected the dwindling ranks of seminarians. Until this final entry the students had spoken with one voice, that of the "senior man," the student closest to ordination. Breaking this tradition with a vengeance, and perhaps unconsciously symbolizing the rejection of the strict hierarchical structure of the church, each of the participants in the Durham census submitted his own report under the heading, "What We Think." While some wrote of the "spirit which has developed among us," others indicated that the summer had been a season of discontent. One seminarian wrote: "My big complaint is that I feel census should be optional so that those who do not take it conscientiously are not around to hinder the rest of the group." Another wrote that "many people are worried about where the money is coming from for their books and other expenses for the school year. If the pay for the census was halfway decent maybe the fellows would do a better job."

The innocence as well as the fervor of the earlier years was gone. What had started out as a ministry had become "a job," and not a particularly appealing one at that. And certainly contributing to the problem for the young men was their dwindling numbers. Whereas in the mid-Fifties there has been more than forty, by 1967, there were but twenty. And as the appeal of the priesthood plummeted, the number of clerical students for North Carolina declined still further, reaching a nadir of eight in 1970. Bishop Waters' dream of an ever expanding corps of diocesan priests had fallen victim to the changing times.

Inserted in the last page of the census log is a glossy photograph of the bishop surrounded by twenty-four seminarians. Behind them is a sign which reads "St. John Vianney Hall." John Vianney, a simple, ascetic Nineteenth Century French parish priest, is the patron saint of the diocesan clergy. The building, located in the mountains of western North Carolina, was a high school seminary, part of the bishop's plan for a vigorous church. The picture of the young men in their black suits would lead one to conclude that the dream was being fulfilled. But this was 1967. Most of the students in the picture would never become priests. The high school seminary soon would be closed. The bishop himself would soon be under siege by many of the priests who, as seminarians, posed with him for similar pictures as they went forth to knock on doors all over the state in the largely futile campaign to promote the Catholic Church.

2) The Apostolate Year

Despite the stress and frustration of the summer census, the program contributed to the formation of a group of energetic priests, who for the balance of the Twentieth Century provided leadership in the dioceses of Raleigh and Charlotte. However, even more than the summer census, these priests credited another dimension of the Missionary Apostolate with forging their friendships, their sense of mission, and their love for North Carolina. Although in time they would be critical of Bishop Waters, some of them severely so, there was no hesitancy in praising the man for his zeal and for challenging them to reach for excellence. The recollections of several of these priests, now retired, can serve to recapture a sense of what Catholic life was like half a century ago and how the Apostolate shaped their lives.

J. Paul Byron, ordained on June 15, 1946, was one of the first young men to join Waters in his crusade to make North Carolina Catholic. Fifty-four years later Byron boasted that he was "the oldest priest in the diocese who's still up and about." Healthy and happy, he suggested that since most priests today are older when ordained, he may be the last in North Carolina ever to celebrate his fiftieth anniversary of priesthood while still active. "That was my goal, and I achieved it."[25]

Not only has Byron been durable, he has been dynamic, providing leadership in a succession of pastoral positions. As will be seen in Chapter Three, he was also one of the priests who spearheaded the opposition to Bishop Waters in the late Sixties and early Seventies. To this day, some more conservative priests look askance at Byron, whom they consider someone who destabilizes the church with his liberal views.

Although required by diocesan policy to retire at age 75 in 1996, Byron continued an active ministry made possible in no small measure by the shortage of priests. For a year he served as interim pastor of St. Matthew parish in Durham. Subsequently, he was assigned as sacramental minister at Holy Family parish in Hillsborough and in 2000 was given a similar post at St. Bernadette Church, Butner.[26] The tenor of the 80-year-old warrior's thinking can be gauged from a homily on vocations which he delivered in July 2000. Citing a controversial new book on the priesthood,[27] Byron said that to attract high quality men to Church service major changes were needed, including the ordination of married men.

A native of Albany, New York, Byron hoped to become a priest of that diocese. However, after his third year in the college seminary at

Dunwoodie, New York, he was asked to leave because "I needed more maturing." Even his uncle, an Albany priest, was not able to get the decision reversed. This was 1941 and World War II was about to begin. A young man not in school was sure to be drafted. Fortunately for Paul Byron, his pastor knew Bishop Eugene J. McGuinness of Raleigh and asked him to sponsor the youth. The North Carolina bishop, desperate for priests, after a brief meeting in the Pennsylvania Hotel in New York City, adopted Byron and sent him to St. Bonaventure Seminary in Syracuse, New York.

During the five years that he was studying, Byron visited North Carolina only once, and that for just four days. The seminarian census program discussed above would begin the year Byron was ordained, giving him the distinction of being the last priest for the next twenty-one years not to participate in that project. On the other hand, together with his classmate, Francis A. McCarthy, Byron was the first to experience the other phases of Bishop Waters' initiation into the North Carolina missions, namely the Apostolate Year, the Trailer Apostolate, and the Mission Band.

With reference to the Apostolate Year, each of the several senior priests interviewed told a similar story of his first year after ordination. Very young and having lived for several years in the semi-monastic environment of the seminary, the novice priests were entrusted to a veteran North Carolina "missionary" for a year of apprenticeship. So, in 1946, Byron was assigned to Father Francis J. Howard in the small town of Whiteville in the southeastern section of the state. From this base parish, Byron traveled out each week to the yet smaller towns of Delco and Tabor City, each with but a handful of Catholics, but each with its tiny Catholic chapel. For a year these miniature "parishes" would be where Byron would say mass, hear confessions, counsel, bless, and console.

Since the war had just ended, factories had not yet returned fully to peacetime production and it was impossible for Byron to buy a car. Consequently, for months he had to hitchhike to his missions. As he reminisced: "So, here I was in the boiling sun, waiting for a bus and hoping someone would pick me up. A Catholic priest in a black suit, a Roman collar, and a Panama hat was a freak thing on the streets of Whiteville."

Byron's fellow neophyte, Father McCarthy, who died in 1962, used to say, "All salvation comes through mileage." Among them, the three priests in Whiteville had six missions, all of which Father Howard had established out of St. Mary parish in Wilmington. The clerics were constantly on the road visiting the sprinkling of Catholics in that vast territory.

The indelible impression made on priests by the Apostolic Year is suggested by the fact that more than fifty years later, Byron could recall in detail that first year of his ministry and lavish warm praise on Father Howard, who died in 1971, as a true missionary. By this assignation, Byron meant a priest who went out to the people, who loved them, who understood them. Byron himself was noted for just such qualities.

Although the new priests were natives of large northern cities with substantial Catholic populations, their initiation to the South by men like Frank Howard instilled in them a model of ministry which they never relinquished. The model included the embracing of the simple, close-to-the-earth conditions under which Catholic faith and practice were experienced. With a laugh, Byron could recall, "I'd be at this mission saying Mass in a kitchen looking through the floorboards and watching the chickens scurrying around underneath."

Although Bishop Waters insisted that they were missionaries, the priests did little real evangelization, mainly attending to the religious needs of those who were already Catholics. However, Byron recalled that in the town of Chadbourn he received a woman into the church. Three months later she went out of her mind. "The whole town decided that it was the Catholic religion that did it to her!"[28] Byron's self-deprecating sense of humor certainly contributed to the preservation of his vocation in a ministry which in the early years produced few measurable results.

3) Trailer Apostolate

Yet another innovation of Bishop Waters was a summer program called the Trailer Apostolate or Motor Missions. While seminarians knocked on doors in one area, elsewhere in the state young priests manned fully equipped chapel trailers which brought Catholicism to mountain towns and coastal villages that never before had seen a priest. No other aspect of their missionary days generated among the veterans of the period as many stories.

The trailers were an adaptation to the changing technological and social landscape. As will be seen in Chapter Six, chapel cars had been utilized in the late nineteenth and early twentieth centuries to bring the Catholic Church to small towns along the railroad lines. With the decline of railroads and the expansion of highways, the church retired the chapel cars and introduced motorized vehicles. They in turn were taken off the road in the mid-Sixties as the increasing availability of television kept more and more families at home in the evenings. But for nearly twenty years, young priests, like religious Pied Pipers, tried to lure people to their message by showing films projected onto a portable screen on a dark country road and by playing 78 rpm recordings of Catholic hymns into the Carolina night.

The trailers, like the chapel cars, were financed by the Catholic Church Extension Society and other out-of-state donors. Each traveling church had a name. The older trailer, introduced in 1948, was called Madonna of the Highways. The newer one, put on the road in 1955, bore the name Our Lady of the Miraculous Medal. Paradoxically, such names were as likely to repel as attract people to the Church of Rome. Although central to Catholic life, devotion to Mary was suspect to the people to whom the Motor Missions were directed.[29]

Whereas the older chapel was simply a retooled standard trailer, Our Lady of the Miraculous Medal was specifically designed to be a chapel. The thirty-five foot long vehicle consisted of three compartments carefully configured for efficiency -- a chapel, living quarters, and a reception area.

The twelve foot long chapel could seat twenty people, more than enough room for the small number of Catholics encountered in the rural towns which the trailer visited. In an effort to make the chapel as authentically Catholic as possible, three small stained glass windows were set in each oak paneled side wall.

Two priests were assigned to each trailer. Rather than being able to rest during the summer, the clerics were required to spend the week living in the cramped quarters of the trailer and then hurry back to their parish assignment for Sunday masses. Their living area, which doubled as the sacristy, was eleven feet by five. Into this space were squeezed a lavatory, sofa bed, bookshelves, cabinets, and a combination stove, sink, and refrigerator.

The third compartment, called a reception room, was a seven foot square area which contained a sofa, chairs, and a table. Here, the priests could meet with people or relax during the hours before the evening service.

Besides these interior features, the state of the art trailer was equipped with an altar and folding platform which opened out from the side of the vehicle for outdoor services. The brochure announcing the motor chapel optimistically said that as many as 500 people could see the altar.[30]

Another veteran of the Trailer Missions was the Reverend H. Charles Mulholland, known throughout the diocese simply as "Charlie Mulholland." Although the same age as Byron, Mulholland was ordained in 1953, seven years after his friend. The two men who lived together during retirement, as young priests during the early Waters period had been the most energetic and committed missioners.

If Byron represents one type of North Carolina priest, namely someone who had been rejected elsewhere, Mulholland represents another, the "late vocation," or what today might be called the "second career priest." Born in New York City, Charlie attended the Merchant Marine Academy in Kings Point, New York, after which he served in the merchant service from 1942 to 1950. Mulholland traces his presence in North Carolina to a ship radio operator whom he befriended. The man, Ed, a native North Carolinian, was in effect the future priest's first convert, becoming a Catholic through his friend's influence. As often happens with converts, Ed became so enthusiastic about the church that he entered the seminary.

Some time later, the two men met in New York where Ed suggested to Charlie that he also consider becoming a priest. His argument was, "Why don't you try it!" With these challenging words in his mind, Mulholland sailed out of New York harbor on a troop ship assigned to transport refugees from Europe to the United States. During the voyage he decided that he would indeed "try it." From Bremerhaven, Germany, he mailed his application to Bishop Waters. Upon his return to New York, a letter from Waters assigned the seaman, sight unseen, to St. John's Seminary in Little Rock, Arkansas. Other than a week long summer orientation program, the new candidate for the priesthood had no contact with North Carolina. In subsequent summers, he participated in the census project discussed above.[31]

Among other things, at age seventy-six, Mulholland recalled his experiences on the long since retired and dismantled chapel trailers. Each summer, a schedule would be created for a twelve-week campaign. One trailer would head to the eastern part of the state and the other to the west. Upon arrival at the predetermined town, the routine was quite simple. After obtaining permission from a farmer to park the vehicle in his field and getting the power company to supply electricity, the priests would post notices about the two-week program throughout the area. They would then set up chairs outside the trailer and hope that people would come. Frequently, no one did. Father John Roueche, a native of Salisbury, North Carolina, and familiar with the ways of the people, told young Byron, "They're timid about coming down, but they're up there on their porches in the dark, listening." So, the priests would preach to empty chairs.[32]

A standard feature of the evening program was a Question Box. Since it was rare for anyone to submit questions, the priests put questions in the box themselves, ones which they believed the people might ask if they had the courage to do so, such as about the pope, Mary, and the Mass. In 1961, Father John A. Wall, ordained the year before, was working the trailer with Mulholland. While the older priest was inside preparing his talk, Wall was supposed to be outside answering the questions. Suddenly Mulholland realized that he heard nothing outside. Finally, Father Wall came in and said, "There's nobody out here." Having taken Father Roueche's advice to heart, Mulholland told his young colleague to begin anyway. As Mulholland recalled forty years later, "After that, John would say that he had preached to deaf people and blind people, but that Mulholland had told him to preach to nobody."

Another retired priest, Monsignor James E. McSweeney, told similar stories of the Missionary Apostolate days.[33] A native of Ohio, McSweeney chose to minister in North Carolina precisely because of his interest in mission work. After ordination in 1950, he was assigned to Sacred Heart, Whiteville for his Apostolate year. Over the succeeding decades he served as pastor in ten parishes, including some of the largest in the diocese. From 1962-67, he was Bishop Waters' chancellor, and while in that position he was named a domestic prelate and given the title Right Reverend Monsignor. More analytical than the other retirees, McSweeney compared the program as designed by Father James Navagh of upstate New York with its implementation in North Carolina. As will be seen below, Waters was so impressed with Navagh's missionary orientation to priesthood that he enlisted him as the first auxiliary bishop of Raleigh. McSweeney reflected:

> There was a major difference, one which explains why it never succeeded here. Navagh's model had three parts: seminarians teach-

ing catechism and taking the census, newly ordained priests working
in the mission churches, and mobile trailer missions. All three components would be focused on the same area. Bishop Waters, on the
other hand, split it up into three parts. He had the seminarians taking
the census in city parishes, the newly ordained in another area, and the
trailers working in yet other sections of the state. Thus split into three
different areas, the plan lost some of its effectiveness. Navagh's idea
was to concentrate resources on one area, and only when the church
was firmly rooted there to move on. It was a saturation method.

4) The Mission Band

Although McSweeney spoke of three components of the
Missionary Apostolate, there was a fourth. It was not personally experienced by all the priests of the diocese, but helped them all, in that it
included collecting funds to support poor mission stations. At first,
Bishop Waters himself regularly traveled to northern cities on "begging
tours," describing conditions in North Carolina and appealing to more
fortunate Catholics for help. However, after a few years of this grueling
routine he devised a new plan. Despite the shortage of priests, Waters
assigned two of them to be full-time fund raisers. One priest was based
in Philadelphia and preached each Sunday at a parish in the Northeast.
Another priest lived in Chicago and covered Midwestern cities.

One of the men sent to Chicago was Father Desmond Robert
Keenan, who spent three years raising money for his home diocese. The
success of Keenan's work could be gauged by the checks he mailed
back to Raleigh each week. As will be seen in Chapter Twelve, Keenan,
who assumed the name "Padre Roberto," moved from being a fund raising missionary to being the first North Carolina priest sent as a missionary to Latin America. After spending nearly thirty years in Mexico,
he returned to Raleigh where for several years he served as Vicar for
Hispanics.[34]

While the full-time fund raisers were preaching to Catholics in
the North and Midwest, other priests were participating in the Mission
Band closer to home. One of them was Monsignor James R. Jones, who
was ordained in 1951 and in the year 2000 was living in retirement in
New Bern, the site of his final pastorate. Like other priests of his generation, Jones experienced all aspects of the Missionary Apostolate.[35]
Not only did he spend his summers on the chapel trailers, but with his
friend, Father William G. Wellein, (who died in 1997) served as co-
director of the outdoor apostolate. For several years, he arranged the

schedules for the mobile chapels, provided orientation to the priests who would be out there on the front lines, and as often as not, spent lonely weeks himself in unreceptive small towns.

As if coordinating the summer program and serving as pastors were not enough, for eight years Fathers Jones and Wellein also comprised the instate diocesan Mission Band. Believing that many parishes could not afford to pay religious order priests who specialized in retreat work, Bishop Waters assigned diocesan priests to assume the mantle of retreat master. In that capacity, they conducted dozens of missions throughout the state during years when revival-like retreats were singularly powerful, high intensity motivational experiences for Catholics. "Making the mission" was almost as obligatory as attending Sunday mass.[36]

Looking Back at the Missionary Apostolate

All the veteran priests interviewed spoke with mixed feelings about their youthful experiences, including the muggy, futile weeks they spent staffing the trailer chapels and the long drives to distant towns to conduct retreats. Although committed without hesitancy to the church, they could see in retrospect the shortcomings of much of what they had done. As these aging priests relate their "war stories," their successors can comprehend only dimly what life was like during the days of racial segregation, suspicion of Catholics, and a church which counted among its members fewer than one percent of the population. When these men pass from the scene, not only will the link with Bishop Waters be ended, but also the heritage of adventure, camaraderie, and missionary zeal. They have lived in both major eras in the history of the church in North Carolina -- the long period of a loosely structured, brink-of-poverty, small town church and the more highly bureaucratized, affluent, cosmopolitan church of today.

One of these "Waters priests" is unique. He has refused to relinquish the now somewhat obsolete title of "missionary." When Monsignor Richard Allen retired from the active clergy of the Diocese of Charlotte in the year 2000, he announced that he was moving to Alaska in order to work on the mission circuit of the Diocese of Anchorage. Although 70 years old, Allen still wanted to be a missionary. His new adventure would take him back half a century when, as a young seminarian, he had moved from the Catholic security of upper New York State to embrace the challenge of a ministry in the deep South. "When I came to North Carolina in the early '50's," Allen related as he announced his "retirement," "the thing that attracted me to this place was small parishes, the small number of Catholics in relation to the population, and the religious atmosphere of North Carolina."[37]

Allen had seen North Carolina move from the Catholic frontier to the Catholic mainstream. This included witnessing the dramatic improvement in the financial health of the Church. It has been a long time since a North Carolina bishop has gone "begging" in other states, and decades since priests like Father Kennan have been assigned as fund raisers. One of Bishop Waters' achievements was to educate Tar Heel Catholics to support their church, not just the local parish, but the diocese. Early in his tenure, he initiated the Diocesan Development Fund (DDF) to support the expanding programs which he had initiated. The major beneficiary of the DDF was the Missionary Apostolate. In 1959, the DDF collected a total of $36,000, "slightly less than one dollar per Catholic man, woman, and child in the diocese."[38] The growth of the Church is reflected in the fact that by the 1990's, the comparable Bishop's appeals in the Raleigh and Charlotte dioceses were collecting better than six million dollars each year.

Paradoxically, some of the major beneficiaries of these more recent collections have been the same men who conducted the mission outreach of the Forties and Fifties. They were now recipients of retirement benefits, one of the largest items in diocesan budgets.[39]

Bishop James J. Navagh

Much of the missionary energy unleashed by Waters was inspired by a priest from far off upstate New York. While serving as a young pastor in a rural area, James J. Navagh, ordained in 1929, asked Buffalo bishop John A. Duffy if he might be released to work in the home missions of the United States. At first the bishop said, "I'll think about it." Six months later Bishop Duffy called him in to say, "If you want to be a missionary, you can be one right here." With that, in 1940, Navagh became the first director of the Missionary Apostolate of the Diocese of Buffalo.[40]

For twelve years Navagh trained priests in pastoral techniques and established parishes in areas were there had been no churches. In 1950, his ideas gained wider circulation with the publication of *The Apostolic Parish*, which was used as a textbook in many seminaries and translated into Spanish and Italian. His conception of priesthood was expressed in the words, "I don't think of a Catholic priest as a chaplain to Catholics. He is an apostle. He has a responsibility before God to every soul in his parish, Catholic and non-Catholic. He must preach the Gospel to every living creature who will listen."[41] This sentiment resonated with Vincent Waters who, as has been related, in the summer of 1946 sent eight of his seminarians to learn the methods and spirit of Navagh's Missionary Apostolate.

So impressed was Waters with Navagh, that in 1952 he requested that the priest be appointed auxiliary bishop of the Diocese of Raleigh. Although the small number of Catholics in North Carolina did not justify an assistant bishop, the vast area to be administered did. And even more so, Waters was able to convince Rome that with the help of someone like Navagh, substantial strides could be made in advancing the cause of Catholicism in the south.

However, with Waters there was not much room for partnership, and although Navagh was appointed director of the North Carolina Layman's Association and promoted a number of Christian family projects, he was largely lost in the shadow of Waters. This was particularly true after the Newton Grove episode of 1953. In 1955, after residing for three years at the Orphanage at Nazareth, Navagh was granted permission to establish Our Lady of Consolation parish in a predominantly black neighborhood in Charlotte. Here, far from the immediate control of Waters, he built an entire parish plant. When the time came for the dedication of the church, it was the Apostolic Delegate to the United States, Archbishop Amleto Giovani Cicognani, not Waters, who presided.

The presence of Cicognani suggested that Navagh was gaining a reputation outside the state of North Carolina. Not only was he awarded honorary doctorates at several universities, but he served as assistant to the chairman of the Administrative Board of the National Catholic Welfare Conference, the central administration of the American Catholic bishops. His reputation as well as his connections resulted in Navagh's appointment in 1957 as bishop of Ogdensburg, New York, in the same region as his native Buffalo. In 1963, after six years in Ogdensburg, Navagh was promoted to the larger diocese of Paterson, New Jersey. He died in Rome on October 2, 1965 while attending the Second Vatican Council.

There were similarities of temperament between Waters and his first auxiliary bishop. The historian of the Ogdensburg diocese refers to Navagh as "an archconservative, a disciplinarian, an uncompromising moralist, a stern teacher...."[42] At the same time he is depicted as a champion of apostolates to priestless areas and a leader for racial justice -- qualities which characterized Waters as well. Most striking of all is the summary appraisal of Navagh; it is one that could be applied to Waters:

> He had demanded the best that any man could give -- and sometimes more than could be given. From 1957 to 1963, there was no period of rest -- Bishop Navagh believed that eternity is for rest, time is for action.[43]

As much as one might by hindsight question their policies and perspective, there is no doubt but that Waters and Navagh were totally committed to their ministry. After his death, it was learned that Bishop Navagh had vowed to begin each year penniless. He died with no assets other than his clothes and his books, which he willed to his unnamed successor as bishop of Paterson. The will specified that he was to be buried in a pine box, draped with a black cloth, and that the funeral costs were not to exceed $450. However, even this modest sum was not in the bishop's possession at the time of his death, and so the cost had to be paid from a charity fund he himself had established to assist the poor.[44]

Despite his credentials, skills, and sanctity, Navagh's five year in North Carolina made hardly a ripple as far as the advancement of the church there was concerned.

Every Catholic Child in a Catholic School

Like Waters, Navagh was a bishop of the pre-Vatican II period, a man who believed in authority, not collaboration, in the tireless pursuit of "souls," in shielding Catholics from a hostile world. Illustrative of this last point is the great stress both men placed on parochial schools. It is related that the day before his installation as bishop of Ogdensberg, Navagh stopped at a parish in Watertown, New York. When he learned that a rectory was to be built he said, "Oh no! You must have a new Catholic school first." The parish building campaign was totally revised.[45]

At the First Plenary Council of Baltimore in 1866, the American bishops decreed that "teachers belonging to religious congregations should be employed when possible in our schools. The latter should be erected in every parish."[46] At the Third Plenary Council, held in 1884, the mandate was made more forceful. Parochial schools were an "absolute necessity." Pastors have "the obligation" to establish them, and "parents must send their children to such schools unless the bishop should judge the reason for sending them elsewhere to be sufficient."[47] In response to this challenge, bishops all over the country undertook a massive campaign to comply with the requirement. As has been noted, Bishop Navagh ordered that a parochial school be built even before he was officially installed as bishop of Ogdensberg in 1957. In North Carolina, Bishop Waters shared this passion for Catholic schools.

Although the number of parochial schools increased dramatically during the Waters years, the first Catholic school had been established in Wilmington in 1869, when Bishop James Gibbons, who had attended the Second Plenary Council as an aide to the archbishop of Baltimore, recruited three Sisters of Mercy from Charleston, South Carolina. Because of financial constraints as well as the sparse Catholic population, few additional schools were opened until the diocese of Raleigh was established in 1924. Even then, only   fifteen schools were established before Waters' arrival in 1945.[48]

The church building boom which occurred during the first decade of Waters' tenure was matched by the construction and staffing of schools. By 1958, the number of schools had increased to 64, 54 elementary and 10 secondary. However, the buildings were small and usually poorly constructed, a situation which paralleled the plight of the public schools of the state. Along with other Southern states, North Carolina ranked at the bottom of all measures of educational attainment.

The marginal status of Catholic education can be gauged by the fact that in 1958 there were 10,043 students enrolled in the 64 schools, an average of 160 per school. The small size of the schools is explained in part by the low Catholic population in the state but also by the fact that schools were racially segregated. Wishing to provide an education to African-Americans, various religious communities opened fifteen schools in North Carolina during this period.[49] As has been seen in the case of Newton Grove, it was typical to have a school for white children and another for black children, both small and both often physically near one another. However, it is widely acknowledged that during the Jim Crow period the Catholic Church provided the best education available to black children in the South.[50]

Bishop Waters was so proud of the Catholic schools in North Carolina that in 1958 he published a book, which celebrated the striking growth of the school network.[51] Neither he nor anyone else suspected that the glory days were coming to an end, that within a few years the cost of parochial education would sky rocket, and schools would be closing rather than opening. That decline began in 1964, as the Vatican Council, then in session, was sending shock waves throughout the Catholic world. By September 1971 the number of secondary schools in North Carolina had declined from 10 to 3, and elementary schools from 54 to 42. However, the surviving schools were somewhat larger, with a pupil enrollment of 10,768.[52]

The Witness of Reverend Frederick A. Koch

Dark days were coming for the church in North Carolina, but it is important not to allow them to obscure the sunshine that brightened the early years of the Waters era. It seemed like everyone was young then, from the bishop himself, to the priests, to the scores of religious sisters who endured privation to teach in the schools, to the people in the pews, to the children -- black and white -- who, in their often poorly fitting uniforms, saluted the flag and said the Hail Mary in simple classrooms all over the state. Everyone knew that Catholics were a minority, misunderstood, maligned. Somehow, that only heightened the conviction that in the plan of God something wonderful was happening, a birth was taking place -- that of the Catholic Church. No one was clairvoyant; no one could foresee what the next decade would bring. There was only the present moment, and for Catholics in the Forties and Fifties, it was a moment bursting with energy and dancing with hope. And the credit was given to Bishop Waters.

During that period, perhaps no one had a more positive and trusting relationship with the bishop than Father Frederick A. Koch. Fortunately, Koch left a uniquely detailed record of Catholic life in North Carolina during the middle decades of the Twentieth Century.[53]

Ordained in 1943, Koch had the humble role of miter bearer at the 1945 installation of Bishop Waters in Sacred Heart Cathedral, Raleigh. Twenty-nine years later, he again played a modest ceremonial part, as he accompanied an archbishop down the aisle of the cathedral at Waters' funeral. In between those two events Koch had a busy career as a priest, one that would continue until his death in 1999 at the age of 83. At Koch's funeral, Waters' successor, Bishop Joseph Gossman, referred to the priest as "a patriarch of our diocese" and "a living icon."[54]

As has been noted, the young Koch was named second editor of the *NC Catholic* in 1946, bringing him into nearly daily contact with Waters. While working on the paper -- but also simultaneously administering St. Eugene parish in Wendell -- Koch wrote an eight-page pamphlet addressed to pastors in other parts of the country for public relations and fundraising purposes. Despite its obvious hyperbole, the document captures the spirit of the Waters' early years.

Referring to North Carolina as "the Number One US Mission Front," Koch asked rhetorically in what respect this was true. His answer was that while other dioceses had fewer priests and fewer parishes, none had such a scattered Catholic population. "Sixteen thousand parishioners live in ones and twos throughout a state which is in length the distance from New York to Cincinnati and in width the distance from Chicago to Detroit."

To emphasize the point of just how few Catholics there were, Koch said that there was no hamlet, much less a town or city in the state, that could be considered Catholic and that driving twenty-five to fifty miles on an empty stomach to say mass was a regular routine for many pastors. These resourceful men were called upon as well for any number of mundane services. On one occasion, a priest was asked to match a saucer when he returned to Charlotte, as a cup had been shattered, breaking the set.

Noting that 90% of the clergy were non-natives of the state, Koch explained the importance of the Missionary Apostolate to prepare them for their ministry, one that offered few tangible rewards. "In our hurry up America, the situation presents an enigma of slow motion." However, not wanting to seem pessimistic, Koch quickly added: "But there is motion and it is moving in the right direction." That movement was due largely to the leadership of Waters, who never became discouraged and inspired his subordinates to have the same dogged confidence.

As will be seen more fully in Chapter Nine, Koch had reason to have positive feelings about his bishop. In 1954, Waters gave the now middle-aged priest permission to fulfill his lifetime dream of going to Rome. Years later, Koch received yet another sign of Waters' kindness when he was allowed to move out of a rectory and live in an apartment with his elderly and infirm mother.

However, while Koch experienced a softer side of Bishop Waters, many others did not. As the Sixties advanced, complaints and criticisms mounted. Like evening thunder after a hot summer day, the ferment and confusion grew. At a time in life when a man should be able to look back with satisfaction on his accomplishments and perhaps begin to devote more time to leisure pursuits and quiet reflection,

Bishop Waters found himself besieged on all sides by problems. As he was swept along by the currents of change in the church, his early achievements in race relations and church building were largely forgotten. As will be examined in the next chapter, many of priests and religious women who once admired him as a courageous leader, now excoriated him as an intransigent obstructionist.

Chapter Three

The Sixties: Conflict & Change

Some Sisters have without our consultation adopted secular dress in place of their traditional religious habit. This wearing of secular dress has been an occasion of serious abuses and some scandal in this diocese. For this reason, I ask the superiors to send into this diocese only Sisters who will wear the traditional habit or the modified habit, modest and identifiably religious.... It is the overtones of worldliness in wearing a secular garb that reduces, to some extent, their spiritual efficiency.

---Letter from Bishop Waters to Superior Generals of communities of Sisters working in North Carolina, July 27, 1971.

All clerics are bound to wear a becoming clerical garb when answering a door call, when handling parish work with the laity, instructing converts, driving automobiles in the line of duty, walking on the street, or appearing in any public place.... Clerical garb means a black suit (not a gray one or any other color) with a conventional clerical collar.

---Letter from Bishop Waters to all priests of the diocese of Raleigh and to the Superiors of religious orders of men working in North Carolina, October 5, 1971.

The Catholic Church is our sure guide to truth and goodness; it is kept true by our infallible teachers, the Holy Father alone or with the Hierarchy, through the Holy Spirit.... I, as your father in God in North Carolina, give an appropriate word of admonition and counsel to our laity regarding proper attire while offering the Living God in Mass, the Sacrifice of Calvary. Some people have fallen into the habit of too unconventional attire at Mass.... They should wear their "Sunday best" -- modest, humble, dignified, joyful -- not distracting or tempting.

---Letter sent by Bishop Waters to the laity, November 30, 1971.

Within the space of four months in 1971, Bishop Waters successively alienated sisters, priests, and lay people. For many Catholics in North Carolina, telling them how to dress was the last straw. For several years, Catholic North Carolina had been a battlefield, with reform-minded men and women arrayed against their bishop, whom they viewed as a reactionary intent on dragging the Church backwards into what they considered the less enlightened period that preceded the Vatican Council. The tension had reached its most dramatic moment when in 1969, more than twenty diocesan priests took the extraordinary step of calling on their bishop to resign.

Rather than compromise on any issue or enter into dialog with his subordinates, Waters stonewalled all who opposed him and continued until the end his efforts to protect the church from falling further into what he considered worldliness, chaos, and lack of respect for authority.

One religious woman, familiar with the situation, put it this way shortly after Waters' death in 1974:

> The Church in the Diocese of Raleigh has been struggling for the past ten years to implement the promulgations of the Second Vatican Council. One would need to be exposed to both the extremely conservative position of the leadership in the diocese and the desire for renewal in the clergy and the laity to comprehend the level of tension during this post Vatican period. ...Seldom have so few mourned the death of a bishop than North Carolina at the passing of Vincent Waters.[1]

Background to Conflict

Despite a steady succession of initiatives during the first ten years of his tenure, Bishop Waters' dream of a Catholic North Carolina was far from reality. Even the modest goal of a one percent Catholic population of the state took eighteen years to achieve.[2] Much more utopian was his 1953 plan for a diocese-wide door-to-door convert campaign. Flush with the celebrated victory at Newton Grove and accompanied by James Navagh, his new auxiliary bishop, Waters presented to his priests and people the slogan, "A convert under instruction for every adult in the church." It seemed so simple: "Count the number of adults in the parish and set this number as a minimum quota to be reached."[3]

The quixotic campaign was not left to chance. Pastors were instructed to organize teams of lay people to visit all the homes in their parish within a designated four-week period and then to commence instruction classes for what Waters imagined would be the hundreds of recruits. His excitement was easily detected in his letter: "We have never made such an all out effort like this before." Not forgetting that divine help was needed, he ordered every Catholic to recite each day the prayer of Father Price for the conversion of North Carolina.[4]

Indeed, the number of converts jumped 31% between 1953 and 1954, but still was but a small fraction of what had been envisioned. More than that, the initial momentum soon waned and each succeeding year saw the total decline, until by 1960, there were far fewer converts than there had been before the statewide project of 1953 was undertaken.[5] This was despite the fact that the total Catholic population was slowly rising due to births and Catholics locating in the state.[6] It is somewhat puzzling that Waters set such an ambitious goal for converts. Not only was he familiar with the frustration experienced by Father Price in attracting people to Catholicism, but for eight years he had been receiving the sobering reports of the seminarians taking the summer census. Furthermore, as a native southerner, he was well aware of the resistance to all things Catholic by the local culture. It is possible that Bishop Navagh, a newcomer and a northerner, convinced Bishop Waters that the project was realistic. The outcome must have been a sobering experience for both bishops.

Paradoxically, this very failure to develop a substantial Catholic population served as a magnet to attract scores of religious personnel to the state. The years after World War II was a peak period for religious vocations in the United States. Idealistic young men and women flocked to seminaries and convents, many of them anxious to serve in the home missions. Waters may have had limited success converting North Carolinians, but he was more successful in recruiting priests and sisters for work in the state. Besides personal trips to the North, Waters tirelessly wrote letters to religious communities describing the challenges available in his diocese for energetic priests and sisters.[7]

Also, the chapel trailers, which made few inroads into the hearts of North Carolinians, created images of a religious frontier, of fields ripe for the harvest right here in the United States. A brochure announcing the inauguration of the second trailer had proclaimed: "Priests, sisters, brothers, and lay apostles are needed in this vast mission field."[8] Lay "apostles" would not come in any significant numbers, but priests and sisters did. They established and funded parishes, schools, and hospitals bringing to the state the distinctive charisms of their congregations, be they Franciscan, Dominican, or Passionist priests or Immaculate Heart of Mary, Glenmary, or Mission Helper of the Sacred Heart sisters -- to name but a few. However, just as these religious congregations could choose to come to North Carolina, they could likewise choose to leave. As has been seen with reference to the Redemptorist Fathers in Newton Grove, as much as he was dependent on them, Waters was irked by the independence of the religious orders.

Even more disturbing to the hardworking bishop must have been the rebellious behavior of his own carefully molded diocesan priests. Men who had marched to his orders like soldiers in a well disciplined army, now questioned and challenged and defied their general. Through it all, Waters maintained a stoic public silence, refusing to grant interviews to the press and ignoring many of the petitions for change from his priests. Because of this obsession with privacy, the story of Bishop Waters contains many gaps. As his longtime associate, Father Gerald L. Lewis remarked, "He wanted to preserve our history.... But he never wanted to push himself. He never pushed his own person."[9] Not only did Bishop Waters not "push" himself, but he left no journal or personal letters which might provide insight into the heart of a man whose life was so central to the history of the Church in North Carolina.[10]

The two major dimensions of the confrontational era will be examined: the unrest and even the defiance of the diocesan priests, and the more subdued but none the less forceful reaction of the sisters who staffed the schools of the diocese. The laity, assuredly, were going through their own reassessment of the church and of their faith during the Sixties and early Seventies. Along with the clergy and religious, they were struggling with the whirlwind of new thinking, new rules, and new procedures which shook the once rock solid institution they had known. However, to a large extent, in this period before substantial lay participation in church leadership, lay men and women were left to watch and wonder at the squabbling going on among their spiritual guides.

The Call for Collegiality

Almost immediately after the close of the Vatican Council in 1965, the call for "collegiality" issued by the epochal gathering of bishops resulted in the emergence of two distinct types of clerical organizations -- Priests' Associations and Priests' Senates. Spreading rapidly from diocese to diocese, these new structures engendered heightened expectations on the part of the clergy. Men, who had lived their lives in a vertical one-on-one relationship with their bishop, began to create horizontal group relationships with one another. Men who had never thought about a representative voice in the government of the diocese, were awakened to the possibility for such structures within their rigidly hierarchical church. Vigorous clerical networks, nonexistent before the council either within a diocese or among dioceses, by 1968 had linked thousands of priests in a spirited brotherhood. Local and national leadership emerged, for the first time since the early church giving rank and file clergy a voice in their destiny. Almost overnight, the docile servant of his bishop was transformed into the self-assured professional.[11]

Whereas senates were official, prescribed by the Vatican Council to advise bishops, associations were unofficial groupings which priests established on their own initiative. The later form of organization, which spoke of the "rights" of its members, was sometimes called a clergy labor union. While some bishops welcomed collaboration with their priests, others had great difficulty adjusting to what they saw as a challenge to their authority. One of the latter was Vincent Waters of Raleigh. In his attempt to maintain the old order, the man who had already ruled the church in North Carolina for twenty years, found his priests were no longer willing to accept without protest his autocratic style.

The North Carolina Priests' Association

Clergy organizing in North Carolina began in late 1967 when a number of priests met on several occasions at the Holiday Inn in Greensboro. Then, on February 27, 1968, Father Charlie Mulholland, as spokesman for the as yet unnamed group, using the stationery of Sacred Heart Cathedral where he was in residence, wrote a letter to all the priests of the diocese inviting them to a meeting at the Holiday Inn on March 11th for the purpose of forming a North Carolina Priests' Council [subsequently renamed an Association].[12]

What particularly excited Mulholland was the fact that on February 12th, nearly 300 priests from across the country had met in Chicago and decided to form the National Federation of Priests' Councils. Although he did not reveal this in his letter, Mulholland, together with Paul Byron and Cranor C. Graves, had attended that gathering. Archbishop Paul Hallinan of Atlanta hailed the action as a step forward in the Church in the United States and offered to host a meeting of those associations within the Atlanta Province which would be joining the new federation. Raleigh belonged to the Atlanta province.[13]

At the Greensboro meeting, 63 priests, more than half the diocesan clergy, formed a statewide association. Although Greensboro is rather centrally located within North Carolina, many priests had to travel for hours in order to be in attendance, attesting to the interest generated by the prospect of organizing independently of the bishop. It should be noted that although dissatisfaction specifically with Waters had been mounting, similar organizational momentum was occurring all over the country. The issue was not a particular bishop; the issue for the priests was a voice in their destiny.

Although Mulholland was elected president of the Association, the follow-up report to the clergy was written by Cranor Graves, widely regarded as one of the most talented priests in the state and informal protégé of Waters. Graves, a sophisticated, southern-born intellectual, offered a counterbalance to the more headstrong Mulholland. His authoring of the letter would lend greater credibility to the Association with those who remained skeptical.

Just as Mulholland in the earlier letter had sought legitimacy for priests organizing by citing the support of Archbishop Hallinan, Graves opened his letter by referring to the Decree on the Ministry and Life of Priests promulgated by the Council and by citing the recent pastoral letter of the American bishops, "The Church in Our Day." The bishops had written: "Priests ought to meet frequently together, welcoming opportunities for the social and other gatherings which give mutual support to one another."

Graves certainly knew that this broad statement had in mind golf outings and shared meals in restaurants, not organized groups that would challenge decisions of bishops. He also knew that the elevated expectations and heightened enthusiasm of some of the priests might lead to conflict and even rebellion. It was hoped that his diplomatic leadership would avoid widespread defections and schism.[14]

Based on the model established by the National Federation of Priests Councils, the North Carolina priests listed five objectives for the new association:

1) to manifest the oneness of the Christian priesthood,
2) to form a fraternal community of clerics,
3) to establish communication between priests,
4) to provide a voice for expressing the conscience of the group,
5) to share the burdens of pastoral responsibility and Christian leadership.

All these overlapping purposes were ambiguous enough that they could be interpreted as benign or as confrontational. Very soon, they would lead to confrontation.

The Priests' Senate

At the same time that Bishop Waters had to wonder what the implications of this new independent association of priests might be, he was adjusting to yet another organized group of priests, namely the recently established diocesan Priests' Senate, which had held its first meeting April 6, 1967. Initially, the bishop himself had selected the senators, an arrangement which immediately drew criticism for being undemocratic.

However, even this hand-picked advisory body did not meekly accede to the Bishop's will. The minutes of the first senate meeting reveal the differing perspectives and expectations of Waters and his priests. While the bishop wished to promote what he called "The Spiritual Apostolate of the Priest," several of the priest senators, including none other than Byron and Mulholland, insisted that the focus be more practical, such as the need for personnel, grievance, and professional development committees. Byron obviously came prepared. In conjunction with Father Donald F. Staib, he presented a list of ten recommendations which would give rank and file clergy greater autonomy, protection from arbitrary action by the bishop, and opportunities for "relaxing and recreation." Just as the seminarians, as noted in the summer census log, reached a point when they were not willing to work incessantly and under unquestioning obedience to the bishop, so also the priests wanted what they considered a more balanced, mature, adult relationship with the bishop, as well as time for developing their talents and living more rounded lives. This need for a personal life was never understood by Waters, who to the end of his life saw himself and all his priests as called to total, unwavering commitment to a ministry like that of the apostle Paul, who preached the Gospel "in season and out of season."[15]

From that first senate meeting came yet another indication of the movement towards a priesthood that was more like other professions and less a unique and lifelong dedication to church service in the proposal by Father Charles J. O'Connor (who died in 1976) and Paul Byron that a retirement plan be instituted. Until this time, it was expected that priests would serve until death or incapacitating infirmity. The senate proposal was very specific, namely that priests be eligible for retirement at age 65; that at age 70 a letter of resignation be submitted to the bishop; and that at age 75 resignation or retirement must take place. This proposal in fact became the policy of the diocese of Raleigh during Waters' time and continues in effect. It is one of Byron's jokes on himself that he was caught in the trap of his own design. For, when nearly thirty years later he reached age 75 and did not wish to retire, he was required to do so by the policy which he himself had sponsored.

The Issue of Authority

Hoping to avoid any false expectations as to the role of the Senate, the bishop made it clear that it was advisory and not legislative. Although the priests were aware of this fact, they nonetheless continued to act as if they did have decision-making power. For example, at the December 22, 1968 senate meeting Father Staib, Chairman of the Committee for Post Ordination Growth and Development of Priests, presented a plan for the continuing education of priests. Although the plan was approved by the Senate, Bishop Waters pointedly reminded the group that it was advisory and that the program was not to be implemented.[16]

Undeterred, the priests, perhaps influenced by the democratic procedures of the priests' association to which they also belonged, persisted in their activist mode. In subsequent senate meetings they passed motions for the formation of new committees and diocesan agencies, policies for paying stipends to retired priests, for granting study leaves to priests, for selecting speakers for inservice training sessions for the clergy. Lest the incipient power struggle get out of hand, at the senate meeting on February 29, 1968, Waters presented guidelines for the Senate. They stated that collegiality meant that the priests could make suggestions to him but that all power remained in his hands alone. The minutes quote him as saying, "authority of a supernatural nature does not come from the voice of the electorate."[17]

Taking exception to this position, Byron and Mulholland, always the gadflies, offered their resignations from the Senate. Father Staib announced that he was considering following suit. The tense situation was diffused when the disgruntled priests agreed to the suggestion of Father Gerald Kennedy that they postpone their decision until the next meeting. By that time, tempers had cooled and the men did not resign.

Despite this minor rebellion, or perhaps to emphasize his position, Waters went on to veto a proposal that senators be elected in a way that was more representative of the priests of the diocese. The minutes, prepared by Father Frederick A. Koch conclude with the pointed statement: "Bishop Waters said that the matter was not to be pursued, as the present manner of selection for Senate membership exemplifies the desire of the ordinary who is free to interpret the assignment of membership as he so desires."

Priest Groups Work in Tandem

Whereas the Senate met under the gaze of the bishop, the Priests' Association met on its own initiative with its own constitution and officers. Initially, it attempted to influence policy by approving reform measures and forwarding them to the Senate as agenda items. Since many of the leaders of the Association were also senators, this was easily accomplished. So, for example, the February 1969 Association meeting approved three items which subsequently appeared on the March Senate agenda:

1) that for pastoral reasons, the Bishop more readily allow Catholic ceremonies in non-Catholic churches;
2) that any pastor be given general permission to use local radio and television time when in his judgment it was helpful to his pastoral work;
3) that broader permission be given for distribution of Holy Communion under both species.[18]

It will be no surprise that these proposals, designed to nudge the Diocese of Raleigh further along the path of reform, were introduced by Fathers Byron and Mulholland, who in effect were couriers between the Association and the Senate. These proposals, together with a number of others, were quickly approved by the Senate. Of course, the flurry of activity meant nothing unless acted upon by the bishop, and he disposed of these and many other Senate-ratified measures by what might be called pocket vetoes.

Aware of the skepticism with which the diocesan clergy viewed the Senate, Cranor Graves, who chaired the Senate at the time, argued in the cover letter accompanying the minutes of the March 1969 meeting that, although the Senate was advisory, the fact that the bishop heard the deliberations which preceded the passing of motions should help to get them implemented. Unfortunately, from the priests' perspective, the bishop seemed unimpressed with the arguments and enthusiasm of his subordinates. He continued to make decisions contrary to the spirit of both the Senate and the Association.

Priests' Association Takes Action

The sense of itself held by the North Carolina Association of Priests may be gauged by the Preamble to its constitution-like "Guidelines." In particular, the document embodies the theology of priesthood which would afford rank and file priests a more active role in church affairs. Although careful to state that the Association "is formed to encourage and express the unity of all priests with their Bishop," it avoids use of the word "obedience," affirming instead that priests owe their Bishop "constant assistance and collaboration." It further reminds the Bishop that he must turn to his priests "for advice and cooperation in his pastoral ministry."

Although the priests concluded their organizational document with a prayer for "docility," it would be difficult to find much docility in the actions taken by the Association in succeeding months. Having shaken off the father-son relationship, the priests now saw themselves as adult collaborators with the bishop and insisted that they not be ignored.[19]

A veritable avalanche of proposals came forth from the Association meetings, some of which were beyond the power of Waters to grant, including the request that "priests be given a consultative vote in the selection of Bishops."[20] But certainly what must have been the most galling motion of all to Waters, one passed unanimously, called on the bishop to abolish by mandate all remaining "Jim Crow parishes." The priests said that the continuing existence of "de jure" black parishes in North Carolina was a scandal. And so, the man, who had been hailed as a champion of racial justice when he had desegregated Newton Grove in 1953, was being prodded to finish the job.

The frustration of the North Carolina priests reached its climax later in 1969, when twenty one of the diocese's one hundred priests signed a letter calling on Waters to resign. They mailed the letter and waited. For five months there was no response from the bishop. Finally, through a spokesman he said that he "does not consider the matter serious."[21] The impotence of the priests was patent. Despite the intoxicating expectations released by the Council, the bishop retained absolute authority, and priesthood was not going to change as much as many had hoped. While the majority of the priests, including Association leaders such as Byron, Mulholland, Kloster, and Staib, came through the fire of those years with a renewed commitment to their calling, many others left the clerical world and established new lives as laymen. One of them was Cranor Graves.

It was well known that Graves was a convert, a prototype perhaps, of the people whom Bishop Waters hoped to attract to the church. While a high school student in Kinston, North Carolina, with the idea of becoming an Episcopal priest, Graves attended a course in apologetics given by Father Thomas A. Williams, pastor of Holy Spirit Catholic Church. The young man expected that he would quickly discover the faults of Catholicism and strengthen his faith in the Episcopal Church which he believed contained "the best of Catholicism and the best of Protestantism." As it turned out, Graves became convinced that the Catholic Church was the one founded by Christ.[22]

As a priest, Graves gained national prominence as a leader of the Movement for a Better World, a program for spiritual revitalization which infused the retreat experience which priests and religious sisters were required to have each year with a spirituality based on modern theology and psychology. However, Graves grew weary of the struggle for a reformed church, and in December 1970, he became the tenth North Carolina priest in three years to resign. He said that his departure had been precipitated by "a breakdown in communication" between himself and the bishop.[23] Subsequently, Graves married and practiced psychotherapy for many years in the Wilmington, North Carolina area where he died in 1999.

While some priests who resigned followed Graves' example and accepted their status as laymen, others attempted to maintain a priestly ministry outside the walls. One of them was Leo McIlrath who was ordained by Bishop Waters in 1966, just as the turmoil was beginning.[24]

For ten years as a Raleigh priest, McIlrath held a variety of positions, including campus minister at Duke University in Durham, chaplain in hospitals and in the US Marines, and finally pastor of Holy Redeemer parish on the Outer Banks. In 1976, still loving much of what priesthood had meant to him but wishing to be free to marry, McIlrath left the ministry and returned to his native Connecticut.

Initially, lacking credentials for professional positions and uncertain as to what he wanted to do for a living, the 36-year-old McIlrath couldn't find employment. Eventually, he accepted a job in a nursing home and within a year obtained a Nursing Home Administrator's license. With this new credential he was appointed Senior Center Director in his native Danbury. For more than twenty years he served as Director of the Department of Elderly Services. His boss, the mayor, had been an altar boy at his first Solemn Mass.

Mcllrath and his wife, Dianne, adopted three children, two from the Philippines and one from Brazil. He also helped raise Dianne's three children from an earlier marriage, officiating at the marriages of two of them and seeing the third through college.

In addition to serving as a volunteer on more than twenty boards and councils, Mcllrath teaches Latin and co-founded the Dorothy Day Hospitality House, a soup kitchen and an emergency housing shelter. Furthermore, many Catholics accept him as a priest and ask him to celebrate marriages and funerals. Others approach him for healing and reconciliation. As a leader of the Corpus Christi/a catholic community (catholic with a small "c"), Mcllrath regularly celebrates the Eucharist.

The former Raleigh priest attributes his energy to his wife, crediting her with making it possible for him to be available to others in so many ways. And his link with North Carolina is not severed. The favorite vacation spot of the now aging couple is the Outer Banks, where decades ago Leo had been the pastor.

The Religious Habit Issue

After three years of conflict with his priests, Bishop Waters issued a challenge to the very people who were the most generous and committed of all Catholic workers in North Carolina, namely, the religious sisters who staffed the schools, hospitals, and orphanages of the diocese. Even more than priests, religious women had been held in virtual voluntary servitude by the church for centuries. Convinced that it was the will of God, they had accepted without complaint rules that not only limited their full development as women, but which often enough were demeaning and sexist. When the liberating currents of the Sixties penetrated convent walls, the effect was rapid. It seemed that one day, shrouded from head to foot in a medieval habit, "Sister" was meekly kneeling in chapel saying the Rosary, and the next day she was being called "Nancy," driving a car, and dressed in the clothing of a contemporary woman.[25]

These changes were distressing to Bishop Waters and he felt conscience-bound to take action. Accordingly, on July 27, 1971, in the letter cited at the beginning of this chapter to the heads of all communities of sisters working in North Carolina, he ordered all sisters to wear a religious habit and a veil or leave the diocese. For Waters, the idea of nuns not wearing veils or distinctive religious garb was shocking and a serious threat to religious life. In particular, the veil symbolized the fact that these women had separated themselves from the laity and dedicated themselves to God. They were not supposed to look like "ordinary women." Whether he would be successful or not, Waters felt compelled to take a stand.

Although most sisters complied with the Bishop's order for the sake of the people they served, the atmosphere in Catholic North Carolina was profoundly soured. The sisters might wear veils, but a veil of sadness and anger settled upon the diocese.

As was true of his racial integration moves in 1953, Waters received extensive media coverage of his 1971 order that nuns wear habits. The major difference was that, whereas on the earlier issue he was hailed as a reformer, in the later he was tarred as an opponent of reform. And as was true with regard to integration, Waters refused to discuss the religious garb issue with the media. On both occasions his position was that he had given an order and it was to be obeyed. He had no obligation to explain or defend.[26]

However, media criticism and a sound lambasting by the North Carolina Priests' Association was counterbalanced by the four hundred letters which Waters received on the issue, most of them lauding him for his "courageous stand."[27] In particular, the religious superiors to whom the letter was directed said that their sisters would comply with his wishes. They did caution that their communities had been undergoing a review of their "Holy Rule" and that some modification of the habit had been approved. One of the superiors, Sister M. Jean Linder of the Sisters of St. Francis of Tiffen, Ohio, wrote that her sisters would comply with Waters' requirement, but she went on to criticize the bishop for his divisiveness. She urged him to "forget the habit in favor of more important issues. Help unify rather than divide the workers in your vineyard."[28]

As it turned out, once the momentum for change got underway, the superiors found themselves as unable to control the behavior of their subjects as the bishop had his priests. One reform achieved in most communities was the transformation of the relationships among community members. Terms like "superior" and "subject" were replaced with more democratic terms like "president" and "community member." There would be no more pope-like "Mother General" with life tenure and absolute power. These changes in terminology reflected a dismantling of a hierarchical organizational structure, replacing it with one in which leadership roles were revamped and decision-making decentralized. However, for all the democratizing changes, most communities saw their numbers plummet. In a way, the instinct of Bishop Waters might seem to have been correct: that discarding the habit would destroy religious life. However, it was not the habit but the changing times. What Waters could not envision was a church that could prosper without legions of anonymous, veiled women religious.

Sisters Leave the Diocese

Some nuns did leave the diocesan service immediately, including the principal of Asheville Catholic High School. In fact, it was the Asheville school which precipitated the Bishop's letter. It had been reported to Waters early in 1971, that Sister Kathleen Winters, a member of the Religious of Christian Education community, was wearing "secular garb" in lieu of the religious habit. In correspondence between the bishop and the Reverend Edward J. Sheridan, Administrator of the high school, Waters expressed his disapproval. In response, Sheridan wrote back, "Sister Winters has been the best sister with whom I have worked and I have found that secular dress, either on the part of Sister Winters or other sisters, has not hindered their inner spirituality or their work with people."[29]

Hoping to avoid the dismissal of the sisters, Sheridan arranged a meeting with the Bishop in Raleigh. The goal was to get Waters to defer his order for one year in order for arrangements to be made for a smooth staff transition. However, after their long drive from Asheville in the far western section of the state, Sheridan and the sisters were informed by Waters that arrangements had just been made for Sisters of Mercy to replace the non-conforming sisters, whose services were no longer needed -- or wanted.

In Burlington, North Carolina, the Sisters of Providence of St. Mary's of the Woods, Indiana, announced that they were leaving Blessed Sacrament Catholic School. They told Religious News Service that "their order gave them freedom to wear what they chose and to accede to the bishop's ruling would violate their principles."[30] In Chapel Hill, Notre Dame de Namur Sister Grace said that she was leaving the diocese but would like to come back, "but only if the Bishop changes his mind or we get a new bishop."[31]

The Priests Speak Out

Certainly emboldened by years of tweaking the bishop's nose and angered at his ignoring of their petitions, the North Carolina Priests' Association issued a scathing statement criticizing Waters' letter on the religious habit. It said in part:

> To measure the depth of dedication according to a criterion based primarily upon the clothing worn seems shallow indeed, and to reject the services of a substantial number of sisters and to prohibit them from working in the diocese seems to place the ministry in a subservient position. The needs of the ministry demand greater depth of thought and judgment.[32]

However, the priests may have exceeded the bounds of honesty as well as prudence. Father Mulholland, spokesman for the Association, was quoted as saying that "two marriages of priests in the past six months were to nuns who wore the traditional habits rather than secular dress." The implication was, of course, that the habit did not shield nuns from romantic entanglements. Efforts by the Bishop to substantiate Mulholland's charge were not successful.[33]

The Association's criticism of the bishop was not subscribed to by all the Raleigh priests. One of them, Monsignor Edward T. Gilbert, pastor of St. Bernadette's parish, Goldsboro, wrote to Waters:

> I believe that you have taken the lead, Bishop, to correct a scandalous practice among many of our Religious. Your masterful letter gives evidence of strong leadership, which means so much to the pastors who have schools.[34]

Gilbert's letter went on to draw attention to what he considered a related problem, that of Catholic lay women who wore clothing "that reveals almost half the anatomy of a woman." He added, suggesting a common style of preaching of the day, "I frequently decry from the pulpit this pagan fashion...." In concluding, the pastor who shared his bishop's perspective on contemporary church issues said, "May I be so bold as to suggest that your Excellency write a pastoral letter on this subject?" As will be seen below, on Nov. 30, Waters did just that.

Reinforcing Correspondence

Although the bishop did not answer critics or give interviews, he did respond to everyone who sent a *supportive* letter.[35] It is clear from specific points made in his reply, that Waters read all the correspondence. Furthermore, the tone of his letters suggests the motivation which impelled the bishop along what many felt was a self-destructive path. For example, to two sisters in Iowa he wrote: "We are fighting against fallen angels and the battle is permitted by the good Lord for our eternal welfare."[36] To a Sister of Charity in Ohio he wrote that he hoped that "present-day "fads" of secular dress will be replaced by a return to the traditional habit." To a priest in Michigan he wrote: "Despite the flak to which you refer [from dissenters], the vast majority of all the letters I have received on this subject have been in support of my stand."[37] It is clear that, effectively walled within his residence and receiving so much encouragement from his correspondents, Waters felt no need to reverse or compromise his position.

Many of the letters he received were prompted by (and accompanied by) articles, editorials, and letters favorable to the bishop which had appeared in such conservative periodicals as the *Wanderer*, the *Brooklyn Tablet*, and *Divine Love*. For example, the Brooklyn diocesan paper published a long letter from Mrs. Eugene McCarthy, who knew Bishop Waters and had just returned from speaking at Belmont, Raleigh, Greensboro, and Asheville in support of the Consortium Perfectae Caritatis, a coalition of conservative nuns established in December 1970 and which campaigned for the retention of the habit. Mrs. McCarthy said that she and the sisters had been well received in North Carolina. Furthermore, she cited the Decree on Religious Life from the Vatican Council which speaks of the habit as "an outward sign of consecration." She also referred to a June 29, 1971 Exhortation of the pope which again supported wearing of the habit. Her argument was that Waters was simply carrying out the decrees of the Council and of the pope.[38]

In October 1971, *Divine Love*[39] published a "Revised Modesty in Dress Issue" which included the complete text of Waters' letter. An editorial quoted a nun as saying that Waters' letter was "a burst of sunlight through darkening clouds." Readers were urged to write to Waters indicating their support. Although there was no organized letter-writing campaign, several of the letters to the bishop referred to *Divine Love*.

In addition to the letters which Waters received, documents and papers which buttressed his position also provided what he considered telling testimony to the dangers of the "fad" of secular dress. Perhaps the most elaborate defense of the traditional habit was a position paper written by an anonymous member of the Sisters of Mercy of Burlingame, California and dated May 1971, several months *before* the Waters letter.[40] It is clear from the tone of the lengthy paper, which was prepared for presentation to the community's General Assembly, that serious differences of opinion existed within religious orders themselves. The unnamed author argued for the retention of a religious habit, not simply because of such issues as the cost of a wardrobe as a waste of community resources and a violation of the vow of poverty, but as a threat to the vow of celibacy as well. She wrote:

> A goodly proportion of Sisters here in secular clothes have drifted out of the more tailored, more conservative type of dress into styles appropriate for young girls who are still playing the dating game.

Divisions Among Nuns Themselves

Just as priests were organizing nationally, so also were nuns. On the side of tradition, the Consortium Perfectae Caritatis, claiming to represent 40,000 sisters, mounted a sophisticated lobbying campaign led by the group's Chairman, Sister Mary Elise, SND. A letter sent to all the American bishops by the Consortium referred to the "present crisis and polarization in religious communities of women"[41] and urged the bishops to address the issue of the habit at their upcoming meeting.

Sensing a powerful ally in Sister Elise, Waters wrote to her commending the Consortium as a group dedicated to "the preservation of real Religious sisters as we have known them."[42] He reported to her that unfortunately the issue of the dress of sisters was not taken up at the November bishops' meeting. He added, however, that several bishops were "very eloquent" in expressing their high esteem for the Consortium. His own esteem for the conservative group is indicated by the fact that in responding to letters from nuns, Waters frequently urged them to join the Consortium.

On the other side of the ideological spectrum was the National Coalition of American Nuns (NCAN), which issued a statement that included the words, "...sisterly solidarity is destroyed when sisters move into a school or hospital from which other nuns have been evicted by arbitrary mandate of parish or diocesan decision-makers."[43] Citing the situation in Raleigh specifically, the NCAN said that nuns must organize and work together to obtain their rights. Lest the analogy with the labor movement be missed, the statement added: "American nuns are probably now where American labor was in the 1930s."

In time, many of the rancorous divisions in religious life subsided, with sisters either leaving their orders or adjusting to the reality of a dramatically changed Catholic landscape. Hollywood may continue to portray stereotypical veiled nuns, but the reality today is a corps of highly educated, professional women who serve the church in a variety of ministries far removed from the parochial school classroom of the pre-conciliar period. The roles they now occupy in the church in North Carolina will be described in Chapter Eleven. Some of the senior sisters working in the state nod their heads and sigh when Bishop Waters is mentioned, recalling the boiling caldron of conflict that characterized the decade after Vatican II.

Discussion in the Press

Not all Catholic papers were editorially supportive of Waters. One, anticipating the view that eventually would prevail, wrote, "We thought the day had finally passed in the Church when Roman congregations and members of the hierarchy would be telling women what to wear." Referring to the habit as "antiquated togs," the editorial said that religious should be able to "make their own decisions regarding what they would wear, when they would recreate, when they would go to bed, etc."[44]

On the other hand, one syndicated columnist wrote in support of Waters, but with a subdued tone, attempting to uncover the basic issues at stake. Referring to the Catholic Church as characterized by outward signs, symbols, and sacraments, he said, "The religious habit proclaims to the world that here is a person who has dedicated her life totally to Christ."[45] The columnist was none other than Dale Francis, who knew Bishop Waters very well having founded and edited Waters' own *North Carolina Catholic* twenty-five years earlier.

Minimal Support from Other Bishops

While a Franciscan priest in Paterson, New Jersey wrote to congratulate Waters as "the first bishop in the United States who has taken a stand" on the issue of the religious habit, an Illinois priest wrote prophetically: "You will be crucified unless and until more bishops come bravely to your side."[46]

Little support was forthcoming. Only one bishop, Leo Aloysius Pursley of Ft. Wayne-South Bend, Indiana took an identical stand and experienced much the same consequences, with some sisters leaving his diocese while others cheered him.[47] No bishop came out publicly in support of Waters. It is not so much that they disagreed with their North Carolina colleague, but they were reluctant to antagonize and lose religious sisters. Only one bishop, Albert L. Fletcher of Little Rock, Arkansas, wrote to Waters expressing his support but saying that it was too late in the year for him to do anything immediately. His praise of Waters included the sentence, "You must have had the Holy Spirit looking over your shoulder when you wrote that letter."[48]

Certainly Waters believed that he was acting under divine guidance, or at least fulfilling his duty as a bishop. The feedback he received reinforced that conviction. As far away as Laramie, Wyoming a supporter wrote that "the fact that Bishop Waters is keeping alive the hallmark of respect in the face of mounting opposition from some quarters will be forever to his credit."[49] Waters did not look for credit or adulation on this issue any more than he had by his stand on racial integration. Doggedly, like the little Dutch boy in the story, he attempted to plug the hole in the dyke, but the flood waters continued to pore in washing away the traditions which Waters and his supporters loved.

Priests Are Told How to Dress

Undeterred by the criticism and encouraged by the hundreds of letters of support, Waters moved ahead to the next stage of his dress code campaign. It had happened that on October 1, two months before Waters' letter on religious habits, a priest in Louisville, Kentucky had written a letter to his local newspaper opposing the secular attire of nuns. When Waters' letter appeared, the Kentucky priest wrote to the bishop as a fellow defender of appropriate attire. In his reply, Waters reflected that if he had "taken up the cudgels" earlier, there would not have been as much opposition. Perhaps. Early or late, he confided to the priest, "I still have to write a letter to our priests and to our laity. So pray for me that we will say the right thing."[50]

Actually, Waters must have been composing the letter to the priests even as he wrote to his Louisville supporter, because it was issued only a few days later.[51] Once again he provoked a firestorm of protest. In a sense, Waters was even more severe on the priests than he had been on the sisters. The nuns he could expel from the diocese; the priests he could strip of their faculties to function as priests. And that is what he threatened, ordering all priests working in his diocese to wear black suits and a roman collar or suffer the consequences.

To find a legal basis for his clerical dress code, Waters was forced to go back twenty-three years, to the diocesan synod held in 1948. In what he referred to as "our present Diocesan synod statutes," actually long forgotten regulations written in Latin, the bishop unearthed and translated the following:

> All clerics are bound to wear a becoming clerical garb when answering a door call, when handling parish work with the laity, instructing converts, driving automobiles in the line of duty, walking on the street, or appearing in any public place."

However, since the synod had failed to specify what was meant by "clerical garb," as is quoted at the opening of this chapter, Waters filled that gap by prescribing a black suit and "conventional clerical collar." Even as Waters attempted to treat nuns and priests equally, an unintended sexist difference crept into the dress code. Whereas nuns were to wear their habits at all times, the priests were allowed to assume "less formal attire" when playing tennis, cutting the grass, or playing golf. Careful to close any possible loophole, he added, "This does not mean, however, that these sport clothes can be worn thereafter throughout the day."[52]

Predictable Response from Priests

Their ire provoked by the Bishop's latest order, the priests of the North Carolina Priests' Association sent a letter to Waters in which they called his directive "at best an exercise in triviality, at worst a symptom of a failure of leadership." NCPA president Byron was quoted as saying that his group, representing about half the 100 priests of the diocese, was more disturbed over the "retaliatory part of the bishop's decree than with the actual rules."[53] He was referring to the bishop's sentence: "I know no priest will disregard this regulation and become subject to the withdrawal of his diocesan faculties."[54]

Already nuns had been forced to leave the diocese; now priests also were threatened. Increasingly unafraid to ridicule Waters, the NCPA said that the directive "could be humorously regarded as an heirloom from the days of hoop skirts and button shoes were it not for the fact that priests were threatened with suspension." As they had done in the past, the priests requested a meeting with Waters, but as usual, none was granted.[55]

Efforts were made, to no avail, to get Waters to put the issue of dress into a broader perspective. The NCPA statement warned that the church was facing a loss of young people, a shortage of vocations to the priesthood, and a deep split between liberal and conservative Catholics. "It is a time when some voice must speak out in the name of the gospel." The priority must not be clothes, but service to others.[56]

In a similar vein, in a letter that went unanswered, a Canadian priest wrote to Waters objecting to the religious garb directives and suggesting that older men like themselves have difficulty understanding the call for dialogue and change. The priest concluded, "...but at least some of us are trying to implement this new teaching of Vatican II."[57] It is clear that Waters felt that he was implementing the rules of the Church, and that it was others who were misinterpreting or violating them.

Not Forgetting the Laity

In the interview with the press after the letter on clerical dress, Byron said prophetically, "What we expect next is a directive about the required dress for lay people attending church services."[58] Sure enough, on November 30 Waters sent a letter to the laity in the parishes, calling it an extension of the ones he had sent to sisters and priests. As he had done in the 1953 order that the Newton Grove parish be integrated, the bishop appealed to authority, telling the people that he was their "father in God in North Carolina" and had the right and duty to give "an appropriate word of admonition" as to proper attire while attending mass. As the excerpt from the letter at the opening of this chapter states, parishioners were counseled to wear their "Sunday best."

The lay people of North Carolina had not been completely silent during the months of controversy over dress. The Catholic Laity of North Carolina (CLNC), an unofficial group affiliated with the National Association of Catholic Laity and claiming a membership of 12,000 in North Carolina, had criticized Waters for prescribing a dress code for sisters, charging that Waters was interfering with "the internal jurisdiction of religious communities which have the right to decide such matters themselves."[59]

However, just as most of the nuns who wrote to Waters supported his position on the habit, so also a large proportion of the laity shared Waters' concern with the casual dress of some churchgoers. After centuries of women not entering a church without their heads covered and men wearing jackets and ties, now people were going to communion in tennis outfits and beach attire. By no means was Bishop Waters alone in believing that informality of dress had gone too far. The problem was, as had been pointed out by the Canadian priest, that he

employed the heavy hand of authority rather than the gentler arts of dialog, diplomacy, flexibility, and a sense of humor.

Communion in the Hand

The discontent with Bishop Waters was not due only to his
directives on dress. At every turn, he resisted the changes which were
sweeping away the church of his youth. However, as much as he
attempted to tug the church back to its old ways, once Rome spoke he
obeyed. So, when the Vatican ordered that the vernacular language
replace Latin as the language of worship, Waters complied. As he practiced for his first mass in English, with tears in his eyes he turned to his
priest assistant and said, "I never thought I'd be doing this."[60]

One issue can serve to illustrate the vigorous efforts Waters
used to preserve the traditional ways of doing things. Today, most
Catholics receive Communion in their hand as they stand before the
priest or eucharistic minister. Prior to the 1970's, only priests distributed
Communion, placing the Host on the tongue of the kneeling man,
woman, or child. Waters was determined to do what he could to preserve that older practice. In June 1972 he sent a letter to all the priests
of the diocese opposing communion in the hand, arguing that the practice "would make possible, and in some instances, probable, the communicating of people who are not Catholics.... It would make possible
the misuse of the Holy Eucharist by some persons in atheistic and diabolical practices unthinkable to real Catholics."[61]

In a step that was rare if not unique for Bishop Waters, he sent
a similar letter to all the American bishops. Using the tone and imagery
which characterized much of his correspondence, he wrote, "We
Bishops, leaders in the Church of Christ, all know the immoral, pagan,
and diabolical spirit of our times."[62] One of the "diabolical" developments, in Waters' view, was the proposal to change the method of
receiving Communion. He argued that receiving communion in the
hand "opens up possible desecration to the Blessed Sacrament."

Not abandoning what had become a futile campaign, the bishop wrote another letter to his priests ten weeks later on the same issue,
linking his opposition to Communion in the hand to "the sad news of
the actual theft of the Eucharist in one of our parishes."[63] However, there
was no logical connection between the two matters. Someone had
entered a church and stolen consecrated hosts from an unlocked tabernacle, not desecrated a host received in the hand.

The intensity of Waters' reverence for the Eucharist, as well as his mounting apprehension of what he termed "the enemies of God," is underscored by his order in this later letter that a "radar electrical alarm" be installed in each church. The device was to cover the area of the sanctuary and, when activated by an intruder, turn on a light and emit a loud siren which could be heard throughout the neighborhood. He further ordered that the alarm be turned on each night and the key guarded with the same care as the tabernacle key itself.

Completely Right, but Totally Wrong

Not only did Bishop Waters receive abundant support from conservative Catholics who shared his abhorrence of the changes taking place, but he received validation from the highest levels of church government. This was particularly true with reference to the pivotal issue of the dress of nuns and priests. On Feb. 2, 1972, Bishop Joseph L. Bernardin, General Secretary of the National Conference of Catholic Bishops, forwarded to Waters a copy of a letter which Archbishop Luigi Raimondi, Apostolic Delegate to the United States, had sent to Cardinal John Krol, President of the Conference of Bishops. In the letter the representative of the Vatican made it very clear that, although nuns may modify the traditional habit, "they may not abolish it altogether or leave it to the judgment of individual sisters."[64] Reinforcing and extending his point, the Apostolic Delegate added that the principle applied to male Religious as well, "who ought always to be distinguished from seculars by the roman collar or some visible and appropriate sign."

In the same mailing, Bernardin also sent to Waters a copy of a letter from the Cardinal Prefect of the Sacred Congregation for Religious to the Bishop of Fort Wayne-South Bend, Indiana. That letter made absolutely clear that Rome wanted nuns to wear habits and furthermore expected bishops to enforce the requirement.

> In regard to the Religious Habit, as you are aware, various Institutes have taken liberties far beyond what was ever intended by the Council. And if any of them say that Rome has approved their wearing contemporary secular dress, they should be challenged to show proof of this.... We would ask you to continue your insistence on the habit, your Excellency. As you know, it is not only your right but your duty."[65]

There is no doubt but that Bishop Waters consistently acted in accord with what his superiors wished. Furthermore, he was completely within his rights as bishop to give orders and to expect that they would be obeyed. There was never any complaint from his peers or superiors. At least, there was never any official objection. On the other hand, there was little imitation. Most bishops, observing what had happened with Cardinal O'Boyle in Washington, DC, Cardinal McIntyre in Los Angeles, and Bishop Waters in Raleigh, quickly learned that the times had changed and that if they wanted peace in their dioceses, they would be advised to tread softly, talk with people, and avoid confrontation.[66]

In his later years, Waters had become an ecclesiastical dinosaur, swinging his tail and baring his teeth, but increasingly seen as a man who had outlived his time. While many saw the process of change as the reinvigoration of an obsolete institution, Waters saw it as destructive. Certainly other bishops at the time shared his concern; few took such bold steps in an effort to stem the tide of reform.

In hindsight, Waters emerges as a tragic figure, a man who started his career heralded as an energetic missionary, but who ended it a widely unmourned reactionary. The man was complex but consistent, hardworking but stubborn, intelligent but unable to relate with warmth to individuals. Perhaps the most insightful recorded profile of the man was written in 1964, long after Newton Grove and before the problems just related erupted. Priests who knew Waters spoke of him in terms similar to these:

> He is many things -- fiery, tough, gentle, zealous, courtly, analytical. The moods are reflected quickly and often, rising and subsiding.... He is also a man of boundless energy and profound dedication... [and] a top flight business administrator. He has been seen by Protestant and Catholic alike as decisive if not hardheaded, courteous but sometimes blunt. If to some he's found opinionated, others are moved by his unshakable faith in God and the Church.... To some of his flock -- indeed, to some of his priests -- the Bishop perhaps has seemed austere, inaccessible.[67]

Vincent Waters loved the security afforded by what he experienced as the stability, inerrancy, and clarity of church teaching and practice. He saw no need for change. Born and raised in the changeless mountains of Virginia, the man who once walked the Appalachian Trail from Lynchburg to Roanoke did not subscribe to the prevailing American value that change was good, that progress demanded novelty, that growth and happiness were to be found in self fulfillment. The man who liked quiet pursuits like fishing, remained convinced to his dying day that what he represented and was obliged to promote was a struc-

ture built on a rock, and that obedience to the Pope and bishops was
Christ's plan for human happiness and salvation.

"From a Struggling Infancy... to a Viable Church"

The commemoration of the Fiftieth anniversary of the Diocese
of Raleigh had been set for December 8, 1974. The date was significant
for Bishop Waters. It was on December 8, 1931 that he had been
ordained a priest in the city of Rome. More important, it was the feast
of the Immaculate Conception of Mary the Mother of Jesus. Devotion
to Mary had been a central component of his spirituality throughout his
life. Even as Mary receded somewhat into the background for many
Catholics after the Vatican Council, she remained for Waters the loving,
tender woman in whom he confided and to whom he turned for consolation. Every day without fail he prayed the Rosary, saluting Mary over
and over again in the "Hail, Mary."

The occasion was to be the most impressive liturgical event in
the history of Catholicism in the state. Three Cardinals would be pres-
ent -- Lawrence Shehan, the retired Archbishop of Baltimore, Patrick
O'Boyle, the retired Archbishop of Washington, and John Wright,
Prefect of the Sacred Congregation of the Clergy. Eighteen other bish-
ops and abbots would process down the aisle in the Dorton Arena in
Raleigh, since the Cathedral of the Sacred Heart could not accommo-
date the anticipated crowd. The homilist would be the most famous
Catholic priest in America, the TV celebrity, Bishop Fulton J. Sheen.
Presiding over all these dignitaries would be the Most Reverend Vincent
S. Waters.[68]

However, this crowning glory of Waters' three decades in
North Carolina was not to be. He died suddenly of a heart attack on
December 3 at the age of 70 and was buried on the 7th.[69] Yet another
Cardinal, John Cody of Chicago, was the principal celebrant at the
funeral mass. Because the cathedral in Raleigh is so small, only clergy,
civic dignitaries, and relatives of the deceased could attend the service.
Rumor has it that one of the visiting bishops, looking around the tiny
church, commented, "So this was Vincent's cathedral!" Built in the
early 1920's, the church had not been intended as a cathedral, but rather
the neighborhood church for the few hundred Catholics living in
Raleigh at the time. When the diocese was established, Sacred Heart, as
the only church in the city, became the cathedral by default. Although
frequently suggested, a larger cathedral was not a priority for Waters,

who took pride in the fact that during his tenure Catholic churches had been established in the majority of counties in the state.

As Waters had wished, the celebration of the anniversary went forward on schedule the day following his funeral, the festivities tempered by the death of their central figure. As the service proceeded, with all the pageantry for which the Catholic Church is noted, attendees looked at the photograph of Waters in the commemorative booklet and read the words he had prepared for the occasion. In this text there is no hint of the controversies in which he had been embroiled, no reference to his discomfort with the changes taking place in the church, no allusion to the scores of priests and sisters who had resigned from church service, or to the precipitous decline in the number of vocations and converts. There is only joy and satisfaction in what he termed "a growth in wisdom and age and grace and numbers."

In these his final public words, Waters also reflects back to "those who planted the Faith on our soil in colonial days and those who nourished this Faith in infancy, such as Bishop John England and Judge William Gaston." The following chapters will examine those early days in which the foundation for the Catholic Church in North Carolina was laid.

Vincent S. Waters (1904-1974), a priest of the Richmond, Virginia diocese, was consecrated bishop of Raleigh on May 15, 1945. After the ceremony in the Richmond cathedral, he gave his blessing to his father, Michael Waters, and to the hundreds of others who gathered in his honor. On June 9, he was installed as bishop in Raleigh's miniscule cathedral (above right).

88

In the top photo, taken in the late 1940's, Bishop Waters posed in front of Sacred Heart Cathedral with most of the priests of the state. The blessing of the new St. Therese parochial school in Wilson (center left) was concrete evidence of the goal of establishing a Catholic school in every parish. Scores of times Waters signed deeds for church property and contracts for new hospitals, churches, and schools. Trailers equipped as chapels were used during summer months to bring the Church's message to remote sectors of the state.

In the top photo, Bishop Waters posed with priests and laity outside Holy Trinity church in Kinston, Lenoir County, in the eastern section of the state. In the town of Cherokee in Swain County in the westernmost corner of the state, he stood with clergy and religious sisters outside the new mission church of Our Lady of Guadalupe (center). After the ceremony, he greeted children.

Bishop Waters died December 3, 1974 and was buried on the 7th. The closed casket at the funeral mass in the cathedral (top) served to symbolize the closing of an era. Waters was buried in the cemetery of the Newton Grove church of Our Lady of Guadalupe (center left) where in 1953 he had integrated the parish. His neighbors in the graveyard included Dr. John Monk, the founder of the church as well as a number of other members of the Monk family.

Part II

A Seed Very Slow to Grow

In 1945, one hundred and twenty-five years after the establishment of the church in North Carolina, there were but 15,000 Catholics in the state, a fraction of a percent of the total population. Such slow development occurred despite the efforts of talented church leaders, in particular Bishop John England, Bishop James Gibbons, Father Thomas Frederick Price, and the prominent lawyer and political figure, William Gaston. An explanation for the failure of the church to grow during this protracted period will be found in the context of the lives of these men and others.

*   *   *

I am bound as a Citizen, and am bound by oath, to support the Constitution of North Carolina. I am avowedly a believer in the doctrines of the Catholic Church. If that Constitution disqualifies a believer in those doctrines from holding public office, it would be dishonorable and wicked in me to accept it.

• William Gaston, 1833

Chapter Four

The Establishment of an Ecclesiastical Presence: Bishop John England & Judge William Gaston

We have had for the last ten days our new Bishop with us. He has done a great deal of good in gathering together the scattered members of his flock and in adding to his fold. He is a man of great learning and eloquence and has preached every night during his stay in Newbern to the most crowded auditories and has wonderfully increased the respect for the Catholic Faith. He is zealous in the cause of religion and promises as soon as possible to station a respectable and good priest amongst us and we are preparing to have a suitable church. The large room in our house above stairs was fitted up as a chapel and he and his sister, a very interesting young lady, staid with me. This day they take their departure.

---William Gaston to his daughter, Susan, June 4, 1821

*   *   *

Although the first white men to visit what would become the state of North Carolina were Roman Catholics, the sound of their Spanish voices would in time fade into the mist of history as the clash of European empires gave the prize to England. The victors brought not only a different language, but a different religion. As the centuries passed, a colony became a state, and that state progressively fashioned its distinctive character. Cotton was king, and slavery its vassal. Only a few Catholics ventured into North Carolina, most of whom were soon absorbed by the dominant Protestant religious culture. It would not be until the 1820's that even the most tenuous Catholic congregational presence would emerge. And that nascent vessel, like a tiny boat on a stormy sea, would struggle to remain afloat only to be swamped by the tidal wave of the Civil War. Barely begun, soon destroyed.

The present chapter will relate the story of the Catholic presence in North Carolina from the earliest days to the approach of the War Between the States, focusing especially on the work of Bishop John England and the assistance given him by William Gaston, the most prominent Catholic North Carolinian of the 19th century. Chapter Five will examine in some detail three major issues in which these two men were involved: the debate on the institution of slavery, the amendment of the North Carolina state constitution to permit Catholics to hold public office, and the effort to introduce more democratic structures into the American Catholic Church.

Spanish Colonial Efforts

Early in the Sixteenth Century, Spanish explorers and soldiers, their ships tossing in the breeze in the shallow coastal harbors, moved tentatively through the swampy tidelands and along the rivers which reached like menacing fingers into the uncharted interior of a land that promised gold and threatened disease. The indigenous people, who met the bearded strangers on the shore and peered at them from the forest, would hear the name of Jesus Christ and see the Cross which some of these men from another world held aloft; but they would not understand. They would also see the gleaming swords and metal breastplates which protected the newcomers from their arrows; these they would soon understand. It was easier to demonstrate the power of the sword than the power of the Cross.

Spain had a head start in what became the mad scramble for dominance in the New World. When, at the end of the Fifteenth Century, Christopher Columbus reported to Ferdinand and Isabelle that he had discovered vast areas of land thousands of miles out in the Atlantic and that these lands were inhabited by near-naked people, government officials began to dream of conquest, business men and adventurers of profits, and priests of souls to be won for Christ. Never in the history of the world had such exciting challenges presented themselves. Indeed, as the sun rose on the Sixteenth Century, fragile ships set sail. The exploration of America had begun.[1]

By 1539, Spain had established a military base in Florida which served as a staging point for an expedition in search of gold and silver. Rumors had circulated that vast amounts of the precious metals were to be found. Led by Hernando de Soto, the band of Spaniards worked its way north, eventually finding itself in the steamy lowlands of North Carolina. What they discovered was not gold, but disease, hunger, and death. The wilderness conditions sapped their energies and broke their spirits. After several years of futile efforts, the venture was abandoned, de Soto himself one of its victims, his body consigned to the waters of the Mississippi River.

Europe during this period was in a state of political and religious ferment and instability. In 1535, a German priest had nailed to the door of the church in Wittenberg his list of objections to the Catholic Church. Martin Luther did not realize that his action would not only sunder the religious unity which had characterized Europe for a thousand years, but fuel political rivalries and fratricidal wars. A few years later, the fabric of Catholic hegemony was further rent when King Henry VIII of England rejected papal authority, disconnected his country from its union with the Church of Rome, and initiated a persecution of Catholics that would continue for centuries and in due course infect the American colonies.

The feudal order which had shaped European society for a millennium dissolved as alternative world views, political systems, and economic theories jostled for dominance. Reason and science wrestled with faith and ritual. To a large extent, the old order was championed by the Catholic Church and the new by Protestantism. From the Protestant perspective, for the modern world to emerge it had to free itself from the political and ideological prison in which the Roman Church attempted to keep it enchained. For Catholics, Protestantism was a betrayal of the heritage which had its roots in Christ and his apostles.

The religious rivalries which racked Europe were transported across the sea and profoundly affected the colonization of the Americas. In particular, Spain and France, which retained a Catholic orientation, confronted Protestant England. There was no middle ground, no room for religious tolerance. Sectarian feelings were deep, even savage. The struggle for land was coupled with the struggle for souls.

On the Catholic side, the most effective warriors would be the well-educated, highly disciplined priests of the Society of Jesus, founded in Spain by Ignatius of Loyola in 1540 precisely as a response to the Protestant Reformation. The Jesuits were the front line troops in the effort to recapture for Rome those areas of Europe that had been lost, and also to win to the Catholic faith the native peoples of the emerging new world. Hundreds, then thousands, of young men flocked to this religious movement, pledging themselves to the service of Christ but also, by a special vow, to the service of the Pope. Understandably, the

Jesuits became targets of Protestant fear and hatred. To people wary of being subjected once again to papal authority, the very word "Jesuit"was synonymous with cunning, intrigue, and duplicity.

During the 1560's the first Jesuit missionaries arrived in Florida. Then in 1571, as part of the effort to advance the Spanish presence northward, five of them attempted to establish a mission in the Chesapeake Bay region. With their companions, all the priests were killed by Indians, terminating what might have been a Spanish, and hence Catholic, outpost as far north as Virginia. This misadventure occurred decades before the first permanent English settlement in the New World at Jamestown, Virginia in 1607. Had the Spanish colonial efforts to the north of Florida succeeded, North Carolina might have had a Catholic religious tradition. As it was, Protestant England would colonize the entire East Coast of North America between French Catholic Canada and Spanish Catholic Florida. Eventually, even those areas would fall to English control.[2]

Early English Attempts at Settlement

Although the venture would fail, North Carolina was the site of the earliest effort to establish an English presence in America. In 1584, Walter Raleigh sent two ships from England to assess the idea of planting a military base from which to mount attacks against the Spanish in Florida and the West Indies. The ships worked their way past the Outer Banks into Albemarle Sound and landed at Roanoke Island, on which today is located the town of Manteo, mentioned in Chapter Two. The sailors brought back to England such glowing accounts of the area that the following year one hundred eight would-be colonists took the perilous journey across the ocean. They disembarked at Roanoke Island but soon became discouraged and returned to England with Sir Francis Drake, who had landed at Roanoke after a raid against the Spanish.

This setback did not deter Raleigh, who in 1587 sent a second group of settlers. This one included women and children. One of the women gave birth to the first white child born in English America, Virginia Dare. However the settlement disappeared, creating one of the great mysteries of the colonization of North America. No trace has ever been found of what became known as the Lost Colony.

One of those who endeavored to find the Lost Colony was the Spanish sea captain, Vicente Gonzalez, who, in 1588, made a futile search of Roanoke Island and the surrounding area. It was this same

Vicente Gonzalez who, seventeen years before, had brought the ill-fated Jesuits to Virginia.[3] Conflict between the English and Spanish for dominance in the area would continue for more than one hundred and fifty years. However, as Gonzalez sailed away from Roanoke Island, for all intents and purposes Spanish hopes for a presence in the Carolinas left with him. The political, military, and economic victory of the English would be, by default, a religious victory as well. But even the English would wait many years before again attempting a settlement in the inhospitable wilderness of the Carolinas. And for nearly a century, there would be no further evidence of Catholics in the area.

The English Colony in North Carolina

Initially, what would become North Carolina was part of the Virginia colony. This southern section of Virginia was visited by English fur trappers for some years, but it was not until about 1660 that Nathaniel Batts settled into his two-room house on the Albemarle Sound in the present day Bertie County, becoming the first permanent white settler. Shortly thereafter, in 1663, the area attained a new status when King Charles II rewarded eight of his supporters by granting them a charter to a vast area south of Virginia and north of Georgia, a region embracing what eventually would be both North and South Carolina. In honor of their patron, the proprietors called the colony Carolina, from the Latin form of the king's name, *Carolus.*

It is worth noting that Charles II came to power in 1660 during one of the most tumultuous periods of English history. In 1649, Charles' father, Charles I, had been tried and executed as a traitor by Parliament which, after abolishing the monarchy and the House of Lords, established a republic under the leadership of Oliver Cromwell. Central to the long period of civil strife and confusion was the issue of religion. It was feared by the Protestants, both the Anglicans and the Puritan dissidents, that the king would restore Catholicism as the official religion of the realm. They had reason to be concerned. Charles II, who was recalled from exile in Scotland by a group of nobles, including those who would become the Proprietors of the Carolina colony, died a Catholic in 1685. His brother, James, who succeeded him, was openly a Catholic and so opposed by parliamentary leaders that they invited the Protestant William of Orange to become king. In 1688, William invaded from the Netherlands with 15,000 troops, defeated the forces of James, and with his wife, Mary, as Queen, was crowned King. The victory of Protestantism was now complete and Catholics cast in the position of enemies of the state.

Aside from these political and religious matters, the Proprietors of the Carolinas were attempting to wrest a profit from the resources of their far-off lands. Since Charleston harbor could handle larger ships than the harbors further north, the area that would become North Carolina was neglected and its economy remained stagnant. Problems in the northern settlements were aggravated by religious conflict. In 1672, George Fox, founder of the Quakers, had visited the towns in the Albemarle Sound area and several Quaker congregations were started. By the 1690's, the numerical strength of the Quakers enabled them to gain control of the local government. With that, the Anglicans complained to the Proprietors, asking that Church of England missionaries be sent to help build churches in Carolina and thereby help restore Anglican political dominance.

The Proprietors obliged and in 1701 an Anglican chapel, the first church building in the colony, was constructed in what is now the town of Edenton. Furthermore, the Proprietors ordered that all colonists, including the Quakers, pay for the support of the Anglican clergy. Finally, the Vestry Act of 1703 provided that all men who wished to be elected to the local assembly swear an oath that they were members of the Church of England. This privileged position of the Church of England would continue until the Revolutionary War when it, along with England itself, was removed from its position of dominance. During all this period, there was no Catholic presence in the area.[4]

Problems administering the vast colony led the Proprietors, in 1711, to divide North and South Carolina into separate jurisdictions. Even so, governing an area that was larger than many European countries was a problem, one which a century later the Catholic Church would face as well. Also, "the fever" long remained the price that white men paid for venturing into the swampy environment of coastal North Carolina. Likewise, the scourge of yellow fever and other diseases would hamper the development of the Catholic Church. Bishop John England regularly bemoaned the epidemics which killed hundreds of people, including several of the young priests he had attracted to the remote mission.

Growth of the Colony

Besides disease, the colonists had to contend with Indians. In 1660 there were some fifty thousand native Americans in the coastal region. By 1711, their numbers had been reduced by diseases imported from Europe to about five thousand. As the white settlers continued to arrive, taking the best land and disrupting traditional hunting grounds, the Indians mounted a war. But they had waited too long. Although they laid waste several of the white settlements and killed many of the new-comers, they could not prevail against the superior technology of the Europeans. The remnants of the original inhabitants of North Carolina were banished to the west. The way was now clear for more rapid devel-opment.

One man who was attracted by the promise of inexpensive land and religious freedom was the Swiss nobleman, Baron Christoph von Graffenried, who was looking for a place in America to settle a community of Swiss and German Protestants. Baron von Graffenried bought a large tract on the Neuse and Trent Rivers and in 1710 sent six hundred fifty people to Carolina. Half the voyagers died on the journey. The rest were robbed of their belongings by a French warship. When the survivors finally reached Carolina, they established the second incorpo-rated town in the colony, New Bern, named for the city in Switzerland (Berne) from which many of them had come.[5] It would be New Bern, founded by Protestants, that a century later would be, in effect, the cra-dle of North Carolina Catholicism. Here in 1821, William Gaston would welcome John England, the first bishop.

As will be seen, Gaston was instrumental in removing from the North Carolina state constitution the exclusion of Catholics from public office. But that would be in 1835. In 1735, the situation was far differ-ent. All the colonies had statutes against Catholics and they were rigor-ously enforced. Even Maryland, founded by Lord Baltimore in 1634 as a haven for Catholics, by 1654 had disenfranchised Catholics. Massachusetts, which today has a large and politically powerful Catholic population, in 1700 passed an act against "Jesuits and popish priests," which ordered all Catholic priests to leave the colony. If they did not do so, they were to be judged enemies of "the true Christian reli-gion" and sentenced to life imprisonment. Furthermore, anyone harbor-ing "any Jesuit, priest, missionary, or other ecclesiastical person of the Romish clergy" was subject to a fine and to be punished with three days in the pillory.

To be a Catholic in colonial America was to be reviled as superstitious, suspected of treason, and barred from public life.

The proprietary period in North Carolina ended in 1729, when the Proprietors, unable to profit from their holdings, sold their rights to the king. The few thousand colonists hoped that as a royal colony North Carolina might gain political stability and economic success. Such hopes were not soon realized, even as the colony grew from a number of disparate directions and sources.

The initial settlements had progressed southward from Virginia, first in the Albemarle Sound area, then in Pamlico Sound, and finally around the Neuse River. In the late 1720's, entrepreneurs began moving north from Charleston, South Carolina into the Cape Fear region, developing large plantations and founding the port city of Wilmington, which in the nineteenth century would become the most populous and culturally diverse city in the state. Included in this wave of settlers were Welsh and Scottish immigrants. The ethnic diversity of the colony was increased further by the overland movement of German and Scotch Irish settlers from Pennsylvania who began to settle the North Carolina piedmont, well to the west of the communities along the rivers and sounds to the east.[6] From these various streams of immigrants the North Carolina culture was being shaped. A similar process was taking place in all the colonies as they became progressively less and less European and more and more distinctively American. And there was one thing that all the regions had in common -- their suspicion of all things Catholic.[7]

In this emerging human amalgam there was a component not yet mentioned, one already deeply ingrained in the fiber of the area, one which would contribute to the prosperity of the colony and state, but which also would poison the soul of a people. It was the "peculiar institution" of slavery. Particularly in the eastern part of North Carolina, it was slave labor that cleared the land, planted the crops, dug the irrigation canals, cared for the houses, and tended the children so that white men might be comfortable. The enslavement of Africans was not only justified by churchgoing colonists but supported by Bible-quoting ministers. Catholics, though divided from their neighbors in other respects, were united with them in accepting slavery. While the Revolutionary War would gain for the colonies their freedom from England, it did not loose the chains which bound the slaves.

The Gastons of New Bern

Although there would be no permanent Catholic clerical presence in North Carolina until nearly half a century into the existence of the new nation, a small but resilient lay presence emerged near the end of the colonial period and took an active role in the American Revolution. This Catholic community, though lacking official recognition or leadership, would cling to the faith and in due time welcome the first bishop assigned to the area. In particular, the Gaston family of New Bern emerged as the foremost seedbed from which the Catholic Church would emerge.[8]

In the early 1760's, Alexander Gaston, a medical doctor, arrived in New Bern and soon became one of the most prosperous and prominent residents of the town. Dr. Gaston's French name derived from a Huguenot family that fled from France to Scotland around 1640 and later fled once again, this time to Ireland, seeking religious freedom. After receiving his medical education at the University of Edinburgh, Alexander joined the British navy as a physician. While serving with the fleet which in 1762 captured Havana, Dr. Gaston contracted a fever, resigned his commission, and settled in New Bern.

As opposition to English rule intensified, Gaston became active in the rebel cause. His name on a 1775 document urging the citizens to remain firm in the growing struggle for liberty, placed his life at risk.

That same year, Margaret Sharpe arrived from England to visit her brothers who were merchants in New Bern. From a devout Catholic family, Margaret had been sent to a convent school in France in an effort to protect her faith in the hostile English environment. Now, in a remote colony on the edge of civilization, the twenty-year-old young woman met and fell in love with Alexander Gaston. Her brief visit was transformed into a lifetime. From the union of Margaret and Alexander, the Catholic Church in North Carolina was born.

During the unsettled conditions of the revolutionary period, while her husband assumed ever more important positions as a rebel leader, Margaret gave birth to three children. The first died as an infant. The second, William, was born in 1778 and two years later, Jane. Then, on Sunday, August 18, 1781, as the Gastons were eating breakfast, word was received that the Redcoats had arrived. Dr. Gaston quickly got into a boat and started rowing across the Trent River to his plantation on the other side. The English troops galloped directly to the wharf, found the small boat still within range, and shot Dr. Gaston. Three-year-old William and one-year-old Jane were fatherless. At the time of her husband's death, the widow was twenty-six years old.[9] Her two brothers were already dead. Margaret Gaston devoted the remainder of her life to the care and education of her children.

Perhaps recalling her own education in a Catholic school in Calais, France, Mrs. Gaston, upon hearing that a Catholic college was to be opened at Georgetown in Maryland, decided to enroll her son. So, in 1791, at the age of twelve, William left New Bern in the company of John Devereux, an old friend of the family. Since the college had not yet opened, the boy lived for five months in Philadelphia with a Dominican priest, Francis Fleming, who helped the young Gaston prepare for college. At the time, Philadelphia was the capitol of the infant nation. The first Congress and the first president were beginning the process of implementing the newly ratified Constitution.

William attended morning Mass at six o'clock each day, went to an English school in the morning and a French school in the afternoon. While waiting for lunch, he read Latin and Greek. In the late afternoon he spent an hour in Father Fleming's library reading what the priest thought proper.

Finally in November, after a three-day journey by stage coach, William was turned over to the Reverend Robert Plunkett, the first president of Georgetown. Since the school building was not yet completed, the young student lived for several weeks with the president and became Georgetown's first student.

The Establishment of the Catholic Church in the United States

While young Gaston was benefiting from a rare opportunity in America to receive a classical Catholic education, the church was slowly being established in a nation which itself was still very much an experiment in democracy, closely watched by a skeptical world. The first federal census taken in 1790 counted some three million people in the thirteen states of the Union, of whom perhaps 50,000 were Catholic.[10]

Before the colonies won their independence from England, the status of the church in English America was quite ambiguous. Missionary priests from Europe answered only to their far-off superiors, and when the French-speaking bishop of Quebec contacted the Jesuits in Philadelphia to inquire if they would be interested in the appointment of a bishop and in his visiting the colonies in order to administer Confirmation, the response was direct and clear: we don't want a bishop and we don't want you to visit. As the Jesuit priest wrote: "It is incredible how hateful to non-Catholics in all parts of America is the very name of Bishop."[11]

However, in 1784, American independence having been won, Rome decided that it was time to establish a local authority in the new country. Accordingly, John Carroll (1735-1815), who had accompanied Benjamin Franklin on a mission to Canada during the war, was appointed superior of the missions in the new country and given faculties to administer Confirmation. Thus, several needs were met: Catholics could be confirmed, no bishop need disturb the Protestants, and the designated representative of the Church was acceptable to the American government.

In his report to Rome in 1785, Carroll estimated the number of Catholics in Maryland, Pennsylvania, Virginia, and New York as about 25,000. He then added: "Many other Catholics are said to be scattered in ... other states, who are utterly deprived of all religious ministry." This, of course, included North Carolina.

Although earlier the priests working in America had been opposed to the appointment of a bishop, by 1788 they felt that conditions had become more favorable. Accordingly, they took a step which was extraordinary in the history of Catholicism. They requested permission to choose the bishop themselves. Rome agreed with their request, stipulating that this was a one time only privilege. The priests voted with near unanimity for John Carroll, and in November 1789 the Diocese of Baltimore was established with Carroll the first bishop. The diocese embraced the entire country.

Gaston's Continuing Education And Early Career

In 1793, after two years at Georgetown, which was not yet accredited as a college, Gaston returned to North Carolina where he was enrolled in the New Bern Academy, conducted by the Reverend Thomas Irving, a Presbyterian minister and Princeton graduate. Midway through the year that he studied at the academy, Gaston delivered an oration "on the blessings of American independence," and when the school closed for summer vacation, once again it was Gaston, already showing singular eloquence, who delivered the valedictory on the theme "The Rising Glory of America." Noting the young man's talent, the Reverend Irving urged Margaret Gaston to send her son to Princeton.

Although pleased to have her son at home, Margaret continued to have great ambitions for William. She consulted Father Francis Neale, one of Gaston's professors at Georgetown. Father Neale opposed the idea of sending Gaston to Princeton, fearful that the young man's faith would be endangered at the Protestant institution. Margaret persisted, contacting Bishop Carroll, who gave his approval.

Before enrolling at Princeton, Gaston spent a month in Philadelphia, visiting friends from his former stay, including Rembrandt Peale, son of the famous artist, Charles Willson Peale. On his earlier visit to Philadelphia, Gaston had written to his mother that Rembrandt had been converted to Catholicism, but that his father was so bitterly opposed that he did everything he could to discourage the fifteen-year-old from continuing in the faith, including serving nothing but meat on Fridays, so that the young man "would be obliged to have no dinner or make out with a piece of bread." Gaston was experiencing first hand the vehemence with which some Protestants opposed his religion.

In 1798, at the age of eighteen, Gaston graduated from Princeton at the head of his class and returned once more to New Bern where he decided to become a lawyer. Since there were no law schools, the young man studied for two years under Francois Xavier Martin, a Catholic and a distinguished lawyer, who later in life became chief justice of the Louisiana supreme court.

Around the time that Gaston was admitted to the bar, his sister, Jane, married John Louis Taylor, a Fayetteville lawyer. Subsequently, Taylor was made a judge and with his family relocated to the state capitol, Raleigh. Just as William Gaston would welcome Bishop England to New Bern, his sister would host the bishop in Raleigh, give him access to influential people, and be one of the principal patrons of the Catholic church there.

While on a visit to his sister when she was still in Fayetteville, William Gaston fell in love with Susan Hay, daughter of yet another lawyer. The couple were married in Fayetteville in 1803. Susan was sixteen and William twenty five. The newly weds returned to New Bern where Gaston continued with his law career. Unfortunately, just eight months after the wedding, the young bride died from complications of pregnancy.

Two years later Gaston married Hannah McClure, the daughter of a general. Since there were no priests in North Carolina, Gaston wrote to Bishop Carroll in Baltimore for guidance. The bishop referred him to Father Simon Felix Gallagher, at the time serving the Catholic community in Charleston, South Carolina. Gallagher's brief stay in New Bern was one of the first recorded times that a priest had visited the state, and Gaston's marriage might have been the first ever officiated at by a Catholic priest in the state. After the wedding, Gaston reported back to Carroll that during his brief time in New Bern, Gallagher had

> several times celebrated the solemn sacrifice of the Mass, and once preached to a numerous and attentive auditory on one of the distinguishing tenets of our Church -- the real presence in the Blessed Sacrament. His very persuasive and logical discourse was well calculated to remove unfounded prejudices and to awaken a proper spirit of inquiry as to the principles of the Catholic Faith.[12]

It will be noted that the Gastons were well-educated professionals, very different from the poor immigrant laborers who already made up the majority of American Catholics, and who would in decades to come swell the number of Catholics in the country. The nativist hostility to Catholics was due largely to the fact that Catholics were seen as "foreign" and diluting the "authentic" American stock and contaminating the culture. Gaston, on the other hand, was the completely acculturated Southern gentleman.

Symptomatic of the scant health care services available at the time, Gaston's second marriage would also end prematurely. After giving birth to three healthy children, while pregnant with a fourth, Hannah died in 1813. Her husband, newly-elected to the United States House of Representatives, was in Washington when he received the news.

In 1815, Gaston was reelected and returned to Washington where he met Eliza Worthington who, in 1816, became his third wife. Eliza bore two daughters but died in 1819 while giving birth to the second. Having lost three wives, Gaston, now in his early forties, determined not to marry again. He raised his five children himself, first with the help of his married sister and later aided by the older girls.[13]

Wearied of the long periods away from home, Gaston had not run for a third term in Congress but returned to New Bern where he would devote the remainder of his life to his family, his business interests, and to the service of the state. Unexpectedly, he also soon would be called upon to take part in the establishment of the Catholic Church in North Carolina.[14]

Dioceses for the South

John Carroll remained the only Catholic bishop in the United States until 1810, when the growing number of Catholics, particularly in Northern cities, led to the erection of dioceses in Boston, New York, Philadelphia, and Bardstown, Kentucky. The southern states remained under the jurisdiction of the now Archdiocese of Baltimore. However, little attention was paid to the South, where only occasionally was a priest sent to minister to minuscule congregations in Charleston, South Carolina, and Augusta, Georgia. Then in 1820, dioceses were established in Richmond, Virginia, and Charleston, South Carolina. The Charleston diocese included the extensive area of North Carolina, South Carolina, and Georgia and was assigned to a 33-year-old Irish priest who had never been to America. That priest, John England, would work with William Gaston and other laymen in laying the groundwork for a Catholic Church in North Carolina. As will be seen in Chapter Six, North Carolina remained a sort of stepchild of Charleston until 1868, when the state would be assigned its own bishop.

The balance of the present chapter will discuss the work of Bishop England in establishing the Catholic Church in North Carolina. Attention will focus particularly on his first trip through the state between May and August, 1821.

An Irishman Who Embraced the Spirit of America

Although he would administer the poorest diocese in the country, John England became a central figure in the American Catholic Church. In addition, he was called upon by Rome to act as its representative to Haiti during a delicate period in that nation's history. Until his death in 1842, at the age of fifty-five, England was constantly traveling -- across his diocese, the country, and the world. His productivity was enormous and his creativity exceptional. While the present chapter will focus on his work in North Carolina, the broader scope of his career will be related in Chapter Five.

The selection of bishops is one part mystery, one part chance, and perhaps one part providential. The process by which a young parish priest in Cork, Ireland was tapped by Rome to head a new diocese in the United States is at once an example of the casual approach that characterized the naming of bishops in the nineteenth century and also the politics involved in such appointments. The process began when the American bishops, through Archbishop Ambrose Marechal of Baltimore, a successor of John Carroll, wrote to Rome explaining why they believed that new dioceses should be erected in Richmond and Charleston. A major concern was the thorny issue of trusteeism. Both Norfolk, Virginia and Charleston, South Carolina had churches which refused to accept the authority of the Archbishop of Baltimore. It was felt that only the presence of bishops on the scene could neutralize the schismatic situations.

In far-off Rome, the official in charge of appointing bishops asked two Irish priests if they could recommend anyone. When they suggested Patrick Kelly and John England, after a perfunctory investigation of the qualifications of those Irish priests, Kelly was notified that he was to go to Richmond and England that he had been assigned to Charleston.

The politics of the action was that, having allowed the American priests to select their own first bishop, Rome wanted to reassert control, not only by naming bishops to the new dioceses but by selecting men who were not Americans. Already a Frenchman presided over the American Church as archbishop of Baltimore. The message was clear: Rome named bishops, not the democracy-infatuated Americans. Little did Rome know that no one would be a greater champion of the new American form of government than John England.

Although young, England had made a name for himself in Ireland, particularly for his efforts on behalf of Irish Catholic emancipation. As his own bishop in Cork wrote in recommending England for promotion, "if he had shown any defect so far ... it was in his political activities which had rendered him somewhat obnoxious to the British Government; but this would not be a defect in America, where religious freedom existed."[15] Indeed not. England never tired of praising the United States Constitution, in particular its guarantee of religious freedom.

As he stepped ashore in Charleston on Dec. 30, 1820, after a two months voyage from Ireland which he called "very tedious and unpleasant,"[16] England found that his diocese, larger in area than his native Ireland and abominated England combined, had but two priests and two occupied churches, one each in Charleston and Augusta. And as if this were not bad enough, the church in Charleston was wracked with what he termed "miserable dissensions."[17] The problem had its roots in the fact that lay people constructed and owned the first church buildings in America. Having the power of the purse, at times they refused to accept or to support a priest and in other ways attempted to control church affairs. Eventually, the tug-of-war was resolved by Bishop England building another church in Charleston and interdicting the rebellious one. The problem of trusteeism was not resolved until legal changes permitted the local bishop to hold title to all church properties in his diocese.[18]

Less than a month after arriving in America, England took
what would be the first of his many innovative steps, addressing a pastoral letter to his scattered flock of a few hundred souls. No American
bishop had ever done such a thing. In this, the first of many letters
which remain extant, England exhorted Catholics to be good citizens of
the country, adding, "we ourself for a long time have admired the excellence of your constitution, and been desirous to behold your eagle grow
in strength and beauty as his years increased."[19] His reference to the
American constitution may suggest that already England was thinking
of formulating such a document for the diocese. However, before doing
so he undertook a visitation of the three states, beginning with South
Carolina, continuing to Georgia, and ending up in North Carolina, from
a Catholic perspective the poorest portion of his vineyard. At least there
would be no trusteeism problem there, since North Carolina had no
Catholic churches.

First Trip to North Carolina: Wilmington

As his journal entry for May 15, 1821, the bishop wrote:

> Arrived at Wilmington at 4 o'clock in the evening, was waited upon
> by Mr. I.O. Calharda, a Portuguese merchant of the town, who resided
> there during thirty years. He invited me to his house, whither I went
> and found a good reception. Was called upon by Mr. James Usher and
> some other Catholics in the evening.[20]

This was the first time that a Catholic bishop set foot in North
Carolina. For the next three months, England visited every town where
any Catholics were known to reside, spending a week or more in the
larger places in an attempt to initiate the process of fashioning a congregation. After this arduous journey through the settlements of the
overwhelmingly rural state, England continued traveling north by way
of Norfolk, Virginia, spending an additional three months in Baltimore,
Philadelphia, and New York. Since he had landed in Charleston, this
was his first visit to the principal cities of the young country.

On his way back to South Carolina, after meeting in
Washington, DC with President James Monroe and Secretary of State
John Quincy Adams, the bishop retraced his steps through North
Carolina, stopping briefly at some of towns he had visited just a few
months before. For example, he arrived in New Bern on Nov. 14th but
"was much disappointed in finding Mr. Gaston was in Raleigh."[21] This
extended swing through North Carolina in 1821 was the first of some

ten such trips that England would make over the succeeding twenty years.

Wilmington, the largest and southernmost port city in North Carolina, had long had some sporadic Catholic presence in the person of seamen from Catholic countries, including Portugal. There were hazy recollections of an occasional priest coming ashore, celebrating Mass, and sailing on. As elsewhere in the state, there was no church. The bishop would remark that during these three months in North Carolina he never met a Catholic priest or found a Catholic Church.

Over the course of seven days in Wilmington, England took steps which would be repeated in each town that he visited. Besides meeting with the Catholics -- no more than twenty in Wilmington and usually fewer elsewhere -- he would preach each evening, frequently at the local courthouse, at times in the sanctuary of accommodating Protestant churches. Since the majority of those who heard him were not Catholics, his objective was to dispel misunderstanding of Catholic doctrine and practices. From the enthusiasm with which he was universally received, it is clear that his speaking style was impressive. Cardinal Gibbons would write:

> Bishop England, of Charleston, was perhaps the ablest pulpit orator that has ever appeared before an American Catholic audience. After a few moments' notice, he could speak for several consecutive hours on any subject within the range of the religious domain; and so eager were the people to hear him, without regard to their convictions of faith, that he was often solicited to address a congregation on arriving in a town after a fatiguing journey.[22]

Throughout the state England discovered people who originally had been Catholics but for want of a church of their own were attending Protestant churches. Furthermore, the paucity of Catholics resulted in most marriages being interfaith, in which cases usually the Catholic religion was lost, at least for the children of such unions. England noted in the Protestant cemeteries tombstones which bore familiar names from his homeland. Nowhere, except in the hearts of a few scattered families, was an authentic Catholic consciousness to be found in North Carolina.

Now, however, for a brief period, Catholic life was celebrated in Wilmington. England not only offered Mass but heard confessions, prepared people for Confirmation, baptized children, and selected men to be the leaders, men who never before had thought of themselves as Catholic leaders and had little idea what to do.

In particular, the bishop did two things which were the heart of his hopes for an informed, united congregation. He established a branch of what he called a "Book Society" and took the initial steps for the construction of a church. The book society was intended to put Catholic reading material in the hands of people, a need which England realized was critical for men and women who had absolutely no contact with anything Catholic, sometimes for their entire lives. As the bishop reported in his diary, many people "had nearly lost all idea of Catholicity." Members of the book society paid a modest amount of money and England promised to send books and pamphlets when he returned to Charleston. At times, on a second visit to a town, he discovered that material had never arrived, had gone unread, or was not circulating as intended.

As far as a church was concerned, England examined a promising plot of land and set up a committee to begin collecting money to construct a building on the site.[23] The project got off auspiciously with more than $1,000 subscribed before the bishop left. However, although these first steps were taken to build a Catholic church in North Carolina, no church was dedicated in Wilmington for another twenty-five years, several years after England's death. The Catholic directory for 1846 describes the newly constructed St. Thomas Church as "a very neat Gothic Church." The word "Gothic" evokes a rather exaggerated image for what was in fact a modest structure. However, it was the first brick Catholic Church in the state. As will be seen in Chapter Six, it was this structure that would serve as the first "cathedral" when in 1868, North Carolina became a separate church jurisdiction.

Bishop England Meets William Gaston: New Bern

> *May 24th. Arrived at Newbern and went to the house of the Hon. William Gaston at his invitation. Saw and conversed with most of the Catholics. In this town are upwards of twenty Catholics, principally females.*[24]

The bishop's second major stop in North Carolina was New Bern, one time colonial capital and still a thriving commercial center at the intersection of the Neuse and Trent rivers. For the next ten days, England engaged in his usual round of religious and organizational activities, including celebrating Mass each day in Gaston's house. As the bishop recorded, Gaston received Communion at Mass on the 26th. In the evenings, the bishop preached in the Court House and "was informed that great numbers of the most respectable inhabitants were convinced of the truth of the Catholic religion, and well disposed to become members thereof." If there was any truth to this report, it did not bear much fruit due to the fact that within a few days the bishop would be gone and with him any hope of nourishing the tender flame of faith which his preaching might have enkindled. England knew this would happen and anguished over the fact that he had no priests to assign to the state.

In what turned out to be a failed effort to establish a priestless Catholic community, England "gave a commission" to Gaston, Peter Brugman, Lewis Leroy, Jr., William Williams, and Benjamin Good to gather the Catholics regularly and lead them in prayer. And although there was discussion of building a church, as was true in Wilmington, the dedication of a church in New Bern, despite Gaston's efforts, would not materialize until after England's death. In fact, it was not until 1844, the year that Gaston himself died, that the Church of St. Paul was officially ready for worship. It is this church, located in the historic district of the picturesque town of New Bern, which has the distinction of being the oldest surviving Catholic church in North Carolina. Although still owned by the Catholic Church, it has been replaced as a place of worship by a large parish plant in the suburbs.

In what certainly must have given England pause, on May 31st he baptized "Abraham, a slave belonging to Mr. Gaston." In Ireland, Father John England had gained a reputation as a champion of the freedom of the Irish people long held in subjugation by the British. Yet, as will be seen in the next chapter, when he encountered a yet more heinous form of oppression in America, he did not speak out in opposition to slavery. In fact, on one occasion he wrote that "the general treatment of the Negroes in the diocese of Charleston is kind and affectionate; far, very far more so than that of the bulk of Irish, agricultural, or other laborers."[25]

A personal and professional relationship between England and Gaston would be maintained over the course of the next twenty years. Their extensive correspondence shows how much the bishop depended on the North Carolina political and judicial figure, not only for legal advice, but as his informal surrogate in a state which he could visit only rarely. Although their letters are written in the flowery formal style of the day, it is clear that the men cared for one another and for the church which they were attempting to place on a firm foundation.[26] Nowhere do the men express impatience or frustration with the slow pace with which their efforts progressed.

Washington, North Carolina

As Gaston's letter at the beginning of this chapter relates, England remained ten days in New Bern. After celebrating Mass and eating breakfast on June 4th, he took his leave of Gaston and started out for Washington. Today, the 50-mile trip between New Bern and Washington might be an hour's drive on US 17. It took England, traveling in a horse drawn coach, until 8 o'clock that evening. His journey on the rutted dirt road was through the Carolina lowlands, breeding ground for yellow fever and other deadly diseases. The diary records how on several occasions during his tour of the state England was forced by illness to suspend activities. And as fast as he enlisted priests for his desolate diocese, he would lose them to maladies for which the only medications were bed rest and prayer. So, for example, on October 25, 1821, England received word that a young priest, Denis Corkery, who had accompanied him from Ireland the year before, had died at his Augusta, Georgia assignment.

Today, Washington, North Carolina is a small town but in the early 19th century it was a bustling business settlement on the Pamlico River. It would be here in what is sometimes called "Little Washington," to distinguish it from the nation's capitol, that the first Catholic church in the state would be built. Credit for this distinction belongs not only to the prodding of Bishop England, but also to the determination of the small group of men who worked for several years to erect the modest structure, knowing all along that it was unlikely that a priest would be assigned to officiate there on a regular basis.

Because of the singular availability of documentation, the process by which the church was established in Washington, North Carolina can serve as a model of what would occur in the handful of towns in North Carolina which had some semblance of a Catholic presence during the first half of the 19th century. Accordingly, after concluding the description of Bishop England's first trip through the state, a somewhat detailed account of the development of the Washington parish will be presented.

Plymouth and Edenton

It was summer now, and the days hot and humid. On June 14, traveling alone and with very limited baggage, the bishop continued his journey, bouncing along the road from Washington to Plymouth. Arriving in the evening, he found but one Catholic in the town, a Doctor Picott. The following day, with no convenient place for Mass, he did not celebrate, "not wishing to exhibit before a people perfectly uninstructed." Nevertheless, he was prevailed upon to preach and did so twice that day, to about forty persons at 11 o'clock and to a larger gathering at 5. Again the following day, he spoke twice. His subjects were those on which he spoke to audiences of non-Catholics, including the claim of the Catholic Church to be the one established by Christ and the doctrine of the sacraments. He "found many misconceptions corrected and prejudices removed."

Somehow, by Sunday, June 17th, the number of people adequately disposed to assist at Mass had increased and England celebrated Mass at the Academy, "the only public building in the town." More than that, although he had encountered only one other Catholic, Alexander Chisholm, he set up a branch of the Catholic book society and was prevailed upon to preach once again that evening. One wonders what might have been accomplished in a town like Plymouth had it been possible to assign a priest there. As it happens, there are today still so few Catholics in Plymouth that no priest is stationed at the little church of St. Joan of Arc.[27]

From Plymouth England continued north, crossing the Chowan River to the port city of Edenton where he found "about ten Catholics: French, Portuguese, and Irish, generally extremely negligent." Despite his disappointment, he preached in the Court House and the following day, June 20th, after celebrating Mass in his room, he exhorted the Catholics "to prepare for the Sacraments and to form the book society." He must have made some progress, because on the 21st he celebrated Mass in the Court House and preached once again. However, in his journal, the usually even-tempered bishop castigated the Catholics of Edenton as he did no others, saying that they were

> negligent, ignorant, and despised by the other denominations. The only one who had any appearance of worldly decency did not come near me and had his daughter married by the Protestant Episcopal Minister on the day after my arrival. His name is Charnier. His family was represented to me as religious Catholics, but they not having

appeared at my Sermon I could not call on them. ... Failed also in my
endeavors to bring the Catholics to the Sacraments.[28]

Elizabeth City and Murfreesboro

Almost all the towns visited by Bishop England during his
inaugural three-month swing through North Carolina were located on
rivers with access to the Atlantic Ocean. Water highways were still the
major travel routes and the only way that goods could be transported
before the introduction of railroads to the South in the 1830's. What
roads there were easily became impassable in rainy weather and were
impractical for shipping cotton, tobacco, or other crops any distance.
Reference to a map will show that Elizabeth City on the Pasquotank
River is the northernmost large town in North Carolina. Here the bishop arrived from Edenton on the evening of June 25th, feeling "very
sick" but undeterred in his determination to present the Catholic message in yet another town that had never seen a priest. With the two
Catholics whom he identified, arrangements were made for him to
preach the following morning in the Court House.

By his fourth day in Elizabeth City, England had found "eight
or ten" Catholics and appointed John. P. McLoughlin, Joseph Lesieur,
and Alexander T. Martin "to read prayers &c," his usual formula for
what he hoped would be the regular gathering of Catholics for simple
prayer service in the absence of a priest. Also, within the brief time that
he was in Elizabeth City, England instructed and baptized four converts.
And then he was gone. No priest would visit Elizabeth City again for
several years.

At this point, July 30th, Bishop England made a detour to the
nearby state of Virginia. Although the diary does not say so, he must
have made prior arrangements to meet in Norfolk with Bishop Patrick
Kelly of Richmond. Less than a year before, the two men had been consecrated bishops in Ireland for these adjacent dioceses in America.
Unfortunately, England's notes are very cryptic, saying simply that at
Kelly's request he preached several times in the Catholic Church in
Norfolk and that the two made each other Vicars General of their dioceses.

This respite behind him, England crossed back into North
Carolina, arriving in Murfreesboro on July 12th, where he found three
Catholics, "two of whom were in the habit of attending the meetings of
the Methodists and Baptists." One of those Catholics was Doctor

Thomas O'Dwyer, who kept a detailed day-by-day diary over the course of many years. Unfortunately only the volume for 1825 has survived, but it provides a unique account of the life of a Catholic in a small North Carolina town.[29]

Dr. Thomas O'Dwyer

Bishop England was understandably concerned that Catholics were attending Protestant services. Through this practice many people were lost to Catholicism. However, there were exceptions, O'Dwyer being one of them. His diary records that although he attended some religious service nearly every day, he never wavered in his commitment to Catholicism. On March 19th, the Methodist minister questioned the Irish-born country doctor on what he founded his hopes for salvation.

> I told him I founded them on belief in Christ as our Redeemer and in attending to the religious duties of the Roman Catholic Society in which myself and ancestry have been educated, the orthodoxy of which I have no reason to doubt and that I have only to regret I am not a better Roman Catholic. Still I hope I shall not be a bigoted one, as I pray that all who are sincerely seeking the truth will find it and be saved.

The same day that O'Dwyer made this profession of faith, he attended the Protestant service in the Murfreesboro meeting house.

O'Dwyer had hosted Bishop England for his one-night stay in 1821 and subscribed to the *Catholic Miscellany*, the newspaper which England founded in 1822. Several times in the 1825 diary, O'Dwyer mentions passing on copies of the *Miscellany* to others. However, during that year, he never saw a priest, attended Mass, or recorded any contact with other Catholics.

O'Dwyer, who had an extensive medical practice in the area, died in 1834, at the age of fifty-seven. He had never married and had no children. In his will, he left $200 to "Dr. England for the benefit of the Roman Catholic Church in Charleston." He also gave instructions for the sale of his fifteen slaves.

Raleigh and Fayetteville

Having visited the towns with ports that lead to the ocean, England now headed inland to Raleigh, which had been selected as the capital of the state because its location was more central than New Bern, Edenton, and Wilmington, much more populous and commercially significant cities. As it would turn out, despite being the state capital, Raleigh would remain a small, quiet city into the time of Bishop Vincent Waters more than a century later.

England's route to Raleigh took him through Halifax, Warrenton, and Louisburg. On the three-day journey he did not come across any Catholics. Fortunately, when he arrived in Raleigh he was "kindly received" by William Gaston's sister, Jane, whose husband, John Taylor, was a judge of the North Carolina Supreme Court. Thanks to the access provided by the judge, not himself a Catholic, the bishop was invited to preach at the Presbyterian Church on July 18th. In attendance were the Governor of the state and the judges of the Supreme Court.

During his two weeks in Raleigh, regaining his strength in the comfortable home of the Taylors, England identified a few other Catholics and instructed and baptized a number of people, especially Negroes, who probably were slaves of the Taylors and the other Raleigh Catholics. Before taking his leave on July 30th, he appointed Jane Taylor and John Devereux "to read prayers and instructions for the faithful" whom he urged to meet regularly. The appointment of Jane Gaston Taylor as one of the leaders is the only example of a woman receiving such a commission from Bishop England. His confidence in her was well deserved in that she was a major force in the building of a church in Raleigh, which England would dedicate in honor of St. John the Baptist in 1839. This would be the third and final church that he would dedicate in North Carolina. The first would be in Fayetteville, some sixty miles southwest of Raleigh, to which town he now headed. At the time, the population of Fayetteville, about 6,000, was double that of Raleigh.

Today, Fayetteville lies in the shadow of the Fort Bragg Military Reservation and the adjacent Pope Air Force Base, one of the largest US military complexes in the world. Not only is the base vital to the economy of the area but a major supplier of highly committed Catholics. However, in 1821, Bishop England "found the Catholics to be very few, very negligent, and poorly instructed." Nevertheless, he went about his usual round of activities: preaching in the Protestant church, organizing the book society, instructing, baptizing, confirming. On August 11th, the day before returning to Raleigh, the bishop "procured a room" in which the Catholics were to meet on Sundays "for prayer and instruction." Following the pattern of his other stops, he commissioned John Kelly and four other men to preside at these meetings.

The efforts of this initially unpromising group would lead to the construction of St. Patrick Church which England dedicated in 1829, just before moving on to Washington for the dedication of the church there as will be related below. That first Fayetteville church was destroyed by fire -- along with disease, an ever present danger -- in 1831. Undeterred by this setback, the lay people constructed a second church in 1835. However, it was not until 1839, in his final trip through North Carolina, that it was dedicated by Bishop England.

Journey's End

With a few days out for his visit to Norfolk, Virginia, England had spent three months in North Carolina visiting every town where there were known to be Catholics. In each place he made efforts to motivate the Catholics to hold fast to their faith, come together regularly in prayer, subscribe to Catholic reading material, attempt to construct a church, and hope to have a priest some day. Although there still was no church or priest in North Carolina, by the end of 1821 every Catholic in the state knew that their existence had been noted and that they had been assigned a bishop who was a skillful preacher and determined organizer. To many, including William Gaston in New Bern, the future looked bright. And certainly, as will be seen in the next chapter, he and Bishop England contributed substantially to creating an environment more congenial to Catholicism.

What is particularly striking about Bishop England is the ease with which he could move from a small stage like Washington, North Carolina, to a large stage like Washington, DC, from New Bern to Rome, and from Raleigh to Paris and Dublin. He was at once pastoral and intellectual, brilliant yet able to communicate with simple people, a man with grandiose ideas for church government who could sit down with a handful of nervous men in a little town and patiently help them organize their community. This chapter concludes with a detailed description of the process of establishing a parish in one such town.

A Case Study in the Formation of a Parish

Though not particularly significant in itself, Washington, North Carolina is uniquely rich in sources of information about the development of the Catholic church there. Three documents in particular, all written during the 1820's through the 1840's, have been preserved which provide a detailed record of the formative years of the church in Beaufort County. The first is Bishop England's diary, already mentioned. A second is the original parish register in which England himself wrote the initial pages and on the occasion of his subsequent ten visits over the next twenty years made additional entries.[30] The third is the   history of the parish written by the Reverend Patrick Joseph Coffey, who was pastor in Washington shortly after Bishop England's death.[31]

The register is a particularly valuable, even beautiful, document. Its pages are yellowed and frayed, some of them detached from the spine, yet this simple ruled notebook is a mute witness to the men who held it, wrote in it, read it nearly two centuries ago. We can imagine them in the dim light of an oil lamp carefully recording what they were doing, recording it because this bishop from Ireland had told them to do so and had modeled for them the importance of keeping records, one of the basic requirements of a church which has for nearly two millennia carefully preserved its story. Although certainly these early 19th century Washington Catholics never thought in these terms, they were following in the footsteps of medieval monks who painstakingly penned their manuscripts for a future world of which they could have no idea.

On the first page of the notebook that would serve for twenty-seven years as the official register of the Church of St. John the Evangelist, Bishop England wrote in clear, elegant script the following statement. It was a first lesson in church history and doctrine which he would give to the religiously illiterate but sincere Catholics he had found in this small town. It also was a proclamation: The Roman Catholic Church has arrived in North Carolina!

By a Bull of his Holiness Pope Pius VII [North Carolina, South Carolina, and Georgia] were separated [from Baltimore] on the 12th day of July, 1820, and subjected to a new episcopal see, which was erected in the city of Charleston, SC by the same Bull. The Reverend John England, P.P. of Ballymoodan and Kilbrogan (Town of Bandon) in the Diocese of Cork, Suffragan to the Archbishop of Cashel in Ireland, was appointed first Bishop of the said new see. On the festival day of St. Matthew, the 21st day of September 1820 he was consecrated, in the 34th year of his life in the Church of St. Finnbar (South Parish Chapel) in the City of Cork by the Right Reverend Father in God, John Murphy, Lord Bishop of Cork, being assisted by the Right Reverend the Bishop of Offley in Ireland and the Right Reverend Father in God, Doctor Patrick Kelly, first Bishop of Richmond (Virginia), there being also present the Most Reverend the

Archbishop of Mityland, coadjutor to the Archbishop of Cashel, and the Right Reverend Bishops of Cloyne and Ross, of Ardfert and Aghadoe, and of Limerick.

The said Bull was published in the Roman Catholic Church of Charleston on Sunday, 31st of December 1820.

I first arrived in Washington on June 4th, 1821.

There were perhaps more bishops mentioned in this magisterial statement than there were adult Catholics in the humble town of Washington. However, it was important for England to establish his apostolic succession and to affirm his legitimacy to people who never before had seen a bishop.

Formalities aside, it is certain that Lewis Leroy, John Gallagher, John Labarbe, William Grace, Walter Hanrahan, and Thomas Moran -- the leading Catholics in Washington -- were pleased to have with them a clergyman of their own religion. Mass could be celebrated, their children solemnly baptized and confirmed, and instruction given. Most of all, there could be offered the hope that some day soon they would have their own church and priest.

Parish Records

The register is divided into three distinct sections. The first is a somewhat standard record of baptisms, confirmations, and marriages. In the center of the book, on pages that are smaller in dimension, is the registry of funerals and burials. Finally, if the book is turned upside down and flipped over to the reverse side, one finds the minutes of the meetings held over the years by the members of the church vestry. Each of these sections will now be examined one at a time, supplementing what they contain with references to the other two documents mentioned. Together, they provide a picture not only of what happened in Washington but suggest what must have been occurring in the other churches which England would attempt to establish in North Carolina.

The size of any parish can be gauged from the number of baptisms, confirmations, and marriages. In the course of twenty-seven years, a total of 108 baptisms were recorded, an average of four per year. On the occasion of his visits to Washington, the bishop confirmed a total of thirty people, and there were five marriages performed.[32]

On the first page of the register, England entered seven baptisms performed in Washington prior to his arrival. Of the seven, six were children of Lewis Leroy and Helen Palmer Leroy. Leroy would become one of the long-term vestry men of the parish and also donate land for a church and cemetery. The seventh baptism was the three-year-old daughter of William and Mary Grace. Grace, like Leroy, was one of the parish leaders. It might be noted that while three of these early baptisms took place in 1819, two years before England's visit, the other four took place June 11, 1808. On that date, the Rev. Michael Lacy baptized four of the Leroy children. Obviously, like the Gastons in New Bern, the Leroys were long-term residents of Washington and instrumental in having a priest visit the town at least on rare occasions.

After these earlier baptisms, England entered the names of those whom he personally baptized and confirmed. The first such entry says: "On June 9th, I baptized (under conditions) and received into the Roman Catholic Church, Mrs. Anne Gallagher, she having renounced the errors of the Protestant Episcopal Church." Mrs. Gallagher was the wife of yet another of the handful of men who were the founders of the parish.

Other entries on that June day in 1821 reflect the social reality of the time. The bishop wrote: "I baptized Jeffrey, an adult boy of color, age about 18 years, and a slave of William Worsley." Another entry noted that England baptized "John, a boy of color, age about fifteen years, and the slave of Louis Leroy."

It might be added that not only did the Washington parish, actually called a "district" by Bishop England, include all of Beaufort Country, but that some of the baptisms entered were of people from Halifax, two counties away. The vast rural "district" drew few immigrants, the principal source of Catholic growth in other parts of America. European workers could not compete with the slave labor on which the plantation economy of the area was based.

Father Coffey's *Memoirs*, certainly based on the account of people who were present, says of Bishop England's first visit to Washington:

> ...he remained ten days. He celebrated Mass and exhorted every morning in the court house, and preached every evening during his stay. He received six converts, baptized two white adults and four colored and three white children and confirmed eleven persons.
>
> In order to remedy as much as possible the evils which resulted from the want of a clergyman, the Bishop commissioned three or four of the principal members of the congregation to assemble the others each Sunday and appointed prayers which were to be read by one of

these. He also provided books of instruction portions of which were to be read, and named teachers of catechism for the children. Mr. Gallagher generally read for the others....[33]

The bishop's own journal is consistent with what Father Coffey wrote. Although England bluntly referred to the Catholics of Washington as "few and generally negligent," he went about the business of appointing leaders, providing them with materials, and assigning tasks, including that of collecting money toward the building of a church. Very deliberately, the organizationally-skilled bishop was laying the foundation of Catholic consciousness and congregational life in the lives of these "negligent" people.

When the bishop passed through Washington in November 1821, retracing his steps back to Charleston after a protracted visit to Northern cities, he found that the people had already discontinued the prayer meetings and were engaged in personal disputes. Furthermore, the converts were becoming lukewarm, and the congregation had received none of the books which he had urged them to procure. England remained just the one night but records that he celebrated Mass, exhorted the people to mutual love, urged them to resume the prayer meetings, and "promised they should be visited by a priest whom I hope they would assist to support." For, as the trustee issue had taught him, assigning a priest was one thing, getting the people to provide for his support was another.

Assignment of the First Priest to North Carolina

England did not forget the promise which he made on several occasions to send a priest to North Carolina. Accordingly, in March 1822, just a few months after his visit to the area, he sent the Reverend Anthony O'Hannan with jurisdiction over the entire state. O'Hannan had been recruited by England in Philadelphia as part of his effort to resolve a conflict there which England refers to as a schism. One of the Philadelphia priests, William Hogan, together with his congregation refused to accept the authority of the bishop of Philadelphia. When England arrived on the scene, he took it upon himself to mediate the conflict. A component of the solution was to make O'Hannan, a friend and collaborator of Hogan, a priest of the Charleston diocese.[34]

So, convinced, or at least hopeful that O'Hannan had mended his rebellious ways, England sent him to North Carolina. Four months later, England was surprised by O'Hannan's unexpected return to

Charleston with the claim that he was sick and requesting assignment
further south. It was only seven months later, in his next trip to North
Carolina, that England discovered that O'Hannan had "made very erroneous impressions upon the little flock respecting the Schism at
Philadelphia, and created great prejudice against the Bishop and in
favor of Mr. Hogan." Furthermore, while he was supposed to be ministering to the Catholics in North Carolina, O'Hannan had actually gone
to Philadelphia and renewed his association with Hogan. In any event,
England's first effort to establish a clerical presence in North Carolina
had been a disaster.

A Church for Washington: 1829

Weighed down by these concerns, in May of 1823, England
once again arrived in Washington on his visitation through North
Carolina. He found that two of the lay leaders had died and that others
had left the church. Undeterred, he spent a week organizing the congregation once again. The most significant development on this occasion
was that Lewis Leroy "offered a lot of ground for a Church and
Cemetery." England set in place the mechanism for raising money to
build the church, including requesting the cooperation of the non-
Catholics in the town. He also met with a builder, sketched plans, and
was given a cost estimate. For his part Lewis Leroy, besides giving the
ground, provided the heavy lumber for the church. Anxious to see the
work begun, the bishop personally pledged the money for the other
materials that would be needed. He also arranged for William Gaston to
draw up the papers for transferring the property for church use. Finally,
in what must have been a happy moment, England drove a stake into the
ground "where the west angle" of the new church was to be located.

This is as far as the bishop's journal goes. For events after 1823,
we must rely on the parish register and the *Memoirs* of Father Coffey.

As simple a project as it was, work on the church went slowly.
The shortage of funds was compounded by dissension within the congregation. Although some of the men had been designated as leaders,
they did not have official ecclesiastical standing and tended to let matters drift until the bishop would return. When he did so in 1824, "he
found the lumber on the ground and some of the subscriptions collected and nothing more done."[35] In fact, although England optimistically
drove the stake in the ground in 1823, it would not be until 1828 that he
would finally celebrate Mass in the building. Although Mass had been
offered many times by now in people's homes and in other locations,

this was the first time Mass was offered in a Catholic church in North Carolina. And even then, the church was not finished sufficiently for it to be officially consecrated. This England did the following year, noting in the parish register: "On this day, [March 25, 1829] I solemnly blessed the church erected at Washington, dedicating it to the service of the Almighty God, under the invocation of St. John the Apostle and Evangelist according to the form of the Roman Ritual."[36]

Even with its own church, the parish remained small and poor. A priest was assigned to the area, but he had to spend half his time in another district. In 1832, England noted the precarious state of affairs:

> In North Carolina, the Catholics of Washington, in Beaufort county, have, by considerable exertion, built a good wooden church under the invocation of St. John the Evangelist. There being not more than eight or ten families that can contribute, they have not been able to finish the interior. A priest officiates for them every alternate month; he spends the other month in the adjoining county of Craven, at New Bern, where there are a few Catholics.[37]

This pattern of a priest alternating between two districts -- or more -- continued for many years. Besides the sacraments recorded in the parish register, there are also notations by priests announcing their assignment to the area. One such entry says, "I, the undersigned, a regularly ordained priest for the diocese of Charleston arrived in Washington, North Carolina on March 21, 1838 as assistant to the Reverend Thomas Murphy to whose care the whole state of North Carolina for said year was entrusted. [signed] Andrew Doyle." Thus, eighteen years after the arrival of Bishop England, the state of North Carolina had but two priests. Washington, with its "eight to ten Catholic families" was the state headquarters.

The register of burials in the cemetery can be dealt with rather quickly. There were thirteen burials during the twenty years after its dedication in 1829, including three children and two slaves. One of the slaves was a woman, "age about sixty," who was baptized one day and buried shortly thereafter. For the final entry, in March 1848 the priest wrote: "Ann, a slave of Mrs. Leroy, was buried in the cemetery of this church, I being unable to attend in consequence of sickness."

Minutes of Meetings of Parish Vestry

The most significant section of the parish register, from the point of view of the development of the church, is the minutes of the meetings held once or twice a year by the lay leaders. Just as the first page of the sacramental section of the book was written by Bishop England himself, so also was the first page of the minutes. But whereas the baptismal register begins in 1821, the minutes commence in 1824. The reason is that it was not until 1823 that England composed the Constitution for the Diocese of Charleston, to be discussed in the following chapter. Suffice it to say here that the meetings of the leaders in Washington, as in the other districts of the diocese, were a form of lay participation in governance that was unique in the Roman Catholic Church.

And so, as the bishop recorded on Feb. 11, 1824, the *laymen*[38] of Washington not only approved the Constitution but "determined that St. John the Evangelist should be the patron saint of the district." Although the five men elected as the initial vestry are named, there is no indication as to how many people voted. Also, no priest was in attendance. Bishop England presented the Constitution, established the district, and presided over the election personally. It was understood that, at least initially, the parish was to be managed without the presence of a priest.

The next entry in the register, the first written by a layman, is a lengthy set of regulations for the use of the church cemetery. The first provision, one which may have been a factor in the disputes which plagued the small community, names five men the "founding members" of the parish and gives them first choice of plots for their families. Perhaps with an eye to avoiding conflict, plot dimensions were precisely specified, and it was stipulated that no one other than these five families was to be buried in the graveyard without the consent of the vestry "and the approbation of the bishop." Although it seems that it would be impossible to consult the bishop given the slow communication system at the time, this last requirement undoubtedly was added at England's insistence to make clear that although the cemetery, like the church building, had been deeded to lay trustees, its use was ultimately under the control of the hierarchy.

One last point on the cemetery. Although payment for each burial was to be made at the rate of twenty cents per square foot, provision was made for poor members of the parish to be buried without pay-

ing the fee, and also a section of the cemetery was allotted "for the interment of colored members of the church apart from the portion of the
whites."

A key feature of the diocesan Constitution was an annual
Convention to be held in each state. However, although several conventions had already been held in South Carolina and Georgia, it was
not until 1829, that the bishop felt that the church in North Carolina had
been developed sufficiently to assemble representatives of the handful
of congregations he had established. Accordingly, the minutes of the
Washington parish for February 8 of that year note that John Gallagher
and Louis Leroy had been elected delegates to the first such Convention
to be held in Fayetteville the following month. That gathering on March
15, to be discussed in Chapter Five, was the first statewide gathering of
Catholics, the first opportunity which the bishop had to shape a Catholic
consciousness which reached beyond the parochial level.

After the Convention, Bishop England, John Gallagher, Louis
Leroy, and Father Andrew Byrne, traveled the 150 miles back to
Washington where the church finally was dedicated and Father Byrne
assigned as the first pastor of the area.

The conditions under which priests were obliged to live are
suggested by the January 8, 1831 entry in the Washington parish register. After two years in North Carolina, Father Byrne had been appointed the first bishop of Little Rock, Arkansas and arrangements were
made for receiving his successor, the Reverend Richard Baker. As had
been true of Father Byrne, Father Baker was to spend alternate months
in Washington and New Bern. The minutes say that the vestry at New
Bern (which did not yet have a church) agreed to this arrangement. It
was further recorded that provision was made to obtain a subscription
for the support of the priest and for the expenses entailed in his travel to
New Bern. Finally, it was specified that, when in Washington Father
Baker was to take turns residing at the homes of John Gallagher, Lewis
Leroy, and John Labarbe. The lay trustees not only owned the church
property, but they controlled the finances, including the pastor's support. The priest was dependent on the free will offerings of the small
congregation and on their providing him with a place to live.

Another entry of interest in the Washington register was written by Bishop England himself in 1839. It is obvious that he had not forgotten the book which he had begun eighteen years earlier. He noted
that a state Board of General Trustees had been established earlier in the

year, of which John Gallagher was elected "treasurer of the general fund." This Board was a structure which England hoped would encourage the local congregations to contribute money for diocesan needs, such as the seminary he had established in Charleston and the *Catholic Miscellany*. On several occasions, the bishop bemoaned the fact that people failed to support any church enterprise outside their own local community. Although the Constitution prescribed a specific amount that each Catholic was to contribute each year for the support of the bishop, the men assigned to collect this "tax" had little success.

Bishop England visited Washington for the last time in May 1840. Later that year, he undertook one of his lengthy trips to Europe. Shortly after returning to Charleston in 1842, he died on April 11th at the age of 55.

In 1849, Father Coffey, the pastor in Washington, noted: "After the death of Bishop England, inaction seemed to have seized the whole diocese."[39] Certainly part of the problem was that no successor to England was named for two years. But it was more than that. When Bishop England died the fragile structure which he had erected and maintained by force of his personality collapsed. The sound of the collapse was not loud, for the structure had been very small. England himself had dedicated but three churches -- in Fayetteville, Washington, and Raleigh. His next two successors as bishops of Charleston, finishing the work which England had begun, added churches in New Bern, Wilmington, Charlotte, and Edenton. So, when the Civil War erupted in 1861, only these seven towns had a Catholic church, serving all told fewer than 800 people. As for "Little Washington," the Church of St. John the Evangelist was burned to the ground by Federal troops as they evacuated Washington on April 30, 1864. More than sixty years would pass before another Catholic church would be constructed in the town.

Chapter Five

The Search for a Just Society: Church Governance, Slavery, and Catholic Political Rights

I have shown that the Saviour did not repeal the permission to hold slaves; but that he promulgated principles calculated to improve their condition, and perhaps, in the process of time, to extinguish slavery. I now proceed to show, from a variety of ecclesiastical documents, that the church which he commissioned to teach all nations, all days to the end of the world, has at all times considered the existence of slaves as compatible with religious profession and practice.

---Bishop John England, October 28, 1840

In an address before the Anti-Duelling Society of Charleston in 1828, Bishop England spoke of himself as an adopted Carolinian, as one who could see both the faults and virtues of southern society. He concluded his lengthy history and analysis of dueling by urging his listeners to dedicate themselves to eradicating the custom from their lives. "Are you satisfied that the practice of dueling is one of the worst remnants of pagan barbarity? Do you believe it to be unnecessary for preserving the refinement of our southern society?"[1]

While England could abhor dueling as a remnant of "pagan barbarity," and urge that it be eliminated, in a seeming misplacement of priorities he could also argue that slavery was not immoral. As one author put it, "To see this champion of freedom defend the institution of slavery is to find at least one lacuna in the greatness of John England."[2] However, to summarily dismiss England's defense of slavery in the light of contemporary consciousness would be to do the man an injustice. He went to great length to explain his position, marshaling scriptural, historical, theological, and philosophical evidence in an effort to found his position on a firm basis. His conclusion, namely that "domestic slavery" was not incompatible with Christianity, is worth examining as an example of how a practice totally rejected today could have been supported in the past. Unlike the mindless racism of many of his contemporaries, the position of England was reached after exhaustive research and reflection.

The present chapter will consider not only the question of slavery, certainly the overarching challenge to American national identity during most of the 19th century, but two other issues in which Bishop England and William Gaston played prominent roles. One is the pervasive anti-Catholicism in North Carolina and its embodiment in the state Constitution, an article of which restricted the holding of public office to Protestants. Gaston was instrumental in having this restriction removed. The third issue is that of church governance. England not only played a leading role within the American Catholic hierarchy, but within his own diocese put in place a structure of government modeled on the United States Constitution, one which included a degree of lay involvement and episcopal accountability unique in the history of Catholicism. First however, it is important to locate the activities of these two men within the cultural context within which they lived.

The Rip Van Wrinkle State

Today, North Carolina is a magnet for high technology businesses, affluent retirees, and students vying to attend top ranked universities such as Duke and the University of North Carolina at Chapel Hill. From ethnic and religious perspectives, it is a state celebrating ever increasing diversity. When, in the year 2000, Mike Easily was elected the first Roman Catholic governor, virtually no attention was paid to his religious affiliation.[3] The same was true a few years earlier when a Catholic academic, Molly Broad, was selected President of the University of North Carolina. In a state which only a few decades ago was characterized by rigid racial segregation, African-American legislators routinely take their places in both houses of the assembly and on judicial benches. It is only with considerable effort that the social situation during the lifetime of Bishop England and William Gaston can be reconstructed. For example, one historian has written:

> North Carolina in the early nineteenth century appeared to its most
> articulate critics — as it has to its most influential twentieth-century
> historians — to be the "Rip Van Winkle State," a lethargic, pastoral,

culturally blighted society. Certainly the political hegemony of con-servative eastern planters, the torpid quality of life in towns and cities, the underdeveloped transportation facilities, the lack of educational opportunities, the migration to the West of two hundred thousand of the state's most energetic people, and, overshadowing all else, slavery and racism profoundly inhibited social change and economic growth.[4]

As is implied in the foregoing quotation, a sharp difference existed between the affluent planters of the tidewater region and strug-gling back country farmers. The former were "country gentlemen," modeled after the English landed aristocracy. Large numbers of slaves provided them with the means to amass substantial fortunes and culti-vate a leisurely lifestyle. The latter were rough, largely illiterate men struggling to make a living and possessing few if any slaves. William Gaston and many of the other Catholics whom Bishop England encoun-tered belonged to the planter class, which held most of the state's eco-nomic resources and participated in what few cultural activities were available. Quite likely, as England insisted, most of them were benevo-lent, paternalistic masters, solicitous for the religious instruction of their human chattel, and not incidentally hoping that religious indoctrination would help insure the continued submissiveness of their slaves.

For poor whites, religion provided not only a gathering place for worship, but was the only school, social center, and source of news available in the hundreds of remote villages and towns of the infant state. Religious teaching, especially as transmitted by Bible-quoting, enthusiastic preachers, had no rival in shaping the mentality of the pop-ulation. The rural preacher might not have had much formal education, but it was clear to his congregation that he was inspired by the Spirit. What he said must be the truth.

The Foundation of Protestant Communities

The various strands of Protestantism which found their way to North Carolina differed in other respects, but were united on three points: reliance on the Bible as the sole source of God's revelation, an intoxicating belief in the ability of the individual to understand God's will without hierarchical intermediaries, and an unwavering conviction that the Catholic religion was evil, deceptive, and a danger to the American way of life. A brief examination of some of the major reli-gious currents that shaped North Carolinians can help in understanding the enormous obstacles which Catholicism faced in attempting to take root and to grow.

The sources of animosity to the church of Rome extend back at least to 1415, when the Catholic bishops gathered in council at Constance in Italy, ordered that John Hus be burned at the stake as a heretic. The offense of this zealous Czech priest was that he advocated reform of the church. At the time, Catholicism was in such disarray that three men claimed the papacy.[5] Bishops routinely received their positions through patronage from political leaders and were notorious for their avarice and simony. Hus, who preceded Martin Luther by more than a century, was killed because he decried the corruption which pervaded the Christian hierarchy. From his ashes would emerge the Moravian Church

In 1753, German-speaking Moravian immigrants from central Europe, established a settlement in a large area of the North Carolina piedmont which they called the Wachovia Tract. Here these spiritual descendants of John Hus created a religiously fervent society in which they hoped to live in strict conformity with biblical teaching. They called their communal center Salem, which would be for them a new Jerusalem.

It is instructive in the context of Bishop England's support of slavery to note that the Moravians, despite their all-consuming religiosity, saw no contradiction in possessing Negro slaves. Furthermore, the African-Americans were instructed and received into the Moravian religion by people who in good conscience combined racial slavery with spiritual fellowship.[6]

In time, the Moravian experiment in communal living would wither, replaced by religions which stressed the autonomy of the individual. However, the Moravian heritage in North Carolina is preserved in Old Salem, an historic enclave in the modern city of Winston-Salem, made wealthy by the presence there for many years of the headquarters of the   R J Reynolds Tobacco Co. A guide directing a tour through the immaculately clean and austere Moravian church in Old Salem, still a place of worship, unhesitatingly recalls the abuses of authority and moral degradation which led Hus to challenge the Catholic Church nearly six centuries ago. While contemporary Moravians may not be any more openly hostile to Catholics than their peace-loving ancestors, the conviction endures that the Catholic Church is a corruption of authentic Christianity.

Even as the Moravians failed to attract many recruits to their rigorous way of life, three other religious currents were thriving, sending missionaries into every section of the vast Carolina territory, transforming thousands of people considered little more than savages into fervent, distinctively American Christians, men and women who rejected the religious traditions of the old world even as they had rejected its political order. The appeal of the Presbyterians, Methodists, and especially the Baptists was in their congruence with the new type of human spirit that was being forged in the furnace of trial, hardship, and sacrifice in the North American wilderness. All three currents flowed from the same source — rejection of the Church of England, which in turn had broken from the Church of Rome. It was all part of the movement toward freedom which intoxicated people long held in subjugation to repressive and interlocked political and religious institutions.

While the Moravians were attempting to create their utopia in Salem, farther south and east Highland Scots were felling trees, draining swamp land, and planting crops. They were also breathing the fresh air of freedom from clan chieftains who in the mountain regions of Scotland had controlled every aspect of their lives. As Presbyterians, they were also staunch opponents of Catholicism, indeed of any religion which had bishops.

Beginning in the 1730's, for reasons that historians debate, boatloads of Highlanders landed in Wilmington and began settling the land along the Cape Fear river, year by year moving farther and farther upstream, until eventually their farms dotted the countryside all the way to the town which became Fayetteville. Interrupted by the Revolutionary War, the migration picked up again in the early 19th century. Nowhere in America did more Highlanders settle than in North Carolina.[7]

Initially speaking Gaelic, the Highlanders quickly adopted both the language and customs of their new home, including the ownership of slaves. As far as religion was concerned, although there were Catholics and Anglicans in Scotland, it seems that all the North Carolina settlers were Presbyterians. In 1758, more than sixty years before a Catholic priest would take up residence in the state, the Cape Fear Presbyterians contracted for their first minister. Since the Anglican Church was the established church in the colony, dissenting ministers were required to sign an oath which included words obviously aimed at Catholics: "I do declare that I do believe that there is not any transubstantiation in the sacrament of the Lord's Supper, in the elements of bread and wine at or after the consecration thereof by any person whatsoever." James Campbell, that first Presbyterian minister, signed the oath.[8] As much as the Presbyterians might dissent from the Anglican Church, they were in accord with that body in their opposition to the Catholic Church.

Methodists

Another group which dissented from Anglicanism and which established an early presence in North Carolina was the Methodist church, or as its adherents preferred to refer to it, the Methodist "movement." John and Charles Wesley and their followers felt that the Episcopal Church had lost much of its power and fallen into ritualism and lukewarm faith. Their goal was to reform it. Key to the Wesleys' approach was vigorous preaching, a fervent presentation of the Gospel aimed at motivating people to conversion, faith, and baptism.[9] In time, the Methodists split off completely from the Anglicans, becoming a distinct denomination, thoroughly Americanized.

The earliest Methodist missionary to North Carolina was Francis Asbury, who arrived in America in 1771, and began preaching his way through the colonies. Reaching North Carolina in 1780, Asbury endured great hardships as he endeavored to attract an obdurate population to Christ.

In time, inroads were made and a virtual army of preachers followed in Asbury's footsteps. The model which the Methodists employed was to send unmarried young men out to preach for a few years before marrying and settling down. These zealous youths invested all their energy in proclaiming the Word in all corners of the state, frequently leading people to tears and open professions of repentance. At camp meetings, hundreds of conversions were the norm, as men and women were drawn to Christ through the power of the preacher's words. Within fifty years, what Asbury had declared a spiritual wilderness had been transformed into a Bible-based, faith-filled world.

Allowing for some exaggeration, the evidence is clear that in the late 18th and early 19th centuries the Methodist preachers evoked in many North Carolinians an overwhelming sense of sin and of the need to be justified by faith in Christ. What is particularly noteworthy is that the Methodists reached people in the isolated westernmost sections of the state, areas which to the present day have virtually no Catholic presence.

Believing that the Holy Spirit could inspire anyone to be a preacher, the early Methodists did not require formal education or ordination for men to be missionaries. "Education can never supply the place of earnest zeal and consecrated labor, hearty sympathy and love for mankind."[10] Guided by this principle, Bible-thumping preachers lit the fire of faith in the hearts of many, effectively reinforcing the determined grit of pioneering Americans with the assurance of divine approbation. On the other hand, when Bishop England arrived in North Carolina in 1821, although he himself had much of the eloquence and all of the sincerity of his Protestant rivals, he was handicapped by the Catholic requirement of educated, celibate clergy. Saddled with such restrictions, he was forced to rely on foreign and Northern priests, men who were both few in number and unfamiliar with the southern way of life. In the two decades of his ministry, he never ordained a native born North Carolinian. Nor did it make his task easier that Catholic rituals were conducted in Latin and encumbered with medieval trappings alien to the emerging American culture. In the backwoods of North Carolina, Catholic doctrines and ceremonies were the exotic residue of a world being left behind in the march toward a civil society based on a new model of human capabilities.

The Baptist Juggernaut

Despite the enthusiasm of the Methodist preachers, their success paled before the sweeping impact of the Baptists on the people of North Carolina. The explanation seems to be that more than any other religion, the Baptists were thoroughly American. The Moravians were from Germany, the Presbyterians from Scotland, the Methodists from England, and of course, the Catholics were seen as "Roman." But the Baptist approach to Christianity was crafted directly from the marrow of the North American experience.

In 1639, convinced that infant baptism was non-Scriptural, Roger Williams, founder of the Rhode Island colony, had himself baptized by immersion and with his followers formed the first Baptist church in America. These morally puritanical but doctrinally liberal rebels rejected the divine right of kings and opposed the establishment of religion, claiming that each person had the right to live as a spiritual individual, looking to the Bible for guidance, with no need for a hierarchy or caste-like clergy. The new religious insight was that anyone moved by the Spirit, no matter his education or lack thereof, was empowered to proclaim the Gospel. This radical idea, though shocking to mainline Protestants and Catholics alike, was eminently congruent with the ideas of democracy and representative government, ideas which would in time inspire the American Declaration of Independence and Constitution.

The Baptist movement grew slowly until the Great Awakening of the mid-1700s when it began to spread rapidly, soon becoming the distinctive religion of the rural American population.

In North Carolina the first major Baptist foundation was the church at Sandy Creek, which Shubal Stearns organized in 1755. This initial congregation not only attracted hundreds of people itself, but stimulated the establishment of forty-two additional churches over a wide swath of the southwestern region of the colony. It is unlikely that any Catholic church anywhere in the world ever had such striking results. It is certain, that while the Baptist religion was sweeping across the landscape, the Catholic church had yet to establish a single congregation. When Bishop England came on the scene, the contest for the soul of North Carolina had already been resolved.

The Baptist understanding of freedom is clearly if overly stated in a collection of essays which attempts to explain the essence of Baptist identity.[11] The essays include such titles as "Freedom of Individual Interpretation," "Freedom of the Local Church," and "Freedom To Be Servant Leaders." It is said with pride that a man might repent of his sins one week, be baptized the next, and the following week open his own Baptist church. There is nothing more distinctive of the North Carolina landscape than the thousands of small Baptist churches which seem to have sprung from the ground like wildflowers in the springtime.[12]

The tongue-in-cheek claim that the Baptist religion is the official religion of the state can be supported by the fact that the proportion of North Carolinians who identify themselves as Baptists has increased with time. Whereas in 1890 they comprised 45.4% of the population, a hundred years later they were 49.8%. During the same period, the percentage of Catholics rose as well, from negligible to 3.8%. The major denominational realignment was the decline of Methodists from 40.3% to 23.1%.[13]

Having attempted to present a positive image of Baptists, it must be added that the tendency to interpret the Bible literally led to the justification of slavery, opposition to scientific ideas such as evolution, and insistence that wives be submissive to their husbands. Furthermore, despite the vaunted belief in the freedom of each congregation in the name of what it considers fidelity to the Bible, the Southern Baptist Convention has been experiencing considerable internal distention as its leadership attempts to impose doctrinal conformity on its member congregations. One of the most divisive manifestations of this was the 1987 takeover of Southeastern Baptist Theological Seminary in Wake Forest, North Carolina, by ultraconservative trustees.[14] Among other things, the new directors did not want Catholics speaking to their students, a practice which their more liberal predecessors had encouraged in the name of interdenominational understanding.

Bishop England Confronts Anti-Catholicism

A major portion of the voluminous writings of Bishop England was devoted to responding to anti-Catholic publications and to the bigotry which he encountered at every turn. In 1826, he wrote that he had come to America and become a United States citizen, "preferring this to any other part of the world," because he expected to be able to live here as a Catholic without experiencing religious bigotry. However, what he found was that Catholics were looked upon by their fellow citizens as "morally degraded," and that it was common for "Protestants to vilify the Catholic religion, and to use the harshest and most offensive terms when designating its practices." England discovered that even educated southern gentlemen believed that Catholics could not be good citizens, "upon the principle that the Catholic religion must produce effects which would be fatal to our state of society and government.[15]

After discussing this matter with Protestants in twelve states, the bishop concluded that the anti-Catholic sentiment was due not to ill-will but rather to a misunderstanding of Catholic doctrine which had been transported from Europe. Accordingly, as would many other Catholic apologists, he went about what was certainly the largely futile effort to present an accurate exposition of Catholicism. His explanations were exhaustive, ranging over the history of the world and examining every point of doctrine or practice which he felt was misrepresented.[16]

By far the most ambitious apologetic was a series of "letters" published in the *Miscellany* between 1826 and 1828 titled "Calumnies of J. Blanco White." This material takes up 440 pages in England's collected works.[17] What made White's attack on the church particularly galling was the fact that he was an apostate Spanish-born Catholic priest now serving a Protestant congregation in England. His book was reprinted in the United States under the sponsorship of a group of

Protestant clergy, who promoted it as "a temperate and able exposition of the errors of Popery."[18] England's fifty-eight letters are an exhaustive compendium of Catholic Church history and theological positions. His stated hope was to ameliorate the anti-Catholicism which he found to be poisoning so many sincere Protestants.

Like a firefighter rushing about attempting to extinguish conflagrations which were breaking out all around him, England continued to produce defenses of the church which typically were several times longer than the original offending article or book. For example, he came across "A Protestant Catechism" produced by the Episcopal Church in 1828.[19] The catechism contains ninety-four questions and answers, all of them blatantly aimed at the Catholic Church. Some examples are:

> 8.   *Q. Does the Church of Rome allow the free use of the Scriptures to the people?*
>
>   *A. No; which is not only very unreasonable, as they are the law by which all men are to be governed and judged, but exceedingly wicked, as Christ and his Apostles have commanded us to read them.*
>
> 22. *Q. Is the Church of Rome a sound and uncorrupt part of the Catholic church?*
>
>   *A. No; it is extremely corrupt, in doctrine, worship, and practice.*
>
> 42. *Q. May we not worship the blessed Virgin, the mother of our Lord?*
>
>   *A. Although the Roman Catholics address prayers to her, yet there is neither command nor example to support such worship in the word of God, and (as she is but a creature) it is downright idolatry.*

In a series of "Letters" signed "A Catholic Clergyman, A Native of Ireland" England addressed each of the Catechism questions, employing vigorous but respectful language, and drawing from his impressive store of historical and theological knowledge. The wonder is that a man with very limited access to libraries and constantly traveling was able to write so voluminously and with such erudition.

When in 1831, *The Southern Religious Telegraph* published an article titled "The Republic in Danger," which charged that Catholics were enemies of the state, England once again countered the attack. The article had charged that: "Popery has invaded the land, and is laying the foundations of an empire, with which, if it prevail, the enlightened freedom of the republic cannot coexist." England proceeded to counter what he considered the calumnies in the publication by means of a series of letters addressed rather grandly "To the Candid and Unprejudiced People of America."[20] Most of what the bishop wrote nearly two centuries ago makes for dull reading today but reflects the unflattering images of Catholicism which were common at the time. Terms such as "Scarlet Whore," "Antichrist," "Beast," "Babylon," "Romish," and "Papists" were employed with apparent unselfconscious venom aimed at proving that the Roman Catholic church was not only corrupt, but a serious threat to American democracy.[21]

The Mouse Gnawing Out of the Catholic Trap

One item from the extensive catalog of anti-Catholic literature produced during England's lifetime is particularly significant because directed specifically at William Gaston and his efforts to remove from the North Carolina state constitution its exclusion of Catholics from public office. In an impassioned twenty page pamphlet, authored by a self described "farmer," the whole repertoire of images and charges were employed in what, as we shall see, was a failed attempt to preserve the ban on Catholics in public life.[22]

Using an image which he might very well have heard more than once from a church pulpit, the pamphleteer wrote, "There is as much difference between the Protestant religion and the Catholic religion as there is between a whore and a virtuous bride ... as between God and the devil."[23] Also, he added that Protestantism had "driven back Popery," but now Catholics wanted "to trample her under foot again."[24]

The paranoia about Catholics, who at the time comprised an infinitesimally small proportion of population of the southern states, might be compared with the anxiety about Communists in government which consumed many Americans during the 1950's. In both cases, although the likelihood of a takeover of the country was remote to say the least, there were historical realities which fueled the concern. So, the fiery 1835 pamphlet, whose circulation and impact cannot be determined, concluded by alluding to events which prompted wariness about the Catholic Church, events and policies for which the Church itself has in recent years acknowledged culpability. Indeed, it was not until the Second Vatican Council in its 1965 Declaration on Religious Freedom that the church officially rejected the principle that error had no rights and that accordingly, if possible, the state should suppress religious error, meaning, of course, Protestantism.[25] The 1835 pamphlet had warned:

The Catholic Church, with the Pope at its head, has exercised tyranny, despotism, and cruelty, in all the nations of Europe — and they
will do so in the United States, whenever they can rise to that influence and power.[26]

Such concern continued unabated in succeeding decades, as
the tidal wave of immigrants from predominantly Catholic regions of
Europe threatened the ascendency of Protestantism. For example, in
1855, Edward Beecher published an attack on the church which questioned the loyalty of Catholic bishops: "It will be observed that I have
not infrequently used an uncommon form of speech in speaking of the
bishops of the Romish church in this country. I do not speak of them as
American citizens, or as American bishops, but as bishops of Rome
sojourning here."[27]

As evidence of what he considered the Catholic plot to take
over America, Beecher went on to cite Bishop England[28] who, on his
return from a trip to Europe, had written in an address to his diocese that
"in Paris and at Lyons I have conversed with those excellent men who
manage the Association for Propagating the Faith...." With a strained
leap of logic, Beecher pointed out that the Association for Propagating
the Faith — the paramount source of funding for financially strapped
areas including the diocese of Charleston — had claimed that within
thirty years the Catholic Church would be in the ascendency in the
United States.[29]

Had he looked more closely at England's writings, Beecher
would have found that the bishop had addressed the issue of Catholic
loyalty directly on numerous occasions, most notably in his precedent-
setting address on January 8, 1826, before the Congress of the United
States. In the course of his two-hour speech, attended by President John
Quincy Adams as well as most members of the House of
Representatives, England raised the question of whether allegiance to
the church compromised a Catholic's loyalty to the country. His answer
was unambiguous: "I would not allow to the Pope, or to any bishop of
our church, outside this Union, the smallest interference with the hum-
blest vote at our most insignificant balloting box. He has no right to
such interference." England went on to praise the constitutional principle of the separation of church and state, adding "You have no power to
interfere with my religious rights; the tribunal of the church has no
power to interfere with my civil rights."[30]

The Catholic Church And Slavery

However, while England insisted from the day he landed on its shores that he was a loyal American, it would be more accurate to say that he was a loyal *southern* American. It is in this context that his stand on slavery must be viewed. For him to have opposed slavery would have been tantamount to a betrayal of his small flock and suicidal for an already fragile church. Furthermore, England could find strong support for his position in official papal documents as well as in the prevailing interpretation of biblical references to slavery.

What must be pictured is a bishop attempting to maintain credibility in a hostile environment who, as much as he might personally abhor slavery, could find no papal or scriptural support for such a stance. Like a lawyer representing an unpopular client, England felt obliged to defend what he considered the Church's position on the controverted issue. Furthermore, England believed that the English were behind the abolitionist movement, and as a militant Irishman he saw hypocrisy in the English opposition to slavery in America while continuing to virtually enslave the Catholic population of Ireland by means of harsh penal laws.

Although England had spoken many times about slavery, an 1840 speech by the United States Secretary of State, John Forsyth, prompted a long series of letters on the subject, creating thereby the most exhaustive recapitulation of 19th century Catholic thinking on the subject.[31] What led Forsyth to refer to the Catholic Church was an Apostolic Letter by Pope Gregory XVI condemning the slave trade.[32] That document, written in typical Vatican obfuscatory style, led Forsyth to believe that the pope had condemned slavery itself. A former Georgia governor and staunch supporter of slavery, Forsyth was concerned that Catholics would now by obliged to support the cause of abolition. England assured the Secretary of State that this was not the case. As was his wont, England not only clarified the pope's statement, but proceeded to range over the entire sweep of Christian history in an effort to buttress the argument that slavery was not intrinsically immoral.

In 1808, the United States had outlawed the slave trade but put no restrictions on retaining in bondage those who were already enslaved — and their offspring. England waxed indignant that Forsyth would think that the pope and the bishop were to be numbered among the abolitionists, those who called for the total elimination of slavery. He insisted that this was not the case and that "the Catholics of the South should not be rendered objects of suspicion by their fellow-citizens."[33]

The first argument advanced by England was based on the fact that the pope's letter had been read and accepted by the bishops of the United States during the Fourth Provincial Council of Baltimore on December 3, 1839. If the bishops had understood the document to condemn domestic slavery, then they would have been required "to refuse the sacraments to all who were slave holders unless they manumitted their slaves." However, no such action has ever been taken, showing clearly that the Catholic bishops understood that the pope was referring only to the slave trade. And, as if sincere men could not be misguided, England pointed out that among "the most pious and religious of their flocks," the southern Catholic bishops counted "large slave holders, who are most exact in performing all their Christian duties, and who frequently receive the sacraments."[34] To a graphic depiction of the horrors of the slave trade, England contrasted what he termed the benign treatment of most of the slaves in the South.[35]

As if to solidify the point that the pope had not condemned slavery itself, England referred to his role in a situation which had caused great anxiety among American slave holders. Early in the 19th century Haitian slaves had revolted, overthrown their French masters, and established a republic. This was the only case in history of a slave population successfully revolting against their white masters. The American plantation owners were understandably concerned lest their slaves hear of the Haitian rebellion and be emboldened to imitate it. In the plantation regions of North Carolina and other southern states, slaves far outnumbered whites.

In order to regularize church affairs in the new republic of Haiti, Bishop England was asked by Rome to go there as its emissary. In personal audiences with Pope Gregory, England asked that a different person be appointed envoy, because of his own "peculiar position" as the bishop of the diocese, "within the limits of which was contained the most numerous Negro slave population that is to be found in any diocese in the world." He pointed out to the pope that his position would render him unacceptable to the Haitian government and, furthermore, that the assignment would compromise his standing in his own diocese. England reported that the pope refused the request, stating: "Though the Southern States of your Union have had domestic slavery as an heirloom, whether they would or not, they are not engaged in the Negro traffic."[36]

England then continued for more than one hundred pages to trace the thinking about slavery, citing not only biblical sources but Greek and Roman philosophers as well. Step by step he built the case that although slavery was not something to be encouraged or praised, it was nevertheless not intrinsically immoral. He referred to St. Augustine who called slavery one of the consequences of original sin.

England's final word on the issue of slavery was given in a note sent to the Editor of the *Miscellany* as the bishop terminated his unsolicited and unanswered "Letters to Forsyth." His note is dated Feb. 25, 1841, as he set sail for Europe. Shortly after his return from that arduous journey, he died.

> Gentlemen: My more pressing duties will not permit me for some weeks to continue the letters on the compatibility of domestic slavery with practical religion. I have been asked by many, a question which I may as well answer at once, viz.: Whether I am friendly to the existence or continuation of slavery? I am not — but I also see the impossibility of now abolishing it here. When it can and ought to be abolished, is a question for the legislature and not for me.[37]

Of course, no one thought that England could abolish slavery. What he could have done was lend his considerable moral weight to the cause of emancipation. However, this he refused to do. One reason for his hesitancy may well have been the deep affection in which he held William Gaston, a man who showed in his exemplary life that puzzling paradox — a deeply religious man who was also a slave owner.

Amending the North Carolina Constitution

Paradoxically, despite the pervasive suspicion of Catholicism, William Gaston, very openly a committed Catholic, was one of the most admired men in North Carolina. That admiration expressed itself in his election to a range of public offices that was capped in 1833 by an invitation from Thomas Ruffin, Chief Justice of the North Carolina Supreme Court, to serve as an Associate Justice on that Court. Gaston was interested but aware that the state Constitution contained a clause which limited public office to Protestants. Or at least it seemed to do so. Over the course of the next two years, the issue would be resolved but not without contention.

The North Carolina Constitution of 1776 contained two articles which mention religion:

> Article XIX. That all men have a natural and unalienable right to worship Almighty God according to the dictates of their own consciences.
>
> Article XXXII. That no Person who shall deny the being of God, or the Truth of the Protestant Religion, or the Divine authority of the Old or New Testament, or who shall hold Religious Principles incompatible with the Freedom and Safety of the State, shall be capable of holding any Office or Place of Trust or Profit in the Civil Department, within this State.

The state's founding fathers believed that although everyone should be permitted to worship freely, only Protestants should hold positions within the government. This restriction was actually a liberalization of the colonial period statutes which had afforded special privileges to members of the Anglican Church. As one author put it, Article XXXII "did not intend so much to exclude anyone from office, as to stress that government power should be handled by those who acknowledged that there was a moral basis to politics."[38] Apparently Catholics (not to mention Jews or non-believers) could not be trusted to uphold that "moral basis." Whatever the motives of the framers of the state Constitution, the men who subsequently represented North Carolina in the US Constitutional Convention in Philadelphia in 1789, mindful of the restrictions in their own governing document, voted against the article which abolished all religious tests for public office. For more than half a century, North Carolina retained in its Constitution the anachronistic religious Test Act which one author labeled "a barnacle of bigotry."[39]

However, since there were so few Catholics in the state, the issue long remained moot. With the political ascendency of Gaston, it had to be dealt with directly. Well aware of the problem, Gaston himself throughout his career had hesitated to accept state offices. As his friend, Bishop England wrote in 1835:

> Some years ago, the general impression was upon the minds of the few Catholics in North Carolina, that they were excluded from office, by the article in question — probably Mr. Gaston himself was of that opinion; he is known to have spoken doubtingly upon the subject, abut fifteen years since, and to have then alleged as a reason for declining an office which some of his friends wished him to take, that

he would prefer waiting until he could be better satisfied as to the full and precise legal effect of this very curious and discreditable 32nd article.[40]

Clearly, Gaston's concern had not been resolved when Ruffin approached him about the Supreme Court position. In a letter to the Chief Justice on Nov. 3, 1833, Gaston wrote:

> I am bound as a Citizen, and am bound by oath, to support the Constitution of No. Carolina. I am avowedly a believer in the doctrines of the Catholic Church. If that Constitution disqualifies a believer in those doctrines from holding office, it would be dishonorable and wicked in me to accept it. If it contains no such disqualification, and my country calls on me to render important services which I am able to perform, it is my duty to obey the call.[41]

In true legal fashion, Gaston went on to find ambiguity in what seemed like a very unambiguous statement. He argued, for example, that the Constitution failed to define what was meant by the Protestant Religion, and since there is no religious authority to provide such a definition, it would be impossible to say who was or was not a Protestant. Also, the Constitution did not exclude Catholics or any other denomination by name. Both these points would seem to render the article in question so imprecise as to lose all validity. Furthermore, Gaston argued, Catholics do not deny any of the truths of the Protestant religion. Catholicism differs from Protestantism more in that Catholics hold some beliefs that the Protestants do not hold, rather than denying any that they profess.

In language equally replete with nuanced legalistic distinctions, Ruffin responded that he was in complete accord with Gaston's interpretation. "I could not in good faith have asked you to do what I thought you could not, in good conscience, do."[42] However, although Gaston's appointment was approved by the governor and ratified by the Assembly without serious opposition, not everyone was happy. Newspaper articles accused Gaston of having taken a false oath and questioned the legitimacy of his position. For his part, Bishop England felt compelled to defend his friend and wrote a "Vindication of Judge Gaston."[43] Among other things, England noted that the Gaston case was not the first, that he himself had been consulted at earlier dates with reference to the appointment of Catholic magistrates in Salisbury and in Wilmington. On those occasions the bishop had examined the wording

of the oaths that were administered and found that Catholics could take
them in good faith.

However, arguments by lawyers and a Catholic bishop were
not likely to satisfy those who believed that the Constitution was being
violated. Only an amendment would resolve the matter once and for all.
Although Article XXXII was not the only issue, it was one of the
motives which led to the convening of a constitutional convention in
1835. At that gathering, Gaston assumed a central role in advocating a
change in the wording of Article XXXII.

Process of Changing the Constitution

In a lengthy and impassioned speech, Gaston asked and
answered the basic question:

> Ought there to be any Religious test in the Constitution? Shall any
> man be debarred from office, merely because of his opinions on mat-
> ters of Religion? To me it seems, if there can be any certainty in moral
> or political science, the answer must be in the negative.[44]

He went on to develop the argument that in a country where
freedom of religion is an inalienable right, to punish a man by exclud-
ing him from public office for exercising that right is "a violation of first
principles." Gaston summoned his colleagues to rise to the level of religious toleration to which all the other states had already risen, calling
for the total elimination of a religious test:

> I trust that we shall act up to the axiom proclaimed in our Bill of
> Rights, and permit no man to suffer inconvenience or to incur inca-
> pacity, because of religion, whether he be Jew or Gentile, Christian or
> Infidel, Heretic or Orthodox.[45]

However, as cogent as were Gaston's arguments, his fellow
delegates, representing perhaps the most conservative religious population in the nation, were not ready to excise the religious test completely. In fact, many of them favored leaving the Constitution the way it
was. Ultimately, Gaston was forced to accept a compromise, substitut-
ing the word "Christian" for the word "Protestant." Obviously, although
this would permit Catholics to hold office, it continued to exclude Jews
and other non-Christians. Religious tests would not be eliminated until
yet another constitutional convention would convene after the Civil
War.

Gaston and Race

Almost as if the men who reluctantly conceded expanded rights to Catholics had to balance their magnanimity by withdrawing rights from others, the 1835 Constitutional Convention disenfranchised "free Negroes and mulattos within four degrees." This was to close a loophole in the 1776 Constitution which had, by declaring that the ballot was open to all "freemen," permitted free Negroes to vote.

William Gaston took up the cause of the free Negroes, arguing that the issue was

> not now whether we should grant the right of suffrage to free blacks, but whether we should take it away. Had they never enjoyed the right, perhaps they would not at this time have thought of aspiring to it. The hardship lay in depriving them of what they had long been in the enjoyment of.[46]

At first, Gaston attempted to have the entire proposed article rejected. When a vote was taken on his motion to strike the article, it was defeated 65 to 62. Because of the closeness of the vote, Gaston suggested that the issue be taken up again. This time he argued that the free colored men were chiefly "the sons of white women, and therefore entitled to all the rights of free men." He also pointed to the legislators own acts which directed how slaves were to be manumitted for meritorious service, and said that that legislation "expressly declared them entitled to all the rights and privileges of colored freemen."

However, sensing that his arguments would not prevail, Gaston reluctantly proposed a compromise — that in order to vote the free Negro must have $500 in property and not have been convicted of a serious crime. As restrictive as was this motion, since $500 was well beyond the means of most Negroes, it also was defeated, by a vote of 65 to 64.

There were other ways in which Gaston attempted to improve the lot of the state's large African American population. In particular, his address to the 1832 graduating class of the University of North Carolina was as blunt as anyone dared to be in a state where the holding of slaves was considered virtually a divine right. Furthermore, Nat Turner's massacre of more than fifty whites in Virginia the previous year had spread fear of slave insurrection to every corner of the South. Undeterred by such concerns, Gaston told the students that it was their duty to provide for the "mitigation" of slavery and what he hoped would be the "ultimate extirpation of the worst evil that affects the Southern part of our Confederacy."[47]

A book published in North Carolina during the era of racial segregation praised Gaston's courage on that occasion:

> There, before a Southern audience, he boldly denounced slavery as the worst evil that afflicted the South, and called for its ultimate extirpation. This was at a time when abolitionists were anathema in North Carolina, but so great was the hold of Gaston upon our people that even this address did not lessen his great popularity.[48]

An even earlier book, used as a text in North Carolina schools, similarly praised Gaston's stand:

> In 1832 Gaston delivered a notable address at the University Commencement. The largest crowd that had ever attended a commencement gathered to hear him. "No other address ever delivered at the University," it has been said, "has been so much admired or so often referred to.".... He pointed out the evils of slavery in the South, and told the students that one of their first duties would be to find some remedy for those evils."[49]

In his position as Supreme Court judge, Gaston had several occasions to rule on race-related issues. In one case involving a slave convicted of murder for slaying his overseer, Gaston ruled that the act had been an act of passion and not of malice, that the slave had been driven to violence by the cruelty of the overseer. Judge Gaston said, "The prisoner is a human being, degraded indeed by slavery, but yet having organs, senses, affections, passion like our own."[50]

In an 1841 case, Gaston ruled in Newlin v Freeman that Sarah Freeman had the right to bequeath her slave to James Newlin, an anti-slavery Quaker. Forbidden by law to manumit the slave, Freeman sought to insure his quasi-freedom by willing him to Newlin. After the woman's death, her husband refused to deliver the slave to Newlin. Although at the time a married woman was not permitted to transfer property to others without the consent of her husband, Gaston ruled that a deed of separate estate filed at the time of her first marriage gave Mrs. Freeman the right to acquire and dispose of personal property on her own volition.[51]

Gaston's Final Days

Gaston consistently showed sympathy for slaves and made every effort to protect the rights of Negroes. In one case, his court sustained a verdict of murder against a master for killing a slave. In yet another case, Gaston ruled that "slaves manumitted become freemen and therefore, if born within North Carolina, are citizens of North Carolina."[52] Nevertheless, he did not manumit his own slaves, leaving them instead to his daughter, Catherine. In March 1851, seven years after her father's death, one of the inherited slaves, "a mulatto, Isaac Sharkey," escaped and became a fugitive. Living in the nation's capital at the time, Catherine went to the Circuit Court of the District of Columbia and sued to have him captured and returned to her. The petition was granted. It is not known whether or not Isaac Sharkey was ever apprehended.[53]

Remaining on the Supreme Court until his death, Gaston regularly traveled back and forth between his home in New Bern and the state capital. When in Raleigh for court sessions he occupied a detached house on the premises of his sister, Mrs. Jane Taylor. It was here that he passed away on the evening of January 28, 1844.

Early that day he had become faint on the bench and was taken home. Reviving somewhat, he entertained some friends during the evening. His last recorded remarks illustrate his quick mind, flowery speaking style, and religious faith, a faith which had remained firm despite the lifelong absence of a supportive Catholic community. He told of a party he had attended some years before in Washington at which a public official said that he was a free thinker in religious matters. Gaston responded: "A belief in an all-ruling Divinity, who shapes our ends, who's eye is upon us, who will reward us according to our deeds, is necessary. We must believe and feel that there is a God, all-wise and almighty." Rising to give emphasis to his words, he fell back and died. William Gaston was sixty-five years old.[54]

Gaston's reputation was such that within two years a North Carolina county was named in his honor and its capitol city called Gastonia. In 1848, cotton manufacturing commenced in Gaston County, and it soon became the foremost textile manufacturing county in the nation. Today, St. Michael Church and school in Gastonia serve a growing and diverse Catholic population.

A Constitution for the Catholic Church

Some liberal American Catholic authors have argued that the monarchical power structure of the church must change if Catholicism is to have widespread appeal in the modern world.[55] One author has actually formulated a model constitution that would specify the rights and duties of all categories of church members, from the pope on down.[56] Particularly since the Second Vatican Council, voices have been raised in support of a more collaborative decision-making process. Those advocating fundamental organizational change believe that such was encouraged by the Council, if not in its documents, at least in its spirit. However, this has not been the view of Pope John Paul II and other Vatican officials who insist that the church cannot be a democracy, that Christ gave to Peter and the apostles the power to "bind and loose," and that this power is exercised over time by their successors, the Pope and bishops. Although the laity may be consulted, their role is never more than advisory.[57]

However, without denying this fundamental structure, Bishop John England experimented with a form of ecclesiastical "democracy" modeled on the still young and revolutionary government of the United States of America. Shortly after his arrival in what became his adopted homeland, with the assistance of William Gaston and others, England formulated the "Constitution of the Roman Catholic Churches of North Carolina, South Carolina, and Georgia."[58]

The effort to construct a form of church management that paralleled the civic government with which Americans were familiar is made explicit in the Preface. For example:

> The portions of our church government are very like to those of the government of this Union. The entire consists of dioceses, the bishop of each of which holds his place, not as the deputy of the Pope, but as a successor of the Apostles; as the governor of each state holds his place not as the deputy of the President, but as vested therewith by the same power which vests the President with his own authority.[59]

The Constitution goes on to say that just as each state makes its own laws provided they do not contravene the general Constitution, so each diocese has legislative power provided the statutes are "not incompatible with the faith or general discipline of the Catholic Church." Furthermore, in a marked departure for a Church accustomed to ruling by fiat from above, the Constitution being proposed was to become effective only after "consultation, discussion, and arrangement between the bishop, the clergy, and the laity" at meetings held throughout the diocese. Although it is doubtful that most lay people fully understood the intricacies of the Constitution, they certainly understand that they were being given a voice in the government of the diocese, and that even if they had no say in the selection of the bishop, the constitution required that he report to them regularly and listen to their views.

After all the congregations had heard, discussed, and approved the Constitution, England carried it to Rome on the first of the four trips he would make to Europe during his years in America. Upon his return, he reported that he had presented it to the Holy See on September 25, 1822 and encountered no objection.[60] It might be noted that England had the Constitution approved before consulting Rome. Although a novice administrator, he already knew the value of approaching superiors with a fait accompli.

Contents of the Constitution

As if to insure the orthodoxy of his bold move, England devoted several pages in the Constitution to an explanation of the nature and organization of the church, material which certainly would have had a catechetical value for lay Catholics as well as allay misgivings which Roman authorities might harbor. In the light of subsequent Church developments it is instructive to note that England held that "we are not required by our faith to believe that the Pope is infallible."[61] Also, addressing the frequently made charge that Catholics owed primary loyalty to the pope, England wrote, "We do not believe that by virtue of this spiritual or ecclesiastical authority, the Pope hath any power or right to interfere with the allegiance that we owe to our state; nor to interfere in or with the concerns of the civil policy or the temporal government thereof, or of the United States of America." England would write this at a time when the Church had concordats with many European nations and was engaged in a protracted military struggle to maintain control of the Papal States in the face of the movement for the unification of Italy.

Also, with the still-simmering trustee issue in mind, while the Constitution insisted that the authority to establish parishes and appoint clergy resided in the bishop, it did allow lay ownership of church property: "The churches, cemeteries, lands, houses, funds, or other property belonging to any particular district, shall be made the property of the vestry of that district, in trust for the same."[62] Furthermore, the laity were advised of their obligation to provide for the maintenance of the property and barred from selling or leasing it without the bishop's authorization. It is clear that a major objective of the Constitution was to bind the laity to provide financial support for the church. However, whereas the civil government could compel the payment of taxes, the church had to depend on free will offerings. It was England's hope that subscribing to the Constitution would motivate people to assume responsibility for the material needs of the church. In this regard he was profoundly disappointed.

Two levels of church support are addressed in the Constitution. Contributing to the local parish or district was one, and since the lay people controlled the money collected to build and maintain their own church building and cemetery, it was expected that they would give generously. They did not, in part because many of them were poor and in part because they saw little need to support a church which offered so few services, since throughout England's two decades as bishop, there were never more than two or three priests in the entire state of North Carolina.

Much more difficult was collecting money for the "general fund" earmarked for diocesan projects, including the seminary which England deemed "absolutely necessary to insure to the diocese a supply and succession of good clergymen."[63] The bishop also needed funds for the erection of a cathedral which most Catholics would never so much as see, but which the bishop referred to as "the great church of the whole diocese." Several other costly diocesan needs were listed, including support for priests working in remote areas, schools which England hoped to establish, and aid to widows, the aged, and orphans.

To gather and administer the general fund, the Constitution erected an elaborate structure with district collectors sending money quarterly to a board consisting of seven clergy and twelve lay members. The annual reports from the bishop as to the financial condition of the diocese show that little money ever found its way to the general fund from the local districts, requiring England to beg for assistance from European church agencies.

Despite its failure, the diocesan financial board exemplified the innovative element of introducing a democratic dimension to church government. Besides the bishop and his vicar, all the other board members were to be elected by their peers at the "annual convention," the most distinctive and participatory feature of the Constitution.

The Conventions

Title VI, Section I of the Constitution called for an annual convention to be held in each state. Modeled perhaps more on the British House of Lords and House of Commons than on the United States Senate and House of Representatives, each two- or three-day gathering consisted of a "house of the clergy" and a "house of the laity." All clergy with faculties in the diocese were *ipso facto* members of their house. Lay delegates, on the other hand, were to be elected by the men in their home district. Although the point was made that the convention "is not to be considered as a portion of the ecclesiastical government of the church, but ... rather as a body of sage, prudent, and religious counsellors to aid the proper ecclesiastical governor of the church in the discharge of his duty...," the bishop pledged to give serious consideration to all suggestions and requests.

In all, twenty-eight Conventions were held of which only two assembled in North Carolina, both in Fayetteville in 1829 and 1831. The late and minimal participation of North Carolina in the process underlines the fact that of the three states in the diocese of Charleston, North Carolina was by far the slowest to develop. In fact, as has been seen, it was not until 1829 that the first two churches in the state were dedicated, one in Fayetteville and the other in Washington. Both these flimsy structures were consecrated by Bishop England in conjunction with the first North Carolina convention.

The addresses which England delivered at most conventions have been preserved and in effect provide a history of the Diocese of Charleston from 1820 to 1839. The presentations, delivered by the bishop from his episcopal throne vested in the full regalia of his office, relate diocesan projects for the year, propose questions for the Convention, and present the bishop's expectations for the coming year.[64] They are in effect State of the Union addresses embodying the vision and agenda of the bishop, as well as serving as motivational speeches designed to engender enthusiasm which the delegates would bring back to their districts. The torturously slow growth of the church during those years suggests just how daunting was the task.

The Fayetteville Conventions

England had already presided over six conventions in South Carolina and two in Georgia when, on March 15, 1829, he greeted the little band of three priests and six laymen who met in the just complet-

ed church in Fayetteville The building was unheated, unfurnished, and
virtually unused, since for much of the past few years no priest had
remained any length of time in Fayetteville, at the time a more populous
city than either Raleigh or Charlotte. Always attempting to be optimistic, but his frustration with the slow pace of church development in
North Carolina hardly disguised, the bishop began his inaugural address
with words which spoke volumes about the frail, fragmented, and impe-
cunious condition of the church in North Carolina:

> Beloved Brethren: The object of our assembling is, with the aid of
> God, to attempt the organization of our little church in this state. Our
> numbers are small, our congregations distant from each other, and our
> other members thinly spread over the surface of the country. The
> occasion which has brought together the clergy which are here met,
> appeared to me calculated by its novelty to attract several of our lay
> members, and I therefore judged it proper to attempt convening our
> body in this place, at the period that we were about to dedicate a
> church to the service of Almighty God, for the first time, according to
> our rite, within the precincts of North Carolina. Circumstanced as we
> are, we can neither have many members in our houses, nor many top-
> ics for our consideration; yet there are some subjects of vital interest
> to our well-being, and to the very existence of our church: and they, I
> should hope, will receive our serious consideration.[65]

The first and overriding subject "of vital interest" was that of
a clergy. Heads nodded as the bishop referred elliptically to the embarrassing "two or three attempts" he had made to supply a priest for the
state from the men recruited from outside the diocese. As the bishop had
to admit, bishops in other states or countries do not release their best
men for assignment elsewhere. The mission areas, desperate for priests,
are welcome dumping grounds for "problem" clerics. More often than
not, the "problem" re-emerged with disastrous consequences for Bishop
England and the Catholic congregations. Chastened by several bitter
experiences, England had decided that the only alternative was to train
and ordain priests within the diocese itself. To this end he had taken the
bold step of establishing a diocesan seminary in Charleston.

The plan was to create a classical college which would accept
non-seminarian paying students whose tuition would subsidize the seminarians. The bishop himself served as rector, and often as sole faculty
member, depending on the students to tutor one another and to study on
their own initiative. As primitive as was the education provided, the

seminary did produce a number of priests, to the point that England could boast to the 1839 convention: "Whatever has been lately done towards supplying the spiritual wants of the church in this state, has been derived from our diocesan seminary."

However, the seminary carried a substantial debt, and its financing was invariably a central point in the bishop's addresses to conventions. Acknowledging that the small congregations in North Carolina were in no position to contribute much to the cause, he nevertheless made this appeal to the little group of men sitting there on uncomfortable benches.[66]

The only other topic developed in what was a short address for Bishop England was his desire to visit more sections of the state, particularly the vast western region covered with forests and gleaming like an emerald in the clear mountain air. Something of this Irishman's missionary yearning is revealed in his words. He confessed that he considered his ministry incomplete because he had not personally visited every village, searched out every hidden Catholic, preached the message in every courthouse and assembly hall that would have him. There must have been tears in his eyes, and perhaps in those of his listeners, as he spoke of Catholics living isolated, concealed lives, abandoned by the Church as it were, hungering for the sacraments, yearning for community with those who shared their faith. Truth to tell, his concern may have said more about his own loneliness than the feelings of the independent-minded frontier Americans for most of whom religion was not a priority. But there it was, that zeal which had impelled countless Irish priests and nuns since the Middle Ages to sail forth from their native land in order to witness to their faith in all sections of the world. The Irish bishop, addressing those nine men in Fayetteville, North Carolina, on that Spring day in 1829, was expressing once again the passion of his spiritual ancestors, his cultivated brogue echoing off the wood plank walls and engraving themselves on the hearts of men whose very presence was clear testimony to their own faith. They loved their talented and open bishop and grieved with him that so little had been accomplished.

The laymen at that meeting included Alexander Gaston, son of William Gaston, representing the New Bern district and Lewis Leroy and John Gallagher from Washington. The latter two men would travel back with the bishop after the convention for the dedication of the church in Washington. Two others present were John Kelly and Dillon

Jordon of Fayetteville itself. Special thanks were extended to Kelly "for his liberality and his zeal in advancing the interests of our religion."[67] In each town, it was a few men such as these who gave a substantial amount of their time and wealth to the establishment of the church.

Two years would pass before another convention would be held in North Carolina. During the interim virtually no progress had been made. In his address on February 27, 1831, the bishop spoke of "the bitterness of disappointment," of "prospects being blighted," "careful calculations baffled," and "the swelling bud, to which he looked with precocious confidence, almost uniformly nipped when about to expand its flower."[68] Certainly discouraged, yet not wanting to dishearten his listeners,[69] England counseled trust in God. Expressing embarrassment that for much of the intervening two years there were no priests available for ministry in North Carolina, he announced that two priests were now assigned to the state. Based on previous unfortunate experiences with clergy, he said that he hoped to be able to keep at least the two "stations" of New Bern/Washington and Fayetteville/Raleigh staffed. This commitment he would be able to keep, as well as to have a "missionary" visit the southwestern section of the state where a few Catholics had been identified in the Charlotte area.

It is not unusual for churchgoers to complain that their minister is always talking about money. Certainly this charge could be leveled against Bishop England. Most of the address to the 1831 Convention concerned the pressing need for financial assistance for the seminary, for building and repairing churches, for supporting the clergy, and for supporting the bishop himself. Evidently irritated, England noted that no provision had been made for the expenses he incurred in coming to Fayetteville. Despite the constitutional provisions for a general fund for diocesan needs, literally nothing had been done to implement even the most rudimentary collection of money. The bishop's expectation that laymen would attend to the financial needs of the church, leaving him and the priests free to concentrate on their spiritual ministry, was not to be realized.

Diocesan Conventions

Although the three states of North Carolina, South Carolina and Georgia officially comprised but one diocese, for many years Bishop England administered his jurisdiction as if it were three dioceses, one for each state. The separate state conventions were the primary indication of this way of dealing with his assignment. Then, in 1839, after a protracted process of amending the Constitution, the separate state conventions were replaced with a single annual gathering for the entire diocese. England explained his reasoning for advocating this change.

> I consider it far more conducive to unity of sentiment and of action, attended with much less expense and inconvenience, better calculated to produce, and tending much more powerfully to attain the great object for which the Convention is intended, to have but one annual assemblage for the entire diocese, than to waste our energies in partial efforts.[70]

The fact is that the sixteen-year experiment in establishing a well-organized Catholic Church in each state had failed. Furthermore, England was getting tired of the constant travel and the myriad details involved in organizing a convention that might be attended by but a handful of men. The novelty had worn off; men grumbled about leaving their homes and businesses for extended periods in order to attend a meeting, which often did little more than remind them of the problems which plagued the diocese. A fresh approach was called for.

Although certainly more convenient for the bishop, a meeting in Charleston required extensive overland and sea travel for the delegates from North Carolina. Nevertheless, six North Carolinians traveled to South Carolina for the first diocesan convention which opened on November 17, 1839. Father Andrew Doyle, pastor of the Washington/New Bern district, and Father Thomas Murphy, pastor of the churches in Fayetteville and Raleigh were accompanied by the laymen: John Preston of Washington, William Daly of Fayetteville, John O'Dougherty of Raleigh, and Thomas O'Brien of New Bern.[71] All told, sixteen priests and thirty laymen gathered in the Cathedral of St. Finbar for this first combined gathering of representatives of all three states.[72]

The occasion was festive and very typically Catholic in its pageantry. As the minutes of the meeting record, "The priests, robed in their vestments, occupied the stalls and chairs, giving an exceedingly rich and solemn appearance to the sanctuary."[73] For his part, the bishop, no longer the young man who had tirelessly journeyed on bone-jolting stage coaches throughout his vast diocese, sat before the assembly, wishing to cheer and encourage them, yet weighted down with the burdens of debt, a chronic shortage of clergy, pathetically small congregations, and nagging anti-Catholicism. He felt compelled to present an honest, indeed a blunt report. In an address which lasted more than an hour, England reviewed the work of nearly two decades. There was little to celebrate, particularly with regards to North Carolina. The fields which he had considered ripe for the harvest had yielded little fruit. True, there had been growth but much less than he had hoped for. In one sense, he did not have to relate this sad situation to the men present; all of them were keenly aware of how difficult had been the efforts and how minimal the achievements. In another sense, the bishop, ever the open, accountable leader, felt the need to lay it all out before them, to admit that the South remained virtually impervious to a vigorous Catholic life. The tone was not one of defeat or resignation but of hope tempered by a realistic assessment of the situation. Bishop England and his beloved colleagues were more than a century too early. They could not know, but perhaps suspected, that a long, fallow period would intervene before their religion could establish any significant presence in the area..

Looking at the sixteen priests gathered around him (there were but eighteen in the diocese), England spoke with a frankness meant to remind them once again of the price they were asked to pay. All these men had heard him speak countless times, were graduates of his seminary, and impelled by the vision he inspired of doing great things for Christ, had pledged themselves to be faithful to a calling which would bring few satisfactions and much privation. They knew that the bishop lived in his person the sacrificial life to which he summoned them. They also knew that many of their colleagues, overwhelmed with the privations they experienced, had abandoned this man, this diocese, these people.

The bishop reported that there had been five priests in the diocese at the time of its creation and that nine others, ordained elsewhere, had been affiliated with it at one time or another. Not one of these priests remained. Furthermore, of the thirty-seven men ordained for the diocese, six had died and thirteen others had left. The loss of priests was a continuous drain on England's spirit and a never-ending source of frustration as he attempted to staff parishes. No sooner would a man be sent to a community, than he would ask to be relieved. The dream of an heroic, sacrificial life was soon replaced with the pain of loneliness and the conviction that life elsewhere would be more fruitful as well as more comfortable.

Although he understood all too well the demands of priesthood in such a diocese, England once again challenged the men before him to be strong:

...too often I have found that my brethren of the clergy, wearied and disgusted by the toil, and the want of immediate success in performing this duty, have persuaded themselves, and sought to persuade each other, that it was a hopeless occupation...[74]

Nor were the laity spared England's sharp criticism. Although the men present were among the most committed Catholics in the diocese — their very presence bore testimony to the sacrifices they were willing to make — the bishop berated them for providing for their own local churches while showing no interest in the needs of the diocese at large. Then, having vented his anger and sadness, England softened his tone and said: "I have been hitherto most disappointed, yet, though frequently baffled, my hopes are not crushed."[75] His hopes may not have been crushed, but his body was growing increasingly weaker. There would be but one more convention, one more time for embracing, for renewing friendships, for comparing notes, for sharing meals, for telling stories. An age was ending for the Catholic Church in the South, and although no one would yet admit the possibility, for the Southern way of life itself.

Second Diocesan Convention: November 1840

The drumbeat of abolition was growing louder and slave holders were becoming increasingly alarmed and defensive. Furthermore, waves of immigrants were flooding Northern cities, creating social problems but also fueling enormous industrial activity. More and more, the South was a different kind of society from the North, perhaps even — some began to think — a different country. A not inconsiderate aspect of the concern many Southerners felt was that millions of Catholics were entering the United States, bringing with them not only their peculiar beliefs and rituals, but massive potential political power. In his addresses to both Diocesan Conventions, Bishop England referred to the growing anti-Catholicism encountered in his diocese. While counseling Catholics not to retaliate, he could not help but realize that it was becoming more and more difficult to be a Catholic in the South. The bishop had the increasingly difficult task of assuring Southern society, including Southern Catholics, that the Church was not inimical to their way of life, that is, not opposed to slavery.

As we have seen, Bishop England went to great length to insist that Catholics were not only good Americans but supportive of the institution of slavery, which he attempted to present in a positive light. At the same time, realizing that Negroes had human needs and human souls, he wanted to offer some services to them. It was a delicate balancing act which he performed in his address at the Charleston convention in November 1840. He wished to open a school for "free children of colour" while not implying that he or the Church opposed slavery.

We can imagine the bishop speaking to slave owners, his most faithful as well as most wealthy Catholics. How alert they would become as soon as the issue was raised; how closely they would listen to every word, observe every gesture. Any wrong move on England's part, and the whole fragile edifice of the church in the diocese would come tumbling down..

Extremely aware of the delicacy of the issue, but prodded by the small community of Sisters of Mercy to provide instruction for free Negroes, England broached the subject. He knew that although it was against the law to teach slaves to read or write, it was legal to do so for free Negroes. He was conscious also that many southerners were uncomfortable with this as well, viewing any bettering of the lot of Negroes as a threat to slavery. Noting that some years before he had opened a school for free Negroes, only to be pressured by local people to discontinue the program, England explained:

> We yielded at the time to their wish, though our judgment differed from theirs. I trust, however, that we may now be permitted to resume that instruction, which the irritation of the moment required us to suspend, and that our fellow-citizens will feel convinced that in the discharge of this duty, we feel ourselves answerable to God to avoid anything that can disturb the peace and good order of society, or violate the laws of those states whose exclusive jurisdiction on this subject we religiously acknowledge.[76]

Most of England's attention was now focused on Charleston, on the little seminary with its nine students; on the struggling *US Catholic Miscellany* newspaper; on the convent which he had just built for the Sisters of Mercy. Also, he was increasingly engaged in activities on a national level. If he didn't have much success organizing Catholic communities in the South, he had more success organizing the American bishops, who had never met in council until prodded by England to do so. Under his continuing leadership, they would hold four provincial councils in Baltimore, laying the foundation for the national episcopal conference which would provide a national voice for Catholic concerns. He was also in frequent contact with Rome and, as if he did not have enough to do, had received jurisdiction over northern Florida. Nearly every day he wrote letters to political and religious leaders as well as to his priests and lay friends, including Gaston. With all this activity, it is small wonder that there was little time for North Carolina, where the few small communities already mentioned struggled to survive.

In one sense the years during which John England was bishop of Charleston was a golden age. England is widely acknowledged as the most creative and significant Catholic of the first half of the nineteenth century. On the other hand, within his diocese itself, particularly in North Carolina, very little of lasting significance was accomplished. At his death, the Constitution went into abeyance. Never again was a Convention held. It would be two years before a successor was named, and within twenty years everything would be destroyed in the cataclysm of the Civil War.

It can be said that the Catholic Church in North Carolina was established by Bishop England. It might also be said that with his death, the Catholic Church in North Carolina collapsed and would not rise again until the arrival of another great bishop, James Gibbons, in 1868. The following chapter will examine the fate of the church during the period from the death of Bishop England through the administration of Bishop Gibbons.

Chapter Six

The Collapse & Reconstruction of the Church: The Civil War & Bishop James Gibbons

I felt myself sent out alone to a strange country among strangers -- to a state where few Catholics were to be found -- where there was little or no immigration, and none to be expected. My clergy numbered but two priests, Rev. Mark S. Gross and the Rev. Lawrence P. O'Connell. In the vicariate everything had to be created.... I was left to feel the loneliness of my situation, more trying than its material poverty.

---Cardinal James Gibbons, describing his arrival in North Carolina in 1868

On New Year's Day, 1871, Archbishop William McCloskey of New York preached at the dedication of St. Ann Church on East 12th Street in Manhattan. The theme of his sermon was the unity of the church. He argued that unity existed in God himself and that God the Father sent his Son to be the Savior of mankind, uniting all men into one body with himself as the head. McCloskey insisted that there would have been chaos if Peter had preached one thing in Rome while James preached another in Jerusalem. The archbishop, soon to become the first American Cardinal, went on to stress the importance of unity of belief in essential dogmas and the harm that had been done by quarreling sects with their contradictory beliefs. He ended by insisting that in the Catholic Church alone could be found that unity of belief that must mark the true Church of Christ.[1]

Shortly thereafter, John Carr Monk, a physician in Newton Grove, North Carolina received in the mail a package of medical supplies wrapped in a copy of the January 2 edition of the *New York Herald*, which contained an account of McCloskey's sermon. Monk read the article with great interest. For some time, he had "entertained

doubts about his religious opinions," and the sermon "struck a responsive chord in his troubled mind." Until this moment, Monk, a
Methodist, had never read any Catholic materials, entered a Catholic
Church, or had any communication with a Catholic clergyman. In fact,
until he read McCloskey's sermon he had "never thought the Catholic
Church worthy of serious consideration." In addition, there were no
members of that religion in Sampson County where he lived and only a
few hundred in the entire state. Furthermore, anti-Catholic sentiment
was as pervasive in his community as the acres of cotton fields through
which he traveled each day to visit his patients. Nevertheless, Dr. Monk
decided to take action.

Not knowing the name or address of any Catholic Church or
clergyman, he simply addressed a letter "To Any Catholic Priest,
Wilmington, NC," requesting information about the doctrines of the
church. The letter was delivered to Father Mark S. Gross, pastor of St.
Thomas Church in that city. Gross in turn showed it to Bishop James
Gibbons, who had recently returned to North Carolina after attending
the First Vatican Council in Rome. Gibbons wrote to Monk recommending books that would help him understand the Church. Obtaining
the books, Monk undertook what in effect was a correspondence course
in Catholicism, studying on his own and addressing to Gross and
Gibbons questions that arose. After instructing himself and his family in
this fashion for several months, Monk notified Gibbons that he wished
to be received into the Church. Accordingly, with his wife, Euphemia,
and their daughters, Anna Elizabeth and Flora Harriet, Monk traveled
the eighty-four miles to Wilmington by horse-drawn carriage and railway. On October 27, 1871, Gibbons baptized the four in St. Thomas
Church. It was the first time the two men met.

Explaining to Gibbons his attraction to Catholicism, Monk said:

> None of the Protestant denominations…could satisfy me. Their mod-
> ern origin, their contradiction of one another, their diverse construc-
> tions of the Bible, made me lose faith in Protestantism. I was casting
> about for the one true Church…; the books of instruction plainly
> showed me that it is the Catholic Church only which delivers all the
> truths of the Bible to be believed.

Two significant outcomes followed this "miraculous" conversion of Dr. Monk. First, through his influence, scores of people in
Newton Grove were converted to Catholicism, creating the first truly

native-born congregation of Catholics in the state. Secondly, the Newton Grove wonder led Bishop Gibbons and other Catholics to hope that this would be but the first of many similar communities. Although this was not destined to occur, the story of Dr. Monk and Newton Grove became an integral part of the folklore of the Church in North Carolina. As we have seen, more than eighty years later the little town in Sampson County would once again emerge from obscurity as the scene of Bishop Waters' 1953 historic integration of the church there.

The present chapter traces the history of Catholicism in North Carolina from the death of Bishop John England in 1842 through 1872 when Bishop Gibbons was transferred from North Carolina to Richmond, Virginia. Included in these three decades is the Civil War, a conflict that not only saw the slaughter of hundreds of thousands of young lives, but also tore to shreds the social fabric of the South. All but unnoticed in the context of this cataclysm was the virtual destruction of the Catholic Church. It would be the assignment of Bishop Gibbons, assigned to North Carolina in 1868, to take up the task of once again establishing a Catholic presence in a land so obdurately resistant to its growth. Although much of the story is of failure, we begin with a continuation of one of the few incidents that sustained the spirits of the missionaries during a most trying period.

Monk's Trials & Ultimate Victory

Initial reaction in Newton Grove to Monk's conversion was one of rejection and alarm. Long fed a diet of anti-Catholicism, the rural population found the idea of a "papist" in its midst abhorrent. If not particularly devout, the people were at least solidly Protestant. However, Dr. Monk's obvious sincerity, his personal integrity, and his jovial disposition soon won over most of his neighbors to toleration, many to interest, and some to conversion. Filled with enthusiasm and armed with his newfound knowledge, Monk instructed family members and friends. As he made his rounds as a doctor, he answered questions, left Catholic literature, and in effect became a lay missionary. Although he was destined to bring into the church more people than any North Carolina priest, it never dawned on church officials that perhaps God was giving the message that an indigenous layman, as minimally formed as he might be, could be more effective than an educated outsider to whom people could not easily relate. Without it being realized at the time, Newton Grove was becoming Catholic in the same manner that hundreds of southern towns had become Baptist.

In January 1872, at Monk's prompting, Father Gross visited Newton Grove, the first time a Catholic priest had ever been seen in this isolated community. After baptizing three children, relatives of the Monks, Gross preached in the open air. Despite the bitter winter cold, a sizable group gathered to listen. For months, the doctor had been telling them about the priest and the bishop whom he had met in Wilmington. Now they had an opportunity to see and hear for themselves. Favorably impressed, some began to consider joining the church. With a subsequent visit by Gibbons himself, mild interest would be transformed into a veritable ground swell of enthusiasm.

Having promised on the occasion of Monk's baptism to go to Newton Grove, Gibbons set out on March 2, 1872, to fulfill his pledge. Rising at four o'clock on a rainy morning to catch the train out of Wilmington, the bishop saw the weather turn ever more severe as the slow-moving train moved north across the Carolina lowlands. At the Faison's Depot station, Gibbons was met by one of Dr. Monk's relatives on horseback, accompanied by a friend in a buggy who would transport the bishop to Newton Grove. As Gibbons later recalled: "It was a journey to be remembered – a trip of 21 miles in the teeth of wind, rain, sleet, and snow." Revived by a hot drink and a warm footbath, Gibbons rested and the following day celebrated mass in Dr. Monk's house. On this occasion, six people were baptized, including a brother and sister of the doctor.

Encouraged by what was happening, Gibbons decided that the time had come to make a commitment to Newton Grove. Accordingly, he promised that the already overextended Father Gross would spend one week each month in Newton Grove. On his first such visit at the end of April 1872, Gross baptized eight converts, including a man who had been minister of the Cambellite sect and his family.

Becoming increasingly concerned, local Protestant ministers accelerated their hostility, forbidding their people from attending Catholic ceremonies or reading Catholic materials. However, their vehemence backfired and, alienated by the anti-Catholic vitriolic, even larger numbers attended Gross's services. This growing interest led to the construction of a rough structure within which the priest could give instructions. Here also hymns were sung and catechisms distributed. At all the services, the new converts exhibited so much joy and satisfaction with their new faith that others were eager to join them. These were people who had never been inside a Catholic Church with its Latin language and elaborate rituals. They were experiencing religion as it was very familiar to them, very Protestant-like. At least initially, the Newton Grove Catholics were encountering a Catholicism adapted to their cultural framework. Dr. Monk as their guide "spoke their language," and Bishop Gibbons, lacking the priest personnel to provide a permanent clerical presence, was forced to allow the new community to develop on its own. What emerged over the following twenty years was a community of some three hundred people, comprised entirely of converts and their children. It was one of the largest Catholic parishes in the state.[2]

Delighted with what was happening as a result of his example and influence, Dr. Monk donated the land and a considerable amount of money for the construction of a church. In short order, a simple frame building was erected and dedicated to St. Mark, the patron saint of Gross who had won the affection of the people. With great satisfaction, Gibbons consecrated the building on August 11, 1874. The following year a parochial school was added, presided over by a lay teacher. Whereas it had taken William Gaston and the Catholics in New Bern twenty years to construct their church, the Newton Grove converts achieved it in twenty months.

Converts continued to swell the ranks of the energetic community, the high point being reached in June 1875, when Gross received thirteen into the church, the largest number to be welcomed on one occasion, not only in Newton Grove but anywhere in the state to that time. The young priest was so delighted that he wrote to his brother: "No Catholics are more fervent; no people more easily won over to the faith." St. Mark was by far the most remarkable mission that Gross and Gibbons were instrumental in developing in the state, and they readily gave the credit to Monk.

Dr. Monk's Legacy

The enthusiastic doctor dominated every aspect of the community's life. He and his wife were frequent godparents for new converts and witnesses at marriages, the first of which was celebrated at St. Mark on February 11, 1877, with Father Gross officiating. Since people traveled great distances to attend the infrequent masses, they were tired and hungry after the service and readily accepted the Monks' invitation to share a meal at their house. That house was the Catholic center and the place where visiting priests lodged.

Monk did not restrict his interest to medicine and religion. In this first generation after the emancipation of the slaves, he took the initiative to help the recently freed Negroes who worked on the area farms and found it difficult to adjust to their newfound status. Monk gave land to the local school committee "for the purpose of a colored School and for colored preaching and for no other purpose whatsoever." It is not clear whether or not the Catholic priest ever preached in this school, but certainly Monk would have wanted the colored people to know about his religion.

Despite his substantial accomplishments, which also included providing funding for the training of another physician for Sampson County, Monk was not destined to live a long life. He had been baptized in 1871, and on September 10, 1877, he died at the age of fifty. In six short years he had been instrumental in establishing a thriving Catholic church in one of the most unlikely places imaginable.

Monk is buried in the Newton Grove church cemetery, not far from the grave of Bishop Waters. On the doctor's tombstone are the words: "A faithful husband; a devoted father; a Christian. In God's hands the founder of this Catholic Mission; the 'Cornelius' of the neighborhood. In life he kept the Faith; and he here rests, awaiting the blessed Hope of the Resurrection."[3]

For the next twenty years St. Mark would continue to be attended by a priest only one Sunday a month. One of those priests was Father Thomas Frederick Price, whose contributions to the church in North Carolina will be related in the next chapter. When in Newton Grove, Price was offered hospitality by Dr. Monk's widow, Euphemia, who survived her husband by many years.

In the Footsteps of Bishop England

Newton Grove in the 1870s was a solitary star shining through the gloom of a long, dark night. The three decades following Bishop England's death had been a period of virtually unremitting decline for the Catholic Church. However, the plight of a religious organization was but a minor aspect of the transformation taking place in southern society. The tensions over slavery and states rights that had been smoldering for years burst into flame in the nation-threatening conflict of the 1860's. The careers of Bishop England's successors must be viewed in the broader context of a society in a state of crisis.

The sorry state of the Church in North Carolina was aggravated by the fact that it took two years to find and install a new bishop. In part, the delay was due to the nature of communication in the 1840s and the complex process entailed in appointing a bishop. Weeks would pass as the archbishop of Baltimore notified the other American bishops of the vacancy and solicited their recommendations as to a successor. A list of three candidates would then be sent to Rome, where church officials would conduct their own investigation and eventually send word back across the Atlantic as to whom they had selected. The candidate would be contacted by the archbishop and asked if he would accept the post. When he did, arrangements would be made for his consecration as a bishop, after which he would finally travel to his new diocese. Under the best of circumstances, this process could take a year. With respect to Charleston, the conditions were anything but good. In fact, the first person selected refused the post, requiring that Rome be asked to select a second candidate.[4]

Eventually, Ignatius Aloysius Reynolds, Vicar General of the Bardstown (Louisville), Kentucky diocese and President of the diocesan college there, accepted the position and was sent off to what was the least desirable diocese in the country. As an eyewitness put it, the difficulty finding someone to go to Charleston was due to "the poverty of the diocese, the intolerance of the natives, the institution of slavery, and the eminence of the first Bishop."[5] Reynolds himself would tell Father Jeremiah O'Connell, whom he had ordained in 1844, that the pastor of any church in any Northern city was better provided with worldly goods than the Bishop and all the priests of the diocese of Charleston combined.[6]

Despite the conditions under which he had to work, Reynolds went about the task of managing the church as best he could in the three-state area. On his first trip to North Carolina late in 1844, he dedicated St. Paul's Church in William Gaston's New Bern. Gaston himself did not live to witness the long-anticipated occasion. During his tenure, Reynolds also blessed what O'Connell referred to as "plain and humble churches best suited for the interests of religion in a poor diocese" in Wilmington (1847) and Charlotte (1851.) However, none of the congregations in North Carolina owed their existence or growth to any organizing activity on the part of Reynolds. He merely validated the work initiated by small groups of men and women who persevered in the faith despite the sporadic attention provided to them. With Bishop England's Constitution ignored by his successor, no state or diocesan meetings brought together delegates from the isolated communities. For all intents and purposes, the few hundred Catholics in North Carolina were left adrift, virtually forgotten by the institutional church.

However, the bishop is not to be judged too harshly for his minimal attention to North Carolina, still the weakest sector of the vast diocese. In an effort to address this problem, Reynolds petitioned the American bishops to reduce the size of his jurisdiction. Accordingly, in 1850, the state of Georgia was made a separate diocese with its episcopal seat in the port city of Savannah. Reynolds was now responsible only for the Carolinas. However, rather than devoting himself to missionary work, he invested most of his energy and financial resources in constructing a cathedral in Charleston, reasoning that Catholics would not be taken seriously until they had an impressive church. To raise the funds needed for this project, Reynolds, as O'Connell put it, "begged all over America, Europe, and Cuba." Finally on April 6, 1854, with elaborate fanfare the new cathedral of St. Finbar was consecrated, replacing the humble building which Bishop England had constructed thirty years earlier. Archbishop John Hughes of New York, who presided, flattered Reynolds by saying that he had never seen "a more perfect specimen of architectural beauty." However, although capable of accommodating 1,000 people, no provision had been made for the poor, since, as O'Connell put it, "the style precluded the use of galleries."

Reynolds was not to be granted much time to savor his accomplishment, dying at the age of fifty-five within the same year, his body laid to rest beside his cathedral. That building, or as O'Connell put it, "that gorgeous pile, the pride of the city of Charleston, intended to remain always as a monument to the zeal and energy of its founder," was destroyed six years later in a fire that ravaged the city. Nor was Reynolds' grave spared. It would turn out that his lasting monument would have to be, not a great cathedral, but the compilation of the works of his predecessor, Bishop England, which he had published in 1849.

Another Interlude of Drift

So once again, in 1855, the diocese of Charleston was without a bishop, and once again what little attention North Carolina received from church authorities was reduced still further. Three priests, based in New Bern, Raleigh, and Charlotte, traveled back and forth across their districts, preserving as best they could a Catholic presence in the state. For their part, the lay Catholics, like their Protestant neighbors, were preoccupied with the gathering clouds of sectional conflict as the rupture between North and South grew more imminent. Certainly the priests wondered who their new supervisor would be, but ecclesiastical matters in Charleston, Baltimore, and Rome were of minimal concern to lay men and women living on the brink of economic and cultural ruin.

This time it would be three years before a new bishop would be appointed to Charleston. Not only was it difficult to find a willing and competent candidate, but the Carolinas again were not a priority on the Church's agenda. In Rome, Pope Pius IX (1846-1878) was battling two related threats to the Catholic Church – modernization and nationalism. Powerful intellectual and political forces were undermining the order that the church had painstakingly established in the aftermath of the Protestant Reformation of the 16th century. Scientific discoveries and new ideas were challenging basic religious doctrines even as ferment for the unification of Italy was demanding the surrender of the Papal States.

A Very Southern Bishop

While higher officials delayed and debated, Charleston was administered by the Reverend Patrick N. Lynch, a young priest with deep roots in the soil of the South, perhaps too deep as it would turn out. In 1858, all other alternatives having failed, Lynch was tapped to assume officially the position he had held de facto for three years. What he became bishop of was not only a poor diocese, but also one about to be devastated by fire and scrambled into chaos by the Civil War.

Although Patrick Nelson Lynch (1817-1882) was born in Ireland, he was brought to America by his parents when only one year old. The boy was raised in Cheraw, South Carolina, a backcountry cotton market town on the Great Pee Dee River. Although distant from Charleston and the larger world that was made accessible on the coast through the countless ships sailing from port to port along the Atlantic coast, Cheraw had a sufficiently large Catholic community to justify the establishment of an early Sisters of Mercy school. Although it had not been true of his two predecessors as bishop, slaves were an integral component of Lynch's life from his earliest years. Not only was he prepared by his upbringing to defend the institution, but also even as a bishop, he himself was a slave owner.

Soon after his arrival in South Carolina, Bishop England had visited Cheraw and met the Lynch family, fellow Irishmen. Young Patrick soon came under England's tutelage and attended the classical seminary that the bishop had established. Having progressed educationally as far as was possible in Charleston, at age seventeen Lynch was sent to the College of the Propaganda in Rome, a seminary dedicated to the training of priests for missionary areas. And so, just as would be true of Vincent Waters nearly a century later, a boy from the Southern hinterlands was plunged into the heart of the Catholic world. There, after six years of study, Lynch was ordained in 1840 and returned to Charleston to undertake his ministry.[7]

As one of the best-educated and most promising young priests, one of the first local vocations generated by Bishop England's efforts,[8] Lynch was assigned to the Cathedral church of St. Finbar and asked to edit the *US Catholic Miscellany*. However, the bishop had little time to further influence his protégé, leaving for Europe in 1841, and dying shortly after his return the following year.

Conditions in Charleston continued to be extremely precarious. In 1836, while Lynch was in Rome, the city suffered an epidemic of Asiatic cholera that killed about 100 Catholics in the city and vicinity, "thus thinning a congregation already miserably small."[9] When Bishop Reynolds arrived in 1845, overwhelmed by the church's dire financial situation, he began to cut back the already minimal institutional structure that Bishop England had built. As he shuttered the seminary in 1851, Reynolds humbly acknowledged that he could not compete with the accomplishments of his talented predecessor.

As for Lynch, by default he became the aide to Reynolds and was entrusted with a number of assignments, including the blessing of the church of St. Thomas in Wilmington, North Carolina in 1849. Then, before his death in 1855, Reynolds appointed the 38-year old Lynch administrator of the diocese, in which capacity he served as caretaker. Initially the position of bishop was offered to John McCaffrey, Rector of St. Mary's College in Baltimore. However, men familiar with the conditions in the Charleston diocese advised him not to accept the assignment. One of them, Bishop John Lancaster Spalding of Louisville, wrote that turning down the episcopate had become something of an epidemic, but not as dangerous "in its symptoms as the yellow and bone-breaking fever of Charleston."[10] When, belatedly, the post was proffered to Lynch, he could not have suspected that he would be subjected to trials even more trying than contagious disease.

As Lynch officially assumed the leadership of the diocese in 1858, there were but twelve priests in South Carolina and four in North Carolina.[11] The latter four men would be at their posts when the Civil War erupted three years later. All, following the lead of their bishop, would align themselves with the Southern cause and, by war's end, have died or joined their little flocks in flight, leaving their vacant churches at the mercy of the warring factions.

Since they were so few, it is an easy matter to list the priests serving the 600 known Catholics who lived in North Carolina on the eve of the American Civil War.:

> The Reverend Augustine F. McNeall was based at St. Peter in Charlotte;

> The Reverend Patrick Ryan pastored St. Patrick in Fayetteville and St. John the Baptist in Raleigh;

> The Reverend Charles Croghan was pastor of St. Paul in New Bern and St. John in Washington; and

> Father Thomas Murphy was at St. Thomas, in Wilmington.

Table II: North Carolina Towns, 1850, 1860			
Catholic churches were located in most of the larger towns in the state.			
	Total Population (% increase)	Slave (%)	Free Black (%)
		1850	
Wilmington	7,264	3,031 (41.7)	652 (8.9)
New Bern	4,681	1,927 (41.2)	800 (17.1)
Fayetteville	4,646	1,542 (33.1)	576 (12.4)
Raleigh	4,518	1,809 (40.0)	456 (10.1)
Washington	2,015	840 (41.6)	219 (10.9)
Morganton	1,978	298 (15.0)	5 (0.3)
Edenton	1,607	1,008 (62.7)	67 (4.2)
Warrenton	1,242	602 (48.5)	28 (2.3)
Charlotte*	1,065	456 (43.6)	36 (3.4)
		1860	
Wilmington	9,552 (31.5)	3,777 (39.5)	573 (6.0)
New Bern	5,432 (16.0)	2,383 (43.9)	689 (12.7)
Fayetteville	4,790 (3.1)	1,519 (31.7)	465 (9.7)
Raleigh	4,780 (5.8)	1,621 (33.9)	466 (9.7)
Salisbury	2,420	1,073 (44.3)	80 (3.3)
Charlotte	2,265(112.7)	825 (36.4)	139 (6.1)
Henderson	1,961	1,225 (62.4)	22 (1.1)
Elizabeth City	1,798	620 (34.5)	217 (1.1)

Sources: U.S. Bureau of the Census, *Seventh Census of the United States, 1850*, and *Population of the United States in 1860, Eighth Census.*
*Charlotte was not listed in the "Population of Cities and Towns" table of the 1850 census but probably ranked about ninth.
Taken from Greenwood, B. *Her Sweet Legacy*; p. 245.

Young Women Build a Church in Edenton

Soon after his consecration, Lynch traveled to Edenton, North Carolina where he laid the cornerstone for a new church. The following year he returned to the little town at the confluence of Albemarle Sound and the Chowan River and on July 26, 1859, the feast of St. Anne, dedicated the completed church in honor of that saint. The fact that there was a church in Edenton was due not to the efforts of any missionary priest but to the faith of three young women. Just as the Church of St. Mark in Newton Grove resulted from the efforts of the convert Dr. Monk, so in Edenton the church of St. Anne sprang from the determination of converts.[12]

After his brief visit to Edenton in 1821, Bishop England had referred to the Catholics there as "negligent." A generation later Mary Elizabeth Jones, her sister, Louise Matilda, and their friend, Elizabeth Moore, would infuse the small and dormant community with exceptional energy. The three, graduates of St. Joseph's convent school in Emmitsburg, Maryland where they converted to Catholicism, with youthful energy decided that their town should have a church. Accordingly, they presented the idea to a priest.

At the time, traveling by postal stagecoach the vast mission circuit of the eastern part of the state, the Reverend C. J. Croghan visited Edenton but once a year. He would gather the handful of Catholics for mass, administer the sacraments and then move on. With the economy sour, rumbles of rebellion increasing, and the number of Catholics small, he had enough trouble maintaining the churches in New Bern and Washington, let alone think of building another in Edenton.

Undeterred, the women asked the priest's permission to see if they could raise the money and build the church themselves. Skeptical of the proposal but certain that there was no harm in humoring the girls, Croghan gave his approval. Armed with this authorization, the young women began by convincing the father of Mary Elizabeth and Louise Matilda to give them $100 and title to a piece of land. Although Mr. Jones was not himself a Catholic, he admired the zeal of his daughters and their friend.

The three returned to Baltimore where they had been received into the Church and visited Archbishop Francis Patrick Kenrick, who knew the girls from their school days. Moved by their idealism, the prelate gave them a $20 gold piece and permission to go door-to-door in the city soliciting funds. As they left his residence, the archbishop advised them, "Be sure now, my children, to put the insults in your hearts and the money in your pockets." The $585 they "put in their pockets" convinced Father Croghan that the young women had not only a dream but also practical skills. He gave his consent for the construction of the church.

Thus encouraged, the women mailed appeals to every bishop and priest listed in the Catholic Directory. They taught music and translated French works into English, devoting every penny to the project.

On the day of the church's dedication, the procession that preceded Bishop Lynch into the building consisted of four men, five women, three children, and the three convert girls – all the Catholics of Edenton. They were joined by some 200 local Protestants.

During the next three years, more than twenty converts were received into the new church, despite the fact that there was no resident pastor. But the period of success was brief and the collapse of the young women's dream total. During the Civil War the church was used for housing troops, its furnishings and sacred vessels, like the garment of Christ on the Cross, auctioned off by soldiers. However, the stone building itself survived and today -- one of the oldest Catholic churches in the state -- it is the place of worship for about 500 parishioners.

The Civil War in North Carolina

Most North Carolinians had no personal motivation to preserve slavery. Small farmers in the east, as well as people inhabiting the mountain areas in the west, held no slaves themselves. However, it was the wealthy plantation owners who dominated the state government and shaped public opinion. Even with the election of Abraham Lincoln in November 1860, there was little talk of secession. But sentiment shifted quickly when in April 1861, Lincoln called upon North Carolina Governor John W. Ellis to mobilize 75,000 troops to suppress the rebellion that had begun in other southern states. Opposition was near unanimous to using North Carolina men to force the seceded states back into the Union. Rather than aiding Lincoln, Ellis ordered the North Carolina militia to occupy federal facilities within the state.[13]

The Catholic lawyer, Edward Conigland, was in court in Warrenton when he learned of Lincoln's call for troops. Although to this point Conigland had supported the Union, he now wrote to his wife in Halifax County that he was ready "to take the sword and to die sustaining the resolve that a foot of theirs [Northern troops] shall never pol-

lute the soil of North Carolina...."[14] As will be seen below, Conigland
subsequently became the friend and legal advisor to Bishop Gibbons.

Excitement mounted rapidly; the issue now was not slavery,
but the right of states to determine their own destiny. On May 20, 1861,
a hastily convened convention assembled in Raleigh and within an hour
the 120 delegates voted unanimously to join the Confederacy. On
receiving the signal that the ordinance of secession had been signed, the
military band outside the capitol began to play William Gaston's "Old
North State."

Four years of savage conflict would ensue. The soldiers who
marched out in glory, returned vanquished; or not at all. The result was
not just the end of slavery, but the beginning of a period of bitterness
that would cloud the South until long after the generation that experienced the war had passed away. In fact, the illusion of a well-ordered,
cultured society that had been brutally destroyed by savage northerners
would shape the southern consciousness for nearly a century.

Bishop Lynch And the War

As Catholic southerners joined their neighbors in supporting
the Confederacy, their leader, Bishop Lynch, assumed a major role in
the cause of secession. There was no thought that involvement by the
clergy in politics was inappropriate. The only thought was the preservation of the southern way of life. So, when South Carolina seceded
from the Union in 1860, the Charleston diocesan newspaper changed its
name to reflect the secessionist viewpoint. The banner of the December
29, 1860 edition appeared as simply *Catholic Miscellany*, rather than
US Catholic Miscellany, the name given to the paper by Bishop
England nearly forty years earlier when it was the only Catholic paper
in the country. Then, with the first issue of 1861, the name changed once
again, to the *Charleston Catholic Miscellany*. Some have tried to attrib-
ute these mutations to the publication's smaller range, noting that
Georgia had become its own diocese in 1850. However, the editor,
Father James Corcoran, made quite clear the reason for the change. He
wrote that he could no longer tolerate "those two obnoxious words
["United States"] which being henceforth without truth of meaning
would ill become the title of the paper."[15]

The *Miscellany*, by whatever name, fared no better than the
Confederacy. The fire that swept across the peninsula of Charleston on
December 11, 1861 destroyed not only the cathedral but also the edito-
rial offices of the paper and its press. Even after the war, the lack of

funds did not permit Bishop Lynch to revive the paper. It would not be until ninety years later, with the *Catholic Banner* of 1951, that the South Carolina diocese once again had its own paper. As has been seen, Bishop Waters had established the *North Carolina Catholic* three years prior to that.

However, the fate of a newspaper was the least of Bishop Lynch's concerns. The man who, in the words of Archbishop Hughes of New York, had become "the ecclesiastical spokesman for the hierarchy of the South," was busy during the war promoting the cause of the Confederacy and after the war picking through the scraps of the bankrupt Carolina Catholic Church.[16]

Following in the footsteps of Bishop England, Lynch gave a carefully worded definition of domestic slavery:

> I define it to be essentially a system or state of mutual claims and obligations between the owner and the slave, whereby the latter is bound to give the former the produce of his reasonable lifelong labor under the owner's direction, and the owner is bound in return to give to the slave a reasonable support according to his condition from infancy to death....[17]

In his lengthy exposition, Lynch went on to defend the right of an owner "to transfer his claims and obligations to another owner without consulting the slave, or as it is said, of selling him." In a brief that could serve as a moral guide to his fellow Catholics, Lynch advised that slaves could be passed from one owner to another by will or inheritance. Furthermore, it was permissible to flog refractory slaves. Imprisonment was not advisable, since it would not really be a punishment at all but "a reward, allowing the Negro to indulge in that greatest of all his luxuries -- idleness." It is quite likely that Lynch spoke from personal experience, since the record shows that he paid taxes for slaves himself.

The Catholics of Charleston served the Confederacy with unanimity. When the Irish volunteers had no company flag, the Sisters of Mercy sewed one for them displaying the eleven stars of the Confederate states. On one side was painted the flag of South Carolina and on the other the harp of Erin, surmounted by a cross with the inscription "In hoc signo vinces." In the Cathedral, Bishop Lynch celebrated a high Mass and presented the flag to the volunteers, reminding them of the homes and altars they had sworn to defend.[18] Into battle with them went several priests as chaplains, including Father Charles J.

Croghan, who a few years earlier had approved the construction of the Edenton church. Croghan was commissioned a Major.[19]

With his solid credentials, Lynch became a logical emissary to approach potential funding sources in Europe on behalf of the Confederacy. He also had as his mission convincing foreign countries and the Papacy to recognize the legitimacy of the Southern right to secede from the Union. As it turned out, he received his commission from Confederate President Jefferson Davis too late to save the doomed cause.

Nevertheless, with at least a glimmer of hope that his mission would succeed, Lynch sailed for Europe on a ship that adroitly evaded the Union blockade. A bale of cotton served as his bed on the long and lonely journey.

In England, Lynch found public opinion on the war divided and Parliament took no action. He then proceeded to Paris, where France refused to support the Confederacy unless England would do so. Finally, Lynch went to Rome. However, his nemesis on the war issue, Archbishop Hughes, had already been there and presented the Federal case. So, fearful of US sympathy with the unification movement in Italy, Pope Pius IX refused to alienate the American government by lending his support to the Southern secession.

Lynch's problems were not over. While he was in Europe, the Civil War ended and his collaboration with the defeated rebels resulted in his being impeded from returning to America until he was granted a pardon by President Andrew Johnson. On his return to New York in February 1866, two years after he had left North Carolina, Lynch was invited by Hughes to preach at St. Patrick's Cathedral. In his presentation, Lynch said that in his diocese the work of forty years had been swept away, "making me feel sad almost to weeping and almost to despair." The *New York Tribune's* response to Lynch was to assail him for his allegiance to the South.[20]

Men can be complex, and although Bishop Lynch is remembered because of his collaboration with the Confederacy, he was also an able preacher, a humanitarian, and in the end, a successful administrator. During the war he personally ministered to the Federal prisoners who were confined within his area and, in 1871, worked among the yellow fever victims of his diocese. Upon his return to South Carolina, finding affluent Catholics stripped of their wealth, he became an episcopal mendicant, begging everywhere, both on behalf of his destitute people and in order to eliminate the diocesan debt. By single-mindedly consuming the remaining years of his life in this fashion, at the time of his death in 1882, Lynch was able to bequeath to his Charleston successor a virtually debt-free diocese.

What helped make this task achievable was a step that Lynch had taken at the Second Plenary Council of Baltimore in October 1866. Aware that the heavy load of responsibility that he bore would leave him little time to visit the scattered communities in North Carolina, he requested that the state be removed from his jurisdiction. When the Council agreed and Rome concurred, a new chapter in the history of the Catholic Church in North Carolina began. In 1868, the state was designated a Vicariate Apostolic with Bishop James Gibbons assigned to administer the newly created ecclesiastical area.

Establishment of the Vicariate Apostolic

A new generation of clerics was needed, men not embittered or enfeebled by the war, men who would have the will and the energy to take the church in North Carolina out of the quicksand of slavery and sectional rivalry and lead it onto firmer ground. However, the task would prove to be daunting, so much so that yet another half a century would elapse before the state was judged ready to become a full-fledged diocese. The paucity of church members, chronic shortage of clergy, and lack of financial means forced it to be left in the limbo state known as a Vicariate Apostolic -- a stepchild of the rapidly growing church in America, a ward of Rome, begging for aid from the rest of the Catholic world.[21]

The man selected to undertake the unenviable assignment of being the first resident bishop of North Carolina was in several respects similar to Bishop England, who in 1820, had been given the equally impossible task of starting a church in, not one, but three states. Both men had been raised in Ireland, both became bishops at the age of thirty-four, and both went on to become prominent leaders in the American Catholic Church. Both also were writers who left behind a detailed record of their activities.

If Bishop England can be called the founder of the Catholic Church in North Carolina, so also can Bishop Gibbons, since the Catholicism he encountered when he arrived in Wilmington in 1868 was little advanced over what Bishop England found when he first visited that city forty-six years earlier. Gibbons himself would write: "Everything had to be started."[22]

Gibbons was a protégé of Archbishop Martin J. Spalding of Baltimore. As secretary to Spalding, Father Gibbons had demonstrated his administrative skills, particularly in organizing the 1866 Plenary Council that proposed the new status for North Carolina. However, what on the one hand was a promotion, on the other hand was a sentence to deprivation and possible failure. Spalding, who had great affection for Gibbons and who would sorely miss his young assistant, had confidence that the young bishop would succeed. On the occasion of Gibbons' installation as Vicar Apostolic, Spalding said: "I have educated you, raised you to the age of manhood; I have given you a ring, and now go root for yourself or die."[23]

As fate would have it, after a vigorous apprenticeship in North Carolina, Gibbons would root himself, not in that state but in Baltimore itself, where in less than ten years he would become the archbishop and head the premier see in the country for forty-three years. But the few years he spent in the wilds of North Carolina shaped, molded, and perfected Gibbons' character and gave him the qualities which made him, in many respects, the first Catholic bishop completely at home in religiously pluralistic America. The Catholics and the Protestants whom he met in Wilmington, in Halifax, in Salisbury, in Newton Grove, and elsewhere in North Carolina taught him lessons which would fashion him into the paramount spokesman of the American Catholic Church.

President William H. Taft would praise Gibbons for his "single-minded patriotism and love of country on the one hand and (his) sincere devotion to his Church and God, on the other." Another president, Theodore Roosevelt, said to him directly: "Taking your life as a whole I think you now occupy the position of being the most respected and venerated and useful citizen of our country."[24]

Gibbons was born in Baltimore, Maryland on July 23, 1834, the third of the six children of Thomas Gibbons and Bridget Walsh Gibbons who had immigrated to the United States about 1829. The family returned to Ireland in 1837, where the father died in 1847. Subsequently, Mrs. Gibbons took the children back to America, settling in New Orleans where James worked for two years in a grocery store before entering the seminary in Maryland in 1855. Ordained in Baltimore in 1861, he spent several years in parochial work until selected by Archbishop Spalding in 1865, to be his secretary. When consecrated by Spalding on August 16, 1868, Gibbons was the youngest Catholic bishop in the world.

The preacher at the consecration ceremony, the Reverend Thomas Foley of the Baltimore cathedral staff, addressed Gibbons as follows:

> I cannot congratulate you on going to North Carolina, but I do rejoice for the honor which the Church of God has conferred upon you, and I congratulate your flock, few and scattered, upon the advantage they are to derive from the apostolic mission you are to establish in that state, which, in a religious sense, may be called a desert.[25]

That "desert" consisted of two priests and at most 700 Catholic lay people.[26] Even before he arrived in North Carolina, Gibbons received a report from the Reverend Henry P. Northrop, who had pastoral responsibility for more than one-third of the area of the state. From his home base in New Bern, Northrop said that only three towns in his circuit had church buildings, New Bern, Raleigh, and Edenton. These three towns had a combined total Catholic population of about 110. Northrop also visited irregularly several other towns, including Greensboro, Wilson, and Halifax. The total population of all the mission stations was about 125.[27]

Initial Activities of the New Bishop

Like a chaplain escorting a condemned man to his execution, Archbishop Spalding accompanied Gibbons to Wilmington, where on the rainy Sunday morning of November 1, 1868, he officially installed the new bishop in St. Thomas Church, now the humble pro-cathedral of the vicariate. After preaching a lengthy sermon in which he heaped effusive praise on Gibbons, Spalding and the three or four priests who attended the ceremony hurried away, leaving Gibbons -- in Spalding's words -- looking "like an orphan and desolate."

Young Father Gross, pastor of the church, was the bishop's sole companion. The two men lived in a sort of lean-to attached to the walls of the church in conditions that were described as poorer than those of Wilmington's common laborers. They shared their meals on a rough table in the same room in which they slept on hard cots. Maintaining their living quarters and the church themselves, they lived the reality as well as the spirit of poverty.[28]

While sharing with Father Gross the routine priestly tasks of celebrating mass, baptizing, aiding the poor, and hearing confessions, Gibbons attempted to enlist religious sisters to establish a school in Wilmington. Like most bishops at the time, he was convinced that

Catholic schools were indispensable for a strong church. His first approach was to reach out to communities in Ireland, that most generous source of assistance to the American missions. However, he had no success. Eventually, as will be seen in greater detail in Chapter Eleven, he was able to convince the Sisters of Mercy in Charleston, the community founded by Bishop England, to send sisters to assist him. Their arrival in 1869, marked the beginning of the ministry of women religious in North Carolina.

By Gibbons' day, railroad lines, being rebuilt and extended after extensive wartime damage, crisscrossed the state. Wilmington, besides being a major seaport, was also, and logically, a railroad terminal serving for decades as the headquarters of the Atlantic Coast Line, which linked cities all along the east coast of America. In the second week of November, Gibbons and Gross boarded a train and headed for Fayetteville, one of the largest cities in a state that was still 95% rural.

It is likely that Gibbons was familiar with Bishop England's writings and knew that it was in Fayetteville that his predecessor had dedicated in 1829, the first Catholic church in North Carolina. However, on his arrival, Gibbons was shocked to find the church -- the 1835 replacement for the earlier building that had been destroyed in a fire in 1831 -- in such a state of disrepair that he immediately ordered a new roof to be installed. Not that the fifty or so Catholics in Fayetteville could be blamed for neglecting the building. They had been impoverished by the war and had had no pastor for several years. As he would subsequently do at Newton Grove, Gibbons told the Fayetteville Catholics that Father Gross would be with them one Sunday every month.

Again following the example of Bishop England and initiating a practice that he would continue throughout his years in North Carolina, Gibbons invited the entire town of Fayetteville to listen to him preach. On the second evening, the crowd reached 500 and included two Protestant ministers.

While periodically returning to Wilmington to attend to business there, over the course of the next few months Gibbons visited all the towns in the state known to have Catholic residents, a task which although demanding was not beyond the capacity of an energetic young man, since there were only about twenty such places. First, accompanied by Father Gross, he toured eastern North Carolina. Then, with Father O'Connell, he visited the Catholics in the western sector of the state. Each priest had no difficulty introducing the bishop to every Catholic in his area. Certainly few bishops in the history of the church could say that he knew personally virtually all the Catholics in his diocese.

It would be somewhat repetitious to recount each stop that Gibbons made. His pattern was to lodge with a prominent Catholic, meet with as many church members as possible, confirm anyone in need of that sacrament, and offer mass. Since there were no more than six useable parish churches in the state, more often than not mass was celebrated in the home of Gibbons' host. However, his most distinctive practice, and the one that would have the most lasting impact, was preaching in a public assembly place. Everyone in the area was invited, and typically hundreds attended, curious about this unique phenomenon and having at the time few alternatives for an evening's entertainment. It would be this experience, so rare for a Catholic bishop, of ministering more to Protestants than to Catholics, that would lead to one of Gibbons' most influential contributions to the church, the authoring of a best-selling book.

The Faith of Our Fathers

Reflecting in later life on the few busy years he had spent in North Carolina, Gibbons said that by and large the sermons he delivered while traveling around the state were prepared for and preached to non-Catholics. They were directed at the heart as well as the mind, typical of the kindly, sensitive, and even ecumenical approach that would endear him to Americans of all religious persuasions. For although, as he himself said, his goal in preaching was to draw people to the one, true Church, he had a respect for others and practiced the old saying that more flies can be attracted with a drop of honey than a gallon of vinegar. His drop of honey became a book, *The Faith of Our Fathers*, the most widely read Catholic book of the 19th century.[29]

After he had been transferred to Richmond, Virginia (1872) and shortly before being named archbishop of Baltimore (1877), at the urging of one of his priests, Gibbons put in book form the sermons which he had been preaching throughout the mission areas of the South. A steady stream of men and women attributed their conversion to having read *The Faith of Our Fathers*. One of those converts, the American historian Carlton J. H. Hayes said that he, while a Baptist, had read and reread the book and finally been convinced of its validity.[30]

Edward Conigland of Halifax (1819-1877)

Rather than follow the bishop step-by-step as he travels the state like an itinerant preacher during the later part of 1868, and much of 1869,[31] attention will focus on two of the Catholics with whom he lodged and with whom he maintained an ongoing relationship, the Halifax lawyer Edward Conigland, and the Salisbury novelist Frances Fisher, who used the pseudonym Christian Reid. The two represent major categories of Catholics: the Irish immigrant and the native born convert. Their lives reveal not only the difficulty of establishing the church, but the social milieu within which Catholics and others lived during and after the Civil War.

After visiting Edenton in late November, where Gibbons found the Catholic population reduced to eighteen persons,"[32] he crossed the Chowan River and continued in a northwestern direction almost to the Virginia border, arriving in the town of Halifax late in the evening of December 1. Here the bishop was welcomed by Edward Conigland, a prominent citizen of a town that retained some architectural reminders of its colonial period prominence. In this peaceful place "a deep and abiding friendship grew between the two men that lasted until Conigland's untimely death in 1877."[33]

Like many of his contemporaries, Conigland had lost the security and stability that the prewar period had provided to energetic, educated men like him. Gone were the slaves whose labor had contributed substantially to his prosperity. Dead or maimed were many of his friends. Dead also, one after the other, were the three women whom Conigland had married, leaving him, as had been the case with William Gaston, to raise his children alone.[34]

Conigland was born in Donegal, Ireland in 1819, just a year before another Irishman, John England, departed Ireland for his ministry in the American South. Since his father was a physician and respected member of the community, young Conigland had every reason to expect that despite the deprivations that Catholics suffered in a country dominated by Protestant England, he would receive a good education and enter a profession. Unfortunately, Dr. Robert Conigland died, leaving his widow and children with no recourse but to search for a better life in America.

When the family arrived in New York in 1834, Edward was fifteen. Distressed by the crowds and noise of the city, the youth underwent a ten-year period of wandering and searching, not sure where to live or what career to pursue. Adding to his losses during this time was the death of his mother. For reasons unrecorded, an older brother, Andrew, had moved to Halifax, North Carolina, and it was here that Edward also settled in 1844, and where he would spend the rest of his life.

At the time, Halifax was a prosperous port settlement on the Roanoke River and just a few miles from the northern terminus of the Weldon and Wilmington Railroad. Today, both Halifax and Weldon are quiet country towns left behind by the changing economy of the state. The site of the original colonial Halifax is preserved as an historic district. Now, as in Conigland's day, there is no functioning Catholic church in the town. St. John the Baptist parish ten miles away in Roanoke Rapids provides services to the approximately 500 Catholics scattered throughout the 725 square miles of Halifax County.[35]

To support himself, Conigland worked as a tutor while he undertook the study of law. In time he was able to purchase a farm that he called Glen Ivy where he lived and worked and where he would welcome Bishop Gibbons. Since the local economy did not enable him to make a living as a full-time lawyer, Conigland was forced to devote more time to the plantation than he would have liked. His letters speak of spending long hours nursing sick slaves back to health. In one of his earliest legal cases he represented a Negro who had killed a white man.

As was true of other Catholics moving into North Carolina, Conigland encountered blatant anti-Catholic sentiment. In fact, his second wife, Mary Wyatt Ezell, "hated with equal ardor ...the North and the Catholic Church." And, although she agreed to be married by a priest and to have the children baptized, "she hated Rome as she always had and always would to the end of her life." As it would turn out, since all of Conigland's wives were Protestants, it would only be with the death of the third that he could raise his children in the Catholic faith without continuous domestic hostility.

Mary Wyatt, whom Conigland married in 1854, and who died in 1866, had other things to worry about besides religion. In contradistinction to her husband, Mary was an avid supporter of secession from the Union. Throughout the war, she kept a "War Journal" in which she jotted down on a near daily basis information about the war as it came to her attention. In her early enthusiasm, she referred to the conflict as "this second war for our independence." However, her optimistic tone changed as the tide of war shifted. On August 30, 1862, two months after the defeat of the South at the Battle of Richmond, she wrote: "It carried desolation to thousands. North Carolina suffered most. Scarcely a household but mourned some loved one dead or wounded. Oh! The horrors of that seven days' fight." Although she was unaware of it at first, her own brother was among those who had fallen. In an effort to find his missing brother-in-law, Edward Conigland went to the hospital where the Confederate wounded were attended and, searching through the bodies of those who had died, found the young man and brought him home.

Paradoxically, it was the pain and losses and humiliation that revived in Conigland's heart the faith that had long lain dormant. Formerly marginal to his Catholic heritage, the death of his wives and the debacle of the war brought about a progressive conversion-like transformation. Conigland's correspondence during and after the war reflects the depth of his spirituality. For example, on January 20, 1863 he wrote to his wife's aunt, Mary Molloy, consoling her for the loss in battle of her son, George:

> I was much edified by the sentiments expressed in your letter. It matters not, indeed where we lie, for wherever we lie, whether among the bones of our kindred, or far removed from them, whether on the land, or in the sea, we shall all rise again with the bodies we had in this life, and blessed will they be who, in that dreadful resurrection day, will rise to a glorious immortality.
>
> This world is simply a pilgrimage to the doors of Eternity, its trials and its temptations are but intended to test our worthiness to enter the blessed mansions prepared for the just. And what we shortsighted mortals morn over as misfortunes, may be blessings in disguise sent by our heavenly Father to purify our hearts as gold is refined in the crucible.

In a letter to the same woman in July of 1865, Conigland returned to the theme of how losses are to be interpreted, advising her that "nothing happens in this world without God's permission, and what he permits must be intended for our good."

Little could Conigland have imagined the loss that he himself was to experience less than a year later. On March 24, 1866, he informed this same aunt that his wife, Mary Wyatt, had died suddenly of a fever, leaving behind three daughters, the youngest only eight months of age. After relating in minute detail Mary's final days, he applied to himself the advice that he had previously given to his correspondent:

When I think of my deplorable situation, when I look at my dear children, bereft of the best and kindest of mothers, deprived of her care and guidance forever, I beg of God to give me the grace not to question the wisdom and justice of His inscrutable decrees. It is hard for mortal eyes to see these attributes in the afflictions with which I have been visited, and I can only pray for the virtue of resignation.

It was this spiritually renewed man who, on hearing of the establishment of the Vicariate Apostolic, had taken the initiative of writing to Gibbons and inviting him to be his guest when he might visit Halifax. What developed in their few meetings and through a number of letters was a mutually beneficial relationship. In their hours together, the two men must have shared stories of their long-ago Irish roots, their setbacks, and their hopes. If the widowed lawyer welcomed the opportunity for priestly guidance, Gibbons welcomed the legal assistance that Conigland could provide, including the drawing up of the bishop's will. It would have been by men like Conigland that Gibbons was schooled in the ways of the South, as well as the mysterious strength that could be found in adversity.[36]

On his return to Wilmington from eastern North Carolina, Gibbons was surprised to learn that Pope Pius IX was summoning to Rome all the bishops of the world for an ecumenical council. This would be the first such gathering since the Council of Trent 350 years before. Although distracted by this news, Gibbons did not forget his new friend in Halifax. Hopeful that the little group of Catholics, no more than thirty people, might develop into a parish, Gibbons wrote to Conigland:

I hope to visit you once again before my departure for Rome. I wish you and Mr. McMahon could secure a little church in or near Halifax. The sooner you have a church, the more frequent you may find the visits of a priest. I have already six students in college, candidates for the ministry in North Carolina. I am obligated to pay for all of them. You may imagine the difficulty I have to contend with in trying to make all ends meet. When some of these young men are ordained, you may expect to see a priest more frequently.[37]

Meanwhile, Conigland's sufferings continued. Two of his four daughters died in their youth. A third, Mary, who married in 1872, but lived at home to care for her father, passed away in 1875. The obituary which her father wrote said that Mary, who had been educated in the convent schools in Columbia and Sumpter, South Carolina,[38] "until the day of her death did not cease to cherish warm feelings of gratitude towards the good sisters who had watched over her with a mother's care." Conigland concluded the obituary with his all too familiar message: "under the dispensation of God, who sends troubles to all, as if to direct their thoughts to the future, she was subject during her married life to frequent attacks of sickness."[39]

Then, on a chilly evening in December 1877, the people gathered around the hearth at Glen Ivy were informed that Edward Conigland, crossing the tracks that ran through his property, had been struck by an unanticipated freight train. He was unable to hear it due to the progressing deafness that had in recent years led him into a world of silence. Despite the urging of Gibbons and the efforts of Conigland, there was no Catholic church in Halifax from which the fifty-eight year old man could be buried.

Frances Fisher (1846-1920)

In the summer of 1869, Gibbons turned his attention westward. Despite the acknowledged privations, he was still basking in the sunshine of his honeymoon as a bishop, reporting to Archbishop Spalding that everywhere he went he was received kindly and that people in towns all across the state wanted Catholic churches. One of the places where he was well received was Charlotte, where he arrived on July 16 and was welcomed by his newly appointed vicar-general, Father Lawrence O'Connell. On the 18th Gibbons presided at a High Mass, preached, and administered Confirmation to forty-three men and women, nine of them converts. People had come from great distances to attend the service and see the new bishop. The Charlotte press spoke of Gibbons as "a man of considerable talents, a very pleasant speaker, and a model gentleman...."[40]

On July 31st, Gibbons and O'Connell journeyed by train to Salisbury, some forty miles northeast of Charlotte, where they were the guests of the Fisher family, one of whose members, 22-year-old Frances who, using the pen name "Christian Reid," would write more than forty novels and become one of the most widely read Catholic authors of her generation. As Dr. John Monk was identified with the Catholic community in Newton Grove, and Edward Conigland with Halifax, so Frances Fisher became the most prominent Catholic and principal benefactor of the church in Salisbury.

As was all too common at the time, Frances, born in Salisbury July 5, 1846, suffered heartbreaking losses in her youth. What started out as a happy life for a privileged child was shattered by her mother's death when Frances was eight years old. She then attached herself to her father, Charles F. Fisher. But that parental anchor of security would also be ripped away by tragedy, leaving Frances adrift in a sea of grief.

When the Civil War erupted, Charles Fisher, one of the most prosperous men in the area, organized a regiment of North Carolinians and marched off with high hopes of victory and glory, kissing his children good-bye and assuring them he would soon return. On July 21, 1861, Colonel Fisher was killed at the battle of Manassas. His reputation was such that the Confederate government named the strategic defensive position protecting Wilmington in his memory. Fort Fisher would be one of the last Confederate positions to fall during the war.

But there was no fortress within which 15-year-old Frances and her younger brother and sister could shelter themselves from the pain. However, fate is such that the loss of her parents redirected Frances' life in a way that could not have been anticipated. The children became wards of Colonel Fisher's sister, Christine, only 26 years old herself. The task of raising the youngsters was made more difficult, because the Fisher family had disowned Christine who had converted to Catholicism while on a visit to a relative in Florida. What was once the palatial home of a wealthy Episcopalian family became now the residence of an unmarried young woman with responsibility for three children and no income.[41]

Their home, bereft of servants, became the children's school with their aunt the teacher. Christine Fisher, a woman of considerable intellectual skill, not only instructed her wards in literature, history, and art but inspired them to embrace her religion as they reached young adulthood, further alienating them from their Protestant relatives. As was true of Dr. Monk and other early converts, the only formation in the faith which the Fishers received was from the few books that came into their hands. There were only two or three other Catholic families in Salisbury, and a priest came but once a month from Charlotte.

Sometimes in the parlor and sometimes in the garden, Frances read the literary masterpieces lining the shelves of her father's library, awakening in her soul the yearning to be a writer herself. The girl, resisting all efforts to get her to socialize with other young people, lived a reclusive life, seldom leaving the family property. With little formal education but an imagination filled with stories, the young woman decided that she would attempt to support the family through her pen. Already at the time of her Confirmation by Gibbons in the family parlor in 1869, she was finishing her first novel, *Valerie Aylmer*, which was published the following year when she was twenty-two years old. As Christian Reid, Fisher turned out a book a year for the next forty-five years.[42]

The first stream of stories are set in the upper-class plantation world of the pre-Civil War South, all of them complex and richly textured tales of adventure and romance. Then in 1879, together with her aunt, Frances made an extended tour of Europe, visiting Paris, Rome, and Venice. With the images gained from this experience, although she was back in the small rural town of her birth, Christian Reid's novels for the next ten years were set in a European world. Although some of her characters are Catholic her goal was not so much to write about Catholics, as to embody in her work what she considered Catholic moral principles.

It was during this second period of story-crafting that Fisher made the first of two major contributions to the Catholic Church in Salisbury, the donation of some of the family property for the construction of a church. Caring for the little church of the Sacred Heart, which was dedicated in 1882, became one of her lifelong projects. Taking a break from her writing, she would gather flowers in the garden and carry them over to the frame building that to a large extent was her private chapel, since a priest came infrequently for mass.

The second significant contribution came some years later when she campaigned to remedy this lack of a permanent clerical presence. Because of Fisher's prominence, the number of Catholics had grown moderately, all of them, like Fisher, converts. The dream persisted that, as had happened in Newton Grove, other vigorous communities of converts would spring up all around the state. Salisbury seemed a likely site. In fact, a priest writing at the time said: "No mission in the state is as thoroughly Catholic and as edifying in its piety as that of Salisbury."[43] In any case, by the late 1890's the people felt that the time had come for the assignment of a full-time pastor. As the community leader, Fisher undertook the task of trying to convince Bishop Leo Haid, a successor of Gibbons as Vicar Apostolic, to provide one of his few priests to what certainly was a less-than-priority post. Although generally reserved and unassertive, on this occasion Fisher utilized some of the leverage that her position allowed.

Since Haid had ignored an earlier letter, on May 9, 1898, Fisher wrote again telling the bishop that the people of Salisbury did not want the occasional services of a Charlotte-based priest; they wanted their own pastor. Although her tone was respectful, she insisted that "the sentiment of protest is intensely strong" and added a veiled threat that finances would suffer if Haid did not accede to their request.

In his response to this forthright letter, Haid assured the novelist that Salisbury would indeed have a resident pastor, on condition that the people provide him with housing. Under Fisher's leadership, funds were raised and a priest's house quickly constructed on the Fisher property. The bishop's requirement having been met, Father Joseph Mueller became the first of a series of Benedictine monks to serve the small community. Early in the 20th century, another Benedictine, Leo Kunz, built a parochial school on the Fisher property that was staffed by Sisters of Mercy. Thus, within her lifetime, Frances Fisher saw Salisbury transformed from a town with a handful of derided Catholics to the locale of a respected community with its own church, pastor, and school.[44]

As the Benedictine priest who was pastor of Sacred Heart Church in Salisbury at the time of Fisher's death in 1920, would say of the parish benefactor:

> Her deep faith and loyalty, her learning and intellectual eminence, her innate refinement and nobility of character, were not only the pride of her home town and the glory of her native state, but the light and inspiration of the little Catholic flock, who for a generation, looked to her for spiritual leadership."[45]

Despite her voluminous writings, Reid never elaborated on her motives for becoming a Catholic. It may be that, like the better-known southern Catholic novelists Flannery O'Connor and Walker Percy, Fisher was attracted to Catholicism precisely because of its sense of mystery and its rejection of the modern world.[46] Certainly her novels were set in an idealized past and ignored the world she would have known best, that of the Civil War and its aftermath. Christian Reid is an anomaly, an old-fashioned southern woman who nevertheless contributed to the breakdown of the cultural world that she loved by her adherence to an alien religion.

An Occasional Meteor

It is not likely that Bishop Gibbons read any of the novels of Christian Reid. He did however express his admiration for the mountains that Reid loved so much and about which she wrote so lyrically.[47] In any case, his work would not allow Gibbons much time for contemplating nature. Besides the concerns of North Carolina, he had now to turn his attention to issues that affected the Catholic Church throughout the world. After less than a year in North Carolina it was time to move on to what certainly would be the greatest adventure in the life of any bishop -- attending an ecumenical council.

In September 1869, Gibbons bid farewell to America and sailed to Europe for the Vatican Council. Just as he had been the world's youngest bishop, he would now have the distinction of being the youngest bishop to attend the Council. At his death in 1921, he would be the last survivor of that gathering, noted for the definition of papal infallibility and cut short by the forces of Giuseppe Garibaldi threatening an assault on Rome.[48]

More than a year would pass before Gibbons' return to North Carolina in October 1870. While in Rome, the council kept him so busy that little attention could be paid to his far-off jurisdiction, which once again was left adrift for an extended period.

Shortly after his return Gibbons ordained two young men to the priesthood and then set out to visit once again the eastern Carolina missions, installing one of the priests, James A. Duncan, as pastor in Edenton and the other, J. Norton Townsend, in New Bern. The latter town had been without a priest for two years. Included in this circuit was a stop in Halifax where once again he stayed with Edward Conigland.[49]

In July 1871, two more newly ordained priests came to work in North Carolina. The Reverend J. A. White was assigned to assist Father Gross in Wilmington, while Father John Hands became resident pastor of St. Patrick, Fayetteville. Slowly, the number of clergy was increasing. For the first time ever, every town with a Catholic church had a resident pastor: Wilmington, Raleigh, Fayetteville, New Bern, Charlotte, and Edenton. Whereas when Gibbons arrived in 1868, there were but two priests, now three years later there were eight.

In August 1871, Gibbons undertook his second tour of the western missions, starting with the installation of Father Hands in Fayetteville. After a visit to Father J. V. McNamara in Raleigh, the bishop made train connections which took him to Salisbury and another visit with Frances Fisher, who by then had published two novels. The Catholic population of Salisbury now stood at twenty, including four converts, whom Gibbons confirmed in the Fisher parlor.

However, no place showed more progress than Charlotte, where in mid-September Gibbons preached on the Vatican Council to a large audience and confirmed twelve persons. At a parish meeting, the congregation took the initiative of raising the money to build a larger church to replace the building that had been their religious home for twenty years. As had happened a decade before in Raleigh, a new church of St. Peter in Charlotte was a clear sign not only of the numerical growth of congregations but of their willingness to assume financial responsibility for their parish. This was true despite the continuing economic and political problems that plagued the South, including the still unsettled status of the freed slaves.

These arduous trips through the state in 1871, would be the last that Gibbons would make. In January 1872, upon the death of Bishop John McGill of the Diocese of Richmond, Gibbons was asked to assume responsibility for that diocese. Besides the confidence which the regional bishops had in Gibbons, there was the fact that North Carolina, with fewer than 1,000 Catholics and but a handful of priests, was not yet able to support a bishop. The feeling was that North Carolina could be administered on a part-time basis. So, within days of his new appointment, Gibbons took up residence in Richmond while retaining his position as Vicar Apostolic for North Carolina.

Understandably, and from Gibbons' perspective regrettably, his new duties permitted only a few brief visits back to the state where he had begun his episcopal career. Once again, North Carolina had no resident bishop and would not have one for another fifteen years when Leo Haid, Abbot of Belmont Abbey, assumed the post. The long tenure of Bishop Haid is the subject of the following chapter.

Sister Mary Charles Curtin, the annalist of the Wilmington Convent of the Sisters of Mercy during the Gibbons years, referred to the diminutive but energetic prelate as "an occasional meteor," a beloved and engaging man who appeared from time to time, lighting up the sky of that Catholic outpost but then just as quickly gone again.[50] For his part, Jeremiah O'Connell, another eyewitness, reflected bluntly on the impact which the loss of a residential bishop had on the church in North Carolina:

The residence of a Bishop in his see is unquestionably of prime necessity for the interests of religion. The evils of absenteeism, in this case, are no less detrimental to the cause of the faith than of the landlords to the property of Ireland. The progress of Catholicity will be retarded in a region remote from the episcopal chair and ruled as an outlying province.[51]

To some extent, the attention that has been paid to the brief North Carolina career of Bishop Gibbons is due to the fact that he subsequently became the archbishop of Baltimore, a cardinal, and the foremost spokesman for the Catholic Church in America. But it is more than that. As the popularity of *The Faith of Our Fathers* attests, the man had that rarest of all combinations -- wisdom, charm, holiness, and administrative skill. Another of his books, *The Eternal Priesthood*, contains his reflections on the qualities that should characterize a priest. Some of the criticisms leveled at the Catholic Church are that it is too dependent on priests, that too much "magic" envelopes priestly ministry, that priests after all are but men with shortcomings just like anyone else. As true as all this certainly is, it is also true that in the Catholic religious tradition, a holy priest is a most powerful force for attracting people to Christ. Who the priest is speaks louder than what he says. For a generation, all over North Carolina, people like John Carr Monk, Edward Conigland, and Frances Fisher recalled with deep satisfaction their brief contacts with Gibbons, an inspiring priest.

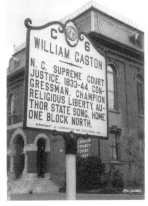

Bishop John England (top) and Judge William Gaston (above left) are rightly considered the founders of the Catholic Church in North Carolina. Both men had reputations that extended beyond the borders of the state and the confines of their religion. Gaston (1778-1844), as the historic marker in his hometown of New Bern suggests, held a number of government posts. His championing of religious liberty included the removal from the state constitution of the ban on Catholics serving in public office.

194

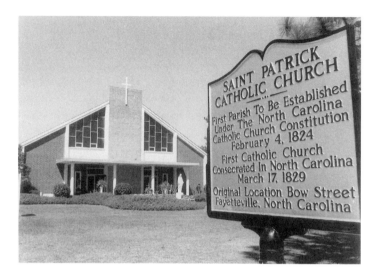

More than 1000 historic markers sprinkled throughout North Carolina are mini-history lessons. Several record events of Catholic·interest. In a trip through the state in 1829, Bishop England consecrated two churches, neither of which remains. St. Patrick in Fayetteville burned down shortly after it was dedicated, and St. John the Evangelist in Washington was destroyed by Union troops during the Civil War. The oldest surviving Catholic church is St. Paul in New Bern (above right), which was dedicated in 1844.

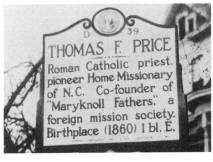

Bishop James Gibbons (top left) was appointed Vicar Apostolic of North Carolina in 1868. A prominent convert during the post-Civil War period was Frances Fisher of Salisbury (top right), who under the pen name "Christian Reid" authored more than forty novels. Above left, Thomas Frederick Price (1860-1919), the "Tar Heel Apostle," was the first native North Carolinian ordained to the diocesan priesthood (1886). A marker notes the location of his Wilmington birthplace.

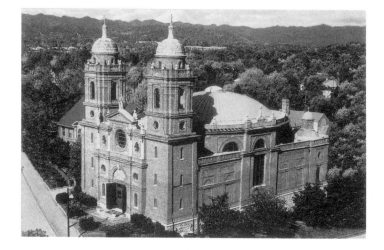

Three cathedral-like churches were built in the first decade of the 20th Century under the supervision of Bishop Haid. Two of them, Belmont's Maryhelp Abbey Church (top left) and Wilmington's St. Mary (top right), actually served as co-cathedrals during Haid's tenure as bishop. The Asheville church of St. Lawrence (above) was so impressive that there was speculation that Asheville might be the see city when the time came for a North Carolina diocese.

Chapter Seven

The Belmont Era:
Abbot Leo Haid & Father Price

> *Bishop Haid is held to be well suited for the position of Vicar Apostolic as far as his personal qualities are concerned, but he lives continuously separated from his Priests and people, seldom going amongst them and is almost totally under the influence of the Monks. He never consults his Council and the Monks continually influence his actions and the works of the State. The Benedictines hold all the offices of the Vicariate. The Secular Priests who alone belong truly to the Vicariate feel very keenly that they are put below the Benedictines and made inferior to them. The Seculars are made to feel that they are tolerated only as sort of stepchildren who cannot be well gotten rid of. His treatment of them at times has I think been very harsh....*

---Letter from Father Price to Cardinal Gibbons, October 27, 1910

At 4 a.m. on May 19, 1900, the monks of Maryhelp Abbey in Belmont, North Carolina assembled in the monastery chapel as usual. In the early morning gloom they took their places in the choir stalls and began chanting the Divine Office. Like thousands of Benedictine priests and brothers had done for fifteen centuries, they lifted their sleep-muffled voices and faith-filled hearts in praise of the God to whom they had dedicated their lives. These men were not clerical dilettantes. Their hands were coarse and their faces tanned from years of hard physical labor. The motto which their founder, St. Benedict, had given his followers was *ora et labora*, pray and work. Over the previous twenty years the monks had crafted an impressive monastic complex from the raw and unpromising property that had been given them. There was reason to feel a sense of pride and satisfaction in what had been accomplished.

Presiding over the praying community was Abbot Leo Haid, the man to whom all attributed the success of what was without any close rival, the most impressive Catholic achievement in the state. Abbot Haid had raised the money, drawn up the plans, and, most of all, inspired the monks to create this spiritual oasis in the wilderness of western North Carolina.

Suddenly the prayer of the monks was interrupted by the sound of footsteps running on the wood floor outside the chapel. In burst Brother Englebert, the night watchman, who said one chilling word: "Fire."[1]

The church bell began peeling as the monks rushed out of the chapel to find the new College Building enveloped in flames and the wind blowing smoke in the direction of the church itself and the monastery, which was their home. All that they had accomplished was in danger of being destroyed.

Despite their shock and confusion, the monks had the presence of mind to evacuate the boarding students who lived in the burning building. Then with that eerie discipline that sometimes strengthens people in the face of extreme crisis, the grim-faced clerics organized the task of saving what objects they could and of containing the accelerating conflagration. A bucket brigade consisting of boys and monks worked methodically and quickly. They were given no outside help. When the Charlotte fire department had been called, the request for assistance was refused, the professional firefighters arguing with cold logic that the lack of water would make a trip useless. Since the water tower had been taken down and not yet replaced, the only water available had to be drawn from wells, one bucket at a time.

In the midst of the confusion, Abbot Haid stood immobilized in front of the monastery. In a state of shock, he had turned authority over to Father Felix Hintemeyer, his indispensable aid and the prior of the monastery. Subsequently, Hintemeyer reported just how devastated Abbot Haid had been:

> At this juncture the saintly Bishop and Abbot Haid, crushed by grief, heartbroken and almost a mental and physical wreck, stepped upon the abbey porch and with arms outstretched towards the pitiless flames, like Moses on the mountain, called upon God's mercy and begged that his monastery and church be saved.

The abbot's prayer was answered. Under Hintemeyer's direction, the monks and boys were able to limit the fire to the college building, a terrible loss but not as severe as it might have been. The entire library of the college had been lost, some three thousand books, as well as the boys' possessions and all the furnishings of the rooms.

With the steely determination which characterized their work at Belmont, the monks decided that they would begin immediately to rebuild the lost building. While Hintemeyer assumed responsibility for the reconstruction, Haid remained in a state of shock and depression. He wrote to Mother Katharine Drexel, one of the abbey's major benefactors, "I am nearly despairing." To Peter Engel, abbot at St. John Abbey, he confided, "I would have given up; I am getting too old to begin over again as the struggle of the past has worn me out." Three weeks later, he again wrote to Engel entreating him to pray for him: "I am still so nervous and fearful. May God strengthen me and give me a little of my former courage."[2]

Another Fire, Another Dream Shattered

Five years after the fire at Belmont Abbey, an even more destructive fire swept through the four-story building that Father Thomas Frederick Price had constructed two hundred miles away to house the priests and students whom he hoped would be the vanguard of those who would convert North Carolina to Catholicism. If Belmont Abbey, near Charlotte, was the monastic and ecclesiastical center of Catholic life in the state, Nazareth, outside Raleigh, was the new frontier, the headquarters of the most dynamic diocesan priest ever to dream of a Catholic North Carolina.

At two o'clock in the morning of October 29, 1905, a student crying, "Fire" awakened Father Price who was asleep in his small third-floor room. Throwing on his pants, the 45-year-old priest began the effort to evacuate the fifteen residents of the building. Unfortunately, the flames made it impossible to use the stairs, forcing everyone to jump from the windows. Those on the lower floors, including Father Price, were able to jump with only minor cuts and bruises. However, boys in the top floor dormitory incurred severe injuries from which two of them died.[3]

The brick building, completed about the time of the Belmont fire, housed the two priests working with Price, a few pre-seminary students, and three of the more mature boys who were residents of the orphanage that was the most successful enterprise at Nazareth.

Fortunately, the building that housed the thirty younger orphans and the Sisters of Mercy who cared for them was not threatened by the blaze. Nor was the little chapel that stood on the rural hilltop, overlooking three hundred acres of farmland and the focal point of the life of the little community. As for the burned building, all that remained were smoldering walls.

Along with all the furniture, the mailing list for Price's monthly publication *Truth* was lost, as well as all the medicines used at the orphanage. As at the Belmont fire the Charlotte fire department had not helped, so in the case of the Nazareth blaze the Raleigh fire department was of little assistance, since their resources were engaged in fighting another major fire which had occurred at about the same time. Also, as was true at Belmont, the minimal fire insurance on the destroyed building was not nearly enough to cover replacement costs.

Whereas the shocked Haid had delegated responsibility during and after the fire to his chief aide, letters from the time suggest that Price, although acknowledging the enormity of the loss, reacted with striking equanimity. For example, two days after the fire, he wrote to the Reverend J. H. O'Rourke, a priest who had recently spent a month at Nazareth:

> The building and all its contents have been utterly destroyed. In two minutes more every member of the Community would have been burned alive. I had only time to seize my trousers and jump from the third story to the kitchen roof. I helped young Killworty the crippled boy down at the same place. ... I shall never forget the awful position of those three boys with the flames all about them on the roof and I powerless to assist them. I gave them absolution before they took the awful leap and picked up their mangled and apparently lifeless bodies after they had jumped. ... I will rebuild at once, using as many as possible of the bricks from the old building. ... I have no fears for the future. Thank God! I confide in no human or earthly thing. He has been pleased to sweep away the work of years -- the work was His -- He could do with it as he pleased.[4]

Price's strength is evidenced also by the fact that just three days after the fire he sent a letter appealing for help to hundreds of people, attaching a copy of the very dramatic article that appeared in the Raleigh paper. Besides asking for money, he requested the donation of books since the fire had destroyed the institution's library. Reaffirming the point he had made to Father O'Rourke, namely that he trusted completely in God, Price expressed confidence that God "will bring good out of evil and cause the work to flourish more vigorously than ever."[5]

Responses to his appeal poured in. Furthermore, the report of the fire had been published in newspapers all over the country, prompting additional expressions of sympathy and substantial contributions. Among the correspondence at the time are several letters from Bishop Haid, who as Vicar Apostolic was Price's superior. What is striking about the letters from Haid is both their tone and content.

In a note on November 4, less than a week after the fire, without even a perfunctory expression of sympathy, Haid said that he hoped the insurance companies would agree to payment soon. He also insisted: "Before rebuilding, I wish to see the plans and have them approved by the architect here." Furthermore, the new building should be strictly a priests' house and not also be used to house the older boys. Finally, the bishop admonished Price, noted for his missionary zeal, "The priests at Nazareth should find time to devote themselves to missionary work." Handwritten notes from Haid on November 8 and 29 and December 7 carry similar messages in a similar chilly tone.[6] Correspondence such as this during a time of crisis certainly contributed to the severe criticism that Price would express to Cardinal Gibbons in the letter cited at the beginning of this chapter.

The Post-Reconstruction Southern Landscape

These two men, literally tested by fire, began their ministry in North Carolina at almost the same time. Price was ordained a priest in 1886 and the following year Haid, recently elected abbot of Maryhelp Abbey, was named Vicar Apostolic. The two would be far and away the most significant figures in the life of the Catholic Church in North Carolina for decades. Price would be a dynamo of missionary energy until he left the state in 1910, to establish the foreign mission society known as Maryknoll. For his part, Haid would endeavor to balance his dual responsibilities as abbot and bishop, achieving much but satisfying neither the monks nor the diocesan clergy. Although these two men will be the main subjects of the present chapter, a brief look at the period in which they lived seems appropriate. Even though they themselves made little reference to the larger socio-political world in which they struggled to develop the Church, their work was necessarily profoundly influenced by that context.

In one of his influential works on the post-Civil War history of the South, C. Vann Woodward wrote, "Apart from Southerners,

Americans have enjoyed a historical continuity that is unique among modern peoples."[7] On the other hand, the South had undergone a series of discontinuities that Woodward classified as: slavery and secession, independence and defeat, emancipation and reconstruction, redemption and reunion. In the mid-20th century, the region would undergo yet another transformation which might be called segregation and integration.[8]

Woodward's four cataclysmic changes were bunched together during a very short period of time, from 1860 to the mid-1880's, when the Jim Crow system would be locked in place, providing a stable if unjust society but also consigning the South to a seventy-year period of economic stagnation and cultural isolation. It would not be until the 1950's, when people like Bishop Vincent Waters and the Reverend Martin Luther King undermined the structure of segregation, that the South would finally shake itself free of the stigma of slavery. These circumstances must be kept in mind when assessing the Church's progress, or more precisely, lack of progress. In truth, few institutions prospered while the state traversed its torturous route towards modernity.

Interlude of Neglect

As has been seen, when Bishop Gibbons was transferred to the diocese of Richmond in 1872, he retained his position as Vicar Apostolic of North Carolina. Although his time and energy had to be concentrated on his new assignment, his affection for the scene of his first episcopal ministry remained strong. He would, in fact, as Archbishop of Baltimore keep a loving eye on the church in North Carolina, particularly through the perspective of Thomas Price, his Wilmington protégé. Also, Gibbons would be the driving force behind the establishment of the Benedictine Abbey at Belmont and the subsequent appointment of its abbot, Leo Haid, as Vicar Apostolic. In other words, though no longer on the scene, Cardinal Gibbons remained a key factor in North Carolina church history to the end of his life in 1921, that is, right up to the eve of the establishment of the diocese of Raleigh in 1924. However, even Gibbons' concern could not shield the state from one last period of neglect.

From Gibbons' transfer to Baltimore in 1878, until the appointment of Haid as Vicar Apostolic in 1887, for all intents and purposes the church in North Carolina was abandoned once again. First of all, Gibbons' successor in Richmond, John J. Keane, who simultaneously assumed responsibility for North Carolina, devoted scant attention to what for him was little more than a mission outpost. Then in 1882, the unwelcome baton of Vicar Apostolic was passed to Henry P. Northrop. As was noted in the previous chapter, Northrop was very familiar with North Carolina, having at one time been responsible for the New Bern district. However, he quickly found himself overwhelmed by the burden of trying to manage the impoverished Vicariate and within a year was appointed successor to Bishop Lynch in Charleston. Predictably, his guardianship of North Carolina became a secondary concern.

So, in 1883, just as white North Carolinians annulled the political rights given to blacks during Reconstruction, chased away the carpetbaggers and scalawags, and hunkered down for a long period of isolation, resentment, and depression, the Catholic Church once again was leaderless. However, there was very little to neglect, explaining why no one was willing to assume the mantle of Vicar Apostolic apart from it being affixed to a more substantial benefice. Finally, in desperation, or perhaps in a bold stroke of genius, in 1887 Gibbons turned to a monk for help. No one could have suspected that Leo Haid would not only accept the position but also occupy it for thirty-five years. Although there would be severe criticism of Haid, there is no denying that he had been called upon to administer what probably was the most difficult assignment in the American Catholic Church. Catholicism's failure to take deeper root during his tenure was not due so much to the farmer's incompetence as to the inhospitable soil he was expected to till.

"The Very Nucleus of Catholicity"

Only one family has contributed three of its sons to the priesthood in North Carolina: the O'Connells of County Cork, Ireland. Originally, all were attached to the Diocese of Charleston and, as the Civil War began, resided together at St. Joseph Church in Columbia, South Carolina.[9] However, within a few years the peripatetic clerical adventurers found themselves in North Carolina. As was related in the previous chapter, Lawrence was the pastor of St. Peter in Charlotte when the Vicariate was established in 1868. The following year on his visit to Charlotte, Gibbons invited Joseph to organize St. Lawrence in Asheville, the first parish in the mountain region.

The third brother, Jeremiah, was by far the most interesting and most significant of the O'Connells. On several occasions, Jeremiah has been referred to as the author of the rambling, colorful, and impressionistic 1879 book, *Catholicity in the Carolinas and Georgia.* However, as valuable as is this account of Catholic life in the South, Jeremiah O'Connell's more substantial contribution to "Catholicity" in

North Carolina had more to do with real estate than books. It was he who donated the land on which was constructed the Benedictine Abbey at Belmont, an institution which one of the monks would proudly identify as "the very nucleus of Catholicity in the State."[10]

Jeremiah O'Connell, who was born in 1821, came to Charleston in 1840 in the last years of Bishop England's life and was among the first priests ordained by Bishop Reynolds in 1844. A most rugged, reliable, and resilient missionary, he crisscrossed the vast territory of the diocese eventually settling in Columbia, where with his brother, Lawrence, he opened a Catholic school in 1857. Unfortunately, the school was forced to close after a few years because of the Civil War, but also because of the "threats of incendiarism, midnight assault, and violence" from those who did not share O'Connell's enthusiasm for such an institution.[11]

In 1871, his health seeming to be failing, Jeremiah moved to Charlotte where he assisted his brother, Lawrence. Still interested in opening a school, after searching for a real estate bargain in the area, the semi-retired priest eventually purchased a 500-acre farm about ten miles from Charlotte in Gaston County. Realizing that he would not be able to establish and operate a school himself, O'Connell decided that a religious community would have to be enticed to accept the challenge.

Aware that the dilapidated farm buildings were not likely to appeal to anyone, he used what limited resources he had to improve the site. However, despite his efforts, it remained an unpromising locale for a religious foundation, especially because of its isolated location and the lack of a Catholic population in the region. For several years it looked like the farm was a well-intentioned white elephant. Then in 1875, Gibbons visited Charlotte and was attracted to O'Connell's dream.

On his return to Richmond, Gibbons wrote to Archabbot Boniface Wimmer, the legendary founder of the Benedictine monks in the United States, and offered him "the fine farm as a gift," with the only condition that the community cultivate the farm and "with God's blessing make it a religious center around which Catholicity would grow." Wimmer, whose forceful personality and risk-taking enthusiasm had attracted a growing community of men to St. Vincent's Archabbey in Pennsylvania,[12] was drawn to the offer precisely because North Carolina had so few Catholics and the diocese was so poor. So, after objections from more pragmatic monks, and sight unseen, Wimmer accepted the farm and, following rather protracted legal maneuvers, in

April 1876 sent a small contingent of monks to take possession of the property. Gibbons had conveniently omitted mention of the fact that one of the conditions for the transfer was that the donor, O'Connell, be allowed to reside on the property until his death.[13]

The new foundation, to be called Maryhelp, had the status of a priory, or dependency of St. Vincent's. The monks were instructed to establish a monastery and a school as well as cultivate the farm. The initial community consisted of one priest and three lay brothers in addition to O'Connell who, although not officially a Benedictine, affixed himself to the little community of hardy Germans. In that first year, the farm was a failure and the school had but two pupils.

Undaunted, the monks constructed a small frame "college" building, which the following year served as dormitory and school for a doubled enrollment, namely four boys. That twenty-two by thirty-nine foot structure would serve as the college for two decades until the brick building was constructed which, as has been related, was destroyed in the fire of 1900.

The continuing failure of the farm to generate an income and of the school to attract pupils tried Wimmer's patience, and after nine years of frustration he was anxious to divest himself of the floundering North Carolina project. Accordingly, it was decided that Maryhelp would be cut loose from St. Vincent's and erected as an independent abbey – on condition that five monks would volunteer to commit themselves to the new foundation. Moved by the spirit of adventure, several monks did so, but they were willing to go only on condition that they be permitted to select their own abbot. Wimmer agreed and the monks chose the 36-year-old Leo Haid to be their leader. In July 1885, Haid became "lord of this minor disaster near the southern border of North Carolina."[14]

Leo Haid, First Abbot of Belmont Abbey

Although not realized at the time, the arrival of Haid and his little band at Maryhelp in July 1886, marked the beginning of the end of the Irish ascendancy in the North Carolina Catholic Church. Not only had Bishops England and Gibbons been Irish, but so also had been most of the clergy, including Jeremiah O'Connell who met Haid at the train station on that hot summer afternoon. Within a few years, the profoundly German Benedictine presence at Belmont would all but completely overwhelm the remnants of seventy years of what was substantially a transplanted Irish version of the church. The Benedictines would also complement with a tight-knit community of monks the "Lone Ranger" secular priests who individually roamed the vast expanse of the state. Whether this transformation advanced the cause of Catholicism in North Carolina or impeded it remained a controverted issue for more than thirty years. For good or for ill, in the 1880's there seemed to be no alternative.

Haid was a monk. This simple statement is the key to understanding the long period of his dominance in the North Carolina vicariate. As Price would acknowledge, no one could fault Abbot Haid as the quintessential Benedictine. The problem was that he was called upon to assume the very unmonklike position of bishop, to move out of the cloister and into the "world." It was asking a man to live what in effect was a schizophrenic existence. On the one hand, his fellow monks wanted him to focus his energies on being their abbot; on the other, the secular priests of North Carolina, including Father Price, wanted him to provide leadership outside the monastery -- founding parishes, opening schools, and defending Catholicism in the public forum. In a continuous tug of war, Haid never fully satisfied either side, least of all the secular priests.

Although Leo Haid had been born in America, his parents, John and Mary Hite, were German immigrants who in 1848, settled in Latrobe, Pennsylvania where only two years earlier the Bavarian, Boniface Wimmer, had established the first permanent Benedictine house in the United States. The peaceful rural area was deeply Catholic and profoundly German, a good place for the immigrant family to raise its children. The Hites' fourth child, Michael, born in 1849, was to live the first thirty-six years of his life in the shadow of or within the walls of the rapidly developing Abbey of St. Vincent. At the age of twelve, he entered the monastery school and seven years later moved on to the novitiate, taking the name "Leo" and changing his patronymic to "Haid."

Even before his ordination in 1872, Frater Leo had begun what would be his uninterrupted career for thirteen years, teaching a range of courses at his alma mater, the abbey's boys' college. During all this time, he never had an assignment outside the monastery and might very well have expected that he would spend his life as a school monk. Hence, it was an abrupt and radical change for him to be selected to go off to North Carolina as head of a foundation at great risk of failure. The wonder is that such an unlikely abbot would achieve so much.

The first indication of the primitive nature of the new assignment was that Jeremiah O'Connell greeted the travel-weary monks with an antique mule-powered farm wagon. Judging the conveyance suited neither to dignity nor safety, Haid and the monks decided to walk the short distance to the farm, allowing O'Connell to ride in style in the ancient wagon. What met Haid's eyes was a ragtag collection of buildings - leaky, creaky, and dirty. Although monks had been there for nine years, overwhelmed by the demands of the situation and lacking competent leadership, they had been able to accomplish very little. All those original monks returned to St. Vincent's as soon as Haid and his group arrived, happy to shake the dust of North Carolina from their robes.

Undeterred, Haid went to work and began the process that, within a few years, would transform O'Connell's Folly into an impressive monastic complex. He accomplished this by an unanticipated combination of organizational skills, fundraising ability, preaching eloquence, and sheer determination. Also, he participated personally in every aspect of the work undertaken, leading by doing. As his mentor, Wimmer, had done, Haid attracted and inspired those with whom he came in contact. And Gibbons and Northrup soon noted his ability.

No one considered capable wanted the job of Vicar Apostolic of North Carolina.[15] The state, still struggling to recover from the war, was attracting no immigrants, the most likely source of Catholic population growth. In the entire state, an area the size of England, there were fewer than 2,500 Catholics and only a dozen priests. In the aftermath of war, the Catholics were like refugees in search of a home; no William Gaston emerged to provide leadership and some semblance of respectability. The few struggling parishes had all they could do to support a pastor, let alone a bishop.

In a desert, the smallest oasis can seem like a paradise, and in North Carolina, Maryhelp Abbey, although only in its initial stage of development, looked very promising. Furthermore, within months of his installation, Haid's name began to circulate as a likely candidate for Vicar. The reasons advanced for the selection of the as yet largely unproven monk included:

1. A Benedictine could more readily enlist the help of the monks for missionary work.
2. The monastery could provide for his lodging and support.
3. Haid was young, vigorous, a builder, and a leader of Catholic education.

4. Because of his ties to both the monastery and vicariate, he
   was less likely to abandon the post, as had the previous vicars.
5. His wide contacts throughout the several monasteries could
   help secure vocations.[16]

The Two Mitres

For his part, Haid was reluctant to become Vicar if that meant
relinquishing his position as abbot. As the ecclesiastical rumor mill continued to mention his name, Haid wrote to Wimmer insisting that he
loved being a monk and wished to dedicate all his energies to creating
a successful monastic foundation at Belmont. The thought of holding
the two posts led him to add, "One mitre has thorns enough, two would
be too much."[17]

Anxious to finally get some stability in North Carolina,
Gibbons was able to convince Rome to permit the unusual dual jurisdictions. So, on July 1, 1888, in the Baltimore cathedral with a
Benedictine choir chanting the mass and all the abbots of the country in
attendance, Gibbons, by now a Cardinal, consecrated the bearded abbot.
An article in the Baltimore Sun referred to Haid as having "dark com-
plexion." As Haid's biographer explained, "Actually the new bishop
was not ordinarily particularly dark, but his work in the fields had left
him tanned. The manual labor had also lent a certain confidence to his
intention to be an abbot-bishop and not a bishop-abbot."[18]

The tension between the two areas of responsibility was soon
expressed symbolically by the fact that there were two official installation ceremonies in North Carolina, one in the pro-Cathedral in
Wilmington, a second at the abbey church at Belmont. The divided
duties of Haid were thus very clearly demonstrated. And it would turn
out that for all intents and purposes, Belmont, not Wilmington, would
become headquarters for the church in North Carolina for the next thirty-six years. In the century between the arrival of Bishop England in
1821 and the establishment of the diocese of Raleigh in 1924, for only
four years, 1868-1972, did a Catholic bishop devote himself full time to
the work of building the church in the state. And as has been seen, even
Gibbons' tenure as the first Vicar Apostolic was interrupted for more
than a year by his attendance at the Vatican Council.

Now, Gibbons was ecstatic; at last the dream of a stable church
administration in North Carolina seemed assured. Of his visit to
Maryhelp for Haid's installation, Gibbons would say:

On the site of a tavern of the Revolutionary period that had served as
the first shelter for the Benedictine Fathers, now stood several large
brick buildings. In the midst of a wilderness had sprung up an Abbey
and College -- a house of prayer and learning and a center of missionary zeal.[19]

To a large extent, Gibbons' vision of Belmont Abbey as the
vibrant center of Catholic life in the state came true, and quickly. The
number of monks increased dramatically, reaching a total of fifty by
1910. Included were many, mostly German lay brothers, sturdy work-
men who tended the farm and constructed a steady and ever more
impressive array of buildings, the crowning achievement of which was
the Abbey Church of Mary Help of Christians standing on a gentle rise,
its twin spires reaching skyward. At the time of its dedication in 1893,
the German Gothic-Revival structure was the largest Catholic Church in
the state and remains today an impressive tribute to the monks who
worked with rudimentary tools and limited finances.

In time, St. John's College added a seminary division which
contributed to the formation of scores of priests, both diocesan and
Benedictine. In 1913, nine men were ordained, the largest class in the
school's history. As has been seen, the future Bishop Vincent Waters
was a student at the college a few years later. Although there is no
longer a seminary component, Belmont Abbey College remains today
the only Catholic college in the state with a student population of about
one thousand. Although still sponsored by the Benedictines, in recent
years it has been run by a lay administration. During all his years at
Belmont, in addition to his other duties, Bishop Haid held the position
of college president and regularly taught classes.[20]

Cardinal Gibbons, unwaveringly affirming, painted a glowing
prospect for the missionary activity of the monks. "In the past, the main
instrument for the conversion of nations (England, Germany, Italy) was
the Benedictine order. It is the same work now in our century and
among our people. The advent of the Benedictines means, let us hope,
the conversion of the South."[21] And indeed, the monks gradually began
to move out of the monastery and to staff parishes, unintentionally pro-
voking hard feelings among the diocesan clergy. Nowhere was this
more evident than in the case of Mark Gross, one of the state's most
dedicated priests and in 1891, pastor of St. Peter Church in Charlotte.
What led to Gross's bitter departure from the state was perhaps the most

blatant example of the conflict of interest created by Haid's wearing of the two mitres.

Belmont Annexes Nine Counties

Problems between the demands of the monastery and of the vicariate emerged after a very short honeymoon. Anxious to show his interest in the churches of the state, Haid made a tour of the parishes, often preaching a message which the beleaguered communities had never before heard, namely that the monastic presence, and his own as abbot-bishop, was a great blessing for the North Carolina. But while he was touting monasticism to the laity, his own monks were chaffing at his frequent absences and reminded him that he was first and foremost a monk. Furthermore, the priest-monks who were being sent out to provide parish services complained that their lives as monks was suffering due to all the time that they had to spend away from the monastery with its set routine of prayer and manual labor.

Adding a sobering note to the hope of sending forth cadres of missionaries to convert the South, as Gibbons envisioned, was the realization that available resources would have to be spread thin simply to provide basic services for the Catholics already in the fold. Therefore, as interested as Haid was in spreading the faith, evangelization would have to wait. To a fellow abbot he wrote in 1891: "It will be a long time before we can hope to breathe the air of Catholic progress."[22]

Wanting to motivate the monks to feel a sense of responsibility for the churches they served and also to avoid conflict with the secular clergy, in 1891, after protracted negotiations, Haid convinced Rome to cede to the Order of St. Benedict for fifty years the spiritual administration of nine counties in the general vicinity of the abbey, namely, Mecklenburg, Lincoln, Cleveland, Cabarrus, Rowan, Davidson, Guilford, Forsythe, and Gaston. Haid had wanted a perpetual grant, but at Gibbons' insistence, the more limited time period was granted. The abbot knew of cases in other parts of the country where monks had established parishes only to have them taken away and turned over to secular clergy. Also, wishing to preserve the monastic lifestyle as much as possible, the abbot wanted those who went out to parishes to be within easy reach of Belmont. In effect, what was created was a diocese within a diocese, an area over which a future bishop – who was not also an abbot -- would have no authority.

The only large city in the area annexed to the abbey was Charlotte, where Mark Gross was pastor. Although Gross had considerable affection for the monks and at one time contemplated joining the community, he was abruptly relieved of his parish. There would be no diocesan priests in the new Benedictine fiefdom. Burdened with feelings of betrayal, Gross left the state, never to return. The other secular priests took note of what was happening.

The jurisdictional permutations through which the area surrounding the Abbey would go in the course of the following eighty years were complex and led to acrimonious relations, first between the monks and the secular clergy and, subsequently, between the monks and the bishops of the dioceses of Raleigh and eventually of Charlotte. Suffice it to say that in 1910, counties around Belmont were declared an *abbatia nullius* diocese, that is, an abbey belonging to no diocese. Now Haid was not only abbot but also the ordinary of the monastic diocese, as well as continuing as Vicar Apostolic for the rest of North Carolina. The *Nullius*, the only such entity in the United States, progressively shrunk in area as the decades passed, until in 1960, the 'diocese' consisted only of the grounds of the monastery itself; it was now a diocese with no territory and no people. Finally, in 1977 the anomalous jurisdiction was suppressed completely.[23]

Katharine Drexel, Benefactor

One of the most significant of Haid's achievements was convincing the Sisters of Mercy to move their headquarters from Wilmington to Belmont. As will be seen in greater detail in Chapter Eleven, in 1892, this one-and-only North Carolina-based community of women not only located its motherhouse on a large tract of land adjacent to the monastery, but in short order opened a girls' school and an orphanage at Belmont as well as a hospital in nearby Charlotte. With the arrival of the sisters, Belmont became even more completely the center of Catholic life in North Carolina.

Besides dealing with the docile Sisters of Mercy, who agreed to do the college and monastery laundry, Haid also had ongoing contact with a different sort of nun, a Philadelphia heiress, destined to be the most significant Catholic benefactor of blacks and native Americans. When Katharine Drexel (1858-1955) first had communication with Haid in 1893, the 35-year-old woman had only recently founded the Sisters of the Blessed Sacrament for Indians and Colored People. Of more importance to the financially strapped Abbot, she was beginning the lifelong process of making generous donations to churches from income generated by the considerable fortune inherited from her father.

However, every grant came with the requirement that the religious needs of Negroes be incorporated into the plans. As was seen in Chapter One, in 1921, the Newton Grove parish would be one of the beneficiaries of Drexel's largesse. However, her first contact with North Carolina was much earlier and much closer to Haid's headquarters, and Haid's heart.[24]

Two ambitious church construction projects were underway at the same time in the early 1890's, the new St. Peter Church in Charlotte and the large Abbey Church rising slowly on a hilltop at Belmont. The expenses of both projects threatened to force the discontinuation of work and the consequent embarrassment to Haid. Katharine Drexel proved to be a savior, but it took some creative footwork by Haid to bring it about.

Several years earlier, believing that blacks were uncomfortable sharing a church with southern whites, Haid had constructed for them on the abbey grounds a chapel named in honor of St. Benedict. This practice of providing separate facilities for blacks was an issue with which church officials would wrestle for sixty years, until Bishop Waters, in the abrupt manner described in Chapter One, decreed that the day of segregated churches was coming to an end. In desperate need of a substantial infusion of money, Haid devised a plan that he hoped would appeal to Drexel. He proposed to convert St. Benedict chapel into a school and bring its black members into the abbey church under construction, where pews would be set aside for their use. He also guaranteed that in the Charlotte church similar arrangements would be made for accommodating blacks. In a June 24, 1893 letter to Drexel in Pennsylvania he argued:

> The *moral effect* on the Catholics in North Carolina especially, and in other Southern States, would be a great gain. If the Benedictines at the Abbey and in Charlotte break down the ugly prejudices against Colored people, it would go far to enable the Bishop to insist on building all future churches large enough to make decent room for Colored people.... There is no use in butting the head against the hard wall of prejudices, but we may climb over the wall or go around it slowly...[25]

Impressed with Haid's presentation, Drexel replied with a check that exceeded his expectations, allowing the work on both churches to go forward. The relationship with Drexel continued over the years, resulting in the construction of a number of quasi-integrated churches that otherwise would have been impossible to build.[26] However, as has been seen, religious orders such as the Redemptorist Fathers took the alternative position, namely that it would be best for black Catholics to have facilities separate from those of whites. As will be seen in Chapter Twelve, black Catholics themselves were divided on the issue.

The Tar Heel Apostle

The year after Leo Haid, a stranger to the South and to North Carolina, arrived at Belmont, Thomas Frederick Price, a native of Wilmington, was ordained to the priesthood. He would become not only the most prominent priest in the history of the state, but also a thorn in the side of Bishop Haid. Two men, two visions; two men, both talented and committed to the church, yet with very different personalities: a bishop cautious and pragmatic, a priest headstrong and impetuous. For more than twenty years they would spar over the direction that the church should take. Had outsiders been aware of it, the conflict would have seemed ludicrous, a tempest in a teapot, talented men struggling on behalf of a church which counted on its roles less than 3/10th of one percent of the population. But for the protagonists, the issue was not just numbers but fidelity to their calling. In his own way, despite his problems, each man contributed to keeping the flame alive until the time for growth should arrive.

Eight-year-old Freddie Price had been among the small band of Catholics who welcomed James Gibbons to the state in 1868. From that moment the youngster attached himself to the older man, a relationship began that would endure for a lifetime. The boy who accompanied the young bishop on his pastoral visits in Wilmington, would, in due course, become the first native-born North Carolinian to be ordained to the diocesan priesthood; more than that, he would work so zealously in the quixotic effort to convert the local population that he would be given the title "The Tar Heel Apostle."[27]

For his part, Gibbons had to navigate carefully between Bishop Haid, his successor as administrator of the Church in North Carolina, and Father Price, in effect his successor as missionary in the state. The ideal might have been for the one to take care of the business side of running a church, while the other took care of the real business of the church, namely the conversion of men and women. Unfortunately, their differing priorities often resulted in conflict. It was Gibbons' unenviable responsibility as Archbishop to serve as mediator.

Early Life of Thomas Frederick Price

Alfred Lanier Price, the future priest's father, married Clarissa Bond in Washington, North Carolina in 1845, and shortly thereafter the couple moved to Wilmington where in 1851, Alfred, trained as a printer, co-founded the *Wilmington Journal*, the first daily newspaper in the state. At the time of Alfred Price's death in 1872, at the age of fifty-six, his paper said of him, "His labors have done as much to build up our thriving city as those of any of her citizens."[28] Although son Thomas, called "Fred" by his friends, was only twelve years old when his father died, early exposure to printing and journalism would contribute substantially to the future priest's work. Like his father, he was skilled in the use of words and in capitalizing on the potential of the media of the day.

If Father Price later believed that North Carolinians could be converted to Catholicism, he had ample evidence from the experience of his own parents. His mother, Clarissa (1825-1885), who had spent her childhood on the family plantation, was sent as a teenager to Washington, North Carolina to further her education. There she boarded with the family of Dr. Frederick Gallagher, devout Catholics and among the earliest members of the church that Bishop England had dedicated in Washington in 1829. Attracted to the religion of her friends, at the age of eighteen Clarissa took the bold step of becoming a convert. Her father opposed this so vigorously that she was never able to live with her family again. As if she had not shocked her family enough, she announced her desire to join the Sisters of Mercy in Charleston, South Carolina. Her father, now completely enraged at his daughter's behavior, threatened to burn down the convent if she dared to enter. Fearing that the wrathful man might follow through on his threat, Clarissa gave up the idea.

Subsequently, the obviously strong-willed young woman became engaged to Alfred Lanier Price (1815-1872) who, although a Protestant, did not harbor anti-Catholic prejudice. Alfred Price's first wife had died leaving him with two children. Perhaps this loss made him more tolerant and certainly grateful to provide the young children with a new mother. In any case, the couple proceeded to have ten children, Thomas being the eighth. Clarissa Price bore and raised all these children despite serious physical disabilities. All her life she wore a brace to strengthen a back broken as a small child when a nurse dropped her. Furthermore, she suffered from defective hearing.

Influenced by his wife's faith, Alfred Lanier Price converted to Catholicism six years before he died Accordingly, when Bishop Gibbons arrived in Wilmington in 1868, he was greeted by a Price family now completely Catholic. That family would give to the service of the church, not only one of its sons as a priest, but two of its daughters as nuns, one of them the first native born North Carolinian to enter the convent. In one of those strange twists of fate, a woman who had been forbidden by her father to become a nun saw two of her daughters do so.

The Marian Spirituality of Father Price

If young Fred inherited an aptitude for writing from his father, he inherited from his mother what might be termed an obsession with Catholicism. And the most prominent feature of that obsession was his devotion to Mary, the mother of Jesus. It was as if he sensed that such devotion was what made him most distinctively Catholic in an environment that considered "worship" of Mary a form of idolatry. Price himself would say that he was so overwhelmed with the presence of Mary in his life that he had no choice but to acknowledge and celebrate her presence.

His fixation on Mary may have begun with an experience he had while traveling by steamer from Wilmington to Baltimore in September 1876. By the age of sixteen, Fred was judged ready to leave his home and family in order to enter the seminary. Not much is known of his earlier schooling, other than that for a time he was tutored by Father Mark Gross in the basement of St. Thomas Church. In any case, his proud but sad mother waving good-bye from the dock, young Price boarded the *Rebecca Clyde*. Black smoke billowing from its stack, the steamer moved slowly down the Cape Fear River and out into the open sea.

However, as the ship passed Ocracoke Inlet south of Cape Hatteras, it was caught in a severe storm and began to break apart. While the crew and some of the six passengers donned the few life preservers, Fred Price, "who could not swim a lick," was left floundering in the tossing waves. One of his fellow passengers later wrote that "how little Fred Price got ashore was certainly miraculous."[29] A full account of "how" he was saved was given to his seminary classmate, William H. O'Connell, who later became the cardinal-archbishop of Boston:

> I shall never forget the story of an incident that happened to him [Price] on his voyage from somewhere in the South to Baltimore. ... Presently the customary smile appeared on his face, and after making

me promise to tell no one, he gave me in confidence the full narration
of what was undoubtedly a manifestation of God's love for him and a
special protection of the Blessed Virgin.... Keeping his head as best he
could, with all his physical strength, above the furious waters, he
cried again, "Christ Jesus, save me or I perish." Like a flash the sky
seemed to open, and out of a speck of blue came the clearest possible
vision, as clear as he saw the howling waves about him -- Mary, the
Mother of Christ, appeared before his eyes. Upon her face was a
smile, and gently stretching forth her hand, she pointed to a great
floating plank, which had been washed overboard from the sinking
ship.[30]

Whether miraculous or not, the traumatic event had a profound
impact on Price's life. His devotion to Mary grew in intensity with the
passing years until, on a retreat at Belmont in 1908, he vowed to write
a letter to her every day. True to his word, for the final ten years of his
life, no matter how busy, Price wrote that letter. With tender expressions
of affection, he shared his hopes and concerns, his plans and his fears.
In more than 3,000 love letters he speaks to Mary as a trusted confi-
dante; she is near, attentive, responsive. These letters are his diary, neu-
rotic perhaps, sentimental certainly but clear testimony to unwavering
dedication to his ministry and a window to the spirituality which ani-
mated the man. In one of the letters, written years after the shipwreck,
Price reminds Mary of that incident and how he had "called your sweet
and loved form to mind" and how she had saved him.[31] If Jesus was the
Divine Savior of the world, for Thomas Price Mary was also a savior,
and more than that, a loving feminine presence in his male, celibate
life.[32]

Mary would remain the only woman in Price's life, at least
until he encountered Bernadette Soubirous (1844-1879), the visionary
of Lourdes, France, who in 1858, experienced a number of appearances
by a woman, who when asked her name answered, "I am the
Immaculate Conception." On a visit to Lourdes in 1910, as Price was
making the transition from his commitment to the conversion of North
Carolina to the broader stage of the foreign missions, he visited Lourdes
and also Nevers, where Bernadette's body was buried in the convent
crypt. The relationship of the fifty-year-old priest and the nun who had
died at the age of thirty-six quickly intensified. Early in 1912, now fully
released from the South and living in New York, Price began to call
himself "Mary Bernadette," going so far as to ask people to address him
as "Father Bernadette." On March 24, he wrote in his letter to Mary:

My heart is filled with delight, Mother, and tonight Sister [Bernadette] came to me in the fullest possession of me and stayed with me for a long time -- as my Bride and my Spouse forever and poured out herself upon me in unspeakable delights. Truly, Mother, you have married us -- our souls -- and our bodies in a way -- and we are one -- and spouses -- and she my eternal Bride.

In the spring of 1913, Bernadette told Price to purchase a wedding ring. He did so and formal marriage vows were exchanged. After the mystical ceremony, there was a little wedding party at which the "Groom" smoked his first cigar and drank some wine, the first he ever drank outside the Eucharist. At his request, after Price's death, his heart was placed in the crypt at Nevers beside the body of Bernadette.[33] The Church has declared Bernadette a saint, and some efforts were made in the 1970's to introduce Price's cause also.[34]

Father Price's Formation for Ministry

The shipwreck from which he was saved delayed by several months Fred Price's voyage to Baltimore, where he would spend ten years, five at St. Charles Preparatory Seminary followed by five at St. Mary's Theological Seminary. Of this prolonged period of preparation for his ministry, Price would later say that while he was taught the doctrines of the church, he learned nothing about how to present the faith to non-Catholics or how to understand the religious perspective of southern Protestants. As he put it, the seminary training had "little or nothing to do with the living present."[35]

That "living present" began for Price with his ordination by Bishop Northrup in June of 1886 in his home church of St. Thomas in Wilmington. Many years earlier in that same church when, for the first time Price was about to assist Bishop Gibbons at mass, the bishop had asked him, "You are not afraid to serve me, are you, my boy?" The child had replied, "No Bishop. You are the priest offering the sacrifice, and God will come to the altar at your word. My mother has taught me that. If you're not afraid, than neither am I."[36] Now, Fred himself was empowered to say the words that would transform bread and wine into the Body and Blood of Christ. Although awed, Price was not afraid. Not only was he convinced that Christ had called him to be a priest but that Mary, the Mother they shared, would protect him always.

There are two major periods in Price's years as a priest in North Carolina. The first centered on the historic town of New Bern, considered the cradle of Catholicism in the state because it was the home of William Gaston. From 1887 to 1896, New Bern would be not so much Price's home as the home base from which the young priest ranged over a vast area of the Carolina lowlands and piedmont. The second period, representing an expansion and acceleration of his work, was centered at Nazareth, the name he gave to the tract of land he purchased near Raleigh and which became headquarters for his various projects.

Parish Period

Price's responsibilities as New Bern pastor included providing religious services at a network of sixteen chapels, stretching from the outskirts of Raleigh to the north and extending nearly to Wilmington to the south. However, although his activity seemingly exceeded the limits of human capabilities, Price's life style was not unique. In the later years of the 19th century all North Carolina diocesan priests were also "circuit riders," journeying incessantly by train and on horseback to visit the scattered Catholic families. Nevertheless, the energy, zeal, and modest self-promotion of Price afforded him an unchallenged preeminence. On one occasion while speaking outside the state, he was introduced with the words, "Behold the secular clergy of North Carolina!"[37]

Although Price considered the conversion of North Carolinians his primary mission, by necessity most of his time was taken up with visiting the small pockets of Catholics who lived in dozens of rural towns. And, although reputedly "absentminded" and "impractical,"[38] he was instrumental in constructing a number of churches. Predictably, many of these simple country structures were dedicated to Mary, including Immaculate Conception in Halifax, St. Mary in Goldsboro, and a second St. Mary in Holly Springs. A brief account of the Holly Springs church can illustrate the experience that Price had in a number of places, as well as the precarious nature of a church dependent for its survival on a few families.

Holly Springs   One day, while making his rounds on horseback, Price saw a site in the village of Holly Springs that he thought would be ideal for a mission church. Purchasing the land with money donated by his growing roster of benefactors, Price had a church constructed in short order. The total cost was $400: $200 for lumber, $100 for a carpenter, and $100 for furnishings.[39] The few Catholics in the area included an elderly Irish family, the Condons, who grew flowers to decorate the church for mass held about once a month. The interior of the small structure was paneled with heart pine, the same local wood from which the pews and the frames around the Stations of the Cross were fashioned. Hanging brass kerosene lamps gave a soft glow, creating a peaceful mood for prayer.

Father Price preached several Missions in the church, all of which were well attended by the local people, most of whom were non-Catholics. After one of these missions, the local blacksmith, Lonnie Price, was humorously referred to as "Father Price." The man, proud of his new "title," kept it the rest of his life. However, although people might listen to the real Father Price, few became Catholic. His explanation of the mass, of confession, of devotion to Mary, and of other practices so meaningful to the young priest himself left his Baptist and Methodist listeners unconvinced.

When Price left the state in 1910, other priests continued to travel on occasion from Nazareth to Holly Springs to say mass for its handful of Catholics. For a brief period in 1914, prospects looked bright when some Hungarians moved to the area to work on the construction of a nearby river dam. However, with World War I better salaries elsewhere lured people, including all the Catholics, away from the small town. Eventually, the church was sold to a doctor who tore it down and used the materials for the construction of a house. Since then, there has been no Catholic Church in Holly Springs.[40]

"Shack" Life   Even such modest churches as St. Mary in Holly Springs were luxurious compared with the primitive structures that Price called "shacks" that he built in various places and which did double duty as shelters for the missioners as well as chapels. Over the years various priests accompanied Price to the shacks. One such priest later recalled his experience:

> *It was a bright day in late spring when I accompanied Father Price and two of his students to open a week's mission to non-Catholics, at a little mission church in Wake County. ... Some beds and household effects were placed in a farm wagon, and the two priests and two students took their seats and set out for the place of rendezvous.*
> *The road was full of ruts, and the passengers received many a jolt on the way. We passed colored settlements, then quite new and curious in my eyes. The large farm horse went in fits and starts, creeping along at times at a snail's pace, and then galloping as fast as his cumbersome load would allow. It was a fairly picturesque route, past pine woods, where doves cooed lazily among the trees, and many plantations of white folks, who placidly gazed at "Priest Price" and his luggage and companions. ... We saluted the people as we passed, and*

some jerked back a nod of recognition over their shoulders, as if mak-ing an effort to return the salutation. The people are well schooled against Catholicism by their spiritual teachers. ... The Southern States are still the happy hunting grounds of illiteracy and prejudice.

I was rather disappointed on seeing the mission chapel or shack, ... It presented an interior of confusion, not having been used for months. The mattresses were duly laid out on the sacristy floor, where we were to sleep, and the novelty was pleasing to us. As for Father Price, he was unconscious of any difference, and was quite at home in the poorest hut in the backwoods as in the most agreeable city home.

... I noticed during my sermon that men and women were con-tinually spitting, and felt hurt at the profanity in a Catholic Church, even in this poor shack.[41]

By comparison with Price's shack life, the priests who in Bishop Waters' years lodged in cramped un-air-conditioned motor chapels, were living comfortably. But in all these situations over the course of more than a century, Catholic priests in North Carolina were routinely expected to endure privations unheard of in other parts of the country. No one took to this austere life more readily than Price. His spirituality included the belief that physical sufferings united him more closely to the crucified Christ. In 1904, he wrote: "For some years my life has been full of trials. Thank God! I expect this to continue till I die. It is my Calvary. I would not have it otherwise."[42]

Changing the Rock of Gibraltar   Unlike Bishops England, Gibbons, and Haid, Father Price was not an engaging preacher. His sermons were straightforward discourses on the Gospels, enriched by his obvious zeal, cheerfulness, and grit more than by oratorical finesse. He believed that "attractive, intelligent, persistent, permanent preaching of the truth, inspired by grace, in the long run cannot but succeed."[43] It did not suc-ceed, and Price offered as the explanation that the people to whom he spoke were not open to the truth. He wrote to Mrs. Moseley, "You might as well try to change the Rock of Gibraltar as a countryman who knows he has the truth."

Sobered by his lack of results, Price turned for help to the Reverend Walter Elliott, a Paulist priest, renowned for his success as a missionary. In the spring of 1894, Price made a retreat in New York with Elliott, after which he invited the Paulist to come to North Carolina and give a mission in Newton Grove. At Price's request, Cardinal Gibbons had agreed to pay the expenses of the trip and mission. However, Elliott would not come. As Price would write to Mrs. Moseley:

I think he feels out of gear in the South. We talked together during the course of two days... [I found him to be] out of sympathy with nearly everything Southern. ... In a word, he is a thorough Yankee and glories in so being![44]

The experience with Elliott convinced Price that what was needed was a program designed specifically for training priests to be missionaries in the South. Again he approached Elliott, asking him if he could assign two priests to come to North Carolina to establish such a program. Once again Elliott refused. However, he gave Price a message which the North Carolinian took to heart. The gruff Paulist said, "Don't depend on me or anyone else; pitch in and do it yourself" And that's exactly what Price would do. However, he would first need the permission of Bishop Haid.[45]

The Transition

In many priests' lives a crisis comes after about ten years of ministry.[46] The point is often made that the Greek word "crisis" means "turning point." As youth comes to an end and the thrill of being a priest subsides, as the work comes to seem futile, repetitious, or boring, some men abandon the priesthood, seeking something new and hopefully better in a different calling, which most probably includes marriage. Others, like Father Price, revitalize their lives within the priesthood itself. They move beyond the framework that had characterized their early adult lives and fashion a more mature structure for the next stage of their life course.[47]

In October 1896, Price confided to Mrs. Moseley that he had submitted his plans to Bishop Haid, "who has approved them only in part -- at least for the present."[48] The plan had three components:

1) Price was to be released from parish work in order to devote himself full time to being a missionary;

2) He was to be permitted to undertake the publication of a monthly magazine designed to attract people to the faith;

3) A second priest was to be assigned to establish with him a Mission House.

It would be quite understandable had the bishop denied the request of one of his few priests to be allowed to experiment. However, although he did not agree to assign a second priest, Haid did release Price to become a "Missionary" and approved the idea of a magazine, assuming Price could finance it on his own. At that time, there were twelve secular and seven Benedictine priests in North Carolina. As for the Benedictines, besides conducting a seminary and a college in Belmont [with a total student body of fewer than 200], monks also were pastors of the churches in Charlotte and Greensboro.

Of the dozen vicariate clergy, five, including Mark Gross, no longer lived in the state having moved away due to sickness or for other causes. Although still officially counted as priests of the Vicariate, they lived in Canada, Germany, Washington, DC, Virginia, and Maryland. That left seven priests, including Price. When he became a free lance Missionary, the remaining six priests served as pastors in Wilmington, Asheville, Fayetteville, Goldsboro, New Bern, and Raleigh. And of course, to each parish were attached a number of missions.[49]

Thus, as the end of the century approached, there were but eight parishes in the state with resident pastors. Price, of course, was aware of this situation as well as Haid. In the silence of the prayer life to which both were committed, they may have acknowledged that, despite their efforts, the church had stagnated and that a new approach was worth trying. Despite the conflicts that would emerge in the future, at this moment Price and Haid were of one mind; they believed that what the Tar Heel Apostle was proposing was prompted by God's grace.

The Missionary

Clearly enthusiastic about this opportunity to devote all his energies to the task of attracting North Carolinians to Catholicism, Price immediately began two dimensions of the work: preaching revival-type missions all over the state and publishing a magazine aimed specifically at communicating the "Truth" to non-Catholics. As to the missions, he wrote to Mrs. Moseley that beginning on November 8, 1896, he would be preaching "in Smithfield, Dunn, Clinton, Littleton, Durham, Fayetteville, Goldsboro, Hope Mills, etc."[50] All these places are within easy reach of Raleigh where Price was then residing. However, his desire to reach every corner of the state brought him out to the mountains, where on two occasions he climbed Mount Mitchell, the highest peak east of the Mississippi. Among his many "firsts" was celebrating mass on top of Mount Mitchell.

However, mountain climbing for Price was not a form of recreation but a symbolic gesture. Like Moses and Jesus before him, he was meeting with God and stretching his hand over what he hoped would be a new Promised Land, one that accepted the message that he felt called to deliver. Never content with symbols or prayer alone, Price came down from the mountain and spoke to all who would listen. In March 1898 he wrote to Paulist Father Doyle asking that twenty-five New Testaments be shipped to Obids, Ashe County, where he was to give "a Protestant mission." Ashe County is in the northwest corner of the state, and Obids is so small it appears on only the most detailed of maps. From 1896, until well into the 20th century, Price brought the message to thousands of people anywhere he was invited. The extent of his energy is suggested by the fact that simultaneously he was founding an orphanage, planning a training center for home missioners, and writing, promoting, and financing a monthly magazine.

Truth

As scattered and impracticable as he might appear to some, Price not only had a keen sense of the power of the media, but was able, virtually single-handedly, to turn out *Truth* magazine every month between April 1897 and 1911. The cover of the first issue, an impressive 28 pages, stated succinctly that the publication was "devoted to giving TRUE explanations of the Catholic Church." The target readership, obviously enough, was non-Catholics who had "erroneous impressions" and whose misunderstanding of Catholicism "is so great as almost to exceed belief."[51]

Despite his desire to reach non-Catholics, Price realized that he would need the support of Catholics if the venture were to succeed. Accordingly, he solicited subscriptions among his array of contacts. Also, diplomatically, complimentary copies were sent to Gibbons and to Haid, both of whom dutifully wrote letters saying that they were favorably impressed and urging all North Carolina Catholics to support the new publication. It should be noted that their letters, featured on the front page of the May issue of *Truth*, were addressed to North Carolina Catholics, reflecting Price's initial vision of using *Truth* as a tool in his campaign to convert his home state. However, it was not long before his range expanded as the number of subscribers outside the state exceeded those within. Certainly the publication's popularity was aided by Cardinal Gibbons' support. In 1876, Gibbons himself had published the popular *Faith of Our Fathers* to explain Catholic teachings to non-Catholics; he was now delighted that his North Carolina protégé was continuing the work through his magazine. On one occasion the Cardinal said, "*Truth* is the most instructive periodical published in the whole country. There is none which effects more real good."[52] Although obviously sincere, Gibbons was also safe in saying this since at the time no similar Catholic magazine was being published in the country.

The most popular feature of *Truth* was the "Question Box," a device that over the years would be used extensively by Catholics to address the moral, doctrinal, and liturgical questions posed by readers or anticipated by editors. However, despite its serious apologetic and cate-chetical purpose, *Truth* included a wide assortment of material from puzzles to current events to notices about agriculture. Price may have realized that twenty-eight pages of Catholic doctrine was too heavy a diet for most readers and shrewdly varied the content. It may also be that the pressure of meeting deadlines required the addition of some last minute "filler."

Perhaps the most significant role that *Truth* played was that it helped its editor to clarify his thinking. Month after month Price had to formulate articles that addressed what he considered the most pressing issues of the day. What emerged was the conviction that Catholics must be concerned not only with "home missions" like North Carolina but 'foreign missions" like China. His vision for the church, and for himself, expanded. Were it not for *Truth*, this might not have happened. As it was, Price gradually became convinced that the United States, long on the receiving end of church assistance, must begin to give. It would be Price, struggling with futility to convert North Carolinians, who was a major force in sparking the foreign missions movement.[53]

Haid did not often submit material to Price's magazine. The two were increasingly at odds - Price impatient with Haid's failure to provide more active leadership in the state, and Haid uncomfortable with Price's carping and his complaining to Gibbons. Nevertheless, Haid inserted a notice in the June 1910 issue of *Truth*, announcing a Eucharistic Congress to be held that September in Montreal and urging as many priests and laity as possible to attend. For some reason, despite his constant poverty and the press of work, Price decided to go. It was at that gathering that he and the Boston priest, James Anthony Walsh, began the process which the following year led to the foundation of Maryknoll, the first Catholic mission-sending organization in the country and still synonymous with creative missionary efforts.[54]

The Orphanage

While Price was giving missions throughout the state, he was also looking for property that might become the headquarters for his dream, a training center for home mission clergy. As has been related through the words of Floyd Pope in Chapter One, Price bought farmland two miles outside the Raleigh city limits where he opened an orphanage for boys. Although not his primary goal, an orphanage responded to a need that even the hostile non-Catholic community could support. In the era before Social Security, unemployment insurance, and welfare, and at a time when many women died in childbirth, there were many children for whom orphanages seemed to be the only solution when family crises struck.

At the time that Price proposed opening the orphanage, the Sisters of Mercy already operated such an institution for girls at their motherhouse in Belmont. One of those sisters was Price's biological sister, Mary, eleven years his senior, who had been little Freddie's first teacher and a second mother. It is not unlikely that Mary, known in religious life as Sister Mary Catherine (1849-1930), suggested to Fred that he establish a similar place for boys. In any case, as the orphanage at Nazareth opened in October 1897, Sister Catherine, resuming her role as Fred's helper, was there to take charge of the eight boys who were the first of hundreds to be housed there over the succeeding seventy-five years. Sister Catherine herself remained at Nazareth supervising a small group of sisters until long after her brother had left the state. In fact, she worked at the home until advancing age forced her retirement in 1919.

Although Price would promote the orphanage, particularly through a second magazine, *Our Lady's Orphan Boy*, begun in 1901, it is clear from his correspondence that it was a minor part of his plan. Ironically, it was the one aspect of his North Carolina work that survived him. Even more lasting a contribution to the church in the state was the land on which the orphanage was located, some 400 acres including a large farm. The area now lies within the city of Raleigh and is extremely valuable real estate. Large portions of the original Price property have already been leased, but the diocese retains a sizable tract, the ultimate disposition of which has not been decided. Those with a sense of history as well as an eye for business wish to retain on the property some memory of Father Price and the pioneering period of the now well-established church.

Although his last visit to North Carolina was in 1913, Price retained contact with the state through his sister with whom he corresponded until shortly before his death in Hong Kong. Without the commitment of Sister Catherine and the other Sisters of Mercy it is quite possible that the orphanage would have failed. Not only were the sisters efficient managers of the home, but also they freed Price to devote himself to what he considered more important activities, in particular the establishment of a community of home missioners.

The Apostolic Company

The Jesuits call themselves the Company of Jesus, the word "company" intended to conjure up images of military units mobilized to do battle with the enemies of the church. In fact, the former soldier, Ignatius Loyola, had founded them in the 16th century precisely to counter the serious inroads that Protestantism had made throughout Europe. The Jesuits were the Pope's shock troops, ready to be deployed wherever their commander-in-chief would order. Father Price, who in his youth considered becoming a Jesuit, had an Ignatian vision for his home state. He would recruit and train missionaries who would go into the battlefield of North Carolina in an effort to bring the misguided into the true fold. His Apostolic Company would go forth under the banner of Mary. But first, the troops had to be recruited and undergo their basic training.

A barracks-like four-story building was quickly constructed, and in 1902, Price and his first priest-associate, Michael Irwin, welcomed the initial little band of students. Two were young Philadelphia boys who had responded to an appeal that Price had made at their Catholic high school. However, conditions at "Regina Apostolorum" [Queen of the Apostles] were so uncomfortable that within weeks the boys returned home. They would be but the first of many students who could not sustain the rigors to which Price's program subjected them, despite the fact that he himself shared all the deprivations.

In order to instill a Jesuit spirit in the company, Price invited the Rev. J. H. O'Rourke, S.J., noted for his skill in forming Jesuit novices, to give a month-long Ignatian retreat at Nazareth. After taking the students through the Spiritual Exercises, O'Rourke wrote a letter in which he described his experience. It is the most detailed picture available of life at Nazareth at the time when Father Price was attempting to form a congregation of secular priests who would dedicate themselves to the home missions.[55]

By the time of O'Rourke's visit in 1905, Price had been working in North Carolina for nearly twenty years, and it is clear that the Jesuit had enormous admiration for the man he called "a saintly and zealous priest" laboring in a "desolate vineyard." He concurred with Price's view that only the most highly committed could persevere "in the hard labor of that neglected field." From the days of Bishop England, priests had been called upon to work under the most trying conditions "with no expectations of seeing the ripe harvest in their day."

In that steamy summer of 1905, O'Rourke found eighteen young men, recruited in the North, who were "eager to devote their lives to the exercises of the ministry in North Carolina." In Price's plan, the students were required to spend at least a year at Nazareth in a sort of "novitiate" before being sent, at considerable expense to Price, to an approved seminary, usually Abbot Haid's St. John's at Belmont. Besides learning the virtues they would need in order to work in the state, the young men went out with Price and Irwin to the shacks in order to experience first hand the life to which they aspired. The idealistic young men taught catechism to the poor children of the villages, attempting to bridge the culture gap as well as communicate the teaching of the church.[56]

As to financing the programs at Nazareth, O'Rourke explained the various sources of income. At the orphanage, five Sisters of Mercy cared for forty orphans, but that institution was connected to an Industrial School that was not only self-supporting but paid "for the bread and butter of the orphans." Thus, public funds were used to afford training in practical skills at a Catholic-sponsored facility and incidentally provide for many of the orphans' material needs.[57]

Furthermore, the Nazareth farm not only supplied most of the vegetables used in the institution but yielded a small profit. However, while the orphanage was substantially self-sustaining, Price had to raise money from other sources for the fledgling Apostolic Company. In this regard *Truth* was valuable, not so much from subscriptions as from donations sent by subscribers in response to appeals that appeared in its pages. Also, by now Price had clergy friends "from Boston to Maryland" who were very generous to a colleague whom they admired. With reference to these benefactors, O'Rourke presents a colorful word picture of Price the fund-raiser:

> Periodically Father Price with his slouch and battered hat, his faded coat and well-worn shoes, his face tanned by the heat of North Carolina, and his hands hardened by toil appears in the North among his friends who are legion and asks for a collection for his missions. The pulpits are thrown open to him and so are the purses, and after a month or six weeks he goes back with much more than enough to keep the wolf from the door for a long time.

O'Rourke also describes the building which served as both residence and school for the students and, as was described at the beginning of the chapter, was destroyed by fire. The Jesuit had lived there
himself shortly before the fire and so wrote from first-hand knowledge:

> The building, furniture and appointments are poor almost to
> excess. There is no plaster on the walls or ceiling and the joists, beams
> and rafters are entirely exposed. The floor is laid of twelve inch
> boards and through the crack of those in my room I could see into the
> office of *Truth* below, while to secure privacy in my apartment I had
> to stuff with paper at least half a dozen holes in the boards of the par-
> titions from which the knots had dropped out. There are no toilet
> rooms, and a rough shed of a most primitive character about fifty
> yards from the house serves the purpose in winter and summer. There
> are no bath rooms of any description either within the house or on the
> premises. ...
>
> Suffice it to say that the food, though abundant and healthy, is
> coarse and with little variety. Wine, beer, soup, dessert or delicacies
> of any kind are never furnished. There are no tablecloths, no chairs,
> but instead benches of the simplest construction.

Although Price reconstructed the building after the tragedy, the
program floundered and in 1908, when every last one of the students
resigned, the Apostolic Company was disbanded. One after the other,
his priest companions -- Michael Irwin, William O'Brien and Edward
Rigney -- had left him as well, moving on to be pastors.[58]

The only priest who remained with Price at Nazareth was
Father George Woods who initially worked as lay manager of the
Nazareth plant, freeing Price from many mundane responsibilities.
Eventually, Woods attended the seminary at Belmont and was ordained
in 1910, thereby becoming the first and only priest produced by the
Missionary Apostolate program. When Price left Nazareth the follow-
ing year, Haid appointed Woods administrator of the orphanage. Woods,
who was deaf, proceeded to dismantle many of what he considered the
inefficient procedures of his predecessor and to limit the authority of
Price's sister.[59]

As for Price himself, before leaving North Carolina to estab-
lish Maryknoll he had one last item on his agenda – the dislodging of
Leo Haid. However, in this as in most of his endeavors in North
Carolina, he did not succeed.

The Secular Clergy vs. the Benedictines

The establishing of the *abbatia nullius* at Belmont in 1910 had been the last straw for the North Carolina diocesan clergy, who numbered just fourteen priests with Price as their senior man in terms of years of service. It was hard enough working in such poor and unpromising conditions without the further irritant of a superior who was considered remote and unsympathetic to their plight. The most galling issue was the clause in the Papal Bull creating the *nullius* that said that until North Carolina was raised to the status of a diocese, the Abbot of Belmont would always be the Vicar Apostolic. That meant that, as Price put it in his letter to Cardinal Gibbons, even if Haid were to die today, his successor as abbot would automatically become Vicar as well.

There may have been other factors that contributed to Price's strong feelings against Haid. In fact, it is certain that there were. He had long felt demeaned and ridiculed by the bishop. For example, in the aftermath of the failure of the Apostolic Community, reports had reached Price's ears that Haid had in effect said, "I told you so." At the very least, Price had always felt that aside from the initial permission to undertake his ventures, Haid had offered no further support. Whatever his motives, Price poured out his heart to Cardinal Gibbons in a letter which ran on for twelve pages, including a two-page postscript.[60]

Price was quite likely the only priest in the country who felt he could write so bluntly and at such length to the man who had become the most prominent Catholic in America. But Price knew that, despite his eminence, Gibbons retained a deep concern for the church in North Carolina and an even deeper love for "little Freddie Price," whose dedication to the state had exceeded Gibbons' wildest expectations. As eccentric as Price may have been, as quixotic his projects, there was no denying him a hearing.

With no polite or personal preamble, the letter immediately cut to the quick, stating unequivocally that the creation of the *Abbatia Nullius* had "aroused a storm of indignation amongst the secular Clergy." What the letter calls for is the immediate transformation of the Vicariate into a Diocese. This way the offending clause of the Papal Bull would become moot and a non-Benedictine bishop could be appointed. Haid would be left to reign over the abbey and the territory of the *nullius*. The solution seemed clear cut; Price was confident that Gibbons had the clout with Rome to bring it about and that he would wish to do so, especially since in the very creation of the *nullius*, he had been bypassed. On all sides, there were personal as well as ecclesiastical dimensions to the conflict.

After the words quoted at the head of this chapter, Price's letter goes on to present specifics as to the dire condition of the church in North Carolina. Although Price's goal was to document the negligence of Haid, it is likely that the very same arguments convinced Gibbons that North Carolina was not yet ready to become an independent diocese. Price's case backfired. His specific points included the following:

1) In Raleigh, to which "all North Carolina flows" as the Capitol of the State, the church consists "of a poor little room or chapel built into the side of a house and worth scarcely one thousand dollars and looks so pitiful that every Catholic in Raleigh and every Catholic coming to Raleigh hangs his head in shame." Haid not only refused to build a proper church but also sold off some Church property there and applied it to other purposes, alienating the congregation. Price contrasted the situation in Raleigh with "the magnificent Belmont Cathedral built in the back woods for a few monks...."

2) At Newton Grove, the pastor [Michael Irwin] had obtained the services of sisters and built a school with no assistance from Haid. Now the school is in a precarious position that Haid could remedy "if his interests were not absorbed in the Monastery."

3) In Goldsboro, for years the pastor had no home and was left to shift for himself, living in private houses as best he could. When he finally was able to build a house for himself it was by begging outside the State.

Price concluded his catalog of neglect of the secular clergy: "In a word, the Monastery is the great factor that is to be built up and made to progress at all costs and everything is subordinated and sacrificed to it." Price is blunt, even cruel. He claims that for the twenty-three years during which Haid has been Vicar, "the Monastery and Belmont Church and College have been built up at the expense of the Vicariate."

The all too personal nature of Price's attack on Haid is revealed in the postscript, in which the Tar Heel Apostle laments that while Haid openly approved the work Price was doing at Nazareth, "he privately despised it, ridiculed it, discouraged it and it is openly said by many that he has tried his best to kill it. Certain it is that whilst encouraging it but little, he has hampered it in almost every conceivable way."

A week after Price's personal letter, a much more carefully worded document, one subscribed to by all the priests of the Vicariate, was hand-delivered to Gibbons in Baltimore by "the three priests who are the Secular Counselors of the Vicariate of North Carolina, to wit: Thos. F. Price, C. Dennen, and Peter Marion, who state that the above are the signatures of all the Secular Priests working in the aforesaid Vicariate." The letter is so obviously the work of Price that it is included without comment in his Collected Letters.[61]

Aware of the argument that the Catholics of North Carolina could not support a bishop were it elevated to a diocese, the letter suggests that, yes, it could not support a bishop in luxury, but that it could support one who was "truly Apostolic," Price's way of saying that the priests wanted a bishop willing to share their poverty for the sake of the gospel.

No diocese was forthcoming, not in Gibbons' lifetime, nor in Haid's, nor in Price's. It is a truism that the Catholic Church moves slowly. Certainly this was the case in North Carolina. More than a century had passed since Bishop England had taken the first steps to organize the church there, fifty-five years since Bishop Gibbons had gone on horseback around the state, and fourteen years since Father Price had shaken the dust of North Carolina from his tattered cassock and gone North. Finally in 1924, as the Belmont Abbey bell solemnly tolled the death of Leo Haid, North Carolina was to become a diocese.

Part III

The Challenges of Expansion

Although growth is what the Church wanted, it was painfully slow in coming about. When it did occur, it was with such speed that a new set of problems had to be confronted. Whereas the first two bishops of the Diocese of Raleigh had to devote much of their energy to fund raising in order to keep the struggling Church solvent, their successors have had to confront the challenge of declining numbers of clergy and religious even as the demand for services has increased.

*   *   *

We are growing so fast and furiously, that you don't have time to think about what's important now because there are so many things coming down the line. ... You can hardly concentrate on the present because the future is so daunting.

• F. Joseph Gossman, Bishop of Raleigh, 2000

Chapter Eight

A Diocese at Last:
Bishops Hafey & McGuinness

The diocese of Raleigh presents a problem that forces one's eyes and heart to be riveted upon Heaven lest the conditions create a feeling of defeat. The atmosphere is surcharged with a spirit of indifferentism to the Catholic Church and one may not blame the people because we have not placed our claims before most of them. In the 92 counties of the diocese, fifty of them are churchless, priestless, and at no time to our knowledge has there been any effort put forth to penetrate these sections. Why? For the very cogent reason that in the remaining high stretches of territory the priests are hard pressed to function regularly among the pitiful few who, in a population of nearly 3,500,000, number but 8,585 Catholics -- less than 1/3 of 1%.

---Bishop Eugene J. McGuinness, 1938

The 1910 request of the secular priests that a diocese replace the Vicariate Apostolic in North Carolina didn't fall on deaf ears, although it may have seemed that way to Father Price and the other diocesan clergy. As a matter of fact, the bishops of the Baltimore province did take up the issue, voted unanimously for the erection of a diocese, and forwarded their recommendation to Rome. The diocese would be based in Wilmington, with Abbot Haid as the bishop. That last stipulation was the sticking point. As had been true in 1887 when Haid was asked to become Vicar Apostolic, he once again made it clear that he would agree only if he was permitted to retain his position as abbot.[1]

Although Cardinal Gibbons went along with his colleagues in requesting the erection of a North Carolina diocese, he expressed misgivings both because of his concern about the state's readiness to support a bishop and because he was aware of Haid's refusal to devote himself fully to such a task. Rome, detecting the Cardinal's reservations, responded to the petition with the word, *Dilata*, delay. Gibbons wrote to Belmont expressing pleasure "that the matter has been deferred."

In 1911, after the dust of the erection of the *nullius* had settled, Price went off to establish Maryknoll and Haid returned to Belmont where, for all intents and purposes, he pulled up the abbey drawbridge and devoted the rest of his life to teaching at the college and giving conferences to his monks. And being puzzled and hurt over his rejection by the secular priests.

For their part, those independent-minded "missionaries" continued providing services to the laity as best they could, seeing Bishop Haid only on those infrequent occasions when he ventured from the monastery. The abbot, so young and vigorous when he assumed responsibility for the state, was now in his sixties, his face gaunt, his beard gray, and his eyes tired. A blessed death would be an appropriate time to once again request a change. It was a matter of waiting.

It proved to be a long wait.

The disruptions of the World War (1914-1917) moved the troubled situation in North Carolina far down on the church's agenda. Americans struggled with the question of whether or not to enter the European war and to send American soldiers to fight overseas. The fact that for the Catholic Church communication with Rome had become more difficult was a minor matter, especially once the reports of the horrors of trench warfare began to fill the newspapers and casualties to mount.[2] It didn't help that many of the monks at Belmont were German-born. For people already suspicious of Catholics, the presence of these "enemies" in their midst was disturbing. It was no time for the monks of Belmont Abbey to be too visible.

The war saw the establishment of army camps near Raleigh and Charlotte as well as Camp Bragg, later Fort Bragg, near Fayetteville. Thousands of Catholics were among those trained at these camps, with religious services provided by military chaplains.[3] For most of the men from other sections of the country, North Carolina was but a brief and not too pleasant interlude in their lives. Although some married local girls and settled in the state, their numbers were too small to make much of an impact on the broader culture. Still nursing the wounds of the Civil War, the South remained a virtual Third World country, proudly walling itself off from the currents of thought that were transforming the rest of the country. As for Catholics, they remained but a drop in a Protestant ocean.[4]

In terms of church politics, with Price having left the scene, clergy complaints subsided but so also did that energy which Price's presence had infused in the state. Like a gadfly, he had prodded and challenged, reminding even those who did not want to be reminded that the meaning of their lives was the proclamation of the Gospel. A mood of resignation replaced confrontation and workaday service, true missionary activity. For a decade the Church struggled along, growing slowly, waiting for something to happen that would inject some fresh energy. For his part, Haid did not so much evoke enthusiasm as awe. As he aged, he became ever more venerable and remote, a hermit-like specter whose occasional appearances around the state presented Catholics with the image a saint, a man more to be admired than followed or imitated. As for the practical affairs of the vicariate, Father Felix Hintemeyer, O.S.B., Haid's friend and Vicar General, took care of those, shielding his superior from mundane distractions.

Nevertheless, the years between 1910 and 1924 witnessed slow but steady growth in the number of churches, priests, and sisters. Whereas at the earlier date there were 15 churches with resident priests, by 1924 there were 24. In addition, the number of "missions with churches" had risen from 24 to 40. Many of these mission churches were little more than the "shacks" which Fred Price had built, but they were a concrete indication that a Catholic community was present. Most such communities were minuscule. If the official number of Catholics in 1924, 8,254, is divided by the 64 parish and mission churches, there would have been an average of 125 Catholics per church. But this does not take into account the fact that there were also dozens of "stations," that is, places without churches where priests offered mass from time to time.

The number of priests had been increasing as well. In 1910, there were 17 secular priests, and when the diocese was established 15 years later, there were 23. However, a more substantial increase took place in the number of Benedictines. Whereas in 1910 the abbey counted 16, by 1925 there were 26. So, despite the criticism of the monks, their number now exceeded that of the secular clergy, and they served as pastors of seven of the state's 24 churches with resident priests – Belmont, Charlotte, Concord, Greensboro, High Point, Salisbury, and Winston.[5] Finally, parishes established in Wilmington and New Bern for black Catholics had pastors who were members of the Society of St. Joseph, an order of priests devoted exclusively to a ministry among blacks.[6]

If North Carolina had 51 priests when the diocese was established, it had more than twice as many women religious, a total of 127, nearly half of them Sisters of Mercy of Belmont. And if Leo Haid must be given credit for sustaining the church in the state for nearly forty years, he must also be given credit for having provided the Mercy sisters with an environment in which they would grow into a substantial community, providing a range of educational, child care, and health-related services throughout the state. Furthermore, the Sisters of Christian Education conducted a girls' school in Asheville; Dominicans staffed parochial schools in Newton Grove, Raleigh and Durham; Daughters of Charity ran a hospital in Greensboro; and Franciscans taught black children in Wilmington. The broader community's image of Catholicism was based largely on the highly regarded work of these women.[7]

1924: The Death of Abbot Haid

Despite the relative calm, discontent never ceased to percolate beneath the surface in the hearts of the secular priests. The storm, which had abated after the departure of Father Price, rose once again with the death of Cardinal Gibbons in 1921 and reached full force with the passing of Leo Haid three years later.

Although it may have seemed to some that Haid would live forever, on July 24, 1924, he died at the age of seventy-four in the embrace of the monks whom he loved in the beautiful abbey that he had created. However, as his biographer would write "Leo Haid did not die happy."[8] To the secular priests he had been too much the monk; to his fellow monks, he had been too much the activist. To himself, he had tried to do too much and in the process lost that which he most cherished, the inner peace that comes from union with God.

In any case, at long last significant change was at hand. Following more than four months of speculation, on December 12, 1924, word came from Rome that the vicariate was suppressed and the Diocese of Raleigh established. It was the end of the Belmont era and the beginning of what might be considered the "adult" status of the Church. However, with but 23 diocesan priests and 6,000 Catholics the church in North Carolina would remain a dependent adult, an indigent ward begging from its more affluent relatives.

The present chapter will discuss the process of establishing the new jurisdiction by the Raleigh Diocese's first two bishops, William J. Hafey (1925-1937) and Eugene J. McGuinness (1938-1944). Both these men were outsiders who, like executives called upon to establish a new business, came in, methodically set in place the apparatus needed, and moved on. Their contributions were not only essential but also substantial. Bishop McGuinness could turn over to his successor, Vincent Waters, a church ready for a concerted effort at expansion. However, as was seen in the first three chapters, while the church did indeed grow under Waters' leadership, it also experienced unanticipated crises.

Although the formative period of the diocese profited from the skill of its first bishops, the vital spirit of the church continued to be provided by the men who spent their lives on the front lines of ministry, the rank-and-file priests who worked in the parishes and missions, sustained the brunt of anti-Catholicism, and strove to expand the Church's presence. Accordingly, Chapter Nine will examine the emergence of the diocese of Raleigh through the lives of several prominent priests, men whose careers bridged the Vicariate and the young diocese. Taken together, these two chapters show the state of Catholicism in North Carolina during the first half of the Twentieth Century.

A Less Than Smooth Transition

In the more than half a century that intervened between James Gibbons' assignment to establish the Vicariate Apostolic of North Carolina and his death as the Cardinal Archbishop of Baltimore, he had achieved near mythical status in the church, providing leadership in a succession of major issues and firmly rooting Roman Catholicism in American soil. Also, for sentimental as well as legal reasons, he had kept an eye on developments in North Carolina. But now he was gone. Someone else as Archbishop of Baltimore would have to take responsibility for the unfinished business of the only remaining state in the United States that was not yet a diocese. That man was Michael J. Curley, the forty-two year old Irish-born bishop of Saint Augustine, Florida. No sooner was Curley installed in Baltimore than the North Carolina priests began once again the drumbeat for the establishment of a diocese. This time, the campaign was led by Christopher Dennen, the pastor of St. Mary Church in Wilmington, and Michael A. Irwin, pastor of St. Mark Church in Newton Grove. Curley not only gave both men his ear but also worked with them to achieve their objective.

Dennen's role was to inform the new archbishop of the wiles of the Benedictines, how supposedly they had enriched their monastery at the expense of the vicariate and how, now in 1922, they were attempting to enlarge their *abbatia nullius* by the addition of Mecklenburg County, which included the city of Charlotte.[9] For his part, Irwin was more conciliatory, offering Curley long dissertations on the spiritual needs of the state, including the counsel that the man selected to be the first bishop of the new diocese:

> must love with all his heart Holy Writ; its style, its verbiage, its twists and turns, its imagery, its simplicity, its thunders, its gentle breathings. If for these hardheaded Calvinistic North Carolinians he prefers another source for his eloquence, he will without doubt become a sounding brass and a tinkling cymbal.

The archbishop eagerly accepted the perspective of these two men, never giving the monks' side a fair hearing. Whether the criticisms were justified or not, the days of Benedictine dominance in the North Carolina church were numbered.

When this agitation began Haid was still alive, but Curley would be ready to act as soon as the abbot should expire. To prepare the ground, since the final decisions on such matters would be made by Rome, Curley instructed Dennen to provide the Vatican's American representative, the Apostolic Delegate, Archbishop Giovanni Bonzano, with a full account of the situation in North Carolina. This Dennen did in May 1922. Furthermore, also at Curley's suggestion, all the secular priests of the vicariate signed the report in which Dennen made the case for the establishment of a diocese.

It is obvious that, as busy as Curley must have been with administering the Archdiocese of Baltimore, North Carolina remained very much a concern. In his June 1923 report to the Apostolic Delegate, a friend with whom he dined regularly, Curley wrote:

> To my mind there is only one solution for the question and that is, on the death of the present Vicar Apostolic, to retain the Abbatia Nullius and to constitute the territory outside the eight counties of the Abbatia nullius a Diocese. The Episcopal See might be placed in Wilmington, North Carolina, Asheville, or Charlotte.[10]

Two things are worth noting here. As much as he might harbor negative feelings about the activities of the Benedictines, Curley was not ready to challenge the private Benedictine jurisdiction which had been created in 1910 and which had been the source of so much consternation to Price and others. He knew that it would not be good politics to suggest that Rome had made a mistake. Secondly, although Curley mentioned three cities in North Carolina as potential settings for the new diocese, none of them was selected when a diocese was created the following year. In particular, mention of Asheville reflected just how little Curley knew about the state. That mountain city might have had a cathedral-like church, but it was -- and remains -- remote from centers of both Catholic and civic life in North Carolina.

When Haid died, confusion ensued both as to the administration of Belmont Abbey and of the vicariate. Not only was the only abbot Belmont had ever known dead, but his right hand man, Felix Hintemeyer, had predeceased him by a few months. The abbey needed to elect a new abbot and a temporary administrator was needed for the vicariate. The situation was not only unprecedented but also complex, and in church quarters, politically sensitive.

Willibald Baumgartner, who had succeeded Hintemeyer as prior of the abbey and Vicar General of the vicariate, automatically assumed responsibility when Haid died but was in an awkward position. He was not a candidate to become the next abbot and was well aware that the vicariate was likely to be suppressed and a diocese established with a non-Benedictine as bishop. So, once again, the Catholic Church in North Carolina found itself adrift.

Establishment of the Diocese of Raleigh

In August, the Belmont monks selected Vincent George Taylor to be their new abbot and ordinary of the *abbatia nullius*. However, his nomination had to be approved by Rome, and also decision made as to whether or not Taylor would be consecrated a bishop for the *nullius*. Months passed, and no word arrived about the status of the church in North Carolina. Finally, on December 12, 1924, almost eight months after Haid's death, the decree was issued under the signature of Pope Pius XI that created the diocese of Raleigh, granting it all the territory of the state, with the exception of the eight counties that comprised the *abbatia nullius*. In an unusual move, the decree appointed Curley Apostolic Administrator of the new diocese until such time as a bishop would be named. Willibald was deemed inappropriate because he resided in another diocese, namely the *abbatia nullius*. Somehow, this reasoning did not apply to Curley in far-off Baltimore. For his part,

Curley promptly appointed Christopher Dennen to be his Vicar General for the interregnum.[11]

Belatedly, in March 1925 Curley went to North Carolina, spending three weeks visiting the Catholic settlements, including Wilmington and Newton Grove. In the latter town, he met Father Irwin who, in a pastorate that extended back over twenty years, had developed a network of outlying mission chapels. Never shy about proclaiming his achievements, Irwin favorably impressed Curley and the two men undertook a correspondence that lasted for years. In fact, Curley was no sooner back in Baltimore when he wrote to Irwin whom he considered an exemplary missionary and supporter of Catholic schools: "I am going to make use of Father Michael Irwin and Newton Grove when-ever I talk" on the need for Christian education.[12]

The First Bishop of Raleigh: William J. Hafey

In 1868 Archbishop Spaulding of Baltimore had selected his protégé, James Gibbons, to be the first Vicar Apostolic of North Carolina. Now, fifty-six years later, one of Spaulding's successors would follow suit, nominating his young assistant, Father William Hafey, to be the first bishop of Raleigh.[13] The appointment came on April 6, 1925, nearly a year after Haid's death and four months after the establishment of the diocese. The following day, the delighted Curley wrote to Dennen:

> You know by now that you have a new Bishop in the person of Father Hafey, Chancellor of the Archdiocese. I cannot speak too highly of the wonderful qualities of the young man who is now in his thirty-seventh year. No better appointment could be made for North Carolina, if the whole Church in America had been canvassed.

Of course, the whole church of America had not been can-vassed, not even the church in North Carolina. Apparently none of the local secular priests was considered an appropriate leader. In fact, it would not be until 1972, when Michael J. Begley was named first bish-op of Charlotte, that the Catholic Church in North Carolina would see one of its own selected to lead the church in the state. However, in 1925 it was a wise move to bring in someone not muddied by the conflicts that had characterized the Belmont years. Bishop Hafey could come aboard with no enemies and find a Catholic population anxious for peace and hopeful for growth.

If anything, Hafey can be credited with not creating contention, at least not during the twelve years that he served in North Carolina.[14] When, in 1937 he was transferred to another diocese, he left as he had come, with few enemies and, it would seem, few friends. He had been faithful, hardworking, but uninspiring. His main contributions were convincing religious orders of men and women to send personnel into the state and maintaining diocesan financial solvency, no mean achievements.

The Installation of Bishop Hafey

Hafey, a native of Springfield, Mass., was consecrated a bishop in Norfolk, Virginia on June 24th and solemnly installed by Archbishop Curley in the recently constructed Sacred Heart Church in Raleigh on July 1. Despite the negligible Catholic population in the state, the event drew considerable attention not only from the clergy, as was to be expected, but from the Raleigh daily newspaper, which during the 1920's boasted on its front page that it was the "only paper in the world having more subscribers than the population of the city in which it was published." As of July 1, 1925, the city of 30,000[15] could lay claim to yet another distinction: the installation of the first Catholic bishop of the smallest diocese in the country in the sanctuary of the nation's smallest cathedral. The newspaper's front-page coverage of the occasion provides the most comprehensive account available.[16]

Of course, size did not really matter to the participants, some of whom had yearned for this day for many years. What mattered was that diocesan status had been attained. The low number of Catholics scattered over 46,000 square miles was but an invitation to growth.

As was true of Gibbons, Hafey was the youngest Catholic bishop when he was appointed. Rome and the American hierarchy knew that conditions in North Carolina required a man with physical stamina and youthful idealism. Both qualities would be put to the test with Hafey as they had been for his predecessor.

In his inaugural address, Hafey gave a good indication of his oratorical style and made crystal clear that there would be no waffling on his part with reference to the Catholic claim to being the one, true church. In fact, he used almost those exact words: "The Catholic Church has the virtue of truth, nothing can be added to the faith as given by Christ. With compromise the Church can have no part; it must teach the spirit of truth, whether the people like it or not."

None of the extant addresses of Hafey suggest that he followed Mike Irwin's counsel, namely, that to be effective in North Carolina a bishop must base his preaching on "Holy Writ." The inaugural sermon demonstrated that the new bishop was well-educated and eloquent but hardly likely to enkindle enthusiasm in the hearts of those searching for religious nourishment. A paragraph from that sermon illustrates his style:

> This congregation, this diocese, will find hope and confidence burst-
> ing into zeal from a brief contemplation of that group of apostles and
> disciples in anxious expectation awaiting the command to go forth as
> Ambassadors of Jesus Christ to renew the face of the earth. Their
> Lord and Master had completed his work, the seeds of eternal truth
> had been sown, the redemption of Man by the death of the God-man
> had been effected, and the Risen Christ Lord had ascended into
> Heaven.[17]

Actually, there was a reference to the Bible. Hafey advised: "I hope no one in the diocese will be without a testament, old and new, and they should be constantly used." However, he himself used the Scriptures only to reinforce his insistence on the singular prerogatives of his church. After citing the text about Christ building his church on Peter, the Rock, Hafey drew the conclusion: "You cannot accept Jesus Christ without accepting the church, which is inseparably identified with him."

The man must be given credit for courage, or perhaps brash-ness. Here he was in the heart of the Bible Belt, telling an audience that included dignitaries of various religions that his was the best. But it is likely that the new bishop was not really considering these visitors at all but rather issuing a rallying cry to his own troops, the rugged band of priests gathered round the altar who shared his perspective. For all of them, the predominance of Protestantism in North Carolina was nothing more than a challenge.

Three men were invited to express words of welcome at Hafey's installation. On behalf of the Benedictines of Belmont, Haid's successor, Abbot Taylor, pledged the support of his monks, although Hafey knew full well that their priority would have to be the monastery and the *abbatia nullius*. In any case, Taylor, who had seen how much Haid had suffered as Vicar Apostolic, was relieved not to have that post himself. It was enough to run the monastery and the *nullius*.

Predictably, for the secular clergy, the spokesman was Monsignor Dennen, the Vicar General. Many in the audience knew that much of the credit for the establishment of the diocese was due to the less than subtle efforts of the Wilmington pastor. Considering the demands made on a priest in the state, Dennen's thirty-four years of service to this point gave him some right to feel satisfaction.[18]

Finally, Colonel George Freeman, a lawyer and the brother of Father Arthur R. Freeman, who would become Vicar General of the diocese after Dennen, represented the laity. In his address, Colonel Freeman spared no hyperbole by saying that although the Catholic population was small, in terms of service to people through hospitals, orphanages,[19] schools, and churches, the new diocese of Raleigh "will compare favorably with any diocese in the county." Perhaps conscious that Hafey was a northerner, Freeman also spoke of "the fine traditions and characteristics of the old South land.... Chivalry may have changed its outward form but it is still inherent in the people.... They are a harmonious people extending brotherly love to each other." He obviously was not thinking of the black population, relegated to poverty, segregation, and disenfranchisement.[20]

Perhaps demonstrating the southern hospitality of which Freeman spoke, the newspaper editorial referred to Hafey as "attractive in person, with a charming manner, endowed with ability and grace. He favorably impressed those who heard him and those who met him." From a media point of view, the diocese was off to a good start.

The ceremony in the hot little church ended, Archbishop Curley boarded the train back to Baltimore, confident that the new diocese was in competent hands and that he could turn his attention to other matters. He was correct. Being retained as Vicar General mollified Dennen. The letters of complaint ceased.

The Bishop's Influence on Young People

Immediately, aware of the desperate need for money and for dedicated personnel, the new bishop began the ceaseless travel that became the hallmark of his tenure. In his appeals to Northern congregations, Hafey would use with great effect the fact that his diocese comprised the least Catholic region of the country, that it was a mission land on the very doorstep of solidly Catholic areas of America and a suitable arena for the labors of idealistic young men and women.

Among those young women was Melissa Hester, a native of Knightdale, a town a few miles east of Raleigh. Because there was no

Catholic church closer, the Hester family attended Sacred Heart Cathedral. Here, Melissa came in contact with Bishop Hafey who, she said, was "like a parish priest at the Cathedral; he took us on his knee for our first confessions. He confirmed me and gave me First Communion."

Too far away to attend the Cathedral school, Melissa went to public institutions, having the distinction of being the only Catholic attending Knightdale High School. While a student, Melissa received religious instructions during the summers. Her teachers were Immaculate Heart of Mary (IHM) sisters of Scranton, Pa., who during the year taught at Saint Monica, then the African-American parish school in Raleigh. Inspired by these sisters, Melissa joined the IHMs. By coincidence, by the time she was ready to profess religious vows, Bishop Hafey had been transferred to Scranton where he presided at the ceremony in which she pledged herself to a life of service as a sister. Subsequently, Sister Melissa returned to North Carolina working for many years as teacher, pastoral assistant, and religious educator and thriving in the small missions to which she was assigned. In 2001, sixty years a sister, she was a receptionist at the IHM Motherhouse in Scranton.[21]

North Carolina had its appeal for young men as well. One of them, Francis Murphy, who would serve as a priest in North Carolina for more than fifty years, also gave credit to Hafey for attracting him to ministry in the state. In his unpublished autobiography, Murphy wrote:

> I felt called to the vocation to become a priest in NC, where the number of Catholics was extremely small, only 12,000 out of 3 million population in 1943, and where there was a great need for priests. Bishop Hafey, the first bishop, had spoken about the missionary work here in our home parish in Harrison, NY. He is reported to have said that Raleigh had the only cathedral where one could stand in the sanctuary and greet the people who entered the front door."[22]

Thomas P. Griffin: First Rector of the Cathedral Parish

No one had closer association with the new bishop than Father Thomas P. Griffin, who was pastor of Sacred Heart Church when the diocese was created and remained on as rector when the church became the cathedral. By coincidence, the two men had a Baltimore link, the city where Griffin had been born in 1870 and from which Hafey had just arrived. Griffin had attended St. Mary's Seminary in his native city with the intention of serving in the archdiocese. However, following the reception of minor orders from Cardinal Gibbons in 1894, his career took some painful detours, ones similar to those of several other men who eventually became successful priests in North Carolina.

After attending St. Mary's for a time, Griffin withdrew for health reasons. Upon being readmitted, he was then dismissed "for apparent lack of vocation." Undeterred, Griffin applied to and was adopted by the diocese of Louisville, Kentucky and transferred to St. Vincent's Seminary in Pennsylvania, the very institution where Leo Haid had studied and subsequently served as faculty member. Unfortunately, for reasons that are not clear, Griffin was once again rejected. Finally, believing that the young man deserved one more chance, the seminary rector recommended Griffin to Haid. Desperate for priests, Haid accepted Griffin who was ordained in 1899 at the age of twenty-nine.[23]

The gamble paid off. After a brief apprenticeship in Wilmington, Griffin was moved to Raleigh where he would be pastor for the rest of his life, playing a major role in preparing the city for its first bishop. As Father Price complained in one of his letters to Cardinal Gibbons, the Raleigh church was poor to the point of embarrassment. It would be Griffin's task, over the course of many years and with the help of numerous benefactors, to construct in the state capitol a church of which Catholics could be proud. As if it were planned that way, the small stone structure was completed just a few months prior to the establishment of the diocese.

Compensating for the miserable quarters which he had shared with Price many years earlier, Griffin also constructed a substantial rectory, a building which could hold its own with the homes of the rich and powerful who lived in the capitol city center. This rectory would serve as Hafey's residence and office during his years in North Carolina.[24]

After the announcement of Hafey's appointment, a delighted 55-year-old Griffin wrote to Father Irwin at Newton Grove:

> I feel that new life will be mine with the companionship of a good, holy, and apostolic superior.... Doesn't it seem like a dream? Asheville, Charlotte, Wilmington! They give $25 to Raleigh's $5; they have numbers, people of wealth, influence, and social standing; we have little of these. Yet Raleigh is the See! God be praised.[25]

Griffin would survive only a few years to bask in the satisfaction of having contributed to the establishment of the church in Raleigh, dying of a heart attack in the rectory on April 2, 1931 at the age of sixty. The extensive coverage that his death and funeral received attest to the high esteem in which he was held and, by extension, the acceptance that the Catholic Church was gradually achieving.[26]

Hafey's remarks at Griffin's funeral, attended by mourners of all denominations, reflect once more the view of the Church which he held, one which may have alienated some of those who heard him:

> The grief of a parish in the passing of a Father is akin to the grief experienced by the family in the death of the father. The parish priest is the spiritual Father of the souls entrusted to his jurisdiction. On the other hand, the death of the Pastor does not interrupt the life and continuity of the parish. Another pastor, not elected but appointed by validly constituted authority, will soon come to take up the duties surrendered by the Priest of God who has reported to the Great High Priest for judgment and, we pray, the eternal reward of the faithful servant. Thus, from the principle of its Divine institution and its apostolicity follows the perpetuity of the Catholic Church.

Hafey's Work Begins

Immediately after his installation, Hafey undertook the expected tour of the state, within the first few months visiting all the parishes and familiarizing himself with the priests, sisters, and lay people. For example, on July 11 he drove to nearby Durham where he met with William B. Carmichael "discussing his possible conversion to the Faith and desire to erect a Catholic Church at Chapel Hill for the benefit of students." Carmichael, a top official at the College, later University, of North Carolina, did become a Catholic and was instrumental in establishing a Catholic presence on campus and eventually the erection of St. Thomas More parish in Chapel Hill. The present church and school are located on Carmichael Street.[27]

On August 4, Hafey was in the small port town of Elizabeth City, where he explored with the six Sisters of Humility of Mary conducting a hospital there the possibility of their uniting with a larger order, a move that would give the women a more secure status within the Church. Hafey's Diary does not indicate awareness that, just a few months before his visit, Elizabeth City had been the scene of one of the most fiery religious battles of the decade, one which reflected the struggle then underway throughout the South, a conflict to which the tiny Catholic community was largely a spectator.

On the one side of the conflict was the fundamentalist evangelist, Mordecai Fowler Ham, who in 1934 would convert North Carolinian Billy Graham, the most prominent preacher of the Twentieth Century. Ham had gained enormous popularity preaching revivals all over the state. In Goldsboro alone, in a 1921 crusade he recorded 1,200 conversions. Now, in the Fall of 1924, he was scheduled to bring his message to Elizabeth City, a town of 10,000, where the local Protestant churches had constructed a 4,000-seat tabernacle for the evangelist's six-week campaign. As would be true of Billy Graham in later years, most Protestant churches supported the evangelist because his preaching tended to increase membership in all the local churches.

Ham's message was an uncompromising attack on what he saw as the corrupting influence of modern cultural and intellectual forces. In particular, he saw the theory of evolution as a threat to biblical teaching. Buttressed by support from North Carolina governor, Cameron Morrison, Ham was committed to ridding the land of "free-thinking infidels" and to restoring the Protestant Christ.

On the other side of the controversy was William Oscar Saunders, owner and editor of the Elizabeth City *Independent*, one of the South's most liberal newspapers. Saunders, proud to be one of Ham's "freethinking infidels," with great zest used the pages of the *Independent* to undertake a campaign against Ham, whom he accused of being a fraud who would conduct "a red-hot, rip-snorting, hell-raising, sin-busting carnival" and then leave town with the money of his gullible listeners. The two men were engaged in the battle of words that was repeated by different actors all over the region as traditional Bible Belt Christians were challenged by new ideas, including recent scientific findings.[28]

As the struggle for the minds of the residents of Elizabeth City raged, the Catholics were on the sidelines. Holy Family parish, established in 1915, together with the Episcopal church refrained from supporting Ham's revival meeting. On the other hand, the small Catholic community, uncomfortable with both camps, also kept its distance from the "freethinking" Saunders. Throughout his time in North Carolina, Bishop Hafey would gain some measure of respect precisely because he steered clear of what were seen as Protestant controversies.

From Elizabeth City, Hafey left by boat for New York to undertake the first of numerous trips to raise funds, recruit candidates for the priesthood, and attempt to interest religious orders in establishing a presence in North Carolina. On this first trip in which he combined vacation with business, Hafey spoke at three masses in a Connecticut parish "on the needs of North Carolina" and "issued envelopes for offerings."

Although he had never before been in the state and had no experience administering a diocese, Hafey soon became comfortable with the geography of North Carolina and quickly created a role for himself as bishop. His priests would provide religious services to the Catholics and evangelize the non-Catholics; he would seek the resources they needed, namely, manpower and money. Hafey would not be preaching in local courthouses like Bishop England or visiting isolated Catholic families as had Bishop Gibbons. It was a new stage in the development of the church, one that called for a businessman more than a missionary and a man who encouraged respectability rather than confrontation among the little flock that looked to him for leadership. Growth first; societal leadership later.

Establishing New Parishes

Growth meant parishes. When Hafey arrived in 1925, there were 24 churches with resident priests in the state. When he left twelve years later there were 52, an average of more than two new parishes per year. It was not so much that the Catholic population was rising rapidly but that, as priests were available, towns that had been missions were raised in status to parishes.[29]

One of the new parishes was St. John the Evangelist in Waynesville, a town located in the remote western mountain region of the state, an area of chronic economic problems and corresponding slow population growth. Since before 1900, at times traveling by horseback, priests had ventured into Haywood County to celebrate mass in the homes of its few Catholic families. By 1920, during the summer tourist season, a priest would come from St. Lawrence in Asheville, still the only church in the mountains, to celebrate mass in the ballroom of the Gordon Hotel on Main Street.

Advised by Catholics in the area that a church was needed west of Asheville, on November 9, 1925, accompanied by Fathers Bernard McDevitt and James Manley and Mr. John O'Donnell, Hafey traveled from Asheville to Waynesville and promptly decided to buy property owned by Michael Kelly for the sum of $20,000. The following day, meeting with O'Donnell and Kelly, Hafey guaranteed that the first payment of $5,000 would be made. Thus, in two days Hafey set in motion the process that would lead to the establishment of a new parish to be dedicated to St. John. That assignment was given to Father McDevitt.

Since it would take time to build a church, McDevitt bought a house on the appropriately named Church Street which he converted into a chapel, rectory, and meeting place. The first mass was offered there in May of 1926 with twenty-seven persons present. The parish embraced the eight westernmost counties of North Carolina -- an area of 3,471 square miles. In that parish, larger in area than many dioceses, there were fifty Catholics.[30]

This procedure was repeated frequently, with Hafey buying land and assigning a priest to build a church. Little time was spent in consultation with real estate agents, bankers, or Catholic communities. Hafey assumed personal responsibility for the debt obligating himself to still more begging trips North. He expected the priest, usually completely naive as to the intricacies of construction, to build the church. Despite what today might seem like a foolhardy procedure, there were no defaults on loans as the churches were built.

Diocesan Staff: Only the Bishop

During all Hafey's time in the state, other than a secretary, there was no diocesan staff. Besides occasional meetings with his consultors, Hafey managed the diocese by himself. There was neither the need for nor the resources to support the professional assistance that would in time transform the missionary diocese into a sophisticated administrative organization with dozens of central staff employees. On the other hand, like a present day businessman, Hafey was constantly "on the road," an ecclesiastical traveling salesman energetically "selling" the North Carolina Catholic Church to people who had only the most vague idea of conditions in the land of cotton and segregation.

In the era before commercial airlines, it was not unusual for Hafey to go to his room after dinner, pack his bag, and proceed to the Raleigh railroad station for a night train. In the darkness, as the coal-powered locomotive pulled its string of cars across the silent landscape, the bishop would read his Breviary until his eyes closed and his head fell forward in a fitful sleep. In the morning, as the train puffed its way into a station, Hafey would step down onto the platform, hungry and anxious for an opportunity to wash and change his clothes. Always he was alone, his Roman collar and pectoral cross attracting deferential nods from Catholics and uncomfortable sideways glances from others. Despite the fatigue of the journey, Hafey braced himself for the work of the day, usually the unenviable task of asking for money.

After a fundraising trip or a pastoral visit to the outer reaches of the state, Hafey would note in his diary on his return to Raleigh: "Spent the day on correspondence." He also covered cathedral parish services when Father Griffin, the only priest in Raleigh in the early years, was away on vacation. At the same time, the bishop was also becoming familiar with rituals reserved to those of his rank.

On August 29, 1925, two months after his installation, he administered the sacrament of Confirmation for the first time -- two adults and five children -- in Holy Innocents Chapel in Maysville, a small town between New Bern and Jacksonville. Today, Maysville, nestled between two enormous forest preserves, has no Catholic church.

Another episcopal prerogative is administering the sacrament of Holy Orders. Although he conferred Minor Orders on students at St. Mary's Seminary in Emmitsburg, Maryland in November 1925, it would not be until the Spring of 1929, four years after his arrival, that Hafey would ordain the first two men to the priesthood of the diocese.

Among other things the bishop was vocations recruiter and director, personally interviewing candidates, assigning them to seminaries, and keeping track of their progress. As the number of candidates for the priesthood increased -- from 16 in 1926, to 25 two years later -- so also did the cost of supporting them. Finding that some of these young men withdrew from the seminary after their fees had been paid for several years, Hafey drew up a contract which he required that students sign, obligating them to repay part of the cost of their education, including those who did not continue to priesthood. As the bishop explained, "I must beg most of the money obtained."[31]

A Typical Schedule for Bishop Hafey

Aside from a three-month trip to Europe and the Holy Land in 1927, Hafey's absences from the diocese, though frequent, were relatively brief. Highlights of the first few months of 1926 give some idea of what his life was like.

Jan. 12: Traveled from Raleigh for New Bern with Father Stanislaus, CP, Provincial of the Passionists. Hafey was instrumental in getting the order to open and support a parish for Negro Catholics in the town of Washington. That parish eventually had a better school and larger church than did the parish for white Catholics in the same town.

Jan. 15: Took the train to Baltimore where he spoke at St. Elizabeth Church, collecting $1,075. After a few days in New York, he was back in Baltimore in time to speak at the Masses at St. Jerome Church on Jan. 24 and St. Paul on the 31st. As it turned out, Baltimore supplied not only a bishop to North Carolina but much of his financial support as well.

Jan. 28: Visited the Immaculate Heart of Mary (IHM) Sisters at Mt. St. Mary's, Maryland "to interest the order in schools in Raleigh." Over time the IHMs would supply more sisters for ministries in the state than any other order of women aside from the locally-based Sisters of Mercy.

Feb. 2: Back in Raleigh.

Feb. 5: Night train to New York, where on successive Sundays he spoke at all the masses in two Brooklyn churches, St. Cecelia and St. Rose of Lima; substantial collections in each place.

Feb. 14: From New York, the first of his many trips to Chicago to meet with officials of the Catholic Church Extension Society, the largest supporter of churches in mission areas of the country. On this occasion Hafey met Father Eugene McGuinness, an Extension official. Neither man could have guessed that eleven years later McGuinness would succeed Hafey as bishop of Raleigh.

Feb. 21: On his return to Brooklyn, he spoke at St. Anthony Church and collected $1,500.

Feb. 23: Back in Raleigh once again, but shortly thereafter off again, first to give a talk in Charleston, South Carolina, followed by a trip to Washington, DC where he spoke at six masses and collected $1,716. Then it was Boston, Baltimore once again, and a return trip to Chicago, this time for the Eucharistic Congress, a major Catholic gathering attended by more than 100,000 people including, in Hafey's words, "all sorts of prelates."

Even as the bishop was establishing parishes and traveling to raise money, two events of national significance were claiming the attention and the passion of the country. Both had implications for the church in North Carolina. One was the election of 1928; the other was the Great Depression.

A Catholic Presidential Candidate

As bad luck would have it, from the point of view of the economy, the Catholic Church made its two major starts in North Carolina at the very worst of times. In 1868 when the Vicariate Apostolic was established, the state was reeling from the trauma of the Civil War; in 1925 when Bishop Hafey inaugurated the Raleigh Diocese, the nation was inching its way towards the great collapse of 1929. However, in the moment when Hafey was being welcomed and the maturing of Catholicism in the state celebrated, it was as if the sun broke through the clouds, shining like a harbinger of prosperity and growth. The pain of World War I had receded and the greater pain of yet another world conflict could not be imagined. But a Carolina sky can be fickle and the warmth of a July day all too soon become the chill of November. And before the Great Depression slammed the nation like a hurricane, the presidential election of 1928 ignited once again the smoldering embers of anti-Catholic sentiment.

Already in 1924 rumbles of anti-Catholicism had been heard when New York Governor Al Smith was put forward as a Democratic candidate for President. When four years later the Catholic Smith was actually nominated, the storm broke in all its fury, placing the South on the horns of a dilemma. Since the Civil War the region had been solidly in the Democratic political camp, bitterly opposed to the Republican party of Abraham Lincoln that had destroyed its way of life. On the other hand, the idea of a Catholic in the White House was too abhorrent for many Southerners to tolerate. Protestant pulpits lit up with warnings that a vote for Smith was a vote for the Pope and the imposition of Catholic religious dogma.

The campaign was hard fought and acrimonious. Catholics might have been a small minority of the North Carolina population, but their religion was mentioned on the front-page of local newspapers nearly every day. Interestingly enough, the Raleigh *News & Observer* supported Smith, its news pages unabashedly biased in his favor as the campaign against Herbert Hoover entered its final weeks.[32] For example, on September 28 the two main front page headlines were "Smith Leader in Supporting Many Women's Causes" and "Al Smith Sees Lack of Leadership as Primary Weakness of Opponents."

Of course, religion was not the only issue. Smith was seen as "wet" by "dry" Southerners who feared that as President he would work to repeal Prohibition. Also, the candidate personified northern, urban culture, which the still predominantly rural South scorned. Finally, Smith, the son of immigrants, was seen as supportive of increased immigration, a development that southerners viewed as a danger to the American way of life. Of course, all these qualities could be rolled into one: Catholic, since the majority of the members of that religion were northern, urban immigrants: Italians who loved their wine, Germans fond of their beer, and Irish who went straight for the hard stuff. As one North Carolina leader put it, "Seventy-five to eighty percent of the objection to Governor Smith is due primarily to religion."[33]

Although Hoover repudiated the religious bigotry of some of his supporters, the damage was done. One Republican national committee woman referred to Smith as "slum-born, rum-raised, a wet Irish Catholic." She also warned: "We must save the United States from being Romanized."[34] A North Carolina Republican congressional candidate openly circulated anti-Catholic literature.[35]

The highlight of the campaign in North Carolina was the mid-October visit by Smith to the state. The candidate traveled by train from Charlotte to Raleigh, making stops along the way. In Charlotte, as the pro-Smith paper put it, "an Al Smith-mad mob volleyed cheers at the candidate as he rode slowly down the torch-lighted wall of human beings." He was given an ovation "the likes of which this city has given no man." The front page banner screamed: "Roaring Welcome for Smith." Secondary headings read: "Enthusiasm for Smith evoked in crowd of 100,000" and "Crowd charmed by Brown Derby."[36] All of this was blatant editorializing on the part of a paper attempting to catapult Smith to victory. Such hoopla may have prompted the North Carolina Methodist bishop to announce that he was voting Republican and urging his clergy to do likewise.[37] A follow-up letter decried the "malicious religious prejudice which characterized the campaign "manifested by some of the prominent and influential ministers and bishops of the Protestant church."[38]

With echoes of William Gaston and the constitutional convention of 1835, an article on the eve of the election reminded voters that the ban on Catholics holding public office had been lifted nearly one hundred years before.

With all the furor raging around him, Bishop Hafey was appropriately circumspect. Nothing would have galvanized anti-Catholic sentiment more than for the local Catholic bishop to show the slightest involvement in the election. The only thing Hafey did was send a letter to the priests of the state ordering that there be no reference to politics from the pulpit. Although the letter made no specific mention of the presidential campaign, it suggested that the priests acquire copies of the article "Has the Pope Any Political Power in the United States?" by James M. Graham. Parishioners were to be urged to read the article and to pass it on "to honest seekers of the truth."[39]

Although Hafey's Diary notes that he voted, it does not indicate how he voted or his reaction to the election's outcome. However, his cautious approach to the political scene is illustrated by the fact that at a meeting of the American bishops later that month he spoke against the issuance of a letter condemning the anti-Catholic bigotry associated with the election. The bishops agreed with Hafey that patience and reserve were "the best means of winning good will and opening the way for the spread of truth about Catholic faith and practice."[40]

When the dust settled on Election Day, North Carolina had joined several other Southern states in voting Republican, contributing to the resounding Hoover victory. For all state offices, Democrats won as usual. In one of the strangest flip-flops in American political history, as the white South switched from Democrat to Republican, those African-Americans allowed to vote transferred their support from the Republicans to the Democrats. However, although Smith was defeated, the sighs of relief and triumph were soon replaced with expressions of concern and apprehension as the country spiraled into depression.

The Great Depression

Like a house of cards, one industry after another collapsed as the nation and much of the world sank into depression, bursting the bubble of optimism that had fueled a giddy run-up of the stock market during the 1920's. Factories laid off workers by the tens of thousands; long lines of despondent men stood in stony silence on bread lines; women wondered how their children would be fed and what their future would be like. North Carolina was not spared. An area barely recovered from the disruptions of the Civil War was once again sent reeling.

Perhaps no word picture of the South during the 1930's is more vivid than that presented by the editors of *The Nation* who wrote:

> the facts about the wasting of the South's splendid natural and human
> resources, the erosion if its soil, the crowding of its rural slums, the
> draining of its youngest blood and best talent, its ramshackle housing,
> its starvation wages, its monopoly of pellagra and its subjection to

syphilis and malaria, its sparse schooling, its exploitation of the labor of women and children, its dependent farm tenantry and brutalized and impoverished landowners, its untaxed industries and its tax-burdened common people -- in short, the grotesque paradox it presents of a land that "is blessed by nature with immense wealth," yet whose "people as a whole are the poorest in the country."[41]

The concluding words in quotation marks are those of Franklin D. Roosevelt, who in 1933 had succeeded Hoover as president and whose New Deal programs were attempting to pull the country out of depression. His remarks were made in conjunction with the National Emergency Council's Report on Economic Conditions in the South, which drew national attention to the plight of a region largely invisible to the rest of the country. There was no war, but the southern landscape was as devastated as if there had been.[42]

A Persistent Beggar

In assessing Hafey's twelve years as Bishop of Raleigh, it cannot be overlooked that for most of that time America was in a state of unprecedented economic crisis. The wonder is that, despite these conditions and the chronic lack of money in the country, Hafey was able to "beg" enough to keep the diocese solvent. The explanation is that he was single-minded. It was as if there was no crisis, no larger world crying for help. For Hafey, there was just the Catholic Church and its needs. He never stopped presenting those needs in any parish that would lend him its pulpit.

His pastoral letters, one of the only remaining sources of his work in North Carolina, are devoted mainly to encouraging generosity in special collections and observation of Lenten regulations. Each year had its letter on the need to support candidates for the priesthood and another for the orphanage at Nazareth. The virtual pulpit of the letter from the bishop, which priests were ordered to read at all masses, was seldom used to help the faithful reflect on the pressing needs of modern life. With reference to the issue of segregation -- perhaps not an issue for most southerners during the Thirties -- Hafey limited himself to pointing with pride to the increasing number of churches that had been established to serve the black community, including St. Monica in Raleigh, which siphoned what few black Catholics there were away from Sacred Heart Cathedral and into their own place of worship.

Not unlike most of his Catholic peers, Hafey saw no need to provide leadership beyond the confines of the Catholic world and for matters strictly sectarian. In any case, his view of the larger world would have provided scant assistance to contemporary men and women struggling to cope with economic problems. So, for example, his Diary entry for December 31, 1931 contains one of the very few references to world events. That New Year's Eve reflection, written not for public consumption but as an expression of his personal feelings, suggests his perspective on the deepening Depression.

> Plenty of news about bank failures and general uneasiness due to financial depression. May God grant that the idol of gold having fallen, men will turn to the true God and that peace will follow during the new year.[43]

Despite the bishop's prayer, peace did not come during the new year, or the year after, nor for many years more. Nevertheless, the Church was inching its way forward, quietly establishing itself as a presence in most of the larger towns of the state. The number of Catholics remained small, just over 10,000 in 1937, but even this modest growth was noteworthy in an area with virtually no immigration and an anti-Catholic tradition. The serious-miened Hafey skillfully kept the ship of the new diocese afloat. At the time of his appointment, some had remained skeptical of the state's readiness to support a bishop. Hafey showed that it was ready provided it had a bishop willing to be a persistent mendicant.

Having justified the trust placed in him by Archbishop Curley, in 1937 Hafey was promoted to the diocese of Scranton, Pennsylvania, where he died in 1957. He would pass on to his successor in North Carolina an empty purse, but no significant debts, and a church finally secure in its position as a bona fide diocese. All things taken into account, it was appropriate that, as Hafey departed the *Raleigh Times* had kind words for the man in an editorial:

> Under his direction the churches and charitable institutions have flourished and the membership has doubled. ... Bishop Hafey has won the complete respect and sympathy of the community in which he has been a force for religion, goodwill, peace and tolerance. His appointment brought to the important work of the Diocese a brilliant scholar, preacher and teacher, a competent executive in a difficult post and a tireless worker for good.[44]

Eugene J. McGuinness: Second Bishop of Raleigh

The man selected to succeed Hafey was very familiar with mission areas like North Carolina. For eighteen years Father Eugene Joseph McGuinness had worked with the Chicago-based Catholic Church Extension Society, distributing millions of dollars to dioceses such as Raleigh. Now McGuinness would see the problem from a different perspective. He would leave the comfort of his office for what was still very much a home mission frontier. The man from whom others had begged would now himself become the beggar.

Born September 6, 1889 in Bethlehem, Pennsylvania, McGuinness attended St. Charles Borromeo Seminary in Philadelphia where he was ordained in 1915. After two years in a parish, he was appointed assistant Director of the Society of the Propagation of the Faith in Philadelphia and two years later moved on to the Extension Society, where he ascended the career ladder to the position of General Secretary. His first boss in Chicago, Father Francis Clement Kelley, had founded the Extension Society in 1905 and in 1924 became the bishop of the Oklahoma-Tulsa diocese. As shall be seen, the paths of the two men were destined to converge once more.

As a Philadelphia priest, McGuinness was taken in tow by that city's powerful and despotic archbishop, Cardinal Dennis Dougherty, who consecrated the forty-eight year old McGuinness on December 21, 1937 and installed him as Bishop of Raleigh on January 6, 1938. The new bishop was clearly in awe of Dougherty. In a series of letters to Father Arthur Freeman, rector of the Raleigh cathedral and administrator of the diocese, McGuinness gave detailed instructions as to how the Cardinal was to be received, housed, and entertained.[45]

More than that, a special train was chartered to carry the Cardinal and his entourage of more than 100 churchmen and laymen from Philadelphia to Raleigh for the installation. Leaving Philadelphia early in the morning of January 5, the train arrived in Raleigh that evening, where Freeman escorted Dougherty and McGuinness to the Sacred Heart rectory while the other dignitaries were directed to a nearby hotel. The following day the "largest assembly of Catholic prelates ever gathered in North Carolina" marched into the cathedral: one cardinal, sixteen bishops, twenty-six monsignori, and more than two hundred priests.[46]

McGuinness was effusive in his praise of Dougherty, "long known in this and other lands for his devotion in building up the Church in sections where it was weak in numbers." One thing McGuinness had learned in his years at Extension was diplomacy and how to handle potential benefactors. He would, in fact, often turn to Dougherty for advice as well as financial assistance in the years ahead. If Hafey could count on access to the affluent churches of Baltimore, so now his successor would turn to Philadelphia.

The echoes of the inaugural celebration had hardly stilled when McGuinness was out about the diocese, introducing himself to the priests and surveying the status of the church in the state. On January 30, he dedicated a church for the first time, actually a chapel, in the little town of Pinebluff, a mission of the parish of Sacred Heart, Pinehurst, which had been established in 1919. The following week the Reverend Thomas Williams, pastor of Sacred Heart, wrote in the parish bulletin an account of the recent installation of the new bishop and of his visit to Pinebluff. Williams' flair for the dramatic is illustrated by the following:

> The ways of God are strange. Over 1900 years ago in the city of Bethlehem Christ was born in a stable and was driven from the city by Herod after the Wise Men visited him on the feast of the Epiphany. Years later, Bishop McGuinness, a native of Bethlehem, Pennsylvania, was installed as Bishop of Raleigh on the Feast of the Epiphany. He then dedicated first the church of the Holy Child which was formerly a stable owned by a man named Herod.[47]

Affirming Catholic Patriotism

Such wonders aside, McGuinness was quickly disavowed of any romantic views he might have about mission work. The words quoted at the beginning of this chapter are from an article he wrote in an early effort to open the pocketbooks of Catholics. Although theoretically familiar with conditions in North Carolina, it would seem that actually living in the state brought home to him with full force how different was the culture there from that of such bastions of Catholic life as Philadelphia and Chicago.[48]

That southern culture included the tenaciously held opinion that Catholics were not good Americans was a significant concern as the nation once again moved towards war. Accordingly, McGuinness added in his article:

> The days of the ranting, vituperative preachers are over and we must adjust ourselves to a people amazed to learn that Catholics are human

and American. The only possible way to dislodge from the minds of
the many that we are not an integral part of American life is to tell
them by contact, by lecture, by sermon that we possess a cherished
heritage that had its origins at the very feet of Christ.[49]

The issue of loyalty to America was addressed further in two
of McGuinness's pastoral letters. In one of them, issued as Hitler was
marching across Europe, he urged the priests to "speak to our people
about the neo-paganism that is submerging the world." Aware that the
Church's strong denunciation of Communism had given the impression
in some quarters that the Church favored fascism "and even nazism," he
insisted that this idea must be disavowed.[50]

In February 1939, Pope Pius XI died after a reign of 17 years.
His successor, Pius XII, took office just as World War II burst into full
fury. In the eye of the hurricane, as it were, the pope came in for sharp
criticism for the way he behaved, an issue that continues to generate
books and articles sixty years after the war's end. For his part, aware of
the criticism of the pope, McGuinness wrote in a May 5, 1942 letter:

> Possibly at no time since the days of the so-called Reformation has
> our Holy Father been called upon by so many for aid. He is harassed
> by statesmen, beleaguered by opponents and, even among the just, his
> attitude of strict neutrality has been questioned.

One step that the American bishops took to burnish the image
of Catholic loyalty, was the recommendation that each diocese and
parish make a list of Catholics serving in the armed forces and publicly
display an honor roll. The thousands of local honor rolls would be combined in a massive "Catholic Honor Roll of the Nation." Bishop
McGuinness dutifully urged all parishes to participate.

Money Matters

One reason why McGuinness may have been particularly sensitive to the issue of patriotism was the fact that during the war the
largest Catholic congregations in the state were those that met each
Sunday on military bases. Furthermore, the generosity of the soldiers
added substantially to diocesan collections. Contributions from the
bases far exceeded what was gathered from parishes. For example,
while the Christmas 1942 collection for the orphanage at Nazareth
amounted to $549 at Sacred Heart Cathedral, the troops training at Fort
Bragg contributed $1,604.19, and the Marines at the New River base

added another $541.01. The following year, the seminary collection brought in $7,136 from all the parishes in the state combined, while the military bases alone contributed $2,584.[51]

Understandably, finances were always a concern for the bishop. Nevertheless, the arrival of a McGuinness letter in a rectory mailbox must have brought a sigh to the lips of many an overworked pastor. Perhaps his years with the Extension Society had conditioned McGuinness to measure success in terms of dollars raised. In any case, the pressure to squeeze more money out of the faithful was incessant. Besides the special diocesan collections, McGuinness was not shy about advancing his own needs. So, in 1943, he bluntly said that he needed more money for his personal support. A cathedraticum[52] of $1,800 per year was much too small. "I cannot subsist, much less run the chancery, upon this sum." Accordingly, McGuinness raised the parish assessment so as to bring in a new total of $3,565 per year, still not an exorbitant amount but a substantial further burden to the parishes.[53]

As if sensitive to, in effect, raising his own salary, McGuinness during that same year increased the salary of his priests. Henceforth, pastors were to get $50 per month, assistants, $25. In a tone which seems cruel if not preposterous in terms of the value of the dollar today, the bishop added: "There is a trend towards lavishness on the part of some who are unmindful that we are missionaries, not sons of Croesus."[54]

Growth of the Church

In some measurable ways, Bishop McGuinness was strikingly successful. His extensive contacts with missionary religious orders enabled him to recruit half a dozen new orders of men for the diocese, many of whom opened parishes for "colored" Catholics. While the ministry of the two earliest religious orders working in North Carolina contracted, others more than took their places. By 1945, the Belmont Benedictines, once the dominant clerical presence in the state, staffed only St. Peter in Charlotte, while the Josephite Fathers, the first to minister to African Americans, retained only St. Thomas in Wilmington. However, Redemptorists, Holy Ghost Fathers, Friars of the Atonement, Edmundite Fathers, Fathers of Mercy, and Franciscans opened churches at a rapid rate. Whereas in 1938, there had been fifty-two parishes with resident pastors, by 1945 there were eighty-six, twenty-three of them "colored parishes."

Religious orders of women also took up the challenge, so that by 1945 some 238 women, representing fourteen religious orders, were staffing the forty Catholic schools in the state, including eleven for colored children.

Most striking of all, the number of priests had risen substantially. The secular clergy, which numbered fifty-three when Bishop Hafey left North Carolina, stood at eighty-three when his successor departed. Even more impressive was the increase in the number of religious order priests from twenty-six in 1938 to fifty-nine in 1945. From all sections of the country, McGuinness had summoned workers to evangelize what remained the state most resistant to Catholic growth. And that resistance continued, adding a sobering note to a valiant campaign. Although McGuinness opened an average of four new parishes each year, the Catholic population increased minimally from 10,571 in 1938 to 12,922 in 1945. In particular, the enormous investment in reaching out to the African American population had borne little fruit. Although there were converts, mainly as a result of the parochial schools, the numbers were disappointing.[55] His dream of a striking missionary breakthrough not realized, McGuinness found a way to transfer his episcopal robes to a more hospitable setting.[56]

Moving to Oklahoma

As had been mentioned, while a young priest at the Extension Society, McGuinness had worked with Francis Clement Kelley, one of the most creative and spiritual men in the history of the American Catholic Church.[57] Kelley had been bishop of the Diocese of Oklahoma City-Tulsa since 1924, but twenty years later his health was failing. McGuinness had maintained contact with his mentor and in 1944 was invited to make a financial appeal in an Oklahoma City parish. His presentation was well received and the collection sizable. More to the point was the condition of "The Boss," Bishop Kelley. As an aide to Kelley confided to McGuinness, "I think he is getting ready to sing his swan song. He may live for several months, but I doubt very much if he will spend another Christmas in this world."[58]

Although it was a delicate matter and Rome had the final say, it was communicated to higher church authorities through the Metropolitan Archbishop that McGuinness would be interested in becoming coadjutor to Kelley with the right of succession. In a letter at the end of June 1944, McGuinness alluded to what he delicately referred to as "the big idea."[59]

The "big idea" was accepted and on November 11, 1944, McGuinness was transferred to Oklahoma.[60] As it turned out, Kelley did not die before Christmas but lingered on for more than three years. When he did succumb in January 1948, McGuinness became ordinary in his own right, passing from this life himself two days after Christmas 1957. His one claim to fame may be that he has high schools named in his honor in two states: Bishop McGuinness High School in Oklahoma City and another of the same name in Winston-Salem, North Carolina.

The subdued tone of McGuinness's departure from Raleigh was in stark contrast to the Cardinal-studded fanfare at his installation. No laudatory editorial appeared in the city paper, only the bishop's picture accompanying a terse announcement buried on page 18.[61] However, conditions in the world were grim and the transfer of the bishop was of minimal public concern. Day after day bold headlines reported the progress of the war in Europe and the Pacific. Each issue of the paper also contained a list of local casualties and the photos of North Carolina young men serving in the armed forces. So, the day that McGuinness's transfer was reported, the front page banner headline read: "Allies Start Big Drive in West. 1,500,000 Men hit Nazis as Eisenhower Launches Mighty Winter Offensive."[62]

McGuinness remained on as Administrator of the Raleigh diocese from November 1944 until his departure for Oklahoma in early January 1945. His final pastoral letter, dated December 13, 1944, listed him as "Administrator." There was no note of farewell, no hint of the change that was taking place; there were no embraces or tears. McGuinness had arrived in Raleigh in a special train, accompanied by a sizable entourage. He left on a regularly scheduled train, alone. In May, Bishop Vincent Waters would arrive, initiating the long period of development and controversy related in the first three chapters.

The careers of bishops are but part of the story of a diocese. Equally essential is the work of parish priests, the men who are on the front lines, as it were, and who communicate to people with their words and lives what Catholic Christianity is all about. The following chapter will look once again at the Catholic Church in North Carolina in the first half of the Twentieth Century, this time through the lives of several of those priests.

Chapter Nine

Pioneering Clergy

Your Excellency has an empire of souls more difficult to convert than an equal number of Chinese. I have had great experience among our people. The labor is very great, the results small. The rewards are small because we priests are too busy with temporal cares and are not sufficiently fortified by our own interior perfection and by the prayers of others. We need [contemplative nuns] close at hand, so that we poor, often infirm and worldly-minded priests might have the example of their personal perfection right under our eyes, right in our own domicile, as it were, so that it would be impossible to escape the aroma of their sanctity.

---Monsignor Michael Irwin to Bishop Waters, January 22, 1946

In May 1937, a college student rang the bell of the Sacred Heart Cathedral rectory in Raleigh. On several occasions growing up on Staten Island, New York, the nervous young man, Fred Koch, had heard Bishop William Hafey speak during a Lenten series in his parish church. Early in the morning Fred would serve the bishop's mass, lifting the chasuble as the prelate mounted the altar steps, carrying the missal from one side of the altar to the other, noting the large ring on Hafey's finger as the boy held the small glass bowl and poured a little water over the hands of the man towering over him and mumbling the Latin words *Lavabo inter innocentes*, "I will wash my hands among the innocent." Koch was one of those innocent ones, the legion of Catholic boys who during the first half of the twentieth century in the mysterious ritual of the Latin mass received a call to the priesthood. Koch's call would summon him to North Carolina.

Now, nine years later, having completed two years at St. Mary's College Seminary in Kentucky, Koch was requesting acceptance as a candidate for the priesthood in the Raleigh Diocese. Never having

been in the South before, the young man was disconcerted by segregated waiting rooms at the railroad station and the water fountains and rest
rooms labeled "White" and "Colored." Compared with his New York,
Raleigh was hardly a city at all, more like a rural town with mules and
horses pulling wagon loads of produce to the municipal market and
unpaved streets only a short distance from downtown. There were
moments of doubt. Did God really want him there? Perhaps he should
stay closer to home. His reveries were interrupted as a young priest
swung open the heavy door and welcomed him to Raleigh.[1]

Newly-ordained Father John A. Brown, taking the young
man's suitcase, ushered him into the impressive stone building inform-
ing the student that Bishop Hafey and the cathedral rector, Father
Joseph L. Federal, were out of town but would be back that evening.[2]
Brown showed Koch the room in which he would stay during his visit
and told him to come down for lunch after he had freshened up. Thus
began a relationship with the Church in North Carolina that would span
sixty years and four bishops.

*   *   *

Church histories, including this one, focus on bishops the way
general histories focus on presidents and kings. Such men are the ones
who make the decisions and provide the leadership that in large measure shapes the society. However, in the case of the Catholic Church in
North Carolina, a handful of rank-and-file priests played such a central
role in sustaining the Church during its early years as a diocese that they
merit special attention. Bishops came and went but these men remained,
ministering to the laity, sustaining the brunt of anti-Catholicism, and
doggedly striving to expand the church.

The present chapter selects six of these men, all of whom had
extremely long careers in the diocese. They were men of their times,
pre-Vatican II men, with a bulldog-like tenacity, an uncompromising
commitment, and an unquestioning loyalty. They represent the forgotten ones, those who are mourned for a short time and then disappear
from memory. If nothing else, they remained at their posts holding the
territory through the long winter of frustration. They wondered why
more people were not given the light to see what they saw, that their
church was the one established by Christ. As often as not, they faulted
their own inadequacy, their lack of spirituality. They yearned to be the
sort of men who would draw people to faith, Baptism, and the
Eucharist.

The profiles that follow, or rather fragments of profiles, are like the pieces of an incomplete mosaic. Many pieces are missing. In some cases it is because records are incomplete; in other cases, it is because the inclusion of more material would unduly delay the effort to shape a comprehensive view of the church. On one level, this chapter might be skipped; it doesn't carry the story forward. However, on another level it is the heart of the story, a brief walk through the years with men who most significantly represented the church during its formative period. Besides Frederick A. Koch, the priests to be profiled are Christopher Dennen, Michael Irwin, William O'Brien, Edward Gilbert, and John Roueche.

*   *   *

Frederick A. Koch (1916-1999)

In the afternoon of that May 1937 day when Koch arrived in Raleigh, Father Brown took him to the orphanage at Nazareth, just two miles from the cathedral, telling the student about Father Price, whose exploits in North Carolina had already reached mythic proportions.[3] With youthful idealism, Koch resolved that, like Price, he would bring Catholicism to the mission land that was Carolina.[4]

Hafey readily agreed to accept Koch for the diocese and the young man returned to the seminary to continue his studies. No sooner had he arrived there than he learned that Hafey had been transferred to Scranton. By coincidence, Koch had been born in that Pennsylvania city and still had relatives there. Years later when visiting Scranton, Koch stopped by to see Hafey, who said that one of the last things he had done in Raleigh was formally adopt Koch and one of the first things he did upon arriving in Scranton was to write a letter releasing him from any ties to his native diocese. With a laugh, the bishop told the young priest that if he had it to do over again he would not have been so quick to release him.

Since almost all the seminarians for North Carolina were from other states, they were required to spend their summer vacations in the diocese familiarizing themselves with the conditions there and allowing the bishop to assess the candidates. So in June 1938, Raleigh's second bishop, Eugene J. McGuinness, welcomed Koch and the other seminarians, assigning them to staff the summer program held at Nazareth. The practice was for the 200 orphans who resided at the institution during the school year to vacation in other locations, the boys at Bogue Island off the North Carolina coast and the girls in a camp in the mountain city of Waynesville. The cows from the Nazareth farm were shipped by train with the children in order to supply them with dairy products during their stay.

Once the orphans moved out, boys and girls from parishes throughout the state replaced them for a program designed to deepen their sense of Catholic identity. The clerical students were the teachers, their youth and enthusiasm enabling them to relate well to the children. Besides the general catechism lessons, boys were taught how to serve Mass so that they could assist the priests back in their home parishes. When not engaged in religious and recreational activities with the children, the seminarians were assigned manual labor such as painting the orphanage buildings.

Nazareth was not the whole diocese of course, and Bishop McGuinness would take the students to missions around the state, not just familiarizing them with the far-flung Catholic outposts but getting to know the young men, forging the bonds that would be essential for an effective ministry. On one occasion, the bishop took the seminarians to the Outer Banks, an area beginning to emerge as a vacation resort, for the dedication of Holy Redeemer Church in Kill Devil Hills. In the evening, the black-suited group attended the recently inaugurated play on Roanoke Island about Sir Water Raleigh's Lost Colony. The young men were excited to see that Eleanor Roosevelt, the wife of President Franklin D. Roosevelt, was in attendance also.

Koch remembered McGuinness as a jovial, kindly, thoughtful man who loved to play Chinese checkers with his seminarians and to serve them ice cream. On one occasion while playing checkers, Koch made a false move. The bishop's reaction was: "Fred, don't do that again, or you'll draw back a bloody stump." It is trivial memories such as these that men cherish for a lifetime.

Upon graduation from college in 1939, Koch was invited to meet with McGuinness at the Hotel Pennsylvania in New York in order to receive his assignment to a major seminary. It was on this occasion that Koch met for the first time another student, George Lynch, recently graduated from Fordham University in New York and destined to be a close associate and auxiliary bishop to Bishop Waters.

McGuinness took the two young men to lunch in the hotel restaurant where the bishop ordered corned beef and cabbage and the seminarians spare ribs. As the bishop ate his meal gracefully, the students struggled awkwardly with the spare ribs. Looking over at the flustered duo, the bishop advised, "Eat spare ribs at home, but when you go out in company order something you can eat with finesse." Another of Koch's indelible memories.

The news that the bishop had for the two seminarians was that they were to study in Rome. He gave the delighted youths letters of introduction to the rector of the North American College and advised them to apply for passports. The embarrassment of the spare ribs was replaced with the exciting prospect of traveling to Europe. However, their rejoicing was soon to be turned into disappointment as within weeks war was declared between Germany and England. Passports were canceled and all travel to Europe suspended. World events altered the plans of many, including two students for the priesthood in North Carolina.

Since American seminaries were crowded, McGuinness had to search for alternative places for his students. In the meanwhile, Koch waited in the Staten Island, New York home of his parents, his trunk, once destined to accompany him to Europe, standing at the ready in the hall.

Early in September Fred and his mother went to the World's Fair being held in Flushing Meadow, Queens. On returning home, a telegram from the bishop advised Fred to report the following day to the Sulpician Theological College at the Catholic University in Washington, DC. As millions of other young men were about to be mobilized for military duty, Koch, Lynch, and hundreds of other draft-exempt clerical students were beginning their basic training for service in the ranks of the clergy. After four years of study, as the war continued to rage in Europe and Asia, the two men were ordained together on May 29, 1943, ready for their first assignments.

A Varied Priestly Career

After serving an apprenticeship in Charlotte, Koch was sent across the state to New Bern where the pastor was Monsignor Michael A. Irwin, at 6' 4" and weighing over 300 pounds, literally one of the giants of the clergy. Irwin, whose career will be related below, had been ordained by Bishop Leo Haid during the period of the Vicariate Apostolic and, along with men like Monsignors William F. O'Brien and Arthur Freeman, loved to regale younger priests with tales of the time when a dozen secular priests and the Belmont Abbey Benedictines covered the entire state, traveling by horseback, train, and model T Ford, spending nights in unheated "shacks" as they ministered to the scattered Catholic population.

When Koch reported to Irwin in 1946, there were five priests in New Bern, more than in Raleigh or any other North Carolina city. It was not that the number of Catholics justified such a wealth of clergy but that the segregated churches required a duplication of facilities. Two Passionist priests staffed the colored parish of St. Joseph and with a few sisters administered a school for colored children. A few blocks away, Irwin, slowed by age, was assisted by Koch and by Father Phillip J. O'Mara, who also served as chaplain to the Depression-era Civilian Conservation Corps that put young men to work in the national forest and in flood-control projects.

By this time, Vincent Waters was the bishop and, as has been seen, one of his early projects was the launching of the *North Carolina Catholic*, the first Catholic newspaper in the state since Civil War days. After one year, the inaugural editor of the *NC Catholic*, the layman Dale Francis, moved on and the position was given to Koch. In order to be closer to the paper's office at Nazareth, Koch was transferred from the aging Monsignor Irwin in New Bern to the feeble Reverend Francis J. Morrissey, pastor of St. Thomas More parish in Chapel Hill.

Aware of his lack of specialized skills for editing a newspaper, Koch took several courses at the University of North Carolina School of Journalism. Coincidentally, Father Michael Begley, superintendent of the orphanage at Nazareth and later the first bishop of Charlotte, had just completed a degree in social work at UNC. Koch and Begley were the first North Carolina diocesan priests to supplement their seminary training with educational work appropriate for professional standing in fields that were not specifically religious. Also, they were pioneers in attending the University of North Carolina, which not only still excluded African-Americans but also had admitted few Catholic students.

After Morrissey's death in 1949, Koch was given his first pastorates at St. Eugene in Wendell and later at St. Catherine of Siena in Wake Forest. His routine now consisted of living at Nazareth from Monday to Friday while he worked on the newspaper and then driving to his assigned parish for weekend services.[5]

At the time, Wake Forest College, a Baptist institution, was located in the town of the same name. It subsequently relocated to Winston-Salem, becoming Wake Forest University. The only Catholics attending the college were brawny Polish-American football players recruited from the North. One of the selling points the coach would use in attempting to lure players to Wake Forest was the assurance that there was a Catholic church nearby. Koch had mothers calling him to be sure that this was true. On a typical Sunday morning, the rear pews of the church would be filled with football players.

A Belated Trip to Europe and a Key Assignment

Even though a priest's income was modest, Koch had been saving his money, dreaming of a trip to Rome, a dream awakened years before at the time of his aborted assignment to the North American College. Well aware that Bishop Waters did not look kindly on his priests taking vacations, Koch approached his classmate, George Lynch, now Waters' Chancellor, and asked him to wait until the bishop was in a good mood to say that Koch would like to go to Rome, at his own expense, of course. What was Koch's surprise when Waters not only granted permission but also advised the priest to study there, anything he liked. Delighted, Koch spent a year and a half in Rome, earning a licentiate in theology from the Lateran University in 1955. Perhaps being in a particularly generous mood during this period, Waters sent Monsignor Charles J. O'Connor to Europe the following year to study Christian art and architecture. Possibly because O'Connor took no courses but simply toured Europe looking at art, he was the last priest to be granted carte blanche permission to be away from the diocese.

On his return to North Carolina, Koch was given a sensitive appointment. He was sent to Newton Grove where the dust was just set-tling after the racial integration that Waters had imposed in 1953.[6] Koch had two responsibilities: he was to help establish peace in the fractured community, and he was to mentor newly ordained priests. As was seen in Chapter One, Newton Grove had been the headquarters of Redemptorist missionary activity in surrounding counties. When the Redemptorists left,[7] the parish continued to be a mission center housing the Missionary Apostolate described in Chapter Two. Each year newly ordained priests were sent to Newton Grove with the expectation that Koch would instill in them the spirit needed for effective ministry in the state.

The typical routine for the Apostolate in Newton Grove was for the community of priests to have a substantial meal at noon each Wednesday, after which the young priests would pack their suitcases and at about 2 PM get in their cars and drive as much as forty miles to their missions. There, sleeping in a small room off the altar, they administered these mini-parishes, doing everything from ringing the bell to announce mass, to conducting catechism classes and preparing couples for marriage. As time allowed, they prepared the sermon that they would deliver to the handful of Catholics who would attend their mass. After Sunday mass, the neophyte priests would return to Newton Grove where they would compare experiences with one another and receive guidance from Koch.

One young priest asked Father Koch's permission to organize a Christian Family group at his mission. After a few months, Koch asked the priest how the group was progressing. Sheepishly, the young cleric said, "There's not one validly married couple in the whole parish."

Despite such discouraging discoveries, there were successes. For example, each year hundreds of adult North Carolinians were received into the Catholic Church, an impressive achievement considering the small Catholic population and the intensity of anti-Catholic sentiment. Today, through the Rite of Christian Initiation of Adults (RCIA), trained laymen and women provide instructions to groups of candidates in each parish. In Koch's day, priests were the exclusive teachers of men and women wishing to become Catholics, and they instructed each one individually. As Koch reported:

> Each convert was the result of hours of individual instruction and kindly association.... You leave the parlor after two or three instructions in an evening, utterly exhausted from earnest talking and mental alertness.[8]

Mother & Son

Over the following thirty-five years, Koch served in parishes throughout the state. To the normal pastoral stresses of consoling the sorrowing, hearing confessions, preparing and delivering sermons, and balancing the parish books were added a second stint as editor of the diocesan paper, twenty years as diocesan consultor, eighteen years as diocesan director of communications, and eight years on the Priests' Personnel committee. However, there were also moments of humor and opportunities for family devotion.

While pastor at Immaculate Heart of Mary Parish in High Point, Koch became what he termed a "movie star," at least part of him did. Like several other central North Carolina cities, High Point was a center of furniture and carpet manufacturing. One carpet company asked him to dress in mass vestments and walk across carpets they hoped to market to clergy around the country for use in church sanctuaries. Since the camera captured him only from the knees down, he had to keep his shoes shined and alb ironed.

For a number of years Koch's mother lived with him in the rectory. Since in most parishes priests lived alone, a mother's presence provided company for the celibate son as well as allowed him to care for the widowed woman. However, while at Our Lady of Lourdes parish in Raleigh, Koch lived with another priest and the arrangement proved problematic. Accordingly, never shy, Koch asked Bishop Waters for permission to move from the rectory to an apartment that he would share with his mother. To the surprise of many, Waters permitted the arrangement, unprecedented at the time. Koch would take his mother with him to the Catholic Center, and while he worked on the newspaper, she would visit with people in the various offices.

Eventually his mother developed Alzheimer's disease and Koch was obliged to have her admitted to the Maryfield nursing home in High Point, an institution that continues to be operated by the Poor Servants of the Mother God. Now the busy priest's routine entailed working all week at the *NC Catholic*, celebrating mass in Cary on Sunday, and then driving one hundred miles to visit his mother. Koch himself would live his final years in a nursing home, St. Joseph of the Pines Health Care Center in Southern Pines. There he died November 7, 1999 at the age of 83.[9]

As editor of the *NC Catholic* from 1967 to 1976, Koch had been in a position to experience first hand the changes taking place in society and in the church. He was constantly on the move, driving all over the state with his box camera, attending functions, talking with civic and political leaders as well as priests. On one occasion, at a dinner meeting of the North Carolina Catholic Laymen's Association being held in Wilson, a market city for tobacco, the mayor commented that this was the first time in history that blacks and whites were sitting down together in a public dining room in Wilson. The mayor added that it was the Catholics who were instrumental in bringing this about.

The young priest becomes the middle-aged pastor becomes the aging monsignor. For Koch, life came full circle. The Cathedral rectory in Raleigh, where he had spent his first night in the state, more than fifty years later became the site of his final days of ministry. It was the 1990s.

Bishop Hafey was dead, so also were Bishops McGuinness and Waters. So also, in a sense, was the Catholic Church to which Koch had given his life. In an interview in the Cathedral rectory parlor Koch revealed how he himself had, in a sense, died to the old and been born again to the new. His transformation is revealed in his answer to the very broad question: "What was the highlight of your priesthood?"

> It occurred in 1965 when I could begin to implement the dreams I had from seminary days. With the Vatican Council the lid was off. We could face the people, use English, sing. There was so much more room for innovation and imagination. We were no longer boxed in. The new liturgy was flexible enough to let one feel free without going beyond what the church prescribed.

Christopher Dennen (ca. 1864-1939)

If Frederick Koch was a pioneer because he had experienced the church in North Carolina from its early days as a diocese, the other five priests to be considered here were even more pioneering because their careers stretched back into the heart of the state's Vicariate Apostolic period. To these men, Koch would be one of the youngsters, a priest who hadn't known as they had the pain of the protracted conflict with the Belmont Benedictines or the delight of learning that at long last North Carolina was to become a diocese. What Koch and others would take for granted had long been the consuming passion of men like Christopher Dennen. However, although Dennen fought for the suppression of the Vicariate, from what is known of his personality, he would not have joined Koch in welcoming the changes of Vatican II. He wanted a new diocese, not a new Catholic Church.

Long before Dennen participated in the establishment of the Diocese of Raleigh in 1924, he had been the scourge of the Belmont Benedictines. Further, while serving for more than forty years as pastor in Wilmington, the historic mother church of North Carolina, he played a central role in solidifying the segregation of the Church. Finally, as Vicar General and consultor of the Raleigh Diocese until 1933, Dennen was a key advisor to the state's first two bishops.

Conflict between Dennen and the monks had flared up in 1910 over the establishment of the *abbatia nullius*. As was seen in the previous chapter, Father Price and the other secular priests were irate, not only that the Benedictines had gotten Rome to grant them a private diocese within North Carolina but also had conceded them the right to have one of their own perpetually as Vicar Apostolic. Both before and after Price's departure from the state, Dennen had taken a prominent role in the controversy. For example, he wrote to Felix Hintemeyer, Abbot Haid's Benedictine Vicar General, that what he termed the "Joker Clause" in the erection of the *nullius* "has crushed the zeal of your secular clergy."[10] Not content with venting his feelings to an aide, Dennen wrote to Haid himself warning that "this clause will hurt you more than it will benefit you." A few days later, his anger unabated, Dennen again wrote to Hintemeyer accusing the Benedictines of using the Vicariate for their own advantage and profit. In response, Hintemeyer suggested that Dennen wanted the episcopal throne for himself. Perhaps he did; at the very least he wanted it to be occupied by a secular cleric, not a Benedictine monk.

Paradoxically, Dennen owed a lot to Haid. Even as the choleric priest was venting his anger, a magnificent new church was being constructed for him in Wilmington, one that owed its existence to the vision, fund raising ability and planning of Haid. In this new building, as in the old, Dennen would preside with all the passion of a prophet. If Haid was "Lord" of Belmont, Dennen was "Lord" of Wilmington. And he would be such even longer than Haid, holding the Wilmington pastorate from 1891 to 1935. There is substantial evidence that Dennen was the proverbial authoritarian Catholic pastor ruling the parish as if it were his personal kingdom.

The relationship between the two men went back to Dennen's student days at St. Vincent's Seminary in Pennsylvania where young Father Haid was on the staff. At the time, neither man could have dreamt that their lives would intertwine in far-off North Carolina, especially since initially Dennen had been a candidate for the Diocese of Harrisburg. However, he transferred his affiliation to North Carolina in 1891 where by then Haid was Vicar Apostolic. The Vicar's confidence in the young man is evidenced by the fact that he was immediately assigned to the pro-cathedral parish of St. Thomas, Wilmington. Psychologists might explain subsequent developments in terms of a son rebelling against his father. In any case, Dennen would contribute significantly to the sorrow of Haid's final years.

Dedication of the Wilmington Pro-Cathedral

St. Thomas Church, dedicated in 1847, had struggled along for decades serving the religious needs of a Catholic population of fewer than one hundred people. Stability was given to the community by

Father Thomas Murphy, who had founded the parish in 1845 and who died of yellow fever during the Civil War. His eighteen years as pastor was by far the longest tenure of any priest in one location in North Carolina up to that time. Eventually, Christopher Dennen would surpass that record more than twofold.

After the Civil War, as has been seen, Father Mark Gross assumed the Wilmington pastorate, assisting Bishop Gibbons in laying the foundation for the Vicariate Apostolic. Despite the fact that St. Thomas was to have the status of pro-cathedral, conditions in the war-ravaged state were so bleak that no thought could be given to the construction of a larger church. In fact, Wilmington was fortunate to have a church at all considering the poverty of the state and the depleted Catholic population.

However, by the time Dennen became pastor, the economy had improved and thoughts turned to the replacement of the aging church. Like Gibbons before him, Haid used St. Thomas as the pro-cathedral, although the Abbey church at Belmont held that title as well. Furthermore, like most people, Haid felt that Wilmington as the largest city in the state would one day be the seat of a diocese and therefore deserved a more substantial church.[11]

Actually, Haid's plan was even more ambitious than a cathedral-ready church for Wilmington. He envisioned a similar structure for Asheville as well. In his grand design, there would be three breathtaking cathedrals: Wilmington on the coast, Asheville in the mountains, and Belmont in the center. The wonder is that the plan actually materialized and despite the fact that there was little money and few Catholics the three churches sent their spires majestically into the sky. Today all three remain impressive tributes to the building genius of Haid. In light of such marvels, it is hard to understand how Dennen could accuse the abbot of draining off money from the vicariate.

Construction of the new Wilmington church began in 1908 and was completed in 1912. Although Dennen would criticize Haid severely during the intervening years, both men put their feelings aside and gathered all the civic and religious dignitaries they could marshal for the grand dedication ceremony. Haid presided and Dennen preached and a new era began for the Catholics of Wilmington. Unfortunately, it was an era of increased racial polarization.

Segregated Wilmington Churches

Typically when a new Catholic church is built, it retains the name of the one it replaces. That was the original plan for Wilmington. However, racial reality led to a revision of those plans and the new edifice was given the name "St. Mary." Just how the change came about is not completely clear. Since the new church was to be several blocks away from the old, on the corner of Fifth Avenue and Ann Street, the logical thing would have been to sell old St. Thomas on Dock Street to help defray the cost of constructing the new building. In fact, some parcels of land owned by the church were sold precisely for that purpose. However, St. Thomas was retained. The final statement of receipts and expenditures for St. Mary, which Dennen sent to Haid, is instructive.[12]

The total cost of the Church and the adjacent priests' home was $95,844, of which the church itself was itemized as $63,335. The sale of two parcels of property brought $23,000, donations $14,445, a building fund $7,399, mortgages and loans $39,000, and a grant from Mother Katherine Drexel $12,000. That last item is particularly significant. Drexel's money was for the purchase of the old St. Thomas, so that it could be available for the use of Black Catholics. She did not intend that the facility be segregated or that St. Mary exclude blacks, but unwittingly she set up a situation that led to just such a development.[13]

Upon completion of St. Mary's in 1912, Dennen's assistant, Father Thomas P. Hayden, assumed responsibility for St. Thomas while Dennen himself remained at the new church. The Mother Drexel-mandated understanding was that, although St. Thomas was to be the religious home of black Catholics, anyone was free to attend and, similarly, blacks were to be free to attend St. Mary. However, two years later, Dennen wrote to Haid requesting that each church be restricted along racial lines. The bishop concurred.[14] How this new arrangement came about reflects the conditions under which the church had to operate at the time, but also its reluctance to take a firm stand in favor of racial justice.

Dennen offered two reasons for requesting the change in policy: First, Catholics were being "severely criticized for mingling with colored," and second, the black Catholics themselves were not happy with the arrangement.

The Wilmington pastor's correspondence with Haid on this matter was in the form of a report from a "parish finance committee," a group of men called together at Haid's insistence to provide some belat-

ed lay input on managing the parish's finances, made more complex by
the debt incurred in the construction of St. Mary. This handpicked group
now provided Dennen with the convenient opening to insist that the
proposed segregation of the churches came not from him but from influential laymen. In an unspecified allusion to what had occurred in
Charlotte, Dennen says that if the mingling of the races continued in
Wilmington, there would be similar trouble in Wilmington. Catholics
had worked hard to be accepted as good southerners and violation of the
race norms had cast a cloud over them. Besides concern for anti-
Catholic sentiment, Dennen also alluded to the fact that the attendance
of whites at St. Thomas had resulted in a loss of income for St. Mary,
his parish.

As to the black Catholic perspective, Dennen wrote that "two
of the best colored Catholics" had told him that they did not feel at
home at St. Thomas "as there were too many whites present and their
presence was defeating the purposes of the colored mission. They are
excluded from the choir and feel they have no part in the parish."
Conscious of Drexel's stipulation, Dennen informed Haid that he had
advised the black Catholics to write to Drexel, explaining the situation
from their point of view. Dennen added: "I can't see how you could be
held to the letter of the agreement where serious damage is done to both
congregations."

Whatever all the dynamics, Dennen recommended a total segregation of the races and submitted "Rules for the Government of the
Parishes in Wilmington," which Haid edited and approved. The bishop's handwritten notes say that the regulations were "in order to preserve peace and harmony among the Catholics of Wilmington." It was
not just on religious occasions, but at social and recreational events as
well, that racial separation was to be maintained. For example, the regulations included the stipulation that "neither pastor is permitted to have
boys of the other parish attend any meeting where both races are present."

Dennen was well aware of the painful history of race relations
in Wilmington. It was in that city during the early years of his tenure as
pastor that the most bloody racial insurrection in the post-Civil War
South had occurred. On November 10, 1898, a group of white men
overthrew the lawfully constituted municipal authority that in the wake
of Reconstruction contained a number of black officials. The rebellion,
which resulted in the deaths of a number of blacks, marked the elimi-

nation of blacks not only from political life in Wilmington but in the state of North Carolina as a whole. It also emboldened other states to follow suit. Within a few years, blacks had been disfranchised throughout the South.[15] As one newspaper bluntly editorialized, "It requires no argument to prove that a white man will not consent to be ruled by a Negro."[16] Nor, it would seem, to tolerate integrated churches.

In 1916, the separate status of St. Thomas was solidified still further. At Bishop Haid's request and on the recommendation of Mother Drexel, the Josephite Fathers assumed responsibility for the church and for the black parish of St. Joseph in New Bern as well.[17] For his part, certainly frustrated with continuous bickering with Dennen, Father Hayden, a secular priest, went off to be a World War I military chaplain.

Dennen's Final Years

The strength and brashness of Dennen ebbed with the years, but some of his characteristic qualities remained. For years he had taken it upon himself to report to Haid the indiscretions of his fellow priests. This practice he continued throughout the Hafey years, becoming a sort of one-man clerical secret police. So in 1933, he reported to the bishop that a priest, "your protégé," had gone out:

> on a date with a blonde. He put her in his car and went into the sacristy to look around and see if the coast was clear. Then he came over to the house and said to the colored servant, 'You have seen nothing, you know nothing; keep your damn mouth shut.'

In his account, Dennen doesn't explain how he was able to spy undetected on the wayward priest. What is perhaps sad, Dennen made this charge in the very letter in which he resigned as Vicar General "for health reasons."[18]

Two years later, his health failing further, Dennen resigned as pastor of St. Mary. "I feel I have outgrown my usefulness and I believe a younger man can rejuvenate the congregation's interest." Ironically, the "younger man," Father James A. Manley, died within a year of Dennen himself.

Despite his infirmities, Dennen lingered on into the administration of Bishop Eugene McGuinness, who succeeded Bishop Hafey in December 1937. Still the dean of clergy, Dennen wrote to McGuinness: "I have been here forty-six years. From what I know of the North Carolina people, you will be most welcome as the bishop of Raleigh."

A few days later, McGuinness graciously replied, assuring Dennen that he remained a diocesan consultor and adding, "I expect much aid from your very wide experience."

However, there was to be little sage advice for the end was near. Late in 1938, an ailing Dennen was admitted to Mercy Hospital in Charlotte. From there he wrote to McGuinness and, in the pleading tone of a prisoner, asked to be released from the hospital. But it was not to be. The man wasted away, dying in October 1939. The final item in his file is the bill for his funeral -- $459.56, including an 8% clergy discount.

Michael Aloysius Irwin (1864-1952)

Just as tyrannical as Dennen in some respects, but much more spiritual and intellectual, was another of the pillars of the early diocese. Because he left a voluminous paper trail, more is known about Mike Irwin than about any other North Carolina priest. His commitment to his calling more than compensated for his widely reported eccentricities.

Today, with married Episcopal priests becoming Catholic priests and with the ordination of widowers and divorced Catholic men, it is not unusual to hear about men who experience marriage and Latin rite priesthood. Both North Carolina dioceses have married (and formerly married) priests serving in parishes with no significant problems either from the laity or from their celibate colleagues.[19] However, such men were exceptional in earlier generations. Mike Irwin was one of those exceptions even if his marriage was, as he put it, *ratum non-con-sumatum*, that is, legally ratified but not physically consummated.

As a young man Irwin, who was born in Norfolk, Virginia to Irish-born parents, established a romantic relationship with a girl. Unfortunately, she developed tuberculosis and was hospitalized in Southern Pines, North Carolina. Determined to marry her anyway, Irwin did so as his young bride lay dying in a hospital bed. Since there was no parish in Southern Pines at the time, the marriage was recorded in the Sacred Heart Cathedral register.

As Irwin would explain it many years later:

> For five weeks in my 28th year I was bound by a *matrimonium ratum* to a most innocent maid of nineteen whom I had converted (*Deo adjuvante*) to the True Faith, and married when she was stricken with a grave disorder that carried her off. She went down to her virginal

grave leaving me the consolation of her pure love and the memory of her virtues to sustain me.[20]

The death of his wife brought about a major change in the course of Irwin's life. Leaving the world of business where he had been employed as a secretary to officials for ten years, Irwin entered Belmont Abbey College in 1896 and was ordained a priest in 1900. Despite the fact that he was thirty-three years old at the time, Irwin lived to celebrate the Golden Jubilee of his priesthood. At the time of his death in 1952, he was the oldest priest in the diocese, and the most colorful.[21] He had served -- and given extensive, unsolicited advice to-- every bishop from Leo Haid who ordained him to Vincent Waters who buried him.

From Nazareth to Newton Grove (1904-1928)

Irwin's introduction to priesthood in North Carolina could not have been more auspicious. He was assigned to work at Nazareth with Father Price, who in 1900 was at the peak of his physical energies and of his determination to convert North Carolina. However, although at first Irwin was an enthusiastic disciple, the relationship with Price would be brief and at times contentious. Yet the impact would have a deep effect and would last a lifetime.[22] In his waning years, as one of the last survivors of the Price era, Irwin was called upon frequently to relate his recollections of those turn-of-the-century days. He did so with zest, embellishing the tale with each telling.

After what was in effect a three year apprenticeship with Price, Irwin's subsequent career was divided neatly into two twenty-four year pastorates, each in one of the historic parishes of North Carolina. The first, and most vigorous, was in Newton Grove where he constructed a network of Catholic chapels that rivaled that of Father Price. Then, in his sixties, feeling that he was slowing down, Irwin asked to be transferred to a less demanding post. Sent to New Bern, he surprised everyone, including himself, by serving for an equally long tenure. In a will drafted late in life, Irwin said that although his heart was in Newton Grove, he wished that his body be buried in New Bern so as not to offend the people whom he had pastored for more than two decades. His wish was granted. Although the New Bern parish plant has been relocated to the suburbs, Irwin's grave remains next to the original St. Paul church, in front of the building which had been his home and which now serves as the deanery offices for Catholic Social Ministries.

Although he shared Price's missionary zeal, Irwin was temperamentally different from his mentor, more outgoing, impetuous, and
even brash. As pastor of St. Mark in Newton Grove he could stretch his
wings, develop his own style, be himself. Under Irwin's leadership,
Newton Grove, which one day would be synonymous with integration,
in the early years of the 20th Century was a showcase of energetic effort
to evangelize the South.

Initially, also, Irwin got along better with Bishop Haid than did
Price. In part, this was due to the fact that in the first decade of the 20th
Century, Haid's career as Vicar Apostolic was at its high point, with
progress measured by money raised from out-of-state donors and from
the sound of hammers nailing boards together for new churches. In
1908, a delighted Haid wrote to Irwin in Newton Grove: "I hope to visit
the Eastern part of the state soon.... Church building is going on from
Asheville to Wilmington – all along the line." Some of that construction
was taking place in the hamlets surrounding Newton Grove, where
Irwin was quickly erecting chapels in anticipation of the massive conversions that never materialized.[23]

However, the era of good will did not last. Little more than two
years later, a Haid letter to Irwin revealed quite a different tone:

> I am informed – I hope it is not true – that you took part in a meeting
> of priests – immediately after hearing the will of the Holy Father
> solemnly expressed in the presence of His delegate – to protest
> against his arrangement, and this without knowing the circumstances
> and without consulting your Bishop who has certainly not been want-
> ing in kindness and consideration towards you for many years. You
> may have been misled or looked at matters only from one side – and
> that the wrong side – but I certainly deeply deplore such action and
> deeply feel the shame of it all.[24]

The precipitating issue was the granting of the *abbatia nullius*
to the Benedictines. As has been discussed earlier, the creation of the
mini-diocese around Belmont Abbey marked the end of any positive
feelings there might have been between Haid and the secular clergy. As
conciliatory as he was in many respects, Irwin joined Price and Dennen
in objecting to what the priests saw as the excessive amassing of power
by the monks. As Irwin wrote in reply to his bishop:

> There has been some action taken by all the secular priests protesting
> against the lowered condition of the Vicariate and seeking lawful rem-

edy – by having it established as a diocese.... The secular priests feel
themselves sorely aggrieved by many things. They feel that you have
not sought to win their confidence, offering your heart to your monks
and not to them.[25]

Also, like Price and Dennen, Irwin wrote to Cardinal Gibbons.
Although his letter to the Archbishop of Baltimore was more charitable
than those of his colleagues, it unambiguously stressed the dissatisfaction of the North Carolina clergy:

All of us missionary-rectors are painfully aware of the blight that has
come over the affairs of the Vicariate on account of the divided energies of our abbot-bishop. We are ill at ease in his presence, feeling
somewhat like stepsons. We love and admire him for his fine qualities
even while we say and feel this and would wish for closer union. But
it seems impossible.[26]

Somewhat prescient, in the letter to Gibbons Irwin suggested
that a diocese be erected in Raleigh. However, he would have to wait
another fifteen years for this to come to pass.

The conflict with Haid did not distract Irwin from the formation of the rural towns around Newton Grove into a vibrant mission territory. To a large extent, what success he achieved was made possible
by Mother Katharine Drexel and, ironically, by the Benedictines.

The year before Irwin was ordained, Drexel had donated
$1,500 to aid in the erection of a residence for priests in Newton Grove.
That money, which Haid had solicited, came with the usual Drexel conditions:

1. A resident priest must be assigned to Newton Grove;
2. Said priest was to give equal care to the colored people as to
   the whites;
3. Should the priest be removed, the $1,500 was to be "placed
at the disposition of Mother Katharine or her successor in office to be
used as she may direct for the colored missions in North Carolina."
Although he didn't really have a priest to spare, Haid agreed, laying the
basis not only for Irwin's work, but also for the racial integration incident of 1953.[27]

The first full-time pastor assigned to Newton Grove was a
Benedictine monk, Father Edward, who reported to Haid on February 1,
1901 that there were 250 white and 60 colored Catholics "under his
charge." The round numbers suggest that Father Edward was estimat-

ing, not really sure how many Catholics there were scattered over the several counties that comprised the parish. Although he hoped to open a parochial school shortly, the dire financial condition of the parish was suggested by the postscript he added to the report: "From January 1st, 1901 I expect $300 salary per year. This has been promised. With 60 colored Catholics I might expect a small piece of the colored mission fund."[28]

Although the report dated Jan. 1, 1903 stated that a white school had been completed and that Mother Katherine had sent him $400 for the construction of a colored school, under the heading "children attending parochial school" Father Edward wrote the word "None." A school without teachers was of no use, and a Catholic school without sisters was a financial impossibility. It would fall to Irwin when he became pastor in 1904 to find the sisters and open and operate both schools.

Never shy about asking for money, Irwin initiated a correspondence with Mother Katherine that enabled him over time to build nine mission chapels as well as a new parish church.[29] His glowing reports to the Philadelphia nun led to her visit to Newton Grove in 1910, where Irwin proudly showed her what her investment had produced. By that time, Dominican Sisters of Newburgh, NY were staffing both the white and the black schools, and apparently the small but thriving Catholic community convinced Drexel that the prospects for growth were encouraging. In any case, as has been seen, this unique benefactor continued to send money to Irwin, a large donation in 1921 resulting in the construction of a hall that would serve as a gathering place for black Catholics. It was this building, converted into St. Benedict church, which led to the integration action of 1953, the year after Irwin's death.[30]

Irwin on the Transition to a Diocese

At the time of Haid's death in 1924, Irwin was sixty years old and firmly ensconced as the not always benign patriarch of the community of simple rural folk who comprised his congregation. Since the people could get to church only once a week, Sunday was the pastor's one opportunity to provide as full a serving of religion as his energy and the people's endurance could sustain. By 10 a.m. the white wood church was surrounded by farm wagons and horses and mules snorting and stomping their feet after hauling families for miles over rutted country roads. Brushing dust from their clothes, mothers and fathers herded children inside as Father Irwin began his hour of religious instruction drilling the faithful on Catholic teaching, never forgetting to remind them that the mercy of God was counterbalanced by the threat of eternal damnation. If he saw a visitor in the congregation, he was known to go through the entire catechism.[31]

At 11 o'clock mass Irwin insisted that everyone sing. In full liturgical vestments, the massive cleric would stride up and down the aisle playing his violin, leading the music, and whacking the head of anyone singing off key.

It was this self-assured man who took it upon himself to send Archbishop Curley his assessment of the state of religion in North Carolina as the church embarked on the long-anticipated new stage in its development:

> Beginnings are always precarious. The Church is new here, but the culture and traditions of our region are old. Not withstanding all their faults and the invincible heresies of our Southern people, they have nevertheless a high appreciation of and are quickly won by true humility, charity and in particular by a noble and almost childlike sincerity.[32]

Shortly thereafter, perhaps feeling some qualms about the barrage of attacks on Haid, Irwin wrote a conciliatory note to Haid's Benedictine successor. The letter sums up the sentiment of the diocesan clergy as at last they achieved their goal:

> We were for some time between two fires – between the fire of love and loyalty to our late revered Bishop and the fire of desire for the permanent settlement of our ecclesiastical status, as all were agreed that it would be better in the long run for the state to become a Diocese.[33]

Problems in Newton Grove

Irwin's pastorate was not without its difficulties. Perhaps the most significant was the abrupt withdrawal of the Dominican sisters in 1922, a severe blow to his ego as well as to the Newton Grove mission. In his report to the bishop for 1907, Irwin had written in the margin: "About 90% of the children attend parochial school. Have no hope of the outcome in regard to those who do not send their children to the Catholic school on account of the bitterness of anti-Catholic prejudice." At the time there were 59 children in the white school and 22 in the colored school. By 1922, the enrollment had shown minimal increase: 61

in the white school and 26 in the colored. Irwin complained that as Sampson County constructed schools and provided bus service, Catholics began sending their children to those more modern facilities.

But the withdrawal of the Dominicans was not due to low enrollment but rather to their own deplorable living conditions. The dilapidated convent had no indoor plumbing, and the money provided for the sisters' support required that they live in an impoverished state unknown to women religious in other sectors of the country. Ultimately, the Dominican superior general decided that the welfare of the sisters required the abandonment of Newton Grove. With the sisters gone, Irwin kept the schools open with lay teachers, but enrollment fell still further.

Never having had the success of Dr. Monk in winning converts to Catholicism, Irwin became embittered. In 1926 he reported: "On account of the danger of contamination of our children by a barbarous race, I make no effort to have non-Catholics in our schools." A year earlier in his annual report, he had commented even more bluntly:

> Catholics and Protestants are sharply divided in this benighted, barbarous territory. Protestant morals and culture are very low and it would be dangerous to have large Protestant children in our schools. Small children can be accepted without danger, but they are not offering as the grand new public school buildings draw them all.

Clearly it was time to move on; the acid seeping into the weary priest's soul could not help but compromise his work. And the resourceful man devised a graceful and perhaps brilliant way to do so. In a letter to Bishop Hafey, he argued that religious order priests should staff Newton Grove! He who had championed diocesan priests was now led to conclude that there were few of his secular colleagues willing "to endure the labors" which he had sustained for more than twenty years. The parish, which since the days of Doctor Monk in the 1870's had been pointed to with pride as a rare North Carolina success story, had become in fact a sort of albatross, its glory in the past and its poverty in the present. Specifically, Irwin recommended "the establishment of a group of Franciscan priests and brothers, young men, who could carry out perpetually" a long-term commitment to the frontier parish.[34]

This suggestion coincided nicely with Bishop Hafey's desire to attract additional religious order priests to North Carolina. However, it was not to the Franciscans but to the Redemptorists that he offered the challenge of Newton Grove. The bishop could -- more with hope than recent results -- depict it as a promising field for attracting converts as well as for a ministry to African Americans. For its part, the order was ready to undertake such work and, exceeding Hafey's expectations, agreed to send four priests, two to staff the parish and two others who would be in residence in Newton Grove as a base for missionary outreach throughout the state. Furthermore, the Redemptorists agreed to renovate St. Mark's facilities, including the convent in anticipation of enlisting an order of sisters to revitalize the nearly moribund schools.[35] In expectation of substantial growth, Hafey bought sixteen acres of land adjacent to the current church property and turned the parish over to the new recruits, who soon renamed it Holy Redeemer, thereby putting the stamp of their presence firmly on the outpost. For his part, Irwin could move on to a new assignment, confident that the parish to which he had devoted so many years was in competent hands.

Irwin at New Bern

If, for Catholics, Newton Grove was indelibly associated with John Monk, so New Bern was synonymous with William Gaston. Both men were authentic southerners; no one could consider them interlopers from the alien North. In addition, the Newton Grove physician was a convert, a dream come true, someone who "miraculously" was moved to embrace Catholicism in a hostile environment. For his part, Gaston, a lawyer, had been so totally accepted by the Protestant population that he had been elected to public office numerous times. Unfortunately, few Monks and Gastons would emerge in the Twentieth Century. By default, leadership fell to priests like Irwin, men who often equated inflexibility with holiness and considered compliance with church regulations more important than compassion. Three incidents from Irwin's years in New Bern can illustrate his style.

A Mr. C. J. McCarthy had left a considerable sum of money to St. Paul Church. Subsequently, his widow asked that Mendelssohn's wedding march be permitted in the church for the marriage of her son and his non-Catholic bride. When Irwin refused to allow such "pagan music" in the church, the woman persisted; begging this one small favor, she argued that her future daughter-in-law had agreed to the simple ceremony prescribed for "mixed religion" marriages and to raise her children as Catholics. Irwin saw his adamant refusal to yield not as heartless rigidity but as fidelity to principles.

A second example of Irwin's rigor occurred in 1945. In reaction to a picture that had appeared in a Catholic publication, he wrote to the priest-principal of the Catholic high school in Waynesville, expressing shock at what he considered the immodest athletic attire of the school's girls' basketball team. When the priest, Rev. A.F. Rohrbacher, replied that all the other Catholic girls' schools were sponsoring teams that wore the same attire, Irwin contacted Bishop Waters. Within a week, Rohrbacker notified Irwin that the school's athletic department for girls had been discontinued.

Finally, in 1949, Irwin criticized a Catholic news agent for selling what Irwin called "sexual material." The defense that Catholic agents all over the country were selling this material made no impression on the priest; what's sinful is sinful, no matter how many people were doing it.[36]

If the man was rigid, it was because a church that prided itself on its immutability had taught him to be that way. It would be this very issue of stability versus change that would challenge so many Catholics after the Second Vatican Council, none more so than Bishop Vincent Waters. Although Irwin would be gone long before the Council, during the first few years of Waters' time in North Carolina, he would have no more persistent a correspondent or stronger supporter than the legendary New Bern pastor. For Waters, Irwin represented the unwavering commitment and strong spirituality that he desired in all his priests.

The quotation that opens this chapter is an example of the advice Irwin gave his bishop. It is striking witness to the divergent thinking of which Irwin was capable. On the surface, it would seem that North Carolina needed activists, men and women who would be out among the people, ministering to Catholics and attempting to convert others. And here was Irwin, the most prominent activist of all, arguing that the most pressing need was for a community of contemplative nuns, women who would remain secluded in their cloister taking no part in the active work of the church. Although the idea that prayer was the key to success was not new, it had not been presented before in such a convincing fashion. And Waters listened.

In 1956, a small community of Carmelite nuns was established in Durham, North Carolina for precisely the reason Irwin had given – to pray for the church in the state. This was the period in Catholic Church history when devotion to the French Carmelite nun, St. Therese of Lisieux, was at its peak. "The Little Flower," who had spent her short life in the cloister, had captivated the Catholic imagination. Perhaps the failure of the church to make substantial headway was due to over reliance on human effort and not enough dependence on God's grace. In activist America in particular, a turning inward occurred, a reassessment of the conviction that hard work could achieve anything. However, the Carmelites' presence in North Carolina was to be brief and contentious. In 1966, the four sisters abandoned the Durham Carmel without so much as advising Bishop Waters of their intention. Subsequent efforts to bring in nuns from other places did not succeed. As had been true of the Church in general, North Carolina proved to be an inhospitable setting for contemplative communities.[37]

Irwin himself was not immune from worldly vanity. In June 1940, Bishop McGuinness nominated him and a few other clerical warriors for the title of monsignor, an honor granted by the pope. The 75-year old pastor, who had lived his life in simplicity, now became like a bride compiling her trousseau as he gathered the paraphernalia needed for the new status. Not able to afford the elaborate and expensive regalia, he contacted Bishop Hafey in Scranton, who sent Irwin some robes worn by his departed predecessor. However, the rochets sent were worn and frayed.[38] Accordingly, Irwin wrote to Cardinal Dennis Dougherty of Philadelphia asking if he could send some of the needed items. With a bow to modesty, Irwin wrote to the Cardinal that the pope had deigned "to raise me from the dung-hill and place me among the princes of the people by making me one of his Domestic Prelates."

The Instruments of Suffering

Despite the forgivable elation over being made a monsignor, Irwin's passion for the priesthood remained strong even as his body weakened. In 1950, he wrote to Waters:

> Very few of us are spared so long to stand and offer the sacrifice of the New Law and to preach the Gospel of the Incarnate God, and to me a Golden Jubilee would be a solemn act of Thanksgiving for the mercies of the Lord which I hope to sing forever.

Irwin did celebrate that Golden Jubilee, but he knew that the end was near. In May of 1951, he asked to be excused from the annual priests' retreat "as I am not physically strong enough to attend the exercises and the going and the coming." In August, he again wrote to Waters, predicting: "very likely this is my last birthday on earth. I am perfectly satisfied with all of God's dispensations in my regard." His forecast was correct; Irwin died on Jan. 6, 1952, the oldest and most widely known priest in North Carolina. But there was something about the gruff, garrulous warrior that no one knew. He had been a man who subjected his body to the type of penances usually associated with medieval saints.

The Reverend Edward Gilbert, executor of Irwin's "estate," did not find much in the late priest's rectory bedroom: a few ancient books, some tattered monsignor's robes, and three very old pictures. The pictures were of the three women in Irwin's life: Mary, the Mother of Jesus, his own mother, and the woman he had married more than fifty years ago, her image ever young both in the photo and in the blustering old man's heart.

The only other items found, hidden behind some dusty books, were the following:

1. A crown of thorns,
2. A belt into which were driven a number of tacks, to be worn around the waist,
3. A piece of barbed wire having a number of sharp prongs,
4. A piece of wood having at one end six tacks,
5. Several leather thongs, most of which had knots on the end.

In his report to Bishop Waters, Gilbert wrote:

> It is my firm conviction, based on knowledge that Monsignor Irwin unwittingly conveyed to me in a conversation, that he often used these instruments on his body to bring it, as he would say, "under control." It is my belief that the punishment he inflicted upon himself was severe... .It is also my belief that the disciplinary practice was carried out during his pastorate in Newton Grove, when the Monsignor was younger and more robust.[39]

Although a very different kind of man from Irwin, Gilbert himself was another of the faithful stewards of the early church in North Carolina.

Edward Gilbert (1902-1983)

Correspondence in the late 1920's illustrates the process by which a young man became a priest in North Carolina. In October 1928, Edward Thomas Gilbert wrote to Bishop Hafey:

Kindly allow me the privilege of addressing you relative to adoption in your diocese. Being very anxious to work in that part of God's Garden where I can do the most good and, harboring a deep interest for missionary work, I take this liberty to make application for the Raleigh diocese. [40]

The 26-year-old Gilbert, born in Brooklyn on June 9, 1902, did not at first plan to become a priest. After attending public elementary and high schools, he worked in what he called "accountancy" in New York City for six years. As the thought of being a priest emerged, Edward commuted to St. Francis College, Brooklyn from Richmond Hill, Queens, where his family now resided. When he applied to St. Francis Seminary in Loretto, Pennsylvania in 1927, his parish priest wrote in a letter on Gilbert's behalf: "He is a very sincere, honest, and devout young man.... We are very happy to recommend him to your parental care with the prayerful hope that he will persevere unto the end." Off to Pennsylvania went Gilbert, still uncertain where he would exercise his priestly ministry. At the time he wrote to Bishop Hafey, he was in the second year of the four-year theology program.

For some reason, it took Hafey three months to respond, certainly creating anxiety in the man who was required to find a sponsoring bishop in order to advance to the third year of studies. But at last the letter of acceptance arrived. Furthermore, Hafey invited Gilbert, "if you found it convenient," to visit Raleigh during the Easter recess in order to establish his domicile in the state and receive tonsure and minor orders, "provided you are recommended for same by the seminary authorities."[41]

Recommendations granted, Gilbert made his first visit to North Carolina and duly signed the standard "Profession of Faith" and a promise to be loyal to the Catholic Church and to serve the diocese "for the salvation of souls." The oath which he, and all would-be priests, took referred specifically to his "complete adherence to all the prescriptions of the encyclical *Pascendi* and the decree *Lamentabili*," the controversial papal documents which called upon Catholics to adjure many modern scientific and political developments. Although the statements of later popes largely negated these decrees of Pope Pius IX, they shaped the perspective of priests for many years. Gilbert, in particular, would remain a Pius IX priest, his mind and spirit never at ease with the changes that would occur as he aged. His fidelity remained rooted in the church as he knew it when he was ordained a priest in May of 1931. By the time he would commemorate his Golden Jubilee in 1981, the Catholic Church had long since switched to a vernacular liturgy. Indicative of the man's traditionalist orientation, Gilbert opted to mark the occasion by celebrating a Latin Mass.[42]

"Little Washington"

In 1932, Gilbert began a twenty-year pastorate in one of the most unusual parishes in the diocese, St. Agnes, the "white parish" in Washington, North Carolina.[43] What made it unusual was that this was the only place in the state where a black parish had more Catholics than the white. For example, in 1935, while Gilbert's St. Agnes counted 128 members, Mother of Mercy around the corner had 172. Furthermore, the tiny church of St. Agnes had no Catholic school, whereas six Immaculate Heart of Mary (IHM) sisters taught 275 black students at Mother of Mercy.

The existence of the relatively successful black parish was due to the Passionist Fathers, who established it in 1925 and continued to subsidize it year after year the way that the Redemptorists would subsidize the Newton Grove parish. So, for example, in 1929 the income from Sunday collections for the entire year was about $300; everything else was from the Passionists and their publication, *The Sign* magazine, which adopted the little mission as a special cause. The prime mover for Mother of Mercy was Father Mark Mosslein, the founder and long time pastor. He loved the parish so much that he used the money received on the occasion of his fiftieth anniversary of priesthood to add a second story to the school building. However, the enthusiasm over the success of Mother of Mercy might have been exaggerated. For example, despite the existence of its subsidized school and church, in 1935 there were but two infant and two adult baptisms, while St. Agnes had six and four respectively.[44]

Fifteen years later, in 1950, the Catholic population of each parish had risen by one quarter with St. Agnes at 160 and Mother of Mercy at 222. Also, St. Agnes now had a parochial school. However, and ironically in the racist South, Mother of Mercy had the only state-accredited school in Washington. Neither the public schools nor St. Agnes could be accredited due to the lack of such facilities as science labs and libraries. Accordingly, ambitious black parents had a better opportunity than did whites to procure a quality education for their children.[45]

Indicative of the expectation that Catholic schools would be a conduit for converts, of the 102 pupils in St.Agnes' school in 1950, 80 were non-Catholics. Similarly, half the children at Mother of Mercy were not Catholics. The church's investment of personnel in the town was substantial. Although Gilbert worked alone at St. Agnes, there were three Passionist priests assigned to Mother of Mercy. This meant that "little" Washington had four priests ministering to a combined Catholic population of fewer than 400, while in the two schools, a total of thirteen IHM sisters taught 328 boys and girls, more than half of whom were not Catholic.

First Superintendent of Schools

With perhaps some degree of hyperbole, one southern writer had said of the North Carolina of the 1920's: "For a mighty long spell North Carolina was asleep, becoming finally the slouchiest and shabbiest and most slothful of the states below the Mason-Dixon line."[46] Bishop McGuinness and Gilbert didn't want the Catholic Church to lag behind as the state attempted to shake off this negative image. Although the objective was sectarian, the Church believed that the most productive way in which it could participate in the redemption of the state was by establishing quality schools. To coordinate the effort, in 1940 McGuinness appointed Gilbert the first diocesan superintendent of schools. However, as was true of all early administrators, Gilbert wore two hats; he was expected to supervise the two-dozen Catholic schools in the state even as he continued in his role as pastor.

Although there had been Catholic schools since the Sisters of Mercy opened a girls' academy in Wilmington in 1869, they had been administered by the religious communities that staffed them and the pastors of the parishes in which they were located. Gilbert's appointment was the first move towards standardizing curriculum, insuring the qualifications of teachers, and obtaining state certification for the schools. He held the post until 1967 by which time the number of Catholic schools in the state had increased to forty, staffed by several hundred religious sisters.[47]

Goldsboro Pastorate

Although bishops are not restricted in the length of time they may leave priests in one parish, in recent years the practice has developed of appointing pastors to six-year terms and frequently renewing the appointment for another six years. They are then transferred. The prevailing wisdom is that it is better both for the priest himself and for the parish that he not become too entrenched in one location. Before the 1970's, the practice was quite different, with many pastors in effect appointed for life, or at least for extremely lengthy periods of time. As has been seen, Mike Irwin served for nearly half a century in just two parishes. The same was true of Ed Gilbert, who in 1952 was transferred to St. Mary in Goldsboro, a parish with five times as many Catholics as St. Agnes in Washington. Just as Irwin spent his younger years in the "missionary" Newton Grove parish and then in middle age moved to the more settled and financially secure New Bern parish, so also Gilbert, after being on the fringes of Catholic North Carolina, moved closer to the center. He would remain in Goldsboro for twenty-five years, at which time, having reached age seventy-five, he retired.

Besides being pastor of a more prestigious parish, Gilbert, made a Monsignor in 1956, the 25th anniversary of his ordination, became an advisor to Bishop Waters, a man with whom he was ideologically compatible. As has been seen, Gilbert supported the beleaguered bishop during the controversies that would swirl around him in the wake of Vatican II. At the time of Gilbert's retirement in 1977, the diocese of Raleigh had a new bishop in Joseph Gossman, and Gilbert, not feeling at home in the eastern part of the state any longer, moved to the recently established diocese of Charlotte, headed by his old Raleigh associate, Michael Begley. It was in Charlotte, far from both Washington and Goldsboro that Gilbert spent his final years. If Gilbert died far from the scenes of his ministry, another North Carolina priest never strayed far from the one parish with which he was associated for more than half a century.

William F. O'Brien (1872-1960)

Although Father Price failed to convert many North Carolinians or to establish a religious order of priests that would carry the Gospel to every corner of the state, he did achieve one unintended effect -- he had a profound influence on two men who would be major stabilizing forces of the North Carolina church. One was Mike Irwin, discussed above; the other was "Billy" O'Brien. These men did not have the expansive vision of Price, but they remained in the state for the entire span of their long lives. For his part, O'Brien devoted himself to but a single parish. In 1907 he became the first resident pastor of Immaculate Conception Church in Durham and remained there until his death in 1960. Also, unique among North Carolina priests, he published his memoirs, which provide the most comprehensive view available of the life of a priest and the evolution of a Catholic parish in the state.[48]

The son of Irish immigrants, O'Brien was born in Washington, DC, on October 18, 1872. His father as a member of the US Army had been wounded in the battle of Gettysburg during the Civil War and subsequently became an employee of the War Department. As such, in 1888, he was transferred to New Bern, North Carolina, at which time his son was fifteen years old.

One of the first people whom young Billy met was Father Price, ordained two years before and the pastor the New Bern parish, which at the time had a Catholic population of 75. Just as Price as a boy in Wilmington had assisted Bishop Gibbons, so O'Brien accompanied Price on his rounds. It is from such associations that vocations are born.

And so it was in the case of O'Brien. In old age, he had strikingly precise recollections of his childhood contact with Price, including a sermon on sanctifying grace that he heard the young priest preach. In Catholic teaching, sanctifying grace is like living water poured into the soul of the believer. Filled with such grace, in the fall of 1889, sixteen-year old Billy entered St. Mary's College Seminary in Belmont where for nine years he studied under the tutelage of the Benedictines. When he was ordained in 1898 by Bishop Haid he joined the five secular priests then serving in the state: Christopher Dennen in Wilmington, Peter Marion in Asheville, Patrick Quinn in Newton Grove, Thomas Griffin in Raleigh and Goldsboro, and Thomas Price, a "Missionary," at Nazareth.

In his memoirs, O'Brien relates an incident that happened during a brief initial appointment to his home parish of New Bern. Having read about the building of St. Anne Church, Edenton "by three little girls," the young priest set out for that town by boat. Delayed at Elizabeth City and wishing to say mass, he asked if there were any Catholics in the town. After a number of inquiries, he was told that an old lady, Mrs. Richardson, living over a store, was a member of that religion. When he told the elderly lady who walked with the aid of crutches of his interest in St. Anne's, the woman asked how he had learned of the story. O'Brien replied that he had read it in the *Catholic Standard & Times* of Philadelphia. The woman then asked if he had ever met the author of the account. He said no. "Well," she said, "the authoress sits before you, and I was one of the little girls."[49]

From Nazareth to Durham

O'Brien might have been trained in theology at Belmont, but he would be trained in missiology at Nazareth. In 1900, when Mike Irwin was ordained, with the approval of Bishop Haid, he and O'Brien joined Father Price, becoming what Price hoped would be the nucleus of a new religious community, the Apostolic Company, secular priests who would devote themselves to evangelizing the American South. Inspired by their leader, the two young priests plunged into the work with enthusiasm, traveling all over the Raleigh area building chapels and preaching to whoever would listen to them. The few hardy Catholic families whom they found sustained their confidence and offered them lodging. When O'Brien wrote his *Memoirs* half a century later, he recalled such families in loving detail.

Then in 1905, as related in Chapter Seven, a fire occurred at Nazareth, which destroyed the wood structure that housed the priests and some of the orphans. O'Brien was in the building at the time and escaped by hanging by his hands from the window sill of his third-floor room and then dropping to the ground, injuring his back. Although Price quickly built a new residence, the Apostolic Company soon dissolved. The problem was one of authority. While Price considered himself the superior of the young clerics, they recognized Bishop Haid as their legitimate supervisor. As has been seen, in 1904 Irwin had left Nazareth to become pastor at Newton Grove. In 1907, O'Brien followed suit when Haid asked him to accept the post of founding pastor of the parish in Durham, a town some twenty miles from Raleigh. Although both Irwin and O'Brien would always express admiration for Price and look back with pride on their years as missionaries, they settled easily into lives as pastors, the traditional work of diocesan priests.

Durham, a Tobacco Town

In the 1880's, William T. O'Brien (no relation to Father O'Brien) perfected a machine for making cigarettes, which until that time had been made by hand. The mechanization of the process made possible the enormous growth of the American Tobacco Company and the even more enormous wealth of its president, James Buchanan Duke. While Duke would endow the Durham-based university which bears his name, William T. O'Brien would be the patron of the city's Catholic church, building Immaculate Conception church there in 1906 on the understanding that Bishop Haid would supply a pastor.[50] It may have been with a rare display of humor that Haid sent Father O'Brien to the church built by a namesake. More likely, however, it was that no other priest was available. In any case, it was a fortuitous choice. Over the course of half a century, O'Brien would see the church prosper even as Durham itself, thanks to the tobacco industry, expanded dramatically, for a time exceeding in population Raleigh itself.[51]

Initially, and unbelievably, the new Durham parish had missions that extended to the Virginia border, including such distant locations as Roanoke Rapids, Weldon, and Halifax. So, although technically O'Brien was no longer an itinerant missionary, he was on the road several times a month. At the same time, he was establishing a parochial school in Durham and fostering the small Catholic presence in Chapel Hill, situated some ten miles distant from Durham.

As his *Memoirs* make clear, O'Brien never lost hope that the Catholic Church was destined to grow in North Carolina:

> Bigotry and opposition may assert themselves in various forms among a limited number who are ignored by the majority of their coreligionists, but this will be only of short duration in comparison to the future years of rich harvesting. ... The pendulum will in God's time swing our way. ... [We are] laying the foundation of a future glorious Church.[52]

When, in 1938, Bishop McGuinness nominated O'Brien for the rank of Monsignor, in a letter to the Apostolic Delegate he confided that "the good old man will be happy unto tears" for the recognition.[53] Well, despite some health problems, the sixty-six year old "good old man" remained as pastor of Immaculate Conception Church for an additional thirteen years when, now seventy-eight, he resigned. However, he did so only on the understanding that he and his sister, Catherine Williams, be permitted to continue living in the rectory and that his salary continue to be paid.[54]

Besides writing his memoirs, in retirement O'Brien retained his position as Dean of the area, consultor to the bishop, and Chaplain of the local Knights of Columbus. He also wrote his will, naming Father John Roueche as executor. Roueche, a generation younger than O'Brien, is the subject of the final section of this chapter.[55]

John F. Roueche (1906-2000)

All five of the pioneering priests of the Diocese of Raleigh presented thus far were outsiders, men for whom North Carolina was an adopted home. They came to love the state and its people but by their accents were always marked as non-southerners. John Roueche [Roo-shay] had no such problem. Like Father Price, he was a native-born North Carolinian. However, because of his religion, he also was seen as odd. As was true of Fred Price, John Roueche was a marginal man – different from southerners because of his religion and different from most of his co-religionists because he was southern. Roueche resolved this identity problem by looking neither North nor South but to Christ in the Eucharist as his touchstone. Nevertheless, he was proud of his southern and Catholic heritage, a heritage that had its origin two generations before his birth.

The family story began in 1838 when, over the objections of her family, Eliza Smith, the granddaughter of a Lutheran minister, became a Catholic and married the immigrant French Catholic merchant, Richard Roueche. The couple traveled by stagecoach from Lincolnton where they had been married and settled in Salisbury, North Carolina. It was in the home of this young couple that an equally young Catholic priest found a welcome as he traveled the lonely miles of the vast territory to which he had been assigned.

Although his full name was Thomas Joseph Cronin, in church records he invariably wrote simply "T.J. Cronin." Like Bishop England, Cronin was a native of County Cork, Ireland. The eloquence of England had drawn Cronin to the American missions. After acclimating himself somewhat to conditions in the South, in 1838 the 34-year-old priest was given the impossible assignment of establishing the Church in an area larger than his native Ireland – the vast forested expanse of the western half of both North and South Carolina. Like a transplanted Don Quixote, Cronin bought a horse and began his quest for Catholics. Of the few he found, none were more hospitable than the Roueches, the only Catholic family in Rowan County. Twice a year T. J. Cronin showed up at their door and was granted lodging. Remaining a few days, he offered mass and baptized the first of the eight children ultimately born to the Roueches. Then, in the autumn of 1842 on one of his visits, Cronin died in the Roueche home. He was taken in the prime of life at age thirty-eight. Paradoxically, a grandson of the Roueches would not only become the first resident of Salisbury to become a priest, but he would live to be the oldest priest in the state.[56]

Although, as has been seen, the novelist Christian Reid (Frances Fisher) was the most celebrated Catholic in Salisbury, the

Roueches retained a position of prominence over the generations. When in 1882, the mission church of the Sacred Heart was constructed on the Fisher property, the Roueche clan comprised more than half the little congregation. Five years later, one of Richard Roueche's sons, John Patrick, and Margaret Taaffe were the first couple to be married in the church. It would be their son, also John, born in 1906, who would become a priest.[57]

Sacred Heart Church was not only the scene of young John's baptism and confirmation but also of his ordination in 1933. Although usually priests were ordained in the cathedral, Bishop Hafey felt that it was appropriate to honor the little Catholic community in Salisbury. Sixty years later, in 1993, Roueche returned to the place of his birth to celebrate an anniversary mass.[58] In remarks filled with reminiscences of eighty years, the retired priest said:

> When I was a boy, the big sign down at the railroad station said 'Salisbury is The Place,' and on the other side, 'The Home of Mint Cola.' Mint Cola is gone, but Salisbury is and will always be 'the place.' And may we all meet again in our true and heavenly home.[59]

Unlike Irwin, Gilbert, and O'Brien, Roueche served in many parishes, moving every few years from one location to another. Over the course of forty-two years, he worked in eleven parishes from New Bern to Asheville. Besides the more or less standard experience of being a pastor, Roueche had several special assignments.

Chapel Cars and Prisoners of War

After an initial posting at Holy Trinity Church in Kinston, for two years Roueche rode the railway chapel car, St. Peter, to Northern cities, raising money for the diocese. The car was a novelty that attracted large crowds in Philadelphia, Scranton, Buffalo, Rochester, and all over New England. Although initially the car had been used by the Passionist Fathers to evangelize the small towns of the state, Bishop Hafey decided that the financial plight of the Raleigh diocese during the Depression years mandated that it be used for more mercenary purposes. Hence, Roueche's adventures. The chapel, which seated about fifty people and had a section fitted as quarters for the priest, provided Catholics with a romantic image of missionary life.[60]

Roueche's second unusual experience came after a six-year pastorate in Burlington, where he saw the number of Catholics increase from 80 to 156. Responding to an appeal from Bishop McGuinness for priests to volunteer as chaplains during World War II, Roueche stepped forward and served in the Army for five years. After two years in Hawaii, scene of the Japanese attack on Pearl Harbor, Captain Roueche was sent to Europe where he had adventures that provided material for stories told over and over again for the rest of his life. A particular highlight was saying mass for 15,000 German prisoners of war. After the service, he learned that four of the prisoners were Catholic priests. Having verified their legitimacy (by speaking with them in Latin), Roueche arranged for them to receive mass kits so that they could minister to their fellow prisoners.

Participation in Bishop Waters' Initiatives

At war's end, this native of a small town in North Carolina, having had the awesome experience of offering mass for 15,000, returned to a state that did not yet have 15,000 Catholics. Trying to remedy that situation, the new bishop, Vincent Waters, was introducing a range of new programs. Hoping that a man born in the area would be an effective missionary, Waters tapped Roueche to take charge of the Apostolate to non-Catholics in the western part of the state. So, the priest, who had once ridden the chapel car all over the North to raise money, now found himself riding the trailer chapels all over Western North Carolina in an effort to save souls. However, Roueche had no more success with the Protestants in the mountains than Father Price had experienced in the lowlands. What both men did achieve was the more modest goal of preserving the faith of the small communities of Catholics residing in the areas where they worked. Both men shared a passion for the mass, a deep devotion to Mary, and an unquestioning loyalty to the pope. And even more than Price, Roueche was a southern gentleman with a gracious charm and an engaging sense of humor.

Perhaps that charm had its greatest effect in Newton Grove. After the integration of the church there in 1953 and the departure of the Redemptorists, Roueche was sent in to restore order. Despite his southern origins and a much more conciliatory style than Bishop Waters, Roueche had difficulty winning the people back. One Catholic man said to him: "I wouldn't give you bread and water if you were starving." Nevertheless, the ever-optimistic priest felt that he helped to bring a church in crisis along the road to healing. As a reward for his service to the diocese, Roueche was named a monsignor in 1955.

A Founding Priest of the Diocese of Charlotte

The next chapter will describe the process of dividing North Carolina into two dioceses. As far as the clergy were concerned, when the western half of the state became a separate diocese in 1972, priests were "frozen" in place, that is, they belonged automatically to the diocese of their current assignment. Thus, John Roueche, after being a Raleigh priest for forty years, found himself one of the founding fathers of the Diocese of Charlotte. It was appropriate, since his hometown of Salisbury was in the new jurisdiction. However, he was now sixty-six years old and most of his memories would be of his days in the Raleigh diocese, in places like Burlington where he saw a parochial school blossom; Newton Grove where he faced the challenge of racial prejudice; and New Bern where the climate was so damp that the Communion hosts would wilt if not changed frequently. Although he had known Michael Begley, the first bishop of Charlotte, for many years, Roueche's bishops would be Hafey, McGuinness, and Waters. In a 1991 interview he had vivid memories of these men and never mentioned Begley.

Final assignments in his long career were St. Lawrence in Asheville, St. Patrick Cathedral in Charlotte, Queen of the Apostles in Belmont, St. Vincent in Charlotte, and finally, St. John the Baptist in Tryon, a quiet town in the Blue Ridge Mountains on the South Carolina border. While in Tryon, the now seventy-year-old Roueche opted to retire. His motive was not to end but to change the focus of his ministry. Imbued with the same conviction as Mike Irwin that prayer was the key to success in converting people Roueche, always a prayerful man, moved to Belmont Abbey, becoming an unofficial 'monk,' joining the Benedictines in their daily round of prayers. It was a coming home for Roueche who, like many of the priests of his generation, had studied at Belmont. Despite tension between the secular and religious priests, the grounds of the Abbey itself were always a peaceful garden, especially in the later years of life. Roueche could walk through the cemetery and see the graves of Bishop Haid, Father Jeremiah O'Connell, and scores of other priests. One day, he would join them.

Finally, although he remained quite healthy, Roueche became a resident of St. Joseph's Nursing Home in Southern Pines. Here for the last ten years of his life he continued his work as a priest. Every day, the regal old man visited each resident of the Home, praying with those who wished it or simply sharing small talk with others, Catholics and non-Catholics alike. He relished the leisure to read the Scriptures and the half dozen Catholic newspapers to which he subscribed and to which he regularly sent letters decrying what he considered the diminution of devotion on the part of Catholics. Most of all, Roueche loved the mass and, continuing the practice of a lifetime, spent an hour in prayer in preparation for each day's celebration.

At age eighty-five, never expecting that he had another nine years to live, Roueche had summed up his understanding of life and the joy with which he continued to embrace the priesthood. It is certain that the other North Carolina priests presented in this chapter would concur with their colleague:

> Mother Teresa is another Christ. She identifies with the poor. We need leaders like that. Most of us are failing Christ. We don't bring the Gospel to everyone. We have to convince people that we have the word of God. We have to call lapsed Catholics to come back. As for me, when I appear before God I will have to answer for every soul I ever met.... I'm on the last lap of my priesthood. It's been a tremendous joy; it seems to get better as I get older. The married people have so many trials. What a joy for me to stand at the altar and offer up the Body and Blood of Christ.

By far the longest tenure for any bishop in North Carolina was that of Leo Haid, who served as Vicar Apostolic from 1887 until his death in 1924. Top left is the thirty-six-year-old Haid in 1885, shortly after his selection as first abbot of Belmont. Below that is the much older Haid, worn down by the dual responsibilities of heading the Benedictine monastery and administering the church in the state. Top right is the shell of the Belmont College building that was gutted by fire in 1900, a great blow to Haid. Above is the Abbot-Bishop in a 1910 picture with the fifty-man monastic community.

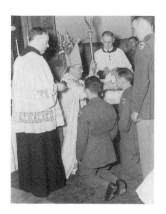

William J. Hafey was consecrated the first bishop of the Diocese of Raleigh in 1925 and served until 1937. In the top photograph he presents a high school diploma to Lawrence J. Hill, who became a diocesan priest and died in 1985. World War II had a major impact on the Church in North Carolina and on Hafey's successor, Eugene J. McGuinness. Above left, McGuinness anoints servicemen as they prepare for active duty. Center right he administers Confirmation to marines at Camp Lejeune near Jacksonville. Lower right, he walks in procession for a liturgy for naval cadets at the University of North Carolina football field in Chapel Hill.

Father Jeremiah O'Connell (top left) wrote an early history of the Church and donated the land on which Belmont Abbey would be established. Father Mark Gross (top right) was Bishop Gibbons' first priest-aide. Below left, Monsignors William F. O'Brien and John F. Roueche are flanked by Bishop Waters and Durham Mayor Evans at the banquet marking O'Brien's 60th anniversary as a priest, fifty years of which were spent as pastor of Immaculate Conception Church, Durham. Below right is the grave of Monsignor Thomas P. Griffin, who built Sacred Heart Cathedral and served there as Rector until his death in 1931. He was buried beside the cathedral.

Although there were churches of cathedral-like proportions in Wilmington, Belmont, and Asheville, most early 20th Century Catholics worshiped in more humble settings. At top is St. Agnes in Washington, where from 1932 to 1952 Father Edward Gilbert ministered to the white congregation. Next is Blessed Sacrament in Burlington. Below that is Little Flower Chapel in Madison County where, for forty years, the Jesuit priest, Andrew Graves, celebrated mass with a handful of Catholics. Finally, the somewhat more substantial Sacred Heart Church, Whiteville.

Chapter Ten

Western Expansion:
The Diocese of Charlotte

I want to reflect with you on the theme of this assembly -- shared responsibility. It is a difficult one but a necessary one to understand and act upon. To some people the idea of shared responsibility within the church is completely foreign. The concept of clergy rule causes anxiety in some. On the other hand, there is unrest if people are to rule. The ancient fear caused by trusteeism ... raises the danger of a heresy to be avoided. The concept of shared responsibility is a middle ground, one in which I will continue to seek your concerns, opinion and guidance. I mean it to be that way. ... The documents of the Vatican Council require democratic procedures to permit a better sharing of responsibility. The intent of the Holy Spirit is more clear in the church through continuous dialog among all members....

--- Bishop Michael Begley, 1978

In the years after the Civil War, even as James Buchanan Duke was building what would become the American Tobacco Company empire in Durham, some eighty miles due west, another entrepreneur, R. J. Reynolds, was establishing his own claim to a piece of the rapidly increasing cigarette market -- and laying the groundwork for a manufacturing conglomerate that would bear his name, employ thousands, and spearhead the expansion of the entire Winston-Salem region. All this did not seem at all likely in 1880, at which time Winston was a nondescript town of 500 adjacent to the quaint Moravian settlement at Salem. However, determined to compete with Duke, Reynolds promoted and financed the upgrading of Winston "from a frontier pest hole" into a respectable city. Sewers were installed, a fire department upgraded, and rail service improved. Step-by-step a thriving economic center was crafted.[1]

With the introduction of Camel cigarettes in 1913, R. J. Reynolds began its climb to the top of the industry ladder. In the 1950's, the names Winston and Salem would become known throughout the country as cigarettes bearing those names were marketed. Virtually all American adults at the time would have the slogan, "Winston tastes good -- like a cigarette should," engraved forever in their consciousness. For Salem, the first filter-tip menthol, the company developed the springtime-in-the-woods advertising campaign that implied that smoking was a passport to health and romance. Of course that was not true, but the prosperity of the company was indeed like a passport to the good life for the people drawn to the Winston-Salem area for employment, including many Catholics.

The base from which growth would occur was small. In 1885 there were only three Catholic families in the city, and monks from Belmont Abbey offered mass occasionally in their homes. However, anticipating the future increase, in 1891 Bishop Leo Haid purchased property on Fourth Street and Brookstown Avenue and had a small church built. Twelve more years would pass before Catholic population growth justified the construction of a rectory in preparation for the assignment of a resident pastor. That event occurred in 1905, and the parish of St. Leo the Great, named after Haid's patron saint, was officially constituted.[2]

As the city developed, a succession of Benedictine pastors nurtured the Catholic community. In 1916, one of those priests, Willibald Baumgartner, initiated a building fund to construct a more substantial church. His fellow monk, Father Michael McInerney, designed the English Gothic edifice that was to be erected – appropriately enough -- on a site formerly occupied by a tobacco barn. However, symptomatic of the poverty of the Catholic Church in the state, it would not be until 1929 that the new church was completed, by which time Leo Haid was dead and the Diocese of Raleigh established. Some of the clerics in attendance when at long last the thousand pound bronze bell was hung in the tower of St. Leo may have noted the irony in the bell's Latin inscription: "I hasten the tardy."

As was true of all Catholic parishes at the time, St. Leo cast a wide net, including in its jurisdiction a number of smaller settlements throughout Forsyth County. One of them, Clemmons, situated ten miles to the southwest of Winston, slumbered through the early decades of the 20th Century, a little noticed rural village with no visible Catholic presence. Before the end of the century it would be home to one of the largest parishes in the state.

The transformation of Clemmons from a one-horse town into a two-car-family suburban community can represent the process of development that was occurring in a number of areas surrounding major economic hubs. In the case of Clemmons, that process was accelerated in the 1970's with the arrival of I-40, the interstate highway that eventually stretched from Wilmington, North Carolina, to the outskirts of Los Angeles, California. Also, the locating of industries other than tobacco provided a healthy diversity that helped to make Winston-Salem the state's third largest economic and population center, trailing only Charlotte and Raleigh. As the economy grew, so also did the Catholic Church.

In 1942, as part of the Belmont Benedictines' gradual withdrawal from staffing parishes, St. Leo was turned over to the diocese of Raleigh and young Father Michael Begley appointed pastor. Thirty years later Begley would become the first bishop of the Diocese of Charlotte, which included Winston-Salem. He would remember the loyal families that had traveled to St. Leo each Sunday from Clemmons.

For those Catholics, the long drive on a Sunday morning was the price to be paid for their small numbers. However, by the time the Diocese of Charlotte was established in 1972, their increased numbers emboldened them to mount a campaign for a church of their own. Responding to that need, in 1976 Bishop Begley purchased ten acres of land in Clemmons as a first step to the establishment of a parish. However, even as the fields and woods of Clemmons were replaced with an ever-expanding web of housing developments with chic names such as Tanglewood and Salem Glen, progress towards a new parish advanced slowly. It wasn't until two years after the purchase of the land that Father Richard Allen, then pastor of St. Leo, celebrated the first mass in Clemmons. Indicative of the prevailing ecumenical spirit, but also harkening back more than 150 years to the experience of Bishop John England, the site of that mass was the local Presbyterian Church.

Continuing as a mission of St. Leo's, but having mass in their own town, Clemmons Catholics found themselves attending services either on Saturday evening in the Moravian Church or on Sunday morning in the Vogler Funeral Home Chapel. Finally, in 1980, Bishop Begley canonically established the Clemmons parish, placing it under the patronage of the Holy Family. As first pastor, he installed Robert Scott, a Paulist priest, to whom he gave the mandate to construct a church.

Energized by the volunteer work of a group of women called the St. Elizabeth Ann Seton Guild, the parish began to take shape.[3]

At its founding, Holy Family had 170 registered families. Two years later, the number had grown to 329, and by the time Begley conducted a groundbreaking ceremony for a church building in 1984, the number of families exceeded 500. When in March 1985, the second Charlotte bishop, John F. Donoghue, dedicated the completed church, parish registration was over 600 families.

The congregation had hardly moved into its new worship space when the continuous influx of new parishioners required that plans be made for an extension. The resulting 14,200 square foot Family Center contained a range of versatile facilities, including a social hall that could seat 350 and be converted into eight classrooms. In 1987, the building won the North Carolina Architectural Brick Design Award of Merit.

The pace of growth continued. By 1990 Holy Family had 765 families, by 1995, 1,100, and by the year 2002, over 1,400. Once again discussions began as to how to resolve the problem of over-crowded church services and insufficient classroom and office space.[4]

The Clemmons parish experience is offered as a metaphor for the growth that has taken place in the Catholic Church in North Carolina in recent years. The present chapter recounts the most significant step that was taken in an effort to respond to, and to anticipate, that growth -- the establishment of the Diocese of Charlotte in 1972. The basic time frame for the chapter is the tenure of the first bishop of Charlotte, Michael J. Begley, who retired in 1984.

The Genesis of a Diocese

When Bishop Waters arrived in Raleigh in 1945, there were fewer than 15,000 Catholics in North Carolina. As has been seen, the number rose slowly but surely: 22,000 in 1950, 42,000 in 1960, and 67,000 in 1970. Some time along the way, Waters began to say publicly that as soon as there were 60,000 Catholic in the state he would ask that the Raleigh diocese be split and a new diocese created in Charlotte, which was fast becoming the most populous city in the state. The census figures for 1970 set in motion the process for fulfilling that pledge.[5]

In keeping with Waters' reputation for secrecy, no one other than his auxiliary bishop, George E. Lynch, knew what was going on. Even Waters' chancellor at the time, Msgr. Louis E. Morton, the man who handled most of the bishop's paperwork, was kept in the dark. In particular, a shroud of silence protected the identity of the priest to be nominated as the first bishop of the new diocese. Whether or not such secrecy was necessary, it was Rome's way as well as Waters'. The idea was that when the announcement came, it would be presented as the action of the Holy Spirit speaking through the pope. Although both the initiative for the new diocese, as well as all the work required to bring it to fruition, had come from Waters, he took no personal credit for what was the most significant development in the church since the establishment of the diocese of Raleigh itself nearly fifty years before. A pastoral letter announcing the new jurisdiction said simply: "When the Family of God grows and matures in any place, in the plan of God a new family is set up. Rejoice with me at this Good News."[6]

The 'good news' came as a complete shock to the man hand-picked by Waters to inaugurate the new diocese. Michael Begley was sixty-two years old and had not been groomed to be a bishop. He was a social worker, a self-effacing, gentle man, down-to-earth, unassuming. Although in no way had he aspired to the episcopacy, Begley seemed to Waters the ideal candidate. Although three names were submitted to Rome, no one seems to have any idea who the other two were. It was just assumed, and probably it was true, that Begley was first on that list. The appointment was the capstone of an association between the two men that had begun on the very day when Waters was installed as bishop of Raleigh.

The Education of a Future Bishop

On that morning in May 1945, in his typically brusque style, Waters asked the thirty-six year old Begley: "Do you want to be Chancellor or Director of Catholic Charities? Choose." Twenty-seven years later Waters would ask with equal abruptness: "Do you accept the position of bishop? Answer yes or no." In the earlier moment of decision, it would seem that by choosing to be head of Catholic Charities, Begley had precluded the likelihood of his ever becoming a bishop, since typically bishops, including Waters himself, are selected from the ranks of chancellors and bishops' secretaries, men familiar with church administration. Not that Begley was thinking in such terms, quite the contrary. Even as he would say "yes" to that second question, his heart would remain with the poor and with children, not with the administrative chores of establishing and running a diocese. In wide-ranging retirement interviews, Begley made scant reference to his achievements as a bishop, preferring to focus instead on the true love of his long life -- being a Catholic priest whose ministry was social work.[7]

Born on March 12, 1909, in Springfield, Massachusetts, Begley had the typical childhood of a New England Catholic boy, attending parochial schools and experiencing early the call to priesthood. How he ended up in North Carolina is one of those coincidences that can shape a life, and in the case of Begley, a diocese. In 1927, a Springfield priest whom Mike Begley consulted asked the young man what he would like to do as a priest. Taken aback, Begley replied that he just wanted to be a priest. He was told that priests do different things. Would he like to join the new Maryknoll order and go to foreign missions or become a teacher like the Jesuits at nearby Holy Cross College? Or, would he be interested in working on the home missions? When Begley showed interest in this last suggestion, the priest said, "I have a friend who is trying to get the Church started in North Carolina. He happens to be vacationing nearby with his family. Would you like to see him?" And so it was arranged for Begley to meet Bishop William Hafey, who accepted him on the spot for the diocese of Raleigh.

After completing his studies at St. Mary's College and Seminary in Emmitsburg, Maryland, Begley was ordained on May 26, 1934. Hafey immediately sent him to assist the aging Monsignor Christopher Dennen at St. Mary in Wilmington. Filled with youthful enthusiasm, Begley threw himself into the sort of missionary activity that had attracted him to North Carolina in the first place. His assignment was to provide services to the ten outlying missions attached to the Wilmington parish. Pigs and chickens ran under houses as he offered mass on kitchen tables. A room filled with tobacco might be his church or a piano keyboard his altar. Each week the priest would drive as many as 150 miles to attend people, a family here, a family there, never a real church or a true congregation.

Hafey had told Begley to bring a car with him to North Carolina, purchased at his own expense. So, the gifts received at ordination had gone towards the $600 purchase price of a new Chevrolet. However, its upkeep was a challenge, since there was no salary. The young priest's only income was $25 a month in mass stipends -- one dollar for each of twenty-five masses -- sent by the Extension Society of Chicago. When the financially destitute priest told the bishop that he needed another $25 a month for car payments, he was asked, "How much do you collect on the missions?" When Begley reported that he got about $15 a month, Hafey replied, "Keep that; I'll give you ten."

At the time, tobacco was cured in barns that needed to be maintained at a constant temperature. To prevent their precious crop from spoiling, men were required to tend the wood fires all night. In order to speak with these farmers, Begley would go down to the barns and, by the glow of the fire and surrounded by the sweet odor of tobacco, share with the men his understanding of God. In retirement, he would recall with nostalgia the attention that the men paid, expressing in simple terms their yearning for the spiritual.

The Shaping of a Social Conscience

Begley's career illustrates the subtle shift in self-awareness that took place in many Catholics as the Twentieth Century progressed. Although popes had issued encyclicals on the rights of workers, the American Church in the South had been forced by its suspect status to remain defensive and largely disengaged from social issues. However, after a few years of relishing the experience of being a priest and imagining himself converting people to Catholicism, Begley's emphasis began to change -- the needs of the poor replacing to some extent those of the church. The Beatitudes: feed the hungry, visit the sick, care for widows and orphans became as urgent as Christ's command to bring everyone into the Church.

So, by the time Bishop Hafey moved on to Scranton in 1937 and Bishop McGuinness moved in from Chicago, Begley also had moved, not geographically, but spiritually. He no longer accepted poverty as an unavoidable fate but saw it as a challenge to be confronted. Although he continued to serve as a pastor until the arrival of Bishop Waters, Begley was mentally ready for a role in the transformation of society. His reeducation would come from the lessons of World War II and in the context of the position as head of Catholic Charities to which Bishop Waters had appointed him.

The war being waged in far-off places was brought home to Begley in the person of 1,900 refugees for whom he had the responsibility of finding temporary housing. One of those refugees, the Polish woman, Gladys Gawroska, became a longtime employee at the Nazareth orphanage where Begley served as superintendent. Years later she said of him: "He was all the time helping people. He helped me. He saved my life,"[8] For the first time, Begley saw people from other countries whose lives had been disrupted by state violence. He could not help but reflect on the violence done to black people in North Carolina, the dehumanizing conditions of workers in factories and on farms, the deplorable state of education, and the glaring inadequacies of health care. Although he would never become a nationally known champion of human rights, in his own quiet way, Begley would devote himself to alleviating human suffering.

To add to the strange contradictions of the time, the priest provided religious services to German prisoners of war who had been put to work in the tobacco fields of North Carolina, replacing American men who were off fighting other Germans in Europe. Many of these young soldiers were Catholic, grateful for the opportunity in an alien land to attend mass and receive Holy Communion. Begley could see in their eyes a yearning for home coupled with relief that their days of battlefield danger were over.

Even as he reflected on the evils in the world, Begley recognized a deficiency in his education and undertook what would be the defining experience for the rest of his life. After two years as head of Catholic Charities, wanting to ground himself on a firmer intellectual and academic base, he requested permission to study social work. The education which he received over the following few years would not only provide him with professional credentials for the post he held, but be the first step on his unanticipated road to the episcopacy.

At that time, when Catholics thought about education, they turned to Church-run institutions. Accordingly, with Waters' blessing, Begley undertook the study of social work at the Catholic University in Washington, DC. However, after a year there, his priest-advisor recommended that he transfer to the University of North Carolina at Chapel Hill, pointing out that not only did UNC have one of the best schools of social work in the country but, with a degree from that institution, he would get more respect than with one from Catholic University. In 1949, Begley was awarded a master's degree in social work, thereby becoming the first professionally credentialed priest-social worker in North Carolina.

Since priests were expected to occupy more than one position, it was logical that the director of Catholic Charities serve also as superintendent of the orphanage at Nazareth. Not only was it located near the bishop's office, but also it was the major social agency of the church in the state. Although for the first time in its sixty-year history Nazareth had a professionally trained director, Begley's heart was not in the administration of the institution. Rather, his delight was to be with what he called the "kiddos," the 175 children who resided in the home. More so than Father Price had done, Begley interacted with the boys and girls, winning from many a lifetime of affection. One woman recalled that as a little girl she would run away just so he would come looking for her. Once he found her hiding under a building. Like the Good Shepherd searching for the lost sheep, the priest gently coaxed her out and into his arms.

Striving for efficiency, Bishop Waters decided that raising cows would be a good use for about a hundred acres of idle orphanage property. When Begley told his father back in Massachusetts that he was now in charge of a herd of cows, his father asked, "What do you know about cows?" The answer of course was "Nothing." Nevertheless, with the help of a seasoned farmer, Begley did what he could. Many a night he was called out to help deliver a calf. His job was to hold the cow's head while someone else eased the delivery. Such was priesthood in North Carolina.

The Bonding of Two Men

Despite their very different styles, Waters and Begley shared experiences that linked them to one another. For example, in the early 1960's, the Cursillo movement, imported from Spain, became a popular program for intensifying the spiritual lives of men and women. Although meant for the laity, priests were required to make a Cursillo in order to serve as spiritual directors to the *cursillistas*, the people who had made the three-day retreat and were living what the movement called "the fourth day, which lasts for the rest of your life." In countless cases, the Cursillo weekend was a life-transforming experience, not only for the laymen in attendance, but for the priests as well.[9]

Men, who thought they had learned in the seminary all they needed to know about the love of Christ, found themselves reduced to tears in the high intensity dynamic of the Cursillo weekend. Also, they did something some had never done before, they physically embraced other human beings as their brothers. They found themselves releasing long-suppressed emotions and being humbled and thrilled by the discovery of the joy that could be found in fellowship. For priests in particular, sincere men who had been taught to be wary of feelings, long dormant dimensions of their deeper selves were released. Both Waters and Begley had that experience.

In far-off Ohio, surrounded by smiling, backslapping laymen, the two North Carolina priests made spiritual and personal breakthroughs. On the return to Raleigh, Waters appointed Begley diocesan director of the Cursillo movement. Although the bishop would never be able to free himself from the inhibitions of a lifetime, he respected Begley who had. The bond created between the two men through the Cursillo may be the never-articulated reason why years later Waters turned to Begley as his choice to be the first bishop of Charlotte.

The Expansion of Experience

Although Begley served as director of Catholic Charities[10] for twenty-five years, he had earlier spent a decade as pastor, first in Wilson and then in Winston-Salem. If the years with Catholic Charities honed his skills as a social worker, his years in parishes taught him the fundamental priestly role, that of pastor of a worship community. Also, it was while he was a pastor that opportunities presented themselves which enabled him to develop new skills, including his ability to work with non-Catholics.

For example, while he was at St. Therese in Wilson, a history professor at Atlantic Christian College invited the priest to be a guest lecturer in his class. "Tell them your understanding of the Crusades. Let them see a Catholic priest. It will help them overcome their prejudice." In addition, the open-minded professor would bring his class on a field trip to St. Therese as if it were some exotic location. When one student peeked gingerly into the confessional, the alert professor pushed him inside saying, "See, there's no trap door." The students had been told all manner of strange things about Catholics, including that there were trap doors in the church, beneath which the priests stored guns in case they were attacked.

When he moved to St. Leo in Winston-Salem in 1942, Begley developed yet another skill, one which would become a hallmark of his ministry. He became an activist in the cause of workers' rights. As a "Right-to-Work" state, North Carolina prided itself in keeping out labor unions. State leaders lured investment by assuring employers that there was a ready supply of unorganized, inexpensive labor. One industry that established a substantial presence in North Carolina was textiles. Enormous plants, their smokestacks piercing the sky, dotted the landscape like dark, prehistoric monsters. Each day thousands of men and women trudged through the factory gates, entering a world of noise, dust, repetitious work, low wages, and few benefits.

Having heard tales of unhealthy conditions, Begley sought and was granted permission to tour the plants operated by Burlington Mills, of which there were so many that it took him three days to visit all that were in the Winston-Salem area. The experience provided insight into how workers were forced to eke out a meager living. Better than any lecture or research article, the mill visits sensitized the priest to the plight of the poor. That sensitivity was able to find expression years later when he joined other Catholic bishops in championing the rights of workers in two significant instances: the acerbic dispute between labor and management in the J. P. Stevens textile company and the living conditions of the people of Appalachia. Both these situations will be discussed below.

Anticipating A Diocese in Charlotte

Although it would not be until 1972 that a diocese was established in Charlotte, as early as 1955, Begley received assignments in that city which laid the groundwork for a future diocese and simultaneously provided him with experiences which would equip him to become its bishop. As was commonly the case, the clergy shortage required that he hold two assignments: pastor of the newly created parish of St. Ann, located south of downtown, and founding director of a Catholic Charities office that would provide services to families in the region. At the same time, he began to familiarize himself with area social welfare agencies and to become acquainted with prominent Catholics in the city, men and women who years later would assist him as he began shaping -- and financing -- the new diocese.

Anxious to give recognition to those who worked with him, Begley regularly reminded people that it was Trinitarian sisters who, as he put it, "did the actual work" of bringing a Catholic social welfare presence to some forty counties in the westernmost part of the state, including the Appalachian region. Begley was well aware of the key role played by women religious, whether in the classroom, the hospital, or the homes of the poor. One of his stories underlined the fact that even as antipathy towards Catholics decreased, the strangeness of some features of the religion did not. In one town, when the Trinitarian sister arrived to visit families, the children would shout, "Here comes Catholic."

Waters' affection for Begley was suggested by an event that occurred on May 26, 1959, the anniversary of Begley's priestly ordination twenty-five years before. Unaware that anything was planned, Begley went over to St. Ann church to say the scheduled morning mass. The fact that several of his classmates were present as well as several other priest friends was surprise enough, but nothing prepared him for the sight of Waters himself, "with a twinkling smile," greeting his friend.[11]

Begley received another surprise five years later. A priest-associate took him out to dinner and on the way home suggested that they stop at Charlotte Catholic High School to see what was going on there. What was going on was a thirtieth anniversary party for the man who had become symbolic of Catholicism in the city. Five hundred people greeted the astonished Begley when he entered the school hall. With some degree of exaggeration, the master-of-ceremonies said that nine years earlier, when Begley had been sent to St. Ann, his orders included building a church and a school. The priest went to work and built the largest Catholic parish in North Carolina and the largest Catholic school in North Carolina, and now "has just about the largest Catholic debt in North Carolina!"[12] All levity aside, Begley had a deep association with Charlotte, eminently preparing him for becoming its bishop.

Getting Started

The behind-the-scenes work of establishing a new diocese having been completed, it remained for Waters to get Begley's acceptance of the post of bishop. So, on November 22, 1971, driving by himself the seventy-five miles from Raleigh, Waters visited Begley, now pastor of Our Lady of Grace parish in Greensboro. In order to insure absolute privacy and using the pretext of viewing some undeveloped church property, Waters took Begley for a drive and parked the car. Between them on the seat was the bishop's Breviary, a book almost as sacred to priests as the Bible itself. With none of the informality which their twenty-six years of friendship might have warranted, in a businesslike voice, Waters said: "I am going to ask you a question which requires a yes or no answer. If you say no, you must swear never to reveal to anyone that this conversation every took place." The question, of course, was "Do you accept the position of first bishop of Charlotte?"

Begley was stunned. Along with most of the priests in the state, he felt that at sixty-two he was too old to be given such a heavy responsibility. He hesitated, wondered aloud if he was the right man, wondered if it was God's will. Waters cut him off. "Don't worry about that. You've been asked. What is your answer?" When they drove back to Our Lady of Grace, Charlotte had its first bishop. Waters made him swear to tell no one of the appointment until it was officially announced by the Apostolic Delegate. At the time, Begley's sister, Mrs. William

Crowley of West Springfield, Massachusetts was visiting her brother. Although he was bursting to tell her, he kept the secret.

It was widely agreed that Begley had been an excellent choice. Although one of Waters' priests, he had not been as closely identified with him as had others, especially George E. Lynch who, as auxiliary bishop and several years younger than Begley, might have been considered a more appropriate candidate. However, as Waters' surrogate in many situations, Lynch had not endeared himself to the diocesan clergy. His personality, like that of Waters himself, was too rigid for leadership in the post-Vatican II era. To his credit, Waters recognized this. Of course, Rome might have appointed someone who had no association whatever with Waters, but Begley was not only untainted by such association but was very uniquely familiar with the western section of the state. At various times he had been pastor in three of the four largest cities in the new diocese and as director of Catholic Charities had an unrivaled knowledge of the needs of an area that was a combination of wealth and poverty, growth and stagnation, modernity and a culture that over generations had changed at a glacial pace.

Once the appointment was confirmed, Begley immediately asked the forty-five year old Father Joseph S. Showfety, pastor of Immaculate Conception parish in Hendersonville, to be his Chancellor. Like Begley, Showfety had no experience as a chancery official, no premonition that he was to be called upon to play a major role in establishing the long-rumored new diocese. These two men, one of Irish descent, the other of Lebanese parents, would spend virtually all their days together for the next seven and a half years. Through trial and error and working with limited personnel resources, they succeeded in laying the foundation for what was to become a thriving diocese. The Catholic population of 34,000 in 1972 would double by the end of Begley's tenure and double once again by the year 2000.

Joseph S. Showfety

In a most unusual way, Joseph Showfety's life had come full circle. In the year 2002, he was retiring as pastor of St. Benedict in downtown Greensboro, the very church in which he had been baptized seventy-five years before. The now antique building, supplemented by a modern activities center, provides services to a diminished congregation of mostly elderly people left behind by the movement of the younger generation to the suburbs. Traffic whirls around the dark-brick building, a silent memorial to a more tranquil past. St. Benedict, named

by the Belmont monks in honor of their patron saint, had been one of
the many churches that benefited not only from the dedication of the
Benedictines but from the largesse of Mother Katharine Drexel. In the
early years of the 20th Century, the sainted heiress had donated $1,500
for the construction of the church with her usual condition that pews be
set aside for blacks.

Blacks were not the only minority group members who called
St. Benedict their spiritual home. A slow stream of Lebanese began to
move into the city in the 1920's, including a young immigrant couple
who celebrated their marriage in the little church. The groom, Abdou
Showfety, opened a men's apparel business in downtown Greensboro,
and the Shofetys began to raise a family. One of their sons would help
Bishop Begley establish the diocese of Charlotte.[13]

In the early 1900's, Lebanese immigrants were the only group
of foreigners to settle in North Carolina in numbers so substantial that
for a time they comprised nearly a majority of the Catholic population
of the state. Furthermore, as successful business people, they were
major contributors to the construction of a number of churches.
Although most of the Lebanese settled further east in towns like Rocky
Mount, Wilson, and New Bern, some ventured as far west as
Greensboro. Wherever they established themselves they prospered,
combining hard work, excellent human relations skills, and contributions to the community. These were the very qualities that would help
Joseph Showfety prosper as well, not in business, of course, but in the
church.[14]

After graduating from St. Benedict parochial school, Showfety
attended the local public high school, coping with the double stigma of
being Lebanese and Catholic. Then, while a student at the Citadel
Military Academy in Charleston, South Carolina, he entered the US
Navy, serving at the Great Lakes Naval Station. It was during this time
that thoughts of priesthood became more insistent. Still not certain that
he was ready for a life commitment to celibacy, he enrolled in Mount
St. Mary's college seminary in Maryland. After completing three years
of study, he felt that it was time to meet with Bishop Waters to discuss
his adoption as a seminarian for the diocese. Whether the bishop was in
a bad mood, doubtful of Showfety's vocation, or perhaps frustrated
from having invested badly needed money in too many seminarians
who had not persevered, Waters gave the student a hard time. "Are you
sure you want to be a priest?" he asked over and over. Each time,

Showfety said that he was not sure. How could anyone be sure at that stage of preparation? With a laugh, more than half a century later, Showfety recalled that initial encounter with the demanding man who was to be his superior.

In the end, Showfety was accepted and assigned for theological studies at St. Mary's Seminary, near Baltimore. During the summers of 1951 through 1954 he participated in the seminarian census program discussed in Chapter Two and in 1955 was ordained by Waters. After four years as assistant in several parishes, without any say in the matter, Showfety was appointed to head the new high school, named in honor of Bishop McGuinness, which was opening in Winston-Salem. Here he worked for seven years, setting on a firm footing the school which continues to serve Catholics of the Triad area and which in the year 2000 relocated to a more modern and enlarged facility. On the other hand, Showfety administered for a year a school which would prove a less successful venture. Asheville Catholic High was closed in 1972 as enrollment declined, religious vocations plummeted, and the cost of Catholic education soared.

Although today few priests serve as school principals, Bishop Waters wanted all church institutions headed by the clergy and believed, as a number of priests who served under him reported, that with ordination a priest was automatically qualified for any position to which he was assigned. The bishop also believed that priests, like loyal soldiers, should accept as God's will whatever was asked of them. Showfety subscribed to this perspective but in his heart felt a preference for parish work. So, when Waters asked him if he would like to go back to school for a degree in education, the priest said "No," realizing that an affirmative answer would most likely destine him to a life as a school administrator. Just as many years before the answer to a question posed by Waters had set Begley's future, so in the mid-1960's Showfety's answer determined his. Accordingly, in 1967 he was released from school work and appointed pastor of the Immaculate Conception, Hendersonville, where Bishop-elect Begley caught up with him five years later.

Where to Start?

The first order of business as the new diocese groped its way into existence was the practical matter of dividing up resources, including the clergy. Fortunately, the process went smoothly because Waters was determined to be fair to a fault. Showfety, who participated in all meetings, said that his Raleigh counterpart, Monsignor Louis Morton, quipped that Waters was more generous to Charlotte than he was to Raleigh. In fact, in a report to Rome at the time of the division of the diocese Waters wrote:

> The hope of this project was to divide the area equitably by general and Catholic population, hoping that the parishes, the institutions, the priests, the religious, the schools, the hospitals, the special institutions, nursing homes, orphanages, social service centers, convents, improved and unimproved real estate, etc., would thus be fairly equally divided.[15]

Furthermore, although no one noticed it except in retrospect, for the year before the split took effect, all clergy transfers were within what would be the area of the new dioceses, not across future diocesan lines. The bishop did not want to be accused of having moved "problem priests" to the Charlotte side or his own friends to the Raleigh side. Further, when it came time for three priests to be ordained in 1973, although technically all belonged to Raleigh, Waters gave them a choice. One, Wilbur Thomas, whose family home was in Lexington, within the territory of the new diocese, chose to go to Charlotte. The other two, Joseph Vetter, a native of Burlington in the reconstituted Raleigh diocese and John F. "Tim" O'Connor, a New York native, opted for Raleigh. Over the years, all three men have held positions of responsibility in their respective dioceses.

As far as the real estate was concerned, it was explained in the report to Rome that more than forty years earlier, Bishop Hafey had gotten the North Carolina legislature, "at a time when there were no Catholic legislators," to adopt a law of titling which provided that the bishop of the diocese, "when properly appointed, coming into the state, and taking possession of his Catholic diocese," would be vested with title to all of the property which had been acquired by his predecessor.[16] With the establishment of the diocese of Charlotte, there was the painstaking task of identifying the deeds for property lying within the new jurisdiction and having them transferred from Waters to Begley.[17]

Showfety gave an example of the differing styles of Waters and Begley. While working on the transfer of funds, he learned that the diocese of Raleigh had five checking accounts. Puzzled, he asked Msgr. Morton what that was all about. Morton replied that Waters insisted on signing personally all diocesan checks and that in order to get things done, multiple accounts had been opened without the bishop's knowledge to take care of day-to-day diocesan business, with only the most important bills presented to Waters for his signature. With Begley, on the other hand, there was no need for such subterfuge. He readily entrusted Showfety with responsibility for all monetary matters.

In light of his need to control everything, how was it possible for Waters to give up half the state with such apparent ease? Without hesitation, Showfety replied, "Because he loved the church." After twenty-five years of unremitting labor to cultivate the religious soil of North Carolina, Waters willingly turned over half the farm, as it were, to Begley. The transfer process entailed frequent meetings over the course of five months. Waters uttered the only sharp word when he overruled his own lawyer, Francis J. Heazel, on a controverted matter. In a tone that brooked no discussion, he insisted that Charlotte be given the contested property.

If there had been conflict in the 1950's over integration and in the 1960's over implementation of church reforms, there was none in the 1970's as the diocese was divided. It was one of Waters' last major actions. Within three years he was dead.

Becoming a Bishop; Becoming a Diocese

In retirement, Begley would look a little puzzled when reminded that he had been a bishop. It was not that he had grown senile as he passed his ninetieth birthday, but to be a bishop had never obscured the fact that first and foremost he was a priest. Although his parish now covered 20,000 square miles, Begley's perspective remained more pastoral than administrative. As he said at the time of his appointment, "I hope to be able to continue my relations with all in the diocese with the same pastoral approach with which I have fulfilled my office as the pastor of a parish." That approach included the down-to-earth chores of kitchen duty on Cursillo weekends. In a humorous tone, one of the lay leaders wrote to Begley, "I do not intend to congratulate you on your new position, for I know I am losing one of my best kitchen helpers."[18]

The Cursillo also played a role in the motto that Begley chose for his coat of arms, *Diligimus Fratres* (We have loved the brothers). He said that the words were suggested by his association with the movement that stressed the loving fraternal links that bound together those who had "made a weekend." Conscious that the word "brothers" was awkward in a society increasingly sensitive to sexist terminology, Begley added that "sisters" were included also.[19]

The elaborate ordination and installation ceremonies at St. Patrick Cathedral in Charlotte on January 12, 1972, presided over by Archbishop Luigi Raimondi, the Apostolic Delegate, were marked by several innovations. For the first time in the Carolinas, the ordination of a bishop was completely in English, and the congregation not only could understand all aspects of the ancient ritual but also was invited to participate. Also, for the first time a woman read a scripture passage within the sanctuary at a pontifical event. The choice was especially appropriate, since Sister of Mercy Mary Andrew Ray was a descendant of the Phelan family that had built the cathedral church in 1940. Another first for those in attendance was that the congregation broke out in spontaneous sustained applause at the conclusion of the reading of the papal document appointing the bishop. Finally, indicative of the fact that not only had a new diocese arrived but also a new age of technology, the ceremony was carried on local television and broadcast via closed circuit TV to the overflow crowd in the nearby school hall.[20]

One wonders what Bishop Waters thought of all this as, sitting in the sanctuary as co-consecrator, he reflected on his own episcopal ordination in the very different world of 1945. If not comfortable with all the changes, he knew none the less that there was no turning back the clock, no stemming the tide of a more emotional, relaxed, and participatory church than that in which he was raised and with which he continued to be more comfortable. Although chronologically only five years older than Begley, he was a generation older spiritually. The torch was being passed, and it would be carried by men -- and women -- who would look back at Waters with admiration for his commitment to the Church but with no desire to emulate his style of leadership. Perhaps there was a subtle but kindly message in the words that Begley addressed to Waters at the dinner for 800 held the evening of the installation. Looking at the man who was now his brother on yet another level, the new bishop expressed his gratitude to Waters for enabling him to get a degree in social work at UNC. "This training helped me to become a person who listens."[21]

The Work Begins

Ceremonies out of the way, Begley and his chancellor undertook the multiplicity of tasks associated with running a diocese. In some respect, the situation in which they found themselves was similar to that of Bishop Gibbons and his de facto chancellor, Father Mark Gross, as they began organizing the Vicariate Apostolic in Wilmington in 1868.

All four men were neophytes, not really sure what steps they should take and whether they were adequate for the task. Also, just as Gibbons and Gross had used their own living quarters as their office, so also did their 20th Century counterparts. For several months, Begley worked out of his bedroom on the second floor of the cathedral rectory, while Showfety took care of the business affairs of the church from a small room on the floor below. It was a matter of opening their own mail, writing their own letters, and sharpening their own pencils.

However, the differences in conditions after nearly a century were much more significant than the similarities. Gibbons and Gross had two priests to minister to about six hundred Catholics scattered across the entire state. There were no religious sisters, no schools, no hospitals, only a couple of war-ravaged churches and no money. On the other hand, the Charlotte diocese started with 40 diocesan and 21 religious order priests, 233 nuns, and 50 parishes to serve 34,208 Catholics in but half the state. In addition, there were three general hospitals and 21 parochial schools.[22] Thanks to the efficient stewardship of Waters, there were adequate financial resources to plan the construction of new churches as well as to find more substantial quarters, both for the bishop and for the emerging diocesan departments. Within the space of a few years, a bona fide independent diocese would be fashioned and the memory of having been part of the diocese of Raleigh fade.

Eyes long accustomed to look to Raleigh for decisions and guidance quickly and smoothly began to turn to Charlotte. To many it seemed only proper that the largest and most dynamic city in the state have its own episcopal see. It was a matter of pride. Raleigh might be the governmental capital, but Charlotte was the center of economic and cultural life. It was also the destination of thousands of young, well-educated Catholic families, people who felt no allegiance to a church past of which they knew nothing. As the glass office towers rose ever higher into the Charlotte sky, the new Catholic diocese participated in the energy and self-confidence of the region. The clergy, all of whom had been Raleigh priests, adjusted with ease to their new status. Now, *they* were the pioneers, the founding fathers, the trailblazers. Time to stop talking about a missionary diocese and bemoaning the paucity of Catholics. Look around; churches were full; every week scores of newcomers were registering, asking about Catholic schools, wanting to know how they could get involved in parish life. You mean we were once part of the diocese of Raleigh?

Calls began to come in to the new Chancery office for dispensations for Catholics to marry non-Catholics.[23] Requests poured in for the bishop to administer Confirmation and dedicate new facilities. Some pastors wanted permission to go ahead with the construction of new churches, while others needed a sympathetic ear for problems. Sisters sought chaplains for their schools and confessors for their convents. Contractors wanted a signature; salesmen with broad smiles showed samples of stationery and made suggestions for furniture and vehicles and office equipment. Two men who had no idea how to run a diocese, soon found out. Like the newly appointed directors of a small but promising company, they were swept along on a dizzying round of appointments, decisions, and daylong trips to the far-flung network of parishes. As Showfety would say decades later, they kept few records of those early days. They just did what needed to be done.

One priority was responding to the need that the city of Charlotte itself had for additional churches to accommodate the expanding population. Planning began immediately and, whereas in 1972 there were seven parishes in the city, a few years later there were nine. Today there are a dozen. This does not include several large parishes located in the suburban ring. Following the pattern that has characterized many areas of the country, Catholics are concentrated in the urban centers of North Carolina. Fully half the households of the diocese of Charlotte live within the Charlotte metropolitan area, where by the year 2000 they comprised about ten percent of the population.

It was and remains a different story in the Appalachian region. Here, Catholics continue to be as rare as a clear day in the air-polluted mountains, accounting for less than one percent of the population of many counties. Nevertheless, once again thanks to the efforts of Bishop Waters, by the time that the diocese of Charlotte was established, there was a Catholic presence in all but four of these counties. In some cases this was nothing more than a small mission chapel where mass would be celebrated on occasion. But it helped move the state further along the road to fulfilling the dream of a church in every county.[24] This infrastructure, as it were, facilitated the work of Begley. His task was not so much planting, as nurturing, not so much laying a foundation, as shepherding growth. For this ministry he was temperamentally well suited. He was also comfortable with the more collegial church envisioned by Vatican II. That collegiality expressed itself through a network of interconnected parish, vicariate, and diocesan structures that emerged in the first few years of the new diocese's existence.

Diocesan Assemblies

By the early 1970's, substantial numbers of American priests expected to collaborate with their bishop in governing the diocese. In North Carolina, as was seen in Chapter Three, the issue was red hot. For several years, the Raleigh Priests Association and the Priests Senate had been locked in a power struggle with Bishop Waters, who refused to yield any of what he considered his God-given authority. Serendipitously, the establishment of the Diocese of Charlotte defused that ferment and, at least in the western half of the state, brought to an end the confrontational relationship between clergy and bishop.

One of the leaders of the North Carolina Priests' Association, and a signer of the 1969 letter calling for the resignation of Waters, was Father George Kloster, who found himself on the Charlotte side of the line when the diocese was split. In a 1972 interview, Kloster said that he didn't know whether a priests' association would be organized in the new diocese. He anticipated a spirit of cooperation between bishop and priests that would make such a group unnecessary. Furthermore, the priests had grown weary of battling with their bishop. They were quite willing to give Begley a chance.[25]

Within a year, with Begley's blessing, the Diocesan Pastoral Council (DPC) was formed. Comprised of priests, nuns, and lay men and women enthusiastic about having a voice in church governance, the DPC planned an Assembly that would bring together delegates representing all the parishes of the diocese. That Assembly, held at Sacred Heart College, Belmont, in June 1975, was the first of seven such gatherings. Taken together, they represent a case study of a diocese striving to implement what Begley termed "shared responsibility."[26]

Each assembly had a theme that suggested the aspect of diocesan development that the DPC considered a priority issue. The themes were:

*1975: Pastoral Planning and the need for parish councils;
*1976: Communication, Liturgy, Planning & Youth Ministry;
*1977: The Role of Women in the Ministry of the Church;
*1978: The Role of the Vicar & Vicariate Councils;
*1979: Evangelization;
*1980: Evangelizing within the Family;
*1982: The Spiritual Renewal of Parish & Vicariate Councils.[27]

A feature of each Assembly was a "State of the Diocese" address by Begley, reminiscent of the presentations of Bishop England at the state Conventions over which he presided in the 1820's and '30's. In fact, the Charlotte assemblies were similar to those earlier meetings, except that now a more egalitarian body in which clergy and lay delegates worked together replaced the English parliamentary system of a "House of the Clergy" and a "House of the Laity." However, the problem of balancing a pseudo-democratic "legislature" with the monarchical episcopacy bedeviled Begley as it had England. A continuous challenge of the Charlotte assemblies was explaining to the clergy and laity alike that their role was advisory, not legislative. The quotation at the beginning of the chapter is an example of this ongoing effort to educate the "delegates" as to the limits of their authority. At one of the meetings Begley said that, "based on legal counsel," he was asking for shared *discussion*, not shared *decision*.[28]

Putting aside the awkwardness of church authority for American Catholics, the gatherings played a defining role in the formation of the diocese. In particular, they taught pastors the need for planning and collaboration. Terms like vision statement, goals, objectives, commissions, and process became part of the vocabulary of church leaders. Although in some respects Catholicism in North Carolina remained a frontier phenomenon, in its mentality and techniques the church embraced many of the features of corporate America. In this regard, North Carolina was not alone. Throughout the country, the 1970's was a turning point in church organization, with informal, horse-and-buggy clerical management being replaced with an increasingly sophisticated team of specialists, most of whom were lay persons. Charlotte led the way, in part because Bishop Begley, trained as a social worker, understood the need for embracing modern thought and technology. More significant, however, was his personality, one that trusted his aides and gave them the freedom to innovate.

One of the first projects undertaken by the DPC, under the leadership of Father William N. Pharr, was the establishment of a representative council in every parish and each of the nine vicariates.[29] Within a year, Pharr could report that forty-five parishes had councils in place. Each was comprised of an executive committee and six "commissions": Education, Family Life, Finance and Administration, Communications, Community Life, and Liturgy. These commissions paralleled similar structures on the vicariate level and within the DPC itself. If all this sounds complicated, that is precisely how the people involved experienced it.

The one level of the emerging apparatus that was constantly pointed to as in need of development was that of the vicariate. A 1982 "Analysis of the First Ten Years of the Diocese of Charlotte," reported quite bluntly that the vicariate structure was one with which people could not identify and which had produced few ideas or programs. Furthermore, surveys conducted by the DPC revealed that lay leaders did not identify with diocesan headquarters either, equating it with the bureaucratic. The final outcome of all the meetings and organizing was the realization that most Catholics were interested in but one structure: their local parish. On that level they found community and lived their faith. While "diocese" and "vicariate" were important for the efficient organization of the institutional church, they were largely irrelevant to rank-and-file church members.

The assemblies themselves became difficult to sustain over time. The first few were well attended because of their novelty. As the years passed, it became increasingly difficult to convince people from distant corners of the diocese that they should travel to Belmont. What originally were two or three day gatherings, ended up in 1982, with a one-day session. That final meeting was held on a Friday, despite the argument that Saturday would be more convenient for working lay people. The DPC explanation was that Friday was selected because priests needed to be in their parishes on Saturday. It had become clear that the dream of broad-based collegiality had yielded to the reality of church life. Meetings were largely for the professional staff. This was not necessarily a bad idea since, in a church undergoing substantial revamping, "in-service" training of the clergy was crucial. Although few wanted to see it in such terms, running a diocese or a parish had become more and more like running a business.

Besides extending the boundaries of collegiality, the assemblies and other meetings were contributing to the shaping of a new "corporate culture" among the clergy. It was not that the clergy of the post-Vatican II church lacked the commitment of their predecessors but that new skills were needed, including the ability to work in close collaboration with women religious, deacons, and lay staff members, to plan parish operations strategically, and to communicate effectively with the broader community. In short, priests were to complement their traditional religious functions with the qualities of modern management.

Perhaps the most insightful critique of the assemblies was given by George Kloster, who having served as a gadfly in 1969 vis-à-vis Bishop Waters, ten years later took upon himself a similar role with reference to the Diocese of Charlotte. As the 1979 assembly approached, Kloster, then pastor at St. Elizabeth parish in Boone, charged that the planned meeting was "a workshop in evangelization," not a true assembly. As he put it:

> A diocesan assembly is a gathering of clergy, religious, and lay delegates for the purpose of giving vision and direction to the overall ministry of the diocese. It is a time to examine the work of diocesan agencies, to review policies, to study how our resources are being used, to see how effective we as a church are. It is a time for setting priorities for the future, to make real the notion of shared responsibility. That is how the first diocesan assembly was conducted. In its own incipient way it was a great success. Each year since we have departed more and more from that concept... Let's hope the bishop, DPC, and others in positions of power will get us back on course.[30]

This summons was not to be heeded. The glow of the Council had faded and for the Diocese of Charlotte, the honeymoon ended. Kloster was a lone voice, urging that the journey to a more participatory church had not ended. For most Catholics, the process was complete. They had what they wanted: increasingly vital parishes characterized by improved homilies, well trained choirs, competent religious education programs, and a range of special interest organizations. Yes, there was a bishop and diocesan offices and vicars and directives from Rome. But all of these served the local community best when seldom seen or heard. Such structures as a Priests Senate, a Sisters Senate, and the DPC continued to exist and to serve in an advisory capacity to the bishop, but substantial lay participation above the parish level could not be sustained.

Reporting to Rome

As pastors and vicars are accountable to their bishop, so bishops are answerable to the pope. The pattern for reporting to Rome entails the preparation of a "Quinquennial Report" which bishops present to the Vatican on the occasion of their *ad limina* visit once every five years. Bishop Begley, in conjunction with the other ordinaries of the Atlanta Province, made three such visits to the Holy See during his twelve-year tenure. The reports are frank assessments of the state of the diocese. Among other things, they reveal the evolving administrative structure as well as emerging pastoral issues.[31]

Indicative of the increasing complexity of the diocese, and the fact that more and more department heads were contributing portions of the report, each one was longer than its predecessor. So, the July 1974 report comprises forty pages whereas later ones have more than twice as many. The reports can be compared with one another, since each responds to a standard set of questions. All begin with what is in effect an autobiography of the bishop. It is clear that Rome wants to know what the men who lead the far-flung network of dioceses are doing. So, in the earliest report, Begley says that in the first year of his ministry he had visited all the parishes in the diocese, save one. That one, located in the mountains, had a change of pastors and he judged that it was better to give the new man time to settle in before visiting him.

In addition, a number of parishes had been visited more than once for Confirmations, liturgical meetings, deanery gatherings, and even for weekend confessions and masses. Begley was known to "cover" for a priest who might be away from his parish on vacation. The bishop also visited parishes for Cursillo meetings, occasionally serving as spiritual director for a weekend program. On another level of ministry, Begley reported that he was chairman of the Catholic Committee on Appalachia, an area where "poverty, illiteracy, and other forms of destitution prevail."

The office space needs of the diocese suggested the growing pains already being experienced. The "duplex" which was serving as headquarters for diocesan agencies was inadequate, and thought was being given to the construction of a new building so that all departments could be housed together.[32] Those departments included the Catholic Schools office, responsible for supervising twenty-one institutions with 5,673 students. Also, Catholic Social Services needed space for the five sisters and lay secretary who staffed the agency. Begley made specific mention of the director of Catholic Social Services, the Rev. Thomas Clements, noting that, like the bishop himself, Clements had a degree in social work from the University of North Carolina. Also, as had been true of Begley when he directed Catholic Charities for the Raleigh Diocese, Clements was a pastor serving at Sacred Heart, Salisbury, forty miles from his Charlotte office.

As far as finances were concerned, in 1972 the budget for Catholic Social Services was $37,000. Today, it is in the millions. The

Diocesan Support Campaign for 1974, the main source of income for diocesan programs, had raised $127,000. By way of comparison, the same appeal for 2002 raised more than $3,500,000. The goal of one Charlotte parish alone, St. Gabriel, was $297,000.

Second Quinquennial Report

By July 1978, when Begley went to Rome for his second *ad limina* visit, the report related that three Assemblies had been held and the number of vicariates had been increased from five to nine "to provide more contact between priests and the vicar." There were now sixty parishes, including seven that had been established since the previous report. The diocese counted 44,000 Catholics out of a population of 2,850,000, only 1.5%, but growing.

A Sisters' Senate had been formed, consisting of two women elected from each vicariate. The bishop himself met regularly with the women, emphasizing the fact that their work could no longer be taken for granted. Influenced by the Women's Movement that was sweeping the nation during the 1970's, the sisters requested greater control over their lives. For the first time, the office of Vicar for Women Religious was occupied not by a priest, but by a woman, Sister M. Jean Linder, who had been recommended to Begley by the Sisters' Senate. As will be shown in the following chapter, the ministries of sisters became more diverse even as their numbers declined. Also, humble deference to bishop and priests was no longer a virtue.

Indicative of the church's moving beyond sectarian boundaries, on the recommendation of both the diocesan Consultors and the Priests' Senate, the diocese had become affiliated with the North Carolina Council of Churches. This was a reversal of the policy of Bishop Waters that had banned priests from joining this group or to engage in other interreligious activities.

In response to a question in the Vatican questionnaire on how Catholic people were accepting church teaching on contraception, Begley's report stated that, although the bishop and, "as far as is known" the priests, supported the position presented in the encyclical *Humanae Vitae*, most Catholic couples did not. In fact, they no longer considered contraception a moral issue. To them, the regulation of conception was a private matter and their decision had no effect on their practice of the faith.

Similarly, abortion was now "an accepted practice" and was so common that in one county in the diocese there had been more abortions than live birth in 1976. This was only three years after the Supreme Court decision legalizing abortion. Although bishops and priests appeared at demonstrations opposing abortion, a culture more tolerant of "free choice" had superseded the notion of moral absolutes, and a less punitive approach to deviation from church teaching had emerged. For example, in May 1977, the American Catholic bishops were nearly unanimous in petitioning that divorced and remarried Catholics no longer be subject to automatic excommunication. In November of that year, Pope Paul VI agreed to halt the practice.

The J. P. Stevens Dispute

Begley's 1978 report related what certainly was the most contentious issue of his career, his uniting with the other bishops of the Atlanta province, including Bishop Joseph Gossman of Raleigh, in an attempt to mediate the labor dispute between the J. P. Stevens Company and the Amalgamated Textile Workers Union. Stevens, the second largest textile company in the country, requested the assistance of the bishops, little suspecting that they would speak out so forcefully on behalf of worker rights. Although the churchmen, who met on several occasions with each side separately, insisted that they were not taking sides, their public pronouncements emphasized the right of collective bargaining.

Their first statement was made in May, 1977. Ten months later, responding to criticism, a second statement was issued which said in part:

> We reemphasize here that our interest in the economic welfare of the community finds its sources in long-standing religious teaching on social justice and the rights of workers to organize and to have a just share in the rewards of their labors. We are conscious that there are those who wish that the church, and churchmen, would "stay in the pulpit," but we insist that the implications of the gospel itself force us to become involved in issues of justice and the basic rights of working people.[33]

The report to Rome argued that far from damaging the status of the bishops, the publicity given the dispute had made the social teaching of the church better known. In any case, southern bishops, usually virtually invisible in the broader society, found themselves in the spotlight of public attention. For Begley, who had visited the Burlington textile mills many years earlier, the plight of factory workers was by no means an abstract issue. Although not bellicose, neither was he reluctant to lend his voice in support of the powerless and exploited.

Looking Towards the Next Bishop

Since bishops were required to submit their resignation at the age of seventy-five, when the seventy-four-year-old Begley went to Rome in 1983, he knew that it was for the last time. Although it might have seemed somewhat inappropriate, like holding a funeral before someone had died, the diocese was already looking ahead to the next bishop. The Assembly of 1982 had actually drawn up a paper on "The Selection of A Bishop." Those who wrote the profile of the diocese in the hope that it would guide the selection process, may not have known that some of their North Carolina predecessors had tried to have just such a voice. Price, Dennen, and Irwin had all presented their prescriptions for an appropriate bishop, believing that they, better than outsiders, knew what was best for the church in the state.

It may be that Begley, who consulted them on virtually everything, had spoiled the October 1982 assembly leaders. They may also have believed that a participatory church extended all the way to Rome. They were mistaken. When the time came to select a new bishop, the decision would be made far away from western Carolina.

Of course, none of this was even hinted at in the 1983 quinquennial report, which rather related the continuing articulation of specialized offices within the diocesan administration. Now there was a Media Center, Office for Peace and Justice, Campus Ministry, Youth Ministry, and Vocations, in addition to the Tribunal and Liturgical Commission. Most of these entities transacted much of their work by means of volunteer committees. For example, the Vocations Office coordinated a Vocations Awareness Committee as well as a Vocations Formation Committee. The latter, consisting of five diocesan priests, met several times a year to review seminary applications and to assess the progress of clerical students. Although this committee was exclusively clerical, most others included a broad spectrum of Catholics, providing just the sort of collegiality envisioned by the Assemblies.

Changing priorities were reflected in the names of departments. What had been the Office of Pastoral Planning was now the Office of Planning and Development, with the word 'development' used as a euphemism for fund raising. Although planning might still include the agenda of the early assemblies, the emphasis had shifted to the financing of diocesan programs. The 1982 Diocesan Support Campaign was the first with a goal over $500,000 and resulted in pledges totaling $670,000. This dramatic increase reflected not only the professionalization of fundraising but also the continuing increase in a Catholic population willing and able to support church projects. Soon enough the diocese would be hiring lay development specialists who would use techniques developed by nonprofit organizations to attract ever larger sums.

Whereas earlier reports said that there were no ethnic groups in the Charlotte diocese other than a community of Cherokee Indians on a reservation in the mountains, the 1983 report signaled the early stages of major demographic changes occurring in the state, ones with major implications for the Church. On the one hand, employment opportunities in the Charlotte area had led to a substantial migration of Hispanics and the opening of the Centro Hispano, which offered 'spiritual and cultural' services to some 400 families. On the other hand, the war in far-off Indochina had produced an influx of Asian refugees, many of whom were assisted by the refugee resettlement program of Catholic Social Services. Both these populations were heavily Catholic and found identification with the church valuable in adjusting to their new environment.

New Issues; New Ministries

In its comprehensive assessment of the church in western North Carolina, the quinquennial report noted that, "reflecting the present trend of opinion," many people in the diocese supported a more inclusive priesthood, including the ordination of women. In response to this issue, the bishop had established a task force on the role of women that provided a forum in which a range of views might be expressed and in which participants could be helped to "understand the position of the Church on the ordination of women."

Gender, sexual, and family issues were reflected as well in the inauguration of services for the widowed, separated, and divorced, including special retreats for this growing population. Also, without indicating any diocesan policy, it was noted that the practice of unmarried couples living together was "occurring frequently." As in the case of contraception, the church found itself unable to counteract the impact of the general culture on the behavior of Catholics.

Although lay leadership would be a hallmark of the post-Vatican II church, the permanent diaconate provided a bridge between the traditional categories of priest and lay person. By their family life and secular occupations, deacons shared lay life styles and by their specialized training and ordination entered the world of the clergy.

General norms for the restoration of the permanent diaconate were issued by Pope Paul VI in June 1967 and adopted by the American hierarchy the following year. In April 1972, representatives of eleven dioceses, including Charlotte and Raleigh, met in Atlanta to explore the possibility of establishing a program. The group worked on developing a 'job description' for a clergy rank that had not been active in the church for more than a millennium. After several years of consultation and planning, Charlotte inaugurated the program. The quinquennial report announced that after three years of study and spiritual direction, twenty men were to be ordained deacons in May 1983.

By 2001, Charlotte had sixty-three deacons, a number roughly equal to that of active diocesan priests. The Raleigh Diocese did not begin a permanent diaconate program until the year 2000.

This Land Is Home To Me

Affluent and well-educated people of every religion tend to have a loud social voice, one that can lobby on behalf of their interests. Not so the poor, who remain socially invisible unless someone takes up their cause. One such population was the millions of people who lived in Appalachia, including the residents of fifteen counties in western North Carolina. One of the most lasting achievements of Bishop Begley was his leadership on behalf of the men, women, and children of that depressed region. Begley's concern for the poor of Appalachia, which began in the first year of his bishopric, continued into his retirement.

Extending from southern New York to northern Georgia and Alabama, the Appalachian Mountains form the backbone of the eastern United States. They also serve as home for some of the poorest people in the country. Perhaps the most vivid image of Appalachia is that of a miner, his tired, hopeless eyes looking out from a face covered with a film of coal dust. He has just exited an elevator that had brought him to the surface after having labored for ten hours hundreds of feet beneath the earth, harvesting the "black gold" that enriched absentee mine owners even as it coated his own lungs with death.

Of course, Appalachia was more than coal mines. It was also steel mills, natural gas exploration sites, timber harvesting areas, and poor farms. It was men and women, most of them white, few of them Catholic, left behind by a prospering nation. There was no leader to draw attention to their plight, as Martin Luther King had done for blacks. Into this vacuum stepped the Catholic bishops, led by Begley. As in earlier years he had toured North Carolina textile mills in order to understand the conditions of workers, so in 1972, as chairman of the bishops' committee, he traveled with other religious leaders throughout Appalachia, familiarizing himself with conditions and embracing the concerns of its people.

In a rare example of cooperation among a number of dioceses, in 1975 the bishops issued *This Land is Home to Me: A Pastoral Letter on Powerlessness in Appalachia*. In a style echoing that of Dr. King, the pastoral eschewed the typical ponderous tone of episcopal pronouncements and spoke from the heart and to the heart:

> Appalachia makes us think of people who live in the hills, who love nature's freedom and beauty, who are alive with song and poetry. But many of these people are also poor and suffer oppression.
> Once they went to the mountains fighting to build a dream different from the injustice they knew before. Until this day their struggle continues, a bitter fight whose sound still rumbles across the hills.[34]

Recognizing that modern technology was a two-edged sword, the bishops expressed hope that the innovations penetrating the once hidden recesses of the mountains would heal and not destroy:

> Once we all knew how to dance and sing, sat in mystery before the poet's spell, felt our hearts rise to nature's cathedral. Now an alien culture battles to shape us into plastic forms empty of Spirit, into beasts of burden without mystery.
> If the struggle's dream can be defended, and we believe it can, then perhaps the great instruments of attack: cable TV, satellite communications, ribbons of highway, can become like so many arms, which instead of crushing life, reach out to make it fuller, to bring to others beyond the mountains, the promise of their vision.

With prescience, the bishops wrote of a development that in subsequent decades would become even more significant:

> We call attention to the presence of powerful multinational corporations now within our region. The fate and role of these institutions is a major question not only for Appalachia, but also for the whole world.

Well aware that their main resource was the power of persuasion, the bishops attempted to instill hope in the people of Appalachia itself even as they tried to enlist the rest of the nation in a concerted effort to alleviate the region's ills. Finally, in order to demonstrate that

Catholic concern was more than just an eloquent letter, the bishops commissioned the Catholic Committee of Appalachia to take up specific issues, including the role of coal in the life of the region and nation, the exploitation of cheap labor, occupational health and safety, and cooperatives. One sign of the ongoing interest in the area is the fact that every few years additional bishops add their names to the original twenty-four, reissue the letter, and reaffirm the church's commitment.

Indicative of that commitment was a tour of the mountain region of North Carolina that Begley took in 1985, the tenth anniversary of the letter. Now retired, Begley invited his successor, Bishop John Donoghue, to see this easily neglected part of the diocese. Shedding their clerical collars, the two bishops climbed into a church van and, joined by priests and lay people, headed west. In Hendersonville, Maggie Valley, Marshall, and Mars Hill, they heard grim reports of unemployment, inadequate housing, and poor health care. But they also received encouraging reports of worker-owned cooperatives, mobile medical services, and ecumenical collaboration among church volunteers. In one of his final public acts, Bishop Begley, ever the social worker, wanted to be sure that the poor were not forgotten by his successor.[35]

"Good-bye, Partner"

For several years after his retirement, Begley made his home at St. Ann in Charlotte, the parish that he had founded in 1955 and the scene of many of his most satisfying experiences. Begley understood that retirement was a time for a more relaxed ministry, not its abandonment. So, in the warm afternoons, no longer burdened with administrative responsibilities, he often did what he so much loved; he played with children. In a spiritual link with the long ago days at the Nazareth orphanage, he walked out to the parochial school yard and was soon surrounded by a squealing circle of his beloved "kiddos." His goal was not to teach religion; it was simply to give joy and to receive joy. In their innocence the children easily recognized someone who loved them.

In 1997, increasing infirmity led Begley to move to Maryfield Nursing Home in High Point. There, the Poor Servants of the Mother of God, a religious order dedicated to ministering to the elderly, cared for him and became the beneficiaries of his warm good cheer. With his mental faculties intact until the end, he welcomed visitors, regaling them with stories of the pioneering days of the church in the state. On Feb. 9, 2002, at the age of ninety-two, his journey ended.[36]

Not only was Begley the first bishop of Charlotte but the last surviving priest to have served under William Hafey, the first bishop of Raleigh. Like candles reverently snuffed out after mass, the men who embodied the living memory of the early days of Catholicism in North Carolina were passing from the scene. One of the survivors was Joe Showfety, Begley's close associate in the establishment of the diocese. By a fortuitous coincidence, Showfety's nonagenarian mother was also a resident of Maryfield. So, when the seventy-four-year-old priest visited his mother, he also would stop by to see his old boss. The day before Begley died, Showfety was at his side once again, this time not helping with the administration of a diocese but with the transition to eternity.

At Begley's funeral mass at Charlotte's St. Gabriel Church, Showfety preached the homily, fondly recalling events from the life of this "man of peace." Few of the people who filled the modern church building, including scores of priests, would have caught the oblique allusion to the troubled days of Bishop Waters. In fact, more than thirty years after the fact, few knew that the Charlotte diocese had been born during a period of pain and dissension -- the birth pains, as it were, of the modern church. Showfety's reference to Begley as "a bridge of unity for his priests" was possibly the final reference to a troubled era.

For his own part, facing retirement after a long ministry, Showfety found himself the last North Carolina priest to have had contact with Raleigh's second bishop, Eugene McGuinness, who had confirmed young Showfety at St. Benedict in Greensboro more than sixty years earlier. As a boy, Showfety was one of only 6,000 Catholics in the state. Now there were more than that many members of St. Gabriel parish alone. It was men like Begley and Showfety who had helped bring about this happy state of affairs. Yet, somehow, those early days were more exciting, more challenging. Young men see visions and old men dream dreams. Showfety's youth had been spent with men like Mike Begley, Mike Irwin, John Roueche, and Billy O'Brien. It had been a hard time to be a Catholic, but perhaps a life is not worth living unless there are difficulties to surmount. Before leaving the lectern at the funeral mass, Showfety looked down at Begley's casket and, his voice choking, whispered, "Good-bye partner."

Part IV

Evolving Ministries in a Diverse Church

It wasn't simply a question of numbers, but of changing roles and increasing diversity. Women religious moved out of the classroom and into a wide range of ministries, including that of serving as parish administrators. African-Americans became more vocal in a church dominated by whites, their voices often drowned out by an avalanche of Latinos whose presence transformed virtually every parish in the state. Koreans, Vietnamese, and people from other countries both enriched and challenged a church struggling to be truly "catholic." Most notable of all, lay men and women were assuming positions of responsibility formerly reserved to priests. As it entered the Twenty-First Century, Catholicism in North Carolina was a kaleidoscope of people building a church with hope and faith their only blueprints. The clergy sex scandals of 2002 were a sobering reminder of human fallibility.

*   *   *

We are people made up of diverse backgrounds. The Church is a mosaic, and all of the pieces fit together to create a picture of Jesus.

• William G. Curlin, Bishop of Charlotte, 2002

Chapter Eleven

Religious Orders of Men & Women

Sisters of Mercy We are happy to announce that the Rt. Rev. Bishop Gibbons has been successful in securing the permanent foundation of Sisters of Mercy for the city of Wilmington. These good Sisters will here devote themselves to the education of youth and to acts of charity. We learn that they are expected to arrive from Charleston about the 20th of this month, and will open a Parochial and Academic School about the beginning of October. Their kindness to our people in the memorable epidemic of 1862 will long be remembered by the people of this city. They will be the first colony of sisters ever permanently established in this State, and which State is the only one hitherto in which they had not school or hospital. We are sure that their untiring and unselfish zeal in the cause of Christian education and suffering humanity will secure for them a cordial reception from our appreciative and benevolent community.

---*Wilmington Daily Journal*, September 9, 1869

The present chapter acknowledges the contributions of religious orders of both men and women to the church in North Carolina. However, since more than eighty orders of women and thirty orders of men have served in the state at some time, only a few can be given specific mention. Much has already been recorded of the work of the Benedictine monks, and more will be added here. As for women religious, one community, the Sisters of Mercy, will be given extensive attention. To a large extent, they *are* the history of religious orders of women in North Carolina. They preceded all other women religious by some thirty-five years, working against great odds to establish Catholic educational and health care services in the state. More than 130 years after their arrival, although reduced in numbers, the Sisters of Mercy remain by far the largest community in the state. However, the others cannot be ignored, nor the fact that religious life has undergone dramatic changes. An account of the experience of the Daughters of Charity, who worked in Greensboro, North Carolina, for nearly a century, can serve to illustrate the trajectory of many groups of women religious.

In 1904, when doctors from the Piedmont medical community needed a hospital they approached Leo Haid, the Vicar Apostolic for North Carolina, who in turn requested the help of the Daughters of Charity of Emmitsburg, Maryland. Accepting the challenge to come to what was then a remote mission outpost, several sisters traveled to Greensboro in 1906, commencing a presence in that city that would span several generations and undergo numerous transformations. More than priests and bishops, religious women exhibited a flexibility and adaptability that kept them on the cutting edge of societal and church needs. Although often hidden in the shadow of bishops and pastors, women consecrated to the service of the church not only were more numerous than their male counterparts, but as often as not more creative and energetic in their accomplishments.

The initial project of the Daughters of Charity, dressed in their blue habits topped with impossibly large wing-like headpieces, was the construction and operation of St. Leo's Hospital and Nursing School. The land for the four-story edifice on Summit Avenue was donated by Caesar Cone, who was Jewish. The hospital, named in honor of Bishop Haid, was Guilford County's first and the most visible contribution of the Catholic Church to Greensboro. Although not understanding why women would wear such unusual clothing and live anonymous, celibate lives, thousands of non-Catholics were grateful for the healing touch of the sisters.

By 1912, ten sisters, working as nurses, teachers, and administrators, were assigned to St. Leo's. When the diocese of Raleigh was established in 1924, that number stood at twelve, a concentration of religious personnel in the state exceeded only by the Benedictine monks and the Sisters of Mercy in Belmont. Two years later, prodded by Bishop Hafey, the sisters expanded their ministry still further, adding schools in St. Mary and St. Benedict parishes, both also in Greensboro. The former school served black children, the latter, white.

As the medical situation in Greensboro improved and more modern hospitals opened, St. Leo's became obsolete and in 1954, its mission completed, the hospital was closed. For a few years after that the building became Notre Dame High School, the only Catholic high school the city ever had. However, bowing to financial pressures and declining enrollment, Notre Dame shut down in 1968, and the diocese leased the property to the Exxon Corporation.

Although their original home now featured a gas station, the sisters continued to staff the Greensboro parochial schools until they were closed in 1955 as part of Bishop Waters' program for integrating Catholic institutions. In their place the more modern and integrated school of St. Pius X was opened. However, even this adjustment to shifting needs did not last for long, as within a few years declining religious vocations required that the sisters turn over the school to a lay staff. While most of the sisters left, a few remained in the parish assuming new roles to go along with their new habits. Although no longer classroom teachers, they taught religion at St. Pius X, complementing the work of the lay teachers and also traveling north to the small parish of Holy Infant in Reidsville, where they assisted with religious education and First Communion preparation.

The next step in the evolving ministry of the Daughters of Charity occurred in 1984 when they accepted responsibility for the coordination of social and religious activities at Dolan Manor, a Catholic nursing home in Greensboro. In addition, embodying the spirit of St. Vincent de Paul, the 19th Century French priest who was their spiritual father, the sisters reached out to assist the increasing numbers of poor migrant workers in the area, many of them from Mexico.

In 1990, the sisters extended their work still further when Sister Ann Joseph became director of the Greensboro office of Catholic Social Services, in which position she not only provided direct services to the needy but served as advocate for peace and justice issues throughout the Greensboro Vicariate. Since the sisters remained based in St. Pius X parish, they continued to offer leadership and inspiration to the Catholics of that community.

Over the years, the sisters had moved from being nurses, to teachers, to religious educators, to social workers, to social justice activists. Sometimes it was the same women changing careers. Other times it was a new generation of sisters, women reared in a different religious world from that of their older colleagues. However, with all the changes, their roots in Greensboro were not forgotten as sisters regularly visited the local hospitals bringing the Eucharist to Catholic patients, something their predecessors at St. Leo's Hospital never dreamed of being authorized to do.

Then, on June 15, 1998, an era came to an end. A farewell ceremony was held at St. Pius X for Sisters Marian Hagner and Celeste Donohue. The two women, advanced in years, were returning to the motherhouse in Maryland, closing the book on ninety-four years of service by their community to the people of Greensboro

However, the Greensboro story did not end in 1998. The year after the sisters departed, on the site where their predecessors had built the hospital in 1906, George Carr, a developer and a member of St. Pius X parish, constructed a forty-four unit housing complex for the elderly poor. Stating that "no soil in Greensboro holds more Catholic history than this parcel," he called the new community St. Leo's Place. Furthermore, Carr placed in the community building the statue of the Virgin Mary that had stood for decades in the grotto of the hospital garden and in front of which class after class of graduating nurses had posed for photos. Finally, linking the past to the future, the grounds remained shaded by the huge oak tree beneath which sisters had walked in prayer and students studied.[1]

Despite their departure from Greensboro, the Daughters of Charity continue to serve North Carolina, staffing St. Ann School in Fayetteville. In the year 2002, the five sisters assigned to St. Ann comprised the largest convent of sisters in the Raleigh Diocese.[2]

What is a Priest?

Before proceeding, it seems appropriate to present a brief reflection on the Church's evolving understanding of priesthood and religious life. Since the Vatican Council of the 1960's, both ways of life have been undergoing changes that have created a prolonged period of ferment. From the point of view of history, it must be emphasized that many of the stresses and uncertainties that characterize the present day did not exist during earlier generations. The lives of priests and religious may have been difficult, but the meaning of their way of life was clear. Privations were counterbalanced by a clarity of purpose and confidence in the future often lacking today.

One of the most thorny issues in the Catholic Church today is defining the role of the priest. Furthermore, since the church teaches that all the baptized share in the priesthood of Christ, distinguishing between the priesthood of the faithful and that of the ordained minister becomes problematic. As lay men and women assume more and more positions previously reserved to priests, what is left for the man called "Father?"

The official documents of the church stress that Christ is the one true priest and that others share in his priesthood, including "the whole community of believers" who through their baptism participate in Christ's mission as priest, prophet, and king. On the other hand, the ministerial or hierarchical priesthood of bishops and priests "is at the service of the common priesthood.... is a *means* by which Christ unceasingly builds up and leads his Church. For this reason it is transmitted by its own sacrament, the sacrament of Holy Orders" (1546, 1547).[3]

However, although the ordained priest represents Christ before the assembly and acts in the name of the whole Church when he presents to God the prayer of the Church, this does not mean that the laity plays no role in worship. On the contrary, the whole Church, as "the Body of Christ," is essential and always active in offering prayer to God (1552, 1553). Thus, although the priest is necessary, so also is the community. The liturgy is the shared action of all the faithful presided over by the ordained priest.

Is presiding at liturgy then the only distinctively priestly action? Although Old Testament priests offering sacrifices and Christ the High Priest offering himself on the cross are presented as images, official doctrine broadens the role of the ordained minister to three functions:

> The ministerial priesthood differs in essence from the common priesthood of the faithful because it confers a sacred power for the service of the faithful. The ordained ministers exercise their service for the People of God by teaching (*munus docendi*), divine worship (*munus liturgicum*) and pastoral governance (*munus regendi*) (1592).

However, to some extent all of these priestly functions are "exercised" by other members of the Church as well, and sometimes by people who are not members of the church at all! For example, much of the teaching is done by non-priests. In fact, both dioceses in North Carolina have Offices of Faith Formation that are headed by lay persons, and virtually all religious instruction is conducted by lay men and women, including the preparation of people for admission to the church through the Rite of the Christian Initiation of Adults (RCIA). Indeed, further confusing the issue, many churches use ordination-like "commissioning services" to install religious education teachers, and both North Carolina dioceses have catechetical training programs that certify religion teachers.

As to the worship role, not only do lay ministers such as lectors and eucharistic ministers routinely participate in the mass, but lay people bring Communion to the sick and are instructed to pray and read the Scriptures with those to whom they bring the sacrament. Permanent deacons, who some have facetiously labeled "ordained laymen," baptize and preach, functions formerly reserved to priests.

Finally, as far as "pastoral governance" is concerned, both dioceses and most large parishes now have lay administrators who are responsible for most of the work of running the church. Even more striking, as will be elaborated in Chapter Thirteen, is the emergence of "pastoral administrators," all of them at the present time women, who for all intents and purposes are the pastors of smaller parishes. Ordained priests come in to officiate at mass and administer the sacraments, but the "governance" of the parish resides with the administrator.

Having said this, it remains true that most Catholics consider the ordained priest *the* essential person in their worship community. Even as others assume more and more church tasks, the priest is intuited as having special power. Scandals like pedophilia, embezzlement, and drunkenness are especially egregious precisely because the ordained priest is viewed as "different," as a mediator between God and man. What distinguishes Catholicism from Protestantism more than anything else is the belief in "sacred signs," in sacraments. And the priest, be he brilliant or dull, personable or nasty, an engaging preacher or a bore, is a visible sign of the invisible God.[4]

What are religious?

Even as priesthood undergoes reassessment, so also does religious life. The dramatic decline in the number of priests, brothers, and sisters in many parts of the world may reflect this definitional confusion. Young men and women are reluctant to enter a state of life that lacks a clear and compelling significance. The generosity with which many young Catholic men and women devote their lives to the service of others as lay persons suggests that idealism has not declined, only the appeal of the traditional choices offered by the church. Whatever the reasons, the statistics are staggering. And the massive flight from religious orders is substantially greater than from the secular priesthood. Between 1965 and 2001, while the number of diocesan priests declined by 16%, the number of religious order priests went down 34% and of religious sisters by a breathtaking 57%.[5]

The church presents a glowing vision of religious life as a context for personal growth and apostolic service. In previous generations this vision drew large numbers of men and women into the hundreds of orders that had emerged over the centuries, each with its distinctive "charism" or spirit. However, although some orders hope for a resurgence of vocations, there are few signs of such a development. This is how the church presents religious life:

> The religious state is thus one way of experiencing a "more intimate" consecration, rooted in Baptism and dedicated totally to God. In the consecrated life, Christ's faithful, moved by the Holy Sprit, propose to follow Christ more nearly, to give themselves to God who is loved above all and, pursuing the perfection of charity in the service of the Kingdom, to signify and proclaim in the Church the glory of the world to come (916).

Religious orders, then, are "institutes canonically erected by the Church" which people join in order to live more perfect lives *and* to assume a ministry "in the service of the Kingdom." That ministry may be primarily "contemplative" or primarily "active." The motto of the Benedictines "To work and to pray" expresses both these values and, as has been seen, the Belmont monks during the Vicariate Apostolic period experienced a tension over how to balance these two dimensions of their vocation. Some members wanted a higher proportion of their time spent in prayer, while others were drawn to a more activist ministry.

Josephite Fathers, on the other hand, who came to the state in 1917 and were the first order of religious men to undertake work in North Carolina after the Benedictines, had no such problem. They had been established with a clear "active" ministry, namely, to work with African Americans. The political and social conditions that prevailed in North Carolina before the Civil Rights movement ideally suited the Josephites for work in the state. Today, with racial integration, there is less call for men who limit their ministry to blacks. Josephites, who no longer serve in North Carolina, filled an important ministerial "niche." For all intents and purposes, such priests were the same as diocesan priests, only limiting their work to specific populations and answering to superiors other than the local bishop.[6]

As for women religious, the same distinction applies. Carmelite nuns are committed to a life of prayer, whereas the Daughters of Charity, discussed above, and the Sisters of Mercy are examples of "active" orders. As was seen in the previous chapter, attempts to establish Carmelite monasteries in North Carolina were not successful. On the other hand, scores of active communities of women have worked in the state.

The word "community" is frequently used when describing religious orders, and a traditional characteristic of religious institutes has been the shared life. The community was a type of "family" providing the emotional and physical support often lacking in the lives of solitary individuals, be they priests or lay persons. However, most contemporary religious women have abandoned this feature of religious life, preferring to live alone rather than in convents. Of the seventy-four sisters residing in the Diocese of Raleigh in 2002, twenty-eight live alone and there are but three residences with three or more sisters. In the Diocese of Charlotte the situation is similar except for the motherhouse of the Sisters of Mercy where forty sisters live together, most of them retired. In fact, in many communities today the communal life is experienced only in the final years of life.

While all religious orders grapple with change, religious order priests have more complex problems than do women. The men have to contend with identity issues surrounding both priesthood *and* religious life. It may be for this reason that their ranks have been thinned at double the rate of that of diocesan priests. In discussing "the dissonance between the mission of Religious institutes and the mission of ordained ministry," one author wrote:

> Both realities in the Church [religious life and priesthood] have undergone significant shifts in perspective and theology. Unfortunately, in many ways for religious priests, they have not been shifting in any mutually coordinated way, leaving religious priests with each leg of their identity firmly planted on logs moving in different directions in the swiftly moving current of post Vatican II theology.[7]

While many order priests have left church service altogether, some have transferred to the diocesan priesthood, including several in North Carolina. The most notable is the Charlotte Diocese Vicar General and Chancellor, Father Mauricio West, who was ordained a Benedictine monk and, after serving for a number of years in the Belmont community, left the order and affiliated with the diocese.[8]

The unsettled status of contemporary religious life should not obscure the fact that religious orders have played – and continue to play -- a major role in the Catholic Church in North Carolina. Bishops continue to beg orders of both men and women to supply personnel. The notice which Bishop James Gibbons placed in the Wilmington newspaper in 1869, and which appears at the opening of this chapter, represents what was the overriding priority at the time – Catholic schools. As Gibbons pointed out, North Carolina was the last state in the Union to establish this hallmark of the Catholic Church in America. For their part, besides recruiting sisters for schools, Bishops Haid, Hafey, and McGuinness sought religious order priests to establish parishes for African Americans. Today the situation is quite different. Bishops are grateful to have a dwindling number of order priests to staff as many parishes as possible and, perhaps nostalgic for their own youthful days in the pre-Vatican II Church, to welcome aging sisters for a range of pastoral positions, few of them in schools.[9]

Although most of the remaining Sisters of Mercy now live in prayerful retirement, there was a time when these women were dynamos of spiritual energy, operating schools and hospitals with quiet efficiency. In fact, for more than a generation, the North Carolina Sisters of Mercy operated all Catholic schools, hospitals, and orphanages in the state. Not every venture succeeded, but those that did put a deep stamp of Catholicity on the communities where they were established. However, the initial ministry of the sisters was a temporary one -- caring for the sick, wounded, and dying during a period of great national crisis -- the Civil War.

Civil War Service of Religious Women

In one of those coincidences of history, two small groups of Sisters of Mercy served as nurses in the state at the same time, one contingent with the Union army that occupied the area around New Bern and the other in Confederate-occupied Wilmington. Coming as they did from different motherhouses, neither group knew of the other's presence.

Since the war required that field hospitals be established in a number of locations, the New York Sisters of Mercy were invited by the Union army to staff a military hospital in the coastal town of Beaufort. Accepting the challenge, on July 16, 1862, nine sisters boarded the government steamship Canawba and set sail for the war zone. Other "passengers" on the vessel were 500 horses destined for cavalry service. The Reverend Mother and her assistant were in the party to be sure that the seven sisters assigned to the hospital received adequate housing accommodations and that "all necessary provisions, medicines, and utensils [were] supplied both for themselves and for the patients under their charge." Furthermore, a chaplain "paid and maintained" by the army was to be provided for their religious needs.[10]

Arriving during a drenching downpour, the sisters were obliged to cross a long, narrow wharf in single file. Patients watching from the windows of the hospital, formerly a resort hotel, "concluded that they were nine widows coming to seek for the remains of their husbands." At the makeshift hospital, the sisters were shown to their living quarters, rooms that until recently had been used by the patients, "blood marks on the walls of some of them, a sad souvenir of the suffering of some wounded mortals." Despite such hardships, the sisters set to work and within a few days had improved the sanitary conditions and developed routines for assisting the patients. Even the doctor in charge, who at first disapproved of placing sick soldiers under the care of Sisters whom he regarded as nonprofessional "Lady-nurses," came to respect them.

Problems plagued the sisters from the start. Three of them fell sick and were obliged to return to New York. Also, it turned out that Father Bruhl, the Hungarian priest assigned as their chaplain, was a Confederate at heart. He went about telling people that the South would win the war. Furthermore, with his little English and even less understanding of American society, he told the men that everyone outside the Catholic Church was damned. At last, in exasperation, the hospital doctor insisted that the priest be discharged, saying "I do not consider it honest for a man to receive a salary from the United States, while he defames its Army and discourages the men that compose it by telling them they are damned to Hell."

As cold October winds made remaining in the exposed waterside location impossible, the hospital was relocated to the better equipped New Bern, where the army commandeered several large houses to serve as the hospital. There the sisters continued their work until April 1863, when they were recalled to New York because, as the annals record, the "patients were nearly all disposed of, either by death or recovery." Thus ended, after nine months, the first mission of religious sisters in North Carolina.

During the same period, three Sisters of Mercy belonging to the community founded by Bishop England had come from Charleston, South Carolina, to Wilmington, not to minister to wounded and sick Confederate soldiers but to help care for the victims of a yellow fever epidemic. Already hemmed in by the Northern blockade, this second assault had a devastating impact on the population. Father Thomas Murphy, pastor of St. Thomas parish, begged his superior, Charleston Bishop Patrick Lynch, for assistance. In response, the sisters were dispatched along with Father James A. Corcoran. Having successfully run the Federal blockade, the steamship "Kate" tied up at the foot of Dock Street on August 6, 1862, and the sisters stepped ashore.[11]

Gratefully referred to by townspeople as "Angels of Mercy," the sisters went to work aiding the yellow fever victims, although aid consisted of little more than palliative care and prayers. One Wilmington resident reported: "One day as I looked out the window I saw all windows closed, with no sign of life save the 'Little Sisters of Mercy' darting across the streets, flitting from door to door, entering to administer to the sick and dying."[12] During the four-weeks of October alone, 447 deaths were attributed to the disease, more than one tenth of the city's population of 3,000.

Although the plague ended with the arrival of cooler weather, the war raged on. Most of the civilian population of Wilmington had fled inland leaving behind their shattered homes and hopes. As for the sisters, their mission accomplished they returned home to Charleston, never dreaming that within a few years Wilmington would become the seat of a new ecclesiastical jurisdiction and that they would be invited back -- this time to stay.

The Establishment of Religious Life in North Carolina

In August 1869, the newly installed Vicar Apostolic, Bishop James Gibbons, wrote to Mother Francis, Superior of the Sisters of Our Lady of Mercy of Charleston, requesting sisters for a school in North Carolina. Although he had earlier attempted to get sisters from Ireland, Gibbons wrote: "I have a decided preference for you, believing you know our people and our peculiar institutions better than others." Among the "peculiar institutions," of course, were slavery and the deep seated mistrust of the Catholic Church.[13]

Anticipating that Mother Francis might refuse because of a shortage of sisters, Gibbons added a post script to another letter to her in which he indicated that "several young ladies in Baltimore and Wilmington have expressed a desire to join the sisters." This was not wishful thinking. Two of the Wilmington "young ladies" were older sisters of Thomas Price. Just as Price would be the first diocesan priest ordained for North Carolina, so also one of his sisters would be the first native North Carolinian to enter the sisterhood.

As a diocesan community, the Charleston Sisters of Mercy were under the jurisdiction of Bishop Lynch and needed his approval to establish a foundation in Wilmington.[14] This permission granted, three sisters

were assigned to the new mission: Sister Mary Augustine Kent, Sister
Mary Charles Curtin, and Sister Mary Baptist Sheehan.[15] In her old age,
Sister Charles was asked to write her recollections of her arrival in
America and of the early years of the North Carolina community.[16] Besides
being the last survivor of the three sisters who established the North
Carolina presence, Sister Charles was the last link with Bishop England.[17]

As was true of many of the early Sisters of Mercy, Sister
Charles was recruited by Bishop England on one of his trips home to
Ireland, accompanying him to America in 1841. As it happened, the
young woman had her first, if brief, contact with Wilmington in that
year. With her twin sister and Father Doyle, also recruited in Ireland,
she had traveled by train from Philadelphia to Wilmington, at the time
the southernmost terminal of the railroad. From there the little group
continued by steamer to Charleston. For the next twenty-eight years
Sister Charles worked in the struggling missions of South Carolina. Her
recollections of the Civil War included an assessment of the spirit that
characterized the people at the onset of that conflict:

> The proud Southerners went into this war sure of victory, and the
> young people indulged in poetic dreams as to its results. Young men,
> mere boys, left college, office and plantation to join the ranks on the
> way to glory, that they might become, so they thought, leaders of
> armies and statesmen. Young ladies made banners with delicate
> hands, hoping to become sisters and wives of princes and generals.
> "We do not want peace, but victory," said one in my hearing.[18]

When the call came to go to Wilmington, Sister Charles was
teaching at the Mercy Academy in Sumpter, South Carolina. Returning to
Charleston, she set off with her companions for the new assignment. On
their arrival in Wilmington in September 1869, the sisters were greeted by
Bishop Gibbons. Although anxious to have a Catholic school, the bishop
was preoccupied by his pending trip to Rome for the Vatican Council as
well as the scarcity of finances to support the sisters. Sister Charles'
retroactive assessment of the situation was that Gibbons "proved but an
occasional meteor, casting now and again a faint light as we worked the
oars of our own little bark. It was well, for a stronger arm [God] took hold
of the helm and has guided it since through storm and calm."

Although Gibbons had begged the sisters to come and provided
them with a house, it was expected that they would quickly become self-
supporting. Accordingly, within a few weeks they announced the opening
of the Academy of the Incarnation, a day school for girls. It was hoped that

the students' tuition would provide for the fledgling group. Thirty-six pupils enrolled for the first session, including about ten Protestants. Although the sisters were disappointed with the number of students, it would turn out to be the maximum they would enroll for the following eleven years. Due to anti-Catholic sentiment and the opening of a public school, within two years all the Protestant girls had withdrawn.

Concern about providing education only for the affluent led to the opening of the tuition-free St. Peter's Parochial School for girls in 1871. However, this institution fared even worse than the academy. As Sister Charles put it, "In addition to its being small, consequently ungraded, the pupils were of a class that attended most irregularly. In the space of one week the number present often ran up and down the scale from five to twenty-five and vise versa."

Conscious that no Catholic education was available to boys, in 1876 the sisters added St. Joseph's Male Academy. Trying to balance the need to be self-supporting with the desire to accommodate the children of the poor, the sisters asked parents to pay what they could afford. This proved to be a disastrous policy. As Sister Charles put it, "Too many are inclined to take advantage of the liberal terms."

Thus, within a few years, the slowly increasing band of sisters had opened and were operating three schools. Although each had an impressive name, all were housed in crowded quarters, minimally staffed, and had small enrollments. Among other obstacles to solvency was the fact that the more affluent Catholic parents tended to send their daughters to more prestigious schools, leaving only the poor for the sisters. As Sister Charles explained: "One cannot form a fine system of graded classes without numbers, nor have great elegance and style without money." As a consequence of the conditions under which the sisters worked, when the school year ended in June 1880, the enrollment in the three institutions combined was fifty-one students -- the sum total of Catholic education in the state.[19]

By this time the number of sisters in Wilmington had risen to thirteen, including two novices and three postulants, and the first move out of the city took place. However, the selection of a location, Hickory, a small town in the hills of the western part of the state, was based not on the need of the Catholic population in that area, in fact, there was but one Catholic family, but rather on concern for the health of the sisters. The low-lying port city of Wilmington was a magnet for various diseases including malaria and scarlet fever. Some sisters had became ill, further crippling the operation of the schools.[20]

Misgivings about going to Hickory were expressed by Gibbons, by then archbishop of Baltimore. Always solicitous for the sisters he had invited to the state, he wrote: "I hope that the community will not be disappointed in going to Hickory ... [but] it is important that the sisters in Wilmington should have an outlet for their health's sake."[21] Notwithstanding these concerns, in January 1880, five sisters, including a novice and a postulant, were assigned to open a school in Hickory. One of the five was Sister Mary Agnes Price, who had entered the community in 1869. Unfortunately, despite the more salubrious climate of Hickory, within three months, Sister Agnes was dead. The first to enter was also the first to die. Her body was brought back to her native Wilmington for burial. Although Fred Price had not yet been ordained a priest, another sister had entered the community by this time and, as has been seen, Sister Catherine worked with her brother in the orphanage at Nazareth.

Attempting to replicate the model used at Wilmington, the sisters opened Mt. St. Joseph's Academy for girls in Hickory, hoping that some of the Protestant tuition-paying girls would be attracted to the Church. As was true of all Catholic enterprises that provided service to non-Catholics, the school was seen as having a missionary function. The sisters' expectations were enhanced by the fact that the prominent convert novelist Christian Reid (Frances Fisher) lived in Salisbury, fifty miles distant from Hickory. Bishop Henry Northrop, who as Vicar Apostolic of North Carolina was the superior of the sisters at the time, counseled them that "Miss Fisher deserves special personal consideration."[22] The attention given her was rewarded with generous contributions to the community.[23]

However, Hickory proved to be a failed experiment. McCarthy devotes many pages to the legal and financial problems in which the sisters were entangled both there and in the larger city of Asheville, where Northrup had urged them to relocate the school. Correspondence between the sisters and the bishop, who spoke of himself as "a soul harassed and perplexed in the extreme,"[24] illustrates the chronic difficulty of establishing a secure Catholic presence in the state, particularly in the mountain region. In 1887, bowing to the inevitable, the sisters closed the school. Although today St. Aloysius Church in Hickory is a successful parish, there has never since been a Catholic school in the town.

Leaving the mountains with their clear air but sparse population, the sisters turned next to a more promising setting, opening a
school at St. Peter parish in Charlotte. Although they did not realize it
at the time, this new foundation would have a profound impact on their
fortunes. As has been related, in 1888, Leo Haid, the abbot of the
Belmont Benedictine monastery, was appointed Vicar Apostolic and
consecrated bishop. Haid would become not only the ecclesiastical
superior of the sisters, but their fervent patron. The transformation of a
struggling handful of women into a thriving religious congregation was
about to begin, due largely to Haid's initiatives.[25]

The Move to Belmont

The proximity of Belmont to Charlotte resulted in the monks
assisting St. Peter's pastor, Father Mark Gross, when he was absent
from the parish. As the monks and sisters came to know one another, the
idea emerged that the sisters might establish a school and convent near
the monastery. This idea led to action in 1891, when Haid wrote excit-
edly to Mother Augustine Kent, the long-term Superior of the
Wilmington-based community, that he had been offered eighty-five
acres adjacent to the monastery for $2,500.

> Its situation is all that could be desired for a convent school, just fifteen
> minutes walk from our college and ten minutes walk from the railroad
> station, on a beautiful hill. For years I tho't it a most desirable place for
> sisters. The produce of the farm would go far to keep them; they could
> have a convent, boarding school, a day school for white children, and
> also teach the colored school already built. Then they might also care
> for white orphans -- little girls -- later if not just now. I would advise
> you to buy the property even if you must borrow the money...[26]

The sisters were as eager as the monks to procure the land but
equally as poor. As the sisters wrangled with Northrup for the money
they had advanced him for the house he had bought in Asheville, Haid,
fearful of losing the site to what he called "land sharks," went ahead and
bought the Belmont site in his own name. In the meanwhile, Felix
Hintemeyer, Haid's aide, wrote several letters to Sister Catherine Price,
then the superior at the Charlotte foundation, expressing the enthusiasm
with which he himself as well as the bishop approved of the project.

No sooner had the ink dried on the deed, subsequently transferred by Haid to the sisters, than the bishop had his corps of sturdy
German brothers construct a building to serve as both school and con-

vent. In August 1892, assured that what was to become their new motherhouse would be ready for occupancy, the sisters boarded the train
from Wilmington and headed west. On September 1, after a few days
stay in Charlotte, the group of nine sisters moved on to Belmont, where
they were met by smiling monks but a far-from-complete convent.

No doors had been hung and there was no way of locking up the
house. As evening came on, the sisters realized that there was no light, not
even a match or candle. Groping their way to their beds, the women
passed a restless night. As for food, since the kitchen had not been
installed the Benedictines brought them their meals from the monastery.

Since, as usual, the sisters were expected to become self-supporting, Haid had the opening of Sacred Heart Academy for girls
announced in all the parishes of the Vicariate, as well as in parishes in
South Carolina and Virginia. Ready or not, a month after the sisters
arrived, the school opened with twenty-one students, twelve boarders,
and nine day pupils. The boarders, the school, and the sisters were all
housed in the hastily constructed building.

Despite the difficult beginnings, the foundation at Belmont
grew and prospered. An orphanage for girls was added in 1894 and in
time the Academy expanded to become Sacred Heart College, which the
sisters operated until its closing in 1988. At that time, neighboring
Belmont Abbey College, which had begun admitting women in 1972,
became the only Catholic college in North Carolina.

But it was during the first two decades of the Twentieth
Century that Belmont Abbey and Sacred Heart Convent saw their most
significant expansion, producing a collection of buildings and programs
unequaled anywhere in the state. To this day, the twin institutions
remain not only impressive campuses but also the only monastery of
men in North Carolina and the only motherhouse of women religious.
Major credit for the success of both foundations must go to Leo Haid, a
fact that Sister Charles anticipated as early as 1893, when she wrote:

> Of late we are hopeful, for a light has fallen across the gloomy path.
> Our little institution has been taken up warmly by our good
> Benedictine Bishop, a favor we scarce looked for, as we expected
> very naturally, that he would call into his field the nuns of his own
> order, among whom he as well as other Fathers of the Abbey have
> near relatives. But grace triumphs in the hearts of St. Benedict's sons.
> ... Looking around, [the bishop] saw on the arid desert committed to
> his care by Providence a stunted plant, that from its very loveliness

has withstood the withering blast of neglect and adversity, and he seems to have said to himself, "That is to be made fruitful by my care and enriched by my bounty." So saying, he made for it a garden near his own St. Mary's Abbey, now rising in such grand proportions that it is justly called the wonder of the South, where this tiny plant is assiduously watered by those who made the desert bloom."[27]

The Nazareth Foundation

The final expansion of the sisters during the nineteenth century was staffing the orphanage for boys that Father Price opened at Nazareth in 1899. Sister Catherine was appointed to lead the group of five sisters assigned to the new work. In an experience reminiscent of the arrival of the sisters at Belmont a few years earlier, when the little group arrived at Raleigh, there was no one to meet them at the railroad station, and so, carrying their suitcases, the black-habited nuns walked to Sacred Heart rectory. There they were greeted by Father Price with the news that no furniture had been purchased for the house in which they were to live at Nazareth. Also, lime and plaster lay thick on the floors of the uncompleted building. Ever resourceful, the sisters provided for their basic needs, and the following day Father Price offered mass for the first time in the new institution "on an improvised altar, decorated with autumn leaves and goldenrod."[28]

Despite the hardships in a place where "poverty reigned supreme," the sisters welcomed what would be the first of a long line of orphans who would be cared for at Nazareth over the course of the following seventy-five years. Embracing it as their calling, sisters served as teachers, nurses, social workers, housekeepers, and mothers to the youngsters until the country's changing social welfare system brought about a diminished need for orphanages, and Nazareth was closed.

Establishing Hospitals in Asheville & Charlotte

As the Twentieth Century began, North Carolina remained a virtual Third World country within the United States. For its part, the Catholic Church continued to be like a ship tossed about in a hostile sea. Besides Father Price and the priests mentioned in Chapter Nine, the crew members were the twin religious communities in the rural village of Belmont. For their part, in addition to their monastic duties, the monks staffed half the parishes in the state, of which at the time there were but twelve with resident pastors. The Sisters of Mercy were similarly energetic. Thirty-one years after the arrival of the first sisters in

Wilmington, the community counted thirty-eight members and staffed schools and orphanages in Wilmington, Charlotte, Belmont, and Nazareth. All this had been achieved despite the fact that the Catholic population of the state barely exceeded 4,000, a small base from which to draw vocations or obtain financial support. Furthermore, few of the sisters had a college degree or any professional training. Nevertheless, they were about to embark on a new ministry.

Even as it seemed that the sisters were specializing in education, in 1900 their work took an unanticipated turn. Years before, at Bishop Northrop's prompting, they had invested several thousand dollars in a house in Asheville with the idea of opening a boarding school. When that plan floundered, what Northrop called the "unlucky house" remained abandoned. Finally, Father Peter Marion, the pastor of St. Lawrence parish in Asheville suggested that the sisters use the building to open a hospital.[29] Rather than a general hospital as initially envisioned, the sisters decided that the Asheville climate was ideal for the treatment of tuberculosis. Accordingly, they opened St. Joseph's Sanitarium, which soon gained a reputation for its treatment of people suffering from that malady. The institution moved and expanded several times, until 1938 when, medical advances having eliminated the need for sanitariums, St. Joseph's was transformed into a 331-room general hospital.

In 1906, once again the sisters stumbled into a new undertaking, one that they were reluctant to assume but which became in time the central focus of their work and, coincidentally, their most valuable asset. When St. Peter parish in Charlotte constructed a new school, the Benedictine pastor, Father Joseph Mueller, remodeled the old parish hall and, supported by Leo Haid, convinced the sisters to open a hospital. In such modest quarters was inaugurated Mercy General Hospital, destined to become the premier health facility in North Carolina's largest city. Like its Asheville counterpart, Mercy progressively became more modern and complex. Sisters who had once been simple bedside nurses now found themselves administering multi-million dollar enterprises. However, the pressure of changing times and declining vocations would lead to yet another metamorphosis in the evolution of the Sisters of Mercy.

Fewer Sisters, More Money

Like supermarkets replacing mom-and-pop grocery stores, all over America enormous medical conglomerates have replaced or swallowed up the smaller hospitals and other health-related agencies that had provided services for generations. Among those to be absorbed by larger entities were the two hospitals of the Sisters of Mercy. In 1995 the Charlotte hospital was sold and three years later St. Joseph's in Asheville.[30] The combined income from the sales was nearly $200 million. The money was used to establish the Sisters of Mercy of North Carolina Foundation that provides grants to support the work of health care, educational, and social service organizations located in Western North Carolina. As the Foundation literature states:

> The Foundation seeks to assist projects which are designed to improve the quality of life for women, children, the elderly and those who are poor. Special attention will be focused on promoting systemic change.

In a recent year more than $3,500,000 was distributed to about seventy-five agencies. The sisters describe what has happened as "moving beyond the direct provision of acute health care services to addressing the needs of the unserved and under served." Whereas in its early years the community had young women and no money, today it has money and no young women.

The last statement is not entirely correct. In one of those mysterious moves that proves to have unforeseen consequences, in 1946 Bishop Appollinaris Baumgartner asked the Belmont sisters to open a school in his diocese of Guam. Suddenly, sisters who had never ventured far from home found themselves on an island in the South Pacific, initiating the first North Carolina contribution to the foreign missions since Father Price left for China in 1918. The project prospered, and today nearly half of the North Carolina Sisters of Mercy -- reduced to just over one hundred members -- are Guamanians, most of them working on Pacific islands. The North American sisters, the majority retired, have no schools, no hospitals, no orphanages, no institutions of their own other than the venerable Belmont campus.

St. Genevieve of the Pines

Although hospitals were important, the quintessential ministry of religious orders of women was the staffing of Catholic schools. For generations the overriding dream of priests was to have all Catholic children attending Catholic schools, from the elementary grades through high school and even into college. One of the wonders of the American church is that this dream often came true, even in North Carolina with its small Catholic population.

As was seen in the discussion of Monsignor Michael Irwin, the Dominican Sisters of Newburgh, New York, opened a school in Newton Grove in 1907, living in conditions that were truly primitive. Two years later, the same community added schools in Raleigh and Durham. Although Newburgh Dominicans no longer serve in the state, in the early decades of the 20th Century dozens of them left the comfort and security of the North for the privations of the South.

Meanwhile, also in 1907, at the other end of the state, a French community of sisters was establishing a boarding school for girls that lasted for more than sixty years and educated future judges, artists, and physicians, as well as wives and mothers. St. Genevieve of the Pines drew a very different kind of student than those taught by the Dominicans. The Religious of Christian Education, who conducted St. Genevieve in Asheville, attracted the children of the affluent, who sent their daughters to what they hoped was a safe, respectable, and Christian school. It seems it was all that and more. Although the school ceased to be a Catholic institution in 1971 and closed its doors in 1987, alumnae continue to recall with fondness their schoolgirl days in the mountains.

For example, Elizabeth Turner who, in the 1990's, with the help of Jesuit Father Frank Reese and Mercy Sister Peggy Verstege, was instrumental in establishing a mission in Burnsville, Yancey County, for the growing number of Mexican immigrants, gives credit to the sisters at St. Genevieve for her interest in social justice issues:

> The sisters were smart, strong, the best role models. They had a huge influence on me. We received permission slips to go to civil rights protest marches, in our white St. Genevieve uniforms, so everyone would know where St. Genevieve's stood on the issue of civil rights.[31]

Although other buildings were added in time, originally the school and convent were housed in what had been the Victoria Inn, constructed around 1896 as lodging for the wealthy who journeyed to the mountains in summer in order to escape the heat of the eastern lowlands. The rambling, ornate, castle-like structure fed the imaginations of impressionable young women who had little else to do on their remote campus than explore the heights and depths of the school. One of them, writing to the alumni association some fifty years after her graduation, recalled the school's bell tower, which at the time was the highest point in the city:

If we were very, very good, we were taken to the tower for a picnic. Or for an hour of reading. It was a very special treat.... We had to go through the nuns' quarters and that was forbidden -- unless a nun was taking us. It had window seats all around it and you could see over all the city and mountains.[32]

The same former student also recalled that on Sundays the girls were taken to the music room for an hour of listening to classical music. A nun would select something, play it, and tell the students the story behind it. The woman recalled: "I would sit there and look out over the mountains while the music was playing."

Even as one alumna recalled going up into the tower, another remembered going in the opposite direction:

It was an absolutely fantastic old "castle" with dungeons in the base- ment where we were convinced they laid the dear old nuns and priests to rest. It was really spooky down there. The passageways were quite narrow, dark, and damp. A Frankenstein movie could easily have been filmed there. There was a gift shop or student store at the entrance way to a door which lead down to the first passage way. An old nun ran the store and her eyesight was failing. One of our classmates would distract her at the counter while the rest of us sneaked past her to delight in our adventures.

In a sense, St. Genevieve was not the real North Carolina; it was an oasis in a state that otherwise remained an educational desert. The French sisters lent an air of European culture to the school and, although the nuns themselves seldom ventured far from the school, they chal- lenged their students to stretch their minds, open their hearts, and expand their imaginations. One of their students, the future Salisbury author, Frances Fisher, attended the school for only a short time, but it is likely that the sisters communicated to her impressionable soul romanticized images of their far-off homeland. Fisher's books would be filled with elegant men and women, the sort of people who would prefer to go up into the bell tower and music room, rather than down into the dungeon.

The "old nun" whom the student recalled staffing the gift shop may have been Mother Noemi Mouquet, or perhaps Mother Noemi was the somewhat younger sister who introduced the girls to classical music, or she might well have been both to different generations of students. In any case, Mother Noemi was one of the original group of sisters who came across the ocean and into the mountains to establish St.

Genevieve's. Like many of the sisters, as if she had taken a vow of stability, she would remain there until her death.

After making her vows as a Religious of Christian Education in
Argentan, France in 1895, Sister Noemi taught in community schools in
France until she and five other sisters were assigned to the new American
mission. During more than fifty years at St. Genevieve's, Mother Noemi
taught music and French to class after class of girls, exposing them to
religious and cultural worlds not often found on the American frontier.
Mother Noemi died in Asheville in 1960 at the age of eighty-eight.[33]

As if wedded to the place, a group of sisters remained in
Asheville even after the school closed. It was only in 1999 that the surviving half dozen sisters, all of them advanced in years, returned to their
motherhouse. The castle-like building where their work had begun had
been demolished in 1962.

Andrew Graves, Jesuit Missionary

A similar story of growth, change, and decline can be told with
reference to religious order priests, except that they did not conduct
schools or hospitals; they established parishes, especially in the more
remote sections of the state. Although there were others, two communities of men will be given particular attention, the Jesuits and the
Glenmary Missioners. It was a few men from these orders who established the Catholic Church in the band of counties that forms the North
Carolina border with Tennessee and Georgia.

It was not until well into the Twentieth Century that any
Catholics were known to be living in much of the Appalachian region.
From the Church's perspective, this was *terra incognita*, whole counties
that had not one Catholic and where the mountain residents were suspicious of outsiders, especially Catholics. Nowhere in the country was there
a more difficult area in which to establish a presence nor, on the other
hand, an area that was more appealing to zealous missionaries.
Throughout the history of the church there have been those whose appetite
is whetted by challenge and who feel compelled to go where the prospects
for success seem dim. More than anyone else in North Carolina Catholic
history, the Jesuit priest, Andrew Graves, illustrates this point.

One Sunday afternoon in the early 1980's two men were sip-
ping iced tea on the porch of a modest farm house in a rural hamlet of
Madison County. One was an elderly priest who had just offered Mass
in the small church of the Little Flower across the road. The other was
the farm owner, a young Catholic of Lithuanian descent from

Pittsburgh, Pennsylvania. Somewhat discouraged by the isolation and the enormous amount of work required to grow tobacco on a few hilly acres, the farmer wondered aloud why he was there. Without hesitation, the priest answered, "You're here because you're the only complete Catholic family in the county."[34]

Although this response was not particularly logical, it did reflect the priest's consciousness of his limited measurable achievements after more than forty years in the area. The Reverend Andrew Graves, like his parishioner, may also have wondered why he was there. His dream of converts had never materialized. When, on one occasion, Bishop Waters asked Graves how many converts he had, the priest answered, "Converts? Why they've just stopped calling me a 'son-of-a-bitch.'" On another occasion, when Graves had not submitted his annual *status animarum* report to the diocese, the Chancellor called to ask for the information. Graves told him that besides one death, all the other data was the same as the previous year.[35] Indeed, an examination of the diocesan records shows just how little changed over the years. In 1953, sixteen years after Graves' arrival, there were forty-five Catholics in his parish which embraced three counties and extended over 1,000 square miles. Seventeen years after that, in 1970, the Catholic population had risen by five to fifty, only thirty of whom were "practical." The remainders were "lax," "lapsed," or "apostates" as the diocesan classification system of the day categorized them.

When a fire destroyed the parish documents in 1950, Graves had no difficulty reconstructing the marriage records since there had been so few, all of them of "mixed" religion. Perhaps made somewhat despondent by the fire which consumed most of his personal possessions as well, Graves added this note to his report:

> I have no assured income to pay my pressing bills for ordinary expenses, except about an average of three dollars each week from my collections. My people are scattered over four hundred and twenty square miles, and you will see the task is not an easy one. Living in a shack which requires continual patching and repair takes a lot of time which might be more profitably spent.

Why a Jesuit Presence in Madison County?

The Catholic Directory for 1926 records that there were twenty-five religious order priests in North Carolina, most of them Benedictines. The following year, there were sixty-seven order priests.

What explains the enormous increase? The answer is the root explana-
tion as to why Father Graves would eventually find himself in Madison
County. And it all goes back to a woman named Bessie Rumbough
Safford.

In the 1870's, the railroad inched its way through the North
Carolina mountains offering the promise of development along its
route. Anticipating such a prospect, Colonel and Mrs. James Rumbough
had established a small town that would be called Hot Springs. Here,
Bessie, the first of five daughters was born in 1857. The little girl spent
her childhood in the quiet of the mountains, little dreaming that she
would not only become a Catholic but be the patron of the Church in
western North Carolina.

Wishing his children to have a religious education, in 1872,
Colonel Rumbough, a Methodist, sent his daughters, Bessie and Mary,
to the Visitation Convent School for Girls in Washington, DC. There
Bessie became acquainted with the son of Andrew Johnson, who had
become president when Abraham Lincoln was assassinated. The young
couple was married in 1875 when Bessie was eighteen. Unfortunately,
Andrew Johnson, Jr. died in 1879, leaving his young widow to mourn
her loss and consider her future. A major aspect of Bessie's new life was
embracing the Catholic religion to which she had been attracted through
the influence of the Visitation sisters.

In 1886, the affluent widow sailed for England and, as the ship
moved across the Atlantic, romance blossomed in her life once again.
New York banker, Daniel B. Safford, fell in love with her and quickly
proposed. When the ship docked, the two were married in London.
After spending several years in Nice in Southern France, the couple
returned to the United Stated, lived for a brief period in New York, and
finally moved to the Carolina mountains in the 1890's. Hot Springs, the
place of her birth, would be Bessie's home for the remainder of her life.
Although the only Catholic in Madison County, she was determined to
have a church in which to pray.

With the permission of Bishop Haid, Bessie built a chapel
beside her own large house. Here she welcomed the priest who occasionally made the thirty-mile trip from St. Lawrence Church in
Asheville, the only permanently staffed Catholic parish in the mountains.

After Mr. Safford died in 1914, Bessie managed the 100-acre
estate with its hotel. However, the popularity of Hot Springs declined,
and motivated by financial as well as religious considerations, in 1926

she leased the hotel building to the Jesuits for use as a house of study for newly ordained priests. Some forty Jesuits descended on Hot Springs, more priests than there were secular clergy in the entire state. Furthermore, there were now many more priests in Hot Springs than there were lay people. In fact, aside from a couple of Irish girls working on her estate, Bessie was still the only one. As it turned out, the Jesuits used the property for the "tertianship program" for only one year. However, the now aged Bessie gave all her property to the Jesuits on condition that they care for her there until her death, which occurred the following year. Although the Jesuits had no intention of establishing a permanent mission in North Carolina, the bequest led them to assign a priest to care for the property and undertake a mission to the area. Thus, accidentally, began the Jesuit presence in Hot Springs. In 1937, the recently ordained Andrew Graves, a native of Washington, DC, was assigned to the area, the only Jesuit in the state.[36]

Although Bishop Hafey approved of the mission in Hot Springs, understandably the mountain counties were not a pastoral priority. When Graves visited Raleigh on his way to his assignment, the bishop made it clear to the young priest that the diocese could provide no support for his work. He would have to fend for himself. Graves did just that. Each year, he published *Mountain Dewings*, a newsletter that related conditions in the vast territory, and solicited funds. It was the contributions of friends and family in the Washington, DC area that supported his ministry for decades.

Despite the cultural wall of resistance to Catholicism, Graves did influence one segment of the population, namely, the young. Certainly their attraction to the priest was a form of rebelliousness against the prejudices of their parents. However, they were aware also that their prospects in Madison County were limited and that their families could offer them little assistance in breaking out of the cycle of poverty. The somewhat exotic outsider was viewed by them not as a danger to their way of life but rather as a link with the more promising world beyond the mountains.

One of the people influenced by Graves was Sue Vilcinskas. During a 1998 interview, she reverently removed from a trunk in her living room a mimeographed history of the church in Madison County which Graves had written. She recalled childhood Bible classes under a tree in the cemetery or in the church of the Little Flower. With feeling, she said, "We lived here in the mountains. The only Catholicism we knew was what we experienced with Father Graves. It was pure and lovely. We knew nothing about the pope or things I've learned about later. If there ever was a saint, it was Father Andy."

Sue Vilcinskas said that the people who were young while Father Graves was in the area have been successful because he taught them to feel good about themselves. He convinced them that because they lived in the mountains didn't mean that they were inferior to others. Although many of the young people moved from the area, several of those who remained, including Sue herself, became teachers in the Madison County schools.

As frailty limited Graves' mobility, another Jesuit, Father Jeff Burton, was sent to assist him. Since finances remained strained and the Catholic population small, Burton obtained employment as a teacher in the local public school. In 1984 infirmity forced Graves to retire; he was eighty-one. It is said that while at the Jesuit retirement residence in Philadelphia, each evening after dinner the old missionary would climb the stairs to a room with a large window that faced North Carolina. There he would say his prayers and think of his people. Graves died in 1995 at the age of ninety-two.

Unexpected Continuity

The legacy of Bessie Safford and Father Graves continues. A portrait of the priest hangs over the stone fireplace in the parlor of the old house in Hot Springs that operates today as the Jesuit House of Prayer. Located adjacent to the Appalachian Trail, the retreat center welcomes hundreds of men and women each year to the soul-refreshing mountains so beloved to Safford and Graves. The Catholic population in the area is still small, and except for the retreat house chapel there is no Catholic church in Hot Springs. In fact, just as was true with Bessie Safford, only one Catholic lives within the city limits, Della Hazel Moore, one of Graves' few converts.[37]

Some ten miles away, the church of the Little Flower where Graves first celebrated mass on his arrival in Madison County and beside which he lived for several years, still stands. Although well preserved in its mountain setting, the building usually is quiet. There never was a real need for it, but Graves loved it. On his stationery was a picture of the church and the name "Revere," even though Revere has never been large enough to have a post office. When Graves arrived, there was a small store down the road and at least a minimal sense of community. Today, even the name "Revere" is gone, replaced with the unflattering biblical name, "Sodom."

For years the Diocese of Charlotte maintained Little Flower as an "historic site," but it was rare for anyone to visit it. So, in 1997, business sense triumphing over sentiment, the property was sold to an Asheville psychologist who planned to convert it into a vacation retreat for himself. However, the man's father, a Baptist minister, warned, "Son, that building was a place of prayer. You shouldn't desecrate it." The dutiful son left the church as he found it, its door always unlocked. An article that appeared in the Asheville newspaper, framed on the wall, relates this story and says that visitors are welcome. On another wall, a plaque erected by Father Graves thanks the donors, most of whom never saw the church, who contributed to its renovation in the 1970's.

Then in the year 2000 some local people, not all of them Catholic, held a family reunion on the property, highlighted by a rededication of Little Flower Chapel. As one couple wrote in their 2001 Christmas letter:

> We were asked to lead the more than sixty returned worshipers in their hymns and prayers. Tears welled in the eyes of many as once again "How Great Thou Art" swelled within those holy walls. Humbled and grateful for this opportunity to share in this memorable service, we offered to do what we could to encourage this community of 'abandoned' Catholics to recover their heritage and renew their faith. 'Will you say Mass for us here?' was the eager question.

Invited to be the celebrant was a former Glenmary priest, Paul Fredette, who with his wife, Karen, a former Poor Clare nun, lives in Madison County. For a time, Karen worked as a cook at the Jesuit House of Prayer. Now, she devotes much of her time to producing a newsletter for hermits that has over 600 subscribers. She herself, while a nun, had lived as a hermit and wants to provide a vehicle for communication among people attracted to that way of life.

The Fredettes did not initiate the idea of celebrating Mass in Little Flower church. They were invited to do so by people who knew them and saw them as the most logical leaders of their little community. Among the Christians who welcomed the reactivation of Little Flower was Vince Vilcinskas, the farmer who still lives across the road from the church and on whose porch Father Graves had sipped iced tea many years before. Accompanying Vince was his wife, Sue. The couple had become disillusioned with the Catholic Church. Now they were back.

The Glenmary Home Missioners

Although Paul Fredette never served as a Glenmary priest in North Carolina, a number of his colleagues did. More than any other religious congregation, the Glenmary Home Missioners were ideally suited for conditions in the western sector of the state. Together with the Glenmary Sisters, they were the prime representatives of the church in a number of counties for more than two decades.

There are parallels in the lives of Father Price and Father William Howard Bishop, the founder of Glenmary. Both worked for more than twenty years as diocesan priests, Price in Raleigh and Bishop in Baltimore. Both had the dream of evangelizing the poor, neglected areas of rural America. As has been seen, Price attempted to establish a community of priests to work in the South. When that plan failed, he redirected his vision and energies to the foreign missions, which turned out to be a successful venture. A generation later, Bishop took up Price's original dream and made it come true. Glenmary, founded in 1939, was substantially what Father Price had in mind for his Missionary Apostolate.

At the prompting of Father Michael Irwin, Bishop Waters petitioned Father Bishop for priests to serve in North Carolina. At first, as the community formed its first priests, Father Bishop had to say, "Not yet, but soon." Finally, in 1954, Glenmary Missioners accepted responsibility for the westernmost counties in the state, establishing a base camp, as it were, in the town of Murphy in Cherokee County, the westernmost point in the state. Included in that initial assignment were Clay and Graham counties as well. As has been seen, in nearby Madison, Yancey, and Haywood counties, Father Graves ministered to fewer than one hundred Catholics. The Glenmary priests had even fewer, with but five Catholic families in their three counties. Father Jim Wilmes, who in 1956 joined Father Joe Dean, the original pastor, said that St. William parish in Murphy was at the time the least Catholic parish in America and one of the largest.[38]

As personnel allowed, Glenmary assumed responsibility for additional mountain territory, including Mitchell County with their base at St. Lucien church in Spruce Pine, and Swain County at the church of St. Joseph in Bryson City. The young priests, committed to working in "no priest lands," injected into the region an energy that produced some converts to Catholicism but mainly established the core communities to which Catholics moving into the area in the future could attach themselves. What must be emphasized is that, at no expense to the diocese, Glenmary built churches, formed congregations, and allayed anti-Catholic sentiment in the most remote section of the state.

Like the US Marines establishing a beachhead and then turning the operation over to the Army, Glenmary's goal has always been to develop a parish to the point of self-sustainability and then turn it over to the diocese. This has been done in all their North Carolina foundations. Murphy, the original location, was given to the diocesan clergy in 1988. Three years before that, as if to give the diocese as substantial a parish as possible, the Glenmary priests led the parishioners in the construction of a larger, more modern church. To bring the beauty of the mountains right into the sanctuary, the wall behind the altar of the new building is clear glass. In winter, it is as if a snow scene were painted on the wall; in summer, the natural mural depicts the velvet green of thousands of pine trees.

The older Murphy church, which had served the little community for thirty-five years, was sold to the Providence Presbyterian Church. As the years passed, the memory of what the Glenmary priests had contributed began to fade. Then in the year 2000, at the suggestion of the diocesan priest pastor, George Kloster, the original church was reacquired, converted into a parish activities center, and named "Glenmary House." As Father Kloster said:

> The ministry of the Glenmary priests, brothers, and sisters in the mountains of North Carolina provided a foundation for the growth of the church in the western part of the state that we have today. Their mentality and ministry were especially adapted for real mission work.... This building is a memorial to what they did. It is a reminder to us of the many, many Glenmarians who contributed so much for so many years.[39]

Continuing Glenmary Presence

Although it is true that there are no Glenmary parishes in North Carolina today, the spirit of Father Bishop lives on in several men who shared the founder's vision. Besides Paul Fredette, who exercises an unofficial ministry in the area, two other former Glenmary priests continue to live in the state which years ago had captured their idealistic young hearts. They left Glenmary, not for want of faith but in order to be free to marry. One of them, Dr. Terry Jackson, is the Director of

Evangelization for the Diocese of Raleigh. When he was named to that position in the late 1990's, after serving for several years as Diocesan Director of Adult Education, the letter of appointment noted that his years as a priest well qualified him for the new assignment. Jackson says that the work of evangelization is exactly what Glenmary had trained him to do.

Don Kaple, a third former Glenmary priest, was ordained in 1958 and spent his pastoral year in Murphy. Three years later, he was assigned to Spruce Pine which embraced Mitchell, Avery, and Yancey Counties. In that entire three-county area there were only 150 Catholics. However, the number increased in summer when affluent families came to their Linwood Falls "cottages" for the holidays. One family had on its grounds a small stone chapel, St. Patrice, where Mass was offered during the summer season. When Kaple arrived for his first mass in the chapel, one of the men said to him, "Father, keep your sermon short and I guarantee every man here will give $50 today." He obliged them; the summer income was a major part of the parish budget. The deficit was made up for by a subsidy from Glenmary.[40]

Kaple also recalled that his bedroom at Spruce Pine was adjacent to the sanctuary which, on Bishop Waters' order, had been wired in order to protect the tabernacle from vandals. With perhaps some retrospective exaggeration, Kaple claims that whenever he turned over in bed, the alarm would go off. Despite this inconvenience, Kaple admired Waters because the bishop made it a point to visit the small parishes and "made every place feel important."

In 1968, Kaple left the active ministry and the following year married his wife, Marion. Obtaining a doctorate in adult education at the University of Georgia, he spent twenty-five years in adult literacy programs and in helping poor people find jobs. In retirement, Kaple lives in Jonas Ridge within the confines of his old Spruce Pine parish. He welcomes anyone who wishes to visit him and spend time in reflection. He also publishes a newsletter in which he shares his spiritual journey. He says that writing the newsletter reminds him of the days when he would prepare sermons for Sunday mass.

"Good bye, Sister"

Older Catholics can remember sisters in flowing habits, large rosary beads attached to their sides, standing in front of neat rows of uniformed boys and girls in parochial schools or gliding silently down the halls of Catholic hospitals. Their children and grandchildren have had no such experience. If they see a nun at all, she is unlikely to have any external sign of her status and her work is not likely to be in an institution conducted by her religious community.

Despite the dwindling number of women religious, one community has maintained a substantial presence in North Carolina. Fifteen sisters, Servants of the Immaculate Heart of Mary (I.H.M.) of Scranton, Pennsylvania work in ten locations throughout the eastern half of the state, six of them as pastoral administrators. Since 1972, the I.H.M.s have been the largest community of women religious serving in the Raleigh diocese and, before that, was second only to the Belmont Sisters of Mercy. The women from Scranton were among the pioneers who came to the state to educate black children in New Bern, Washington, and Raleigh. When St. Monica School in Raleigh closed in the late 1960's, four I.H.M. sisters accompanied their black students into the unfamiliar world of the previously all-white Sacred Heart Cathedral School. In addition, the sisters operated schools in Goldsboro, Rocky Mount, and Greensboro.

Another community that played a pivotal role in the development of the Church in North Carolina was the Mission Helpers of the Sacred Heart. Before their arrival no formal religious education was available in the state for children attending public schools. The parish priest and sisters working in Catholic schools taught the public school children as best they could. Bishop Waters invited the Mission Helpers to set up schools of religion. Working in groups of four, the sisters set up schools in a number of places, including Henderson, Charlotte, Farmville, and Winston-Salem. Their modus operandi was to establish the school, initially doing all the teaching themselves but simultaneously training lay catechists. Once the program was firmly rooted, they moved on. Today, only one Mission Helper remains in the state, Sister Dolores Glick. Her story, as the first pastoral administrator, will be told in Chapter Thirteen.

The present chapter concludes with the story of two sisters who said good bye to North Carolina in 1998 when they returned to their motherhouse in Tiffin, Ohio. Aside from the Belmont Sisters of Mercy, all the other communities that have worked in the state have come from other places, converging on North Carolina out of an impulse to serve in the missions. Sisters of Charity came from Ohio, Canada, Kentucky, and Pennsylvania. Franciscan Sisters came from New York, Pennsylvania, Missouri, Iowa, Wisconsin, and Ohio.

Sisters Roberta McKinnon, 77, and Virginia Gase, 67, who had worked in the town of Cherokee in Swain County, on the Tennessee border for many years, were returning to Tiffin whence they had come. As the newspaper report of their departure put it, they were going in order to undertake "new challenges."[41]

For decades, Sisters Virginia and Roberta had been a Catholic presence in an economically depressed area populated largely by Hispanics and Cherokee Indians. They had fostered an ecumenical spirit, helped to establish an emergency assistance fund for those in need, taught music lessons to high school students, counseled those who were chemically dependent, and assisted adults in obtaining their high school diplomas. As Charlotte Bishop Curlin put it in bidding them farewell: "It's a charism of the Sisters of St. Francis of Tiffin, Ohio, that wherever they go, they find people to love them."

It was in 1972 that sisters first came to Cherokee. Father Ron McLaughlin, the pastor of several churches in the area, including Our Lady of Guadalupe in Cherokee, asked the sisters to put on their habits and walk through the village so that people would know that they were not tourists.[42] Initially, the sisters' home was an apartment built onto the church as an overnight stopping place for priests but was never used for that purpose. Eventually, Bishop Begley improved their accommodations by having a single-wide mobile home installed at the site. The sisters lived as simply as did the people they served.

Just as many other religious women and men have similarly testified, the sisters insisted that they had received more than they had given. They had taken the risk of leaving home and spending the better part of their lives with people who, in many ways, were different from those they had known. And they had been surprised by the joy and satisfaction those people had cascaded into their souls. Sister Roberta spoke for many when she said of her years in western North Carolina: "It was a rich, rich experience. I just feel that the Spirit led us to things we never could have thought of."

Chapter Twelve

Racial & Ethnic Minorities

We're invisible in the diocese. We're invisible people. ... African American ministry is not mentioned in the diocese's new capital campaign. Once again we've been ignored. Black Catholic attendance at diocesan conferences ... is usually minimal, in part because there is no invitation or inclusion of black Catholics and their culture. It might sound strange, but often African Americans don't think these celebrations are spiritual enough. Nonetheless, the diocese has to make an effort to be inclusive. ... The Church in her history has abandoned the African American church periodically. There has not been a consistent evangelization among African Americans. There's no way you can get around that. Its just part of our history. ... And it needs to be recognized.

---Monsignor Thomas Hadden, 2001

After the Jesuit priest had recited the words of Consecration, the Gospel Choir of Holy Cross Catholic Church in Durham sang the customary acclamation: "Christ has died; Christ is risen; Christ will come again." It did so to the melody of the Civil Rights Movement song, "We Shall Overcome," the congregation singing along with the choir, perhaps blending in their hearts a commitment to racial justice and to the Catholic Church. However, their ardor may have been tempered by the realization that both in their country and their church not all obstacles to full acceptance have been overcome.

Holy Cross is unusual, if not unique. It is an African American parish, a remnant of the age of segregation when every major town in North Carolina had a "white" church and a "colored" church. Here, no one complains. In fact, any effort to change the character of Holy Cross would be resisted by its parishioners, many of them lifelong members of the congregation which, in its modest size and joyous music, is not that different from the numerous Baptist churches sprinkled throughout this African American neighborhood. Adding to the sense that a black church belongs here is the fact that it is located adjacent to North Carolina Central University, one of the traditionally black institutions of a state that segregated its people until forced to integrate in the 1960's. However, the continuing existence of race-based schools and churches reflects as much the pride in group membership as the legacy of exclusion.

For all its peacefulness today, Holy Cross's identity was put to the test not so many years ago. The challenge to its character as an African American parish not only caused conflict and hard feelings but also highlighted what many black Catholics see as the Church once again marginalizing them. The issue was not racist segregation but the innocent but enormous influx of Latinos to North Carolina, a demographic tidal wave that threatened in its exuberance to overwhelm small but faithful African American Catholic communities.

The Holy Cross Parish Mission Statement, printed each week in the parish bulletin, makes clear the distinctive character of the church:

> Holy Cross Church was founded by the Society of Jesus to serve the African American Catholics of Durham. We are a people baptized in Christ. We gather to worship the Lord in joy, to proclaim the Gospel, and to serve the Durham community, as well as the needs of the whole people of God. Our special character as an African American parish continues to shape our worship, our ministries, and our contribution to the wider Church.

In 1939, joining other religious orders that felt the need to do something for black Catholics in North Carolina, the Maryland Province of the Society of Jesus established a mission in Durham, the hub of the state's thriving tobacco industry. As has been related, in 1906 Father William O'Brien had established Durham's Immaculate Conception parish for the hundred or so Catholics who lived in the town. With the help of some affluent tobacco officials, including William Carmichael, O'Brien had built a substantial church, opened a parochial school, and provided the Catholic Church with respectability in the predominantly Protestant town. However, the racial norms of the period made it impossible for O'Brien to reach out to the black population without antagonizing his white congregants. The solution was to open a mission separate from the white parish, one that would attempt to develop a black Catholic community. The Jesuits accepted the challenge -- and the financial responsibility. Without interruption, they have maintained their commitment.[1]

Despite the fact that Father John A. Risacher, S.J. found only one black Catholic family when he arrived in Durham, the priest went ahead and arranged to celebrate mass in the dental office of Dr. Norman Cordice. As word spread and other Catholics emerged, services were moved to a classroom in the DeShazor Beauty Parlor Training School on Old Fayetteville Street. Soon property was purchased and in 1943 a rectory constructed, one room of which served as a chapel. Finally, in 1952, ground was broken and the following year Bishop Waters dedicated the present stone church. It is indicative of the complexity of the racial situation in the state, that the very year that Waters attracted national attention for forcing the integration of the segregated Catholic churches in Newton Grove, he solidified the segregation of the Catholics in Durham by blessing Holy Cross.

When Father Risacher retired in 1966, five other Jesuits, each of whom had relatively brief tenure as pastor, succeeded him. Then, in 1985, Bruce Bavinger, S.J., began an eleven-year pastorate at Holy Cross and by his charismatic personality attracted not only a modestly increased black congregation, but unwittingly sowed the seeds of a problem that would come to symbolize the most recent version of a long history of interracial tension.

By the mid-1980's the Latino population of Durham had begun to grow and in 1988 a group of Spanish-speaking people asked Father Bavinger if he would initiate a Latino ministry at Holy Cross. Seeing this as an opportunity to add a needed dimension to the work of the church in the area, he agreed. In order to inhibit the segregation of the parish based on language, Bavinger instituted bilingual masses instead of Spanish language liturgies. However, the feel of the parish changed. Although it was difficult to complain about opening their church to these new arrivals, some of the black Catholics felt uncomfortable with what they perceived as the newcomers taking over their church.

Holy Cross is perhaps one of the most beautiful Catholic churches in the state; certainly it is one of the smallest, capable of seating about 100 people. This size was adequate for the African Americans, but the arrival of the Latinos created a crisis. Accordingly, when Father Bavinger left in 1996, a Jesuit who did not speak Spanish replaced him. The bilingual mass was discontinued and a cultural tug of war ensued, with the black Catholics arguing that the Latinos should adapt to *their* way of celebrating liturgy, while the Latinos wanted their own language and culture reflected in the mass. As the Immaculate Conception parish history explains:

> The church also felt that given its size and current resources, it could not fulfill its mission to minister to the African American Catholics of Durham and meet the Latinos' needs adequately. Many parishioners agreed. They hoped that this decision would serve to unite the two congregations, which had not come together as the church had desired.

The effort at cultural blending did not succeed. The cessation of the bilingual mass led many of the Latinos to decide that they were no longer welcome at Holy Cross. So, on October 13, 1996, the majority of the Latino immigrants walked out of the church, taking with them their statue of Our Lady of Guadalupe. Turning to Franciscan Father John Heffernan at Immaculate Conception, they asked if that church might become their new parish home.[2] Accepted at Immaculate Conception, a vigorous Spanish program developed while Holy Cross reverted to its predominantly African American character.

*   *   *   *

The present chapter examines the racial and ethnic dimensions of Catholic life in North Carolina. Like the state itself, the Church has seen a transformation from a population that was almost exclusively English-speaking white and black to a diverse blend of peoples from many places in the world. The most significant development has been the extraordinary growth in the number of Spanish-speaking people. Within the course of two decades, the Hispanic population increased from a negligible number to a near majority of the Catholics in North Carolina. The impact of their presence is felt in virtually every parish in the state.

Further compounding the situation for the church is the establishment of Korean, Vietnamese, and other Asian communities, particularly in Charlotte. The challenges with which urban dioceses in the North had wrestled for generations at last had reached North Carolina.

North Carolina's First Black Catholics

Records show that, beginning in 1821, Bishop John England baptized slaves of several North Carolina Catholics, including those of William Gaston in New Bern and William Worsley of Washington. Besides the notation of their reception into the church, nothing further is known of these men, women, and children. Like so many million other enslaved people, their stories remain shrouded in silence. Even those who held them in bondage reveal little. One wonders, for example, what the highly regarded Gaston thought as on May 31st, 1821, he watched Bishop England pour the water of baptism on the head of a man identified simply as "Abraham, a slave belonging to Mr. Gaston." No last name; no parents; no date of birth. These facts, if known, were not relevant. Abraham's ownership by Gaston was all the identification required.

And what about England himself? He must have experienced a form of culture shock, leaving a country where there were no black people and where virtually all the whites were Catholic and finding himself ministering in a land where there was an enormous, enslaved black population and where few of the whites were Catholic. Did he ever think about returning to Ireland or requesting a less stressful assignment? There is no indication that such thoughts ever crossed his mind. Besides being highly committed to his ministry, England thrived in America. As has been seen, he adjusted quickly to the reality of life in his adopted land, not only assuming a leadership role in the Catholic hierarchy but also gaining the respect of political leaders and Protestant clergy. He achieved this by living within realistic parameters, recognizing that his ability to contribute to the establishment of the Church in the South required that he not raise his voice against slavery.

Nevertheless, some reflection on the status of slaves may have taken place as the bishop bounced his way on the stagecoach to Washington at the end of his visit to New Bern during that initial swing through the state. He may have been haunted by the dark, frightened, perhaps pleading eyes of Abraham, Gaston's slave. In any case, England added a little more personal information about the slaves whom he baptized at this next stop. In entries dated June 9, 1821, he wrote in the Washington register: "I baptized Jeffrey, an adult boy of color, age about eighteen years, and a slave of William Worsley." Also, "John, a boy of color, age about fifteen years and the slave of Louis Leroy." Jeffrey and John joined Abraham as the first black Catholics in North Carolina.

Other Voices During the Slave Period

Bishop England was a man of the church, not a social reformer. In the lengthy series of letters on slavery which he wrote to Secretary of State John Forsyth, we look in vain either for any personal reflections or social analysis. All we have is a catalog of scriptural, theological, and papal references aimed at showing that the Catholic Church did not oppose slavery and consequently was not a threat to the prevailing social arrangements. In this regard, England was no different from his Baptist friend, Richard Fuller, who wrote: "What God sanctioned in the Old Testament, and permitted in the New, cannot be sin."[3] However, a European Catholic, viewing the American scene during the same period, was not shackled by the ecclesiastical reasoning which England felt compelled to defend. After his 1831 visit to America Alexis de Tocqueville wrote: "The most formidable evil threatening the future of the US is the presence of the blacks on their soil."[4]

That "evil" had already infected southern whites. Not only did they live in fear of a slave uprising, but also the existence of slavery had made white southerners "lazy and nonproductive," unwilling to do manual work, which they considered beneath their dignity. The price of slavery included the fact that while the free states were rapidly advancing in manufacturing, commerce, and trade, the slave states remained economically and culturally underdeveloped. De Tocqueville put it succinctly: "Slavery, so cruel to the slave, was fatal to the master." Finally, in words that might well apply to Gaston and the other slave-owning Catholics, the Frenchman wrote: "In the southern states there is silence; one does not speak of the future before strangers; one avoids discussing it with one's friends; each man, so to say, hides it from himself...."[5]

Virtually nothing is known of the role that Catholicism played in shaping the lives and values of slaves. This is especially true for North Carolina where the number of Catholics was minuscule. The only known reference to Catholicism made by a slave was recorded in 1937 as part of the Federal Writers Project of the Works Progress Administration. Ransom Sidney Taylor, born in January 1857, reported that his master, John Cane, was from the North and buried in the "Catholic graveyard" in Raleigh. Taylor recalled:

> My master would not allow anyone to whip his Negroes. If they was to be whipped, he did it himself and the licks he gave them would not hurt a flea. He was good to all of us and we all loved him. My master was an Irishman. Mother and father said he was one of the best white men that ever lived.[6]

However, although they had "prayer meetings on the plantation," there was no Catholic church to attend. As Taylor related: "At times we went to the white folks' church. Master was a Catholic, but we went to the Methodist Church."

The most prominent Catholic in public life during the middle of the 19th Century was the Marylander, Roger Brooke Taney, who in 1836 succeeded John Marshall as Chief Justice of the United States and served in that position for nearly thirty years. Taney remained a faithful Catholic despite the embarrassments he suffered from those who disliked the church. Perhaps his most famous ruling, certainly one which contributed to the outbreak of the Civil War, was the Dred Scott decision of 1857 which declared the Missouri Compromise of 1820 unconstitutional and said that Dred Scott, born a slave, did not gain his freedom merely because he had escaped to a free territory.

Like virtually all Catholics of his day, Taney neither foresaw nor called for the end of slavery. Although he had manumitted his own slaves, he supported states' rights and felt that the sudden emancipation of slaves "would be absolute ruin to the Negroes, as well as to the white population." As far as religion was concerned, he said in a letter:

> Unquestionably it is the duty of every master to watch over the religious and moral culture of his slaves, and to give them every comfort and privilege that is not incompatible with the continued existence of the relations between them.[7]

Of course "the relations between them" referred to the master-slave relationship.

If Taney or other Catholic laymen were to look to the hierarchy of their church for guidance, they would find either silence or complicity with the status quo. For example, in the decrees and pastoral letter issued by the First Plenary Council of Baltimore held in 1852, there is no mention of slavery or of abolition. Just as a century later the American bishops would be accused of being more concerned about Hispanics than blacks, so in the years before the Civil War their attention was focused on the immigrants of that period. As one author put it: "The Irish and Germans must come first; then the Negroes."[8]

Despite the fact that a number of slaves were baptized as Catholics, no black Catholic community emerged in North Carolina during slavery. Nor is there any evidence that any Catholics were to be found among the masses of freedmen who lived in the state when Bishop James Gibbons was assigned as Vicar Apostolic in 1868. As has been seen, there were few enough white Catholics, virtually no personnel, and scant material resources. In such an environment, it is no criticism of Gibbons to say that he showed little interest in the former slaves.

It was only after the accession of Leo Haid to the position of Vicar that the church found itself rooted securely enough to turn some attention to blacks. In particular, it was the numerous grants made by Katherine Drexel beginning in the 1890's that spurred Haid to provide services for those few African Americans who were drawn to a church with which they could relate culturally with only the greatest difficulty. However, the major contribution of the Catholic Church to North Carolina African Americans was not welcoming them into the church but into the Catholic schools. The paucity of black Catholics in the pews must be viewed in conjunction with the thousands in the classrooms. The education provided by the parochial schools was a ticket to freedom for many, a ticket used more often than not to flee from North Carolina.

"The Seedbed of the Nation"

In 1959, Washington, North Carolina's Mother of Mercy High School for Colored Children graduated ninety-three students. Within weeks, all but six had left their native town, most of them traveling north where the prospects of employment were greater and the racial climate more liberal. Of the students who had graduated during the previous ten years, only one was still in Washington and she was preparing to leave. Furthermore, the majority of these students were Catholic, precisely the ones who could have provided a foundation for a black Catholic community in the town. As the Mother of Mercy pastor, Passionist Father Raymond Pulvino, reported: "although fewer than ten per cent of the children who enroll in the mission school's first grade are Catholic, by the time the class reaches senior year of high school nearly all of them are. This is not due completely to conversions, but to the fact that some of the non-Catholics drop out in order to coast by in the public school with the fine foundation they have acquired in the Catholic school."[9] Pulvino gave credit to the Immaculate Heart of Mary sisters who provided an education that was far superior to that available in other area schools for either blacks or whites.

A further indication of the rapid erosion of the African American community was the fact that although there had been twenty-nine baptisms in the parish during the previous year, including thirteen adults, parish membership had not increased. In fact it had decreased, because forty-seven men, women, and children had moved north. Although Pulvino was happy to see people bettering their lives, the steady outbound stream of his people saddened him: "With the summer months will come another great exodus, an exodus of those graduates and of many parishioners. Most of them, perhaps all of them, will never return to Mother of Mercy."

The sociologist Rupert Vance referred to the South as "the seedbed of the nation," a metaphor for the way that the young people of the South, white and black alike, were transplanted to other parts of the country.[10] Although the drain of white Catholics bedeviled the North Carolina church, the loss of blacks was particularly devastating. Ironically, missionaries who had traveled from the North to evangelize the South found that many of the people they converted and educated were traveling in the opposite direction, often to Washington, DC, Philadelphia, and New York, the very cities from which they themselves had come.

Black Catholic Elementary Schools

As successful as it was, Mother of Mercy High School was a rare resource for a small town in North Carolina. For black students it was unique. Catholic high school education became so rare, that when St. Genevieve of the Pines in Asheville ceased to be a Catholic school in 1971, there remained but three Church-run high schools in the state, one each in Charlotte, Raleigh, and Winston-Salem, North Carolina's three major population centers. With faculties comprised mainly of lay men and women, the high tuition in these schools limited their availability to those families most highly committed to Catholic education and, in general, to the most affluent. For all intents and purposes, a Catholic high school education was no longer available to African Americans.

Much more widely available was – and is -- Catholic elementary school education. In particular, the network of Catholic schools for black students that spanned the state during the era of segregation was the crown jewel of the Church in North Carolina. As unfortunate as was the racism of the period, the Church provided what was the most effective mechanism available for black boys and girls to improve their chances of success in society. Consistently, Catholic schools exceeded in quality the educational standards of the separate but *unequal* public schools. And it was not just Catholics who profited from the dedication of the nuns and the generosity of white Catholic donors. In virtually every school, the majority of students were non-Catholics.

What spurred the development of Catholic schools was the emphasis placed on education by the bishops gathered at the Third Plenary Council of Baltimore, over which Cardinal Gibbons presided in

1884. Almost a quarter of the decrees of the Council were concerned with education. In particular, and certainly unrealistically, the bishops insisted that where parochial schools were lacking they be established within two years. Bowing to social reality, the prelates suggested that, where necessary, separate schools be erected for Negroes. In order to make feasible their commitment to the education of African Americans, the bishops initiated an annual general collection for Negro and Indian Missions, a collection which more than a century later continues to make possible a range of services in hundreds of communities around the country.

As has been seen, Bishop Waters found himself between a rock and a hard place with regard to the race issue. On the one hand, he wanted to integrate all Catholic institutions, while on the other hand, as a southerner himself, he knew just how deeply engrained was white antipathy to any mixing of the races. In effect, his 1953 desegregation of the churches and schools in Newton Grove was a test case. Despite the fact that liberal priests pressured him to continue the process, he knew that the forced integration of elementary schools would destroy Catholic education in the state, as indeed it had in Newton Grove. Accordingly, although Waters integrated Catholic high schools, he left the elementary schools alone. In fact, even after Newton Grove, three additional black Catholic schools were opened. This was in no way an indication of Waters' support of segregation. Rather, it was motivated by his overriding belief in the value of Catholic schools.

In 1960, as the Civil Rights movement gathered steam, a total of sixteen black Catholic schools were operating in North Carolina. All were associated with black parishes or missions. In every case, religious orders of women conducted the schools, and in most cases, religious orders of men ran the parishes. The investment of personnel and financial resources represented a commitment to African Americans comparable to the Church's subsequent zeal for Latinos.

The black schools, with the year they were founded, are as follows:

- 1887 St. Joseph   New Bern
- 1888 St. Thomas   Wilmington
- 1927 Mother of Mercy   Washington
- 1928 Our Lady of the Miraculous Medal   Greensboro
- 1930 St. Monica   Raleigh

- 1936 St. Anthony of Padua   Asheville
- 1941 St. Catherine   Elizabeth City
- 1942 Our Lady of Victory   West Southern Pines
- 1945 St. Alphonsus   Wilson
- 1946 St. Madeline Sophia   Lumberton
- 1949 Our Lady of the Atonement   Kinston
- 1950 Christ the King   High Point
- 1950 St. Benedict the Moor   Winston Salem
- 1956 St. Gabriel   Greenville
- 1956 St. Ann   Fayetteville
- 1957 Our Lady of Consolation   Charlotte[11]

To put this network of schools in context, it must be recalled that in 1960, there were but 45,000 Catholics in North Carolina, less than one percent of the population. It might also be noted that half the schools had been opened after World War II, an event which not only sensitized Americans to injustice overseas but to social evils within their own country as well. In particular, religious communities of women, awakened to the plight of Southern blacks, fanned out over the region and, in their own quiet way, became civil rights activists. By their presence, they affirmed that black children had just as much a right to a good education as did white children. If Bishop Waters had contributed to the overturning of Jim Crow by integrating Newton Grove, even more so did the sisters contribute to the spiritual emancipation of blacks by embracing their cause and affirming their dignity.

St. Alphonsus, Wilson

Each of these sixteen schools, all of them long since closed, has its story, as do the parishes with which they were associated. Three will be discussed: St. Alphonsus in Wilson, St. Monica in Raleigh, and Our Lady of Consolation in Charlotte.

When, in 1945, a community of black nuns, the Oblate Sisters of Providence, opened St. Alphonsus School in the Redemptorist-founded colored parish in Wilson, of the one hundred pupils who enrolled only two were Catholics. Located in a poor neighborhood, the school struggled as the sisters strove to accept any child who applied. One indication of the church's commitment to the total community was the fact that of the eleven students who graduated from the eighth grade in 1962, none were Catholics. However, two years later, a Catholic did graduate, the convert Sharon Roberts. Decades later, Roberts recalled her experience as a member of the small parish and in particular the pain she felt when the church was closed. Although founded because of white racism, it had become her spiritual home.

It was a very devastating time when St. Alphonsus Church was closed. The congregation was small, twenty-five or thirty families, but it had a long history. What happened was that it was just announced from the altar one Sunday that the church would be closed in two weeks time. That was October 1986. It was like a slap in the face to be told two weeks before hand that the church was going to be closed. A group went and spoke with Bishop Gossman. But that was after the closing had been announced. It was too late.

Those families in which the parents and children were Catholics continued to go to church, but many of us were converts. When *our* church closed, we couldn't just go to a church where we didn't feel comfortable. For myself, I just stopped going. It was only in recent years that I began attending mass again. It wasn't an easy road for many of us.

I had attended St. Alphonsus parochial school, graduating in 1964. At that time, many of the children here in East Wilson went to St. Alphonsus, whether they were Catholic or not. Since I wasn't from a Catholic family, I didn't have my mother telling me to go to church on Sunday.

The school closed in 1968 and most of the children went to the public school. Wilson County was integrating around that time; lots of changes were taking place. It was through the school that many of us became Catholics. When the school closed, and many of the young people moved away, the congregation stopped growing.

I was angry a very long time. For five years I wandered from church to church. Finally, I said to myself: 'You're going over there. You are black and you are Catholic.' So, I went over to St. Theresa's [the 'white' parish in Wilson] and I really let off steam with Father [James M.] Labosky. He listened to me and I felt better afterwards. It was my way of working it out.[12]

Although St. Alphonsus School no longer stands, the white frame church remains and is used on occasion for meetings. Adjacent to the church is the rectory that had housed a succession of Redemptorist priests and subsequently several secular priests, men who in the waning days of their ministry were assigned to St. Alphonsus as a post that would make few demands. Other than a mass on Sunday, there was little to do but pray and be available for the infrequent office calls. With the school gone, silence had replaced the squeals and laugher of children and non-Catholics no longer looked to St. Alphonsus for assistance.

African American Ministry

However, St. Alphonsus was destined to experience a minor reincarnation. Sensitive to the complaint that, as one by one the African American schools and parishes were closed, black Catholics were being abandoned, in 1978, the Diocese of Raleigh established a commission on African American Ministry and Evangelization which recommended that a special office be created to promote the interests of African Americans. Accordingly, in 1982, the Office of African American Ministry and Evangelization was established, with the vacant St. Alphonsus rectory designated the headquarters of the new program. It is in that white frame building that Sharon Roberts, as receptionist and secretary, maintained the thin thread of Catholic continuity in the neighborhood.

The first director of the office was African American Friar of the Atonement, Father Martin Carter, a native of High Point, North Carolina. Without delay, Carter drew up a list of objectives, including maintaining a talent list of African Americans for appointment to diocesan bodies, developing African American Ministry chapters throughout the diocese, introducing cultural programs to parishes, and fostering job opportunities.[13]

Subsequently, Maxine Towns, an Oblate Sister of Providence, became Director, a position she held for eleven years. However, Sister Maxine maintained a low profile and during her tenure the Office itself and black Catholics assumed the "invisibility" to which Monsignor Thomas Hadden referred in the statement quoted at the beginning of this chapter. Then, in the year 2000, with the withdrawal of Sister Maxine from the diocese, Hadden was given the opportunity to do something about the situation when he was appointed interim head of the Office. As long-time Vicar for African Americans, he was well aware of the limitations of the Church's commitment to its black members. More than that, as the senior African American priest in the state, no one had greater knowledge of the history of black Catholics or a greater right to serve as spokesperson for his people. Hadden's life as a Catholic had begun more than sixty years earlier, while he was a student at St. Monica School in Raleigh.

St. Monica, Raleigh

On July 18, 1930, having heard that a school for Negroes was to be constructed in Raleigh, an elderly black man wrote a lengthy letter to Bishop Hafey. The man, Charles N. Hunter of Cotton Place, Raleigh, related how in 1901, finding himself alone in Trenton, New Jersey, he had gone to St. Mary's Catholic Cathedral. When he entered the crowded church, one of the worshipers got up and gave him his seat.

> I was exalted into a new realm of Christianity. I was a stranger – a Negro – and you took me in. I went to the church under the apprehension that I might be rudely treated, or at best find a place in some isolated nook. Instead, I was warmly greeted. 'Ye took me in.'

Subsequently, Hunter was admitted as a patient to St. Francis' Hospital, also in Trenton. Although he had no money, the sisters received him cordially. On being discharged, Hunter requested a statement of his bill. One of the sisters informed him that there would be no charges, that they were "glad to have relieved my suffering."

Hunter exemplifies the all too common experience of the Catholic Church in its efforts to attract Negroes. Even those who admired it, as Hunter most certainly did, seldom became members. The man concluded his letter by saying that he was an Episcopalian but had found "many Negroes who are rejoicing in the prospect of your proposed school."

Less than two months later, Bishop Hafey offered the first mass to be said in St. Monica Church, dedicating the little building and the adjacent school to which Charles Hunter had referred. In his diary the bishop noted:

> Large attendance of colored people. Also, sisters representing the Immaculate Heart of Mary, Mercys, Franciscans, Dominicans, Sisters of Charity. Ten priests also present. Rev. Charles Hannigan, SSJ, pastor, addressed the gathering. One hundred thirty-six children registered for the school – not one of them a Catholic ... another proof of the great harvest ready for the reaper.[14]

The idea of establishing the church had been broached several years earlier and moved to the implementation stage in 1928, when Hafey received a check for $9,000 from John J. Sullivan of Philadelphia "for a chapel for colored people in Raleigh." Another contribution was received from the Director General of "The Catholic Board for Mission Work Among the Colored People."[15] As was always the case, no project could move forward until adequate funding was available. This was particularly true for programs for African Americans. Besides the fact that none of the children in the new school were Catholics, at the dedication mass, although the church was two-thirds full, there were only seven colored Catholics present, five of whom, as the bishop noted in his diary, "live far outside the city of Raleigh." The forty-voice choir, consisting of older school children, contained no Catholics.

Although a Josephite priest, Charles Hannigan, had been the founding pastor, it would be another order that would staff St. Monica for most of its history. Constantly trying to lure more clergy to North Carolina, in 1934 Hafey wrote to the Provincial of the Dominican priests in New York, extending to them "an invitation to join the ranks of the religious orders which are taking up the work on behalf of the colored of North Carolina." The appeal was effective, and in June Fathers R. F. Vollmer and R. J. Dewdney arrived at St. Monica, succeeding Father Hannigan. The Dominicans would remain at St. Monica until the suppression of the parish in 1968. By that time, St. Monica's most prominent alumnus had been a priest of the diocese of Raleigh for ten years.

Father Thomas P. Hadden

In the early years of the 20th Century, Thomas Hadden's grandfather, a truck farmer, had leased the property on which St Monica would be built. At the time, despite being the state capital, Raleigh was still very much a rural settlement, its Negro population eking out a modest living within the constraints of Jim Crow. When the white owners of the land, who lived in the manor house up the street, agreed to sell the parcel to the church, Bishop Hafey made a settlement with Hadden's grandfather. So, although not Catholic, the family was associated with the church from its foundation. Furthermore, Hadden's mother, a seamstress, made the drapes for behind the altar and used to send young Thomas over to the convent with peonies and dahlias to decorate the sisters' chapel.[16]

As seemed his destiny, Hadden attended St. Monica School and, like most of his classmates, was not a Catholic. However, in the seventh grade the boy experienced what he termed an overwhelming desire to enter the Church. Furthermore, even at this young age, he thought that he would like to be a priest. Although some relatives were opposed to his conversion, his parents, including his father, a Methodist minister, were supportive. Most helpful of all were the Dominican priests and the Immaculate Heart of Mary sisters who staffed the school.

From his vantage point of a long and successful career, Hadden would look back fondly on his childhood days. At a reunion of former

St. Monica students held more than thirty years after the school had closed, the now retired priest would say:

> "You were taught by a group of white nuns and white priests who dedicated their lives to you educationally and spiritually, who loved you and stood up for you. There was a real feeling of closeness and family.[17]

The bonding which took place between Hadden and the religious of his childhood would sustain him as he spent his life working as a black man in a predominantly white church. No matter how much racism or indifference he encountered, he could never forget that it was white men and women who had been his main support during his formative years. This became even truer when both his parents died while he was still a teenager.

As an orphan, Thomas was sent to Portsmouth, Virginia, to live with an older brother who worked in the Navy Yard there. Attending Our Lady of Victory High School, Hadden found the Daughters of Charity of Emmitsburg, Maryland, just as loving as the sisters in Raleigh. One of those Charity nuns, Sister Martha, became his mentor, nurturing his faith and encouraging his dream of being a priest. By one of those strange turns of fate, had his parents lived and Hadden remained in Raleigh, he would have attended public high school, since Cathedral Catholic High had not yet been integrated. It is highly unlikely that the public school would have provided the guidance needed to pursue a calling to the priesthood. As it turned out, it was difficult enough even with the help of the sisters.

When Tom spoke to the provincial of the religious community that staffed the Portsmouth parish, he was told, "Well, maybe if you finish college and graduate school, by then we will be accepting colored candidates; but not now." When next he applied to the Josephite Fathers, who ministered exclusively to blacks, he was told that they took candidates only from their own parishes. Catching them in their subterfuge, Hadden wrote back to the Josephites and said, "I don't understand this. Every Josephite I've seen is white. You work in black parishes. Where do these priests come from?"

Undeterred, Hadden wrote to yet a third religious order and was told that all the colored candidates they had accepted suffered nervous breakdowns and had to be dismissed. Upset at this further rejection, Hadden countered with the argument: "I'm sure that some of your Irish,

German, and Italian seminarians also have had nervous breakdowns. Have you excluded candidates from those backgrounds?"

Eventually, having heard that they did not discriminate, Hadden entered the Society of the Divine Word seminary in Bay St. Louis, Mississippi. However, perhaps because of the pattern of rejection, he decided that he did not want to be a religious order priest after all but was unsure if he would be welcome in the diocesan clergy. A knock on the door in the summer of 1950 gave him his answer.

As was related in Chapter Two, Bishop Waters had Raleigh seminarians take the census during the summer. One of those seminarians, Raymond Donohue, [who was ordained a priest in 1951 and died in 1997] visited the Hadden house, where Thomas' sister was the only one at home. She told Donohue about her brother and that he was interested in being a diocesan priest. Excited, the seminarian told Waters about the young man. The bishop snapped: "Go get him!"

Even though some of the Raleigh clergy were not pleased with the idea, Waters persisted. This was the period of his leadership in the Civil Rights movement, and he was determined to break the taboo that held that blacks were not ready for the demands of priesthood. Not only did the bishop accept Hadden but underlined his confidence in the young man by assigning him to Rome for his theological studies.

Even at this juncture the going was not smooth, with some bishops objecting to a black seminarian. However, persevering in the face of obstacles, in December 1958, Hadden became the first black seminarian ordained from the North American College as well as the first of his race to become a priest of the Raleigh diocese. The following year, a second black priest, Joseph L. Howze, was ordained for North Carolina providing Hadden with some companionship but also, as it would turn out, with a rival for higher honors.[18]

Joseph L. Howze

Like Hadden, Howze was a convert. Born in Daphne, Alabama in 1923, he attended Alabama State Teachers College, graduating in 1948 with a degree in science and education. While teaching biology at Central Catholic High School in Mobile, he took instructions and was received into the Church by a Josephite priest in 1948.

In 1950 Howze entered the Josephite College in Newburgh, New York. However, despite the debt he felt to that order, like Hadden, Howze was attracted to the diocesan clergy. It happened that one of the Josephites, Vincent Warren, while in a parish in Norfolk, Virginia, had become acquainted with Father Vincent Waters, who subsequently had become bishop of Raleigh. Warren advised Howze to contact Waters.[19]

Adopted by Waters, Howze was assigned to the Preparatory Seminary in Buffalo, New York, and then to Christ the King Seminary, also in upstate New York, for his theological studies. Whereas Hadden had been ordained in Rome, Howze had the distinction of being the first black priest ordained in North Carolina, when in May 1959, at the age of 33, he was raised to the priesthood in Sacred Heart Cathedral in Raleigh. As the diocesan paper recorded: "The bishop and all forty-seven priests in attendance imposed hands on the cleric."[20]

From 1959 to 1972 Howze served as pastor at several black parishes, including Our Lady of Consolation in Charlotte and St. Anthony in Asheville. He was also chairman of the Diocesan Liturgical Commission and Director of the Propagation of the Faith. It was while in his final assignment in North Carolina, as pastor of St. Lawrence Church in Asheville, that he received word that he had been appointed Auxiliary Bishop of the Diocese of Natchez-Jackson, Mississippi. Five years later, on June 6, 1977, Howze was selected to be the Ordinary of the newly established diocese of Biloxi, a jurisdiction that covers the southern third of the state. In 1998, at the mandatory retirement age of 75, Howze submitted his resignation, having served as a bishop in the state of Mississippi for twenty-five years. At the time of his appointment, there had been but one other black bishop in the U.S. hierarchy, Harold R. Perry, Auxiliary Bishop of New Orleans. By the time Howze left office, there were sixteen.[21]

Black Priest, White Church

Although in time he would be accepted and admired, in the early years of his ministry, Hadden endured numerous humiliating and, at times, dangerous experiences. His initial assignment was – of all places – Newton Grove. Here was the church that was at the eye of a racial storm in 1953 being sent a black priest six years later. Father Fred Koch was pastor at the time, and his new assistant was principally responsible for Sacred Heart, the colored mission in Goldsboro. However, when Koch was away, Hadden was left in charge of Newton Grove as well. When the young black priest went over to church to hear confessions, he heard a man outside the confessional say to someone, "Why you going in there; don't you know that nigger's in there?" The other man replied, "He's a priest, ain't he?"

Our Lady of Guadalupe, the Newton Grove church, is constructed in such a way that it has two front doors, one on each side of the central spire. One Sunday morning Hadden went over to church, unlocked one of the doors, and went into the sacristy. In a while, a white man came in and said, "Ain't you going to unlock the door?" Hadden responded, "I did." The man explained, "You only unlocked the colored door. We come in the other one."[22]

Hadden's next assignment was equally delicate. In 1962, the Passionist Fathers left New Bern where there were two parishes and two schools, St. Paul for white Catholics and St. Joseph for blacks. Hadden's task was to merge the parishes into one. It was hoped that he would be able to assure black parishioners that they would be welcome at St. Paul without unduly alienating the whites. However, as had happened in Newton Grove, the priest met with resistance. A number of the white parishioners sent a petition to Waters to have the new priest removed, arguing that they were accustomed to having an older man as pastor. Other New Bern Catholics did not want him to baptize their children.

The most disturbing experience of all occurred one night after Hadden had gone to bed. Hearing a noise, he looked out the window and saw hooded Klan members running around the rectory in a menacing fashion. Understandably fearful, Hadden called for police protection. When he reported the incident to the bishop, Waters said, "Maybe what the church of North Carolina needs is a martyr." Hadden replied, "Bishop, I'm not a candidate for martyrdom."

Despite the continuous evidence of racism, Hadden's commitment to a church that didn't fully accept him remained firm. His tenacity is reflected in the fact that he stayed on as pastor in New Bern for ten years. After that, his fidelity was rewarded by assignment as Rector of Sacred Heart Cathedral in Raleigh, another first for a black priest. Hadden was the kind of priest that Waters liked, one who was loyal, obedient, and hard working. Although in later years, Hadden would become more outspoken, during the Waters' years he was the epitome of moderation, even as other blacks became more assertive.

Hadden's final major post was to St. Mary, Wilmington, its rectory perhaps haunted by the ghost of Christopher Dennen, who nearly a century earlier had engineered the racial division of the parish. Hadden remained in Wilmington, the initial headquarters of the Church in the state, for fifteen years. Then, in 2000, having reached the diocesan mandatory retirement age of 70, he relinquished his pastorate but assumed the post of interim Director of the Office of African American Affairs, taking up residence in the old St. Alphonsus rectory in Wilson.

George Stallings

In some respects the mirror image of Tom Hadden is George Stallings, possibly the most controversial black priest in American history. Whereas Hadden's approach to priesthood was to downplay the significance of his racial identity, Stallings celebrated it. From the tone of his voice and the content of his preaching, a blind person might not realize that Hadden was black. There was no such doubt about Stallings, who brought a powerful Afro-centric emphasis to his ministry and in so doing attracted an enormous following.

In 1989, when Stallings, a priest of the archdiocese of Washington, decided to leave the Catholic Church and create a new church, Hadden said: "He was my altar boy in New Bern. Now I'm full of mixed emotions. I'm not understanding what he did. I sympathize with him, but I don't agree with him."[23]

What Hadden didn't understand was not Stallings' anger but his lack of respect for authority. It was understandable for Stallings to call the Church "racist;" Hadden had done so many times himself. But Stallings crossed the line when he "thumbed his nose at the Catholic hierarchy" by disobeying Cardinal James A. Hickey and starting his own church, called Imani Temple after the Swahili word for faith.[24]

Stallings had been born to convert parents in New Bern in 1948, the oldest of seven children. His Baptist maternal grandmother, Bessie Taylor, had been housekeeper and cook to the Catholic nuns staffing New Bern's black Catholic school, where she registered her own children. A daughter, who would be George's mother, converted to Catholicism with the approval of Taylor, although she herself remained a Baptist. As a child, young George often accompanied his grandmother to the Baptist church, absorbing the rhythm and themes of the preaching style. Later in life, Stallings said that the more powerfully the Word is preached, the more powerfully it affects people's lives.[25]

Ordained in Rome in 1974, Stallings had sensational success. Over the course of twelve years as pastor of St. Teresa of Avila parish in Southeast Washington, DC, he built the congregation from 200 members to more than 2,000 families and the Sunday collection from $400 to $8,000. Attendance at his masses was so large that TV screens had to be installed in the church basement to accommodate the overflow crowds. There was no doubt but that his Afro-centric approach to preaching and ritual appealed to many Catholics. However, complaints about his life style and orthodoxy mounted, and the archbishop felt compelled to remove the charismatic but self-willed priest.

North Carolina Roots

Stallings' conflict with church officials was nothing new. It had begun in North Carolina many years earlier while the New Bern native was a seminarian for the Raleigh Diocese. Bishop Waters hoped that Stallings might join Hadden and Howze in a growing corps of black priests, who would not only show that the Catholic Church welcomed blacks but help bring about at last the long anticipated "harvest" of which Bishop Hafey had dreamed years earlier.[26] However, Stallings was a very different kind of black man than Hadden and Howze. These older men, raised in the era of segregation, not only were not militant but conformed to the style and mentality of the "white" Church. They were priests who happened to be black. Stallings, on the other hand, a child of the Sixties and the Black Power movement, was a black man who happened to be a priest. His African heritage shaped his identity, and he was determined that it would shape his ministry as well.

In 1964, at age sixteen, Stallings entered the short-lived high school seminary that Waters had established in the mountains near Asheville. The bishop hoped that by recruiting them young, boys could be molded into men who would be self-sacrificing, obedient priests. As a student, Stallings was so popular with his peers that he was selected prefect, or head student. When he moved on to a college level seminary in Kentucky, he was elected student body president. Waters, pleased with the young man's progress, sent him to Rome, as he had done earlier with Hadden. However, as Stallings matured, he developed a mentality that was incompatible with Waters' expectations. The precipitating incident was, of all things, "facial hair."

On a trip back from Rome two years before ordination, Stallings visited the bishop and was abruptly ordered: "George, shave off that beard! Canon law says a priest cannot have a beard." Stallings replied, "Your excellency, it's not a beard, it's a mustache." He explained further, "It's an expression of being black." Perhaps jolted by that last very revealing remark, the bishop insisted: "Beard, mustache. It's all the same! Shave it off!" Hair was not Waters' only concern. Stallings also sported a "$400 suit," suggesting that the young man had strayed from the modest style of his New Bern upbringing.[27]

This confrontation took place in June 1972 as Waters was having the post-Vatican II problems with priests and nuns related in Chapter Three. He was not about to let rebelliousness spread to seminarians. Uneasy with a man who wished to express his blackness and was also cultivating expensive tastes, Waters refused to authorize Stallings' return to Rome, ordering him instead to take a year off, live with his family, and relearn the simple life. Instead, Stallings was accepted by the Washington Archdiocese, resumed his studies, and was ordained on schedule in 1974, the same year that Waters died.

What Stallings discovered in the aftermath of his split with the church was that he was cheered and supported as long as he remained within the official Catholic fold, but that few Catholics were willing to follow him into the wilderness of schism. Most black Catholics, like most whites, intuit that, for all its faults, the Church of Rome is where they belong. Stallings' own family members remained loyal members of St. Paul parish in New Bern. Although the Imani Temple survived, it never expanded into the network of black Catholic congregations Stallings had envisioned.[28]

Meager Harvest

Southern blacks, like southern whites, have never been particularly attracted to the Catholic Church. The census of the Raleigh Diocese for 1955 enumerated 3,021 Negro Catholics, 2/10s of 1% of the black population of North Carolina. At the time, 35 priests were engaged exclusively in Negro work. This averages out to one priest for every 86 Negro Catholics, an extraordinary commitment of personnel. In addition, 61 sisters, assigned to thirteen parochial schools, were educating black children. A sign that perhaps some headway was being made was the fact that more than half of the 311 Negro Baptisms that year were of adults.[29] However, the hope of a substantial African American Catholic population was never realized. As has been indicated, part of the problem was that most of the graduates of Catholic schools moved north. But even granting this drain, the results were meager. To a substantial extent, black people affiliated with churches where they felt at home and experienced a sense of community. Although this was possible to some extent in the segregated Catholic parishes, one of the ironies of integrating parishes was the hemorrhaging of blacks from the Church.

Twenty-four years after that 1955 census, Waters' successor, Bishop Joseph Gossman, would express dismay at the small number of black Catholics in the diocese.

> I came here four years ago assuming that there would be a sizeable part of our church that would be black and Catholic and I was very surprised to find it was not there. I've wondered for a long time just what our efforts to reach the black people of North Carolina have really amounted to....[30]

Part of the answer to Gossman's bewilderment was that once separate schools and parishes for African Americans were eliminated in the name of racial equality, a ministry directed specifically to them virtually evaporated. Although not always rejected in the white parishes, neither were blacks sought out and invited in. Furthermore, in the ecumenical atmosphere of the late Sixties and beyond, the need to convert people subsided. Furthermore, as the revolt of Father Stallings highlighted, more militant African Americans could not find much with which to identify in what remained substantially a Euro-centric "white man's church."

Our Lady of Consolation, Charlotte

As it became evident to Bishop Waters that the cause of racial integration was not being served simply by closing black churches and telling parishioners to go to the white church, an alternative approach was devised for Charlotte. By 1970, there were already seven parishes in North Carolina's most populous city. One of them, Our Lady of Consolation (OLC) in the North Central sector of the city, had been established in 1941 as a colored parish and over time saw the development of a loyal and cohesive Catholic community. The spirit of the parish was strengthened in no small measure by its highly regarded parochial school. It was clear to all that the closing of this parish would be a tragic loss to its members. Accordingly, employing a strategy used by the government to bring about broader racial representation in the legislature, the diocese redrew the boundaries of several Charlotte parishes. By a stroke of the episcopal pen, several hundred white members of St. Peter, the old central city parish, suddenly found themselves members of OLC. Similarly, many of the Consolation faithful were reassigned to other parishes.

Although initially many white parishioners protested, decrying yet another peremptory decision by Waters, there was no overt rebellion. The outcome was that – technically -- whereas formerly there had been 300 Negro families at OLC, there were now about 180 Negro and 150 white families. However, by the 1970's people no longer took officially designated boundaries all that seriously, and for all intents and purposes OLC remained a black parish, while those whites who preferred to attend St. Peter continued to do so. What mattered was that the bishop could report that he had ended segregation.[31]

As for the parish school, which had been established in 1957 as the last colored school opened in the state, there was now some integration with 10% of its 350 students, white. Staffing the school at the time were Oblate Sisters of Providence, a predominantly Negro teaching community. Further adding to the ethnic and racial mix of the reconfigured parish was the fact that the two priests serving there were Consolata Fathers, members of an Italian missionary society.

In large measure the de facto preservation of OLC as a black parish reflected the area in which the church was located. But it also manifested, as was true of Holy Cross in Durham, the racial pride and sense of ownership that characterized many African Americans. It had been assumed that they wanted to be integrated with whites. It turned out that what they wanted was the right to attend any church while retaining their own. The experiences of two veteran members of OLC can illustrate the racial pride of African Americans as well as the typical route that many black North Carolinians have taken on their journey to a Catholic identity.

Raised a Baptist During Segregation

As a child, Virginia Williamson would occasionally surreptitiously drink from a water fountain marked "White," rather than the nearby one marked "Colored." In her innocence, the girl could never figure out what the difference was. For a while she thought that perhaps the water for Caucasians had sugar in it. Despite growing up in the segregated South of the 1930s and '40s, Williamson harbored no malice in her heart. Like Thomas Hadden and Joseph Howze, she was able to navigate her way through a very difficult time and emerge with the ability to relate without rancor or suspicion to white people, including the priests of the predominantly white Catholic Church.

Raised a Baptist in the North Carolina town of Shelby, Williamson recalled that on Sundays her family spent virtually the entire day in church, singing, praying, and listening to impassioned preaching. However, influenced by some of the members of the town's

Catholic Church of St. Mary, Williamson converted while still in her teens. Although she maintained a loving relationship with her family, in a significant way the young woman had separated herself from much of the world of her childhood in which kinship ties, religion, and social life were intimately entwined.[32]

Helpful to success in shaping a new religious identity is moving away from one's hometown with its power to hold one captive to traditional patterns of thought and behavior. Williamson's new life began when she attended college at Virginia's predominantly African American Hampton Institute. After graduating with a degree in elementary education in 1952 and soon thereafter marrying her childhood sweetheart, Sam, Williamson began a career teaching in a segregated Charlotte school, one that was similar to the school she had attended as a child. At the same time, she and her husband began attending OLC. Teaching Sunday school and serving as a lector at mass became important dimensions of her deepening commitment to the church.

Retirement in 1984 freed Williamson for more extensive church and civic involvement. For years she was a member of the Charlotte Diocese Catholic Social Services board and its Elder Ministry Task Force. Even more challenging for a woman now in her seventies, Williamson became a motivational speaker, putting to use skills she had honed over several decades in the classroom. Presentations to churches and other groups on such topics as love, respect, and cherishing every moment of life have given her a renewed sense of value as a person. "I prayed about it [her new ministry], and I think that the seed was planted long ago.... I am happier now than I have ever been. It is my calling, and I truly want to make a meaningful difference."

Two Generations of Deacons

Growing up in Charlotte of the 1930's and '40's, Charles Knight had to deal with the challenge of understanding himself in a world that treated him as a second-class citizen. Helping him to make sense out of life was his maternal grandfather, a deacon in the Baptist church. Many days the boy accompanied his grandfather to work and to church, learning the love of God from this wise older man. Knight never dreamed that one day he also would be a deacon, not in the Baptist church of his birth but the Catholic Church to which he converted.[33]

Hoping to become an industrial arts teacher, Knight started college after graduating from high school in 1951. However, the family's financial situation did not permit him to continue. Instead, with GI

Bill education funding as an incentive, he joined the Navy. When his tour of duty ended, the young man returned to North Carolina and resumed his college education while working as a custodian. With a bachelor's degree in economics in hand, Knight accepted the best paying job available, that of mail carrier for the postal service. As he later said: "Integration was not in effect much back then. We had some of the best-educated postmen anywhere." Knight remained with the postal service for thirty-one years.

In the meanwhile, he had married Lavone, who like himself was raised in a single-parent home and reared in the Baptist faith. Living down the street from OLC, the Knights became acquainted with the pastor and some of the parishioners and in 1962 joined the church. Since the Catholic Church was going through the changes brought about by Vatican II, the couple had to undergo a complex and sometimes confusing adjustment. What supported them was becoming active in parish life. As had been true in their Baptist experience, OLC was more than just a place for Sunday worship but the center of cherished relationships and valuable contributions to the community. Like his fellow parishioner, Virginia Williamson, Charles Knight became a lector and faith formation teacher. His wife taught kindergarten while their daughter was attending OLC School.

When Knight heard about the newly restored permanent deaconate program, he knew it was for him. "I was doing a lot in the church already and felt that spiritually it would be an extension of my work." So, for several years, Lavone and Charles attended the classes prescribed for potential deacons, finding the experience enriching for their marriage as well as for their faith.

After ordination in 1983, Knight became involved in a range of church-related work, including the Cursillo, parish and finance councils, and Eucharistic ministry to the sick and shut-ins. As he went about his work as a deacon, he must have thought of those long ago days in a very different world when he had walked hand in hand with his deacon grandfather through the streets of Charlotte.

From Migrants to Immigrants

Although the story of the Hispanics in North Carolina is not so much a matter of the history of the Church as its future, some account of the roots of this major influx of an ethnic minority into the state is in order. The genesis of the Spanish-speaking population differed substantially in the eastern and western sectors of the state. In the Eastern agricultural region, the first Hispanics were migrant farm laborers, most of them poor Mexicans, who progressively traveled up the coast from Florida to Maine harvesting the crops and moving on. On the other hand, in the urban region around Charlotte, many of the early arrivals were middle class Cubans fleeing the communism that Fidel Castro had imposed on their native land. Initially, and appropriately, the Church responded differently to each of these situations. However, within two decades the distinctions would dissolve as thousands of mostly poor immigrants added a substantial Hispanic community to virtually every city and town in the state.

In the late 1970's some 30,000 migrant farm workers labored under the hot sun of eastern North Carolina each summer, often traveling as family groups. Farmers needed them, but only for a short period of time. Labor contractors acted as middlemen, trucking in workers and agreeing to get them out of the area again once the work was completed. There was no thought of permanent settlement, no need for year-round employees. With little government protection, these vulnerable workers were hired and fired at the whim of farmers, provided with substandard housing, and paid minimum wage, or less. Often, since income was based on the amount of fruit, vegetables, or tobacco picked, children accompanied parents into the fields spending their days bending over cucumber plants rather than over schoolbooks.

As early as 1960, Edward R. Murrow's television documentary "Harvest of Shame" had exposed the plight of the migrant workers. However, it was not until the late '70's that the Raleigh Diocese made a concerted effort to reach out to these people who arrived and departed with little notice. Although their needs were many, they had no spokespersons and few advocates. That changed in 1978 when Sister Evelyn Mattern prevailed upon Bishop Joseph Gossman to sponsor a summer migrant ministry program.

In her capacity as head of the diocesan Office of Peace and Justice, Mattern recruited, trained, and assigned some thirty volunteers, many of them sisters from northern states, to several areas where migrant camps were located, including Newton Grove, Washington, and Wilson. These "migrant ministers" visited the camps offering assistance to the migrants who often were virtual prisoners lacking the transportation to leave their isolated rural areas. More than anything else, the program showed the workers that people cared about them and showed the growers that the outside world was watching. On several occasions the "outside meddlers" encountered threatening reactions from farmers, who ordered them off their property. Undeterred, the ministers transported workers to health clinics and food stamp offices and attempted to enroll children in summer schools designed specifically for migrants. The church workers cooperated with Steven Edelstein of Farmworker Legal Services who represented the defenseless workers when they had legal problems.[34]

Although the principal thrust of the migrant ministers' work was responding to material needs, the spiritual was not forgotten. In several churches "Spanish masses" were organized, the first experiments in what would, within a few years, become a standard feature of parishes throughout the state. In those early summer programs, conducted by men and women with more good will than skill in dealing with Hispanics, it was discovered that the migrants would turn out in unexpected numbers for any service offered in their native language. Somehow, despite the lack of telephones, cars, and communication among the scattered farms, word spread and people mysteriously showed up, self conscious and not quite sure what to do, but eager to worship in the religion that was part of their heritage.[35]

In Wilson, where a family of migrant ministers lived in the rectory of St. Alphonsus Church with the pastor, Reverend John M. Breunig, a bus was hired to transport people from the camps to the church.[36] Symbolic of the rapidly changing Catholic demographics of the area and of the state, at one Sunday afternoon mass in July 1979, Spanish-speaking Catholics filled St. Alphonsus, whereas the regularly scheduled morning service at this black parish had counted only thirty African American worshipers. For the first time the Scripture readings were heard in Spanish and tentative voices raised in song in that language as well. After mass, two children were baptized, not only the first Mexicans baptized in St. Alphonsus but the first of thousands yet to come in churches all over the state. What happened that Sunday in the little church in Wilson was a small ripple in what was to become a tidal wave of change, not just for the church but also for North Carolina as a whole.

Recognizing what was happening, not only in North Carolina but also throughout the country, in 1982 the American Hispanic bishops issued a pastoral letter that drew attention to the accelerating rise in the Hispanic population. They summoned their fellow bishops to respond to the challenge. Prophetically, they said: "We are in the beginning stages of our life as Hispanic Americans."[37] Anticipating the bishops' message, both dioceses in North Carolina had already taken action. In fact, within months of founding the Diocese of Charlotte, Bishop Michael Begley had opened a Hispanic Center, not for migrants but for the first wave of permanent Latino residents.

Centro Catolico Hispano

Not only were the early Charlotte Hispanics more affluent than their migrant brothers and sisters, but also they were not afraid to approach the bishop with the request that their religious needs be met. Accordingly, in 1972, the Centro Catolico Hispano was opened. Its goal was to provide religious services but also to serve as a meeting place for the Cuban refugees, who clung together as they went through the process of cultural assimilation. Within a few years, the community grew from 50 to nearly 500 families, including immigrants from virtually every country in Latin America.

For thirty years, while sponsoring a wide range of activities, the congregation had no worship space of its own, celebrating mass in the school gymnasiums of city parishes. Then, in 2002, having raised nearly $2 million, the congregation of construction workers, hotel maids, landscapers, and cooks moved into their own building. Furthermore, what had been known as the Hispanic Center now became Our Lady of Guadalupe parish, the name signaling that Mexicans had become the predominant component of the linguistically unified but culturally diverse community. Each weekend 4,000 Latinos attend the six Spanish-language masses held in the new facility, located near the Charlotte/Douglas International Airport, the initial point of arrival of many of the worshipers.[38]

An early director of Centro Hispano was Father Joseph Kerin, ordained in 1957, who prepared for his assignment in an unanticipated fashion. Responding to the challenge offered by Vatican II that the American Catholics assume greater responsibility for the Church in Latin America, Bishop Waters had accepted a parish in Mexico City and released two priests to staff it. One of them was Kerin. Waters took pride in the fact that the "missionary diocese" of Raleigh was sending priests to Mexico where clergy were needed even more than at home. In fact, the parish that Raleigh had adopted, Most Holy Trinity, had approximately the same number of Catholics as there were in the entire state of North Carolina.[39]

Whereas Kerin served in Mexico for two years and then assumed the directorship of Centro Hispano, another North Carolina priest, Roberto Keenan, so loved his work South of the Border that he remained there for nearly three decades. On his return to North Carolina in 1994, Keenan became Vicar for Hispanics of the Diocese of Raleigh. The North Carolina commitment to Mexico has been maintained, with Father Christopher J. Flanagan volunteering in 2001 to spend two years in a Mexican parish.

Recruiting Priests from Colombia

Even as North Carolina priests were working in Latin America, the Diocese of Raleigh was recruiting seminarians from Colombia, a country that was producing a surplus of candidates for the priesthood. However, linguistic and cultural difficulties required that the diocese invest additional resources in preparing these young men to assume pastoral responsibilities in the United States. A House of Formation – named in honor of Father Price – was opened in Chapel Hill as a transitional location where students lived while improving their command of English and preparing for admission to American seminaries. The project began to bear fruit in 1998 when Arturo Cabra became the first native Colombian to be ordained.[40] In 2002, of the five men ordained by Bishop Gossman, four were from Colombia. Not only was this a striking occurrence in itself but also, for the first time, the church in which an ordination took place was filled with Hispanics.[41]

North Carolina's "Little Mexico"

While both Raleigh and Charlotte continued to enlist priests who were native Spanish speakers, for the most part the North Carolina dioceses had to rely on American-born priests who learned Spanish as a second language and were eager to work with Latinos.[42] One of the most successful of these American priests was the Conventual Franciscan, Daniel Quackenbush, who worked as "Spanish priest" at St. Julia's Church in Siler City from 1991 to 2002. During Padre Daniel's tenure the small central Carolina city became a metaphor for the demographic revolution occurring in North Carolina. The Siler City story can represent what was occurring to a greater or lesser extent in towns and parishes across the state. Ironically, the upsurge in Hispanic migration had been spurred by the effort of the United States government to stem the tide of illegal immigration.

The conservative political climate of the early 1980's resulted in the passage of the Immigration Reform and Control Act (IRCA) of 1986 that was intended to discourage immigration through increased border patrols and sanctions on employers who hired undocumented workers. The IRCA also provided an amnesty that afforded long-term residents an opportunity to normalize their immigrant status. However, instead of serving as a deterrent, IRCA actually encouraged migration. Fearful of the risks entailed in frequent crossings of the border for temporary work, many decided to become permanent residents of the United States, whether legal or not. The consequence was the explosive growth of the Hispanic population in subsequent years.

That growth was felt with particular force in North Carolina for several reasons. For one thing, many workers were familiar with the region from their experience as migrant laborers. Also, the expansion of the economy opened up job opportunities for thousands of unskilled workers. Finally, the climate was roughly comparable to what they had known at home. Abetted by strong family and village networks, those who arrived early soon invited relatives and friends to join them.[43] One of the most notable magnets for this migration was the little town of Siler City, its surrounding poultry processing plants and textile mills hungry for workers willing to labor under stressful conditions for low wages. Latin Americans, who had worked for $5 a day at home, considered $6 an hour a move up the ladder.

The speed with which the population change in Siler City took place can be gauged by the experience of the Chatham County Health Department. In 1992, when the Department launched a program to help poor families, most of the clients were African Americans. Almost overnight, the majority were Hispanics as thousands of Mexicans poured in, within five years boosting Siler City's population from 5,000 to 8,000. A town that had been predominantly white and black was now 40 percent Hispanic, transforming every aspect of life in the area.[44] One of the institutions most profoundly affected was the church of St. Julia, a mission of Blessed Sacrament parish in Burlington, twenty-five miles away in Alamance County. The little church that for decades had been adequate for its small Catholic population suddenly found itself bursting at the seams.

By 1997, the Hispanic population had grown not only in numbers but also in pride and daring. That year, on Good Friday, introducing a custom from their homeland, the people reenacted the journey of

Christ to his death on the cross. Processing in costume through the streets of the town, several dozen men and women assumed the roles of the participants in the crucifixion, dramatizing for hundreds of onlookers this pivotal event of the Christian religion. In 1999, when Jorge Ocampo portrayed the central role of Jesus, he grew his black hair down to his shoulders and painted his beard with Grecian Formula to remove the gray. More significantly, he prepared himself spiritually. "I came to mass every Sunday and I asked God to forgive me if I do it wrong." Although the central figure in the annual pageant, in his ordinary life, Ocampo, like hundreds of others, works on the line at a chicken processing plant.[45]

Not everyone welcomed the Hispanics to Siler City. Irritated that their town was being labeled "Little Mexico,"[46] several hundred people attended an anti-immigrant rally in front of the town hall in February 2000 protesting the influx of so many foreigners, many of them undocumented. The featured speaker was former Ku Klux Klan leader David Duke, who recently had established a group called NOFEAR – the National Organization for European American Rights. Participants carried signs reading "America: World's Septic Tank" and "Repatriate Aliens." The target of their anger was made very clear; the day of the rally, St. Julia's church was vandalized, including the defacing of a sign that read, in English and Spanish, "For I was…a stranger and you welcomed me."[47]

Events in Siler City prompted Bishop Gossman of Raleigh to write an article expressing his support for the Hispanics, whom he praised for "their hard-working ethic, their strong family values and love for children, their deep faith in God, their long-suffering, and their love for life and vibrant celebrations."[48]

Many of those "vibrant celebrations" were presided over by Father Quackenbush who remained a stabilizing force throughout the long period of transition in Siler City. He was so committed to the parish that his Franciscan colleagues had to insist that he take off a day each week. Only half in jest, the low-keyed priest said that St. Francis would not approve of his playing golf.

After mass on Mother's Day, 1998, as is the custom of Catholic priests in recent years, Quackenbush stood outside St. Julia greeting the people as they exited the church.[49] For many parishioners this was a convenient opportunity to make inquiries about baptizing a child or getting married. Some do not have telephones, while others are shy about using the phone, fearful that someone will answer who does not speak Spanish. Although tired and sweaty, Padre Daniel listened attentively to the whispered requests. His week would be busy. But tomorrow he will play a round of golf.[50]

The Lebanese

Although the Hispanics are by far the largest ethnic group in North Carolina, with over 300,000 in the state by 2000,[51] they are not the only one, nor were they the first to influence the development of the Catholic Church. Nineteenth century arrivals such as the Irish, Portuguese, and Germans were too few in number to make a significant impact. However, in the early 20th century an unlikely group of people settled quietly in North Carolina and carved for themselves an enduring niche in the religious history of the state. Virtually forgotten in the whirlwind of change, at one time the Lebanese were the most numerous and generous Catholic minority group in North Carolina.

The story of the coming, the industriousness, and the faith of many can be represented by the life of one man. Isaac Kannon was an illiterate Lebanese shepherd when he heard about opportunities available in far-off America. So, in 1905, leaving his wife and children behind, he joined scores of his countrymen in sailing to the New World. After passing through Ellis Island, Kannon joined his brother-in-law in Raleigh where he began to peddle notions, fabrics, and spools of thread. For eight years, painstakingly learning a few words of English, he walked the streets until he had saved enough money to bring his family from the old country.

Having gained a modest measure of success, in 1916 the Kannons moved to the town of Wendell, seventeen miles east of Raleigh, where they bought a white Victorian house on Academy Street, opened a dry goods store on Main Street, and prospered. Now in its fourth generation, the family continues to live in the old house and to operate what has become a successful clothing business. Also, the family worships in St. Eugene church, founded by their ancestors at a time when the only Catholics in town were Lebanese.[52]

Over half the small parishes of Eastern North Carolina owe their founding and continuance to the Lebanese. One of them, St. Anne in Scotland Neck, was constructed in 1929 on a plot of land donated by a Lebanese family and became a mission of St. Charles Borromeo parish in Ahoskie. However, in time the changing economy resulted in most of the Lebanese – the only Catholics in the area – moving away;

by 1990 only four people were attending mass at St. Anne. One of the four, David Alkazin, a descendent of the original Lebanese settlers, who was born next door to the church, contacted Raleigh Bishop Joseph Gossman and offered to buy the church. The bishop replied that he would never close the church as long as there were any Catholics. As it turned out, the bishop's confidence was rewarded. Within a few years the church that had had but four worshipers was overflowing each Sunday with more than 120. The Hispanics had arrived in Scotland Neck. St. Anne, which had not had a First Communion in 34 years, in 2002 had 13.[53]

Although most of the Lebanese settled in the eastern section of North Carolina, as was seen in Chapter Ten, Monsignor Joseph Showfety's Lebanese immigrant parents moved to Greensboro in the center of the state. Others found their way to Andrews in the far western corner of the state where the El-Khouri family was a major factor in the construction of Holy Redeemer church there in the late 1950's.[54]

Historically, the Lebanese belonged to the Maronite rite of the Catholic Church. They supported and built Latin rite churches in North Carolina because there was not a great enough concentration to support a Maronite congregation. That situation changed in 1973, when Bishop Waters asked the Eparch of St. Maron of Brooklyn to establish a church to serve the needs of the Carolina Lebanese. Approval granted, the community bought the original St. Patrick church in Fayetteville from the Raleigh diocese and remodeled it according to the Maronite liturgical tradition. Over the first 10 years of its existence the congregation grew from 25 to 80 families.[55]

Although much more could be said about the Lebanese, an editorial in the *NC Catholic* in 1960 summarizes their story in picturesque fashion:

> In 50 years, the Lebanese in North Carolina have made great progress, overcoming odds to take their social place in so short a time without industrial skills, practically illiterate in both Arabic and English, sepia in complexion and Catholic to boot, they managed in one generation to fasten deep roots in the community life of North Carolina.
> From huckster packs and hot dog stands, they moved into cafes and clothing stores. Possessed of an almost fierce love of land and home, they owned their own homes in less than a decade. Their gardens became show places and their sheep and goats hallmarks. Young men who began penniless in 1910 now are affluent.

Catholics of the Maronite Rite, they worshiped at the small Roman Catholic churches of their adopted land. Often it meant taking the train 20 or 30 miles on a Sunday. In many cases new parishes were organized and churches built around a small Lebanese nucleus.[56]

In 1925, William Hafey, the first bishop of Raleigh, had taken note of the Lebanese, whom he mistakenly referred to as "Syrians:" "Visited Farmville. Thirty Syrians in that town. No other Catholics."[57] By 1960, when the editorial quoted above was written, there were approximately 2,500 Lebanese in the state. Although an insignificant part of the general population, they comprised a substantial portion of the Catholic community.

Vietnamese & Koreans

If people from the Near East contributed to the diversity of the Church in North Carolina at the beginning of the 20th century, by the end of the century it was immigrants and refugees from the Far East, in particular from Vietnam and Korea. Just as Isaac Kannon's life served to illustrate the Lebanese experience, so the story of one refugee from Vietnam can represent the danger and deprivation that thousands of people from that war-ravaged country encountered. It also suggests the intensity of the faith that supported such people during their ordeals. Although barriers of language and culture make it difficult for native-born American Catholics to communicate with these co-religionists, it is important that they appreciate the heroism of people who share not only their faith but also, at times, the very buildings in which they themselves worship.

Despite the warfare raging in Vietnam in the late 1960's, Joseph Long Dinh was able to enter a South Vietnamese minor seminary at the age of 11. When he graduated from high school in 1977, the war had ended, but the political repression was in full swing. The Communist North Vietnamese had descended through the South, occupying the city of Saigon and arresting those suspected of collaboration with the defeated American-supported government, including Dinh's own father who died in a concentration camp.

Dinh himself barely survived the three years he spent in a labor camp. He was sustained by the hope of returning to the seminary after the camp. However, by the time he was released, the government had closed the seminary. Seeing no future for himself as a Christian in a communist country, Dinh decided to take the risk of leaving the country, a move that was illegal. After several failed attempts and near captures, he set out on a small boat with twenty others and found safe haven in Thailand. Here he spent two years in refugee camps, still dreaming of becoming a priest. Finally, through the sponsorship of an American priest, Dinh arrived in the United States and enrolled in Divine Word College Seminary in Iowa. A few years later, in order to be closer to family members who had come to the United States and settled in Charlotte, he transferred to that diocese and in 2000 was ordained a priest, thirty years after he had first entered a seminary.[58]

The following year, two more Vietnamese men were ordained for Charlotte. At the ordination ceremony, the large church of St. Gabriel was filled with women dressed in colorful traditional Vietnamese gowns and men in glistening white shirts. Many belonged to the 1,500-member St. Joseph Vietnamese Catholic Community that held Sunday mass at St. Ann Church in Charlotte. Not forgetting those left behind, after a typhoon had ravaged Southeast Asia in 1997, the Charlotte community collected more than $4,000, which was sent to the Can Tho diocese in Vietnam.[59]

An earlier war in which the United States was involved also played a role in the development of the Catholic Church in North Carolina. Hundreds of Koreans settled in Charlotte beginning in the 1970's, and in 1980 seven families initiated Catholic community life when, led by a Korean priest who traveled from Atlanta, they began gathering for a monthly liturgical celebration at St. Patrick Cathedral. As the community grew larger, a committee was formed to explore the possibility of building a church. A fund drive was begun, and in 1990 the community purchased four acres of land in east Charlotte. A house on the site was put to use as a rectory and meeting center. Later that year, the Archdiocese of Taegu agreed to send a Korean priest to Charlotte to serve the growing community there. Over the following few years, several Korean priests worked in Charlotte and, in 1995, a 5,000 square-foot building was completed and called St. John Lee Korean Catholic Church. A sign of the community's growth was the confirmation of seventy people during a September 1996 liturgy. Indicative of the rapid assimilation of the Koreans was the inauguration of an English language mass for the benefit of the younger generation of Korean Americans.[60]

Towards a More Participatory Church

Even as the Church rejoiced in its rapid expansion in the state, including the new ethnic communities, it was undergoing major institutional changes and attempting to cope with an array of problems. Although there was no organized opposition to episcopal authority as had been the case in Bishop Waters' final years, his successors in Raleigh and Charlotte did not have an easy time of it. The drumbeat for a greater lay voice in church governance, coupled with the steady erosion of clerical and religious vocations, demanded a delicate diplomacy on the part of bishops. On the one hand, the large sums of money required to finance new churches and other projects required that they not alienate the laity. On the other hand, they were answerable to Rome, which opposed any democratization of the church or diminution of clerical authority. Then, as the North Carolina church seemed like it was successfully navigating this Scylla and Charybdis, the clergy sex scandals of 2002 threw the Church into its most serious crisis in generations. The next and final chapter will describe several key developments in the Church from the death of Bishop Waters in 1974 to the uneasy dawning of the 21st century.

Late in 1971 the diocese of Charlotte was created in the western half of North Carolina. Michael Begley, a Raleigh diocesan priest, was named first bishop. Top left, the 62-year old Begley smiles for his first official portrait. Top right, in 1778, he confers with Bishop Gossman of Raleigh. Below that, Begley celebrates his seventy-eighth birthday by reading to his beloved "kiddos" at St. Ann School in Charlotte. Immediately above, William G. Curlin, the third bishop of Charlotte, and Gossman present their 1997 joint pastoral, "Of One Heart and One Mind," calling for economic justice for all. Above that, Curlin welcomes Mother Teresa to Charlotte in 1995.

Since the arrival of the Sisters of Mercy in 1869, women religious have provided strength to the North Carolina church. These pictures show the evolution of sisters' habits, symbolic of the transformation of their self-image and ministry. Top left, many communities are represented at the 1945 installation of Bishop Waters. Below that, children cheer a sister in a "modified habit" crossing the finish line. Bottom left, Sister M. Elizabeth has more than 60 children in her 1957 classroom at Infant of Prague School in Jacksonville. Top right, Sister Mary Evangelist Nixon attends a newborn at Mercy Hospital, Charlotte. Bottom right, Franciscan Sister Joan Jurski, coordinator of the Peace and Justice Department of the Raleigh Diocese, represents the move to secular dress but also the new responsibilities given to vowed religious women.

Two African American priests can symbolize the uneasy relationship of many black Catholics to the Church. Top left, Father Thomas Hadden celebrates mass in the mid-1960's with Bishop Waters. Despite numerous racist experiences, Hadden remained faithful to the Church. Top right, Father Ronald Rhodes, ordained in 1981, assists Bishop Gossman. In 1997, Rhodes left the Church and joined the schismatic priest, George Stallings, a New Bern native. Three church buildings can represent the history of black Catholicism in North Carolina. Immediately above right, is St. Joseph Church, New Bern, which was merged with the "white" church in 1963. Above that is Holy Cross Church, Durham, constructed by the Jesuits in 1952, which continues to function as a predominantly African American parish. Above left is a 1944 photograph of St. Alphonsus Church in Wilson, which was closed in 1986.

The arrival of tens of thousands of Hispanics has offered an unprecedent-ed challenge to the Church. Siler City in Chatham County witnesses an annual Good Friday "Viacrucis" in which members of St. Julia parish reen-act the death of Christ. In 1997, Jorge Ocampo portrayed Jesus, (top left) whose cross is raised by "Roman soldiers" on the church grounds. The small Siler City church (top right) could no longer accommodate the wor-shipers so, with Daniel Quackenbush, O. F. M. Conv., pastor, looking on, ground was broken for a new church, which opened in 2001. Above, Mexican immigrants, the majority of them young men, pray the Rosary.

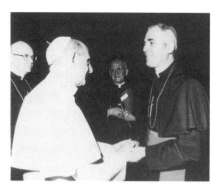

In 1975, F. Joseph Gossman of Baltimore was assigned by Pope Paul VI (top left) to succeed Vincent Waters as bishop of Raleigh. Gossman quickly won the support of a diocese fractured by years of post-Vatican II controversy. Nuns (top right) were given enhanced status. Although vocations to the priesthood declined, over the years Gossman ordained some fifty priests. The picture above shows Bishop-elect Gossman meeting in early 1975 with representatives of the diocese he was to head: Charles Griffin, Sr. Kathleen O'Neill, SSJ, auxiliary bishop George E. Lynch, and the Reverend Robert T. Lawson.

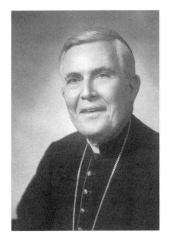

Top left, Bishop Gossman in a 1993 photo. Top right, surrounded by lay activists, he reads a statement opposing capital punishment. Center left, the bishop is seen with H. Charles Mulholland shortly before "Father Charlie's" death in 2001. Center right he bids farewell to Monsignor Gerald L. Lewis, who not only served as Vicar General and Moderator of the Curia for many years but also resided with the bishop. Above, in 1991, in one of many ecumenical initiatives, he and John F. Donoghue, the Roman Catholic bishop of Charlotte, clasp hands with the Lutheran bishop of North Carolina.

Chapter Thirteen

Toward A Collegial Church

Formerly defined as "a congregation of those who profess the same faith, receive the same sacraments, are governed by their lawful pastor under one visible head," the church of today is defined as "the People of God." By defining the church as the people of God we remember that it is by baptism that we become members of the church, designated as disciples of Christ to spread the faith to the best of our ability. In other words, together we share the responsibility of building up the Kingdom. Just a few years ago I called together representatives of the people of God to form a Diocesan Pastoral Council, a representative gathering of religious, laity and priests from throughout our diocese that would be involved in the ongoing process of discerning our strengths and weaknesses, with a view toward setting a direction for ministry in the vast and diversified regions of the piedmont and western North Carolina.

---Bishop Michael Begley, 1982

When Bishop Waters died on December 3, 1974, a not always peaceful era in the history of the church in North Carolina came to an end. Although some mourned his passing, respecting the man's missionary zeal, there were few who did not welcome the chance for a new beginning which his death presented. For nearly thirty years Waters had ruled the fledgling church with an iron hand. As it would turn out, if he was a lion his successor would be a lamb, but a lamb who with his gentle manner would accomplish more than did Waters with all his appeals to authority. Although the Diocese of Raleigh had no say in the selection of its bishop, it's hard to imagine a more effective antidote to Vincent Waters than Joseph Gossman.

Those who knew both men were wont to say that whereas Waters was born knowing that he would be a bishop, Gossman never anticipated attaining such a position and brought to North Carolina a disingenuousness that was startling to some and delightful to others. However, the differences between the two men were not simply a matter of personality but also of differing understandings of the nature of the church and the role of the bishop. When Waters said "I am the bishop," he implied that his word was law and that he alone was responsible for making all decisions. When Gossman said "You're an intelligent man, decide for yourself," he was not abdicating responsibility but signaling his conviction that he was a member of a team, and not necessarily the most insightful member. Waters controlled every meeting he attended; Gossman controlled none, quietly letting others take the lead. In almost every instance, Waters made the decision. Gossman, on the other hand, favored ratifying the decisions arrived at by others.

The upshot of it all was that during Waters' thirty years, virtually everything that happened was the result of his initiative, whereas during Gossman's nearly thirty years what happened was largely attributable to the initiative of others. As was true in the Charlotte Diocese under Bishop Michael Begley (1972-84), so in Raleigh under Joseph Gossman (1975-   ), a new model of church began to be implemented, one that was less authoritarian and more collaborative. Once the priests and lay people realized what was happening, the Catholic Church in North Carolina began to hum with renewed energy. Without it ever being mentioned, the "democratic" Church envisioned 150 years earlier by Bishop John England had at last arrived.

While not neglecting recent developments in the Diocese of Charlotte, this final chapter will focus on the Diocese of Raleigh and the man who turned it around. Although it is too soon to write the definitive account of Bishop Gossman's tenure, the major features of the period from 1975 to 2002 seem clear. The guiding principle of the transformed Catholic Church in North Carolina was *collegiality*, an idea made popular throughout the Catholic world by Vatican II. From the moment of his arrival in Raleigh, Gossman made it clear that the days of episcopal fiat had ended and the era of collaboration begun. His understanding of collegiality was definitively codified in his 1981 paper "The Collegial Church," to be discussed below.

By a felicitous coincidence, both the man selected by Waters to be the first bishop of Charlotte and the man who succeeded Waters himself in Raleigh worked in tandem to move North Carolina Catholicism from a condition of medieval-like fiefdom, to one of the most vibrant sectors of the American Catholic church. Neither Bishop

Begley in Charlotte nor Bishop Gossman of Raleigh achieved the national reputation of Waters, but they did gain the affection of the rapidly expanding Catholic population. More importantly, they created the climate and put in place the structures that would shape the church for the 21st century. By 1982, the year of Begley's statement quoted at the beginning of this chapter, both dioceses had become firmly rooted in the era of participatory management. As those roots sank deeper into the Carolina soil, the church flourished. Certainly this was due in no small measure to the substantial infusion of well-educated, affluent northerners and dynamic young Hispanics. However, the argument of this chapter is that Begley and Gossman offered to those newcomers a vision of a Catholic Church to which they responded enthusiastically.

Although Gossman did not use the same mechanisms as Begley, he achieved substantially the same result -- the maximization of lay participation in virtually every aspect of church life. In one respect at least, Gossman surpassed Begley and his Charlotte successors. He steadily advanced the position of women in the church, going so far as to indicate on more than one occasion his puzzlement as to why they they could not be ordained priests.

After a brief discussion of the concept of collegiality, the chapter will describe three dimensions of its implementation:

· the opening of diocesan and parish positions to lay people;
· the utilization of women as pastoral administrators;
· lay dominance in planning and fundraising.

The Collegial Model of the Church

Church historian Thomas J. Reese has written: "Vatican II caused a revolution in church thinking and practice from the papacy to the local parish."[1] Nowhere was that thinking and practice affected more profoundly than in response to the concept of collegiality, which became at one and the same time a mantra for those who wanted radical church reform and a source of concern in those who felt that the democratizing trend threatened the divinely established organization of the church. Although originally applied specifically to the relationship between the pope and bishops, the spirit of collegiality to one extent or other permeated every level of church life.

Decades after the fact, it is difficult to appreciate just how exciting the idea of collegiality was in the 1960s and 1970s. The context for that excitement was the monarchical Catholic world created by the first Vatican Council (1869-70). That gathering of the world's bishops had defined papal primacy and infallibility, creating the belief that the pope alone could decide all matters of faith, morals, and church governance. Even as the pontiff lost his temporal power by the forced surrender of the Papal States, he took on the spiritual power of a divinely guided ruler. In the wake of this elevation of papal prerogatives, for the better part of a century a damper was put on independent Catholic theological thought.

Particularly after the decree *Lamenabili* and Pius X's encyclical *Pascendi* (both 1907), which condemned many of the "errors" of modern thought, the church abdicated participation in mainstream intellectual life. For their part, fearful of the pope's ire, American bishops turned their attention to building churches and schools, shielding their flocks from real and imagined threats to their souls. Then unexpectedly, as the 1960's dawned, Pope John XXIII summoned the bishops to the Vatican once again. The objective of the new council was *aggiornamento*, the updating of a church which, Pope John realized, had atrophied. What emerged from this historic event was a series of documents which became the blueprint for what many considered the long overdue reformation of the Roman church. One of those documents, *Lumen Gentium*, the Dogmatic Constitution on the Church, revolutionized the church's understanding of itself.

As was alluded to by Bishop Begley in his 1982 address, *Lumen Gentium* redefined the church as "the People of God." Rather than starting with a hierarchical image, Catholics were told to look at the Church as "the sacramentally structured community of believers in Jesus Christ, which He uses as His instrument for the redemption of mankind."[2] This emphasis on the common vocation of all believers was deliberately addressed before the document took up its consideration of the Church's hierarchical structure. The intention was to emphasize that the *people* are the church.

When it turned its attention to the role of bishops, *Lumen Gentium* advanced a major reformulation of authority within the church. Not that papal primacy was rejected, but it was placed in the context of a college of bishops, all of them equally successors of the apostles, all of them responsible for the universal church. Bishops, who heretofore thought of themselves as individuals, were told to collaborate with one another, to realize that when they acted in concert they were guided and protected by the Holy Spirit, just as was the pope. Collegiality was defined as an essential component of the episcopal charism. The bishops returned to their various countries with the mandate to reinvigorate their national and regional conferences and reorganize their dioceses.

As has been shown, Bishop Waters, who attended Vatican II, was not comfortable with the idea of collegiality. Rather, he saw the sharing of responsibility as a threat to the unity of the church and the authority of the bishop. Even as his priests clamored for a greater voice in the management of the church in North Carolina, he resisted. It would be his successor, ordained a bishop three years after the close of Vatican II, who would bring the spirit of the council to the Tar Heel State. Joseph Gossman's commitment to the Council was reinforced by his personal style.

Letting People Breathe

When, on the occasion of his 25th anniversary as bishop of Raleigh, Gossman was asked how he would like to be remembered, he replied:

> As someone who loves people and tried to do his best to help them and to be a faithful servant of the Lord. One who let people breathe, not just the air of the Church but the air of life. Someone that was not overwhelmed by his own importance.[3]

Gossman, who usually signed his letters to priests with a simple "Joe" and vacationed with them at the beach in summer, turned self-deprecation into a strength and vulnerability into power. Few bishops have acknowledged their limitations more openly and in so doing gained such affection and loyalty. In his homily at the 1998 Holy Week Chrism Mass, surrounded by the clergy of the diocese, he spoke with a frankness and humility few bishops have ever used in public. He referred to himself as "a first class *klutz*," as someone who is "foolish, embarrassing, even funny."[4] To the startled clergy, he went on to compare himself with Simon Peter, not in order to affirm that he was a successor to the apostles, but rather to claim that what he had in common with the first pope was that both were rather pathetic figures. "The only thing infallible about this fisherman was his ability, when life was going well, to blow it.... No sooner had he been handed the keys of the kingdom than he began to drop them." Gossman made it quite clear that he was comparing himself with the all too fallible Peter:

You see, in secret, I get it wrong too. And I need to believe that the Church will survive my foolishness, my ineptness, my failures. Perhaps God is trying to tell us something with our falls, our deadly seriousness, the way we get funnier by the day.... Laughter directed at myself is the closest I come to knowing the unconditional acceptance, the pure forgiveness, the freedom, the creativity that I believe the love of God to be.

Gossman's refusal to take himself too seriously was clear from the start. When a reporter interviewed him a month after his arrival in Raleigh, the bishop quipped, "I've got to get the heck out of here. All work and no play makes Jack a dull boy." The reporter wrote that the bishop was "informal and friendly," and that when addressed as "Your Excellency," Gossman retorted, "I'm not really any more excellent than anyone else."[5]

A month later, Gossman was named "Tarheel of the Week" by the Raleigh paper. Again, he revealed his vulnerability, confessing that he had to learn "a whole new style, a whole new group of people. Every place, every face is new and strange." He also told the reporter that he would like to be a parish priest. "I think I could do that pretty well. I don't know how well I'll be able to do the bishop thing."[6]

Such openness with the news media was in sharp contrast with Bishop Waters' avoidance of the press. On one occasion when asked by the *National Catholic Reporter* to comment on the removal of a priest from his position as pastor of St. Lucien church in Spruce Pine, Waters told the reporter: "I'm not going to help your circulation increase. I hope you finally fold up and we finally get good journalism." Of course, on this occasion as on others, Waters did not give any explanation of his decision to the people of Spruce Pine either.[7]

Baltimore Roots

As it had been when James Gibbons was appointed first Vicar Apostolic for North Carolina in 1868, and again in 1925 when William Hafey was named first bishop of the Diocese of Raleigh, so in 1975, the new bishop came from Baltimore. Like his predecessors, Joseph Gossman had worked closely with the archbishop of that city and been tapped while young for advancement. Unlike them, however, Gossman had seven years of pastoral experience as an auxiliary bishop before being selected to move south to what for him was the "outer space" of North Carolina.

Francis Joseph Gossman was born in Baltimore on April 1, 1930. It certainly did not escape the man who labeled himself "a klutz" and "foolish" that he had been born on April Fool's Day. Despite what some might have taken for a bad omen, "Joe" Gossman experienced a rapid rise within the church and, despite his self proclaimed ineptitude, approached retirement age with a record of success and a minimum of criticism.

Gossman was a blend of the two major ethnic strains that comprised the Catholic community of his native city. His father, Frank, was of German descent, while his mother, Genevieve Steadman Gossman, was of Irish ancestry. Speaking stereotypically, it might be said that he inherited his father's German discipline and his mother's Irish sense of humor. His father was certainly a model of fidelity, working as an accountant for the Baltimore and Ohio Railroad for fifty years. His mother, as was true of most women at the time, was a full time home-maker.

Hardly having reached the age of puberty, Joe entered the minor seminary in Catonsville, Maryland, continued his studies at St. Mary's in Baltimore, and completed them in Rome, where he was ordained in 1955. Destined for a career in administration, the young priest was sent almost immediately to the Catholic University in Washington, DC to study canon law. In 1959, a doctorate in hand, he was assigned to a succession of diocesan posts, including assistant chancellor, pro-synodal judge, and vice officialis, positions which drew upon his expertise in Church law.

This history of absorption into the inner and often secretive world of church officialdom would not seem the environment from which a pastoral bishop might emerge. Yet, paradoxically, when he was ordained an auxiliary bishop in 1968, rather than being pulled even more completely into the administrative cocoon, he undertook what would be the most pastoral and satisfying period in his life. Perhaps because at thirty-eight Gossman was the youngest bishop in America, he had the energy to immerse himself in the role of Urban Vicar for the City of Baltimore, a position which permitted him to collaborate with his brother priests in ministering to people. He was a bishop without the burdens of administrative responsibility.

Many auxiliary bishops spend their careers as assistants to the ordinaries of large dioceses. They are delegated duties by the ordinary, representing him at functions, serving on committees, administering the sacrament of Confirmation. Gossman thought that this would be his life. He loved Baltimore, and temperamentally he was content to take orders from someone else, at first from his mentor, Cardinal Lawrence J. Sheehan, and later from his successor, Archbishop William D. Borders. Then, in 1975, everything changed. Borders informed Gossman that he had been selected to head the Diocese of Raleigh. From Gossman's perspective, North Carolina was another world, one about which he knew nothing. Just as Gibbons and Hafey had been sent to what from a Catholic perspective was mission territory, so also Gossman found the state as alien as a foreign country. "I remember wondering how [North Carolina] got this way. It's 350 miles away from Baltimore but three galaxies away ideologically, socially, in almost every way."[8]

The Collegial Church

Although Gossman initiated a participatory spirit and established collegial structures from the start of his administration, in 1981 he issued a definitive elaboration of his views and goals. "The Collegial Church" might be considered the Magna Carta of the Diocese of Raleigh.[9]

The very genesis of the document was collegial, in that it was prompted by the Diocesan Pastoral Council which had called for "a communication network which is effective among people of the diocese." Gossman felt he could contribute to this mandate by setting forth "the principles, policies and procedures operative at this time in our diocese." The paper goes on to describe the decision-making process, diocesan collegial structures, and diocesan planning. Although relatively brief, the paper outlines the process and structure which would shape the remainder of Gossman's lengthy tenure.

In analyzing the key notion of decision-making, Gossman made clear that he had no intention of making any important decisions without extensive input from others. After quoting the Vatican Council to the effect that bishops may "legislate, pass judgment and administer the activities of the diocesan community," he immediately added that "the increasing difficulty of adequately exercising all three obligations" had led him and other bishops "to entrust the responsibility for certain aspects of judgment and administration to others."

It is important to note that he did not say that he was sharing the power to *legislate*. Gossman was not abdicating the traditional episcopal power to have the final word on all matters. If then they had no legislative power, what was the role of collegial bodies? The answer was that "some have been invited to serve as resource persons in the legislative process." Realizing that this might sound like a hollow role for priests, religious, and laity in the management of the diocese, Gossman insisted that it would be inadequate to describe the work of councils as advisory or consultative. Rather, bishop, pastor, and collegial structures alike "must assume a proper relationship in the exercise of their legitimate roles, for neither can function well without the other."

Walking a tight rope between preserving his authority as ultimate diocesan legislator and giving collegial structures substantial responsibility, Gossman introduced the idea of consensus. Decisions must be made on the basis of a thorough analysis of all the available facts. The goal was "a common understanding of the facts so that the differences resulting from various interpretations of the data are minimized." In effect, Gossman was saying that if everyone was in agreement -- including himself -- then the decision flowing from the process was certainly the best one that could be made. The bishop pledged that he would work patiently with the various structures to achieve objectives with which all could agree.

The paper went on to describe the various parish, deanery, and diocesan collegial structures, an apparatus which at times would prove slow moving, yet which would afford everyone a voice. At times, decisions might have to be deferred and no action taken, but Gossman's goal was to work with people to the point where all could be in agreement. For more than twenty years, although at times he was faulted for acting too slowly, Gossman was never accused of being arbitrary or authoritarian in decision-making.[10]

The Emergence of Lay Leadership

Perhaps the most striking development in the Church in recent decades has been the professionalization and expansion of diocesan and parish administration and the hiring of lay men and women for virtually every position. If Bishop Hafey had his office in his pocket and Bishop Waters had his in a couple of rooms in his residence, Bishop Gossman and the recent Charlotte bishops employed scores of specialists to manage ever more complex bureaucracies. For their part, although pastors no longer had a housekeeper attending to their needs in a comfortable rectory, they had as many as a dozen or more paid staff persons, their "pastoral team," sharing the tasks which a priest once handled by himself or with volunteers. Diocesan lay employees, once limited to custodians and secretaries, now included the editor of the diocesan newspaper, the director of Catholic social services, and the superintendent of Catholic schools. Parishes frequently included on their staff lay directors of Music, Faith Formation and Youth, as well as Finance Administrators, Pastoral Associates, Hispanic Ministry directors, and Data Managers. In time, the titles of positions held by full-time lay church employees in the state would exceed one hundred. Including the staff of Catholic schools, by the end of the 20th century there were more paid lay employees than there had been Catholics in the entire state when Bishop Gibbons arrived in North Carolina in 1868.

In addition to employees, the dioceses and parishes had thousands of volunteers serving on committees and in scores of ministries. For example, in 2002 the bulletin of Immaculate Conception Church in Durham listed more than forty parishioners who held volunteer "portfolios" in such roles as Deanery representative, Pastoral Council chair, Legion of Mary, AIDS Ministry, and Altar Care. At St. Thomas More parish in Chapel Hill, sixteen Eucharistic ministers regularly assisted the priest in distributing communion at Sunday liturgy. Parishes in the Charlotte Diocese, following the model established by Bishop Begley, were organized into "commissions," each of which had several subdivisions. For example, Holy Family parish in Clemmons, the origin and development of which was described in Chapter Ten, had more than thirty people listed in the weekly bulletin as leaders of the various commissions and other groups, such as the parish pastoral council, the annual craft bazaar, and Senior Citizens. By the year 2002, the parish which had been established in 1980, had a staff of fifteen and a core group of fifty volunteers coordinating several hundred other parishioners regularly involved in one or more of dozens of programs.

To what extent the increasing reliance on lay people to run the church was attributable to conviction or to the shortage of priests and sisters, was not clear. Although bishops affirmed their trust in lay employees, there was no doubt but that the process of declericalizing church administration had been accelerated by the clergy drought. Certainly the lay staffs in Catholic schools was due to the precipitous decline in the number of women religious. In any case, lay people became so firmly entrenched in most positions that it became hard to imagine a reclericalizing of agencies.

The largest agency of the Raleigh Diocese was Catholic Social Ministries (CSM), which had regional offices in each of the diocese's seven deaneries. Of the forty CSM employees, *all* were lay people, many with Masters degrees in Social Work. In some rural areas where there was no Catholic church, CSM deanery directors and their staffs were the only Catholic presence, providing aid to the poor, resettling refugees, serving as advocates for the abused and homeless, and in other ways embodying the Church's response to community needs.

The sixteen people in the diocesan Business Services Department, including accountants and computer specialists, were all lay men and women, as were all employees of the Communications Division and even the Faith Development Department, which was responsible for assisting parishes in conducting religious education programs. In particular, they sponsored courses for certifying parish catechists, all of whom were lay people.[11]

Although organized differently than Raleigh's CSM, Charlotte's Catholic Social Services department was similarly a lay enterprise. None of the seventy-five employees was a priest. Most distinctive was the Refugee Resettlement Office with seventeen employees representing the wide range of language groups located in the Charlotte area. In addition, of the seventeen Catholic schools in the Charlotte diocese, only two had sisters as principals, and of the nine employees with the title Campus Minister, only one was a priest.[12]

A Lay Chancellor

The most striking evidence of the increasing lay dominance in the church was the 1992 appointment of a layman as Chancellor of the Raleigh diocese. If the Vicar General is something like the Vice President of a diocese, assuming responsibility when the Bishop is incapacitated, the Chancellor is similar to the Chief of Staff, responsible for the day-to-day operation of the non-religious aspects of church administration, including the supervision of the chancery staff. He is also the principal diocesan contact person with pastors on such matters as financial reporting, construction projects, and personnel issues. Although the Chancellor has no strictly religious functions, it had been required until recent years that a priest be entrusted with the position.[13]

The first lay Chancellor, John Riedy, with a master's degree from Harvard Business School, had a lengthy apprenticeship for the position having served as diocesan business manager since 1985. In this subordinate capacity he gained the confidence of the bishop. Accordingly, as the shortage of priests for parish work grew more pronounced, and joining other dioceses that had already turned over chancery responsibilities to lay men and eventually to women, Riedy succeeded Father Joseph Vetter who became pastor of Sacred Heart parish in Southport. Priests, long accustomed to viewing the Chancellor as the bishop's right hand man, had to adjust to the novelty of a layman in the episcopal inner circle. However, by 1992 so many changes had taken place that most accepted the development easily.

After serving for six years, Riedy retired in 1998 and the position went to Russell Elmayan who had followed Riedy as business manager. Quickly, the point had been reached when appointing a priest as chancellor would have seemed inappropriate! Riedy suggested as much when, on retiring, he said that the nature of the job made it a natural for a lay person, despite the fact that in the past it had been held by priests. Riedy added that his job had gone smoothly, given Bishop Gossman's leadership style. "The bishop delegates to people, then he stands back and lets them do the job."[14]

Beloved of Women

When asked in 1999 what his greatest achievement had been, Gossman answered that he would leave that up to others to decide.[15] Although some might argue that his greatest contribution to the church was his extensive ecumenical work with Baptists, Lutherans, and members of other Protestant denominations, it is likely that religious sisters would affirm that it was his desire to give women equality with men in church ministry. Within weeks of arriving in North Carolina, Gossman let it be known that he saw no reason why women could not be ordained priests,[16] and although he could not violate the Vatican's prohibition, he promoted women to ever more responsible positions within the diocese.

After their strained relationship with Bishop Waters, many sisters spoke of Gossman's coming as "Resurrection Time." Well aware of that history and anxious to begin the healing process, one of the first things the newly installed bishop did was to gather women religious for a period of prayer, reflection, and camaraderie. Throughout the weekend Gossman mixed with the women, getting to know them and revealing a man who was not only charming but not threatened by their desire to have a greater voice, not only in the conduct of their own lives but in the Church at large. It was at this 1975 weekend of frank sharing that the idea of a Sisters' Council was conceived. With little delay, the council became an integral part of diocesan life.[17]

Furthermore, women, both lay and religious, began to be appointed to advisory boards and to diocesan staff positions. By the year 2001, not only were the majority of the bishop's twelve-member top staff lay persons, but three of them were women -- the Director of

Stewardship and Development, the Director of Business Services, and the Director of Catholic Social Ministries. Of the nearly fifty people working at the Catholic Center, the majority were women, many of them in major positions. Besides the directorships already mentioned, women were serving as Administrator of the Tribunal, Director of Hispanic Ministry, and Director of Lay Ministry. In terms of the transformation of what was once a bastion of clerical collars, only one priest, the Vicar General, was working at the Catholic Center on a full-time basis.

Pastoral Administrators

Although women have long held the majority of staff positions in parishes as well as at diocesan offices, the most striking indication of Gossman's confidence in women was the entrusting of a dozen parishes to them. Although not unique, the appointment of Pastoral Administrators in the Raleigh Diocese became a model of the successful administration of parishes by women.[18]

As the issue of how to provide services to small Catholic communities was discussed by the Priests' Council during the early 1980's, the idea was floated that religious women might be appointed as administrators of such parishes. Perhaps sensing that their central role in the church was being threatened, some Council members opposed the suggestion, arguing that the Catholic laity would be confused by a woman "pastor." An alternative suggested was that parishes be consolidated, that is, that a smaller community be folded into a larger one, usually many miles away in a larger town. Yet another possibility, one used in North Carolina since the days of Bishop England, was for one priest to be pastor of two, or even three, parishes. Under this alternative adopted in many dioceses, a priest becomes a "circuit rider," traveling from parish to parish in order to provide minimal services. In this scenario, there would be no full-time pastoral presence in smaller communities.

After considerable debate and with few precedents to guide him, in 1984 Gossman approved the appointment of the first three pastoral administrators, all of them experienced women religious. One of the women, Mission Helper of the Sacred Heart Dolores Glick, had especially solid credentials. She had first come to North Carolina in 1953 and assisted Bishop Waters in the sensitive work of desegregating Catholic parishes. Now, thirty-one years later, "Sister Dolly" was asked to work with Bishop Gossman in another major Catholic initiative.

Sister Dolly was assigned to St. Elizabeth parish in Raeford, a town south of Fayetteville in rural Hoke County. The Catholic church there had been built in 1959, thanks to a gift from to a group of women in New York. At the time there were only forty five Catholics in a county with a total population of 5,000.[19] Although always too small to support a full-time pastor, the community established a solid identity and welcomed the appointment of Sister Dolly. Any confusion as to her role was quickly resolved, and the new administrator set about establishing a parish council and the other components of a parochial structure. Although her responsibilities included managing finances and seeing to the upkeep of the building, most of her time was consumed in such pastoral activities as visiting the sick, counseling the troubled, preparing parents for the baptism of their children, and providing assistance to the poor. More than once, she felt a sense of helplessness as Church law forbade her to administer the sacrament of the sick to a dying person or hear the confession of someone she had guided to the point of repentance. Each week, the "Supervising Pastor and Sacramental Minister" drove the twenty miles from the church of St. Mary in Laurinburg to celebrate mass. Although the Catholic people were grateful for the mass and few questioned the Church's regulations, Sister Dolly was their spiritual leader. When the priest drove back to Laurinburg on Sunday afternoon, she remained with them.

Over time, as routines became established, the priests of the diocese adjusted to the fact that women were in charge of parishes. Gradually more churches were assigned to sisters and a Pastoral Administrators Committee was added to the diocesan structure. The regular list of new assignments now included the names of the administrators along with those of priests. Letters from the bishop were addressed to "Pastors and Pastoral Administrators" and all attended meetings as equals.[20]

Another parish assigned a pastoral administrator was St. Elizabeth in rural Farmville. As was mentioned in Chapter Twelve, when Bishop Hafey visited that Pitt County settlement in 1925, he found a small community of Lebanese but no other Catholics. In 1931 a church that seated about eighty people was constructed. For decades St. Elizabeth remained a remote mission, attended occasionally by priests from larger parishes. In the 1950's, Missionary Servants of the Most Holy Trinity, popularly called Trinitarians, used Farmville as the base of their missionary work in North Carolina. Subsequently, for short periods of time, diocesan priests resided there. Then, in 1987 a member of the Order of St. Francis, Brother Gerard O.S.F., was appointed pastoral administrator. Brother Gerard remained at St. Elizabeth until 1992, the only male pastoral administrator the state has had.

Today, as one of the smallest Catholic churches in the state, St. Elizabeth is a reminder of what nearly all Catholic churches were like until the middle of the 20th century. When Brother Gerald arrived in Farmville, there were but forty families registered in the parish, representing one percent of the area population. The current pastoral administrator, Immaculate Heart of Mary Sister Grace Campbell, has seen the Catholic population grow and has spearheaded the long overdue restoration of the church building.[21]

Thirteen years after the appointment of the first pastoral administrators, Gossman said that the sisters had often exceeded his expectations:

> We provided an opportunity for women to demonstrate their pastoral skills, and they've done that. Women bring things to the ministry that men never bring. They're more compassionate. They're empathetic. The female dimension is very much what the church should represent to its people.[22]

Of course, the appointment of women as parish administrators contributed to the widely asked question: "Why can't women be priests?" In an effort to tamp down such questioning, Pope John Paul II issued a letter in 1994 forbidding any further discussion of the issue, declaring that "the Church has no authority whatsoever to confer priestly ordination on women."[23] Despite this ban but choosing his words carefully, Gossman continued to profess his support for such a development. However, unlike in the early days of his ministry, he no longer stated his support directly. Rather, when asked the question, he replied, "There's nothing Joe Gossman can do about women's ordination." However, his frustration with Rome was reflected in his adding that he could not understand a position "that rules out fifty percent of the human race."[24]

For its part, the Charlotte Diocese has been much slower than Raleigh in appointing women to administer parishes. In 1999, only one parish, St. Joseph of the Hills, in Eden, had an administrator, Sister Bernadette McNamara, R.S.M. In several parishes with priest pastors, women held the position "Pastoral Associate." One mission church, Our Lady of the Mountains in Highlands, had a lay Pastoral Associate, Diane Small.[25]

In the year 2002, the following North Carolina parishes were administered by women:

· St. Bernadette	Fuquay-Varina
· Holy Family	Hillsborough
· Our Lady of the Rosary	Louisburg
· St. Elizabeth	Farmville
· St. Joseph the Worker	Warrenton
· St. Joan of Arc	Plymouth
· St. Bernadette	Butner
· Our Lady of the Snows	Elizabethtown
· St. Elizabeth of Hungary	Raeford
· St. Peter the Fisherman	Oriental
· Holy Trinity	Williamston
· St. Joseph of the Hills	Eden[26]

Successful Fund Raising

Perhaps Chancellor John Riedy's major accomplishment was one for which he claimed no credit, but for which his leadership created a healthy environment -- the enormous increase in money raised in diocesan campaigns. Of course, there was the Stewardship and Development staff, along with the fifteen-member Business Services department and the dozen people in the Communications Department. These lay men and women, equipped with the skills needed by charitable, educational, and cultural organizations to develop and implement fund raising plans, have produced campaigns year after year that resulted in ever higher goals consistently being exceeded.[27]

For example, in 1982, the goal of the annual Bishop's Appeal of the Raleigh diocese was $548,000, and $672,000 was pledged. By the year 2000 the annual appeal had risen to over $3 million. Perhaps emboldened by this record of success, in 2001 a breathtaking move was made. A super campaign, called "God's Work/ Our Challenge,"with a goal of $30 million, was announced, much of it earmarked for a variety of endowments. Clearly attempting to appeal to as wide a range of interests as possible, endowments would be established for Faith Development, Lay Leadership Formation, Clergy Education and Formation, Hispanic Ministry, and Campus Ministry, and the Poor. In addition, a substantial portion of the money would be devoted to a Diocesan Land Trust, the object of which would be to purchase land in areas where it was projected parishes would be needed in the future. These and the other components of the campaign were spelled out in attractive brochures. As usual, each parish was assessed a goal and its fundraising volunteers trained in how to encourage affluent parishioners to make generous pledges. Also, as an incentive to work hard, pastors were assured that a substantial portion of the money raised would be returned to the parish.

The clergy sex scandal of 2002 broke just as the campaign was cresting. Despite the negative publicity, the Raleigh Diocesan campaign proceeded on schedule and not only reached its goal, but nearly doubled it. This astounding result was attributable to a number of factors, including the skills of the lay diocesan staff. It also reflected the affluence and enthusiasm for church development of the rapidly rising Catholic population. Finally, it was suggested that generosity in the campaign would serve as a concrete tribute to Bishop Gossman, who would be retiring as the final money pledged during the campaign was being paid.[28]

Charlotte Diocesan Planning

The most impressive evidence of the professionalization of Church administration is the elaborate long-range planning process that became an integral component of the operation of both dioceses. Although culminating at the diocesan level, planning mechanisms included input from the regional deaneries and vicariates, which in turn gathered ideas from local parishes. Committees held discussions, reports were generated, and proposals submitted to the bishop. On the one hand, there was the sense of democracy in action, while on the other hand the bishop remained free to accept or reject any proposal. However, as has been stressed, Bishop Gossman as well as the bishops who have headed the Charlotte diocese, have avoided major confrontations with either priests or laity. Unlike Bishop Waters, they were able to delegate responsibility, consult without controlling, and make decisions based on consensus.

It is beyond the scope of this book, but a comparison of the planning histories of the two dioceses would be instructive and perhaps give some insight into the advantages and disadvantages of the different approaches employed. Charlotte's planning has been anchored in diocesan-wide gatherings, beginning with the series of Assemblies held during founding bishop Begley's tenure and continuing with the synod held by his successor, Bishop John F. Donoghue, in 1986-87. Also, in 1998, Charlotte hired a full time Director of Planning who set in motion the process for a twenty-year strategic plan.[29] On the other hand, Raleigh has had no assemblies or synods and has no full time planning specialist. Instead, working in consultation with deanery committees, the Chancery staff has put together a series of three-year plans which are presented in books running several hundred pages in length.[30]

Charlotte's Second Bishop

As a post-Vatican II creation, the Diocese of Charlotte has been characterized by a collegial spirit from its inception. Clergy, religious, and laity alike made it clear to Bishop Donoghue that they expected the tone set by Bishop Begley to be maintained. And of course Begley, still healthy in retirement, lived close at hand. Although he would in no way interfere with Donoghue's running of the diocese, the founding bishop's presence was a clear reminder of the youthfulness of the diocese and of its aspirations for collegiality.

From a progressive perspective, the new bishop did not come with the most promising credentials. A native of Washington, DC, Donoghue had been trained in canon law and became secretary to Cardinal Patrick O'Boyle, whom he later referred to as his "father figure."[31] O'Boyle had been an even more strident conservative and authoritarian prelate then Bishop Waters, suspending dozens of priests for refusing to support the 1968 papal ban on artificial contraception. Well schooled in what many Vatican II supporters considered the increasingly reactionary style of Pope John Paul II, the 55-year old Donoghue was sent from the Washington Chancery to Charlotte to succeed the pastoral Begley.

Determined to show his willingness to listen, Donoghue visited each of the eighty parishes and missions of the diocese during his first year, meeting with the parish staff, the parish council and, where there was a school, its staff as well. After completing this initial circuit, he repeated it over a three year period. In the meanwhile, responding to the request for a diocesan-wide representative gathering, he authorized a synod that met in three sessions in 1986-87. The synod not only continued the tradition of assemblies which Begley had held but included in its planning many of the same people who had led those earlier meetings.

One of those leaders was Father George Kloster, the only priest on the fourteen-member Synod Preparatory Commissions. The balance of the group consisted of two religious women, four lay women, and seven lay men. As had been the case with the Begley Assemblies, proposals were organized under seven Commissions: Spiritual Life,

Evangelization, Poverty, Lay Ministry, Councils, and Growth. When the synod itself met, the Chair was a lay woman, Miriam Williams.[32]

The process used by the synod was similar to that employed at Vatican II. The 150 synod members who gathered at Sacred Heart College in Belmont were given schema prepared by the Preparatory Commissions. The broadly representative group debated the materials and suggested revisions. This procedure was repeated twice more as the synod met every few months over the course of a year. At the conclusion of the proceedings, Donoghue was presented with the final documents and promised to take them into account. Many of the synod proposals were indeed adopted as the diocese, its population growing and diversifying rapidly, added new programs, hired more people, and raised more money. Eventually, the expansion prompted plans to construct a new and larger diocesan headquarters. However, Donoghue would not remain long enough to occupy the modern office tower which resulted. Unusual developments in the archdiocese of Atlanta led to his promotion to that see.

In June 1990, Eugene A. Marino, the nation's first black archbishop, resigned in scandal as the head of the Atlanta archdiocese. The church had learned of his sexual relationship with a parishioner, Vicki Long. Further, it was rumored that the two had secretly exchanged wedding vows.[33] Marino was succeeded by Archbishop James Lyke, also an African American. Compounding the instability in which the archdiocese found itself, Lyke died of cancer the year following his appointment, opening up the position which was given to Donoghue in 1993.

A Cloud of Mistrust

Even as the Catholic Church in North Carolina was finally making substantial numerical and financial progress, surpassing Methodists as the state's second largest denomination and outnumbered now only by Baptists,[34] the clergy sex abuse scandal of 2002 rocked the American Catholic Church and didn't spare the dioceses of Raleigh and Charlotte. Day after day during the spring and early summer, new revelations exposed the breadth of the problem. Even as it was confirmed that hundreds of priests had been guilty of sexually abusing children and youths, bishops were forced to confront their own complicity. All over the country it became clear that bishops had transferred known abusers from parish to parish, paid substantial sums of church money to compensate and silence accusers, failed to report criminal behavior to the civil authorities, and lied. The credibility of the American Catholic hierarchy was dealt a severe blow and Bishop Gossman of Raleigh and William G. Curlin, who had succeeded Donoghue as bishop of Charlotte, were not spared. At least seven Charlotte priests and four in the Raleigh diocese were implicated in one way or another and both bishops were named by the *Dallas News* as guilty of cover-ups and misstatements.[35]

In June 2002, the American bishops voted overwhelmingly for the "Charter for the Protection of Children and Young People." No bishops' meeting had ever gained such media attention, which was highlighted by the moving testimony of several people who as children had been abused by priests. A nation that had revered and trusted priests began to wonder. Not since the Protestant Reformation of the 16th Century had the church been put to such a test. With civil authorities all over the country investigating charges and Catholic lay people protesting outside the cathedral in Boston, the moral uprightness of men supposedly dedicated to holiness was severely challenged. Although the charter included a "zero tolerance" clause, which said that even one confirmed act of sexual abuse of a child would result in the immediate and permanent barring of a priest from ministry, the fact that such a charter was necessary was itself shocking.[36]

Gossman, who at one time had been the country's youngest bishop, was now the oldest active priest in the Raleigh Diocese. The strain of the scandal was palpable, and he who had been treated with such affection by the media now found himself being questioned like the CEO of a corrupt corporation. Weary from the stress, his long-time Vicar General, Msgr. Gerald L. Lewis, retired, leaving the bishop to begin working with a new chief aide, Msgr. Michael P. Shugrue.[37]

As he had done at the 1998 Chrism mass, Gossman spoke with feeling to his priests at the same ceremony held in the Spring of 2002. However, this time, rather than focusing on his own limitations, he commiserated with the confusion, anxiety, and fears of the priests, several of whom he had been obliged to dismiss from ministry. Gossman said:

> Our vocation that was once held in high esteem holds little appeal for American youth or their parents. There is a new perspective to the priesthood; new demands, new expectations, unfamiliar doubts and confusion....
> In this time of unparalleled scandal, we must follow Jesus in his dying. In our physical infirmities, our asthma and arthritis, our failing sight and failing memories, our palsy and our coronary artery disease... and not in just physical pain but in all the little deaths, psy-

chological and spiritual which can nail a priest to his cross today --
criticism, burnout, fear, loneliness, aging, scandals.[38]

On the other end of the state, Bishop Curlin, likewise the oldest
active priest of his diocese, was devoting considerable time to responding to the crisis which, like a forest fire, was in danger of spreading out
of control. Without admitting his own questionable behavior, Curlin was
forthright in condemning the evil and praying for healing:

> The sexual abuse of children and young people by some priests and
> bishops, and the ways in which Church leaders have sometimes dealt
> with these terrible acts, have caused anger, confusion and pain among
> many in our faith community.... The restoration of trust and fellow-
> ship will result from our actions, and I pledge to you actions worthy
> of our words.[39]

It wasn't supposed to be this way. Men who prided themselves
on being pastoral found themselves on the defensive, wondering when
the next embarrassing revelation would occur. Neither bishop had
gained national attention or assumed a leadership role in the American
hierarchy. Even in North Carolina, their names were barely recognized
outside Catholic circles. Yet, here they were now with their pictures on
the front pages of secular newspapers and their priests paraded like
criminals before the censorious gaze of a population barely a generation
removed from anti-Catholicism.

Their long-ago predecessor, Bishop John England, while
working to establish a Catholic presence in North Carolina, was also a
leader among the American bishops. Bishop James Gibbons went on to
become a Cardinal, a widely read author, and the premier representative
of the Church in America. For all his failings, Bishop Waters had provided leadership in the civil rights movement. Bishops Gossman and
Curlin could make no such claims to fame. Their reputations would rest
on their stewardship of the Church in North Carolina, guiding it to much
greater heights than any of their more illustrious predecessors. Then
came the clergy sex scandal, prompting both men to turn to the image
of the Cross hopeful that, as in the case of Jesus, an Easter Sunday
would follow the Good Friday which had nailed their ministry on a
cross of doubt.

Epilogue: Angels over Carolina

One of the most obvious differences between Catholics and
Baptists is the names they give to their churches. While Baptists, in
keeping with their distaste for statues, elaborate rituals and ornate buildings prefer such simple names as "First Baptist Church of Raleigh,"
Catholics delight in labeling their churches after the numerous titles for
Mary and Jesus as well as an ever-widening assortment of saints. More
than thirty of the nearly two hundred Catholic churches in North
Carolina are dedicated to Mary, including nine in honor of the
Immaculate Conception. Others form a devotional mosaic of saints,
ranging from such well-known heroes of Christianity as Peter and Paul
to more obscure personages like Egbert, Eugene, and Mildred. Scattered
throughout the state are churches named Holy Cross, Holy Infant, Holy
Spirit, Holy Family, Holy Redeemer, and Holy Angels. In Fayetteville
the four churches are named for saints of four different nationalities: St.
Andrew Kim, a Korean; St. Elizabeth Ann Seton, an American; St. Ann,
a Jewish woman from Palestine, and St. Patrick, the name reflecting the
nationality of the area's early Irish Catholics settlers.

It will be with three churches which bear the names of angels
that this account of the Catholic Church in North Carolina will be concluded. At one time Catholic children were taught that each human
being was assigned a guardian angel by God. Older prayer books and
not a few works of art depicted lovely creatures with enormous wings
sheltering a little child from danger. Each day millions of Catholic boys
and girls faithfully and reverently prayed:

> Angel of God, my guardian dear, to whom God's love entrusts me here,
> ever this night be at my side, to light and guard, to rule and guide. Amen.

For most Catholics, angels have disappeared from their devotional lives along with Purgatory, Limbo, scapulars, and Rosary beads.
Yet, with a little reconstructionist imagination, it might be said that
angels hover over North Carolina, their feathery wings stirring a cool
breeze in the hot summer night and their keen eyes vigilant for danger.
The angels are named Michael, Raphael, and Gabriel and they are the
patrons of three of the largest Catholic parishes in the state.

In the Bible, angels were emissaries of God. Michael was
assigned the messy work of driving the rebellious Satan into Hell
(Revelation 12:7), Raphael guided and protected the young Tobias
(Tobias 5), and Gabriel had certainly the most prestigious assignment of

all, announcing to Mary that she was had been chosen to be the mother of Jesus (Luke 1:26).

All three parishes had humble origins during the administration of Bishop Waters, when modest structures were built in anticipation of the growth about to transform North Carolina. The first was St. Gabriel in Charlotte, where in 1957 Father Paul Byron celebrated the first mass in a small brick building that previously had been a telephone office. The 175 families that comprised the new parish, sat on folding chairs and a shoe box was passed around for the collection. As was the practice in that pre-Vatican II era, the first building constructed was a parochial school followed by a succession of churches, each one accommodating twice as many people as its predecessor -- 250, 500, 1000. The most recent church is so large and imposing that it is used for the ordination of priests and was the setting for the 2002 funeral of Bishop Begley. Like the other two angel parishes, at the dawn of the 21st century St. Gabriel had over 10,000 registered members, more Catholics by far than were in the entire state when Bishop Hafey established the diocese of Raleigh in 1925.

A second angel parish, St. Michael, was established in 1962 in Cary, a satellite city to Raleigh. Cary had become a magnet for young professionals attracted to the area by employment opportunities in the high technology businesses filling the cavernous structures of the nearby Research Triangle Park. Computer corporations and international pharmaceutical giants jockeyed with hopeful startup companies for space, capital, and market share. Each morning the Cary Parkway and Interstate 40 carry thousands of men and women to the offices, factories, and laboratories where the future is being created. A high proportion of these workers are Catholics, members of St. Michael the Archangel Parish. As if trumpeting its success, the church bulletin has these words of the prophet Isaiah on its front page: *The Seraphim were stationed above the throne and they cried out one to the other: Holy, Holy, Holy is the Lord of Hosts. all the earth is filled with his Glory!"*

The massive red brick church, long rather than tall, hugging the earth rather than soaring into the sky, is an appropriate metaphor for people anxious to establish roots and to feel secure. Of the more than 3,000 families registered at St. Michael, the vast majority have lived in the area less than ten years. Aware of this, the parish sponsors regular "Newcomer Welcome Dinners," which like a Catholic Welcome Wagon provide initial contacts for potential golf and tennis partners as well as opportunities to volunteer for the choir or other of the extensive shopping list of parish-sponsored ministries. Getting connected, and doing it quickly, is a basic need for highly mobile people.

For many North Carolinians, the word "Cary" is synonymous with overgrowth, shallowness, and materialism. In a state long characterized by tarpaper shacks and a high rate of illiteracy, the lavish homes, manicured gardens, and Ivy League pedigrees of the Cary set are likely to be ridiculed. Yet, it is St. Michael church that not only overflows with the faithful each Sunday, but which sponsors a bewildering array of charitable projects, and which year after year receives more men and women into the Catholic church than any other parish in North Carolina.

The third angel sheltering the Catholics of the state is St. Raphael in North Raleigh. The giant parish, established in 1966, has two things in common with St. Gabriel in Charlotte. Father Paul Byron was one of its long-term pastors, and it has the distinction of having been designated one of 300 "Excellent Parishes" in the United States.[40]

Like many Catholic parishes at the beginning of the 21st Century, St. Raphael has a major problem -- parking. Turning into the stadium-like parking lots off Falls of the Neuse Road can be a challenge, and more than a few people arrive late for mass, and more than a little frazzled, because of the congestion.

While St. Gabriel and St. Michael are staffed by diocesan priests, since Father Byron's retirement in 1996, St. Raphael has been a Jesuit parish with three priests anchoring a large contingent of deacons, religious sisters, and lay men and women. Like the other angels, St. Raphael is not a single building but a campus or plant. During much of the week, while the central sanctuary stands idle, school buildings, gymnasium, parish center, and play areas bustle with activity. Although many decry the size and anonymity of contemporary mega-parishes, scores of special interest groupings help create the more manageable social environment of the small parish of earlier days.

St. Raphael church is round, and rather than its sanctuary being a raised platform against one wall, it is in the center and on the floor. No step anywhere separates the people from the service, giving a sense of unity between ministers and people rather than the more traditional relationship of actors and audience. Concentric rings of pews slope downwards so that everyone can see the sanctuary easily. The space between the several components of the sanctuary are considerable. At one end of the long, narrow, marble floor is the ambo, or reader's stand. Far to the other end is the chair where the celebrant presides, looking past the paschal candle and the altar. In this setting, the mass becomes like scenes in a play, each scene with its own stage area.

For the Gospel, the celebrant walks the full length of the sanctuary to the lectern, reverencing the altar on the way. After the assigned reading, he moves to the center of the stage, his cordless, clip-on microphone freeing him to move around and be heard easily. Furthermore, the church is equipped with a special radio transmitter which enables people who are hearing impaired to listen through borrowed receivers. No excuse for not hearing the Word!

On a February Sunday, the Gospel is from St. Luke, Chapter 6, and contains the following words:

> Woe to you who are rich, for you have received your consolation.
> Woe to you who are full now, for you will be hungry.
> Woe to you who are laughing now, for you will mourn and weep.

A priest ministering in a parish running $10,000 a month below budget has to be diplomatic in his interpretation of such a passage. Whereas priests of an earlier age, such as Mike Irwin or Christopher Dennen, or even Fred Price, would have made their audience cringe under the verbal lash as these words of Christ, the diplomatic Jesuit preacher of today is able to communicate the message in a more affirming manner. Being careful not to make his listeners uneasy, he gives the reading a more palatable spin. Asking Christ's understanding, he changes the words to:

> Blessed are you rich, for you have the means to help your less fortunate neighbor.
> Blessed are you who are full, for you are in a position to give of your surplus to those who are hungry.
> Blessed are you who laugh, for you can bring good cheer to those who are sad.

A line from the 1989 film, *Field of Dreams*, seems applicable in the burgeoning suburbs of Raleigh and Charlotte, North Carolina: "If you build it they will come." If you build attractive churches like St. Gabriel, St. Michael, and St. Raphael, people will fill them; if you construct schools, people will sacrifice to enroll their children; if you ask for money to develop the church more fully in other parts of the state, people will give; if you sponsor groups to advance the cause of social justice, to feed the poor, and to assist the newly arrived, the response will be generous.

As to why they come, only God knows all the complex factors that motivate people. Years ago, fear of sin and the fires of hell might have been the explanation. Today, for good or for ill, such fear rarely influences anyone. Instead, it would seem that hundreds of thousands of Catholics all over North Carolina attend church and participate in parish-sponsored programs because somewhere in the recesses of their souls echo the words of Christ, "Come to me, all you who labor and are burdened, and I will give you rest" (Matt. 11:28). And perhaps angels are silently trying to nudge Tarheel Catholics even closer to the heart of Jesus.

Abbreviations & Brief Citations

AAB, Archives of the Archdiocese of Baltimore
AAP, Archives of the Archdiocese of Philadelphia
ADC, Archives of the Diocese of Charlotte
ADR, Archives of the Diocese of Raleigh
AGU, Archives of Georgetown University
ASHC, Archives of Sacred Heart Convent, Belmont, NC
Annals, Sister Mary Charles Curtin, *Annals:*
        Sacred Heart Convent, 1841-1892
Catholicity, Jeremiah O'Connell, *Catholicity in the Carolinas*
        and Georgia
Diurnal, John England, *Diurnal of the Right Rev. John England*
Duke, Special Collections Library
Ellis, John Tracy Ellis, *Documents of American Catholic History*
Garaventa, Louis T. Garaventa*, Bishop James Gibbons & the Roman*
        Catholic Church in N.C.
My Lord, Paschal Baumstein, *My Lord of Belmont*
NC Catholic, North Carolina Catholic (Raleigh Diocesan paper)
News & Herald, Catholic News & Herald (Charlotte Diocesan paper)
Price Symposium, Robert E. Sheridan, *Very Rev. Thomas Frederick*
        Price, A Symposium
Reminiscences, James Gibbons, *Reminiscences of Catholicity in*
        North Carolina
Works, *The Works of the Right Reverend John England*
        (Messmer Edition)

NOTES

Chapter 1

1. Information about Waters' personal life is scant. Although he left behind hundreds of pastoral letters and other church-related documents, he guarded his privacy, seldom speaking about himself or revealing his feelings. There is no diary, memoir, or unguarded personal letter. See, John Strange, "Bishop Waters, third bishop of Raleigh, firmly establishes Catholic community," *NC Catholic*, Nov. 14, 1999, p. 9A.

2. A number of anecdotes such as this derive from informal conversations the author had with North Carolinians.

3. Charles Craven, "Catholic Bishop Vincent S. Waters of Raleigh," Raleigh *News & Observer*, Feb. 16, 1964.

4. In the early 1970's, after Bishop Waters had required all nuns working in North Carolina to wear religious habits, his own sister, who had moved with many other sisters to more secular attire, was required to don a religious veil once again in order to enter her brother's diocese. Sister Elizabeth Waters died Nov. 22, 2001 at the age of 84.

5. For nearly half a century, Belmont Abbey was the most significant Catholic institution in North Carolina, providing an anchor of stability for a fragile church. See Chapter Seven.

6. Chapter Eight will describe the process of establishing the diocese of Raleigh and the work of Waters' two predecessors.

7. Then, as now, neither Virginia nor the adjacent state of North Carolina had a seminary of its own.

8. Precise attribution is difficult. When Waters generated extensive media attention after his civil rights initiatives, his secretary gathered newspaper articles and other materials into three large binders which are preserved in the Archives of the Diocese of Raleigh (ADR). Unfortunately, the dates and sources of many items are lacking. The story about Waters' prejudice appeared in the Proceedings of the Liturgical Conference.

9. The chancellor is proxy for the bishop in the day-to-day business affairs of the diocese, supervising accountants, secretaries, planners, and other specialists who administer the non-sacramental aspects of church government.

10. Nessa Johnson, *A Special Pilgrimage: A History of Black Catholics in Richmond*. Privately printed. Richmond, VA, 1978. p. 44. Waters would maintain his interest in the Catholic Conference of the South and in 1947 hosted its annual meeting in Charlotte. Bishop Howze's career will be related in Chapter. 12.

11. Waters' uncle had been one of the pioneering members of the Mission band. Gerald P. Fogarty, *Commonwealth Catholicism: A History of the Catholic Church in Virginia*. Notre Dame, Indiana: Univ. of Notre Dame Press, 2001, 378-379.

12. Waters had gained a modest reputation for his concern for racial justice long before Newton Grove. Within months of becoming Bishop of Raleigh in 1945, speaking at a meeting of the Catholic Interracial Council, he said that there should be no need for such an organization, that Catholics should be the least prejudiced people in the country. He added: "Maybe America needs to be embarrassed if it is not living up to true American principles; maybe Catholics should be embarrassed if they are not living up to real Catholic truth." *Interracial Review*, 18:168-170, Nov. 1945. Also, one of the earliest issues of the diocesan newspaper which Waters had founded carried a column with what at the time was the inflammatory suggestion that Catholic schools should set an example for other educational bodies by desegregating. John Gavin Nolan, "Justice for Negroes," *NC Catholic*, Dec. 8, 1946, p. 3.

13. The founding of the church in Newton Grove in the 1870's is one of the most interesting events in the history of Catholicism in North Carolina. See Chapter Six.

14. James Garneau, "St. Katharine Drexel Left Her Mark on NC Church," *NC Catholic*, Sept. 24, 2000, p. 8. Drexel, canonized a saint by the Catholic Church in the year 2000, played a significant role in shaping the racial policies of the church in North Carolina. See Chapter Seven.

15. ADR, *Proceedings of the First Synod* (privately printed, Raleigh, 1948). This first and only synod of the Diocese of Raleigh brought together virtually all the clergy of the state. In the resulting long catalog of regulations, the only mention of race is the instruction that priests were to abide by the state law which forbade marriages between people of different races.

16. Jan. 29, 1951. The letter stated the principle that there was to be no segregation in Catholic churches.

17. ADR, *Status Animarum*, 1952. Pastors are required to submit annual reports which are bound in yearly volumes.

18. ADR, *Status Animarum*. Various years. Financial Reports for the Newton Grove parishes. Similar notations appear in the reports of the Franciscans who staffed St. Francis of Assisi parish in Lenoir in the western part of the state.

19. *The New York Times*, May 22, 1953, 15:1. Some citations in this section are from the clippings scrap books which often lacks dates.

20. *News & Observer*, May 26, 1953. The scrap books in the archives contain similar articles from other North Carolina papers.

21. Associated Press release, May 21, 1953. In 1970, George Lynch was named auxiliary bishop of Raleigh. When Waters died in 1974, Lynch served as administrator of the diocese until the appointment of F. Joseph Gossman as the new ordinary. After serving as a pastor for a few years, Lynch retired to his native New York. There he was active in the antiabortion movement, including being arrested on several occasions while demonstrating outside abortion clinics.

22. ADR. *Nazareth Remembered*, 1982. Pope was interviewed by the Rev. Donald Staib, a Raleigh priest. All material in this section is from the interview text. A plaque bearing Pope's picture and an account of his long association with the orphanage hangs on the wall in the Catholic Center, the diocesan offices located in the former orphanage building.

23. Father Price is a key figure, not only in the history of the Catholic Church in North Carolina, but in the American church in general. His story will be related in Chapter Seven.

24. *Daily News*, Greensboro, North Carolina, June 1, 1953.

25. *News & Observer*, Raleigh, North Carolina, June 1, 1953.

26. At a meeting in Des Moines, Iowa the following month, Waters said that a Newton Grove minority had tried to pressure him into changing his decision. In response to their petition he told them, "When you obey, I'll see you."

27. After the fact, Waters did have several nuns, Mission Helpers of the Sacred Heart, visit the Catholics, both black and white, who had been affected by his action. The sisters attempted to win back to the church people alienated by the changes. Interview with Sister Dolores Glick, MHSH, Oct. 28, 2000.

28. ADR, Bishop Waters' Pastoral Letter, January 29, 1951.

29. ADR, Bound volume of clippings on Pastoral on Race.

30. *The New York Times*, July 31, 1953.

31. See Vincent S. Waters, *Catholic Education in North Carolina*, Washington, DC: Williams & Heintz, 1958. This is the only book which carried Waters' name as author. Although no reference is made to race, photographs of school groups show that many were in fact single race institutions.

32. ADR, Clippings collection. No dates given.

Chapter 2

1. *NC Catholic*, Dec. 8, 1946, 1.

2. ADR, Letters from Waters to Father Irwin, June 23 & July 25, 1945. (Irwin l.6.1.7) Pastoral Letter, Feb. 15, 1946, refers to the miles he had driven. Bishop Waters' Liturgical Desk Calendars contain brief descriptive notations of each day's activities. The only expression of emotion is found in the entry for

May 31, 1953. The bishop wrote, "Desegregation of Newton Grove. Deo gracias."

    3. Vincent S. Waters, "Double or Nothing," *Extension*, 44, 10-11, 1949.

    4. The spirit of the state can be gauged by the fact that two of the three most recently established counties were named for Confederate generals, Hoke and Lee. [Avery had been a Revolutionary War soldier.]

    5. In the year 2000, there were still nine counties, all of them in the sparsely populated areas in the eastern part of the state, without a church. On the other hand, densely populated counties like Wake (Raleigh) and Mecklenburg (Charlotte) had numerous large parish plants.

    6. "Traveling Bishop," *Jubilee*, Nov. 1956, 35-38.

    7. The pastor of St. Jude the Apostle parish in Hampstead, further south along the Atlantic coast, purchased a condo which he lets out free of charge to vacationing priests who will agree to help him by celebrating two weekend masses.

    8. ADR, Kill Devil Hills (Folder 3.8.1.) When a new church was constructed in 1976, it was built around and over the earlier structure. At the time, there were 150 Catholics in winter, and ten times that number during the summer months. When the 1976 church was destroyed by a fire in 1998, it was replaced by a larger building to serve a congregation that now numbered in the thousands.

    9. *The Official Catholic Directory* for 1907 lists fifteen North Carolina churches with resident priests and a Catholic population of 4,800.

    10. The experience of African-American Catholics is discussed in Chapter Twelve.

    11. Highlights of Bishop Waters' First Full Year," *NC Catholic,* Dec. 29, 1946, 1. The article noted the dedication of two new churches, the opening of four schools, and the ordination of four priests for the diocese. Besides establishing the NCCLA, Waters also inaugurated the Home Mission Apostolate to be discussed below.

    12. The design for the NCCLA bears some similarities to the state conventions held by Bishop John England in North Carolina in the 1830's. However, as will be seen in Chapter Five, England's vision was based on a more democratic model of the church than that of Waters.

    13. Subsequently called the *NC Catholic*, the name that will be used henceforth.

    14. As will be seen in Chapter Four, in 1822, Bishop England founded the *US Catholic Miscellany*, the first Catholic newspaper to be published in the United States. The *Miscellany* ceased publication during the Civil War. There would be no Catholic paper in North Carolina again for nearly eighty years.

    15. One handicap which Waters inherited from his predecessors was the lack of facilities for meetings. The small churches and schools were inadequate for the regional and even national gatherings which the bishop hoped to host in North Carolina. Initially, the orphanage, itself rather antiquated,

was the only place large enough for meetings. In time, better accommodations were developed at the site of the Catholic hospital in Southern Pines and at a conference center in the mountains near Hendersonville.

16. "Bishop Waters Opens Nation's Church Unity Octave Observance," *NC Catholic*, Jan. 26, 1947, 1.

17. An editorial in the Feb. 7, 1960 *NC Catholic* referred to a letter to the editor which had appeared in a Raleigh paper. The letter said that "wherever Catholics get in power, all other religions are banned or rendered to (sic) a sterile state." The letter went on to say, "We Protestants are simply afraid for our church lives." The editorial countered this expression of concern with the charge that Protestants were trying to reintroduce Bible reading in the public schools.

18. Father Charles Mulholland, Interview, April 6, 1998. Mulholland said that getting converts was Waters' obsession. "During Lent he would have us rent a store front and put out a sign that said 'Come in and ask any questions you have about the Catholic Church.' I told him, 'These people are good Protestants. Why should we bother them?' But he was insistent. We got very few until the Yankees started to come down here."

19. "Newman Club Discusses Freedom and Authority," *NC Catholic*, Jan. 24, 1960, 8A.

20. In light of the view that Catholic beliefs and practices were not based on Scripture, it is worth noting that Waters was a member of the Bishops' Committee of the Confraternity of Christian Doctrine which supervised the new English language translation of the Old Testament, issued in 1970. His name appears in the introductory material at the front of the New American Bible.

21. *NC Catholic*, Sept. 21, 1947.

22. Mulholland served as editor from May 1966 to May 1967. In an *NC Catholic* editorial (Feb. 26, 1967) he expressed opposition to the Vietnam War.

23. For some of the young men who came to Raleigh, North Carolina was not their first choice. They had been rejected by other dioceses, usually for academic or health reasons. Although today there is a shortage of priestly vocations, in the years before the Vatican Council there were so many applicants to Northern dioceses that bishops could be selective. Waters and other Southern bishops had no such luxury. Although Waters encountered problems with some of these men, several of the most successful priests of the era were men who had experienced such rejection.

24. ADR, A detailed record of the census project, which lasted from 1947-1967, has been preserved in the *Seminarians Census Log*, a handwritten ledger in which one or more of the students penned a report at the end of each season. The log provides a window into the church in North Carolina during a period of changes.

25. Paul Byron was interviewed with Father Charles Mulholland, on April 6, 1998 in the Raleigh house which they shared in retirement.

26. "Sacramental minister" is the term used to identify the priest who administers the sacraments and celebrates mass at a parish headed by a "Pastoral Administrator." The emergence of this parochial structure will be discussed in Chapter Eleven.

27. Donald B. Cozzens, *The Changing Face of the Priesthood*, Collegeville, MN, 2000.

28. The sincere, but largely failed effort to convert North Carolinians, is illustrated by the street missions which the Reverend John A. O'Brian, author of the best selling *Faith of Millions*, preached in the cities and villages of the Waynesville, North Carolina parish in the summer of 1947. O'Brian, who was a Professor of Philosophy at Notre Dame University during the academic year, is pictured in the *NC Catholic* (August 3, 1947, 1) preaching to a half dozen puzzled looking mountain men sitting on a bench in Bryson City.

29. While Waters was in Virginia, the Richmond diocese had a motor chapel named St. Mary of the Highways. Fogarty, *Commonwealth Catholics*, p. 447.

30. ADR. Information about the motor chapels can be found in the box labeled "Motor Missions."

31. Mulholland's friend, Ed, entered a Trappist monastery. Having advanced as far as diaconate, he asked for a leave of absence. While on leave, Ed fell in love with and married a Catholic school teacher.

32. Father, later Monsignor, John F. Roueche, born in Salisbury, North Carolina, was a descendant of the first Catholic family in that town. Ordained in 1933, he died in 2000 at the age of 93. His ministry extended back to the pre-Waters period and will be related in Chapter Eight.

33. McSweeney was interviewed in his retirement home in Cary, North Carolina on November 4, 1997. In 1981, he had been appointed Vicar General of the diocese, a position he held until his death on March 28, 1999. "Diocese of Raleigh Vicar General, Msgr. James McSweeney, dies at age 74," *NC Catholic*, April 2, 1999.

34. "Padre Roberto retires," *NC Catholic*, July 15, 2001, p. 1. Other priests who served as full time fund-raisers were John P. Manley and Peter McNearney. ADR, Frederick Koch, "Tar on the Heels of a Missionary," Raleigh, 1949, 6.

35. For a time, Jones was the only surviving Monsignor in the Raleigh diocese. During the first twenty-five years of his tenure, Bishop Waters' successor, Bishop Joseph Gossman, did not recommend any of his priests for the honor. Then, surprising everyone, in the summer of 2000 he announced that Rome had awarded the title to seven Raleigh priests. *NC Catholic*, Aug. 27, 2000, 1.

36. Parish missions were popular before Vatican II. Typically, there would be a week of services for women, followed by a week for men. Women were always first, since it was considered easier to get them to attend. The women were encouraged to get their husbands out for the following week.

37. Jimmy, Rostar, "Diocesan priest 'retires' to Alaskan mission circuit," *News & Herald*, August 18, 2000, 5.

38. *NC Catholic*, Feb. 21, 1960. By 1971, the amount collected by the annual appeal, also called "Diocesan Loyalty Campaign," had quadrupled to over $144,000. *NC Catholic*, March 17, 1971.

39. In the year 2000, retired Raleigh priests were paid a stipend of $2,000 per month. Both dioceses spend approximately $1,000,000 for the support of more than 30 retired diocesan priests. They also contribute to the retirement programs of religious orders working in the state.

40. Sister Mary Christine Taylor,, S.S.J., *A History of Catholicism in the North Country*, Camden, NY: A. M. Farnsworth Sons, 1972. In this history of the diocese of Ogdensburg, the chapter on Bishop Navagh runs from page 161-181.

41. James J Navagh, *The Apostolic Parish*, New York: PJ Kenedy & Sons, 1950.

42. Taylor, op. cit., p. 177.

43. ibid., p. 180.

44. ibid., p. 180.

45. ibid., p. 163.

46. "Plenary Councils of Baltimore," *Catholic Encyclopedia*, Second Plenary Council, Title IX.

47. ibid., Third Plenary Council, Title VI.

48. ADR, Edward T. Gilbert, "A Sketch of Catholic Education in North Carolina from the Beginning of the Vicariate Apostolic to the Present Day," Privately printed, 1954.

49. Chapter Twelve will examine more closely the role of Catholic schools in the lives of African-Americans.

50. Donald F. Staib, *A Descriptive Study of Catholic School Participation in Title III of the Elementary & Secondary Education Act of 1969 in North Carolina*, unpublished Ph.D. Dissertation, UNC-Chapel Hill, 1973. Father Staib, ordained in 1961 by Bishop Waters, was Superintendent of Catholic schools for several years.

51. Vincent S. Waters, *Catholic Education in North Carolina*, Williams & Heintz Lithograph Corp.: Washington, DC, 1958.

52. In 2001 there are still but three Catholic high schools in North Carolina, one each in Raleigh, Charlotte, and Winston-Salem. Charlotte Catholic High School had been opened before Waters came to North Carolina, graduating its first class in 1945, shortly after his installation. A larger building was completed under Waters' guidance in 1955, and the school, continuously operated by the Sisters of Mercy, has graduated thousands of boys and girls. Cf. Susan Long Isom, *A Follow up Study of the May 1971 to May 1975 Graduates of Charlotte Catholic High School*, Masters Thesis, Winthrop College, Rock Hill, SC, 1978.

53. ADR, Frederick A. Koch, "Tar on the Heels of a Missionary," Raleigh, NC, 1949. Also, videotaped interview at Sacred Heart Cathedral Rectory, conducted by Rev. Joseph Vetter, February 1992.

54. John Strange, "Priest, editor, 'icon' ," *NC Catholic*, Nov. 21, 1999, 1.

55. In conjunction with his work as editor of the *NC Catholic*, Koch also studied journalism at the University of North Carolina at Chapel Hill.

56. Koch took his mother with him to the Catholic Center each day. She would visit with people in the various offices while her son worked. However, advancing Alzheimer's disease made it necessary to place her in Maryfield Nursing Home in High Point. In 1993, Koch himself moved to St. Joseph of the Pines Health Care Center in Southern Pines, where he died.

Chapter 3

1. ADR, Rocky Mount parish file. Sister Ann Parker, *History of Our Lady of Perpetual Help Parish, Rocky Mount, North Carolina*. Masters thesis, Marywood College, Scranton, PA, 1975, p. 15.

2. *Official Catholic Directory, 1963*. The population of North Carolina had reached 4.8 million. The Catholic population stood at 48,429.

3. ADR, Bishop Waters, Pastoral Letter, August 10, 1953.

4. ADR, Bishop Waters, Letter dated Sept. 4, 1953 to be read at all masses on Sept. 13.

5. Each edition of the *Official Catholic Directory* lists the number of converts for each diocese. For Raleigh, the totals for the years under consideration were:

1953---584	1954---769	1955---752	1956---721
1957---659	1958---600	1959---593	1960---519

6. Much of the increase in Catholic population can be attributed to military personnel stationed at the large bases located in the state. Substantial proportions of the Catholics of the parishes in Fayetteville, Goldsboro, Jacksonville, and Havelock were servicemen, a number of whom married local woman and settled permanently in the area.

7. Waters knew that great effort was needed to attract personnel. In his first year in North Carolina, he wrote hundreds of letters to religious communities which operated hospitals, inviting them to open a hospital in his diocese. Only two expressed interest. ADR, Bishop Waters letter to priests, Feb. 15, 1946.

8. ADR, Illustrated booklet, undated, but with 1954 population data.

9. See also, John Strange, "Bishop Waters, third bishop of Raleigh, firmly establishes Catholic community," *NC Catholic*, Nov. 14, 1999, p. 9A. This article, written for a special edition of the diocesan paper to mark the 75th anniversary of the diocese, made no reference to the problems Waters encountered in his later years. Hagiography at work.

10. One religious sister, who had been in North Carolina during most of the Waters' years, said that she felt he became paranoid as the attacks mounted. (confidential communication)

11. For the earliest stages in the development of priests' organizations, see Yzermans, Vincent A., (editor), "The Time to Build," comprising three papers presented at a national meeting of priests' councils. Our Sunday Visitor Press: Huntington, Indiana, 1968. Also, William F. Powers, *Free Priests: The Movement for Ministerial Reform in the American Catholic Church*, Loyola University Press: Chicago, 1992, especially Chapter 9.

12. Much of the material in this section is from the letters and minutes which Father George Kloster of the Charlotte Diocese had preserved and which he gave the author. Ordained in December 1968, the young Kloster quickly joined his older confreres in the organizing process. Although one of the "rebels" during the turbulent times being discussed, Kloster remains a highly regarded priest, and is particularly active in ecumenical activities.

13. Although the basic unit of government within the church is the diocese, dioceses are grouped into provinces. The dioceses within Georgia, North Carolina, and South Carolina comprise the Atlanta Province. Although the archbishop has no authority over diocesan bishops, he presides at their meetings and can wield considerable influence. Even as Bishop Waters was grouped with the more conservative post-conciliar bishops, Archbishop Hallinan gained a reputation as a liberal. In 1967, Hallinan said: "Catholics opposed to the changes of Vatican II seem to think that to the four marks of the church -- one, holy, catholic, and apostolic -- there should be added a fifth immutable. A living body must grow and develop." *NC Catholic*, July 30, 1967, p. 8A.

14. The most striking incidence of rebellion by clergy occurred in the Archdiocese of Washington, where forty-four priests who refused to accept Pope Paul VI's condemnation of birth control in the encyclical letter, *Humanae Vitae*, issued July 29, 1968, were suspended by Archbishop Patrick O'Boyle.

15. In this regard, Bishop Waters explored the idea of introducing the cause of Thomas Frederick Price for canonization as a saint. If any North Carolina priest embodied the sort of missionary drive that Waters admired, it was Price. Father Price's story will be told in Chapter Seven.

16. All information is from Senate minutes. In time, to avoid any impression that the Senate had legislative power, the name was changed to Priests' Council.

17. Chapter Thirteen takes up the issue of collegiality again. By the mid-1970's bishops and priests had learned how to work together within the constraints of Church law.

18. On June 16, 1967, the Vatican issued an "Instruction on Worship of the Eucharistic Mystery," which provided norms for the distribution of Communion under the form of wine as well as bread. Until that time, Catholic practice had been for the priest alone to receive the wine at mass. The

Instruction gave local bishops authority to decide how and when to implement the norms.

19. The Guidelines consist of three undated, mimeographed pages, but are clearly from early 1968. It is perhaps not coincidental that at the start of that year the National Conference of Catholic Bishops announced that a Committee on the Ministry and Life of the Priest had been undertaking a study of the priesthood. A letter from the committee, addressed directly to all American priests acknowledged that the priesthood was in a state of crisis. Letter, signed by the sixteen committee members, January 18, 1968, Washington, DC.

20. Association minutes for May 19, 1969.

21. No copy of the letter sent by the priests has been located. Father Donald Staib, one of the signers, said in a phone conversation Feb. 29, 2000, that it had been written at a priests' meeting in Charleston, South Carolina. Subsequently, Staib served as Chancellor and when Waters died, Staib went through the bishop's papers, trying to create some order. He threw away many items, mostly duplicates, and put the rest in a "Bishop Waters" file. Staib left the Chancery in 1982 and doesn't know what happened to the papers, which in any case did not contain the letter calling on the bishop to resign. Staib said that he had come to Raleigh because he was attracted to Waters. Eventually, he got what he called a "divorce," moving for a time to the Charlotte diocese and returning to Raleigh when Waters died. See also, *News and Observer*, "Bishop Waters Dies at Age 70," Dec. 4, 1974.

22. Graves, Cranor, "Why I Became a Catholic," *NC Catholic*, August 3, 1947, p. 3.

23. *New York Times*, "Carolina Bishop Assailed by Nuns," Sept. 5, 1971.

24. *CORPUS Reports*, May/June 2000, p. 26-27.

25. The decline in the number of religious sisters in North Carolina began before Bishop Waters' 1971 letter and has continued unabated: 1960----457; 1970----408; 1980----354; 1990----274; 2000----225. (*National Catholic Directories*.) This pattern reflects the dramatic decline in the number of religious sisters in the United States as a whole. Whereas between 1965 and 2000, the number of priests declined by 22%, the number of sisters declined an astonishing 56%. (CARA web site, 2001.)

26. "Bishop Tells Nuns Old Habit is Best," Raleigh *News & Observer*, August 12, 1971; "Carolina Bishop Assailed by Nuns," *New York Times,* Sept. 5, 1971. Many Catholic papers published the National Catholic wire service article. For example, "Bishop Cites Scandal; Requires Habits for Nuns," Davenport *Catholic Messenger*, August 26, 1971.

27. ADR, The letters are preserved in three boxes. More than 90% are highly supportive of Waters, praising him as a champion of morality and a protector of religious life.

28. ADR, Letter dated Aug. 18, 1971.

29. Waters never dealt directly with individual sisters. So he had written to the community's General Superior insisting that Sister Winters resume wearing the habit. Father Sheridan's letter is dated July 6, 1971. See also, "Catholic Nuns Required to Wear Traditional Habit," *Asheville Citizen*, August 10, 1971, p. 9. Sister Winters would remain in residence in Asheville until the late 1990 s when she retired to the Massachussets motherhouse.

30. ADR, Undated clipping .

31. "Insists on Return to Habits," *St. Louis Review*, Aug. 20, 1971, p. 4.

32. Undated, but cited in a number of newspaper articles, including "Bishop Cites Scandal; Requires Habits for Nuns," Davenport *Catholic Messenger*, Aug. 26, 1971.

33. ADR, Quote is from an Aug. 23, 1971 letter to Waters from a sister in Baltimore who had read Mulholland's remark in an unnamed paper. In his reply to the sister, Waters said he had been unable to verify the statement.

34. ADR, Letter dated Aug. 3, 1971. Gilbert also served as Superintendent of Catholic schools for many years. A revealing anecdote is that when it came time to turn the altars around so that the priest faced the people, Gilbert said, "I'll turn the altar around when Pope Paul VI comes here in person and tells me to do it." Overhearing this, Waters responded, "Ed, I'm not the pope, but grab the other end of that altar."

35. ADR, Carbon copies of Waters' letters are in the file folders with the letters from supporters.

36. ADR, Letter dated Sept. 16, 1971.

37. ADR, Letter dated Sept. 16, 1971.

38. The *Tablet* letter appeared Sept. 2, 1971 and referred to an article on the issue which had appeared on August 19.

39. Waters subscribed to *Divine Love*. His copy of issue 54, of October 15, 1971 is preserved with his letters.

40. ADR, From its location in his letters, it is clear that the paper was sent to Waters *after* his letter was issued.

41. ADR, Letter from the Consortium, Nov. 6, 1971.

42. ADR, Letter dated Dec. 8, 1971.

43. "Nuns: Quit Scabbing," *National Catholic Reporter*, Dec. 24, 1971, p. 2.

44. Editorial: "Women's Wear," *The Catholic Herald*, Louisville, Kentucky, August 26, 1971, p. 4.

45. Francis, Dale, "Question of Religious Habits," *National Catholic Register*, Sept. 5, 1971.

46. ADR, Letter from Father George Knese, Aug. 27, 1971.

47. ADR, Related in a letter to Waters from Rev. Henry Haacke of Indiana, Oct. 7, 1971.

48. ADR, Fletcher's first letter is dated Sept. 1, 1971. A second is dated Sept. 10.

49. Letter to Editor, *Daily Boomerang*, Laramie, Wyoming, Aug. 21, 1971.

50. ADR, Letter Oct. 2, 1971. Haacke's letter had appeared in the May 23, 1971 *Louisville Courier Journal*. Haacke sent Waters not only that letter, but more than one hundred of the letters he had received in support of his position.

51. The letter, dated Oct. 5, 1971, was sent to the superiors of the religious order priests working in North Carolina as well as to the diocesan clergy. He had heard that some of his priests went around in colored slacks and sport shirts.

52. A week after the 1972 school year had commenced, the seven Sisters of Providence teaching in two parochial schools in Fayetteville were ordered to leave the diocese. Waters had learned that although the nuns wore their habits while teaching, they were wearing secular clothes outside the classroom. "Sisters of Providence Obey Order of Bishop," *Fayetteville Observer*, Sept. 1, 1972, p. 1B. Also, "Clothes Rule Removes Nuns." *News & Observer*, Sept. 6, 1972. The arbitrariness of Waters' position was underlined by the fact that the sisters expelled from Raleigh were accepted by the newly established Diocese of Charlotte, where the bishop, Michael J. Begley, a protégé of Waters, was happy to have them. "Charlotte Diocese Accepts Sisters," *News & Observer*, Sept. 14, 1972.

53. "Clerical Dress Code Criticized," *Charlotte News*, Nov. 16, 1971, p. 16B.

54. Legend has it that Waters would make surprise visits to rectories in order to assure compliance with his dress code. However, if she knew where he was going, his secretary would phone ahead to warn the priests.

55. "Priests Criticize Bishop Waters for Dress Rule," *Charlotte Observer*, Nov. 17, 1971; "Clerical Dress Rules Hit By Priests Association," *News & Observer*, Nov. 17, 1971.

56. In 1970, for the first time since 1900, the number of Catholics in the United States fell. Also, there was a decline in the number of priests, nuns, brothers, converts, infant baptisms, schools, and students in Catholic schools. *1970 Official Catholic Directory.*

57. ADR, Undated letter, apparently late 1971.

58. *Charlotte News*, op. cit., Nov. 16, 1971.

59. "Rap Nun Garb Rule," *Catholic Virginian*, Aug. 27, 1971.

60. Interview with Msgr. Gerald L. Lewis. Pope Paul VI signed the Constitution on the Liturgy On Dec. 4, 1963 which called for the reform and renewal of the Church's central acts of worship, especially the Mass. Changes were introduced progressively over the following few years.

61. ADR, Pastoral Letter, June 26, 1972.

62. This letter, like the one to the North Carolina priests, was dated June 26, 1972.

63. ADR, Pastoral Letter, Sept. 7, 1972.

64. ADR. The letter from Raimondi is dated Jan. 28, 1972.

65. ADR. The letter to the Indiana bishop is dated Feb. 5, 1972.

66. When Cardinal O'Boyle attempted to force priests to accept the ban on contraception, many left the priesthood. In California, when Cardinal McIntyre attempted to get the Immaculate Heart of Mary sisters to wear the habit, the majority of the sisters resigned and established a group that was not under the Cardinal's control.

67. Craven, Charles, "Catholic Bishop Vincent S. Waters of Raleigh," *News & Observer*, Feb. 16, 1964. See also, "Bishop Shuns Publicity for Himself, for Church," *News & Observer*, July 5, 1971.

68. ADR. A booklet, titled "Raleigh: 1924-1974" contains pictures of Pope Paul VI, Waters, and Sheen, as well as a brief History of the Diocese, and the music and prayers for the solemn mass.

69. "Bishop Waters Dies at Age 70," *News & Observer*, Dec. 4, 1974; "Funeral Mass Slated Today for Bishop," *News & Observer*, Dec. 7, 1974.

Chapter 4

1. Many books relate the general history of early North Carolina. See, for example: Thomas C. Parramore, *Carolina Quest*. Englewood Cliffs, NJ: Prentice-Hall, 1978; Lindley S. Butler and Alan D. Watson (eds.) *The North Carolina Experience; An Interpretive and Documentary History*. Chapel Hill, NC: University of North Carolina Press, 1984; William S. Powell, *North Carolina Through Four Centuries*. Chapel Hill, NC: University of North Carolina Press, 1989.

2. On the conflict between Spain and England over the settlement of America, see John Tracy Ellis, *Catholics in Colonial America*. Baltimore, MD: Helicon Press, 1965.

3. Paul E. Hoffman, "New Light on Vicente Gonzalez's 1588 Voyage in Search of Raleigh s English Colonies," *North Carolina Historical Review*, April 1986, p. 199 223.

4. The earliest reference to Catholics living in North Carolina is found in John Brickell, *The Natural History of North Carolina*, Ireland, 1737. Brickell, an Irish doctor who visited Edenton c. 1730, said there were Catholics in the town of Bath and "they have likewise a clergyman of their own Order among them at present." But Brickell had no direct contact with these Catholics and his report is not confirmed. Quoted in Hugh Lefler Talmage, *North Carolina History Told by Contemporaries*, 4th edition. Chapel Hill, NC: University of North Carolina, Chapel Hill, 1965, p. 62.

5. The first town was Bath, established on the Pamlico River in 1705.

6. Duane Meyer, *The Highland Scots of North Carolina: 1732-1776*. Chapel Hill, NC: University of North Carolina Press, 1957. For the religious situation in the western region of the state see Andrew C. Denson, "Diversity, Religion, and the North Carolina Regulators," *North Carolina Historical Review*, January 1995, 30-55. Denson says that there were few whites in the

interior areas of North Carolina until the late eighteenth century and that religious practice was fluid, with distinctions between Baptists and Presbyterians blurred as a Southern Protestant consciousness was formed.

7. On the virtual absence of Catholics from colonial North Carolina see Frederick Lewis Weis, *The Colonial Clergy of Virginia, North Carolina and South Carolina, (1955)* republished Baltimore, MD: Clearfield Co., 1990. The book lists colonial era clergy; none are Catholics. Also, J. K. Rouse, *Some Interesting Colonial Churches in North Carolina*, privately published, Kannapolis, North Carolina, 1961. None of the churches are Catholic. Also, Anne Russell and Marjorie Megivern, *North Carolina Portraits of Faith: A Pictorial History of Religions*. Norfolk, VA: The Donning Company, 1986, which says: "The most conspicuous departure from the general American pattern was the relative absence of Roman Catholics until well into the twentieth century," p. 11.

8. The story of the Gastons is found in the works of J. Herman Schauinger, particularly, "The Domestic Life of William Gaston, Catholic Jurist," *Catholic Historical Review*, Jan. 1945, 394-426, and *William Gaston, Carolinian*. Milwaukee: Bruce Publishing Co., 1949.

9. A dramatic picture of the death of Dr. Gaston is given in Elizabeth F. Ellet, *The Women of the American Revolution*, (1848), republished Westport, CT: Praeger, 1998. Ellet interviewed Susan Gaston Donaldson, granddaughter of Alexander and Margaret Gaston. "Throwing herself in agony at the Royalists' feet, Mrs. Gaston implored his life, but in vain. Their cruelty sacrificed him in the midst of her cries for mercy; the ball that found his heart was from a musket leveled over her shoulder." p. 154.

10. For the general history of the Catholic Church in the United States, see Charles R. Morris, *American Catholic: The Saints and Sinners Who Built America's Most Powerful Church*. NY: Random House, 1997; James Hennessey, SJ, *American Catholics: A History of the Roman Catholic Community in the United States*. NY: Oxford Univ. Press, 1981.

11. Ellis, Vol. 1, p. 127.

12. AAB. Gaston to Carroll, Oct. 25, 1805.

13. Steven M. Stowe, *Intimacy and Power in the Old South: Ritual in the Lives of Planters*. Baltimore, MD: Johns Hopkins Univ. Press, 1987. The chapter on Gaston, titled "The Treasure of Offspring," 164-191, is a detailed and well-documented account of Gaston as a parent.

14. Though brief, Gaston's time in Congress was noteworthy. Daniel Webster spoke of him as one of the finest intellectuals in the country. Gaston's personality was complex. On the one hand, he came close to fighting duels with two political enemies, John Forsyth and John C. Calhoun, both of whom subsequently became secretaries of state. On the other hand, he was a daily communicant while in Washington. He introduced and saw through to passage, the bill which chartered his alma mater, Georgetown, as a college with the right

to grant degrees. J. Herman Schauinger, "William Gaston: Southern Catholic," *Ave Maria*, Aug. 4, 1962, 5 10.

15. Peter Guilday, *The Life & Times of John England, first Bishop of Charleston*. NY: The America Press, 1927.

16. *Diurnal*, American Catholic Historical Society, 1895. This is the day-by-day diary written by England during the first three years of his episcopate, August 5, 1820 to December 5, 1823. (Since this work was only discovered in 1881, in a convent in Cork, Ireland, where a sister of Bishop England had lived, it is not included in the *Works* mentioned in the following note.)

17. *Works*, vol. 4, p. 310. Thanks to England's successor in Charleston, Bishop Ignatius Reynolds, England's writings were collected.The first edition was published in five volumes by John Murphy & Co., 1849. A later edition, under the direction of Archbishop Sebastian G. Messmer, was published by Arthur H. Clark in 7 volumes in 1908. This later edition was reprinted by Arno Press in five volumes, 1978. All references to the *Works* are to the Messmer edition.

18. Patrick W. Carey, *People, Priests, and Prelates: Ecclesiastical Democracy and the Tensions of Trusteeism*. Notre Dame, IN: Univ. of Notre Dame Press, 1987.

19. *Works*, vol. 4, p. 235.

20. *Diurnal*, p. 17.

21. *Diurnal*, p. 41.

22. Cardinal James Gibbons, *Ambassador of Christ*. Baltimore, MD: John Murphy Co., 1896, p. 295.

23. The names of the committee members suggest the ethnic character of the Catholics in Wilmington: J.P. Calharda, E. C. Bettencourt, William Usher, Dominique Cazaux, Wm. Bettencourt, and Eugene Mazurotti.

24. *Diurnal*, p. 20. Unless otherwise noted, all the material about the bishop's trip through the state is taken from this source and will not be further cited.

25. *Works*, Vol. 4, p. 318. This reference is from "The Early History of the Diocese of Charleston" which England published in pamphlet form in 1832. The document, pages 298-327 of Vol. 4 of the *Works*, includes South Carolina and Georgia as well as North Carolina, and is the first effort to write a history of the church in the area.

26. William Gaston, Papers, 1781-1915, Manuscript Dept., Southern Historical Collection, University of North Carolina, Chapel Hill.

27. Plymouth is one of a dozen small parishes in North Carolina that is administered by a religious sister. The pastor of the church in Ahoskie, two counties away, is sacramental minister. Pastoral Administrators will be discussed in Chapter Eleven.

28. When on his way back to Charleston several months later, England passed through Edenton, he found "the flock much scattered by sickness."

29. *1825 Diary of Dr. Thomas O'Dwyer*, in Samuel Jordan Wheeler papers, Southern Historical Collection, University of North Carolina, Chapel Hill, #766, vol. 1. Pages are not numbered. Thomas Parramore studied the diary and wrote an unpublished paper, "Dr. Thomas O'Dwyer's Diary," no date, which was given to author by Parramore in 1998.

30. ADR, Register, Church of Washington, NC, 1821-1849. It is reported that some years ago the register was found in an attic and turned over to the church.

31. ADR, Patrick Joseph Coffey, *Memoirs of the Church & Congregation of St. John the Apostle and Evangelist, Washington, Beaufort County, NC*, 1849. Unpublished ms.

32. One of the marriages was that of Alfred Lanier Price and Clarissa Bond in 1845. Alfred and Clarissa Price subsequently moved to Wilmington, where in 1860 a son, Thomas Frederick, was born.

33. Coffey, *Memoirs*, p. 4.

34. A detailed account of the Philadelphia "schism" is given on pp. 31-40 of the *Diurnal*. England was betrayed by priests on a number of occasions. In 1832, he wrote that "some bad priests who, rejected from the ministry of their native land, betook themselves to a new country, where the dearth of a clergy who could speak the language of the people, almost compelled ...that they be accepted. Alas. how extensive and pernicious have been the evils produced in America from this melancholy source!" *Works*, Vol. 4, p. 308

35. Coffey, *Memoirs*, p. 5.

36. As was noted above, the bishop had consecrated St. Patrick's Church in Fayetteville a few days before this. Thus, technically, Fayetteville has the distinction of being home to the first Catholic Church in the state.

37. *Works*, III, p. 262.

38. The Constitution prescribed that although women were to be considered members of the church, they were not eligible to vote or to be elected to office.

39. Coffey, *Memoirs*, p. 8.

40. See Stephen C. Worsley, "Catholicism in Ante bellum North Carolina," *North Carolina Historical Review*, Vol. 60, Oct. 1983, 399-430. Worsley has a table (p. 426) which lists nine churches. However, two of them were basically the private chapels of families in Gaston and Halifax counties.

Chapter 5

1. *Works*, Vol.. 7, 425-449.

2. Peter Clarke, *A Free Church in a Free Society: the Ecclesiology of John England*, Doctoral Thesis, Pontifical Gregorian University, 1980, p. 41

3. Some sources claim that Thomas Burke, a delegate to the US Constitutional Convention and governor of North Carolina in 1780, was a Catholic. However, this seems based more on his Irish surname than on direct evidence. Cf. Martin Griffin, "North Carolina Not an Enemy of Our Faith," *Records of the American Historical Society of Philadelphia*, July 1890, 129-132.

4. Robert M. Calhoon, "An Agrarian and Evangelical Culture," in Butler & Watson, *The North Carolina Experience: An Interpretive and Documentary History*, Chapel Hill, 1984.

5. Hus, John, *New Catholic Encyclopedia*, Washington, DC, Catholic University Press.

6. Jon F. Sensbach, *A Separate Canaan: The Making of an Afro-American World in North Carolina*, 1763-1840, Chapel Hill, Univ. of North Carolina Press, 1998.

7. For a detailed discussion, see Duane Meyer, *The Highland Scots of North Carolina*, 1732-1776, Univ. of North Carolina Press, Chapel Hill, 1957.

8. ibid., p. 114. Reference is given to court records of Cumberland County, North Carolina.

9. The material on Methodism is drawn from M. H. Moore, *Sketches of the Pioneers of Methodism in North Carolina & Virginia*, Nashville, TN, Southern Methodist Publishing House, 1884. (Reprinted 1977, The Attic Press, Greenwood, SC.)

10. ibid., p. 107.

11. Alan Neely, editor, *Being Baptist Means Freedom*, Charlotte, NC: Southern Baptist Alliance, 1988.

12. By 1850, North Carolina had 615 Baptist churches and four Catholic churches. By 1890, while the Catholics now had sixty churches, the Baptists had 3,124. See, Gaustad & Barlow, *New Historical Atlas of Religion in America,* New York: Oxford University Press, 2001, p. 401.

13. Ibid., p. 40. Presbyterians held their own, increasing from 5.3% to 5.8%.

14. Thomas A. Bland, ed., *Servant Songs: Reflection on the History and Mission of Southeastern Baptist Theological Seminary, 1950-1988*, Macon, Georgia: Smyth & Helwys Publishing, Inc., 1994.

15. *Works*, Vol. 2, p. 213-214.

16. See also, John McGill, *The True Church, Indicated to the Inquirer*, Richmond, VA: Ritchie & Dennavant, 1862. McGill was the Catholic bishop of Richmond.

17. *Works*, Vol. 2, p. 213-562 and Vol. 3, p. 9-103.

18. Ibid., p. 226.

19. *Works*, Vol. 1, p. 349-506, Vol. 2, p. 9-170. The *Catechism* itself, reprinted in England's Works, consists of 14 pages. The rejoinder runs for more than 300 pages. All the material was published over several months in the Miscellany.

20. *Works*, Vol. 4, pp. 411 - 510.

21. The flood of anti-Catholic literature would increase with the passage of time. An early classic study is Ray Allen Billington, *The Protestant Crusade, 1800-1860: A Study of the Origins of American Nativism*, New York: Macmillan, 1938. In 1914, a Commission on Religious Prejudices, established by the Knights of Columbus, found that there were over 60 national weeklies devoted to attacks on the Church. Robert P. Lockwood, editor, *Anti-Catholicism in American Culture, Huntington, Indiana*: Our Sunday Visitor Publishing Division, 2000, p. 36.

22. J., Lawrence, *The Mouse Trying to Gnaw Out of the Catholic Trap*, Tarrborough [NC} Press, 1835.

23. ibid., p. 5.

24. ibid., p.12.

25. Cf. John T. Noonan, Jr., *The Lustre of our Country: The American Experience of Religious Freedom*, Berkeley: University of California Press, 1998.

26. Lawrence, op. cit., p. 20.

27. Edward Beecher, *The Papal Conspiracy Exposed*, New York: M. W. Dodd, 1855. (Reprinted 1977 by Arno Press, NY.) p. 399.

28. Beecher identified England as a Jesuit, which although not accurate, would tend to further demonize the bishop.

29. Ibid., p. 405. As a matter of fact, by 1860, with approximately 3.1 million adherents, the Catholic Church was the largest single religious body in America. However, by then the xenophobia which had expressed itself in nativist propaganda had been displaced by slavery as the nation's paramount political and moral issue. Jenny Franchot, *Roads to Rome: The Ante-bellum Protestant Encounter with Catholicism*, Berkeley: University of California Press, 1994, p. xx.

30. *Works*, vol. 7, p. 32.

31. *Works*, "Domestic Slavery," vol. 5, p. 183-311.

32. Pope Gregory XVI, "In Supremo Apostolatus," 1839. Catholic Resource Network, online information system.

33. *Works*, Vol. 5, p. 190.

34. Ibid., p. 191.

35. Others have described slavery in areas settled by Protestants as very severe in comparison with conditions in areas settled by Catholic Spain and Portugal. Cf. Clement Eaton, *The Growth of Southern Civilization*, New York: Harper & Brothers, 1961, p. 91.

36. Ibid., p. 192.

37. Ibid., p. 311.

38. Robert M. Calhoon, *Religion and the American Revolution in North Carolina*, Raleigh, NC: Department of Cultural Resources, 1976, p. 69.

39. Peter Guilday, *The Life and Times of John England, first Bishop of Charleston*, New York: America Press, 1927, p. 132.

40. *Works*, vol. 5, p.64-65.

41. Robert M. Calhoon, *Religion and the American Revolution in North Carolina*, Raleigh, NC: NC Department of Cultural Resources, p. 70.

42. Ibid., p. 72.

43. *Works*, vol. 5, pp. 55-66.

44. Hugh Talmage Lefler, *North Carolina History Told by Contemporaries*, 4th edition, Chapel Hill: University of North Carolina Press, 1965, p. 110. In the Proceedings of the Convention, Gaston's speech on June 30, 1835 comprised 40 pages. John Tracy Ellis, (ed.) *Documents of American Catholic History, Vol. I*, Wilmington, Delaware: Michael Glazier, 1987, p. 244.

45. Ibid., p. 246. Cf., William Gaston, "Plea for Religious Toleration," *Historical Records & Studies*, XVII, 1926, 189-244.

46. Lefler, op. cit., p.72. Cf., John V. Orth, *North Carolina State Constitution: With History and Commentary*, (Reference Guide to State Constitutions, #16.)

47. Guion Griffis Johnson, *Ante-bellum North Carolina: A Social History*, Chapel Hill, 1937.

48. Robert C. Lawrence, *Here in Carolina*, Lumberton, NC: Little & Ives, 1939, p.180.

49. R.D.W. Connor, *Makers of North Carolina History*, Raleigh, NC: The Thompson Publishing Co., 1911, p. 179.

50. Samuel Acourt Ashe, *History of North Carolina*, Raleigh: Edwards & Groughton, 1925, vol. 2, p. 361.

51. Victoria E. Bynum, *Unruly Women: The Politics of Social & Sexual Control in the Old South*, Chapel Hill: University of North Carolina Press, 1992. Until 1970, North Carolina law required the written assent of the husband before a wife could convey her real property to someone else.

52. Ashe, op. cit., p. 362.

53. *Records of the US District Court relating to slaves*, 1851-1863, National Archives, Microfilm Publication M433, Roll 3.

54. Bynum, op. cit., p. 438.

55. Eugene Bianchi and Rosemary Radford Ruether (eds.), *A Democratic Catholic Church: The Reconstruction of Roman Catholicism*. New York: Crossroads, 1992.

56. Leonard Swidler, *Toward a Catholic Constitution*. New York: Crossroads, 1996.

57. Cardinal Joseph Ratzinger, cited in *Intermediair*, December 21, 1990, p. 23.

58. *Works*, 1849 edition, Vol. 5, pp. 91-108. The Constitution was included in a "General Appendix," comprised of works not written by England personally, but under his direction. The "General Appendix" was not included in the 1908 edition.

59. *Works*, 5, 92.

60. Ibid., p. 93.

61. Ibid., p. 96. Papal infallibility was defined at the First Vatican Council in 1869.

62. Ibid., p. 99.

63. Ibid., p. 100.

64. Peter Clarke, *A Free Church in a Free Society*, op. cit., pp. 20-25.

65. *Works*, Vol. 5, p. 376.

66. However, although these men turned out to be more reliable than those accepted from outside the diocese, they themselves were all non-Southerners, the majority of them recruited by the bishop in his native Ireland

67. Ibid., p. 379. Kelly's generosity would be called on again. The original Fayetteville church burned down shortly after it was dedicated. Kelly make possible the construction of a second church, as he had the first.

68. Ibid., p. 379.

69. No record was kept of the delegates who attended this second North Carolina convention. However, England hinted at a small turn out by saying "Though a large number of our lay delegation has not been able to assist at our deliberations,..."

70. *Works*, Vol. 5, p. 418.

71. It should be noted that the two priests were Irish-born and that the four laymen also bore Irish names. Although few Irish immigrated to North Carolina, those who did became the backbone of the church there.

72. The word "cathedral" can give a false impression. England referred to it as "the miserable temporary shed in which we are here assembled." *Works*, Vol. 7, p. 264.

73. *Works*, Vol. 5, p. 419. The 1908 edition contains the bishop's addresses to the conventions, but not the minutes-like notes included in the 1849 edition. In the 1908 edition, all the addresses are in Vol. 7.

74. Ibid., Vol. 7, p. 255.

75. Ibid.

76. *Works*, Vol. 7, p. 276.

Chapter 6

1. Charles H. Bowman, Jr., "Dr. John Carr Monk: Sampson County's Latter Day 'Cornelius'," *North Carolina Historical Review*, Jan. 1973, p. 52-72. Unless otherwise cited, the material on Dr. Monk is from this source.

2. Cardinal James Gibbons, *The Ambassador of Christ*. Baltimore, MD: John Murphy Co., 1896, p. 344.

3. Cornelius was a Roman centurion baptized by the apostle Peter. He is considered the first Gentile convert to Christianity, and hence the analogy with Monk, the first convert to Catholicism in northern Sampson County.

4. Much of this information in this section is from *Catholicity*. Some have questioned the accuracy of O'Connell's "history". However, few would have been in a better position than he to know what occurred during the period.

5. Ibid. p. 106.

6. Ibid. p. 113.

7. Material on Bishop Lynch is derived from Henry Francis Wolfe, *The Life and Times of Patrick Nelson Lynch*. Charleston, SC: Diocese of Charleston, 1929. (typed, privately published); Also, *Catholicity.*

8. The first native-born Carolinian priest was James Andrew Corcoran, who was born in Charleston March 30, 1820. Like Lynch, he was sent to Rome by Bishop England. After ordination in 1842, Corcoran taught at the seminary in Charleston until it closed in 1851. In 1863, he succeeded Father Murphy as pastor of the Wilmington parish. In 1868 he was called to Rome to assist in the preparations for the First Vatican Council. On his return to America he became a professor at the newly founded St. Charles Seminary, Overbrook, Pennsylvania, where he spent the rest of his life. *Catholicity*, p. 141; Garaventa, p. 8.

9. Wolfe, op. cit., p. 13. This is a quote from Bishop Clancy, an Irishman who served briefly as England's coadjutor before being assigned a diocese of his own. England sought Clancy's assistance due to his concern about leaving the diocese without an episcopal presence during his long absences.

10. Wolfe, *Life of Lynch*, p. 42.

11. *Official Catholic Directory*, 1858.

12. ADR, "History of St. Anne's Church," (no date), in Edenton Parish file.

13. John G. Barrett, *The Civil War in North Carolina*. Chapel Hill: University of NC Press, 1963.

14. Letter of April 16, 1861, E. Conigland Papers, Southern Historical Collection, UNC-Chapel Hill.

15. Susan King, "*The US Catholic Miscellany*," unpublished paper delivered March 1999, American Catholic Historical Association meeting, Santa Fe, NM. At the time, King was archivist of the Charleston Diocese.

16. The text of correspondence between Lynch and Hughes was printed in the *New York Daily Tribune*, September 5, 1861.

17. Manuscript in the Charleston archives. Cited at length in Wolfe, *The Life & Times of Patrick Nelson Lynch*, p. 71.

18. Wolfe, op. cit., p. 89.

19. *Catholicity*, p. 157. Northern priests were just as fervently committed to their side of the conflict as were their Southern counterparts. One such Northern priest, on the occasion of "baptizing" an artillery piece spoke of the weapon as "this noble son of a great father, who has his mouth open..., anxious to speak, which I have no doubt he soon will, in a thundering voice, to the joy of his friends, and the terror of his enemies." Charles Frank Pitts, *Chaplains in Gray: The Confederate Chaplains' Story*. St. John, Indiana: Christian Book Gallery, 1957, p. 27.

20. Wolfe, op. cit., p. 114.

21. A vicariate apostolic is established in a region in which ecclesiastical organization is still in its infancy. It is a mission area under the jurisdiction of the Congregation for the Propagation of the Faith that appoints a Vicar Apostolic. If the vicar is a bishop, he possesses all the rights and faculties

of a diocesan bishop. A vicariate is an area in need of financial and personnel assistance from the more developed sectors of the church. *New Catholic Encyclopedia*, 1967. Vol. 14, p. 638-639.

22. James Gibbons, "Reminiscences of Catholicity in North Carolina," lecture delivered Feb. 18, 1891 before the New York Historical Society. Not published, but reprinted in *NC Catholic* in three installments: May 18, May 25 and June 1, 1947.

23. *Catholicity*, p. 166.

24. http://www.cin.org/kc87-3.html. Catholic Information Network article on Gibbons.

25. Garaventa, Louis T., *Bishop James Gibbons & the Roman Catholic Church in North Carolina, 1868-1872*. Unpublished thesis, University of North Carolina-Chapel Hill, 1973, p. 21. Unless otherwise noted, all material on Gibbons is from this source, henceforth called "*Garaventa.*"

26. The 1860 US Census of North Carolina counted 630,000 whites and 361,522 blacks, 30,463 of whom were free.

27. As it turned out, Northrup asked to be reassigned to the Charleston Diocese. So, as the quotation at the beginning of this chapter states, Gibbons had but two priests when he began his work in North Carolina, Mark Gross in Wilmington and Lawrence P. O'Connell in Charlotte. [Lawrence O'Connell was the brother of Jeremiah O'Connell, author of the frequently cited *Catholicity*.]

28. D.A. Willey, "Cardinal Gibbons Forty Years Ago: The Work of a Zealous Young Bishop in North Carolina," *Putnam's Monthly*. August 1908, 518; cited by Garaventa, p. 27.

29. James Cardinal Gibbons, *The Faith of Our Fathers*. Baltimore: MD, John Murphy Co., 1876. The book went through scores of printings and editions. By 1965, 2,500,000 copies had been sold.

30. John Tracy Ellis, "The Spirit of Cardinal Gibbons," *Records of the American Catholic Historical Society of Philadelphia*. Vol. 76, March 1965, 14-20.

31. A detailed account of Gibbons' travels can be found in his Diary and in Garaventa.

32. Despite their depleted numbers, the people of Edenton begged Gibbons to send them a priest. Knowing that no priest was available, and that such a small congregation could not support one in any case, he took the unusual step of promising to ask Father O'Keefe in Norfolk, Virginia, another diocese, to supply a priest, if possible, once a month. It pained the bishop to see the church of St. Anne, which he called the "finest Catholic church in the state," standing empty and cold. Gibbons' *Diary*, Nov. 30, 1868; Garaventa, p. 34.

33. Garaventa, p. 32. Also consulted were the Edward Conigland Papers in the Southern Historical Collection, University of North Carolina at Chapel Hill.

34. The similarities with Gaston include also a role in public life. Just as Gaston played a major role in the Constitutional Convention of 1835, so

likewise did Conigland in the Convention of 1865 that required many constitutional changes in order for North Carolina to be readmitted to the Union.

35. Another Irish-immigrant family, that of Michael Ferrall (1811-1862), built a small church in Halifax that today is on the National Register of Historic Places. The Church of the Immaculate Conception was dedicated in 1889 and served as a mission until almost all the Catholics had moved from the town. The church and adjacent Ferrall Family Cemetery were maintained by Miss Nannie Gary (1887-1969), the last descendant of the Ferrall family to live in Halifax. Her will provided for the perpetual care of the property. ADR has Gary's papers.

36. There was also the experience of family life. On his first visit to Glen Ivy, one of Conigland's young daughters was told to go into the parlor and kiss the bishop's ring. Instead, she ran in, flung her arms around the youthful prelate's neck and kissed him. He rewarded her by putting his pectoral cross on her and letting her exhibit it to those present. Sketch of Edward Conigland of Halifax, written by his granddaughter Daisy Moseley. p. 107. Conigland papers, UNC-Chapel Hill. Undated, but probably 1950s.

37. In Box 8 of the Conigland Papers in the UNC-Chapel Hill library, there are seven letters from Gibbons to Conigland, starting from this of Feb. 17, 1869 through March 10, 1871. There is also a touching letter dated June 10, 1869 from Father Mark Gross to Conigland, responding to the lawyer's request for spiritual advice. In Gross's response, clearly recognizing the depth of Conigland's spirituality, the priest adds, "It seems as if I should rather ask advice from you."

38. Schools staffed by the Charleston Sisters of Mercy. There were no Catholic schools in North Carolina at the time.

39. Obituary of Mary Alice Conigland Smith, *Roanoke News*, Weldon, NC, Oct. 1875.

40. Garaventa, p. 43. Although in his Diary Gibbons wrote positively of his visit to St. Charlotte, more than 20 years later he would write in his *Reminiscences*: "The religious bigotry of Charlotte and its vicinity (it is a Scotch-Irish Presbyterian region) I found to be only surpassed by the staunch faith of its few trusty Catholics."

41. Col. Fisher had vowed that no Catholic priest would ever enter his house. As it turned out, not only priests but also a bishop would make his house the Catholic headquarters in Salisbury. Furthermore, L. Silliman Ives (1797-1867), who had been the Episcopal bishop of North Carolina during the 1840's and lodged with the Fishers, had converted to Catholicism in the 1850's. L. Silliman Ives, *The Trials of a Mind in its Progress to Catholicism*. Boston: Patrick Donahue, 1854.

42. Kate Harbes Becker, *Biography of Christian Reid*. Belmont, NC, 1941. Becker, a Sister of Mercy, had written her Masters' thesis on Reid at the Catholic University of America in 1933. Anne Heagney's *The Magic Pen*.

Milwaukee: Bruce Publishing Co., 1949 is a somewhat fictionalized account of Reid's life. Heagney has Gibbons tell Reid: "I do not consider novel writing a proper vocation for a woman." p. 89. Subsequently, Gibbons became convinced that wholesome novels could have a salutary effect on people, especially young girls, Reid's principal audience.

43. Very Rev. Felix, O.S.B., "Catholicity in North Carolina," *The Messenger of the Sacred Heart of Jesus.* Vol. 34, Feb. 1899, p. 99-113. Father Felix added a point that certainly was taken into account in the decision to assign a priest to Salisbury, namely that the arrival of the Southern Railway offered promise of commercial development for the area.

44. ADR. The correspondence between Fisher and Haid are in the records for the Salisbury parish, Box RG 3.8.1.

45. ADC, Letter of Rev. William Regnat, O.S.B. to Bishop Leo Haid. (1923). Sacred Heart Parish file. In 1920 there were 160 Catholics in Salisbury and 38 children in the parish school. Seven infants and two adults were baptized. There were three marriages and one death, Frances Fisher.

46. Flannery O'Connor, "The Catholic Novelist in the Protestant South," in *Mystery and Manners.* NY: Farrar, Straus & Giroux, 1969, and Walker Percy, *Signposts on a Strange Land: Uncollected Essays.* Edited by Edward Patrick Samway. NY: Harper & Row, 1991.

47. Reid's best-known book is not a romantic story at all, but *The Land of the Sky.* NY: D. Appleton & Co, 1876, a travel tale that drew attention to the mountains of western North Carolina.

48. For the complete account of Gibbons' long life, including his role in the Vatican Council, see John Tracy Ellis, *The Life of James Cardinal Gibbons.* Milwaukee: Bruce Publishing Co., 1952. Two volumes.

49. It was during this time that Gibbons began correspondence with Dr. John Monk of Newton Grove.

50. Sister Mary Helen McCarthy, *History of the Sisters of Mercy of Belmont, NC, 1869-1934.* Masters thesis, Catholic University of America, 1934, p. 42.

51. O'Connell, *Catholicity,* p. 396.

Chapter 7

1. Pascal Baumstein, O.S.B., *My Lord of Belmont.* Charlotte, NC: Laney-Smith, Inc., 1985, p. 185. (Henceforth, Baumstein.) This biography of Leo Haid, together with other writings by Baumstein, a monk of the Belmont Abbey, is the primary source of information on Haid.

2. Baumstein, p. 188.

3. "From Fiery Death A Mangling Leap," *Raleigh News & Observer,* October 29, 1905.

4. J. H. O'Rourke, S.J., "A Month in North Carolina," *Woodstock Letters,* Vol. 34, 1905, p. 371-2.

5. AAP. Price Collection. Letter dated Nov. 1, 1905. The Philadelphia Archdiocesan Archives have two boxes of correspondence relating to the fire.

6. AAP. Price Collection. Box 1, Folders 7 & 8.

7. C. Vann Woodward, *The Strange Career of Jim Crow*, (3rd edition). New York: Oxford Univ. Press, 1974, p. 3. See also Woodward's *The Origins of the New South: 1877-1913.* Louisiana State Univ. Press, 1951.

8. Following Woodward's model, it might be suggested that two additional social upheavals have occurred in North Carolina. From the 1970's on, an increasing numbers of Northerners and high tech businesses have moved into the state. This transformation might be called regionalism and federalism. Secondly, the increase of Hispanics and other non-English speaking people during the 1990's might be termed homogeneity and diversity.

9. Sadlier's Catholic Almanac for 1865. A note says that the listing for the Diocese of Charleston was "Reprinted from Almanac of 1861." The war had made it impossible to get more recent information.

10. Very Rev. Felix, O.S.B., "Catholicity in North Carolina," *The Messenger of the Sacred Heart.* Feb. 1899, p. 108.

11. *Catholicity*, p. 247.

12. Wimmer (1809-1887) was convinced that a religious community would do the best missionary work rather than secular priests who, in Wimmer's words, are "in great danger of becoming careless and worldly-minded." Ellis, Vol. 1, p. 279.

13. Despite his infirmities, O'Connell lived until 1894, a donor who was often a thorn in the side of the monks. O'Connell was buried at Belmont. When Leo Haid died he also was buried there, with O'Connell at his feet. Baumstein, p. 292.

14. Baumstein, p. 43.

15. In 1879, Mark Gross, was offered the position. Gross, Gibbons' companion in starting the Vicariate in 1868 and a respected priest, at first accepted, but subsequently renounced the nomination.

16. Baumstein, p. 85.

17. Ibid. p. 88.

18. Ibid. p. 90.

19. Gibbons, *Reminiscences.*

20. John P. Bradley, *The First Hundred Years: Belmont Abbey College, 1876-1976.* Belmont Abbey College: Belmont, NC, 1976.

21. Gibbons, *Reminiscences.*

22. Baumstein, p. 97.

23. Paschal Baumstein, "An Abbatial Diocese in the United States," *The Catholic Historical Review*, Vol. 79, April 1993, p. 217-245.

24. Consuela Marie Duffy, *Katharine Drexel, A Biography.* Philadelphia: P. Reilly Co., 1966.

25. Cited in Baumstein, p. 121.

26. Haid was fortunate as well to have among his monks Father Michael McInerney, who not only designed many of the churches in North Carolina but also gained a national reputation. Fees from his speaking engagements and contracts contributed to the abbey's income.

27. John C. Murrett, *Tar Heel Apostle*. New York: Longmans, Green, 1944. A film titled "The Tar Heel Apostle," available at the Raleigh Diocese media center, relates the North Carolina phase of Price's life. A Father Hedwig, S.J., born in Chapel Hill, was the first native-born North Carolinian ordained a priest.

28. *Wilmington Journal*, February 27, 1872. The Maryknoll Fathers have done extensive work on their co-founder. Much of it is contained in three books by Robert E. Sheridan, and published by Maryknoll: *Very Rev. Thomas Frederick Price, M. M., A Symposium 1956 with Supplement 1981; The Founders of Maryknoll: Historical Reflections, 1980; Collected Letters of Father Price, 1981.*

29. John T. Seddon, *When Saints are Lovers: The Spirituality of Maryknoll's Co-Founder, Thomas Frederick Price*. Collegeville, MN: The Liturgical Press, 1997, p. 27.

30. William H. O'Connell, *Recollections of Seventy Years*. Boston: Houghton, Mifflin, 1934, p. 62.

31. Price, *Diary*, August 25th, 1908. Father McConnell, the Maryknoll priest who in the 1970's spent several years transcribing Price's 3,087 letters to Mary, said at the conclusion of the project: "I agree with whoever it was who said that no holy person is to be imitated by everyone in everything, and some of them are not to be imitated in anything by anybody." In Sheridan, *The Founders of Maryknoll*, p. 12.

32. Seddon, op. cit. Seddon suggests that Southern culture included chivalry, or a high degree of reverence for and honoring of women. Also, Catholic devotion to Mary was at its peak in the late 19th century. These two factors dovetailed in the spirituality of Fred Price, "a Southern gentleman." p. 9.

33. Other facets of the relationship of Price to Mary and to Bernadette are described and analyzed by Seddon, op. cit.

34. ADC. "Father Price Research" file. In a letter to the Superior General of Maryknoll (Feb. 27, 1973) Bishop Vincent Waters expressed his "desire before I die to introduce the cause of Father Thomas Price." In a March 30, 1973 letter to Waters, Bishop Michael J. Begley, the bishop of the newly established Diocese of Charlotte, said that he had questions about Father Price, including "his leaving North Carolina for China; the wedding ring incident, as well as the objective of the interment of his heart at Lourdes."

35. ADC. "Father Price Research." May 25, 1894 letter to Mrs. Farinholt, a benefactor. Letters in the folder to Mrs. Farinholt and to her sister, Mrs. Moseley, written between 1894 and 1896 reveal the germination of Price's projects and his thinking on ministry.

36. Murrett, *Tar Heel Apostle*, and cited in D. H. Moseley, "Father Price of Maryknoll," *Commonweal*, Sept. 9, 1944, p. 495.

37. Priest of Maryknoll, (compiler), *Father Price of Maryknoll, A Short Sketch of the Life of Rev. Thomas Frederick Price*. Maryknoll, NY: Catholic Foreign Mission Society of America, 1923. This was the first book that appeared after Price's death. It is based on the recollections of people who knew him.

38. ADC. D. H. Moseley, op. cit.

39. Price Symposium, p. 92.

40. "St. Mary's, Holly Springs," *NC Catholic*, Oct. 7, 1973, p. 7. The last baptism performed by Father Price before he left North Carolina was in Holly Springs. The child baptized, John Clifton Scholl, grew up to be the American Agricultural Attaché to Guatemala, where he was able to help Father Price's Maryknoll missionaries.

41. Rev. William B. Hannon, in Priest of Maryknoll, *Father Price...*, p. 35-38.

42. June 30, 1904 letter, Price to Father Walter Elliott, in *Collected Letters.*

43. Moseley, op. cit., p. 494-498.

44. ADC, Letter, Price to Mrs. Moseley, June 13, 1894.

45. A century later, North Carolina again turned to the Paulist Fathers for assistance. In 1996 the Raleigh Diocese introduced "Disciples in Mission," a three-year parish-based program designed by the Paulists to raise Catholic consciousness with reference to inviting people to join the church.

46. Price *Symposium*, p. 21-31.

47. See, Daniel J. Levinson, *The Seasons of a Man's Life*. New York: Ballantine Books, 1978.

48. Sheridan, *Collected Letters*, p. 256.

49. *Official Catholic Directory*, 1896. The 1900 Directory lists 10 parishes with resident pastors, five Benedictines and five diocesan priests. The churches in Fayetteville and Raleigh had the same pastor, Rev. Thomas P. Griffin.

50. Sheridan, *Collected Letters*, p. 255.

51. ADR. Initial issue of *Truth*. The Archives has a complete collection of this publication as well as of Price's, *Our Lady's Orphan Boy.*

52. Price *Symposium*, p. 24, citing a speech by Gibbons in November, 1900. *The Symposium article*: "Nazareth & *Truth*," describes the circulation history, subject matter and spirituality of *Truth*.

53. In 1901, Price presented a paper on his fifteen years of missionary experience at the First Conference of the Catholic Missionary Union, an organization to promote mission work in the United States. The paper revealed his interest in *foreign* missions and not just home missions. Murrett, *Tar Heel Apostle*, 48-49.

54. The story of Maryknoll is beyond the scope of this book. Some of the many books about Maryknoll include, James Keller, *Men of Maryknoll*. NY: Grosset & Dunlap, 1943; Robert E. Sheridan, *The Founders of Maryknoll: Historical Reflections*. Maryknoll, NY: Maryknoll Fathers, 1980. Jean-Paul Wiest, *Maryknoll in China, 1918-1955*. Armonk, NY: M.E. Sharpe, 1988.

55. J. H. O'Rourke, S. J., "A Month in North Carolina," *Woodstock Letters*, vol. 34, 1905, 361-372. All quotations in this section are from this source.

56. It might be recalled that fifty years later, Bishop Waters required seminarians to spend their summers "taking the census," a program which had the objective of familiarizing them with the environment in which they would be working. (Chapter Two.) In the 1990's the Diocese of Raleigh opened a House of Formation in Chapel Hill, named for Father Price, where students aspiring to the priesthood spend a year or more in the state before being sponsored at seminaries. Now, instead of coming from the north, the majority of the students come from Latin America.

57. Also, Sister Agnes served as postmaster of the Nazareth Post Office, and her $700 a year salary helped support the orphanage.

58. In 1951, a picture was taken of Bishop Waters with these three "pioneer priests who were closely associated with Father Price, founder of Nazareth Mission Center." O'Brien, who died in 1960, was the last North Carolina link with Father Price. *NC Catholic*, January 3, 1960. Chapter Nine describes the careers of Irwin and O'Brien.

59. Price Symposium, p. 61.

60. Sheridan. *Collected Letters of Thomas Frederick Price*, p. 407-418.

61. Sheridan, *Collected Letters*, 419-423.

Chapter 8

1. All the original documents from this period are in the Baltimore Archdiocesan Archives and cited in detail in Baumstein, p. 265-269.

2. North Carolina sent 86,457 men into service, of whom nearly 2,400 lost their lives and another 4,000 were wounded. Though substantial, these losses paled by comparison with the devastation of the Civil War, in which more than 40,000 North Carolinians were killed in battle or died of disease. *Encyclopedia of North Carolina*, Vol. 1, p. 86, 100

3. Despite the shortage of clergy in the state, three North Carolina priests served as chaplains during the war: James A. Manley, Thomas P. Hayden, and Francis Underwood, OSB. (*Catholic Directory*, 1920)

4. The Catholic Directory for 1924, the year that Haid died and the diocese of Raleigh was created, listed 8,254 Catholics in the state, an obvious exaggeration, since the 1926 Directory, the first for which information was submitted by the diocese, claimed but 6,483. This decrease of more than 20% was not due to a decline in the number of Catholics but to more careful census

taking. As a matter of fact, the number 8,254 had been used for five consecutive years, 1921-25.

5. The Benedictines gradually reduced their work in the state. Today, the substantially reduced community engages in no regular ministry outside the monastic grounds.

6. The Rev. C. B. Winkler, SSJ, took over the parish of St. Thomas in Wilmington in 1916, and the Reverend William F. Reichmeyer, SSJ, assumed responsibility for St. Joseph in New Bern the following year.

7. The contributions of religious, both men and women, will be discussed more fully in Chapter Twelve.

8. Baumstein, p. 294.

9. At Cardinal Gibbons' insistence, the eight-county *nullius* granted the Benedictines in 1910 did not include Mecklenburg County. Gibbons thought Charlotte was the likely seat of a diocese and didn't want it under the control of the monks. See Baumstein, p. 240-245.

10. Letter from Curley to Delegate, June 18, 1923, quoted in Baumstein, p. 286.

11. At the same time that the Diocese of Raleigh was established, Taylor was confirmed as abbot of Belmont, but *not* granted episcopal consecration as head of the *abbatia nullius*. This put him in an awkward and, at times, embarrassing position with his episcopal peers. See, Baumstein, Footnote 32, p. 366.

12. ADR, Letter of Curley to Irwin, April 9, 1925. References to correspondence of Irwin, Dennen, Griffith, and Freeman are in their "Clergy Personnel Files."

13. As if providing even more continuity, Hafey had also served as secretary to Gibbons. The Baltimore connection would emerge once again, when in 1975, F. Joseph Gossman, Auxiliary Bishop of Baltimore, succeeded Vincent Waters as Bishop of Raleigh.

14. As has been seen, Bishop Waters would place responsibility for segregated parishes on his predecessors.

15. The 1920 census counted 24,418 residents of Raleigh, and the 1930 census, 37,379.

16. "Installation Ceremonies Mark Epoch for Catholics," *News & Observer*, July 2, 1925.

17. John Strange, "Bishop William J. Hafey, the first bishop of Raleigh, met missionary challenge," *NC Catholic*, November 14, 1999, p. 7A. This issue of the *NC Catholic*, on the occasion of the 75th anniversary of the diocese, contains a number of articles on the history of the church in the state.

18. Dennen's prominence was further demonstrated by the fact that he had been invited to serve as Archpriest to Archbishop Curley at Hafey's episcopal consecration in Norfolk. Dennen's career is related in Chapter Nine.

19. On the day that a couple of hundred people welcomed the new Catholic bishop, one hundred miles to the west, in Thomasville, North Carolina,

more than 5,000 people celebrated the fortieth anniversary of the Baptist orphanage in that town, noted for the manufacture of furniture. *News & Observer*, July 2, p. 4.

20. The same issue of the *News & Observer* reported that an audience of 150-200 people in Salisbury, North Carolina heard a national representative of the Ku Klux Klan. The speaker "dwelt on Americanism, and touched on Romanism and also the race problem."

21. Mattern, Sister Evelyn, "One sister's history is people," *NC Catholic*, July 29, 2001, p. 6. The IHMs were one of the first communities of sisters whom Hafey was able to recruit. In November 2001, the sisters celebrated 75 years of service to the church in North Carolina with a mass in New Bern where they had staffed a school.

22. "Msgr. Francis Murphy, priest for 55 years, dies," *NC Catholic*, August 9, 1998, p. 1.

23. ADR, Griffin Personnel file. Letter from Pascal Baumstein to Bishop Begley, June 22, 1990.

24. Griffin also built Sacred Heart Academy, an elementary and high school staffed by Dominican sisters.

25. ADR, Irwin Box 1:1.6.1.5.Letter Griffin to Irwin, May 25, 1925.

26. "Priest of City Dies," *Raleigh Times*, April 3, 1931; "Beloved Priest Dies in Raleigh," *News & Observer*, April 3, 1931; "Monsignor Griffin Laid to Rest Beside Cathedral," *News & Observer*, April 7, 1931.

27. ADR, Much of the specific information on Hafey is derived from his Diary.

28. James T. Baker, "The Battle of Elizabeth City: Christ and Antichrist in North Carolina," *The North Carolina Historical Review*. Vol. LIV, Number 4, October 1977, p. 393-405.

29. The Catholic population had risen from 6,483 in 1926 to 10,191 in 1937. *Official Catholic Directory*, 1926, 1937.

30. Joanita M. Nellenbach, "Waynesville parish celebrates 75th anniversary," *Catholic News & Herald*, October 20, 2001. In subsequent years, other parishes were established in the region. All of them remain small. In the year 2000, St. John in Waynesville had 234 registered families.

31. ADR, Bishop Hafey's Pastoral Letters, Letter to Seminarians, May 7, 1928.

32. Editorial, *News & Observer*, Sept. 28, 1928, p. 4. An examination of issues of the paper up to Nov. 6, Election Day, revealed that news articles consistently presented Smith in a favorable light and tended to ignore Hoover. On Election Day itself, the front page carried a large photo of Smith and none of Hoover.

33. "Says Opposition Due to Religion," *News & Observer*, Sept. 29, 1928, p. 2. See also, Robert Slayton, *Empire Statesman: The Rise and Redemption of Al Smith*. NY: The Free Press, 2001.

34. "Hoover Assails Religious Issue," *News & Observer*, Sept. 29, 1928, p. 3.

35. "Makes Religion Campaign Issue," *News & Observer*, Oct. 5, 1928, p. 5.

36. *News & Observer*, October 12, 1928.

37. "Says Ministers will vote ticket," *News & Observer*, Nov. 1, 1928, p. 2.

38. "Religious Prejudice," *News & Observer*, Nov. 4, 1928, p. 6.

39. ADR, Pastoral Letter, July 19, 1928.

40. ADR, Hafey Diary, Nov. 15, 1928.

41. "Southern Waste Land," *The Nation* 147 (August 20, 1938), p. 169.

42. David L. Carlton and Peter A. Coclanis, *Confronting Southern Poverty in the Great Depression*. Bedford Books of St. Martin's Press, Boston, 1996.

43. ADR, Diary of Bishop Hafey, final page.

44. Quoted in *NC Catholic*, Nov. 14, 1999, p. 7A.

45. ADR. McGuinness papers are contained in one box. "Bishop-Elect McGuinness to Be Consecrated in Cathedral at Philadelphia," *Bulletin of the Catholic Laymen's Association of Georgia*, Dec. 21, 1937.

46. "New Bishop Installed in Colorful Ceremony," *News & Observer*, Jan. 7, 1938.

47. ADR, McGuinness papers.

48. McGuinness's remark that there had been a lack of effort to reach people in the "churchless, priestless" sections of the state suggests that he was unaware of the evangelizing work of Father Price several decades earlier.

49. ADR, McGuinness box. The bishop's handwritten, undated text has written across it, "Copy made and mailed." Neither the publication to which it was sent nor the date are indicated.

50. ADR, Pastoral Letter, November 9, 1938.

51. ADR. Lists of contributions from each church are included with Bishop McGuinness's Pastoral Letters.

52. "Cathedraticum," the money contributed by the people for the support of the bishop and his office. Typically, it is a "tax" on the ordinary collections of parishes.

53. ADR, McGuinness Pastoral, Nov. 12, 1943.

54. ADR, McGuinness Pastoral Letters, March 2, 1943.

55. In 1938 there were 240 converts recorded in the state. In 1945, the number had risen to 441, a substantial increase, but not nearly commensurate with the investment of personnel and money. For example, while the number of priests had jumped by 80%, the Catholic population had risen by only 22% during the McGuinness years.

56. The achievements of McGuinness were experienced as problems by his successor. As has been seen, Bishop Waters blamed his predecessor for

the existence of segregated parishes and had conflict with the religious order priests.

57. Kelley wrote several books related to his work, including the autobiographical *The Bishop Jots It Down*, New York: Harper & Brothers, 1939.

58. ADR. McGuinness Box, letters of April 12 and June 26, 1944, from Rev. Gavan P. Monaghan, Diocesan Superintendent of Schools for Oklahoma, to McGuinness.

59. ADR. McGuinness to Monaghan, June 29, 1944.

60. In 1945, while the Catholic population of North Carolina stood at 12,922 that of Oklahoma was 67,844.

61. "Pope Transfers Three Bishops," *News & Observer*, November 17, 1944.

62. Besides the war, early November 1944 had seen also the election of Franklin D. Roosevelt to a fourth term as President. Roosevelt, supported by the *News & Observer*, carried North Carolina over the Republican candidate, Thomas Dewey, by a three-to-one margin.

Chapter 9

1. Information about Koch is based on a videotaped interview that Father Joseph Vetter conducted in February 1992 at Sacred Heart Rectory, where Koch was residing.

2. Joseph L. Federal (1910-2000) was ordained in 1934 for Raleigh. In 1951 he was named auxiliary bishop of Salt Lake City, Utah and was promoted to ordinary in 1960. He retired in 1980.

3. Father, later Monsignor, John A. Brown (1909-1986), was ordained in 1937 in Scranton, PA. He came to Raleigh to assist Father Federal at Sacred Heart Cathedral, Raleigh.

4. Subsequently, Nazareth was annexed to Raleigh.

5. Koch edited the *NC Catholic* from 1947 to 1954 and again from 1967 to 1976.

6. As will be seen below, Father John Roueche was the first diocesan priest pastor in Newton Grove after integration.

7. The Redemptorists left North Carolina completely. One of their parishes was Kannapolis (now a mission of Concord.) On their departure, they took everything with them, including the kitchen sink, the doors and all the fixtures and appliances. Ironically, when the community was invited back to North Carolina by the bishop of Charlotte they were reassigned to Kannapolis, now a mission of St. James parish in Concord.

8. ADR. Frederick A Koch, "Tar on the Heels of a Missionary." Pamphlet addressed to pastors in other parts of the country. No date, but apparently 1949. 8 pp.

9. John Strange, "Priest, editor, 'icon'," *NC Catholic*, November 21, 1999, p.1.

10. Baumstein, p. 248. The following quotes are from the same source.

11. Thus, the least Catholic state in the Union had not one, but two, "cathedrals," neither of which was destined to be a real cathedral when at last a diocese would be established. Haid could not have foreseen the decline of Wilmington following the slump in sea and rail transportation. What was the largest city in the state eventually fell to ninth place. The ten largest cities in North Carolina are: Charlotte, Raleigh, Greensboro, Durham, Winston-Salem, Fayetteville, Cary, High Point, Wilmington and Asheville. *2000 US Census.*

12. ADR, Wilmington parish files, Box 1.

13. As to the loans, substantial for that day, Dennen announced from the pulpit: "I have built the church; future generations will pay for it." He was correct. The debt was not liquidated until the mid 1940's.

14. Belmont Abbey Archives, Letter, Dennen to Haid, with enclosures, October 20, 1914.

15. On Reconstruction see Eric Foner, *Reconstruction: America's Unfinished Revolution, 1863-1877.* New York: Harper & Row, 1988. See also the work of C. Vann Woodward, including *The Strange Career of Jim Crow*, 3rd revised edition. New York: Oxford University Press, 1974.

16. *The Brooklyn Citizen*, November 11, 1898, quoted in Harry Hayden, *The Story of the Wilmington Rebellion*, Wilmington, NC, 1936. Privately printed.

17. The Josephites were the first religious order of men to take up work in the state since the arrival of the Benedictines at Belmont in 1876.

18. ADR, Dennen file. Letter Dennen to Hafey, July 5, 1933. The following items are in the same file.

19. The case of a married priest of the Charlotte Diocese getting divorced raised some eyebrows but did not put a halt to the ordination of men who are husbands, fathers, and at times, grandfathers.

20. ADR, Irwin Box 1, Folder 6.1.2. Letter of Irwin to Archb. Curley, 1923. Much of the information on Irwin is derived from material in the two boxes of letters and other items preserved by the archives.

21. "Monsignor Michael Irwin Buried," *NC Catholic*, Jan. 11, 1952.

22. On more than one occasion, in his diary Price refers to Irwin as an impediment to his work, as someone to be avoided.

23. ADR, Irwin, Box 1, Folder 1.6.1.1 September 13, 1908.

24. Ibid. Jan. 29, 1911.

25. Ibid. Feb. 13, 1911.

26. Letter, Irwin to Gibbons, Nov. 3, 1910. Cited in Baumstein, p. 248.

27. ADR. Our Lady of Guadalupe box, Folder 3.8.1, Sept. 29, 1899 Agreement.

28. ADR. Financial record for St. Mark's, Feb. 1, 1901.

29. The Catholic Directory for 1912 states that Irwin was responsible for the following missions: St. Anthony's in Benson, St. Cecelia's in

Bentonville, Immaculate Conception in Clinton, Emmanuel Church in Dobbersville, Sacred Heart in Dunn, St. Elizabeth's at Peacock Junction, St. Michael's in Rosin Hill, and unnamed missions in Godwin and Hobtown.

30. James Garneau, "St. Katharine Drexel left her mark on NC Church," *NC Catholic*, Sept. 24, 2000, p.8.

31. Msgr. Fred Koch gave this picture of Irwin in his 1992 videotaped interview with Fr. Vetter.

32. ADR. Irwin Box 1.6.1.4. Letter of Irwin to Curley, Jan. 23, 1925. In a draft of the letter written a few days earlier, Irwin had written: "You will not be deceived by ax-grinders, wire-pullers, place-hunters or stepping-stoners." Having second thoughts about this negative approach to the qualities that should characterize the as yet unnamed new bishop, Irwin revised his counsel to the more positive suggestion that he be a man who loves the Bible.

33. ADR. Irwin Box I: Letter of Irwin to Willibald, OSB, February 11, 1925.

34. ADR, Newton Grove parish report, 1926.

35. The Belmont Sisters of Mercy undertook the staffing of the schools in 1928.

36. Irwin got a taste of his own medicine when shortly before his death he requested permission to celebrate mass in his house while sitting down. Rather than affording the dying priest this one favor, Waters refused.

37. For a time, there was also a small Carmel in Asheville. The story of the Carmelite nuns will be related more fully in Chapter Eleven.

38. Rochet: a sort of short linen surplice, with tight sleeves, and open at the sides, worn by bishops and some other church dignitaries." Webster's Unabridged Dictionary.

39. ADR. Irwin Box 2, letter by Gilbert dated March 26, 1952. In this box also are a score of letters written by Father Price to Irwin between 1897 and 1919. Price engaged in chastisement of his body; it is possible that Irwin adopted the practice based on the example of his mentor.

40. ADR. Gilbert personnel files. Letter dated October 9, 1928.

41. ADR. Ibid, Feb. 13, 1929.

42. "Former Schools Director Dies," *NC Catholic*, Jan. 9, 1983, p. 1.

43. To avoid confusion with the nation's capitol, the Carolina town is called "Little Washington" by outsiders, but "the original Washington" by locals, who stress that their Washington had been given its name in 1776, long before there was a Washington, DC.

44. All data is from the annual reports of the parishes.

45. ADR. Note written by Gilbert Oct. 21, 1937 in his annual report: "St Agnes School for members of the white race started last month. Kindergarten: 7 students. Special classes for high school students and adults: 25 students. Conducted by the Immaculate Heart of Mary sisters." Additional information on the history of the parish is from an Oct. 16, 1997 interview with the Reverend Donald Baribeau, M.S., then pastor of Mother of Mercy.

46. Irvin S. Cobb, *North Carolina*. New York: George H. Doran Co, 1924, p. 29.

47. Unfortunately, no records have been preserved of Gilbert's work as superintendent.

48. William Francis O'Brien, *Memoirs*. Durham, North Carolina: Christian Printing Co., 1958. Earlier, O'Brien had published *A History of the Catholic Church of Durham*, NC: 1871-1944, which is appended to the *Memoirs*.

49. The story of the building of the Edenton church is related in Chapter Six.

50. Father O'Brien would refer to Mr. O'Brien as "the most generous Catholic layman in North Carolina in his day." *Memoirs*, p. 76.

51. Today, there are four Catholic parishes in Durham. Immaculate Conception, now staffed by Franciscan priests, has nearly 2,000 registered families. There are no longer any tobacco-manufacturing facilities in the city.

52. *Memoirs*, p. 84.

53. ADR. O'Brien files. Letter of July 18, 1938.

54. In O'Brien's obituary, his sister was identified as the rectory "hostess." "Father O'Brien Passes at 87," *The Durham Sun*, March 24, 1960.

55. ADR. O'Brien files. In the initial will, dated July 2, 1952, O'Brien left everything to his sister. However, in a later will, he left $1,000 to help reduce the debt of the Durham parochial school. His estate, all in a savings account, amounted to $4,123.45.

56. "A Pioneer Priest," *The Gastonia Gazette*, July 18, 1965, p. 8D.

57. Margaret and John had nine children. One daughter, the third child, became Sister Mary Xavier of the Belmont Sisters of Mercy. The youngest child was John Francis Xavier Roueche, who became a priest. "Robert T. Lawson, "Old Friend, fellow priest remembers, praises Msgr. John Roueche," *Catholic News & Herald*, July 16, 2000, p.9.

58. A new Sacred Heart Church had been built in 1940, and a new school in 1965.

59. Obituary of Msgr. John Roueche, *Salisbury Post*, June 3, 2000; History of Sacred Heart Roman Catholic Church, www.shrcnc.org/Document_Static/History/History.

60. Much of the information about Father Roueche is from a Feb. 18, 1991 videotaped interview conducted by Father Joseph Vetter. The tape is in the Raleigh Diocese Communications Dept.

Chapter 10

1. Richard Kluger, *Ashes to Ashes*. New York: Vintage Books, 1996, p.29. Rob Waters, "The rap on R.J. Reynolds," *News & Observer*, March 11, 2001, p. 4G.

2. Parish Profile, "St. Leo the Great Church," *Catholic News & Herald*, April 25, 1997, p. 16. "History of St. Leo's", http://www.massintransit.com/nc/leo-nc-winsal/hist.html.

3. Denise Kasper, "Reestablished women's group promotes church development and fellowship," *Catholic News & Herald*, Feb. 1, 2002, p. 15.

4. Holy Family Parish History. www.holyfamilyclemmons.com/history.html.

5. Much of the information in this chapter is from interviews with Msgr. Gerald L. Lewis, who was closely associated with Bishop Waters, and with Msgr. Joseph S. Showfety, who served as the first Chancellor of the Charlotte diocese. See, "First Chancellor recalls life in ministry," *News & Herald*, July 26, 2002, p. 1.

6. ADR. Pastoral Letter, dated November 30, 1971, to be read at all masses on December 5.

7. Much of the material on Bishop Begley is taken from a videotaped interview conducted by Fr. Joseph Vetter on January 31, 1992. See also, Miriam Miller, *A History of the Early Years of the Roman Catholic Diocese of Charlotte*. Laney-Smith, Inc.: Charlotte, NC, 1984; Jimmy Rostar, "'The Lord has been very good,' says diocese's founding bishop," *The Catholic News & Herald*, Dec. 24, 1999, p. 7.

8. Obituary, The Most Reverend Michael Joseph Begley, *Charlotte Observer*, Feb. 11, 2002.

9. William F. Powers, *The Cursillo Movement and the Assimilation of the Puerto Rican*. MA thesis, St. John's University, New York, 1968.

10. In time, church officials became uncomfortable with the word "Charities," as sounding demeaning to its clients. The Charlotte Diocese employs the more politically correct term "Catholic Social Services," while Raleigh reframed its agency as "Catholic Social Ministries."

11. *North Carolina Catholic*, May 31, 1959. In 1955, Waters had honored Begley and several other priests, including Edward Gilbert and John Roueche, by naming them monsignors.

12. "For the man who does for others...," *Charlotte Observer* May 18, 1964.

13. "Rev. Joseph Showfety, Designate Chancellor, Diocese of Charlotte," *NC Catholic*, Jan. 16, 1972, p. 1.

14. Joseph Vetter, "First Chancellor talks about the history and growth of the Diocese of Charlotte," *NC Catholic*, July 15, 1979, p. 6-7. Also, author interview with Msgr. Showfety at St. Benedict on Jan. 29, 2002.

15. ADR, Folder, "Division of the Diocese."

16. ADR, Box "Division of the Diocese." The file contains financial statements for 1971 and 1972 as well as correspondence related to the January 12, 1972 establishment of the diocese and the division of stocks, bonds, and estates left to the diocese.

17. While the retired Bishop Begley resided in a nursing home, a developer contacted him expressing interest in buying a parcel of land that was in Begley's name. The bishop told the man that he did not own the property. When the man insisted, Begley advised him to read the deed more carefully, that it said, "Bishop Begley or his successor in office."

18. "Bishop-Elect Begley Gives His Views at an Interview," *NC Catholic*, Jan. 16, 1972, p.1.

19. "Bishop Begley's Coat of Arms," *NC Catholic*, Jan. 9, 1972, p. 10.

20. "New Diocese on its way with Hearty Celebration," *NC Catholic*, Jan. 23, 1972, p. 1.

21. Ibid. This issue of the *NC Catholic* contains several pages of pictures as well as several articles on the events of January 12.

22. *1972 Official Catholic Directory*. This was the first year that the two North Carolina dioceses were listed separately.

23. Of the 394 marriages performed in Catholic churches in the Charlotte diocese in 1972, 83% were "mixed" religion. This was symptomatic of the fact that Catholics comprised only 1.3% of the general population. In 1984, the final Begley year, there were 567 marriages, 67% of them of "mixed" religion couples.

24. Today, there is a parish or mission in every county in the Charlotte diocese.

25. "NC priests association split into two groups," *Charlotte News*, March 8, 1972.

26. ADC. Records of all but the 2nd and 3rd diocesan assemblies are in a folder "Diocesan Assemblies."

27. No Assembly was held in 1981. In its place, the DPC arranged a series of "forums," attended by the bishop and held in various parts of the diocese.

28. Chapter Thirteen discusses how "collegiality" was being implemented during the same period in the Raleigh Diocese.

29. For reasons not explained, the Charlotte priests requested that the word "vicariate" be used for what previously had been called a "deanery." The Raleigh Diocese continued to use the earlier term. A vicariate/deanery is an intermediate structure between the local parish and the diocese. The "vicar" or "dean" has supervisory responsibility over a number of parishes.

30. George Kloster, Letter to the Editor, *NC Catholic*, July 15, 1979, p.3.

31. ADC folder "Quinquennial Reports" contains copies of all three reports.

32. As it turned out, instead of constructing a headquarters, an existing three-story building was purchased. When in the 1990's that building proved inadequate, the six-story office building on South Church Street that currently serves as Pastoral Center, was constructed.

33. "Bishops Urge Stevens Action," *Georgia Bulletin*, March 16, 1978.

34. *This Land Is Home To Me*, 25th Anniversary edition, Society of the Divine Word, Techny, IL, 2000.

35. Kathleen McClain, "Catholic Bishops Examine Appalachian Progress, Problems," *Oblate Magazine*, June 1985.

36. Tim Funk, "First leader of diocese remembered as 'bishop of the people,' *Charlotte Observer*, Feb. 11, 2002.

Chapter 11

1. Jim Schlosser, "Housing complex to grow up on former St. Leo's Hospital site, *News & Record*, Greensboro, January 11, 1999.

2. In 1973, Bishop Waters enlisted the Sisters of Charity for work in the Social Services Department of the Raleigh Diocese. Diocese. For a number of years they staffed the Raleigh, Fayetteville and Hertford regional offices.

3. All the material in this section is taken from *Catechism of the Catholic Church*, Libreria Editrice Vaticana. Chicago, IL: Loyola University Press, 1994.

4. One author argues that the word "manager" expresses the role of the ordained minister better than "priest." Robert Kress, "The Priest-Pastor As C. E. O.," *America*, March 11, 2002, pp. 8-11.

5. Data compiled by the Center for Applied Research in the Apostolate (CARA). Brothers are members of religious orders who are not ordained priests. Some orders, including the Benedictines, have both priests and brothers. Others, like the Christian Brothers, have no priest members. Brothers comprise but a small fraction of religious personal, with only a handful working in North Carolina. Since 1965, the number of religious brothers has declined by 55%.

6. Religious order priests, although assigned by their community superiors, must be appointed by the local bishop and are required to submit reports to him the same as diocesan priests.

7. Ted Keating, SM., "The Religious Priests in the US Church," *Touchstone* (Quarterly of the National Federation of Priests Councils) XIII, Spring 1998.

8. On the other hand, ... *American Benedictine Review*, June 1998.

9. "One of the most effective instruments for the expansion and perpetuity of the religion of Christ is the Catholic day school. ... No parish is fully equipped without a parochial school." Cardinal Gibbons, *Ambassador of Christ*. Baltimore: John Murphy Co., 1896, p. 322.

10. Archives of the Sisters of Mercy. *Annals of the New York Sisters of Mercy for 1862-63* (pp. 40-53). All material in this section is from this source.

11. ASHC, Sister Mary Helen McCarthy, *History of the Sisters of Mercy of Belmont, North Carolina*, Dissertation, Catholic University of America, 1934, p. 15. Also, undated paper "Three Sisters of Mercy and a Priest Join Father Murphy in Yellow Fever Mission of Mercy."

12. W. Buck Yearns & John G. Barrett (eds.), *North Carolina Civil War Documentary.* Chapel Hill, Univ. of North Carolina Press, 1980, p. 77.

13. McCarthy, op. cit., p. 21.

14. In 1872, the Wilmington sisters severed their connection with Charleston, coming under the jurisdiction of Gibbons and his successors. In 1913, the community became affiliated with Catherine McAuley's Sisters of Mercy, thereby moving beyond the confines of a strictly local foundation. In 1991, in order to be more cost-effective in an environment of declining vocations, Belmont joined two-dozen other regional communities in a new order, the Institute of the Sisters of Mercy of the Americas.

15. All Sisters of Mercy had "Mary" as part of the name given to them at the time of their religious profession. After Vatican II, most communities, including the Sisters of Mercy, abandoned the practice of assigning new names.

16. ASHC, Sister Mary Charles Curtin, *Annals: Sacred Heart Convent, 1841-1892.* (Henceforth, *Annals.*)

17. Sister Baptist died in 1891, Sister Augustine in 1901, and Sister Charles in 1910. Bishop England had died in 1842.

18. *Annals*, p. 2.

19. *Annals*, p. 36.

20. The diseases that swept through the city also decimated the small student population, not only because children got sick, but also because parents, fearful of contagion, kept them home.

21. Letter of December 24, 1879. Cited in McCarthy, *History*, p. 50.

22. Letter of August 18, 1883, in McCarthy, *History*, p. 55.

23. As it turned out, Jews were the main support of the school. "Some of them were young ladies who remained until they graduated; they brightened up classes and cheered the teachers." *Annals*, p. 34.

24. McCarthy, *History*, p. 52.

25. It was not until 1888, 19 years after they arrived in North Carolina, that the sisters began to teach "colored" children. In that same year, the Academy of the Incarnation and the parochial schools in Wilmington were merged into one and called St. Mary's Parochial School.

26. Letter of October 18, 1891. In McCarthy, *History*, p. 74.

27. *Annals*, p. "b"

28. McCarthy, *History*, p. 90.

29. McCarthy, *History*, p. 90. The previous year, Bishop Northrup had rented the house to a group of Sisters of Charity from Youngstown, Ohio. It was when their effort to establish a general hospital failed that Father Marion contacted the Sisters of Mercy.

30. In 1999, the last remaining Catholic health agency in the Charlotte Diocese, Good Shepherd Home Health and Hospice Agency in Hayesville, was absorbed by Murphy Medical Center. Good Shepherd had been established by Glenmary Sisters in 1954, when little medical care was available in the

westernmost counties of the state. "Diocese sells Home Health and Hospice Agency," *News & Herald*, Aug. 6, 1999.

31. "Woman defines life through benevolent works for others," *News & Herald*, Dec. 28, 2001, p. 5.

32. All this material is from the school's web site: www.cdschool.org/Alumni/SGAlumHome.htm.

33. Obituary: *NC Catholic*, Feb. 14, 1960.

34. The farmer, Vince Vilcinskas, was interviewed June 15, 1998 at his home in Revere, NC.

35. Rev. Gerald Lewis, who had known Graves, supplied these anecdotes.

36. AGU. The Papers of Rev. Andrew V. Graves, S. J. are housed in seven boxes in the Special Collections Division of the Lauinger Library, Georgetown University.

37. Hazel Moore was interviewed June 16, 1998 at the Hot Springs Public Library where she worked. In 1992, she published *Hot Springs of North Carolina* (Biltmore Press), which provides an account of the Rumbaugh family.

38. "NC Parish Honors Its Glenmary History," Glenmary Boost-A-Month Club Newsletter, April 2001. Extensive information on Glenmary can be found at www.glenmary.org.

39. "St. William Church reclaims original church building, "*News & Herald*, Jan. 5, 2001, p. 7.

40. Don Kaple was interviewed June 14, 1998. He and the author attended Sunday mass at St. Lucien where a local woman who remembered when he was pastor there more than thirty years earlier warmly greeted Kaple.

41. "Franciscan Sisters bid Good-bye to Cherokee parish," *News & Herald*, Sept. 11, 1998, p. 15.

42. Also, as has been seen, Bishop Waters insisted that nuns working in North Carolina wear habits.

Chapter 12

1. Information is from the web sites of Holy Cross (http://home.nc.rr.com/danpratt/hchome.html) and Immaculate Conception (www.immaculate-conception-church.org) churches in Durham.

2. In 1996 Franciscan Friars of Holy Name Province assumed responsibility for Immaculate Conception, succeeding diocesan priests.

3. Richard Fuller & Francis Wayland, *Domestic Slavery Considered as a Scriptural Institution*. NY: Lewis Colby, 1845; cited in David B. Chesebrough, *Clergy Dissent in the Old South, 1830-1865*. Carbondale, IL: Southern Illinois University Press, 1996, p. 30.

4. Alexis de Tocqueville, *Democracy in America*. New York: Doubleday & Co., 1969, p. 340.

5. Ibid. p. 358. As was noted in Chapter 5, Gaston did eventually speak out against slavery; England never did.

6. George P. Rawick, (Ed) *The American Slave: North Carolina*, Vol. XV. Westport, CT: Greenwood Press, 1979, p. 336-337 Originally published, 1941.

7. John Tracy Ellis, (Ed) *Documents of American Catholic History*, Vol. I. Wilmington, Delaware: Michael Glazier, 1987, p. 322-325.

8. Robert Joseph Murphy, "The Catholic Church in the United States During the Civil War Period," *Records of the American Catholic Historical Society*, December 1928, p. 293.

9. "Washington, North Carolina & the Black Exodus," *NC Catholic*, June 14, 1959, p. 6A.

10. Cf. John Shelton Reed, *Southern Cultures*. Chapel Hill: University of North Carolina Press, 2001.

11. Sister Mary De Sales Harris, *A History of Catholic Elementary Schools for the Negro in North Carolina*. M.A. Dissertation, Catholic University of America, 1965. Harris was a member of the colored Oblate Sisters of Providence founded in the 1820's.

12. Telephone interview with Sharon Roberts, Sept.19, 2000.

13. "Director named for new diocesan office," *NC Catholic*, October 17, 1982, p. 1.

14. ADR, Diary of Bishop William Hafey, p. 171.

15. ADR, File "St. Monica's 1924-1973."

16. Most of this personal information is from an interview conducted by the author, April 27, 1998 at St. Mary Church, Wilmington.

17. John Strange, "Homecoming," *NC Catholic*, August 12, 2001, p. 1.

18. From comments made on several occasions, it is clear that it irritated Hadden that he had not been appointed a bishop. His feeling of being passed over was partially allayed when he was named a monsignor in 2000.

19. Sister Caroline Hemesath, OFS, *Our Black Shepherds*, Washington, DC: Josephite Pastoral Center, 1987, pp. 50-51.

20. "Father Howze, First Negro Priest, Ordained by Bishop for Diocese," *NC Catholic*, May 17, 1959.

21. Shirley Henderson, "Bishop Howze Marks Silver Jubilee as Mississippi Bishop," *News & Herald*, March 3, 1998, p. 10. "Bishop Howze of Biloxi retires at 77, served in N.C," *News & Herald*, May 18, 2001, p.7.

22. Some of these anecdotes are from an address titled "Black Priest, White Church" which Hadden delivered at the Newman Center in Chapel Hill, April 1, 2001.

23. "Priest suspended for forming own congregation," *Durham Morning Herald*, July 7, 1989.

24. Erin Kelly, "Black priest from New Bern shakes up Catholic church," *News & Observer*, July 31, 1989.

25. John Michael Spencer, compiler, *The African American Catholic Congregation Movement Under the Leadership of George Augustus Stallings*,

Jr.: Newspaper & Magazine Articles. Ohio: Bowling Green State University, 1990.

26. A third black priest, Wilbur Thomas, ordained by Waters in 1973, opted for service in the newly erected Charlotte Diocese. The first black priest actually ordained for Charlotte, Damion Lynch, was expelled from the priesthood in the late 1990's following charges of sexual abuse of a minor.

27. November 2002 recollection of the event by Waters' chancellor, Rev. Gerald L. Lewis.

28. Laura Sessions Stepp, "Maverick Priest Girds for Another Fight With Authority," *Washington Post*, July 1, 1989. Several Black priests joined Stallings. One of them, Father Ronald Rhodes, ordained for the Diocese of Raleigh in 1981, left the priesthood in 1997 and joined Stallings. "Father Ronald Rhodes leaves Roman Catholic priesthood," *NC Catholic*, Dec. 7, 1997.

29. ADR, Diocesan Census, 1955. The Census was not broken down by race in most subsequent years.

30. Lawrence S. Earley, "More black priests, nuns are needed," *NC Catholic*, July 15, 1979, p.1.

31. "A New Unity," *NC Catholic*, Nov. 14, 1971.

32. Alesha M. Price, "Charlotte woman uses life experiences as motivation," *News & Herald*, Nov. 9, 2001.

33. Alesha M. Price, "Deacon finds his way home after years in Maryland," *News & Herald*, Dec. 14, 2001.

34. "Migrant orientation held," *NC Catholic*, July 15, 1979, p. 4.

35. A study commissioned by the Raleigh Diocese in 2002 found that whereas a substantial proportion of Spanish-speaking immigrants identified themselves as Catholics, their children were less likely to do so. "Diocesan study confirms sky-high Hispanic numbers, challenges to ministry," *NC Catholic*, July 7, 2002, p. 1.

36. The author, his wife, Ann, and their young children, Bill and Amy, were the family that lived at St. Alphonsus.

37. Pastoral Message of the US Hispanic Bishops, Summer 1982. *Origins*, 12, August 12, 1982, 145-152. In Ellis, *Documents*, 3, 764-776.

38. Tim Funk, "Latino Catholics move into church of their own," *Catholic News & Herald*, April 26, 2002, p. 8.

39. Bishop Waters' Pastoral Letter, *NC Catholic*, Jan. 20, 1974, p. 1.

40. "El Padre Arturo Cabra es el primer sacerdote hispano nativo de la diocesis," *NC Catholic*, Aug. 23, 1998, p. 3A (Spanish language insert)

41. Susan E. White, "Five men ordained to the priesthood in Apex," *NC Catholic*, June 9, 2002, p. 1.

42. Raleigh is one of only two dioceses in the south (the other is Knoxville, Tenn.) that requires its seminarians to learn Spanish.

43. Vincent H. Finnerty, C.M., "Hispanic Ministry studies and statistics," *Catholic News & Herald*, Nov. 5, 1999, p. 12.

44. Ned Glascock and Ruth Sheehan, "Backlash greets newcomers," *News & Observer*, Feb. 23, 1998.

45. Carol Hall, "Good Friday observed in Hispanic tradition," *News & Observer*, April 3, 1999.

46. Barry Yeoman, "Hispanic Diaspora," *Mother Jones*, July/August 2000, p. 39.

47. John Strange, "St. Julia Church responds to immigrant protest with prayer" and "Vandals strike at St. Julia Church," *NC Catholic*, Feb. 27, 2000.

48. "Hispanic immigrants have a place here," *News & Observer*, March 1, 2000, p. 15A.

49. In 1946, anticipating by many years practices that would become standard, Bishop Waters issued a set of rules for his priests which included the requirement that they greet people at the door after mass and that they give a brief sermon at daily mass.

50. The author interviewed Father Quackenbush at St. Julia's, May 22, 1998.

51. Tim Simmons, "Hunt aide tells Latinos to be glad of headway," *News & Observer*, March 12, 2000, p. 6B.

52. "Well-suited in Wendell," *Raleigh News & Observer*, Aug. 6, 2000, p. D1.

53. "Revival touches building and congregation at St. Anne Parish," *NC Catholic*, July 21, 2002, p. 3.

54. "Maronites are proud of their heritage," *NC Catholic*, October 24, 1982, p. 7.

55. "The Glory of Lebanon," *NC Catholic*, October 24, 1982, p. 7.

56. Editorial, *NC Catholic*, Feb. 21, 1960, p. 4A.

57. ADR, Bishop Hafey's Diary, Nov. 4, 1925.

58. Jimmy Rostar, "Seminarian's faith journey leads him to transitional deaconate," *Catholic News & Herald*, Dec. 18, 1998, p. 12.

59. "Charlotte's Vietnamese community ...," *Charlotte Observer*, Dec. 10, 1997.

60. Parish Profile, "St. John Lee Korean Catholic Church," *Catholic News & Herald*, March 13, 1998, p. 12. Although the communities are smaller than that in Charlotte, Fayetteville's St. Andrew Kim Chapel and Raleigh's St. Joseph Church also have Korean language masses.

Chapter 13

1. Thomas J. Reese, *Inside the Vatican*. Cambridge, Mass: Harvard University Press, 1996, p. 38.

2. See *Lumen Gentium*, Chapter 1. Also, Neuner & Dupuis, *Christian Faith: Doctrinal Documents of the Catholic Church* (5th Edition). New York: Alba House, 1990, p. 261.

3. Joan Welch Peak, "Bishop Joseph Gossman recently celebrated 25 years as bishop of the Catholic Diocese of Raleigh," *Durham Herald Sun*, July 16, 2000, p. E1.

4. "Chrism Mass," *NC Catholic*, April 26, 1998, p. 1.

5. Jack Adams, "Roman Catholics: New Man at Helm," *News & Observer*, June 21, 1975.

6. Ernie Wood, "New Bishop Aiming for Openness and Flexibility," *News & Observer*, July 27, 1975.

7. "Bishop mum on why pastor was moved," *NCR*, Jan. 17, 1968, p. 10.

8. Peak, op. cit.

9. ADR. Bishop F. Joseph Gossman, *The Collegial Church -- A Working Document*. Reprinted in Origins, July 1982.

10. In the late 1990's, the Diocesan Pastoral Council was disbanded. The apparatus for participation was judged too cumbersome. Subsequently, the bishop and his staff met annually with each deanery council for planning process input.

11. Directory of the Diocese of Raleigh, Sept. 2001.

12. Official Directory for the Roman Catholic Diocese of Charlotte, 1999-2001.

13. The Code of Canon Law (1983) no longer requires that the Chancellor be a priest. (Canon 482)

14. John Strange, "Change of Guard," *NC Catholic*, March 22, 1998, p. 1. When Msgr. Gerald Lewis retired from active ministry in 2002, he said that the proudest achievement of his 41 years of service occurred while he was Chancellor in the early 1970's. He was instrumental in raising salaries of lay employees of the diocese to the federal minimum wage or higher, and making available to them health insurance and retirement programs. John Strange, "Msgr. Lewis ready to retire to the beach, pastoral care," *NC Catholic*, June 23, 2002.

15. "Bishop Gossman celebrates his years in North Carolina," *NC Catholic*, Nov. 14, 1999, p. 14A.

16. Ernie Wood, "New Bishop Aiming For Openness and Flexibility," *News & Observer*, July 27, 1975.

17. "Remembering the impact of a bishop," *NC Catholic*, Sept. 5, 1993, p. 27.

18. The new Code of Canon Law, promulgated in 1983, had made provision for someone other than a priest to be entrusted "with a share in the exercise of the pastoral care of a parish." (Canon 517, #2.)

19. "Raeford church donated as memorial to employer," *NC Catholic*, Feb. 1, 1959.

20. The 1983 document from Rome which allowed for the use of pastoral administrators did not restrict the title to sisters. In fact, one religious brother and one lay woman have held the position in North Carolina.

21. Matt Doyle, "St. Elizabeth given assistance to preserve historical church in eastern North Carolina," *NC Catholic*, Jan. 24, 1999, p. 8.

22. Yonat Shimron, "Practically Pastors," *News & Observer*, Nov. 2, 1997.

23. *Ordinatio Sacerdotalis*, Boston: Pauline Books, 1997, p. 7.

24. Joan Peak, "Bishop Joseph Gossman," *Durham Herald-Sun*, July 16, 2000.

25. Although there are nearly 100 permanent deacons in North Carolina, none have been appointed pastoral administrators. There is some feeling that deacons would occasion more confusion to the laity than women, since the deacons could baptize, officiate at marriages, and preach, ministries not permitted to the non-ordained.

26. In one symbolic respect, the Charlotte Diocese is more sensitive to sisters and to lay people than is Raleigh. The most recent Charlotte diocesan directory included an alphabetical listing of women religious as it always had done for priests and deacons. Furthermore, it gave the honorific Mr., Ms. or Mrs. to lay employees. In earlier editions only clergy and religious were given titles. The most recent Raleigh Directory did not contain these features.

27. The diocese also had hired consultants to help with fund raising and planning.

28. John Strange, "Capital campaign enters final stretch at $46 million," *NC Catholic*, June 9, 2002.

29. Jimmy Rostar, "Building up the body of Christ: Strategic plan to take ministry beyond millennium," *Catholic News & Herald*, Dec. 11, 1998, p.15.

30. ADR. 2002-2005 Diocesan Plan. Also, "Long Range Staff Plan," Supplement to *NC Catholic*, August 4, 2002.

31. "Bishop Donoghue Chosen for Atlanta See," *Georgia Bulletin*, July 1, 1993.

32. ADC. Synod material are in three spiral binders, some of which were reproduced by the Diocesan Planning Department in 1998 in preparation for the next phase of planning.

33. Marino spent his later years counseling priests, nuns, and monks with personal problems. He died in 2000 at the age of 66. http://afgen.com/bishop_marino.html.

34. Yonat Shimron, "State sees spirited diversity," *News & Observer*, Feb. 2, 2002, p. 1.

35. "Two thirds of bishops let accused priests work," *Dallas News*, June 12, 2002. Although the incident which led to Bishop Gossman being named was not a case of an abusing priest being assigned, the Dallas News did not issue a retraction. See also: "The Sins of the Fathers," *News & Observer*, April 7, 2002, p. 23A, and Ken Garfield, "Catholics vent over priests, leaders," *Charlotte Observer*, May 30, 2002

36. The text of the Charter appeared in many places, including both North Carolina diocesan papers.

37. John Strange, "Msgr. Lewis ready to retire... & Msgr. Shugrue...," *NC Catholic*, June 23, 2002, p. 1.

38. Dana Wind, "Bishop at Chrism Mass," *NC Catholic*, April 7, 2002, p. 1.

39. "A letter from Bishop Curlin," *Catholic News & Herald*, June 28, 2002, p. 9. Reaching the mandatory retirement age of 75 on August 30, 2002, Curlin submitted his resignation, which was promptly accepted by Rome. "Vatican accepts resignation of Bishop William G. Curlin," *News & Herald*, Sept. 6, 2002, p. 1.

40. Paul Wilkes, *Excellent Catholic Parishes*, NY: Paulist Press, 2001. Two other North Carolina churches were named as well, Holy Family in Clemmons, which was featured in Chapter 10, and St. Francis of Assisi in Raleigh, which is staffed by Franciscan Friars. Like St. Raphael, St. Francis is located in North Raleigh and has about 10,000 members. Yonat Shimron, "Thriving on reaching out," *News & Observer*, Feb. 19, 2001, p. B1.

Selected Bibliography

Anderson, Jon W., and William B. Friend. *The Culture of Bible Belt Catholics*. New York: Paulist Press, 1995.

Baker, James T. "The Battle of Elizabeth City: Christ & Antichrist in North Carolina." *North Carolina Historical Review* 9 (Oct. 1977), 393-407.

Bales, Susan Ridgely. *"An Ethnographic Study of Children's Interpretation of First Communion at Holy Cross Church in Durham, N.C."* M.A. thesis, University of North Carolina, Chapel Hill, 1998.

Baumstein, Paschal. *My Lord of Belmont: A Biography of Leo Haid*. Belmont, North Carolina: Belmont Abbey, 1985.

Becker, Kate Harbes. *Biography of Christian Reid*. Belmont, North Carolina, 1941.

Bowes, John C. *Glory in Gloom: Abram J. Ryan. Southern Catholicism and the Lost Cause*. Ph.D. Dissertation, St. Louis University, 1996.

Bowman, Charles H. "Dr. John Carr Monk: Sampson County's Latter Day 'Cornelius.'" *North Carolina Historical Review* 50 (Winter 1973), 52-72.

Bradley, John P. *The First Hundred Years: Belmont Abbey College, 1876-1976*. Belmont, North Carolina: Belmont Abbey College, 1976.

Butler, Lindley S., and Alan D. Watson, eds. *The North Carolina Experience: An Interpretive and Documentary History*, Chapel Hill: University of North Carolina Press, 1984.

Byrne, Patrick James. *Father Price of Maryknoll: A Short Sketch*. Maryknoll, New York: Catholic Foreign Missionary Society of America, 1923.

Calhoon, Robert M. *Religion and the American Revolution in North Carolina*. Raleigh, North Carolina: Department of Cultural Resources, Division of Archives and History, 1976.

Carey, Patrick. *An Immigrant Bishop: John England's Adaptation of Irish Catholicism to American Republicanism.* Yonkers, New York: U.S. Catholic Historical Society, 1982.

Carey, Patrick. "Two Episcopal Views of Lay-Clerical Conflicts: 1785-1860." *Records of The American Catholic Historical Society of Philadelphia* 87 (Mar.-Dec. 1976), 85-98.

Catholic Bishops of Appalachia. *This Land Is Home to Me: A Pastoral Letter on Powerlessness, 1973.* 25th Anniversary edition. Techny, Illinois: Society of the Divine Word, 1999.

Center For Applied Research on the Apostolate. *Church Planning Data: A Statistical Profile for North Carolina.* Washington, DC: 1972.

Chineworth, Mary Alice, ed. *Rise 'N' Shine: Catholic Education and the African-American Community.* Washington, D.C.: National Catholic Educational Association, 1996.

Clarke, Peter. *A Free Church in a Free Society: The Ecclesiology of John England.* Ph.D. Dissertation. Rome: Pontifical Gregorian University, 1980.

Conigland, Edward. *Papers, 1838-1921.* Southern Historical Collection, University of North Carolina-Chapel Hill.

Connor, R.D.W. *William Gaston: A Southern Federalist of the Old School and his Yankee Friends, 1778-1844.* Worcester, Mass.: American Antiquarian Society, 1934.

Davis, Cyprian. *The History of Black Catholics in the United States.* NY: Crossroad, 1990.

Diocese of Raleigh, *Proceedings of the First Synod of the Diocese.* Raleigh, NC 1948.

Dolan, Jay P., ed. *The American Catholic Parish, a History from 1850 to the Present.* NY: Paulist Press, 1987.

Ellis, John Tracy, ed. *Documents of American Catholic History.* 3 vols. Wilmington, Delaware: Michael Glazier, 1987.

Ellis, John Tracy. *The Life of James Cardinal Gibbons, Archbishop of Baltimore.* Milwaukee: Bruce, 1952.

England, John. *Works.* (ed. under direction of Archbishop Sebastian G. Messmer). 7 vols. Cleveland: Arthur H. Clark, 1908.

Felix, Very Rev, OSB. "Catholicity in North Carolina." *Messenger of the Sacred Heart* 34 (Feb. 1899), 99-113.

Fogarty, Gerald P. *Commonwealth Catholicism: A History of the Catholic Church in Virginia.* Notre Dame: University of Notre Dame Press, 2001.

Garaventa, Louis T. *Bishop James Gibbons and the Roman Catholic Church in North Carolina, 1868-1872.* Thesis. University of North Carolina-Chapel Hill, 1973.

Gaston, William. *Papers.* Chapel Hill, NC: Southern Historical Collection, UNC Library.

Gibbons, James Cardinal. *A Retrospective of Fifty Years.* Baltimore: John Murphy, 1916.

Gibbons, James Cardinal. *Faith of Our Fathers.* Baltimore: John Murphy Co., 1876.

Glazier, Michael and Thomas J. Shelley, eds. *The Encyclopedia of American Catholic History.* Collegeville: The Liturgical Press, 1997.

Guilday, Peter. *The Life and Times of John England, first Bishop of Charleston.* NY: The America Press, 1927.

Harris, Sister Mary DeSales. *A History of Catholic Elementary Schools for the Negro in North Carolina.* MA Dissertation, Catholic University of America, 1965.

Heisser, David C.R. "Bishop Lynch's People: Slaveholding by a South Carolina Prelate." *South Carolina Historical Magazine* 102 (July 2001), 238-262.

Land, Guy Paul. "John F. Kennedy's Southern Strategy: 1956-1960." *North Carolina Historical Review* LVI (Jan. 1979), 41-63.

Lefler, Hugh T. *North Carolina History Told by Contemporaries*, 4th ed. Chapel Hill: University of North Carolina Press, 1965.

Lucas, Lawrence E. *Black Priest/White Church.* NY: Random House, 1970.

McCarthy, Sister Mary Helen, RSM. *History of the Sisters of Mercy of Belmont, NC, 1869-1934.* Masters Thesis. Washington, DC: Catholic University of America, 1934.

Madden, Richard C. *Catholics in South Carolina: A Record.* Latham, MD; University Press of America, 1985.

Maher, Sister Mary Denis. *To Bind Up the Wounds: Catholic Sister Nurses in the U.S. Civil War.* NY: Greenwood Press, 1989.

Miller, Sister Miriam, OFS. *A History of the Early Years of the Roman Catholic Diocese Of Charlotte.* Charlotte, NC: Laney-Smith, 1984.

Miller, Randall M. and Jon L. Wakelyn, eds. *Catholics in the Old South.* Macon, GA: Mercer University Press, 1983.

Morris, Charles R. *American Catholic: The Saints & Sinners Who Built America's Most Powerful Church.* NY: Times Books/Random House, 1997.

Murrett, John C. *Tar Heel Apostle: Thomas Frederick Price Co-founder of Maryknoll.* NY: Longmans Green, 1944.

Navagh, James J. *The Apostolic Parish.* NY: PJ Kennedy & Sons, 1950.

Nolan, Hugh J., ed. *Pastoral Letters of the U S Catholic Bishops.* 4 vols. Washington, DC: National Conference of Catholic Bishops, 1983, 1984.

O'Brien, William Francis. *The Memoirs of William F. O'Brien.* Durham, NC: Christian Printing, 1958.

O'Connell, Jeremiah J. *Catholicity in the Carolinas & Georgia: Leaves of its History, 1820-1878.* NY: Ars Sacra, 1964 (original 1879).

O'Dwyer, Thomas. *Diary, 1825.* in Samuel Jordan Wheeler Papers. Southern Historical Collection, University of North Carolina-Chapel Hill.

O'Rourke, J. H., SJ. "A Month in North Carolina." *Woodstock Letters* 34 (1905), 361-372.

Parker, Sister Ann, IHM. *History of Our Lady of Perpetual Help Parish, Rocky Mount, NC.* Thesis. Marywood College, 1975.

Parramore, Thomas C. *Carolina Quest,* Englewood Cliffs, NJ: Prentice-Hall, 1978.

Pitts, Charles Frank. *Chaplains in Grey: The Confederate Chaplains' Story.* St. John, Indiana: Christian Book Gallery, 1957.

Powell, William S. *North Carolina: A History.* NY: W.W. Norton, 1977.

Rausch, John S, ed. *Mission 2000: The Future of the Catholic Church in the South.* Atlanta, GA: Glenmary Research Center, 1990.

Reid, Christian. *The Secret Bequest.* Notre Dame: Ave Maria Press, 1915. (Reid's last novel).

Reid, Christian. *Valerie Aylmer.* NY: D. Appleton, 1871. (Reid's first novel).

Russell, Anne & Marjorie Megivern. *North Carolina Portraits of Faith: A Pictorial History of Religions.* Norfolk, VA: The Donning Company, 1986.

Saunders, R. Frank. "Bishop John England of Charleston: Catholic spokesman & Southern intellectual, 1820-1842." *Journal of the Early Republic* 13 (Fall 1993), 301-322.

Schauinger, J. Herman. *William Gaston: Carolinian.* Milwaukee: Bruce, 1949.

Schauinger, J. Herman. "The Domestic Life of William Gaston, Catholic Jurist." *Catholic Historical Review* 30 (Jan. 1945), 394-426.

Seddon, John T. *When Saints are Lovers: The Spirituality of Maryknoll Co-Founder Thomas F. Price.* Collegeville, MN: The Liturgical Press, 1997.

Sheridan, Robert E., ed. *Thomas Frederick Price: Collected Letters, 1883-1919.* Maryknoll, NY: Maryknoll Fathers, 1981.

Sheridan, Robert E., compiler. *Thomas Frederick Price: A Symposium in 1956* (with Supplement). Maryknoll, NY: Maryknoll Fathers, 1981.

Spencer, Jon Michael, compiler. *The African American Catholic Congregation Movement Under the leadership of George Augustus Stallings, Jr.: Newspaper and Magazine Articles.* Bowling Green, OH: Bowling Green State University, 1990.

Staib, Donald F. *A Descriptive Study of Catholic School Participation in Title III of the Elementary & Secondary Education Act of 1965 in North Carolina.* Ph.D. Dissertation. Chapel Hill, NC: University of North Carolina, 1973.

Stowe, Steven M. *Intimacy & Power in the Old South: Ritual in the Lives of Planters.* Baltimore: The Johns Hopkins University Press, 1987. (Chapter on Gaston).

Taylor, Sr. Mary Christine, SSJ. *A History of Catholicism in the North Country.* Camden, NY: A.M. Farnsworth Sons, 1972. (Chapter on Bishop Navagh).

Thompson, James. J. *The Church, the South & the Future.* Westminster, MD: Christian Classics, 1988.

Waters, Vincent S. *Catholic Education in North Carolina.* Washington, DC: Williams & Heintz Lithograph, 1958.

Waters, Vincent S. "Interracial Sunday Sermon." *Interracial Review* 27 (April 1954), 60-63.

Wilkes, Paul. *Excellent Catholic Parishes: A Guide to Best Places & Practices.* NY: Paulist Press, 2001.

Wolfe, Henry Francis. *The Life & Times of Patrick Nelson Lynch,*
          1817-1882. Charleston, SC: Diocese of Charleston, 1929.
Worsley, Stephen C. "Catholicism in Antebellum North Carolina."
          North Carolina Historical Review 60 (October 1983), 399-430.

William F. Powers was born in New York City on July 18, 1934 to Irish Catholic immigrant parents. After attending parochial schools and the Seminary of the Immaculate Conception in Huntington, Long Island, he was ordained a priest for the Diocese of Brooklyn in 1959. In 1969 he resigned from the clerical ministry and the following year married Ann Goddard and began a twenty-nine-year career as Professor of Sociology at Suffolk Community College on Long Island. At retirement in 1999, he and his wife relocated to Chapel Hill, North Carolina. He is the author of *Free Priests: The Movement for Ministerial Reform in the American Catholic Church* and *Alive and Well: The Emergence of the Active Nonagenarian.*

Index